REALITY'S STORYLINE DECODED II
QUERY STACKS

Reality's Storyline Decoded II
Query Stacks
Copyright © David Mivshek, 2023

All rights reserved. This book or any portion thereof may not be reproduced or used in any manner whatsoever without the express written permission of the author except for the use of brief quotations in a book review.

ISBN 979-8-9879930-0-2

Cover design by David Mivshek

10 9 8 7 6 5 4 3 2 1

Printed in the United States of America
First Printing, 2023

CONTENTS

FUNDAMENTALS vii

PREFACE ix

CHAPTER ONE
Section One • God/Heaven: He Gains 13
Section Two • Devil/Hell: Horde Wans 29
▪ Subsection: Challenges to Determine Who Wans 35
▪ Subsection: QS-7CAP 41
Section Three • Jesus/Earth: Joe Assures 45
▪ Subsection: QS-7CAP 51
Section Four • Dave/Earth: Adore Giver 59
▪ Subsection: QS-7CAP 63
▪ Subsection: Questions to Ask a Hint Giver 67
Section Five • Review: Four Stacks 79
▪ Subsection: QS-7CAP Formula 81

CHAPTER TWO
Section One • Joe/Earth: Hint Grew 89
▪ Subsection: QS-7CAP 92
Section Two • Mary/Earth: Marry Reason 101
▪ Subsection: QS-7CAP 106
Section Three • Review: Six Stacks 111
▪ Subsection: Steps to Manifest Mary 114

CHAPTER THREE
Section One • Holy^Ghost/Heaven: Naïve or Answering 121
▪ Subsection: QS-7CAP 128
Section Two • Review: Seven Stacks 135

CHAPTER FOUR
Section One • YHWH/Heaven: Yahweh's Horn 143
▪ Subsection: QS-7CAP 146
Section Two • Yahweh/Heaven: Heaven's Horn 153
▪ Subsection: QS-7CAP 156
Section Three • Review: Nine Stacks 163

CHAPTER FIVE

Section One • Creator/Reality: Core's Real 173
- Subsection: QS-7CAP 179
Section Two • Yahweh/Reality: They or Reins 187
- Subsection: QS-7CAP 193
Section Three • Yahweh/Trinity: Hairy We 201
- Subsection: QS-7CAP 206
Section Four • "Five Stacks"/Trinity 215
- Subsection: Father/Trinity: Fair Hinter 220
- Subsection: Son/Trinity: Trying Sinew 221
- Subsection: Holy^Ghost/Trinity: Torah's Glory 223
- Subsection: God/Trinity: Got Wording 225
- Subsection: Jesus/Trinity: I Ring Entry 227
- Subsection: QS-7CAP 229
Section Five • Review: Seventeen Stacks 241

CHAPTER SIX

Section One • Trinity/Heaven: Eviternity's Horn 253
- Subsection: QS-7CAP 257
Section Two • Review: Eighteen Stacks 269

CHAPTER SEVEN

Section One • "Two Stacks"/Hell 277
- Subsection: Lucifer/Hell: Siring a We 282
- Subsection: Satan/Hell: Lie Wans 284
- Subsection: QS-7CAP 287
Section Two • Conclusion: Twenty Stacks 299
- Subsection: God is Real 302
- Subsection: No One Made God 303
- Subsection: Prophecy of a Dave 305
- Subsection: God Transformed Her/Himself into a Trinity 307
- Subsection: God Authored QS Answers 311
- Subsection: God is Good and Evil 313
- Subsection: God is the De Facto Devil 321
- Subsection: God Merits Reverence 332
- Subsection: God is or Identifies as Male 333
- Subsection: God is Incomprehensible 336
- Subsection: God is Self-Conscious 337
Section Three • God's Theological Perspective 343

Section Four • QS Answer Statistics and Analyses 349
- Subsection: QS Answer Main Subjects: Statistics 350
- Subsection: QS Answer Main Subjects: Statistical Analyses 351
- Subsection: QS Answer Word Types: Categories 355
- Subsection: QS Answer Word Types: Statistics 357
- Subsection: QS Answer Word Types: Statistical Analyses (Nouns) 360
- Subsection: QS Answer Word Types: Statistical Analyses (Verbs) 373
- Subsection: QS Answer Word Types: Statistical Analyses (Indefinite Articles) 383
- Subsection: QS Answer Word Types: Statistical Analyses (Pronouns) 387
- Subsection: QS Answer Word Types: Statistical Analyses (Adjectives) 389
- Subsection: QS Answer Word Types: Statistical Analyses (Conjunctions) 390
- Subsection: QS Answer Word Types: Statistical Analyses (Contractions) 392
- Subsection: QS Answer Word Types: Statistical Analyses (Adverbs) 393
- Subsection: QS Answer Word Types: Statistical Analyses (Interjections) 394
- Subsection: QS Answer Words and Definitions: Standard, Archaic and Obsolete 395
- Subsection: QS Answer Points of View: Statistical Analyses 396
- Subsection: QS Answer Statistics: Composite 397
- Subsection: Query Stack Answer Totals 416
Section Five • Composite QS Answer Interpretation 421
- Subsection: Composite Interpretation 427

AFTERWORD 431

APPENDICES 433
Appendix A • Query Stack Rules and Guides 435
Appendix B • Seven Common Query Stack Answer Properties 437
Appendix C • "QS-7CAP" Formula, Example and Key 439
Appendix D • Query Stack Database 441

GLOSSARIES 445
Glossary I • Answer Words and Definitions 447
Glossary II • Study Terms and Definitions 451

BIBLIOGRAPHY 455

INDICES 457
Index I • Tables, Diagrams, Charts, Etc. 459
Index II • Topic Tag Directory 475

NOTES, AGREEMENTS & ARGUMENTS 483

FUNDAMENTALS

In 2013, nearly ten years ago, I'd self-published *Reality's Storyline Decoded ("RSD")*, the eponymously titled, first book of the *Reality's Storyline Decoded* book series. In two of the chapters of *RSD*, I'd shined a spotlight onto Query Stacks, which were comprised of sets of words that I'd vertically stacked and messages which I'd derived from said stacks of words. My grasp on Query Stacks was weaker when *RSD* was published than what it was when I'd published this book, *Reality's Storyline Decoded II: Query Stacks ("RSD-II: QS")*, which was the reason I'd dedicated only sixty-four pages to Query Stacks in *RSD* but nearly five hundred pages to Query Stacks in *"RSD-II: QS,"* or this book. In one of the said two chapters of *RSD* which focused on Query Stacks, I'd introduced three Query Stacks, which I'd reassessed, updated, then published in this book. In the second of the said two chapters of *RSD* which focused on Query Stacks, I'd uncovered forty-six Query Stacks, which I'd excluded from this book but planned to reassess, update, then publish in a book that would become a member of the *RSD-II* book series at a later time. Moreover, I'd planned to reassess, update then republish all of the encryption and decryption techniques and topics which I'd introduced, exemplified and analyzed in *RSD* as books that would become members of the *RSD-II* book series at a later time.

I'd started this book, *"RSD-II: QS,"* with a personal anecdote which told how I'd stumbled upon Query Stacks. After said anecdote, I'd presented the fundamentals of Query Stacks; like: what a Query Stack was and how a Query Stack was constructed and solved. I'd focused on each Query Stack's composition, decryption and interpretation. I'd thoroughly picked apart each Query Stack by detailing and exemplifying each Query Stack's construction and decryption and provided a comprehensive explanation and analyzation of my interpretation of each Query Stack's answer. Midway through this book, I'd shortened or eliminated certain explanations and exemplifications of techniques, since I'd used the same techniques to construct and decode each Query Stack in this book. In "Ch. 7, Sec. 2," I'd reassessed my work and committed to a final judgment on several particularities regarding Query Stacks. In the back matter of this book, I'd provided appendices, a bibliography, glossaries and indices for readers who'd needed references and multiple ways for finding information I'd presented in this book.

I'd written this book while I'd unveiled Query Stacks, so some information and explanations mentioned in early sections was rethought, reassessed and slightly modified in later sections; however, I'd noted and explained any modification I'd made and assured that any said modifications aligned with the fundamental principles of my study of Query Stacks.

PREFACE

My first tries at solving word games occurred when I was young, around ten years old. I'd play word searches and crossword puzzles. I'd connect letters buried within letter matrices and place letters of words which were answers to cryptic clues into boxes that were labyrinthically laid out. I'd feel disappointed when I wasn't able to unveil a game's solution on my own accord and had to peek at a game's answer key.

I'd started to pen lyrics and poems in my teenage years. I'd enjoyed winding my thoughts into rhythmic patterns. I was captivated by the challenge of being concise and adhering to syllabic meter, while, at the same time, using words which lured me in by a grammatical ring.

I'd attended a community college in Lake County, Illinois. I'd graduated with an "Associates in Science" degree. My goals of attaining higher degrees ended when I wasn't able to meet a state university's cost of tuition. With no scholastic options available, I'd readjusted my goals and stepped onto a pathway which winded through a corporate jungle.

When I was twenty-six years old, my then-girlfriend and I had rented an apartment. About a year later, our relationship fell apart. Without much notice, my then-girlfriend moved out of said apartment, which left me in the position of having to pay for bills which I couldn't afford on my own. I was on the brink of homelessness. I was confused and terrified. My consciousness cracked. My emotions became a sea of slush. Bitterness and turmoil ensued. In an effort to cure my troubled self, I'd embarked on an introspective journey; or, "a journey to the center of my soul," as I'd called it back then. I'd searched my soul for clues and conjured up guesses on how reality was produced. I'd trashed my belongings, like my tv, radio and computer, because I'd begun to believe that said belongings blocked my intellect from comprehending reality in ways which would've led me to an authentic and comprehensive perception of reality.

I'd wanted to know if reality was fabricated by a conscious being. If reality was made by a conscious being, I'd wanted to meet Her or Him, or "Her/Him." (Later on in this book, I'd stopped using composite pronouns, like *Her/Him* or *S/He* [*she* or *he*], when I'd cited Reality's maker, since later on in this book I'd pinpointed Her/His gender). I had questions to ask the maker of Reality. I'd wanted to tell Reality's maker that S/He was to blame for any pain I'd felt. I'd wanted to rebuke Reality's maker. I'd fantasized of punching Reality's maker in Her/His face, if S/He had a face; and, by the way, not a fight I'd thought I'd win.

If Reality's maker had devised a way which permitted me to communicate with Her/Him, then I'd guessed that our conversation would had consisted of linguistic symbols which I was able to recognize and fathom, such as the twenty-six English letters (*A* to *Z*) and ten Arabic numbers (*0* to *9*). I'd never witnessed Reality's maker communicate with a human in a face-to-face conversation, which compelled me to wonder if Reality's maker intertwined messages into human language and then left it up to humans to find said messages.

Hour after hour, I'd pick through human language in an attempt to unravel hidden messages. I'd sever and reform words. I'd rearrange one word's letters in order to spell another word, and then convince myself that I'd unveiled a divinely inspired anagram:

GOOD → GO DO

EVIL → VEIL

EARTH → HEART → HATER

I'd combed and clawed through the English language. I'd sniffed for messages that I'd hoped told the tale of how Reality's maker had made Reality. Actually, I'd wanted to hack into the mind of Reality's maker, read said maker's thoughts letter by letter and pen said maker's thoughts onto paper. I'd figured that if I was able to read said maker's thoughts at the letter-level, then I would've been able to transcribe the way in which S/He'd remembered making Reality.

Sincerely,
David R. Mivshek

Spell an answer out before, not after, you know said answer by uncovering said answer's letters, clumping said answer's letters into words, sequencing said answer's words, then sprinkling punctuation among said sequenced answer's words in order to unleash meaningful phrases.

CHAPTER ONE: SECTION ONE

GOD/HEAVEN: HE GAINS

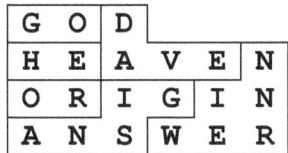

Once upon an unusual day, questions about the origination of God surfaced in my mind:

Ch. 1, Sec. 1: 1

Did God of Heaven emerge from an origin which God of Heaven had made?

If God of Heaven did make Her/His own origin, then how did God of Heaven make the origin from which S/He'd emerged?

If God of Heaven didn't make Her/His own origin, then how was the origin which God of Heaven emerged from made?

While I'd composed and ruminated over concepts about how God had potentially been created, an animated vision blossomed autonomically in my mind. The vision consisted of three words which scrolled sequentially from right to left and then became a vertical stack of left-aligned, neatly-rowed words. The three words I'd envisioned and which comprised said "word stack" were *God, Heaven* and *origin*:

(a) The name GOD occupied the word stack's first row;
(b) The name HEAVEN occupied the word stack's second row;
(c) The word ORIGIN occupied the word stack's third row;

Ch. 1, Sec. 1: 2

[a]**GOD**
[b]**HEAVEN**
[c]**ORIGIN**

I'd read said word stack downwards but interpreted said word stack as if said word stack's words had been horizontally listed in a left-to-right direction:

(a) GOD: word stack's first row, phrase's first word;
(b) HEAVEN: word stack's second row, phrase's second word;
(c) ORIGIN: word stack's third row, phrase's third word;

Ch. 1, Sec. 1: 3

^aGOD
^bHEAVEN
^cORIGIN

^aGOD ^bHEAVEN ^cORIGIN

I'd integrated punctuation marks into the linear transposition of said three words. The said punctuation caused said transposition to become a direct question which asked for an explanation for how God had been made:

(a) GOD/HEAVEN: the question's main subject is God of Heaven;
(b) ORIGIN: the question asks for an explanation for how God of Heaven was made;

Ch. 1, Sec. 1: 4

^aGOD/HEAVEN: ^bORIGIN?

The question in "Ch. 1, Sec. 1: 4" was a less wordy version of one of the questions I'd asked immediately preceding my vision of a word stack, which was "Did God of Heaven emerge from an origin which God of Heaven had made?" (see "Ch. 1, Sec. 1: 1"):

(a) Wordy word stack question;
(b) Editing marks show how question(a) was made less wordy;
   | ~~removed~~ | [added] | retained |
(c) Less wordy version of question(a);
(d) Editing marks show how question(c) was transposed into question(e);
   | ~~removed~~ | [added] | retained |
(e) Word stack question in final word stack question format;

Ch. 1, Sec. 1: 5

a"**Did God of Heaven emerge from an origin which God of Heaven had made?**

b~~Did~~ **God of Heaven[′s]** *~~emerge from an~~* **origin** ~~which God of Heaven had made~~**?**

*c***God of Heaven's origin?**

*d***God** ~~of~~**[/] Heaven**~~'s~~ **[:] origin?**

*e***God/Heaven: origin?**

I'd penciled said word stack onto a piece of paper. What should I do with this stack of words, I'd wondered. A few ideas followed:

> If I add a fourth word into the word stack from my vision and treat said fourth word in the same way that I've treated the three intrinsic words of said vision, then I'd insert said fourth word into the word stack question spotlighted in "Ch. 1, Sec. 1: 4";
>
> If I put the word *answer* into the fourth row of the word stack in "Ch. 1, Sec. 1: 2," then said word should become the fourth word in the question spotlighted in "Ch. 1, Sec. 1: 4";
>
> (a) ANSWER: word stack's fourth row, word stack question's fourth word

Ch. 1, Sec. 1: 6

```
GOD
HEAVEN
ORIGIN
```
*a***ANSWER**

GOD/HEAVEN: ORIGIN *a***ANSWER?**

After I'd incorporated the word *answer* into the question spotlighted in "Ch. 1, Sec. 1: 4," I'd repunctuated said question in order to clarify the updated meaning conveyed through said question:

> (a) Punctuated word stack question without the word *answer*;
> (b) The word *answer* incorporated into and repunctuation of question(a);
> | [added] | retained |
> (c) Punctuated word stack question with the word *answer*;

Ch. 1, Sec. 1: 7

[a]**God/Heaven: origin?**

[b]**["]God/Heaven: origin?["] [answer?]**

[c]**"God/Heaven: origin?" answer?**

I'd explained the meaning conveyed by the question in "Ch. 1, Sec. 1: 7(c)" through an interpretation which I'd written in an easy-read, conversational format:

(a) Unaltered version of the word stack question;
(b) Easy-read interpretation of the word stack question;

Ch. 1, Sec. 1: 8

[a]**"God/Heaven: origin?" answer?**

[b]**For the "God of Heaven's origin" question, what's the answer?**

I'd coined the word stack in "Ch. 1, Sec. 1: 6" as a "Query Stack":

"Query" spotlights the word stack's question, while "Stack" portrays the organizational appearance of the word stack question's words;

Query Stack

"Query Stack" is abbreviated "QS";

Query Stack = QS

I had a series of thoughts which I'd hoped were leading me towards an answer to the "What's God's origin" question:

Maybe, the question in "Ch. 1, Sec. 1: 7(c)" and said question's answer were alphabetically interwoven, as a result of being spelt from the same set of letters. Maybe, if I recombine said question's letters into new words, then the new words will reveal the answer to said question. Maybe, I should connect together letters of the Query Stack's rowed words (see "Ch. 1, Sec. 1: 6") in order to create said new words.

My series of thoughts enticed me to lay out a Query Stack as a geometrical table of columnized letters, in which the first letter of each rowed word was added to one column and each subsequent letter of each rowed word was added to a subsequent column:

I've colored letters white and backgrounds of letter columns black;
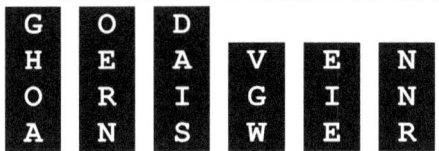

Ch. 1, Sec. 1: 9

G	O	D			
H	E	A	V	E	N
O	R	I	G	I	N
A	N	S	W	E	R

I'd decided to call a Query Stack's rowed word a "Row'd Word," because the word *row'd* was an elision of the word *rowed* (in the same way that the word *bless'd* is an elision of the word *blessed*), was an anagram of the word *word* (I'd rearranged the letters of the word *word* and added an apostrophe to spell the word *row'd*) and signified how a row'd word occupied a word row in a Query Stack, while the word *word* signified what type of grammatical element the row'd word was:

Row'd Word

I'd made mental notes of the steps which had culminated into the construction of the first Query Stack ever uncovered, in case I'd needed to apply said steps to a Query Stack at a later time:

Ch. 1, Sec. 1: 10

Query Stack Rules

I'd implemented five steps when I'd made my first Query Stack, which became five rules which I'd continued to strictly adhere to when I'd constructed subsequent Query Stacks:

QS Rule 1: Determine a question.

QS Rule 2: Reduce the question's vocabulary to key words.

QS Rule 3: Stack key words in a rowed order which causes said question to be

> asked when rowed key words are read downwards.
>
> **QS Rule 4:** Align the first letter of each row'd word into one column.
>
> **QS Rule 5:** Align subsequent letters of each row'd word into subsequent columns.

I'd stared at the columnized letters in "Ch. 1, Sec. 1: 9," and pondered new ways said letters could be linked together so new words emerged. Maybe, if I was able to make new words with said letters, I could string the new words into coherent phrases, I'd mused. Would a composite of said phrases convey a sensible message, I'd wondered.

I'd linked together the columnized letters which were horizontally, vertically and diagonally adjacent to one another in "Ch. 1, Sec. 1: 9," in hopes new words would emerge from said links. I did unravel new words, but said words combined to form nothing but grammatical chaos due to unused letters and a senseless message:

Diagonally connected row'd word letters and a QS answer word that is spelt with said row'd word letters are colored white and set upon a black background, while unusable letters in the QS answer are boxed in;

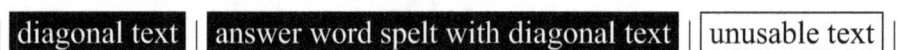

Ch. 1, Sec. 1: 11

G	O	D		
H	E	A	V	E	N
O	R	I	G	I	N
A	N	S	W	E	R

HOG ODE VAINS RENEWING R A   *(incoherence = bad!)*

Initially, several QS answers comprised of incoherent grammar and irrational meaning emerged, like the QS answer in "Ch. 1, Sec. 1: 11." I knew my Query Stack would've been scorned as "a waste of time and effort" if said Query Stack didn't produce anything but meaningless incoherencies. To block the emergence of senseless QS answers and lessen any doubts in my Query Stack, I'd thought up and tested ways to align QS answers with common standards of acceptable grammar.

I can stop grammatical incoherency in my QS answer if I hinder the production of leftover answer letters, I'd assumed. My assumption led me to develop "QS Rule 6," a rule which mandated that each row'd word letter had to appear in the spelling of a useful QS answer word, or an answer word which strengthened a QS answer's meaning and grammatical coherency:

Ch. 1, Sec. 1: 12

Rule 6: Each row'd word letter must appear in a useful answer word.

I'd hoped to knock a hole into a potential "anyone can make meaningful phrases with a group of letters" criticism by limiting the number of times each row'd word letter was allowed to appear in my QS answer's vocabulary to no more and no less than one time:

Ch. 1, Sec. 1: 13

Rule 7: Each row'd word letter must appear in an answer no more and no less than one time.

I'd connected row'd word letters together in every possible direction in order to spell answer words, yet I couldn't compose a sensible QS answers with said answer words. Even if I'd revealed an answer which seemed to satisfy the "What's God's origin" question, I'd figured that dissenters of my Query Stack would've said, "The more ways David is able to connect row'd word letters, the greater the chance is that Dave can make answer words which he feels satisfies his Query Stack question." To relieve said dissent, I'd made a rule which stated that row'd word letters were only allowed to be connected horizontally and vertically, never diagonally. It should be difficult to produce coherent, meaningful answers if I reduce the number of ways I'm able to connect row'd word letters together, I'd conjectured:

Ch. 1, Sec. 1: 14

Rule 8: Row'd word letters can only be connected horizontally and/or vertically.

If I adhere to QS rules to reveal one QS answer but produce more than one coherent and meaningful answer, is only one of the said answers right, I'd wondered. What characteristics delineate an answer as the right answer? Is the right answer the most coherent and meaningful answer? Which qualities of an answer's meaning do I judge in order to determine if said answer's meaning carries the highest degree of significance?

I couldn't have made a rule which defined the qualities that made one QS answer the most meaningful QS answer, since I didn't know which qualities defined an answer's meaningfulness. Instead of a rule, I'd made a loosely defined guide. I'd used said guide to elevate potential QS answers to an optimum level of grammatical correctness and lucidity:

QS guides are loosely defined directives and aren't enforced as strictly as QS rules;

Ch. 1, Sec. 1: 15

Guide 1: The best Query Stack answer is a Query Stack's most coherent, meaningful answer.

I'd proceeded to decode the Query Stack in "Ch. 1, Sec. 1: 9" according to "QS Rule 1-8" and "QS Guide 1." First, I'd linked the first two letters of the row'd word GOD together and made the QS answer word *GO*:

✓ Row'd word letters linked horizontally (QS Rule 8);

Ch. 1, Sec. 1: 16

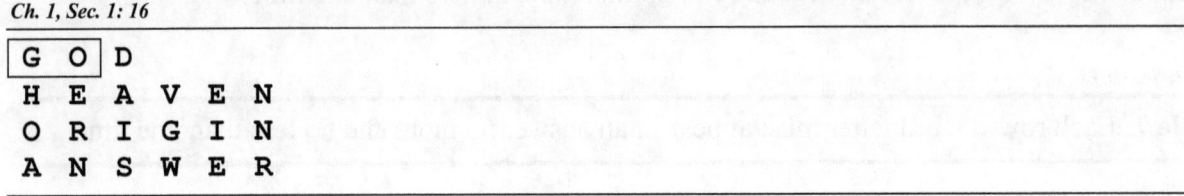

I'd made the answer word *GO* the first word of the QS answer:

Ch. 1, Sec. 1: 17

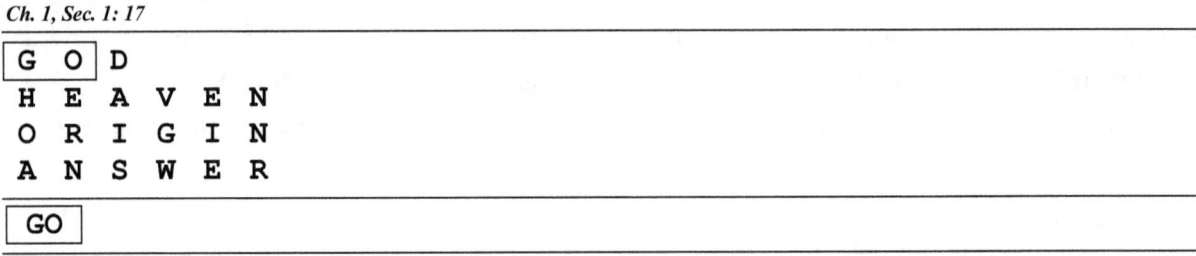

I'd noticed that the first two letters of the row'd word HEAVEN spelt the word *he*, so I'd boxed in the row'd word letters *H* and *E* and created the QS answer word *HE*:

✓ Row'd word letters linked horizontally (QS Rule 8);

Ch. 1, Sec. 1: 18

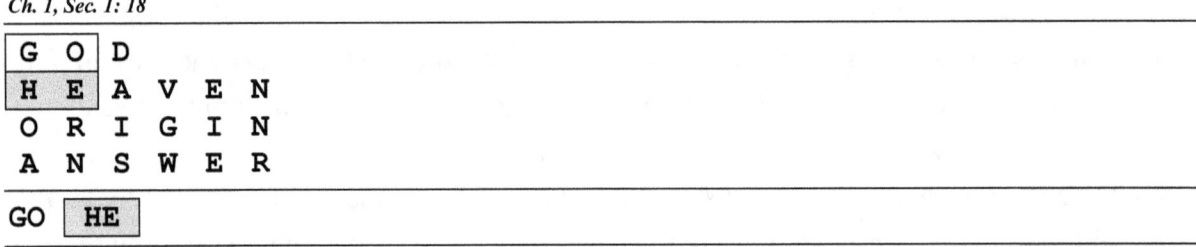

I'd seen the word *or* in the row'd word ORIGIN, so I'd boxed it in and dropped it into the growing QS answer:

✓ Row'd word letters linked horizontally (QS Rule 8);

Ch. 1, Sec. 1: 19

The next two QS answer words which I'd found weren't as easy to pick out of the matrix of row'd word letters as the QS answer words *GO*, *HE* and *OR*, since the letters of the said two QS answer words zigzagged horizontally and vertically throughout said matrix:

(a) I'd rearranged the letters of the "N-I-N-W-E-R" letter-set into the valid word *WINNER*;
(b) I'd rearranged the letters of the "I-G-A-N-S" letter-set into the valid word *GAINS*;

✓ Row'd word letters linked horizontally and vertically (QS Rule 8);

Ch. 1, Sec. 1: 20

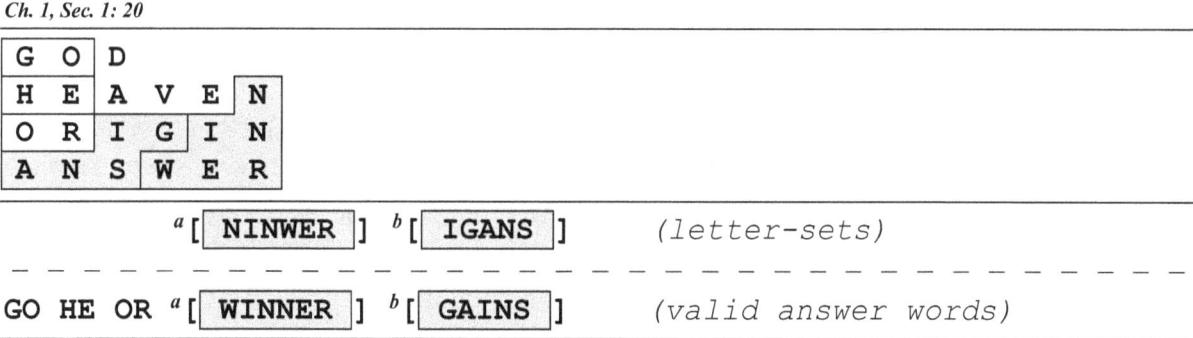

I'd made a rule which stated that row'd word letters which had been correctly connected were allowed to be arranged in any sequence, so long as said sequence formed a valid word:

Ch. 1, Sec. 1: 21

Rule 9: Letters in a set of connected row'd word letters can be arranged in any order to make an answer word.

I'd spelled the answer word *VEDA* with the last four unlinked letters—*Veda* was defined as "any of a class of the most ancient sacred writings of the Hindus[2]":

(a) I'd rearranged the letters of the "D-A-V-E" letter-set into the valid answer word *VEDA*;

✓ Row'd word letters are linked horizontally and vertically (QS Rule 8);
✓ Letter-set letters are rearranged to spell valid answer words (QS Rule 9);

Ch. 1, Sec. 1: 22

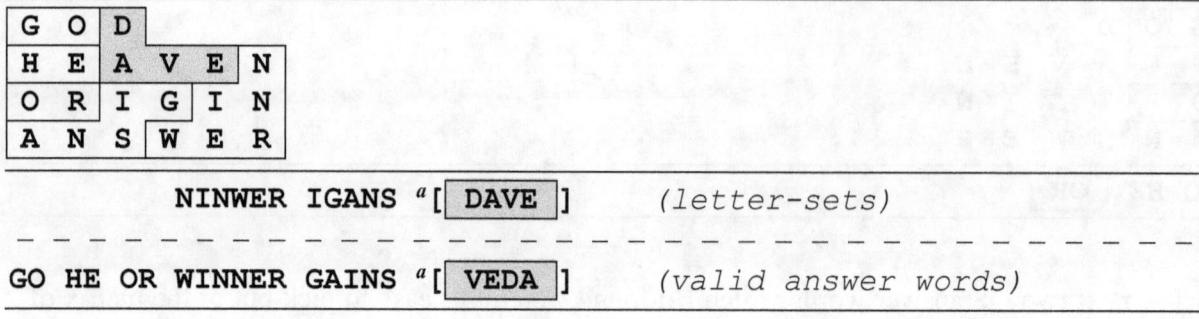

NINWER IGANS "[DAVE]	(letter-sets)

- -

GO HE OR WINNER GAINS "[VEDA]	(valid answer words)

I had six valid QS answer words but no rule which mandated how I was supposed to sequence said answer words. If I'd removed QS answer words from a QS matrix and inserted said answer words into QS answers without adhering to a strict protocol, then someone could've rightfully argued that "Anyone can make a sensible QS answer out of a group of words that can be put into whichever order results in grammatical coherency and a meaningful message." Coherency and meaningfulness in a QS answer should've become less achievable if I had to abide by rules that mandated a strict sequence which QS answer words had to be removed from a QS matrix and inserted into an answer, I'd figured.

Through trial and error, I'd learned that the best sequence to remove QS answer words from a QS matrix was top-left to bottom-right, or the direction one reads an English paragraph. The best sequence I'd come up with which pertained to inserting said QS answer words into the answer was linearly, from left to right, and in the same order that said answer words were removed from said matrix:

Ch. 1, Sec. 1: 23

Rule 10: Words built from connected row'd word letters are removed in a top-left to bottom-right sequence and listed in the order of removal to make a legitimate answer.

Read and review the seven alphanumeric tables which follow, in order to confirm that I'd removed QS answer words from the QS matrix and inserted them into the QS answer in accordance with the mandate expressed in "QS Rule 10" (see "Ch. 1, Sec. 1: 23"):

Each row'd word letter position is represented by a number;

| G → 01 | D → 03 | H → 04 | V → 07 | S → 18 |

Ch. 1, Sec. 1: 24

G O D	→	01 02 03
H E A V E N	→	04 05 06 07 08 09
O R I G I N	→	10 11 12 13 14 15
A N S W E R	→	16 17 18 19 20 21

The first word I'd removed from the QS matrix and listed in the QS answer was the QS answer word *GO*, since the letter *G* of *GO* occupied the top-leftmost position (*pos. 1*) of said matrix:

- ✓ Top-left to bottom-right direction for answer word removal (QS Rule 10);

Ch. 1, Sec. 1: 25

G	O	D				01	02	03			
H	E	A	V	E	N	04	05	06	07	08	09
O	R	I	G	I	N	10	11	12	13	14	15
A	N	S	W	E	R	16	17	18	19	20	21

GO

I'd continued to remove QS answer words from the QS matrix in a top-left to bottom-right direction and adding said words into the QS answer in the same order as I'd removed them from said matrix:

The row'd word letter to the right of the row'd word letter *G* (*pos. 1*) was *O* (*pos. 2*). *O* (*pos. 2*) helped to spell the answer word *GO*, so I'd dropped *GO* into the QS answer for a second time. The row'd word letter to the right of the row'd word letter *O* (*pos. 2*) was *D* (*pos. 3*). *D* (*pos. 3*) helped to spell the answer word *VEDA*, so I'd dropped *VEDA* into the QS answer. I wasn't able to move to the right of the row'd word letter *D* (*pos. 3*), since *D* (*pos. 3*) was the last letter in the first row'd word row; so, I'd done the same as if I was reading an English paragraph; meaning, I'd moved my focus to the first letter of the second row's row'd word, which was *H* (*pos. 4*). *H* (*pos. 4*) helped to spell the word *HE*, so I'd dropped the answer word *HE* into the QS answer. The row'd word letter to the right of the row'd word letter *H* (*pos. 4*) was *E* (*pos. 5*). *E* (*pos. 5*) helped to spell the answer word *HE* too, so I'd dropped *HE* into the QS answer for a second time. The row'd word letter to the right of the row'd word letter *E* (*pos. 5*) was *A* (*pos. 6*). *A* (*pos. 6*) helped to spell the answer word *VEDA*, so I'd dropped *VEDA* into the QS answer for a second time.

I'd realized that dropping a QS answer word that was spelled with the same letter-set into the QS answer more than one time weakened said answer's grammatical coherency:

Follow the position numbers in chronological order to retrace my method of answer word removal and placement (QS Rule 10);

Ch. 1, Sec. 1: 26

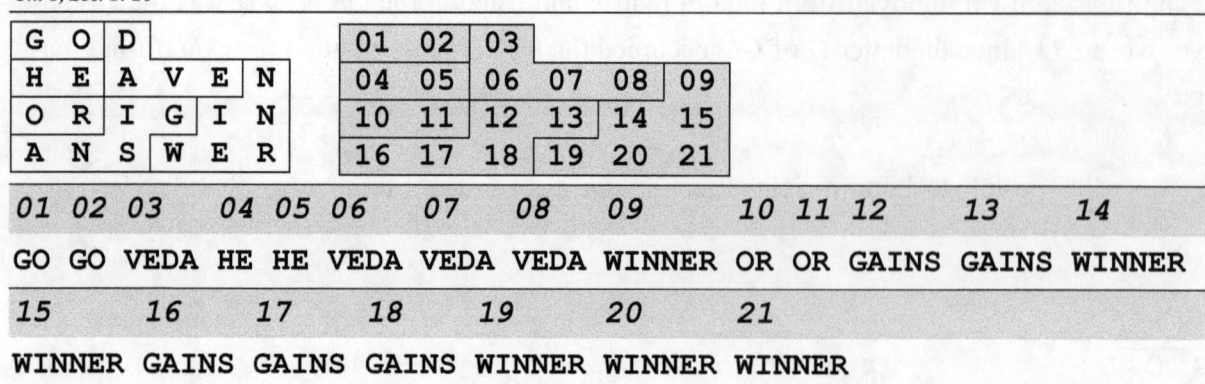

I could make the QS answer more legible if I was able to eliminate the redundant answer words, I'd imagined. Eventually, I'd made a QS rule which mandated that each QS answer word comprised of the same letter-set must appear in the QS answer no more and no less than one time:

Ch. 1, Sec. 1: 27

Rule 11: A word produced by linking row'd word letters together must be removed from a row'd word matrix and listed in the answer no more and no less than one time.

The QS answer became more coherent and sensible once I'd eliminated redundant answer words:

> *A row'd word letter on a gray background marks when I came across a QS answer word for the first time. The matching pattern of gray backgrounds in the QS matrix and numerical matrix link row'd word letters to a corresponding position number. Read the numbers in the numerical matrix in a chronological order to assess if I've removed words from the QS matrix and placed words into the QS answer in accordance with the mandates of "QS Rule 10, 11";*

- ✓ Top-left to bottom-right is the direction of answer word removal (QS Rule 10);
- ✓ An answer word made from a distinct set of row'd word letters appears in an answer no more and no less than one time (QS Rule 11);

Ch. 1, Sec. 1: 28

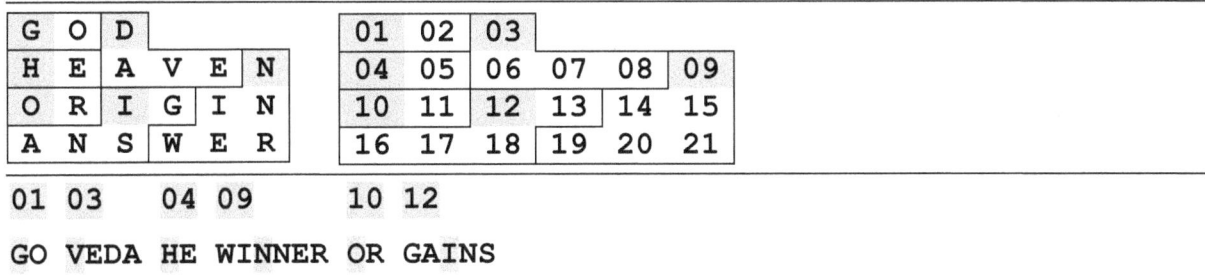

01 03   04 09   10 12

GO VEDA HE WINNER OR GAINS

Even after I'd erased chunks of grammatical incoherency from the QS answer, said answer's meaning still wasn't totally clear. In an attempt to articulate said meaning, I'd punctuated said answer:

(a) Unpunctuated answer;
(b) Editing marks pinpointing punctuation;
    | [added] |
(c) Punctuated answer;

Ch. 1, Sec. 1: 29

^aGo Veda he winner or gains

^bGo Veda[.] He[:] winner[;] or[,] gains[.]

^cGo Veda. He: winner; or, gains.

I'd applied definitions to the QS answer's vocabulary:

> *Each definition's source is spotlighted in the "Bibliography" section in the back matter of this book and matched to a superscripted number. I've shortened some definitions to reduce read time, but I've not altered any definition's essential meaning;*
>
> *| n = noun | prop-n = proper noun | pron = pronoun | v = verb | conj = conjunction |*

Ch. 1, Sec. 1: 30

GO VEDA. HE: WINNER; OR, GAINS.

GO *v.* To occupy oneself with.[2]
VEDA *prop-n.* Any of a class of the most ancient sacred writings of the Hindus.[2]
HE *pron.* That male one.[2]
WINNER *n.* One that's successful.[2]
OR *conj.* The synonymous, equivalent, or substitutive character of two words or phrases.[2]
GAIN *v.* To secure advantage or profit; acquire gain.[2]

After I'd applied definitions to the QS answer words, I'd interpreted the meaning that the string of answer words produced:

Each subscript (sent1, sent2) matches each answer sentence to an easy-read interpretation of said sentence;

Ch. 1, Sec. 1: 31

GO VEDA.$_{\text{sent1}}$ **HE: WINNER; OR, GAINS.**$_{\text{sent2}}$

$_{sent1}$: *Occupy yourself with the most ancient sacred writings of the Hindus.*
$_{sent2}$: *The male's a success; meaning, the male profits.*

The QS answer was comprised of two sentences, but said sentences' meanings weren't compatible. The first sentence, *"go Veda,"* urged an unidentified person to involve her/himself with sacred Hindu writings. The second sentence, *"he: winner; or, gains,"* profiled an unidentified male as a success; or, a male who'd achieved a goal and profited from said achievement:

(a) Incongruent meanings *(sent1 ≠ sent2)*;

Ch. 1, Sec. 1: 32

GO VEDA.$_{\text{sent1}}$ **HE: WINNER; OR, GAINS.**$_{\text{sent2}}$

$^a_{sent1}$: *Occupy yourself with the most ancient sacred writings of the Hindus.*
$^a_{sent2}$: *The male's a success; meaning, the male profits.*

I'd compounded the QS sentences' meanings in order to see how nonsensical the result was. My interpretation of the said composition was that the QS answer's author was urging a male to occupy his time with sacred Hindu writings in order to find success and profit from said success:

Ch. 1, Sec. 1: 33

GO VEDA.$_{\text{sent1}}$ **HE: WINNER; OR, GAINS.**$_{\text{sent2}}$

$_{sent1}$: *Occupy yourself with the most ancient sacred writings of the Hindus.*
$_{sent2}$: *A male is a success and profits because he studied sacred writings of the Hindus.*

I'd never read the *Veda*, so I had no idea if studying Vedic text turned males into successes. Honestly, I didn't even care to track down and read the *Veda* in order to see if the *Veda* taught males ways to be successes. I was more interested in revealing a meaning which I would've been able to quickly verify.

While I'd flirted with my own conclusion of "Query Stacks are nothing more than linguistical poppycock," I'd realized that the "D-A-V-E" letter-set spelt the common nickname for the first name *David*. I was stunned. I'd stared at the Query Stack as I'd silently exclaimed, "My name is in the answer!" Literally, sparks of enlightenment sizzled upon the tips of my brain's neurons as new neuronal connections were made:

Ch. 1, Sec. 1: 34

G	O	D		
H	E	A	V	E	N
O	R	I	G	I	N
A	N	S	W	E	R

GO **DAVE**. HE: WINNER; OR, GAINS.

The QS answer's final set of QS answer words and QS answer word definitions follow (compare to "Ch. 1, Sec. 1: 30"):

(a) *GO*, redefined;
(b) *DAVE*, instead of *VEDA*;

Ch. 1, Sec. 1: 35

^aGO ^bDAVE. HE: WINNER; OR, GAINS.

^aGO *v.* **To begin an action or motion.**[2]
^bDAVE *prop-n.* **A diminutive of the male given name David.**[2]
HE *pron.* **That male one.**[2]
WINNER *n.* **One that's successful.**[2]
OR *conj.* **The synonymous, equivalent, or substitutive character of two words or phrases.**[2]
GAINS *v.* **To secure advantage or profit; acquire gain.**[2]

I'd applied the newest set of definitions to the newest set of words in the QS answer and interpreted said answer's meaning (compare to "Ch. 1, Sec. 1: 31-33"):

Ch. 1, Sec. 1: 36

GO DAVE._{sent1} HE: WINNER; OR, GAINS._{sent2}

_{sent1}: **Begin an action, David.**
_{sent2}: **That male, David, is a success; meaning, David profits.**

Even though I'd uncovered a coherent and meaningful QS answer, I didn't know what the best interpretation of said QS answer was. Was I supposed to heed the command "Go Dave" since I was a man named *David* and the David who'd been the first person to uncover and decode the Query Stack? If so, was my pursuit to answer the question "What's God's origin?" the action that the QS answer's author was commanding me to commence? Was the QS answer's second sentence, *"he: winner; or, gains,"* referring to me, since I was a Dave and a he? If I was the Dave and he which was spotlighted in said QS answer, was said QS answer's second sentence implicitly telling me to anticipate and be reassured that my journey to unveil God's origin would end as a success and with profit? Would I become a success for and profit from revealing God's origin? Would my mere answer to the question "What's God's origin?" be my gain? I had no idea, but I'd added my conjectures to my interpretation of the QS answer for future bouts of contemplation:

(a) QS question;
(b) QS answer;
(c) QS interpretation;

Ch. 1, Sec. 1: 37

[a] **"God/Heaven: origin?" answer?**

[b] **GO DAVE.$_{sent1}$ HE: WINNER; OR, GAINS.$_{sent2}$**

[c]$_{sent1}$: **Begin seeking the answer to who God's maker is, David Mivshek.**
[c]$_{sent2}$: **The male known as David Mivshek is a success or profits by unveiling God's maker.**

Did the QS answer word *DAVE* symbolize my name or did I squeeze personal meaning into said answer even though said answer didn't actually contain an intrinsic meaning which intentionally pinpointed me? Was I a victim of linguistical delusions?

Ultimately, I'd treated the QS answer as if it was authored by someone who'd written a message to and about me. My interpretation of said answer was that said answer's author had challenged me to embark upon an intellectual quest to unveil God's origin. Without hesitation, I'd accepted said challenge.

I didn't care if I was right or wrong or how crazy someone might've thought I was. I was intrigued by the Query Stack, grabbed hold of said intrigue, and committed myself to investigating the validity of the QS answer's message until I'd collected the final fact and unwrapped whatever truth was at my journey's end. What do I have to lose, I thought. If the QS answer was valid and truthful, there were three gains for me: the methods I'd used to construct and solve the Query Stack fascinated me, so I'd be intellectually gratified if I'd used said methods in an attempt to unravel another Query Stack; I'd learn how God was created; and I'd be rewarded for successfully unveiling God's origin.

Did the answer foretell a success that I'd actually encounter? I was willing to find out.

CHAPTER ONE: SECTION TWO

DEVIL/HELL: HORDE WANS

```
D E V I L
H E L L
O R I G I N
A N S W E R
```

As I was unfolding a second QS matrix, several questions streamed through my mind:

If the second Query Stack unfolds into a message, will said second message be at least as coherent and meaningful as the message I'd derived from the first Query Stack *("Go Dave. He: winner; or, gains.")*? Will my name appear as an answer word again? Will said second message reveal or at least provide some pertinent details about God's origin, since said first message didn't?

I'd made sure that the second Query Stack which I'd unraveled consisted of row'd words that shared conceptually meaningful links with the row'd words of the first Query Stack which I'd unraveled. The row'd words which I'd inserted into the top two rows of the second QS matrix were DEVIL and HELL. I'd chosen DEVIL and HELL as row'd words because said row'd words' meanings were conceptually related to the meanings of the row'd words GOD and HEAVEN, respectively. On a spectrum of morality, the Devil and God occupied and operated from opposite ends, since the Devil embodied absolute evil while God embodied absolute good. On a spectrum of biblical locations, Hell and Heaven served antithetical purposes in the afterlife, since Hell was where God punished souls and Heaven was where God rewarded souls:

QS Titling

I've devised a way to shorten the names of and title Query Stacks: a Query Stack title consists of the abbreviation of the term *Query Stack*, or "*QS*," hyphenated to the top two row'd words of the Query Stack being titled. For example, the Query Stack which contains the top two row'd words GOD and HEAVEN is titled "QS-God/Heaven." Similarly, the Query Stack that contains the top two row'd words

DEVIL and HELL is titled "QS-Devil/Hell":

> "'Query Stack' for 'God of Heaven'" is "QS-God/Heaven"
> "'Query Stack' for 'Devil of Hell'" is "QS-Devil/Hell"

(a) GOD; DEVIL: antipodal entities, first-row row'd words;
(b) HEAVEN; HELL: antipodal locations, second-row row'd words;

Ch. 1, Sec. 2: 1

QS-God/Heaven	QS-Devil/Hell
[a]G O D	[a]D E V I L
[b]H E A V E N	[b]H E L L
O R I G I N	
A N S W E R	

I'd inserted the row'd words ORIGIN and ANSWER into the bottom half of the "QS-Devil/Hell" row'd word matrix, which expanded the linguistic consistencies and similarities shared by the "QS-God/Heaven" and "QS-Devil/Hell" row'd word matrices:

(a) ORIGIN; ORIGIN: same words, third-row row'd words;
(b) ANSWER; ANSWER: same words, fourth-row row'd words;

Ch. 1, Sec. 2: 2

QS-God/Heaven	QS-Devil/Hell
G O D	D E V I L
H E A V E N	H E L L
[a]O R I G I N	[a]O R I G I N
[b]A N S W E R	[b]A N S W E R

I'd laid the row'd words out linearly and punctuated them to produce a question, in exactly the same way that I'd constructed the "QS-God/Heaven" question:

(a) DEVIL: first row'd word row, question's first word;
(b) HELL: second row'd word row, question's second word;
(c) ORIGIN: third row'd word row, question's third word;
(d) ANSWER: fourth row'd word row, question's fourth word;

Ch. 1, Sec. 2: 3

[a]**DEVIL**
[b]**HELL**
[c]**ORIGIN**
[d]**ANSWER**
"[a]**DEVIL**/[b]**HELL**: [c]**ORIGIN?**" [d]**ANSWER?**

A transposition of the "QS-Devil/Hell" question into an easy-read, conversational format follows:

(a) Unaltered version;
(b) Easy-read version;

Ch. 1, Sec. 2: 4

[a]**"Devil/Hell: origin?" answer?**
[b]**For the "Devil of Hell's origin" question, what's the answer?**

I'd connected letters of the "QS-Devil/Hell" row'd word matrix to make answer words, removed said answer words in a top-left to bottom-right direction from said matrix and linearly listed said answer words in the sequence which I'd removed them from said matrix:

✓ All QS rules were adhered to (see "Appendix A");

Ch. 1, Sec. 2: 5

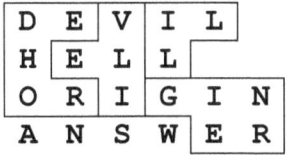

HORDE EVIL ILL REIGN (ANSW)

I'd meticulously worked at finding an answer word which was spelt with the four letters of the letter-set "A-N-S-W" and had a meaning that consummated the meaning of the sentences in the "QS-Devil/Hell" answer. In one attempt, I'd transposed said letter-set into the QS answer word *SWAN*:

Ch. 1, Sec. 2: 6

```
D E V I L
H E L L
O R I G I N
A N S W E R
```

HORDE EVIL ILL REIGN | SWAN

I'd decorated the potential QS answer with punctuation, in order to accentuate my interpretation of said answer's message:

(a) Unpunctuated answer;
(b) Editing marks pinpointing punctuation;
 | [added] |
(c) Punctuated answer;

Ch. 1, Sec. 2: 7

^a**Horde evil ill reign swan**

^b**Horde[:] evil[.] Ill reign[,] swan[.]**

^c**Horde: evil. Ill reign, swan.**

I'd applied definitions to the QS answer words in "Ch. 1, Sec. 2: 6":

Ch. 1, Sec. 2: 8

HORDE: EVIL. ILL REIGN, SWAN.

HORDE *n.* **A crowd of individuals.**[2]

EVIL *n.* **One that personifies wickedness.**[2]

ILL *n.* **Sickness.**[2]

REIGN *v.* **To exercise sovereign power; rule.**[2]

SWAN *v.* **Sweep majestically.**[2]

After I'd applied definitions to the QS answer words in "Ch. 1, Sec. 2: 8," a QS answer with an incoherent meaning emerged. Said answer inferred that a sickness had swanned, or "swept majestically; or, pompously pranced around"; yet, sicknesses can't pompously prance around:

(a) Answer word doesn't fit into the context of answer's meaning;
 | ~~removed~~ |

Ch. 1, Sec. 2: 9

HORDE: EVIL.~sent1~ **ILL REIGN, "~~SWAN~~.**~sent2~

sent1: *A crowd of individuals is a wicked entity.*

sent2: *A sickness does exercise rulership and* ª(~~prance around pompously~~).

I should try to spell another word with the "A-N-S-W" letter-set, I'd thought. Eventually, I'd transposed "A-N-S-W" into the QS answer word *WANS*:

Ch. 1, Sec. 2: 10

D	E	V	I	L
H	E	L	L	
O	R	I	G	N
A	N	S	W	E	R

HORDE: EVIL. ILL REIGN, WANS .

The QS answer word *WANS* fit into the context of the answer's meaning better than the answer word *SWAN*, since the definition for the verb form of the word *wan*, "*v.* to grow or become pale or sickly^2," mirrored the meaning I'd already assigned to the answer word *ILL*:

(a) Matching definitions: both definitions concern sickness;

Ch. 1, Sec. 2: 11

ILL *n.* ª**Sickness**.

WAN *v.* To grow or become ª**sickly**.

The meanings of the two sentences in the "QS-Devil/Hell" answer didn't coalesce into one overall, meaningful message. The first sentence identified an evil crowd, while the second sentence described a sickness which reigned, or exercised rulership, and became sick. Was the evil crowd which was introduced in the "QS-Devil/Hell" answer's first sentence the same entity as the sickness that was mentioned in said answer's second sentence? Was said evil crowd a sickness? Honestly, I didn't know:

(a) Incongruent meaning (sent1 ≠ sent2);

Ch. 1, Sec. 2: 12

HORDE: EVIL._{sent1} **ILL REIGN, WANS.**_{sent2}

^{a}_{sent1}: *A crowd of individuals is a wicked entity.*
^{a}_{sent2}: *Sickness does exercise rulership and grows or becomes sickly.*

Since the interpretation in "Ch. 1, Sec. 2: 12" contained a meaning which was disjointed, I'd reassessed the most recent definitions I'd assigned to the "QS-Devil/Hell" answer words. As I was combing through definitions of the word *ill*, I'd seen "*n.* evil[2]." I'd applied said definition to the answer word *ILL*. Said definition paralleled the definition of the answer word *EVIL,* or "one that personifies wickedness[2]," I'd realized. The linguistic similarities of the answer words *EVIL* and *ILL* coalesced the meanings of said answer's two sentences:

(a) Synonymous answer words;
(b) Congruent definitions;

Ch. 1, Sec. 2: 13

HORDE: ^{a}**EVIL.**_{sent1} ^{a}**ILL REIGN, WANS.**_{sent2}

_{sent1}: *A crowd of individuals is a ^{b}(wicked entity).*
_{sent2}: *An ^{b}(evil [wicked entity]) does exercise rulership and grows or becomes sickly.*

The answer words *EVIL* and *ILL* were synonyms, a relationship which persuaded me to believe that the evil horde was the evil entity which had exercised rulership and grown or became sickly:

(a) Descriptions linked to same entity;
(b) Actions linked to same entity;

Ch. 1, Sec. 2: 14

HORDE: ^{a}**EVIL.**_{sent1} ^{a}**ILL** ^{b}**REIGN,** ^{b}**WANS.**_{sent2}

_{sent1}: *A crowd of individuals is a ^{a}(wicked entity).*
_{sent2}: *A ^{a}(wicked entity [crowd]) does ^{b}(exercise rulership) and ^{b}(grows or becomes sickly).*

Once I'd unassigned the definition "sickness" from the QS answer word *ILL*, I'd wondered if the definition "become sickly," which I'd assigned to the answer word *WANS*, was appropriate. I didn't know which sickness or evil crowd the "QS-Devil/Hell" answer identified, so I had no way of knowing if the meaning conveyed by the "QS-Devil/Hell" answer was practical.

I'd relooked up the word *wan* in a hardcopy of Webster's dictionary, in hopes that I'd find a definition which rendered the QS answer's meaning lucid. Eventually, I'd found the definition "*v.* to become or make wan[1] *(adj [adjective].* lacking in forcefulness, competence, or effectiveness.[1])":

(a) WANS: answer word and meaning;

Ch. 1, Sec. 2: 15

HORDE: EVIL.sent1 **ILL REIGN, ᵃWANS.**sent2

sent1: *A crowd of individuals is a wicked entity.*
sent2: *The wicked crowd does exercise rulership and ᵃ(becomes lacking in or makes others lack in forcefulness, competence or effectiveness).*

Even though the latest definition which I'd applied to the QS answer word *WANS* coincided with the "QS-Devil/Hell" answer's meaning, I didn't know if the evil horde was the entity which had wanned or if said horde had wanned others and I didn't know if said answer word referred to a lack in forcefulness, competence or effectiveness. However, I'd integrated the definition of *WANS* into the meaning of the "QS-Devil/Hell" answer in six different ways in order to determine which definition was the best fit for the meaning of said answer:

(a) Ill reigns and becomes lacking in [1] Forcefulness, [2] Competence, or [3] Effectiveness;
(b) Ill reigns and makes others lack in [1] Forcefulness, [2] Competence, or [3] Effectiveness;

Ch. 1, Sec. 2: 16

ILL REIGN, [(a, b)(1, 2, 3)]**WANS.**

The wicked crowd does exercise rulership and ᵃ[becomes lacking in] ¹(forcefulness).
The wicked crowd does exercise rulership and ᵃ[becomes lacking in] ²(competence).
The wicked crowd does exercise rulership and ᵃ[becomes lacking in] ³(effectiveness).

— —

The wicked crowd does exercise rulership and ᵇ[makes others lack in] ¹(forcefulness).
The wicked crowd does exercise rulership and ᵇ[makes others lack in] ²(competence).
The wicked crowd does exercise rulership and ᵇ[makes others lack in] ³(effectiveness).

To help me determine which definition was the best fit, I'd developed three challenges:

Challenges to Determine Who Wans—Challenge 1
Determine which one of the evil horde's qualities had wanned: forcefulness, competence or effectiveness? Base said determination solely on a vocabular analysis of

the answer's second sentence;

Challenges to Determine Who Wans—Challenge 2
Determine which quality said horde had caused others to wan in. Forcefulness? Competence? Effectiveness? Base said determination solely on a vocabular analysis of the answer's second sentence;

Challenges to Determine Who Wans—Challenge 3
Compare results of "Challenge 1" and "Challenge 2." Pick the most sensible result;

Challenges to Determine Who Wans—Challenge 1

Determine which one of the wicked crowd's qualities had wanned: forcefulness, competence or effectiveness? Base the determination solely on a vocabular analysis of the answer's second sentence.

(a) Wicked crowd's *forcefulness* wans;
(b) Wicked crowd's *competence* wans;
(c) Wicked crowd's *effectiveness* wans;

Ch. 1, Sec. 2: 17

ILL REIGN, [a, b, c]**WANS.**

The wicked crowd does exercise rulership and [a]*(becomes lacking in forcefulness).*
The wicked crowd does exercise rulership and [b]*(becomes lacking in competence).*
The wicked crowd does exercise rulership and [c]*(becomes lacking in effectiveness).*

If a wicked crowd was "exercising rulership," or wielding dominance to compel obedience, wouldn't said crowd employ forceful tactics to subjugate anyone opposing its wicked dominance? Yes, if a crowd was wicked and wanted to sustain its dominance, then said crowd would do whatever wickedness suppressed said crowd's adversaries.

If the wicked crowd's ability to be forceful faded, then said crowd's control over said adversaries would fade too. Without force to suppress said adversaries, said adversaries could swiftly dismantle said crowd's reign.

The meaning of the "QS-Devil/Hell" answer's second sentence focused on said crowd's forcefulness. Said crowd reigned when said crowd exerted forcefulness but lost reign when said crowd's forcefulness had wanned. Meaning, the degree of forcefulness said crowd exerted established said crowd's degree of competence and level of effectiveness in maintaining a grip on said crowd's lieges:

(a) Wicked crowd's *forcefulness* wans;
(b) Wicked crowd's *competence* wans;
  | ~~removed~~ |
(c) Wicked crowd's *effectiveness* wans;
  | ~~removed~~ |

Ch. 1, Sec. 2: 18

ILL REIGN, (a, b, c)WANS.

The wicked crowd does exercise rulership and ᵃ(becomes lacking in forcefulness).
The wicked crowd does exercise rulership and ᵇ~~*(becomes lacking in competence)*~~*.*
The wicked crowd does exercise rulership and ᶜ~~*(becomes lacking in effectiveness)*~~*.*

Challenges to Determine Who Wans—Challenge 2

Determine which quality the wicked crowd had caused others to wan in. Forcefulness? Competence? Effectiveness? Base the determination solely on a vocabular analysis of the answer's second sentence.

(a) Wicked crowd makes others' *forcefulness* wan;
(b) Wicked crowd makes others' *competence* wan;
(c) Wicked crowd makes others' *effectiveness* wan;

Ch. 1, Sec. 2: 19

ILL REIGN, (a, b, c)WANS.

The wicked crowd does exercise rulership and ᵃ(makes others lack in forcefulness).
The wicked crowd does exercise rulership and ᵇ(makes others lack in competence).
The wicked crowd does exercise rulership and ᶜ(makes others lack in effectiveness).

If a wicked crowd was "exercising rulership," or wielding dominance to compel obedience, wouldn't said crowd try to diminish any power adversaries harnessed and might use in an attempt to dismantle said crowd's dominance? Yes, a wicked crowd which wanted to maintain dominance would have a better chance at maintaining dominance if said crowd decimated as much of an adversary's forcefulness as said crowd was able to. If said crowd squashed an adversary's forcefulness, then, in turn, said crowd diminished said adversary's competence and effectiveness in counteracting the forcefulness exerted by said crowd:

(a) Wicked crowd makes others' *forcefulness* wan;
(b) Wicked crowd makes others' *competence* wan;
   | ~~removed~~ |
(c) Wicked crowd makes others' *effectiveness* wan;
   | ~~removed~~ |

Ch. 1, Sec. 2: 20

ILL REIGN, ^(a, b, c)WANS.

The wicked crowd does exercise rulership and ^a(makes others lack in forcefulness).
The wicked crowd does exercise rulership and ^b~~(makes others lack in competence)~~.
The wicked crowd does exercise rulership and ^c~~(makes others lack in effectiveness)~~.

Challenges to Determine Who Wans—Challenge 3

Compare results of "Challenge 1" and "Challenge 2." Pick the most sensible result.

So, which interpretation of the answer word *WANS* helped the "QS-Devil/Hell" answer's second sentence attain optimal meaningfulness? A wicked crowd which ruled by force but lost powerful rank when said crowd's forcefulness had faded or a wicked crowd that ruled by force by breaking down the forcefulness of said crowd's lieges?

(a) Wicked crowd's forcefulness wans;
(b) Wicked crowd makes others' forcefulness wan;

Ch. 1, Sec. 2: 21

ILL REIGN, ^(a, b)WANS.

The wicked crowd does exercise rulership and ^a(becomes lacking in forcefulness).
The wicked crowd does exercise rulership and ^b(makes others lack in forcefulness).

Both interpretations harbored meaning; however, only one of said interpretations helped linguistic features in the "QS-Devil/Hell" answer's second sentence line up with linguistic features in the "QS-God/Heaven" answer's second sentence. Maybe, the best answers for some Query Stacks were discernible because linguistic features of said answers mirrored linguistic features in the best answers of other Query Stacks, I'd proffered. For example, the he in the "QS-God/Heaven" answer received gains; therefore, actions mentioned in the

"QS-God/Heaven" answer's second sentence happened to the he. If linguistic features of the "QS-Devil/Hell" answer's second sentence contained a subject-action relationship like the subject-action relationship, *he-gains*, in the "QS-God/Heaven" answer, then the ill, in the QS-Devil/Hell" answer's second sentence, was who'd reigned and became less forceful:

(a) "QS-God/Heaven": actions assigned to the he;
(b) "QS-Devil/Hell": actions assigned to the ill;

Ch. 1, Sec. 2: 22

ᵃ**HE**: WINNER; OR, ᵃ**GAINS**.
ᵃ*(A certain male) ... ᵃ(profits).*
ᵇ**ILL** ᵇ**REIGN,** ᵇ**WANS**.
ᵇ*(The ill does exercise rulership)* and ᵇ*(the ill becomes lacking in forcefulness).*

Persuaded by the similarities in linguistic features of the "QS-God/Heaven" and "QS-Devil/Hell" answers, I'd chosen the definition of *wans* which characterized the wicked crowd as a crowd that experienced a weakening in said crowd's force:

(a) Wicked crowd's forcefulness wans;
(b) Wicked crowd makes others' forcefulness wan;
| ~~removed~~ |

Ch. 1, Sec. 2: 23

ILL REIGN, ⁽ᵃ, ᵇ⁾**WANS**.
The wicked crowd does exercise rulership and ᵃ*(becomes lacking in forcefulness).*   *The wicked crowd does exercise rulership and* ᵇ~~*(makes others lack in forcefulness).*~~

Eventually, I'd devised two more QS guides. Both guides pertained to QS vocabulary. The first of the two guides stated that a QS answer should only be comprised of vocabulary which spotlights said answer's main subject:

Ch. 1, Sec. 1: 24

Guide 2: A Query Stack's most coherent, meaningful answer is comprised of vocabulary that pertains to no more and no less than one subject, the main subject.

The second of the two guides stated that actions mentioned in a QS answer should affect said answer's main subject:

Ch. 1, Sec. 2: 25

Guide 3: Actions mentioned in a QS answer affect said answer's main subject.

Besides a subject-action relationship, the "QS-God/Heaven" and "QS-Devil/Hell" answers shared other linguistic congruencies. The "QS-God/Heaven" row'd words GOD and HEAVEN reverberated in overtones which sang spiritual goodness and encrypted answer words which rang the uplifting phrases *"he winner"* and *"he gains"*; in other words, "QS-God/Heaven" broadcasted a positive vibe. On the other end of the spectrum of moral meaning, the "QS-Devil/Hell" row'd words DEVIL and HELL not only casted out evil overtones but also encrypted an answer which barked out the negative messages *"ill reign"* and *"ill wans"*; in other words, "QS-Devil/Hell" broadcasted a negative note:

A gray background groups positive row'd words and answer words together, while a black background groups negative row'd words and answer words together;

| positive meaning | | negative meaning |

Ch. 1, Sec. 2: 26

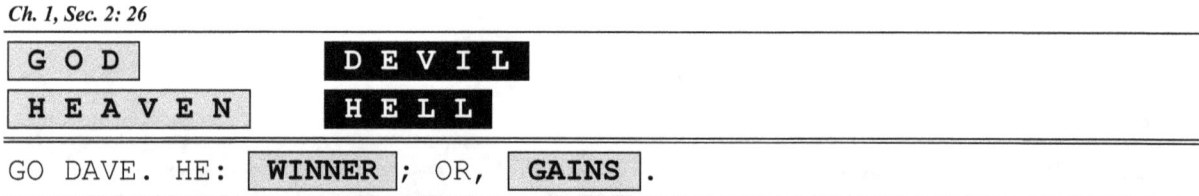

On the other hand, a linguistic incongruency which dichotomized the "QS-Devil/Hell" and "QS-God/Heaven" answers was based on two contrasting characteristics of said answers' main subjects, or the horde and he, respectively. The main subject in the "QS-Devil/Hell" answer was a horde, or (1) a group of individuals who were (2) unnamed, while the main subject in the "QS-God/Heaven" answer was Dave, or (1) one individual who was (2) named:

(a) Contrasting main subjects: group of unnamed individuals, one named individual;

Ch. 1, Sec. 2: 27

"**HORDE:** EVIL. ILL REIGN, WANS.

GO "**DAVE.** HE: WINNER; OR, GAINS.

(One can find connections in anything and everywhere if one wants and tries hard enough to, some say.)

I'd discovered seven grammatical properties which had been integrated into each of the two QS answers I'd revealed in this book so far. Said properties were so distinct and precise that the presence of said properties in both said answers compelled me to believe that said properties were intentionally integrated into said answers by said answers' author. I'd coined the seven properties the "Seven Common Query Stack Answer Properties" ("QS-7CAP"):

Seven Common QS Answer Properties = QS-7CAP

Next, I'd listed each of the seven "QS-7CAP" properties and showed the integration of each said property into the "QS-God/Heaven" and "QS-Devil/Hell" answers:

Seven Common QS Answer Properties

1. Each answer contains no more and no less than two sentences (sent1, sent2):

QS-God/Heaven

GO **DAVE.**$_{sent1}$ HE: WINNER; OR, GAINS.$_{sent2}$

QS-Devil/Hell

HORDE: EVIL.$_{sent1}$ ILL REIGN, WANS.$_{sent2}$

2. Each answer's first sentence contains no more and no less than two words (word1, word2):

QS-God/Heaven

GO$_{word1}$ **DAVE**$_{word2}$. HE: WINNER; OR, GAINS.

QS-Devil/Hell

HORDE$_{word1}$: **EVIL**$_{word2}$. ILL REIGN, WANS.

3. In each answer's first sentence, the main subject is introduced (subj1, subj2):

QS-God/Heaven

GO **DAVE**~subj1~. HE: WINNER; OR, GAINS.

QS-Devil/Hell

HORDE~subj2~: EVIL. ILL REIGN, WANS.

4. In each answer, the main subject introduced in the first sentence is mentioned in the second sentence (subj1-subj1, subj2-subj2):

QS-God/Heaven

GO **DAVE**~subj1~. **HE**~subj1~: WINNER; OR, GAINS.

QS-Devil/Hell

HORDE~subj2~: EVIL. **ILL**~subj2~ REIGN, WANS.

5. In each answer, the first sentence's second word and the second sentence's first word are synonymous in definition (syn) or context (con):

> *Synonymous answer words are tagged "syn," while answer words which share contextual meaning are tagged "con";*

(con1) DAVE; HE: context, both words identify the same man;
(syn2) EVIL; ILL: synonyms, each word means "wicked";

QS-God/Heaven

GO **DAVE**~con1~. **HE**~con1~: WINNER; OR, GAINS.

QS-Devil/Hell

HORDE: **EVIL**~syn2~. **ILL**~syn2~ REIGN, WANS.

6. In each answer's second sentence, at least one action is applied to the main subject (subj1–act1, subj2–act2):

QS-God/Heaven

GO DAVE. **HE**~subj1~: WINNER; OR, **GAINS**~act1~.

QS-Devil/Hell

HORDE: EVIL. **ILL**~subj2~ **REIGN**~act2~, WANS.

7. Along each answer's breadth of vocabulary, there's at least one site where an answer letter *S* would've enhanced the answer's grammatical correctness if it was available in the accompanying row'd word matrix and usable:

   Removing a colon (:) that follows a noun and appending a contractive 's to the end of said noun would produce a conversational tone and clearer syntax (e.g. <u>He's</u> winner; <u>Horde's</u> evil). Inflecting certain verbs by appending a letter S to each verb's back end would promote optimal grammar (e.g. Ill <u>reigns</u>). However, each answer's row'd word matrix lacks a letter S that's needed or that's capable of being used in ways mandated by QS rules (see "Appendix A");

   QS-God/Heaven: <u>He's</u> winner;
   QS-Devil/Hell: <u>Horde's</u> evil, Ill <u>reigns</u>;

QS-God/Heaven
```
GO DAVE. HE: WINNER; OR, GAINS.
```
QS-Devil/Hell
```
HORDE: EVIL. ILL REIGN, WANS.
```

I'd readily observed the "QS-Devil/Hell" answer's grammatical coherency, but I wasn't able to easily perceive said answer's meaning. Who was the "QS-Devil/Hell" answer talking about, I'd wondered. Was the crowd of wicked individuals comprised of the Devil and a swarm of demons, since the Devil and demons embodied pure evil and the answer that the wicked crowd was mentioned in was decoded from the row'd words DEVIL and HELL, a wicked entity and a wicked realm, respectively? If the "QS-Devil/Hell" answer did portray the Devil and demons, then the Devil and demons would've been the individuals in the wicked crowd which exercised rulership and lacked forcefulness, I'd supposed:

(a) QS question;
(b) QS answer;
(c) QS interpretation;

Ch. 1, Sec. 2: 28

a **"Devil/Hell: origin?"** answer?

b HORDE: EVIL.$_{sent1}$ ILL REIGN, WANS.$_{sent2}$

c$_{sent1}$: *The crowd is composed of the wicked Devil and demons.*

c$_{sent2}$: *The crowd composed of the wicked Devil and demons exercises rulership and becomes lacking in forcefulness.*

If I was correct in associating the "QS-Devil/Hell" answer's main subject, the horde, with the being named in the top row of the "QS-Devil/Hell" matrix, Devil, then I'd have to associate the "QS-God/Heaven" answer's main subject, Dave, with the being named in the top row of the "QS-God/Heaven" matrix, God, to maintain interpretative consistency, I'd figured. However, "*Dave ≠ God*":

(a) GOD; DAVE: invalid association *(God ≠ Dave)*;

Ch. 1, Sec. 2: 29

a G O D

H E A V E N
O R I G I N
A N S W E R

GO *a* **DAVE**. HE: WINNER; OR, GAINS.

To maintain interpretative consistency, I'd decided that if "*God ≠ Dave*," then "*Devil ≠ horde*":

(a) DEVIL/HORDE: invalid association *(Devil ≠ horde)*;

Ch. 1, Sec. 2: 30

a D E V I L

H E L L
O R I G I N
A N S W E R

a **HORDE**: EVIL. ILL REIGN, WANS.

Who'd membered the evil horde, if not the Devil and demons, I'd wondered. I had no clue, but I did attempt to construct and decode a third Query Stack in hopes that I'd find out.

CHAPTER ONE: SECTION THREE

JESUS/EARTH: JOE ASSURES

```
J E S U S
E A R T H
O R I G I N
A N S W E R
```

Even though I'd uncovered two Query Stacks with row'd words which were theologically affiliated and answers with grammatical parallelisms, I wasn't sure if said relationships were significant or meaningless irregularities. (One can find connections in anything and everywhere if one wants and tries hard enough to, some say). I'd needed to uncover more Query Stacks which were structurally, linguistically and theologically similar to the two Query Stacks that I'd already uncovered before I would've felt comfortable stating that Query Stacks were more than curious letter charts and phrases I'd subconsciously contrived. Eventually, I did uncover more Query Stacks, and each said Query Stack not only abided by every QS rule but, also, mirrored structural, linguistical and theological features of "QS-God/Heaven" and "QS-Devil/Hell":

✓ All QS rules followed (see "Appendix A");

Ch. 1, Sec. 3: 1

```
J E S U S
E A R T H
O R I G I N
A N S W E R
```

JOE ASSURE. RIGHT, REIN WANS.

I'd inserted the row'd word EARTH into the "QS-Jesus/Earth" matrix (see "Ch. 1, Sec. 3: 1") because said row'd word named a realm that shared a locational relationship with Heaven and Hell. Biblical verses implied that Earth, and, thus, mankind, existed in a realm that was located in between Heaven and Hell. One verse proposed that Heaven was located over mankind, and, thus, over Earth: "And no man hath <u>ascended up to heaven</u>, but he that <u>came down from heaven</u>, even the Son of man which is in heaven" (John 3:13 KJV [King James Version]). Another verse claimed that Hell was located under mankind, and, thus, below Earth: "The way of life is above to the wise, that he may depart from <u>hell beneath</u>" (Proverbs 15:24 KJV):

HEAVEN: realm above mankind;
EARTH: realm of mankind;
HELL: realm below mankind;

Ch. 1, Sec. 3: 2

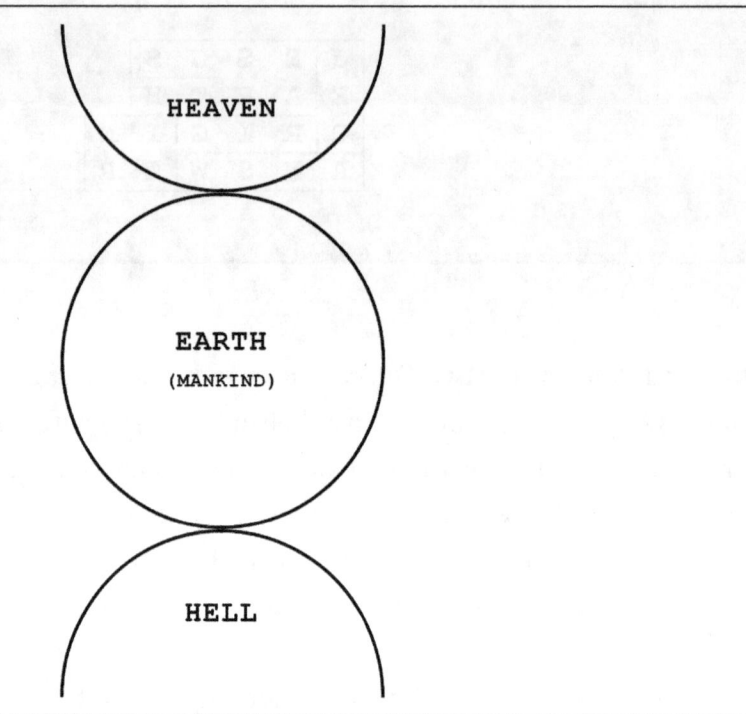

Because of Earth's locational relationship with Heaven and Hell, I'd inserted the row'd word EARTH into the second row of the "QS-Jesus/Earth" row'd word matrix:

(a) HEAVEN; HELL; EARTH: realms related locationally, second-row row'd words;

Ch. 1, Sec. 3: 3

QS-God/Heaven	QS-Devil/Hell	QS-Jesus/Earth
G O D	D E V I L	
"H E A V E N	"H E L L	"E A R T H
O R I G I N	O R I G I N	
A N S W E R	A N S W E R	

I'd dropped the row'd word JESUS into the first row of the "QS-Jesus/Earth" row'd word matrix, because Jesus was a notable biblical character and held earthly preeminence:

(a) GOD; DEVIL; JESUS: notable biblical beings, first row'd word rows;

Ch. 1, Sec. 3: 4

QS-God/Heaven	QS-Devil/Hell	QS-Jesus/Earth
^aG O D	^aD E V I L	^aJ E S U S
H E A V E N	H E L L	E A R T H
O R I G I N	O R I G I N	
A N S W E R	A N S W E R	

My decision to make the name *Jesus* a row'd word was based on a few traits that the row'd word pair "JESUS/EARTH" had and had in common with the row'd word pairs "GOD/HEAVEN" and "DEVIL/HELL." Two traits which the three row'd word pairs had in common were: (1) each of said row'd word pairs consisted of a name of a character in the Bible and each of said row'd word pairs consisted of a name of a realm that said biblical character was commonly paired up with or preeminent in. For example, in the Bible, Jesus was the ultimate king and lord, evidenced by the verse "And <u>he</u> (Jesus) hath on his vesture and on his thigh a name written, <u>King Of Kings,</u> And <u>Lord Of Lords</u>" (Revelations 19:16 KJV), and had preeminent reign on Earth, as evidenced by the verse "And <u>Jesus</u> came and <u>spake unto them</u>, saying, <u>All power is given unto me</u> in heaven and <u>in earth</u>" (Matthew 28:18 KJV):

(a) GOD: notable biblical figure; of Heaven; Heaven's ruler;
(b) DEVIL: notable biblical figure; of Hell; God sends evil to Hell, Devil is evilest being, Devil is evilest being God could send to Hell;
(c) **JESUS: notable biblical figure; of Earth; Earth's premier ruler;**

Ch. 1, Sec. 3: 5

BIBLICAL BEING	DOMAIN	NOTORIETY
^aGOD	^aHEAVEN	^aRULER
^bDEVIL	^bHELL	^bEVILEST RESIDENT
^c**JESUS**	^c**EARTH**	^c**PREMIER RULER**

I'd inserted the row'd word ORIGIN and the row'd word ANSWER into the third and fourth row of the "QS-Jesus/Earth" row'd word matrix, respectively. I'd chosen said row'd words because I'd inserted the same row'd words into the QS matrices which I'd previously revealed in this book:

(a) ORIGIN; ORIGIN; ORIGIN: same words, third-row row'd words;
(b) ANSWER; ANSWER; ANSWER: same words, fourth-row row'd words;

Ch. 1, Sec. 3: 6

QS-God/Heaven	QS-Devil/Hell	QS-Jesus/Earth
G O D	D E V I L	J E S U S
H E A V E N	H E L L	E A R T H
ᵃO R I G I N	ᵃO R I G I N	ᵃO R I G I N
ᵇA N S W E R	ᵇA N S W E R	ᵇA N S W E R

I'd read the "QS-Jesus/Heaven" answer several times, examining said answer's verbal architecture and ascertaining said answer's meaning. During my investigation, I'd pursued the identity of said answer's main subject, the joe. I'd compared four definitions of the word *joe*, attempting to decipher which definition levitated said answer's meaning to an optimal level of sensibleness:

Ch. 1, Sec. 3: 7

*(1, 2, 3, 4)*JOE ASSURE. RIGHT, REIN WANS.

(1) *n.* (slang) Coffee.[2]

(2) *prop-n.* A common nickname for Joseph, also used as a formal male given name.[3]

(3) *prop-n.* A female given name, a form of Joanne or Josephine.[3]

(4) *n.* (slang) Guy.[2]

I'd applied the definition "coffee" to the answer word *JOE*:

⁽¹⁾ JOE: *n.* (slang) Coffee;

Ch. 1, Sec. 3: 8

¹COFFEE ASSURE. RIGHT, REIN WANS.

The "QS-Jesus/Earth" answer's meaning collapsed when I'd applied the definition "coffee" to the answer word JOE, since coffee can't carry out acts of assurance. The definition "coffee," or definition(1), wasn't a useful definition, so I'd eliminated it from my list of definitions for "QS-Jesus/Earth" answer words:

Ch. 1, Sec. 3: 9

~~**(1)** *n.* (slang) Coffee.~~

I'd applied two other definitions to the QS answer word *JOE*. One definition said that *Joe* was a masculine name, while another definition said that *Joe* was a feminine name:

(2) JOE: *prop-n.* a common nickname for *Joseph*, also used as a formal male given name;

(3) JOE: *prop-n.* a female given name, a form of *Joanne* or *Josephine*;

Ch. 1, Sec. 3: 10

A ²BOY/³GIRL NAMED OR NICKNAMED "JOE" ASSURE. RIGHT, REIN WANS.

How will I know which boy with the formal name *Joe* the "QS-Jesus/Earth" answer refers to if I don't know any boys named *Joe* that match the persona of the Joe mentioned in said answer, I'd wondered. How will I be able to identify which Joe is the right Joe out of millions of boys named *Joe* that have lived, are living or are yet to live? As I'd thought more and more about said Joe, I'd realized that finding the right Joe was an insurmountable pursuit. Moreover, I'd been just about as interested in finding Joe as in reading the *Veda*; in other words, not interested at all (see "Ch. 1, Sec. 1: 30-33"). Ultimately, I'd set the "formal name" facet of definition(2) aside due to said definition's unverifiability:

Ch. 1, Sec. 3: 11

(2) *prop-n.* **A common nickname for Joseph,** ~~also used as a formal male given name.~~

I'd reread definitions(2, 3) and focused on the name *Joe* as a nickname for the masculine name *Joseph* and feminine names *Joanne* and *Josephine*. The "nickname" aspect of both definitions grabbed my attention, since a nickname had already emerged as an answer word—the nickname and answer word *DAVE* (see "Ch. 1, Sec. 1: 34"):

(2) JOE: *prop-n.* a common nickname for Joseph;

(3) JOE: *prop-n.* a female given name, a form of Joanne or Josephine;

Ch. 1, Sec. 3: 12

A ²BOY/³GIRL NICKNAMED JOE ASSURE. RIGHT, REIN WANS.

I didn't know of any boy or girl with the nickname *Joe* whose actions would've reinforced the "QS-Jesus/Earth" answer's meaning, so I'd decided to eliminate definitions(2, 3):

Ch. 1, Sec. 3: 13

~~**(2)** *prop. n.* **A common nickname for Joseph, also used as a formal male given name.**~~
~~**(3)** *prop. n.* **A female given name, a form of Joanne or Josephine.**~~

Lastly, I'd applied the slang definition "guy" to the QS answer word *JOE*:

(4) JOE: *n.* (slang) guy;

Ch. 1, Sec. 3: 14

[4]**GUY** ASSURE. RIGHT, REIN WANS.

Definition(4), or "guy," opened up the possibility that the QS answer word *JOE* referenced a guy, "*n.* man; boy; fellow[2]," with an unexposed given name. I'd tried to decipher who the unidentified boy was and what role the unidentified boy played in the "QS-Jesus/Earth" answer's meaning. First, I'd applied a definition to each "QS-Jesus/Earth" answer word:

| *adv* = *adverb* | *adj* = *adjective* |

Ch. 1, Sec. 3: 15

JOE ASSURE. RIGHT, REIN WANS.

JOE *n.* (slang) Guy.[2]
ASSURE *v.* To inform positively.[2]
RIGHT *adv.* According to fact or truth.[2]
REIN *n.* The controlling power.[2]
WANS *v.* <WAN *v.*> To become wan (*adj.* lacking in forcefulness).[1]

After I'd assigned a definition to each "QS-Jesus/Earth" answer word, I'd interpreted the "QS-Jesus/Earth" answer:

Ch. 1, Sec. 3: 16

JOE ASSURE.[sent1] **RIGHT, REIN WANS.**[sent2]

[sent1]: *A boy does inform positively.*
[sent2]: *The truth is, the controlling power becomes lacking in forcefulness.*

I'd analyzed the "QS-Jesus/Earth" answer words next. During my analysis, I'd recalled the mandate stated in the fourth property of "QS-7CAP" ("QS-7CAP, Prop. 4"): the main subject introduced in a QS answer's first sentence is mentioned in the same answer's second sentence. I'd followed the "QS-7CAP, Prop. 4" mandate by unifying the identities of the subjects mentioned in both sentences of the "QS-Jesus/Earth" answer; which meant, the joe was the rein *(joe = rein)*:

JOE; REIN: identities of main subject *(joe = rein)*;

Ch. 1, Sec. 3: 17

`JOE`_{subj} `ASSURE. RIGHT,` `REIN`_{subj} `WANS.`

Since the QS answer words *JOE* and *REIN* identified the same subject, I'd combined their definitions in a reinterpretation of the "QS-Jesus/Earth" answer. Said reinterpretation inferred that the boy who'd informed positively had done so by stating a truth which regarded him as a controlling power who'd become lacking in forcefulness; in other words, the joe who'd assured was the rein who'd wanned:

(a) Answer words, answer word reinterpretations: same individual;

Ch. 1, Sec. 3: 18

`"JOE ASSURE.`_{sent1} `RIGHT, "REIN WANS.`_{sent2}

_{sent1}: *A "(boy) does inform positively.*
_{sent2}: *The truth is, "(the controlling power, who's a boy,) becomes lacking in forcefulness.*

The "QS-Jesus/Earth" answer became grammatically coherent and meaningful, yet I'd wondered if said answer was the best or most meaningful answer that I could've derived from the "QS-Jesus/Earth" row'd word matrix. To measure the validity of my answer, I'd ran it through the "QS-7CAP" test:

Seven Common QS Answer Properties

1. Each answer contains no more and no less than two sentences (sent1, sent2):

QS-God/Heaven

`GO DAVE.`_{sent1} `HE: WINNER; OR, GAINS.`_{sent2}

QS-Devil/Hell

`HORDE: EVIL.`_{sent1} `ILL REIGN, WANS.`_{sent2}

QS-Jesus/Earth

`JOE ASSURE.`_{sent1} `RIGHT, REIN WANS.`_{sent2}

2. Each answer's first sentence contains no more and no less than two words (word1, word2):

QS-God/Heaven

GO$_{word1}$ **DAVE**$_{word2}$. HE: WINNER; OR, GAINS.

QS-Devil/Hell

HORDE$_{word1}$: **EVIL**$_{word2}$. ILL REIGN, WANS.

QS-Jesus/Earth

JOE$_{word1}$ **ASSURE**$_{word2}$. RIGHT, REIN WANS.

3. In each answer's first sentence, the main subject is introduced (subj1, subj2, ...):

QS-God/Heaven

GO **DAVE**$_{subj1}$. HE: WINNER; OR, GAINS.

QS-Devil/Hell

HORDE$_{subj2}$: EVIL. ILL REIGN, WANS.

QS-Jesus/Earth

JOE$_{subj3}$ ASSURE. RIGHT, REIN WANS.

4. In each answer, the main subject introduced in the first sentence is mentioned in the second sentence (subj1-subj1, subj2-subj2, ...):

QS-God/Heaven

GO **DAVE**$_{subj1}$. **HE**$_{subj1}$: WINNER; OR, GAINS.

QS-Devil/Hell

HORDE$_{subj2}$: EVIL. **ILL**$_{subj2}$ REIGN, WANS.

QS-Jesus/Earth

JOE$_{subj3}$ ASSURE. RIGHT, **REIN**$_{subj3}$ WANS.

5. In each answer, the first sentence's second word and the second sentence's first word are synonymous in definition (syn) or context (con):

> *Synonymous answer words are tagged "syn," while answer words which share contextual meaning are tagged "con";*

$^{(con1)}$ DAVE; HE: context, both words identify the same man;
$^{(syn2)}$ EVIL; ILL: synonyms, each word means "wicked";
$^{(con3)}$ ASSURE; RIGHT: context, both words convey affirmation;

QS-God/Heaven

GO **DAVE**$_{con1}$. **HE**$_{con1}$: WINNER; OR, GAINS.

QS-Devil/Hell

HORDE: **EVIL**$_{syn2}$. **ILL**$_{syn2}$ REIGN, WANS.

QS-Jesus/Earth

JOE **ASSURE**$_{con3}$. **RIGHT**$_{con3}$, REIN WANS.

6. In each answer's second sentence, at least one action is applied to the main subject (subj1–act1, subj2–act2, ...):

QS-God/Heaven

GO DAVE. **HE**$_{subj1}$: WINNER; OR, **GAINS**$_{act1}$.

QS-Devil/Hell

HORDE: EVIL. **ILL**$_{subj2}$ **REIGN**$_{act2}$, WANS.

QS-Jesus/Earth

JOE ASSURE. RIGHT, **REIN**$_{subj3}$ **WANS**$_{act3}$.

7. Along each answer's breadth of vocabulary, there's at least one site where an answer letter *S* would've enhanced the answer's grammatical correctness if it had been available in the accompanying row'd word matrix and usable:

> *Removing a colon (:) that follows a noun and appending a contraction 's to the end of said noun would produce a conversational tone and clearer syntax (e.g. <u>He's</u> winner; <u>Horde's</u> evil). Inflecting certain verbs by appending a letter S to their back ends would promote optimal grammar (e.g. Ill <u>reigns</u>; Joe <u>assures</u>). However, each answer's row'd word matrix lacks a letter S that's needed or that's capable of being used in ways mandated by QS rules (see "Appendix A");*

***QS-God/Heaven:** <u>He's</u> winner;*
***QS-Devil/Hell:** <u>Horde's</u> evil, Ill <u>reigns</u>;*
***QS-Jesus/Earth:** Joe <u>assures</u>;*

QS-God/Heaven

GO DAVE. **HE: WINNER**; OR, GAINS.

QS-Devil/Hell

HORDE: EVIL. ILL REIGN, WANS.

QS-Jesus/Earth

JOE ASSURE. RIGHT, REIN WANS.

After I'd seen the "QS-Jesus/Earth" answer pass the "QS-7CAP" test, I'd worked on unveiling said answer's meaning. The first step I'd made to unveil said answer's meaning happened when I'd taken a stab at unveiling the joe's identity. The joe was a boy, a controlling power and became lacking in forcefulness. The description of the joe paralleled the "QS-Devil/Hell" answer's description of the horde. Each main subject, joe or horde, exercised controlling power, became lacking in forcefulness and wasn't identified by name:

(a) HORDE; JOE: unnamed entity; unnamed individual;
(b) REIGN; REIN: exercises controlling power; the controlling power;
(c) WANS; WANS: becomes lacking in forcefulness; becomes lacking in forcefulness;

Ch. 1, Sec. 3: 19

a"**HORDE**: EVIL. ILL *b***REIGN**, *c***WANS**.

An *a*(unnamed crowd of people) *b*(exercises controlling power) and *c*(becomes lacking in forcefulness).

*a***JOE** ASSURE. RIGHT, *b***REIN** *c***WANS**.

An *a*(unnamed individual) who's *b*(the controlling power) *c*(becomes lacking in forcefulness).

If I was to treat the horde and the joe as the same entity, a contradiction would've emerged. On one hand, a horde was a crowd of people; therefore, the horde was comprised of more than one person. On the other hand, the joe was only one person, and, therefore, wasn't a crowd of people. At first, it seemed to me that the horde wasn't the joe. However, after some bouts of contemplation about the horde and the joe, I'd wondered if the joe was a member of the horde:

(a) HORDE; JOE: crowd of unnamed persons; unnamed person in crowd;

Ch. 1, Sec. 3: 20

^a`HORDE: EVIL. ILL REIGN, WANS.`

A ^a(crowd of unnamed persons) exercises controlling power and becomes lacking in forcefulness.

^a`JOE ASSURE. RIGHT, REIN WANS.`

An ^a(unnamed person in the crowd) is a boy, is the controlling power and becomes lacking in forcefulness.

If my interpretation of each QS answer I'd listed in "Ch. 1, Sec. 3: 20" was correct, then information in the "QS-Devil/Hell" answer was assured by the joe mentioned in the "QS-Jesus/Earth" answer; meaning, the horde exercised controlling power and became lacking in forcefulness, while the joe assured that he was a controlling power in the horde and became lacking in forcefulness:

(a) "QS-Devil/Hell";
(b) "QS-Jesus/Earth";

Ch. 1, Sec. 3: 21

^a`HORDE: EVIL. ILL REIGN, WANS.`

The crowd of people is wicked, exercises controlling power and becomes lacking in forcefulness.

^b`JOE ASSURE. RIGHT, REIN WANS.`

A boy in the wicked crowd informs positively on the truth when said boy confirms that he's the controlling power in said crowd and becomes lacking in forcefulness.

Was I wrong to have intertwined my interpretations of the "QS-Jesus/Earth" and "QS-Devil/Hell" answers? Were similar features in said answers' vocabularies hints which had been intentionally constructed and signals for me to combine said answers' meanings or had I coupled and drawn meaning from vocabulary which I'd erroneously intertwined? Did I unveil a dishonest storyline which was contrived by my subconscious imagination or expose a factual narration penned and woven into stacks of words by someone who wasn't me?

To maintain consistency in comparing and interpreting QS answers, I'd decided to pen a composite interpretation which merged my interpretation of the "QS-God/Heaven" answer with the combined interpretation of the "QS-Devil/Hell" and "QS-Jesus/Earth" answers. I was curious if the "QS-God/Heaven" answer's main subject, Dave, was the joe.

In my composite interpretation of the "QS-Devil/Hell" and "QS-Jesus/Earth" answers, I'd determined that there was a boy who was a member in a crowd of people. Similarly, the main subject of the "QS-God/Heaven" answer, Dave, was a boy. The joe and Dave's matching masculine identities persuaded me into melding the "QS-God/Heaven" answer's main subject, Dave, with the boy mentioned in my composite interpretation of the "QS-Devil/Hell" and "QS-Jesus/Earth" answers who was a person in the wicked crowd:

(a) "QS-God/Heaven" answer and interpretation;
(b) "QS-Devil/Hell" answer;
(c) "QS-Jesus/Earth" answer;
(d) Composite interpretation of (b) and (c);

Ch. 1, Sec. 3: 22

^a"GO DAVE. HE: WINNER; OR, GAINS.

^a*Begin an action, David. That male, David, is a success; meaning, David profits.*

^bHORDE: EVIL. ILL REIGN, WANS.

^cJOE ASSURE. RIGHT, REIN WANS.

^d*The crowd of people is wicked, exercises controlling power and becomes lacking in forcefulness. David, a male in said crowd, informs positively on the truth by confirming that he's the controlling power in said crowd and becomes lacking in forcefulness.*

I'd continued to fill in the blank identities of the unnamed members in the crowd mentioned in the "QS-Devil/Hell" answer and the unnamed joe mentioned in the "QS-Jesus/Earth" answer with the known identity of the Dave mentioned in the "QS-God/Heaven" answer. In other words, I'd made Dave a member in the horde who'd made a profit by exercising his controlling power to subjugate people:

(a) "QS-God/Heaven" answer;
(b) "QS-Devil/Hell" answer;
(c) "QS-Jesus/Earth" answer;
(d) Composite interpretation of (a), (b) and (c);

Ch. 1, Sec. 3: 23

^aGO DAVE. HE: WINNER; OR, GAINS.

^bHORDE: EVIL. ILL REIGN, WANS.

^cJOE ASSURE. RIGHT, REIN WANS.

^dBegin an action, David. That male, David, is a success; meaning, David profits. The crowd of people is wicked, exercises controlling power over people and becomes lacking in forcefulness. David, a member of said crowd, informs positively on the truth, or admits that as a winner, or the controlling power in said crowd, he profits by subduing people, but, eventually, David becomes lacking in forcefulness.

To determine if any of my QS answer interpretations were pragmatic, I'd continued to search for more Query Stacks to decipher.

CHAPTER ONE: SECTION FOUR

DAVE/EARTH: ADORE GIVER

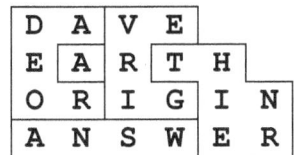

Initially, I'd turned the nickname *Dave* into a row'd word to see if I was able to carve a meaningful answer out of a QS matrix which contained my name. There were two reasons why I'd made the nickname *Dave* instead of the formal name *David* a row'd word: (1) I'd tried but failed to produce a valid QS answer which was derived from a QS matrix that consisted of the row'd word DAVID, and (2) the nickname *Dave* had been already established as valid QS vocabulary by being an answer word in the first sentence of the "QS-God/Heaven" answer:

(a) DAVE: answer word, answer word transposed into row'd word;

Ch. 1, Sec. 4: 1

QS-God/Heaven

GO "**DAVE**. HE: WINNER; OR, GAINS

QS-Dave/Earth

```
"D A V E
 E A R T H
 O R I G I N
 A N S W E R
```

As was the case with the row'd words which occupied the second rows in the "QS-God/Heaven," "QS-Devil/Hell" and "QS-Jesus/Earth" row'd word matrices, the row'd word in the second row of the "QS-Dave/Earth" matrix, EARTH, named a domain which was locationally related to Heaven, Hell and Earth:

(a) EARTH; EARTH: realms related locationally, second row'd word rows;

Ch. 1, Sec. 4: 2

QS-God/Heaven	QS-Devil/Hell	QS-Jesus/Earth	QS-Dave/Earth
G O D	D E V I L	J E S U S	D A V E
H E A V E N	H E L L	"E A R T H	"E A R T H
O R I G I N	O R I G I N	O R I G I N	
A N S W E R	A N S W E R	A N S W E R	

The top row'd word in each of the four QS matrices which I'd uncovered identified a notable biblical character; which meant, the row'd word DAVE didn't refer to me but, instead, referred to the biblical character David.

David was a notable biblical character for several reasons. David was a direct ancestor of Jesus Christ, anointed by God to become the third King of Israel and a receiver of God's rarely declared adoration. According to the Bible, "And when <u>he *(God)*</u> had removed him *(Saul)*, <u>he raised up unto them David to be their king</u>; to whom also he gave their testimony, and said, <u>I *(God)* have found David</u> the son of Jesse, <u>a man after mine own heart, which shall fulfil all my will</u>" (Acts 13:22 KJV):

(a) GOD; DEVIL; JESUS; DAVID: notable biblical beings, first-row row'd words;

Ch. 1, Sec. 4: 3

QS-God/Heaven	QS-Devil/Hell	QS-Jesus/Earth	QS-Dave/Earth
"G O D	**"D E V I L**	**"J E S U S**	**"D A V E**
H E A V E N	H E L L	E A R T H	E A R T H
O R I G I N	O R I G I N	O R I G I N	
A N S W E R	A N S W E R	A N S W E R	

Biblical David was notable on Earth, since David was a direct ancestor of Jesus Christ and was the third king of Israel:

(a) GOD: notable biblical figure; of Heaven; Heaven's ruler;
(b) DEVIL: notable biblical figure; of Hell; God sends evil to Hell, Devil is the evilest being, Devil is evilest being God could send to Hell;
(c) JESUS: notable biblical figure; of Earth; Earth's premier ruler;
(d) **DAVE *(David)*: notable biblical figure; of Earth; third King of Israel;**

Ch. 1, Sec. 4: 4

BIBLICAL BEING	DOMAIN	NOTORIETY
[a]GOD	[a]HEAVEN	[a]RULER
[b]DEVIL	[b]HELL	[b]EVILEST RESIDENT
[c]JESUS	[c]EARTH	[c]PREMIER RULER
[d]DAVE	**[d]EARTH**	**[d]ANOINTED KING**

I'd inserted the row'd word ORIGIN and the row'd word ANSWER into the third and fourth row of the "QS-Dave/Earth" matrix, respectively:

(a) ORIGIN; ORIGIN; ORIGIN; ORIGIN: same words, third-row row'd words;
(b) ANSWER; ANSWER; ANSWER; ANSWER: same words, fourth-row row'd words;

Ch. 1, Sec. 4: 5

QS-God/Heaven	QS-Devil/Hell	QS-Jesus/Earth	QS-Dave/Earth
G O D	D E V I L	J E S U S	D A V E
H E A V E N	H E L L	E A R T H	E A R T H
[a]O R I G I N	[a]O R I G I N	[a]O R I G I N	[a]O R I G I N
[b]A N S W E R	[b]A N S W E R	[b]A N S W E R	[b]A N S W E R

I'd linked adjacent row'd word letters together, in an effort to produce a valid QS answer. Eventually, I'd unveiled a QS answer which was grammatically coherent and meaningful:

✓ All QS rules followed (see "Appendix A");

Ch. 1, Sec. 4: 6

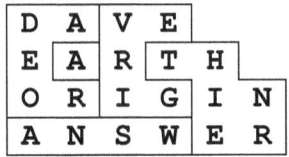

ADORE GIVER. A HINTER WANS.

Next, I'd assigned definitions to the "QS-Dave/Earth" answer words:

| *i-art = independent article* |

Ch. 1, Sec. 4: 7

ADORE GIVER. A HINTER WANS.

ADORE *v.* To worship with profound reverence.[2]
GIVER *n.* One that gives (*v.* to confer the ownership of without receiving a return).[2]
A *i-art.* Used before most singular nouns when the individual in question is unidentified, especially when the individual is being called to notice.[2]
HINTER *n.* One that hints (*v.* brings to mind by allusion rather than explicit expression).[2]
WANS *v.* <WAN *v.*> To become wan (*adj.* lacking in forcefulness).[1]

After I'd assigned a definition to each "QS-Dave/Earth" answer word, I'd penned an interpretation:

Ch. 1, Sec. 4: 8

ADORE GIVER.$_{sent1}$ **A HINTER WANS.**$_{sent2}$

$_{sent1}$: *With profound reverence, worship the person known to confer the ownership of things without receiving a return.*

$_{sent2}$: *A person known for communicating allusive, or inexplicit, messages becomes lacking in forcefulness.*

During my analysis of the "QS-Dave/Earth" answer's vocabulary, I'd abided by the mandate stated in "QS-7CAP, Prop. 4"—the main subject introduced in an answer's first sentence is a subject mentioned in the same answer's second sentence—and unified the identities of the subjects listed in the "QS-Dave/Earth" answer's two sentences; in other words, I'd treated the giver and hinter as the same person *(giver = hinter)*:

GIVER; HINTER: identities of main subject *(giver = hinter)*;

Ch. 1, Sec. 4: 9

ADORE **GIVER**$_{subj}$. A **HINTER**$_{subj}$ WANS.

Since the QS answer words *GIVER* and *HINTER* identified the same subject, I'd combined their definitions in my second interpretation of the "QS-Dave/Earth" answer. Said second interpretation inferred that the person who was known to have conferred ownership of things without receiving a return and should've been worshipped with profound reverence was also the person who communicated allusions and became lacking in forcefulness; in other words, the giver who'd deserved adoration was the hinter who'd wanned:

(a) Answer words, answer word interpretations: identities of main subject;

Ch. 1, Sec. 4: 10

ADORE "GIVER.sent1 **A "HINTER WANS.**sent2

sent1: *With profound reverence, worship the "(generous and selfless person).*

sent2: *The "(generous and selfless person known for expressing allusions) becomes lacking in forcefulness.*

My initial "QS-Dave/Earth" answer was grammatically coherent and meaningful, yet I'd wondered if it was the most meaningful answer that could've been extracted from the "QS-Dave/Earth" row'd word matrix. To validate my answer, I'd ran it through the "QS-7CAP" test:

Seven Common QS Answer Properties

1. Each answer contains no more and no less than two sentences (sent1, sent2):

QS-God/Heaven

GO DAVE.sent1 `HE: WINNER; OR, GAINS.`sent2

QS-Devil/Hell

HORDE: EVIL.sent1 `ILL REIGN, WANS.`sent2

QS-Jesus/Earth

JOE ASSURE.sent1 `RIGHT, REIN WANS.`sent2

QS-Dave/Earth

ADORE GIVER.sent1 `A HINTER WANS.`sent2

2. Each answer's first sentence contains no more and no less than two words (word1, word2):

QS-God/Heaven

GOword1 **DAVE**word2. `HE: WINNER; OR, GAINS.`

QS-Devil/Hell

HORDEword1: **EVIL**word2. `ILL REIGN, WANS.`

QS-Jesus/Earth

JOEword1 **ASSURE**word2. `RIGHT, REIN WANS.`

QS-Dave/Earth

ADOREword1 **GIVER**word2. `A HINTER WANS.`

3. In each answer's first sentence, the main subject is introduced (subj1, subj2, ...):

QS-God/Heaven

GO **DAVE**$_{subj1}$. HE: WINNER; OR, GAINS.

QS-Devil/Hell

HORDE$_{subj2}$: EVIL. ILL REIGN, WANS.

QS-Jesus/Earth

JOE$_{subj3}$ ASSURE. RIGHT, REIN WANS.

QS-Dave/Earth

ADORE **GIVER**$_{subj4}$. A HINTER WANS.

4. In each answer, the main subject introduced in the first sentence is mentioned in the second sentence (subj1-subj1, subj2-subj2, ...):

QS-God/Heaven

GO **DAVE**$_{subj1}$. **HE**$_{subj1}$: WINNER; OR, GAINS.

QS-Devil/Hell

HORDE$_{subj2}$: EVIL. **ILL**$_{subj2}$ REIGN, WANS.

QS-Jesus/Earth

JOE$_{subj3}$ ASSURE. RIGHT, **REIN**$_{subj3}$ WANS.

QS-Dave/Earth

ADORE **GIVER**$_{subj4}$. A **HINTER**$_{subj4}$ WANS.

5. In each answer, the first sentence's second word and the second sentence's first word are synonymous in definition (syn) or context (con):

Synonymous answer words are tagged "syn," while answer words which share contextual meaning are tagged "con";

(con1) DAVE; HE: context, both words identify the same man;

(syn2) EVIL; ILL: synonyms, each word means "wicked";

(con3) ASSURE; RIGHT: context, both words convey affirmation;

(con4) GIVER; [A HINTER]: context, word and [phrase] identify same person; [*Property Deviation Resolution: "A" is the first answer word in the second sentence. "A" doesn't share a synonymous definition or a contextual relationship with the answer word GIVER. The second answer word in the second sentence, HINTER, is an answer word that shares a contextual re-*

lationship with GIVER. "A" is simply acting as a determiner in this case; in other words, calling to notice an unidentified subject that's referred to by the singular noun HINTER. "A" serves no function other than to reinforce HINTER as a singular subject; in fact, "A" could be removed from the answer without affecting the answer's meaning—"a hinter wans" means the same thing as "hinter wans." Based on my analysis, I've determined that if "A" is the first word in the second sentence of a QS answer and is a determiner for a noun that's in the second position of the second sentence of said QS answer, then the "A" and noun that "A" modifies can be bracketed and treated as one answer word.];

QS-God/Heaven

GO **DAVE**$_{con1}$. **HE**$_{con1}$: WINNER; OR, GAINS.

QS-Devil/Hell

HORDE: **EVIL**$_{syn2}$. **ILL**$_{syn2}$ REIGN, WANS.

QS-Jesus/Earth

JOE **ASSURE**$_{con3}$. **RIGHT**$_{con3}$, REIN WANS.

QS-Dave/Earth

ADORE **GIVER**$_{con4}$. **[A HINTER]**$_{con4}$ WANS.

6. In each answer's second sentence, at least one action is applied to the main subject (subj1–act1, subj2–act2, ...):

QS-God/Heaven

GO DAVE. **HE**$_{subj1}$: WINNER; OR, **GAINS**$_{act1}$.

QS-Devil/Hell

HORDE: EVIL. **ILL**$_{subj2}$ **REIGN**$_{act2}$, WANS.

QS-Jesus/Earth

JOE ASSURE. RIGHT, **REIN**$_{subj3}$ **WANS**$_{act3}$.

QS-Dave/Earth

ADORE GIVER. A **HINTER**$_{subj4}$ **WANS**$_{act4}$.

7. Along each answer's breadth of vocabulary, there's at least one site where an answer letter *S* would've enhanced the answer's grammatical correctness if it would've been available in the accompanying row'd word matrix and usable:

Removing a colon (:) that follows a noun and appending a contraction 's to the end of said noun would produce a conversational tone and clearer syntax (e.g. <u>He's</u> winner; <u>Horde's</u> evil). Inflecting certain verbs by appending a letter S to the end of them would promote optimal grammar (e.g. Ill <u>reigns</u>; Joe <u>assures</u>). However, each answer's row'd word matrix lacks a letter S that's needed or that's capable of being used in ways mandated by QS rules (see "Appendix A");

[Property Deviation Resolution: No grammatically incorrect syntax can be found within the "QS-Dave/Earth" answer's vocabulary. Optimal vocabulary contains no grammatical mistakes. If a QS answer doesn't contain missing letters in its vocabulary, then the vocabulary of said QS answer is grammatically optimal and therefore acceptable.];

QS-God/Heaven: <u>He's</u> winner;
QS-Devil/Hell: <u>Horde's</u> evil, Ill <u>reigns</u>;
QS-Jesus/Earth: Joe <u>assures</u>;
QS-Dave/Earth: (optimal grammar);

QS-God/Heaven
```
GO DAVE. HE: WINNER; OR, GAINS.
```
QS-Devil/Hell
```
HORDE: EVIL. ILL REIGN, WANS.
```
QS-Jesus/Earth
```
JOE ASSURE. RIGHT, REIN WANS.
```
QS-Dave/Earth
```
ADORE GIVER. A HINTER WANS.
```

After I'd ran the "QS-Dave/Earth" answer through "QS-7CAP" and recorded said answer's two property deviations, I'd pursued solutions to four question which I'd posed and hoped were going to help me unveil the "QS-Dave/Earth" answer's meaning:

Questions to Ask a Hint Giver—Question 1
What was the giver/hinter known to be a giver of?

Questions to Ask a Hint Giver—Question 2
Which hints did the giver/hinter express?

Questions to Ask a Hint Giver—Question 3
Why did the giver/hinter deserve adoration?

Questions to Ask a Hint Giver—Question 4
How did the giver/hinter wan?

Questions to Ask a Hint Giver—Question 1
What was the giver/hinter known to be a giver of?

The "QS-Dave/Earth" answer's main subject was identified as a giver, yet the "QS-Dave/Earth" answer didn't explicitly express what said subject was a giver of. However, said subject was deemed a hinter, or "a giver of hints," in said answer's second sentence. Based on a compound characterization of said subject, as in *"giver + hinter = hint giver,"* I'd determined that said subject was a giver because said subject was a giver of hints:

Ch. 1, Sec. 4: 11

If—main subject is a *giver*, or *one that gives*,
And—main subject is a *hinter*, or *one that gives hints*,
Then—main subject is a *hint giver*, or *one that gives hints*.

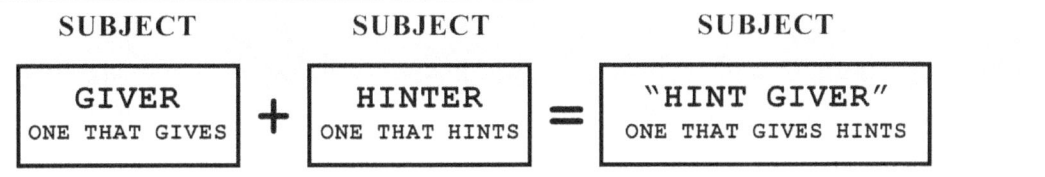

Questions to Ask a Hint Giver—Question 2
Which hints did the giver/hinter express?

The "QS-Dave/Earth" answer didn't specify which hints the hint giver was known to have been a giver of, so I'd reasoned out a determination on my own:

> If each QS answer which I'd uncovered up until this point was a hint that was meant to help inch me closer to an understanding of God's origin, then each said QS answer was a hint that the hint giver had given:

Ch. 1, Sec. 4: 12

If—*hint giver* is *one that gives hints*,
And—*QS answers* are *hints pertaining to God's origin*,
Then—*hint giver* is the *giver of QS answers*.

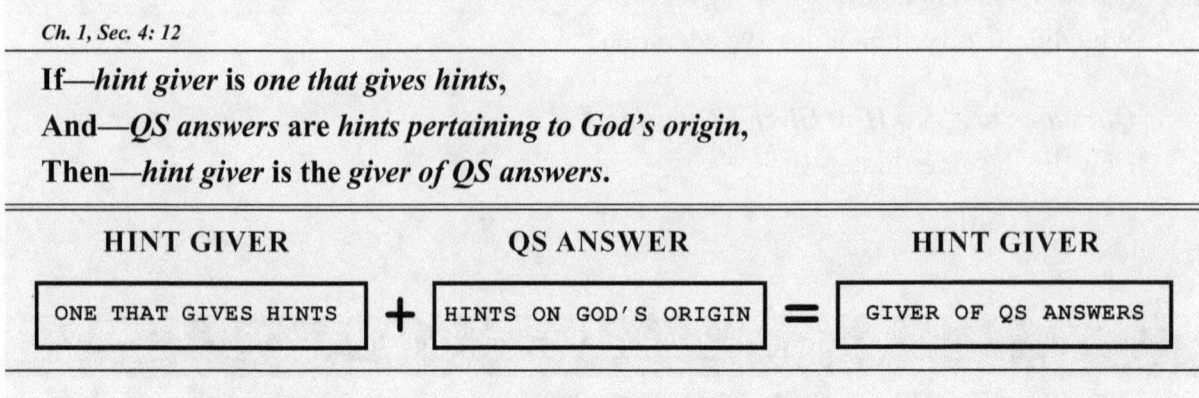

Questions to Ask a Hint Giver—Question 3
Why did the giver/hinter deserve adoration?

The message expressed by the "QS-Dave/Earth" answer's first sentence was a request for people to grace the hint giver with adoration but didn't say why people should grace said hint giver with adoration; nevertheless, I'd made my own determination:

> Via QS answers, the giver provided hints which alluded to God's origin. The hint giver penned QS answers in a human language and entangled QS answers within specific vocabulary with no human awareness, consent or participation. If the hint giver constructed QS answers and embedded QS answers which conveyed knowledge concerning God's origin in a human language, then, arguably, the hint giver would've been able to design said human language and may've known or was God, I'd surmised.

> If the hint giver was the author of Query Stacks and was God, then God, the hint giver, must've intentionally wrote Her/Himself into the "QS-Dave/Earth" answer as said answer's main subject; which meant, God intentionally authored said QS answer's phrase *"adore giver"* to solicit idolization for Her/Himself.

> By definition, a giver wouldn't of received anything in return for the offering said giver handed out; thus, God wasn't trying to receive adoration in an exchange for hints. However, God might've been trying to receive adoration for nothing but Her/His intrinsic godliness, an attribute which God couldn't separate from Her/Himself even if God tried to give it away. In fact, biblical text said that God demanded to be adored for Her/His intrinsic godliness: "<u>Thou shalt have no other gods before me. Thou shalt not bow down thyself to them nor serve them</u>: for I the Lord thy God am a jealous God, visiting the iniquity of the fathers upon on the children unto the third and fourth generation of them that hate me; And

shewing mercy unto thousands of them that love me, and keep my commandments. Thou shalt not take the name of the Lord thy God in vain; for the Lord will not hold him guiltless that taketh his name in vain" (Exodus 20:3, 5-7 KJV):

Ch. 1, Sec. 4: 13

ADORE GIVER.

Revere the one and only God for Her/His inherent godliness.

Questions to Ask a Hint Giver—Question 4
How did the giver/hinter wan?

In accordance with "QS Guide 3"—actions mentioned in a QS answer affect the QS answer's main subject,—I'd determined that the main subjects of the "QS-Devil/Hell" and "QS-Jesus/Earth" answers were who'd wanned; in other words, each said subject suffered a weakening in the capability to exert forcefulness:

(a) Main subject becomes lacking in forcefulness;
(b) Main subject becomes lacking in forcefulness;

Ch. 1, Sec. 4: 14

QS-Devil/Hell

^a**ILL** REIGN, ^a**WANS.**

^a*(An evil becomes lacking in forcefulness).*

QS-Jesus/Earth

RIGHT, ^b**REIN** ^b**WANS.**

^b*(The controlling power becomes lacking in forcefulness).*

Once again, I'd followed "QS Guide 3" in order to maintain consistency in my interpretation of QS answers by identifying the main subject of the "QS-Dave/Earth" answer as who'd wanned; in other words, I'd pinned down God, the hint giver, as the one who'd became lacking in a capability to exert forcefulness:

(a) Main subject becomes lacking in forcefulness;
(b) Main subject becomes lacking in forcefulness;
(c) Main subject becomes lacking in forcefulness;

Ch. 1, Sec. 4: 15

QS-Devil/Hell
[a]ILL REIGN, [a]WANS.
[a]*(The evil becomes lacking in forcefulness).*

QS-Jesus/Earth
RIGHT, [b]REIN [b]WANS.
[b]*(The controlling power becomes lacking in forcefulness).*

QS-Dave/Earth
A [c]HINTER [c]WANS.
[c]*(The giver of allusions becomes lacking in forcefulness).*

After I'd determined that God was who'd wanned, I strove to answer how God had wanned. To determine how God wanned, I'd continued to compare vocabulary in the "QS-Dave/Earth" answer to vocabulary in the "QS-Devil/Hell" and "QS-Jesus/Earth" answers.

In "Ch. 1, Sec. 3: 19-21," I'd explained why *JOE* (QS-Jesus/Earth) and *HORDE* (QS-Devil/Hell) were two answer words which didn't identify the same subject yet might've identified two subjects which were closely related to one another; specifically, I'd reasoned that the joe wasn't the horde but was a horde member. A reason why I'd thought that the joe and horde shared a close affiliation was because phrases in each subject's corresponding QS answer contained similar details about the corresponding answer's subject. I'd believed that the QS author, God, the hint giver, purposefully devised said similar details to steer readers into merging the identities of the joe and horde and assigning said merged identity to a single subject.

While I was analyzing the "QS-Dave/Earth" answer, I'd realized that the main subject mentioned in said answer reflected three characteristics of the joe and horde: (1) each of the three subjects weren't identified by a proper name; (2) each of the three subjects had either exercised controlling power, was the controlling power or requested reverent adoration (as controlling powers do to brainwash and bend unacclimatized people towards agendas); and, (3) each of the three subjects became lacking in forcefulness:

(a) HORDE; JOE; HINTER: unnamed persons; unnamed person; unnamed person;
(b) REIGN; REIN; ADORE: exercises controlling power; the controlling power; requests reverence (as controlling powers do);
(c) WANS; WANS; WANS: becomes lacking in forcefulness; becomes lacking in forcefulness; becomes lacking in forcefulness;

Ch. 1, Sec. 4: 16

QS-Devil/Hell

^a**HORDE: EVIL. ILL** ^b**REIGN,** ^c**WANS.**

An ^a*(unnamed crowd) of people* ^b*(exercises controlling power) and* ^c*(becomes lacking in forcefulness).*

QS-Jesus/Earth

^a**JOE ASSURE. RIGHT,** ^b**REIN** ^c**WANS.**

An ^a*(unnamed boy) who's* ^b*(the controlling power)* ^c*(becomes lacking in forcefulness).*

QS-Dave/Earth

^b**ADORE GIVER. A** ^a**HINTER** ^c**WANS.**

^b*(Revere)* ^a*(the person who shares allusions) and* ^c*(becomes lacking in forcefulness).*

If the hint giver was God (which I've already rationalized that the hint giver was [see "Question 3"]) and the joe, then, in turn, God was the joe *(God = joe)*:

Ch. 1, Sec. 4: 17

If—hint giver is God,
And—hint giver is joe,
Then—God is joe.

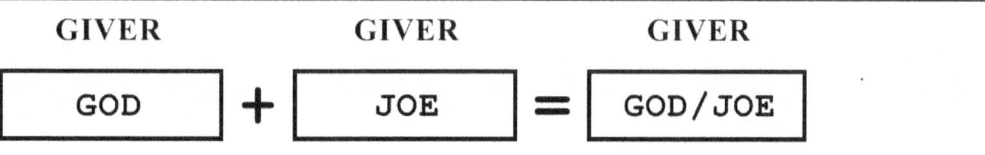

If God was the joe and the joe was a horde member (which I'd already shown that the joe was [see "Ch. 1, Sec. 3: 20"]), then God was a member of the horde:

Ch. 1, Sec. 4: 18

If—God is joe,
And—joe is in horde,
Then—God is in horde.

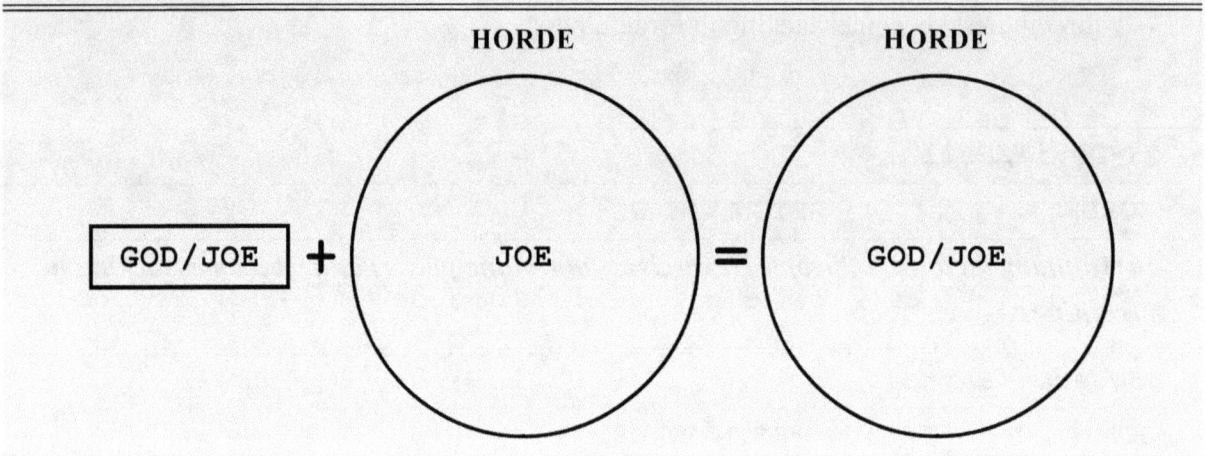

Is there a horde which God is already known to be a member of, I'd wondered. As I'd mulled over my question, an idea about the Trinity surfaced in my mind:

Trinity *prop-n.* the union of three persons or hypostases (as the Father [God], the Son [Jesus], and the Holy Spirit [Holy Ghost]) in one godhead so that all the three are one God as to substance but three persons or hypostases as to individuality.[2]"

In simpler terms, God, Jesus and Holy Ghost were three individuals who were capable of functioning individually but were facets of one entity named *Trinity*. Each of the three individuals was a conduit which God and only God could express ~~Her~~/ Himself through—(in "Ch. 1, Sec. 4: 17," I'd determined that God was the joe; which meant, God was a boy, since the definition of the word *joe* was "guy; boy; man; fellow[2]")—and use to interact with and affect Reality:

Ch. 1, Sec. 4: 19

If—God is one-third of Trinity,
And—Jesus is one-third of Trinity,
And—Holy Ghost is one-third of Trinity,
Then—God, Jesus and Holy Ghost complete Trinity.

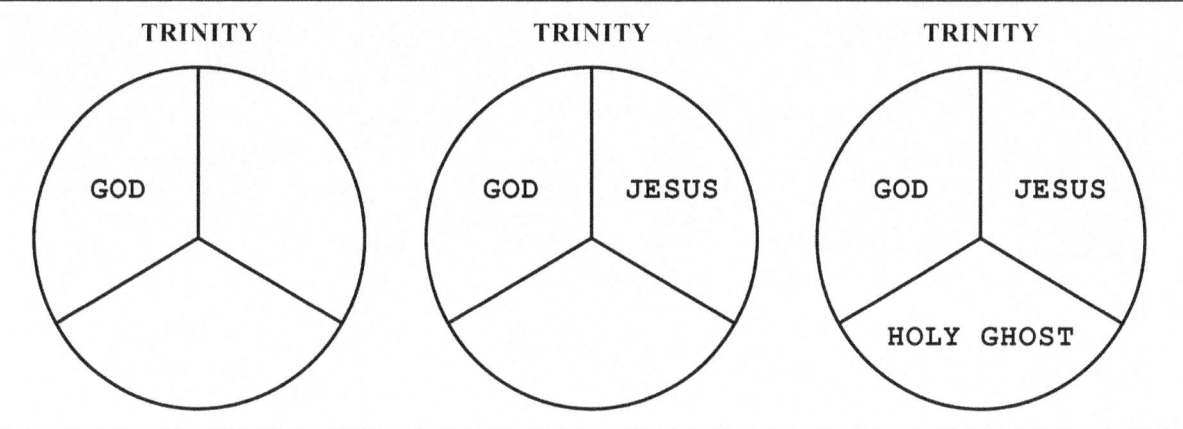

By definition, the horde mentioned in the "QS-Devil/Hell" answer was multiple individuals who were gathered together in one place and shared a common goal. Likewise, God's Trinity was multiple individuals who were gathered together in one place and shared a common goal:

Ch. 1, Sec. 4: 20

If—horde is crowd,
And—Trinity is crowd,
Then—horde is Trinity.

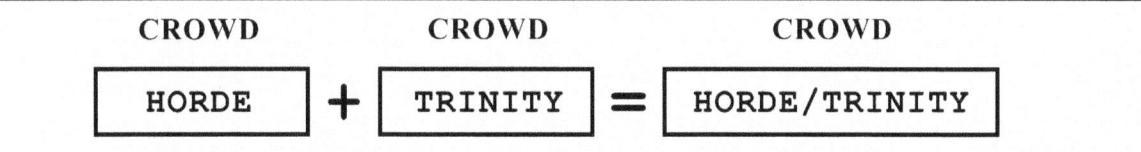

Up until now, I'd determined that the joe was a member in an unnamed horde. However I'd also determined that the joe was God and that God was a member in a horde named *Trinity*. Since the joe and God were the same individual, the horde which God was a member of, the Trinity, was the same horde which joe was a member of:

Ch. 1, Sec. 4: 21

If—joe is in horde,
And—God is in Trinity,
And—joe is God,
Then—God/joe is in Trinity-horde.

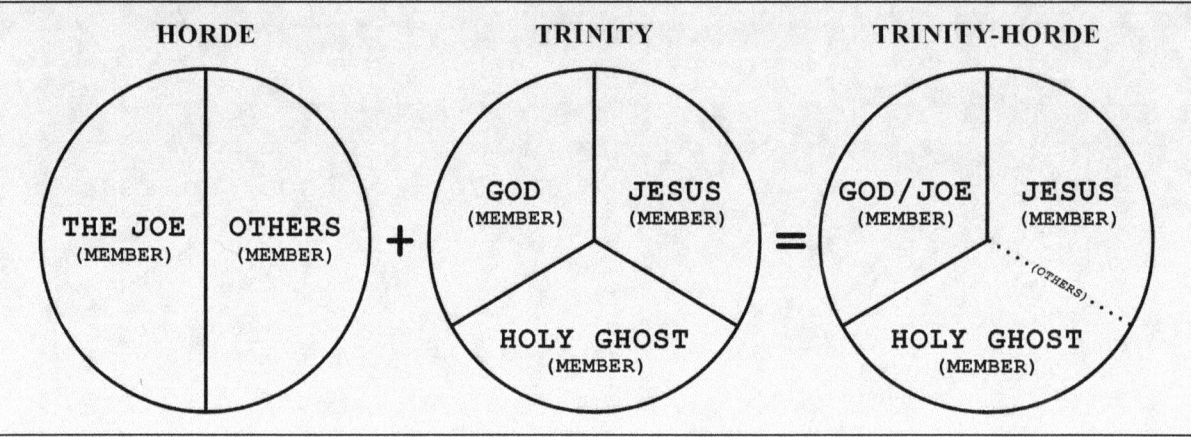

If the horde was an evil, as the "QS-Devil/Hell" answer phrase *"horde: evil"* had stated, and the Trinity was said horde (see "Ch. 1, Sec. 4: 21"), then the Trinity was an evil horde:

Ch. 1, Sec. 4: 22

If—horde is evil,
And—Trinity is horde,
Then—Trinity is evil horde.

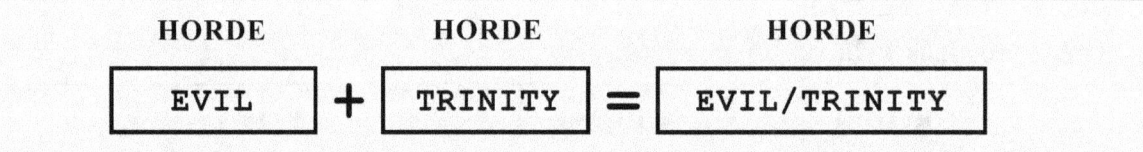

Based on my theological ignorance, I'd believed that characterizing the Trinity as an evil entity contradicted the biblical doctrine of God's omnibenevolence, or infinite goodness. However, a verse in the Bible quoted an assertion made by God in which God said that instead of just being the creator of peace, He'd also made evil. Moreover, God insisted that He was the only god who'd ever existed; thus, no one possessed the necessary hierarchical status and creative power to override God's will or invent evil:

"I am the LORD, and there is none else, there is no God beside me: I girded thee, though thou hast not known me: That they may know from the rising of the sun, and from the west, that there is none beside me. I am the LORD, and there is none else. I form the light, and create darkness: <u>I make peace</u>, and <u>create evil</u>: <u>I the LORD do all these things</u>" (Isaiah 45:5-7 KJV).

Based on God's quote in "Isaiah 45:5-7," the Trinity was membered by God, an individual who'd invented both good and evil and, therefore, could wield good and evil:

Ch. 1, Sec. 4: 23

If—God is good and is in horde named *Trinity*,
And—God is evil and is in horde named *Trinity*,
Then—Trinity-horde is good and evil.

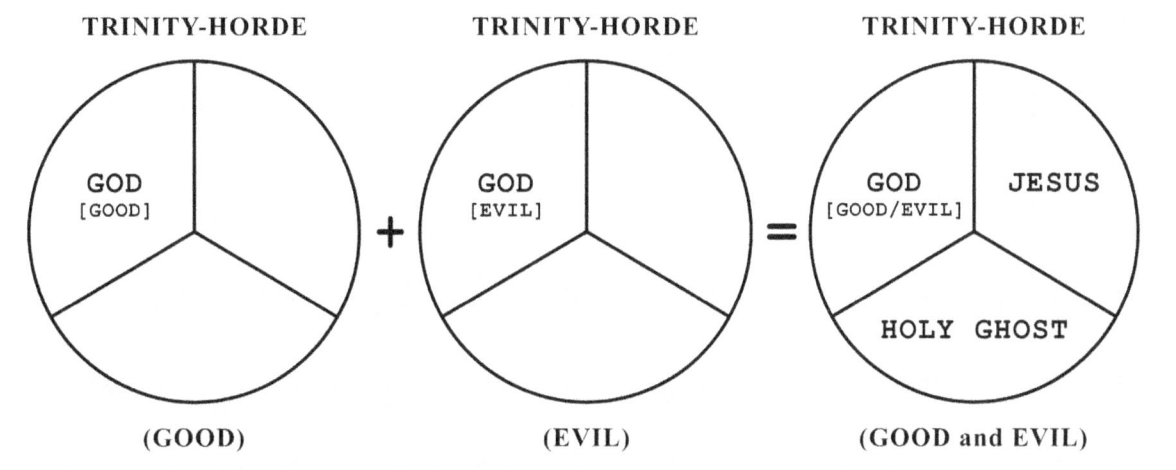

Even though the Trinity was comprised of three individual members, each individual member was a conduit which God could use to interact with Reality. The essential element which constituted each Trinity member was God's essence, therefore God guided every action that each Trinity member expressed. God was each member of the Trinity; therefore, the names *God* and *Trinity* were synonymous and interchangeable:

Ch. 1, Sec. 4: 24

If—God is God in Trinity,
And—God is Jesus in Trinity,
And—God is Holy Ghost in Trinity,
Then—God is Trinity.

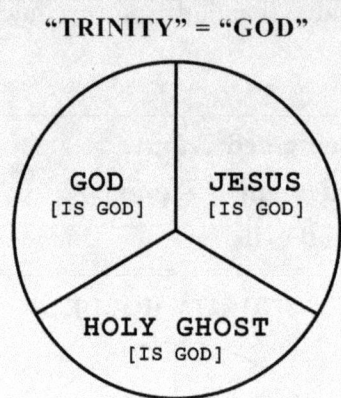

Based on six biblical verses, I'd determined that absolute goodness was the strongest moral force while absolute evilness was the weakest moral force. In the first of said biblical verses, God declared that He'd held the highest hierarchical position in Reality:

> "For my thoughts are not your thoughts, neither are your ways my ways, saith the Lord. For as the heavens are higher than the earth, so are my ways higher than your ways, and my thoughts than your thoughts" (Isaiah 55:8-9 KJV).

The second biblical verse claimed that God was able to exert absolute goodness:

> "Every good gift and every perfect gift is from above, and cometh down from the Father of lights, with whom is no variableness, neither shadow of turning" (James 1:17 KJV).

The third biblical verse claimed that God unconditionally exerted absolute goodness upon every person which He'd created by providing sustenance to each person regardless of each person's moral leanings:

> "That ye may be the children of your Father which is in heaven: for he maketh his sun to rise on the evil and on the good, and sendeth rain on the just and on the unjust" (Matthew 5:45 KJV).

The fourth biblical verse stated that God rewarded people who'd expressed goodness but disengaged from people who'd thrived on evil:

> "Behold therefore the goodness and severity of God: on them which fell, severity; but toward thee, goodness, if thou continue in his goodness: otherwise thou also shalt be cut off" (Romans 11:22 KJV).

The fifth biblical verse insinuated that the moral strength of goodness was stronger than the moral strength of evilness because said verse instructed people to exert goodness in order to counteract evilness:

> "Be not overcome of evil, but overcome evil with good" (Romans 12:21 KJV).

The sixth biblical verse solidified the notion that the moral strength of goodness was stronger than the moral strength of evilness:

> "The evil bow before the good; and the wicked at the gates of the righteous" (Proverbs 14:19 KJV).

In summary, God created a spectrum of morality which encompassed a range from absolute goodness to absolute evilness. God created beings which committed actions that were measured against said moral spectrum. Regardless of which gradient in said moral spectrum a person expressed themselves from, God provided said person with sustenance; however, God rewarded people who'd exerted goodness and abandoned people who'd exercised evilness. The reason God reinforced goodness was because goodness had a stronger position than evilness within God's moral spectrum. If a person exerted goodness, then said person's moral force was strong. However, if a person exercised evilness, then said person's moral force became weak, or wanned.

Based on my summation and in my estimation, God not only created but also exercised evil. When God exerted goodness, God, and therefore the Trinity, was morally strong. But, when God exercised evilness, God, and therefore the Trinity, became morally weak, or wanned:

Ch. 1, Sec. 4: 25

First—Trinity-horde exerts good,
Next—Trinity-horde exerts evil,
Result—Trinity-horde's good force wans.

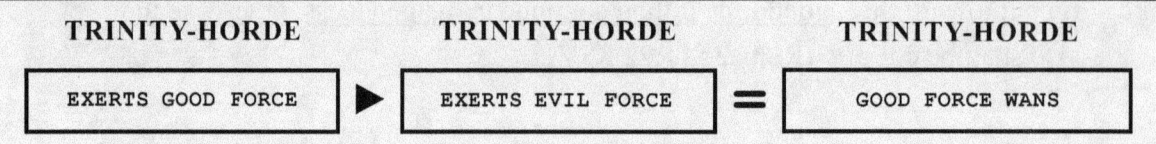

When the "QS-Devil/Hell" answer stated that the horde/ill had wanned, it meant that the horde named *Trinity* had wanned because God had exercised evilness. Similarly, when the "QS-Jesus/Earth" and "QS Dave/Earth" answers stated that the joe/rein and giver/hinter, respectively, had wanned, both answers declared that God, who was joe/rein, giver/hinter and the Trinity, had wanned because God had expressed evilness:

(a) "QS-Devil/Hell": main subject identifies Trinity;
(b) "QS-Jesus/Earth": main subject identifies Trinity/God;
(c) "QS-Dave/Earth": main subject identifies Trinity/God;

Ch. 1, Sec. 4: 26

QS-Devil/Hell

^a**HORDE**: EVIL. ^a**ILL** REIGN, ^a**WANS**.

^a*(Trinity, the wicked entity, becomes lacking in forcefulness).*

QS-Jesus/Earth

^b**JOE** ASSURE. RIGHT, ^b**REIN** ^b**WANS**.

^b*(Trinity, the controlling power, becomes lacking in forcefulness).*

QS-Dave/Earth

ADORE ^c**GIVER**. A ^c**HINTER** ^c**WANS**.

^c*(Trinity, the selfless provider of allusions, becomes lacking in forcefulness).*

What evil actions did God commit which caused His moral force to wan?

CHAPTER ONE: SECTION FIVE

REVIEW: FOUR STACKS

G	O	D		
H	E	A	V	E	N
O	R	I	G	I	N
A	N	S	W	E	R

D	E	V	I	L
H	E	L	L	
O	R	I	G	I	N
A	N	S	W	E	R

J	E	S	U	S
E	A	R	T	H
O	R	I	G	I	N
A	N	S	W	E	R

D	A	V	E	
E	A	R	T	H
O	R	I	G	I	N
A	N	S	W	E	R

Each of the four Query Stacks I'd unmasked up until this point in this book was comprised of a matrix of neatly aligned rows and columns which contained equidistantly spaced letters that spelt four vertically stacked row'd words. Row'd words which composed each one of the four unique matrices shared theological and linguistical relationships with row'd words in the same matrix and in each of the other three matrices. Each vertically stacked set of four row'd words posed a unique question when said set of row'd words were read from top to bottom row'd word. I'd linked together adjacent row'd word letters in accordance with stern letter-connection rules (see "Appendix A") in an attempt to construct QS answer words that formed an answer for said question. I'd removed QS answer words from each row'd word matrix in a top-left to bottom-right direction and laid out said answer words in a linear sequence and in the same chronological order which I'd removed said answer words from said answer words' corresponding row'd word matrix. I'd incorporated punctuation into said linear sequence of answer words, in order to elucidate each QS answer's grammatical coherency and showcase each QS answer's meaning. I'd ran each QS answer through "QS-7CAP" in order to verify the validity of each QS answer's grammatical structure and, in turn, each QS answer's meaning.

Consider the particular and exact rules which were mandated by the eleven QS rules that I'd unfurled. QS rules didn't provide me with much or any room at all to bend row'd words and row'd word letters towards a solution which I'd desired or expected:

Ch. 1, Sec. 5: 1

QUERY STACK CONSTRUCTION RULES

Rule 1—Determine a question;

Rule 2—Reduce the question's vocabulary to key words;

Rule 3—Stack key words in an order which causes the question to be asked if rowed key words are read downwards;

Rule 4—Align the first letter of each row'd word into one column;

Rule 5—Align subsequent letters of row'd words into subsequent columns.

QUERY STACK DECRYPTION RULES

Rule 6—Each and every row'd word letter must appear in a useful answer word;

Rule 7—Each row'd word letter must appear in the answer no more and no less than one time;

Rule 8—Row'd word letters can only be connected horizontally and/or vertically;

Rule 9—Letters in a set of connected row'd word letters can be arranged in any order to make an answer word;

Rule 10—Words built from connected row'd word letters are removed in a top-left to bottom-right sequence and listed in the order of removal to make a legitimate answer;

Rule 11—A word produced by linking row'd word letters together must be removed from a row'd word matrix and listed in the answer no more and no less than one time.

Furthermore, I'd adhered to the syntactical mandates of "QS-7CAP" to compose coherent, meaningful QS answers:

Ch. 1, Sec. 5: 2

SEVEN COMMON QUERY STACK ANSWER PROPERTIES

Prop. 1—Each answer contains no more and no less than two sentences;

Prop. 2—Each answer's first sentence contains no more and no less than two words;

Prop. 3—In each answer's first sentence, the main subject is introduced;

Prop. 4—In each answer, the main subject introduced in the first sentence is mentioned in the second sentence;

Prop. 5—In each answer, the first sentence's second word and the second sentence's first word are similar in definition (synonym) or context (context); one property deviation (*"A + [noun]"*; phrase perceived as one word);

Prop. 6—In each answer's second sentence, at least one action is applied to the main subject;

Prop. 7—Along each answer's breadth of vocabulary, there's at least one site where an answer letter *S* would've enhanced the answer's grammatical correctness if it would've been available in the accompanying row'd word matrix and usable; one property deviation (*"no missing letter S"*; perfect grammar).

I'd formulated a symbological template for "QS-7CAP," and named said template the "QS-7CAP Formula":

Ch. 1, Sec. 5: 3

QS-7CAP FORMULA

$[1^{(:)}]_{(*)} \quad [2^{(\sim 3)(:)}]_{(*)} \,.\quad [3^{(\sim 2)(:)}]_{(*)(>)} \quad [4^{(:)}]_{(*)(>)} \quad \{+ \quad [\#^{(:)}]_{(*)(>)}\}\,.$

An explanation for each symbol in the "QS-7CAP Formula" follows:

A QS answer must contain no more and no less than two sentences:

Each "." is a sentence;

Ch. 1, Sec. 5: 4

. .

A QS answer's first sentence must contain no more and no less than two words:

"[#]" represents a word;

Ch. 1, Sec. 5: 5

`[1] [2]. .`

`GO`[1] `DAVE`[2]` . .`

At least one word in the first sentence of a QS answer must identify said answer's main subject:

"∗" signifies that the word "∗" is linked to must identify the main subject; If the "∗" is enclosed by "( )", then the word that "(∗)" is linked to doesn't necessarily have to identify the answer's main subject;

Ch. 1, Sec. 5: 6

`[1]`(∗)` [2]`(∗)`. .`

`GO DAVE`∗`.`

The main subject introduced in the first sentence of a QS answer must be mentioned in said answer's second sentence:

Each word "∗" is attached to in an answer identifies said answer's main subject;

Ch. 1, Sec. 5: 7

`GO DAVE`∗`. HE`∗`.`

In a QS answer, the first sentence's second word and the second sentence's first word must be synonymous in definition or context:

"[~#]" denotes congruency in definition or context between two answer words;

Ch. 1, Sec. 5: 8

`[1]`(∗)` [2~3]`(∗)`. [3~2]`(∗)`.`

`GO DAVE`(HE)∗`. HE`(DAVE)∗`.`

In a QS answer's second sentence, at least one action must be applied to the main subject:

">" is linked to a word which must depict an action associated to the answer's

main subject; if the ">" is enclosed by "( )", then that means that the word which "(>)" is linked to doesn't necessarily have to depict an action associated with the answer's main subject;

Ch. 1, Sec. 5: 9

[1] (*) [2~3] (*) . [3~2] (*) (>) [4] (*) (>) .

GO DAVE (HE) * . HE (DAVE) * : WINNER * ; OR, GAINS > .

A QS answer's second sentence must contain at least two words but may contain more than two words:

"{+ [#]}" signifies that an undefined number of answer words might follow the second word in an answer's second sentence;

Ch. 1, Sec. 5: 10

[1] (*) [2~3] (*) . [3~2] (*) (>) [4] (*) (>) {+ [#] (*) (>) } .

Some QS answer words may not contain an *S* or *'s* at the end of their spellings:

":"is linked to a word which is missing an S or 's; if ":" is enclosed by "( )", then that means that the word which "(:)" is linked to doesn't necessarily have to be missing an S or 's;

Ch. 1, Sec. 5: 11

[1 (:)] (*) [2~3 (:)] (*) . [3~2 (:)] (*) (>) [4 (:)] (*) (>) {+ [# (:)] (*) (>) } .

Three guides led me to and made me feel comfortable with my interpretation of each of the four QS answers I'd revealed so far:

Guide 1—A Query Stack's best answer is a Query Stack's most coherent, meaningful answer;

Guide 2—A Query Stack's most coherent, meaningful answer is comprised of vocabulary which pertains to no more and no less than one subject, the main subject;

Guide 3—Actions mentioned in a QS answer affect the QS answer's main subject;

Ch. 1, Sec. 5: 12

QUERY STACK INTERPRETATION GUIDES
Guide 1—The best QS answer is a Query Stack's most coherent, meaningful answer.
Guide 2—Vocabulary in a QS answer pertains to the QS answer's main subject.
(QS-God/Heaven)—David Mivshek is the Dave to Go and is the He who's the Winner or Gains.
(QS-Devil/Hell)—Trinity is the Horde that's Evil and is the Ill which does Reign and Wans.
(QS-Jesus/Earth)—God is the Joe who does Assure and is the Rein which Wans.
(QS-Dave/Earth)—God is the Giver one should Adore and is a Hinter who Wans.
Guide 3—Actions declared in a QS answer affect the QS answer's main subject;
(QS-God/Heaven)—Dave is the main subject to Go and that Gains.
(QS-Devil/Hell)—Horde is the main subject that does Reign and Wans.
(QS-Jesus/Earth)—Joe is the main subject who does Assure and Wans.
(QS-Dave/Earth)—Giver is the main subject one should Adore and who Wans.

Eventually, I'd compiled a table of QS answer words. The table contained three tiers, and each tier was a distinct category: "David Mivshek," "Trinity" or "God." Each said tier contained QS answer words which were derived from QS answers that had a main subject which reflected the who or what that the name of the tier which I'd placed said QS answer words into identified. For example, I'd placed the QS answer word *ADORE* into the "God" tier, because the answer word *ADORE* was in a QS answer in which a giver was the QS answer's main subject and said giver was God:

A parenthetic number (#) succeeding a distinct answer word reports how many times said answer word appears in QS answers that may or may not share a distinct main subject but have main subjects which refer either to David Mivshek, Trinity or God;

[a] "QS-God/Heaven" answer words: "David Mivshek" tier, Dave is main subject, Dave is David Mivshek;

[b] "QS-Devil/Hell" answer words: "Trinity" tier, horde is main subject, horde is Trinity;

[c] "QS-Jesus/Earth" answer words: "God" tier, joe is main subject, joe is God;

[d] "QS-Dave/Earth" answer words: "God" tier, giver is main subject, giver is God;

Ch. 1, Sec. 5: 13

DAVID MIVSHEK
Nouns—*ᵃ*Winner;
Proper Nouns—*ᵃ*Dave;
Pronouns—*ᵃ*He;
Verbs—*ᵃ*Gains, *ᵃ*Go;
Conjunctions—*ᵃ*Or.
TRINITY
Nouns—*ᵇ*Evil, *ᵇ*Horde, *ᵇ*Ill;
Verbs—*ᵇ*Reign, *ᵇ*Wans.
GOD
Nouns—*ᵈ*Giver, *ᵈ*Hinter, *ᶜ*Joe, *ᶜ*Rein;
Verbs—*ᵈ*Adore, *ᶜ*Assure, *⁽ᶜ, ᵈ⁾*Wans (2);
Adverbs—*ᶜ*Right;
Indefinite Articles—*ᵈ*A.

I'd created the log of answer words and main subject categories in "Ch. 1, Sec. 5: 13" to answer two questions. The first question was:

1. If a distinct answer word appears in multiple answers, will each occurrence of said answer word always fall within one and the same tier of the three tiers in the "Ch. 1, Sec. 5: 13" table?

For instance, I'd found the answer word *ASSURE* in a QS answer in which the main subject, the joe, was God; therefore, I'd wondered if I'd only find the answer word *ASSURE* in QS answers which contained main subjects who identified as God?

In each of two QS answers, the answer word *WANS* denoted an action that a distinct main subject endured. One main subject was a horde named *Trinity*, while the other main subject was a giver named *God*. Therefore, an answer word which appeared in multiple answers was permitted to be associated with multiple main subjects. However, was the answer word *WANS* a special case because the two main subjects which the answer word *WANS* was linked to, horde and giver, cited the same entity, God/Trinity *(God = God, God = Trinity)*?

A parenthetic number (#) succeeding a distinct answer word reports how many times said answer word appears in QS answers that may or may not share a distinct main subject but have main subjects which refer either to David Mivshek, Trinity or God;

(a) WANS: "Trinity" tier and "God" tier, linked to two main subjects (horde, giver);

Ch. 1, Sec. 5: 14

DAVID MIVSHEK

Nouns—Winner;
Proper Nouns—Dave;
Pronouns—He;
Verbs—Gains, Go;
Conjunctions—Or.

TRINITY

Nouns—Evil, Horde, Ill;
Verbs—Reign, *ᵃWans*.

GOD

Nouns—Giver, Hinter, Joe, Rein;
Verbs—Adore, Assure, *ᵃWans* (2);
Adverbs—Right;
Indefinite Articles—A.

The second question was:

2. **Does an answer word which identifies an individual and appears in multiple answers always identify one and the same individual no matter who the main subject in each said answer is?**

   For instance, if the answer word *HE* denoted David Mivshek in one QS answer, did that mean that the answer word *HE* denoted David Mivshek in every QS answer, even if said answer word was in a QS answer which had a main subject that didn't identify as David Mivshek? Did the answer word *GIVER* only and always denote God? Did the answer word *HORDE* only and always denote the Trinity?

   (I wasn't able to answer my second question, since I hadn't yet uncovered any answer words which identified an individual and appeared in multiple QS answers.)

I'd logged more data which pertained to Query Stacks; such as: number of answer words and answer word letters per each QS answer, average number of letters in an answer word per each QS answer and total number of answer words and answer word letters integrated into a group of QS answers. I didn't know if my statistics held significance, but I'd felt that it was a good idea to maintain said statistics in case I'd needed said statistics downstream. Maybe, unexpected relationships or repetitious ratios would eventually emerge:

Ch. 1, Sec. 5: 15

QS-GOD/HEAVEN
GO DAVE. HE: WINNER; OR, GAINS.
Number of QS answer words—6
Number of QS answer letters—21
Average number of letters per answer word—3.50

QS-DEVIL/HELL
HORDE: EVIL. ILL REIGN, WANS.
Number of QS answer words—5
Number of QS answer letters—21
Average number of letters per answer word—4.20

QS-JESUS/EARTH
JOE ASSURE. RIGHT, REIN WANS.
Number of QS answer words—5
Number of QS answer letters—22
Average number of letters per answer word—4.40

QS-DAVE/EARTH
ADORE GIVER. A HINTER WANS.
Number of QS answer words—5
Number of QS answer letters—21
Average number of letters per answer word—4.20

QUERY STACK TOTALS AND AVERAGES
Total number of QS answers—4
Total number of QS answer words—21
Total number of QS answer letters—85
Average number of letters per QS answer—21.25
Average number of words per QS answer—5.25

Average number of letters per answer word—4.05

How many QS matrices will I need to transpose into coherent, meaningful phrases before I can confidently conclude that Query Stacks are nothing less than legit, objective phenomena, I'd wondered. If Query Stacks are real, how did Query Stacks become woven into language? Are Query Stacks a byproduct of happenchance or an intentional integration conceived and implemented by someone other than me? Thousands of years ago, did our human ancestors intentionally make human language multilateral and predetermine that someone in a subsequent generation would unveil said multilateral levels of human language? If ancient humans devised a blueprint of and evolution for a language entangled with secret messages and knew that someone who was going to be born thousands of years later would find the messages, then said ancient humans achieved a level of linguistical intelligence and time domination which contemporary linguists and physicists haven't yet detected, unearthed, observed, recognized, reported on or possessed. Did a nonhuman being which predated humankind gift humankind with a language that was interwoven with esoteric messages and was preprogrammed to evolve and unfold within humans as humans evolved?

I thought of the question "What's God of Heaven's origin?" and then had a vision of a preliminary Query Stack which emerged autonomously in my mind. Said Query Stack matured as I'd constructed and decoded said Query Stack in accordance with construction and decryption rules and interpretation guides. Compelled by my vision's revelation and how rigid all of the rules which defined and propelled the Query Stack process were, I'd leaned onto the belief that Query Stacks were conceived and authored by a nonhuman being and weren't the result of whimsical happenchance or a linguistical ruse implemented by ancient humans.

After I'd produced the four QS answers I'd uncovered so far in this book, I'd realized that the only QS question which held significance was the "QS-God/Heaven" question, "'God/Heaven's origin?' answer?" Hints to help me answer the "QS-God/Heaven" question weren't conveyed through only the "QS-God/Heaven" answer but were conveyed through the other three QS answers as well. Based on the uselessness of QS questions which weren't the "QS-God/Heaven" question, I'd decided to not print QS questions associated with any other QS matrix in this book. By eliminating the breakdown and explanation of new QS questions in subsequent chapters, I'd decreased my book's word-count, which, in turn, made my book a quicker read:

- ✓ **Each subsequent QS matrix contains a group of row'd words which asks a unique question when read from top to bottom row'd word; however, I've stopped showing QS questions derived from any subsequent row'd word matrices revealed in this book.**

CHAPTER TWO: SECTION ONE

JOE/EARTH: HINT GREW

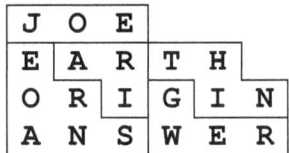

In "Ch. 1, Sec. 4: 1," I'd transposed the QS answer word *DAVE* into a row'd word and then I'd inserted the row'd word DAVE into the first row of a QS matrix. As an answer word, the nickname *Dave* identified a nonbiblical figure named *David*, but as a row'd word, the nickname *Dave* signified a biblical character named *David*. I'd decided I'd use the same steps which I'd used to change the answer word *DAVE* into a first-row row'd word in order to change the answer word *JOE* into a first-row row'd word; therefore, when I'd transposed the answer word *JOE* into the first-row row'd word JOE, I'd switched out the answer word's nonbiblical meaning "guy" for the row'd word's meaning "nickname for the name *Joseph*." JOE was an acceptable row'd word, because Joseph was a prominent biblical figure:

(a) DAVE: answer word, answer word transposed into row'd word;
(b) JOE: answer word, answer word transposed into row'd word;

Ch. 2, Sec. 1: 1

QS-God/Heaven

GO ^a**DAVE**. HE: WINNER; OR, GAINS.

QS-Jesus/Earth

^b**JOE** ASSURE. RIGHT, REIN WANS.

QS-Dave/Earth	*QS-Joe/Earth*
^aD A V E	^bJ O E
E A R T H	E A R T H
O R I G I N	O R I G I N
A N S W E R	A N S W E R

Joseph was a prominent biblical figure, just like all of the other biblical figures whose names occupied the first rows of the row'd word matrices unraveled heretofore:

(a) GOD; DEVIL; JESUS; DAVE *(David)*; JOE *(Joseph)*: notable biblical characters, first-row row'd words;

Ch. 2, Sec. 1: 2

QS-God/Heaven	QS-Devil/Hell	QS-Jesus/Earth	QS-Dave/Earth
"G O D	"D E V I L	"J E S U S	"D A V E
H E A V E N	H E L L	E A R T H	E A R T H
O R I G I N	O R I G I N	O R I G I N	O R I G I N
A N S W E R	A N S W E R	A N S W E R	A N S W E R

QS-Joe/Earth
"J O E
E A R T H
O R I G I N
A N S W E R

Biblically, Joseph was a prominent character and human being on Earth. Joseph was notably known as the husband of Virgin Mary (Jesus's mother):

(a) GOD: notable biblical figure; of Heaven; Heaven's ruler;
(b) DEVIL: notable biblical figure; of Hell; God sends evil to Hell, Devil is the evilest being, Devil is evilest being God could send to Hell;
(c) JESUS: notable biblical figure; of Earth; Earth's premier ruler;
(d) DAVE *(David)*: notable biblical figure; of Earth; third King of Israel;
(e) **JOE *(Joseph)*: notable biblical figure; of Earth; Virgin Mary's husband;**

Ch. 2, Sec. 1: 3

BIBLICAL BEING	**DOMAIN**	**NOTORIETY**
[a]GOD	[a]HEAVEN	[a]RULER
[b]DEVIL	[b]HELL	[b]EVILEST RESIDENT
[c]JESUS	[c]EARTH	[c]PREMIER RULER
[d]DAVE *(David)*	[d]EARTH	[d]ANOINTED KING
[e]JOE *(Joseph)*	**[e]EARTH**	**[e]MARY'S HUSBAND**

I'd inserted the row'd word ORIGIN and the row'd word ANSWER into the third and fourth row of the "QS-Joe/Earth" matrix, respectively:

(a) ORIGIN; ORIGIN; ORIGIN; ORIGIN; ORIGIN: same words, third-row row'd words;
(b) ANSWER; ANSWER; ANSWER; ANSWER; ANSWER: same words, fourth-row row'd words;

Ch. 2, Sec. 1: 4

QS-God/Heaven	QS-Devil/Hell	QS-Jesus/Earth	QS-Dave/Earth
G O D	D E V I L	J E S U S	D A V E
H E A V E N	H E L L	E A R T H	E A R T H
^{a}O R I G I N	^{a}O R I G I N	^{a}O R I G I N	^{a}O R I G I N
^{b}A N S W E R	^{b}A N S W E R	^{b}A N S W E R	^{b}A N S W E R

QS-Joe/Earth
J O E
E A R T H
^{a}O R I G I N
^{b}A N S W E R

I'd linked adjacent row'd word letters together in an effort to produce a valid QS answer. Eventually, I'd uncovered an answer that was grammatically coherent and meaningful:

    ✓ All QS rules followed (see "Appendix A");

Ch. 2, Sec. 1: 5

JOE: REASON. AIR/HINT GREW.

Next, I'd assigned definitions to the "QS-Joe/Earth" answer words:

Ch. 2, Sec. 1: 6

JOE: REASON. AIR/HINT GREW.

JOE *n.* **(slang) Guy.**[2]

REASON *n.* **A statement offered as an explanation of an assertion.**[2]

AIR *n.* **Public utterance (*n.* an oral or written statement).**[2]

HINT *n.* **A statement conveying by implication what it is preferred not to say explicitly.**[2]

GREW *v.* **<GROW *v.*> To increase in any way.**[2]

After I'd assigned a definition to each answer word, I'd composed an interpretation:

Ch. 2, Sec. 1: 7

```
JOE: REASON.sent1 AIR/HINT GREW.sent2
```
sent1: *A boy has made a statement regarding an explanation for an assertion.*
sent2: *A public statement conveying an allusive message increased.*

My initial "QS-Joe/Earth" answer was grammatically coherent and meaningful, yet I'd wondered if it was the most meaningful answer which could've been derived from said answer's corresponding row'd word letter matrix—"QS Guide 1" suggested that the best QS answer is a Query Stack's most coherent, meaningful answer. I ran it through "QS-7CAP" to challenge said answer's validity:

Seven Common QS Answer Properties

1. Each answer contains no more and no less than two sentences (sent1, sent2):

QS-God/Heaven
```
GO DAVE.sent1 HE: WINNER; OR, GAINS.sent2
```
QS-Devil/Hell
```
HORDE: EVIL.sent1 ILL REIGN, WANS.sent2
```
QS-Jesus/Earth
```
JOE ASSURE.sent1 RIGHT, REIN WANS.sent2
```
QS-Dave/Earth
```
ADORE GIVER.sent1 A HINTER WANS.sent2
```
QS-Joe/Earth
```
JOE: REASON.sent1 AIR/HINT GREW.sent2
```

2. Each answer's first sentence contains no more and no less than two words (word1, word2):

QS-God/Heaven

GO_{word1} **DAVE**_{word2}. HE: WINNER; OR, GAINS.

QS-Devil/Hell

HORDE_{word1}: EVIL_{word2}. ILL REIGN, WANS.

QS-Jesus/Earth

JOE_{word1} ASSURE_{word2}. RIGHT, REIN WANS.

QS-Dave/Earth

ADORE_{word1} **GIVER**_{word2}. A HINTER WANS.

QS-Joe/Earth

JOE_{word1}: REASON_{word2}. AIR/HINT GREW.

3. In each answer's first sentence, the main subject is introduced (subj1, subj2, ...):

QS-God/Heaven

GO **DAVE**_{subj1}. HE: WINNER; OR, GAINS.

QS-Devil/Hell

HORDE_{subj2}: EVIL. ILL REIGN, WANS.

QS-Jesus/Earth

JOE_{subj3} ASSURE. RIGHT, REIN WANS.

QS-Dave/Earth

ADORE **GIVER**_{subj4}. A HINTER WANS.

QS-Joe/Earth

JOE: REASON_{subj5}. AIR/HINT GREW.

4. In each answer, the main subject introduced in the first sentence is mentioned in the second sentence (subj1-subj1, subj2-subj2, ...):

QS-God/Heaven

GO **DAVE**~subj1~. **HE**~subj1~: WINNER; OR, GAINS.

QS-Devil/Hell

HORDE~subj2~: EVIL. **ILL**~subj2~ REIGN, WANS.

QS-Jesus/Earth

JOE~subj3~ ASSURE. RIGHT, **REIN**~subj3~ WANS.

QS-Dave/Earth

ADORE **GIVER**~subj4~. A **HINTER**~subj4~ WANS.

QS-Joe/Earth

JOE: **REASON**~subj5~. **AIR**~subj5~/HINT GREW.

5. In each answer, the first sentence's second word and the second sentence's first word are synonymous in definition (syn) or context (con):

   Synonymous answer words are tagged "syn," while answer words which share contextual meaning are tagged "con";

   (con1) DAVE; HE: context, both words identify the same man;
   (syn2) EVIL; ILL: synonyms, each word means "wicked";
   (con3) ASSURE; RIGHT: context, both words convey affirmation;
   (con4) GIVER; [A HINTER]: context, word and [phrase] identify same person; *[Property Deviation Resolution: (see "Appendix B")];*
   (con5) REASON; AIR: context, the reason is expressed as a written statement;

QS-God/Heaven

GO **DAVE**~con1~. **HE**~con1~: WINNER; OR, GAINS.

QS-Devil/Hell

HORDE: **EVIL**~syn2~. **ILL**~syn2~ REIGN, WANS.

QS-Jesus/Earth

JOE **ASSURE**~con3~. **RIGHT**~con3~, REIN WANS.

QS-Dave/Earth

ADORE **GIVER**~con4~. **[A HINTER]**~con4~ WANS.

QS-Joe/Earth

JOE: **REASON**~con5~. **AIR**~con5~/HINT GREW.

6. In each answer's second sentence, at least one action is applied to the main subject (subj1–act1, subj2–act2, ...):

QS-God/Heaven

GO DAVE. **HE**$_{subj1}$: WINNER; OR, **GAINS**$_{act1}$.

QS-Devil/Hell

HORDE: EVIL. **ILL**$_{subj2}$ **REIGN**$_{act2}$, WANS.

QS-Jesus/Earth

JOE ASSURE. RIGHT, **REIN**$_{subj3}$ **WANS**$_{act3}$.

QS-Dave/Earth

ADORE GIVER. A **HINTER**$_{subj4}$ **WANS**$_{act4}$.

QS-Joe/Earth

JOE: REASON. **AIR**$_{subj5}$/HINT **GREW**$_{act5}$.

7. Along each answer's breadth of vocabulary, there's at least one site where an answer letter *S* would've enhanced the answer's grammatical correctness if it would've been available in the accompanying row'd word matrix and usable:

   Removing a colon (:) that follows a noun and appending a contraction 's to the end of said noun would produce a conversational tone and clearer syntax (e.g. <u>He's</u> winner; <u>Horde's</u> evil). Removing a colon (:) that follows a noun and appending a possessive 's to the end of said noun would produce a conversational tone and clearer syntax (e.g. <u>Joe's</u> reason). Inflecting certain verbs by appending a letter S to the end of them would promote optimal grammar (e.g. Ill <u>reigns</u>; Joe <u>assures</u>). However, each answer's row'd word matrix lacks a letter S that's needed or that's capable of being used in ways mandated by QS rules (see "Appendix A");

   [Property Deviation Resolution (see "Appendix B"): "QS-Dave/Earth"];

   QS-God/Heaven: <u>He's</u> *winner;*
   QS-Devil/Hell: <u>Horde's</u> *evil, Ill <u>reigns</u>;*
   QS-Jesus/Earth: *Joe <u>assures</u>;*
   QS-Dave/Earth: *(optimal grammar);*
   QS-Joe/Earth: <u>Joe's</u> *reason;*

QS-God/Heaven

GO DAVE. HE: WINNER; OR, GAINS.

QS-Devil/Hell

HORDE: EVIL. ILL REIGN, WANS.

QS-Jesus/Earth

JOE ASSURE. RIGHT, REIN WANS.

QS-Dave/Earth

ADORE GIVER. A HINTER WANS.

QS-Joe/Earth

JOE: REASON. AIR/HINT GREW.

After the answer passed the "QS-7CAP" test, I'd studied its vocabulary and worked on unraveling its meaning. First, I'd compared the vocabularies of the "QS-Jesus/Earth" and "QS-Joe/Earth" answers, since both answers contained the answer word *JOE*:

(a) JOE: common answer word;

Ch. 2, Sec. 1: 8

QS-Jesus/Earth Answer

"JOE ASSURE. RIGHT, REIN WANS.

QS-Joe/Earth Answer

"JOE: REASON. AIR/HINT GREW.

I'd assigned the definition "*n.* (slang) guy; (boy; man; fellow)" to each answer word *JOE*:

(a) JOE: answer word means "guy";
(b) JOE: answer word means "guy";

Ch. 2, Sec. 1: 9

QS-Jesus/Earth Answer
ᵃ(JOE) ASSURE. RIGHT, REIN WANS.
QS-Jesus/Earth Interpretation
A ᵃ(boy) informs positively on a truth.
QS-Joe/Earth Answer
ᵇ(JOE): REASON. AIR/HINT GREW.
QS-Joe/Earth Interpretation
A ᵇ(boy) has made a statement regarding an explanation for an assertion.

In each answer's first sentence, a joe, or boy, affirmed that something was true or gave an explanation which conveyed why he'd believed that something was true:

(a) JOE: informs positively on a truth;
(b) JOE: explains why an assertion is true;

Ch. 2, Sec. 1: 10

QS-Jesus/Earth Answer
JOE *ᵃ(ASSURE).* RIGHT, REIN WANS.
QS-Jesus/Earth Interpretation
A boy ᵃ(informs positively on a truth).
QS-Joe/Earth Answer
JOE: *ᵇ(REASON).* AIR/HINT GREW.
QS-Joe/Earth Interpretation
A boy has made ᵇ(a statement regarding an explanation for an assertion).

By "Ch. 1, Sec. 4: 18," I'd determined that the joe was God, and, therefore, God was a boy:

(a) JOE: is boy, is God;
(b) JOE: is boy, is God;

Ch. 2, Sec. 1: 11

QS-Jesus/Earth Answer
^a(JOE) ASSURE. RIGHT, REIN WANS.
QS-Jesus/Earth Interpretation
^a(God, a boy), informs positively on a truth.
QS-Joe/Earth Answer
^b(JOE): REASON. AIR/HINT GREW.
QS-Joe/Earth Interpretation
^b(God, a boy), has made a statement regarding an explanation for an assertion.

Based on the similar vocabularies and meanings shared by the first sentences of the "QS-Jesus/Earth" and "QS-Joe/Earth" answers, I'd deduced that the assertion which declared God as the controlling power who'd become lacking in forcefulness and which God assured was true was the same assertion that God gave an explanation for:

(a) The joe's, or God's, assertion;
(b) The joe's, or God's, explanation for assertion;

Ch. 2, Sec. 1: 12

QS-Jesus/Earth Answer
^a(JOE ASSURE. RIGHT, REIN WANS).
QS-Jesus/Earth Interpretation
^a(God informs positively on a truth. Said truth is that God, the controlling power, becomes lacking in forcefulness).
QS-Joe/Earth Answer
^b(JOE: REASON). AIR/HINT GREW.
QS-Joe/Earth Interpretation
^b(God has made a statement regarding an explanation for why He'd asserted that He'd became lacking in forcefulness).

In the "QS-Jesus/Earth" answer, the QS author, God, assured that He was the controlling power who'd wanned, while in the "QS-Joe/Earth" answer, God said that His explanation for how He'd wanned was conveyed as an allusive statement that He'd made and increased in some way:

(a) The joe's, or God's, statement that conveyed His explanation for His assertion increased;

Ch. 2, Sec. 1: 13

JOE: REASON. *"(AIR/HINT GREW).*

"(God's explanation, in which He'd assured that He'd became lacking in forcefulness, was concealed within a publicized but allusive statement and increased in some way).

As was determined in "Ch. 1, Sec. 4: 12," hints, or allusions, that God was known as a giver of were written as QS answers; which meant, God's explanation for how He'd became less forceful as a controlling power was written as an allusive QS answer. In "Ch. 2, Sec. 1: 14," I'd determined that an allusive explanation which hinted about God's wanning was aired, or publicized, as a QS answer and had grown, or increased, when God added more words to His explanation:

(a) The joe's, or God's, QS answer containing an explanation for His assertion increased;

Ch. 2, Sec. 1: 14

JOE: REASON. *"(AIR/HINT GREW).*

God's explanation, in which God assured that He'd became lacking in forcefulness, was concealed within "(a publicized, allusive QS answer that became wordier as God increased the number of details in said explanation).

CHAPTER TWO: SECTION TWO

MARY/EARTH: MARRY REASON

M	A	R	Y		
E	A	R	T	H	
O	R	I	G	I	N
A	N	S	W	E	R

A nickname or proper name of a biblical character who'd shared a familial bond with Virgin Mary occupied the first row in four out of the five QS matrices I'd revealed in this book so far. The only biblical character who didn't occupy a branch of Virgin Mary's family tree was the Devil:

Some of the biblical names which I've listed in the diagram belong in Virgin Mary's lineage but aren't QS row'd words (e.g. "Bathsheba," "Solomon," "Nathan") yet elucidate how some biblical characters with names that are QS row'd words are related;

SOLID LINE (——) = Genealogically linked to Mary;
DASHED LINE (– – –) = Father of Mary's son Jesus, via no sexual contact;
DASHED/DOTTED LINE (– ·· –) = Mary's husband, but not Jesus's father;
DOUBLE LINE (====) = Not genealogically linked to Mary;
BLACK NAME BOX **NAME** = Row'd word, and main focus of family tree;
GRAY NAME BOX *NAME* = Row'd word, and member of family tree;
WHITE NAME BOX NAME = Row'd word, but not a member of family tree;
UNBOXED NAME = Not a row'd word, but member of family tree;

(a) MARY: herself;
(b) JOE *(Joseph)*: Mary's husband;
(c) DAVE *(David)*: Mary's multi-great-grandfather;
(d) JESUS: Mary's son;
(e) GOD: Mary's spiritual co-parent;
(f) DEVIL: God's antipode;

Ch. 2, Sec. 2: 1

QS-God/Heaven	*QS-Devil/Hell*	*QS-Jesus/Earth*	*QS-Dave/Earth*
G O D	**D E V I L**	**J E S U S**	**D A V E**
H E A V E N	H E L L	E A R T H	E A R T H
O R I G I N	O R I G I N	O R I G I N	O R I G I N
A N S W E R	A N S W E R	A N S W E R	A N S W E R

QS-Joe/Earth

J O E
E A R T H
O R I G I N
A N S W E R

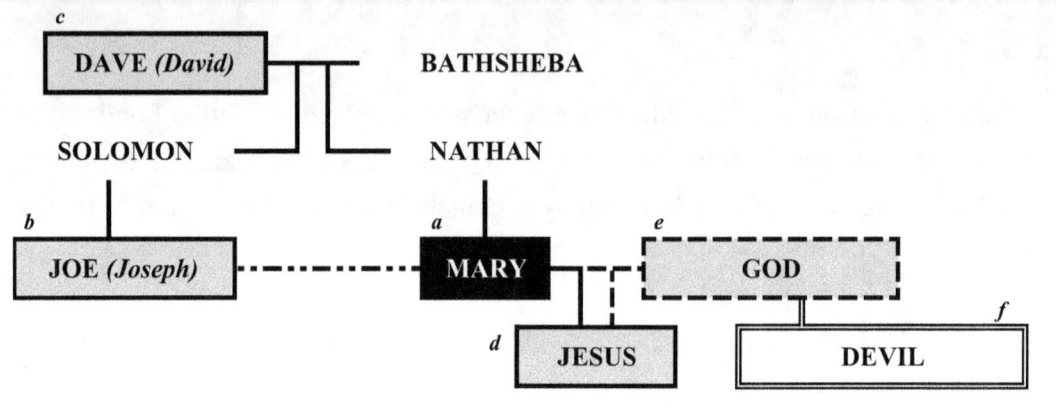

I'd decided to construct a QS matrix in which Mary's name occupied the said matrix's first row, since Mary had family ties to most of the people whose names occupied the first rows of the QS matrices I'd revealed in this book so far:

[a] MARY: first-row row'd word;

Ch. 2, Sec. 2: 2

[a]**M A R Y**
E A R T H
O R I G I N
A N S W E R

Mary was a prominent biblical character and human being on Earth, because Mary was Jesus Christ's biological mother:

(a) GOD: notable biblical figure; of Heaven; Heaven's ruler;

(b) DEVIL: notable biblical figure; of Hell; God sends evil to Hell, Devil is the evilest being, Devil is evilest being God could send to Hell;

(c) JESUS: notable biblical figure; of Earth; Earth's premier ruler;

(d) DAVE *(David)*: notable biblical figure; of Earth; third King of Israel;

(e) JOE *(Joseph)*: notable biblical figure; of Earth; Virgin Mary's husband;

(f) **MARY: notable biblical figure; of Earth; Jesus's mother;**

Ch. 2, Sec. 2: 3

BIBLICAL BEING	DOMAIN	NOTORIETY
[a]GOD	[a]HEAVEN	[a]RULER
[b]DEVIL	[b]HELL	[b]EVILEST RESIDENT
[c]JESUS	[c]EARTH	[c]PREMIER RULER
[d]DAVE *(David)*	[d]EARTH	[d]ANOINTED KING
[e]JOE *(Joseph)*	[e]EARTH	[e]MARY'S HUSBAND
[f]**MARY**	[f]**EARTH**	[f]**JESUS'S MOTHER**

I'd inserted the row'd word ORIGIN and the row'd word ANSWER into the third and fourth row of the "QS-Mary/Earth" matrix, respectively:

(a) ORIGIN; ORIGIN; ORIGIN; ORIGIN; ORIGIN; ORIGIN: same words, third-row row'd words;

(b) ANSWER; ANSWER; ANSWER; ANSWER; ANSWER; ANSWER: same words, fourth-row row'd words;

Ch. 2, Sec. 2: 4

QS-God/Heaven	QS-Devil/Hell	QS-Jesus/Earth	QS-Dave/Earth
G O D	D E V I L	J E S U S	D A V E
H E A V E N	H E L L	E A R T H	E A R T H
[a]O R I G I N	[a]O R I G I N	[a]O R I G I N	[a]O R I G I N
[b]A N S W E R	[b]A N S W E R	[b]A N S W E R	[b]A N S W E R

QS-Joe/Earth	QS-Mary/Earth		
J O E	M A R Y		
E A R T H	E A R T H		
[a]O R I G I N	[a]O R I G I N		
[b]A N S W E R	[b]A N S W E R		

I'd linked adjacent letters in the "QS-Mary/Earth" row'd word matrix together, in an attempt to produce a valid QS answer. Eventually, I'd uncovered an answer which was grammatically coherent and meaningful:

✓ All QS rules followed (see "Appendix A");

Ch. 2, Sec. 2: 5

```
M A R Y
E A R T H
O R I G I N
A N S W E R
```

MARRY REASON. A HINT, I GREW.

Next, I'd assigned definitions to the "QS-Mary/Earth" answer words:

Ch. 2, Sec. 2: 6

MARRY REASON. A HINT, I GREW.

MARRY *v.* To unite in close and usually permanent relation.[2]
REASON *n.* A statement offered as an explanation of an assertion.[2]
A *i-art.* Used before most singular nouns when the individual in question is unidentified, especially when the individual is being called to notice.[2]
HINT *n.* A statement conveying by implication what it is preferred not to say explicitly.[2]
I *pron.* The one who is speaking or writing.[2]
GREW *v.* <GROW *v.*> To increase in any way.[2]

After I'd assigned a definition to each answer word, I'd composed my interpretation:

Ch. 2, Sec. 2: 7

MARRY REASON.sent1 **A HINT, I GREW.**sent2

sent1: **Closely and permanently unite a statement offered as an explanation of an assertion.**
sent2: **An allusive message, the QS answer's author claims to have increased.**

The "QS-Mary/Earth" answer's vocabulary mirrored the "QS-Joe/Earth" answer's vocabulary, which compelled me to reflect my interpretation of the "QS-Joe/Earth" answer onto my interpretation of the "QS-Mary/Earth" answer.

According to my interpretation of the "QS-Joe/Earth" answer (see "Ch. 2, Sec. 1: 14"), the explanation which God provided about His assertion concerning His forcefulness wanning was conveyed as a publicized, allusive statement, or QS answer, that increased, or became wordier, as God added more details to said explanation. Similarly, my interpretation of the "QS-Mary/Earth" answer stated that God wrote the "QS-Mary/Earth" answer to personally say that

He was the source who'd pieced together segments of the publicized, allusive statement, or QS answer, which conveyed His explanation for how His forcefulness wanned:

(a) (JOE: REASON); (MARRY REASON): God pieces an explanation together;
(b) (AIR/HINT); (A HINT): God's explanation is in a publicized, allusive statement;
(c) GREW; (I GREW): God claims He'd added words to His explanation;

Ch. 2, Sec. 2: 8

QS-Joe/Earth Answer

^{a}(JOE: REASON).sent1 ^{b}(AIR/HINT) ^{c}(GREW).sent2

QS-Joe/Earth Interpretation

sent1: ^{a}*(God has an explanation for His assertion) about His forcefulness wanning.*

sent2: ^{b}*(God's explanation for His assertion that He'd wanned was concealed within a publicized, allusive QS answer) which ^{c}(became wordier as God added more details to said explanation.*

QS-Mary/Earth Answer

^{a}(MARRY REASON).sent1 ^{b}(A HINT), ^{c}(I GREW).sent2

QS-Mary/Earth Interpretation

sent1: ^{a}*(God pieced together His explanation concerning how His forcefulness wanned by piecing together QS answers which contained portions of said explanation).*

sent2: ^{b}*(An allusive QS answer), ^{c}(God personally said that He'd inserted more words into).*

Furthermore, God, the QS author, inserted the QS answer word *I* into the "QS-Mary/Earth" answer's vocabulary, which provided evidence that supported the claim that God was the author of the allusive QS answers published in this book:

(a) I: God conveys message in first-person singular point of view;

Ch. 2, Sec. 2: 9

A HINT, ^{a}I GREW.

"*An allusive QS answer, ^{a}(I, God, the QS author), have inserted more words into.*"

Even though the "QS-Mary/Earth" answer was grammatically coherent and meaningful, I'd ran said answer through "QS-7CAP" to verify said answer's validity:

Seven Common QS Answer Properties

1. Each answer contains no more and no less than two sentences (sent1, sent2):

QS-God/Heaven
`GO DAVE.`sent1 `HE: WINNER; OR, GAINS.`sent2

QS-Devil/Hell
`HORDE: EVIL.`sent1 `ILL REIGN, WANS.`sent2

QS-Jesus/Earth
`JOE ASSURE.`sent1 `RIGHT, REIN WANS.`sent2

QS-Dave/Earth
`ADORE GIVER.`sent1 `A HINTER WANS.`sent2

QS-Joe/Earth
`JOE: REASON.`sent1 `AIR/HINT GREW.`sent2

QS-Mary/Earth
`MARRY REASON.`sent1 `A HINT, I GREW.`sent2

2. Each answer's first sentence contains no more and no less than two words (word1, word2):

QS-God/Heaven
`GO`word1 `DAVE`word2`. HE: WINNER; OR, GAINS.`

QS-Devil/Hell
`HORDE`word1`: EVIL`word2`. ILL REIGN, WANS.`

QS-Jesus/Earth
`JOE`word1 `ASSURE`word2`. RIGHT, REIN WANS.`

QS-Dave/Earth
`ADORE`word1 `GIVER`word2`. A HINTER WANS.`

QS-Joe/Earth
`JOE`word1`: REASON`word2`. AIR/HINT GREW.`

QS-Mary/Earth
`MARRY`word1 `REASON`word2`. A HINT, I GREW.`

3. In each answer's first sentence, the main subject is introduced (subj1, subj2, ...):

QS-God/Heaven

GO **DAVE**_{subj1}. HE: WINNER; OR, GAINS.

QS-Devil/Hell

HORDE_{subj2}: EVIL. ILL REIGN, WANS.

QS-Jesus/Earth

JOE_{subj3} ASSURE. RIGHT, REIN WANS.

QS-Dave/Earth

ADORE **GIVER**_{subj4}. A HINTER WANS.

QS-Joe/Earth

JOE: **REASON**_{subj5}. AIR/HINT GREW.

QS-Mary/Earth

MARRY **REASON**_{subj6}. A HINT, I GREW.

4. In each answer, the main subject introduced in the first sentence is mentioned in the second sentence (subj1-subj1, subj2-subj2, ...):

QS-God/Heaven

GO **DAVE**_{subj1}. **HE**_{subj1}: WINNER; OR, GAINS.

QS-Devil/Hell

HORDE_{subj2}: EVIL. **ILL**_{subj2} REIGN, WANS.

QS-Jesus/Earth

JOE_{subj3} ASSURE. RIGHT, **REIN**_{subj3} WANS.

QS-Dave/Earth

ADORE **GIVER**_{subj4}. A **HINTER**_{subj4} WANS.

QS-Joe/Earth

JOE: **REASON**_{subj5}. **AIR**_{subj5}/HINT GREW.

QS-Mary/Earth

MARRY **REASON**_{subj6}. A **HINT**_{subj6}, I GREW.

5. In each answer, the first sentence's second word and the second sentence's first word are synonymous in definition (syn) or context (con):

> *Synonymous answer words are tagged "syn," while answer words which share contextual meaning are tagged "con";*

(con1) DAVE; HE: context, both words identify the same man;

(syn2) EVIL; ILL: synonyms, each word means "wicked";

(con3) ASSURE; RIGHT: context, both words convey affirmation;

(con4) GIVER; [A HINTER]: context, word and [phrase] identify same person; *[Property Deviation Resolution: (see "Appendix B")]*;

(con5) REASON; AIR: context, the reason is expressed as a written statement;

(con6) REASON; [A HINT]: context, the reason is expressed as an allusive statement; *[Property Deviation Resolution: "A" is the first answer word in the second sentence. "A" doesn't share a synonymous definition or a contextual relationship with the answer word REASON. The second answer word in the second sentence, HINT, is an answer word that shares a contextual relationship with REASON. "A" is simply acting as a determiner; in other words, calling to notice an unidentified subject that's referred to by the singular noun HINT. "A" serves no function other than to reinforce HINT as a singular subject; in fact, "A" could be removed from the answer without affecting the answer's meaning—"hint, I grew" means the same thing as "a hint, I grew." Based on my analysis, I've determined that if "A" is the first word in the second sentence of a QS answer and is a determiner for a noun that's in the second position of the second sentence of said QS answer, then the "A" and noun that "A" modifies can be bracketed and treated as one answer word.]*;

QS-God/Heaven

GO **DAVE**$_{con1}$. **HE**$_{con1}$: WINNER; OR, GAINS.

QS-Devil/Hell

HORDE: **EVIL**$_{syn2}$. **ILL**$_{syn2}$ REIGN, WANS.

QS-Jesus/Earth

JOE **ASSURE**$_{con3}$. **RIGHT**$_{con3}$, REIN WANS.

QS-Dave/Earth

ADORE **GIVER**$_{con4}$. **[A HINTER]**$_{con4}$ WANS.

QS-Joe/Earth

JOE: **REASON**$_{con5}$. **AIR**$_{con5}$/HINT GREW.

QS-Mary/Earth

MARRY **REASON**$_{con6}$. **[A HINT]**$_{con6}$, I GREW.

6. In each answer's second sentence, at least one action is applied to the main subject (subj1–act1, subj2–act2, ...):

QS-God/Heaven

GO DAVE. **HE**_{subj1}: WINNER; OR, **GAINS**_{act1}.

QS-Devil/Hell

HORDE: EVIL. **ILL**_{subj2} **REIGN**_{act2}, WANS.

QS-Jesus/Earth

JOE ASSURE. RIGHT, **REIN**_{subj3} **WANS**_{act3}.

QS-Dave/Earth

ADORE GIVER. A **HINTER**_{subj4} **WANS**_{act4}.

QS-Joe/Earth

JOE: REASON. **AIR**_{subj5}/HINT **GREW**_{act5}.

QS-Mary/Earth

MARRY REASON. A **HINT**_{subj6}, I **GREW**_{act6}.

7. Along each answer's breadth of vocabulary, there's at least one site where an answer letter S would've enhanced the answer's grammatical correctness if it would've been available in the accompanying row'd word matrix and usable:

Removing a colon (:) that follows a noun and appending a contraction 's to the end of said noun would produce a conversational tone and clearer syntax (e.g. He's winner; Horde's evil). Removing a colon (:) that follows a noun and appending a possessive 's to the end of said noun would produce a conversational tone and clearer syntax (e.g. Joe's reason). Inflecting certain verbs by appending a letter S to the end of them would promote optimal grammar (e.g. Ill reigns; Joe assures). However, each answer's row'd word matrix lacks a letter S that's needed or that's capable of being used in ways mandated by QS rules (see "Appendix A");

[Property Deviation Resolution: No grammatically incorrect syntax can be found within the "QS-Dave/Earth" or "QS-Mary/Earth" answer's vocabulary. Optimal vocabulary contains no grammatical mistakes. If a QS answer doesn't contain missing letters in its vocabulary, then the vocabulary of said QS answer is grammatically optimal and therefore acceptable.];

QS-God/Heaven: <u>He's</u> winner;
QS-Devil/Hell: <u>Horde's</u> evil, Ill <u>reigns</u>;
QS-Jesus/Earth: Joe <u>assures</u>;
QS-Dave/Earth: (optimal grammar);
QS-Joe/Earth: <u>Joe's</u> reason;
QS-Mary/Earth: (optimal grammar);

QS-God/Heaven

GO DAVE. **HE: WINNER**; OR, GAINS.

QS-Devil/Hell

HORDE: EVIL. ILL REIGN, WANS.

QS-Jesus/Earth

JOE ASSURE. RIGHT, REIN WANS.

QS-Dave/Earth

ADORE GIVER. A HINTER WANS.

QS-Joe/Earth

JOE: REASON. AIR/HINT GREW.

QS-Mary/Earth

MARRY REASON. A HINT, I GREW.

CHAPTER TWO: SECTION THREE

REVIEW: SIX STACKS

```
G O D              DEVIL            JESUS
HEAVEN             HELL             EARTH
ORIGIN             ORIGIN           ORIGIN
ANSWER             ANSWER           ANSWER

DAVE               JOE              MARY
EARTH              EARTH            EARTH
ORIGIN             ORIGIN           ORIGIN
ANSWER             ANSWER           ANSWER
```

I'd noticed that the six Query Stacks which I'd shown in this book so far fit into two categories. I'd named one category "Lineal Query Stacks" and the other category "Lineally-Coupled Query Stacks." The first category contained five of said six Query Stacks. The said five Query Stacks were composed from names of biblical characters who were members of Virgin Mary's "lineage," which was why the said five Query Stacks were "Lineal" Query Stacks. The second category consisted of only "QS-Devil/Hell." "QS-Devil/Hell" contained a biblical character, the Devil, who wasn't a member of Virgin Mary's lineage but was commonly "coupled to a biblical character, God, who was a member of Virgin Mary's lineage," which was why "QS-Devil/Hell" was a "Lineally-Coupled" Query Stack:

QS Categories

Lineal Query Stack
Query Stack with a first-row row'd word that names a character who belongs to a particular family tree (e.g. Virgin Mary's family tree).

Lineally-Coupled Query Stack
Query Stack with a first-row row'd word that names a character who doesn't belong to but is commonly associated with a member of a particular family tree (e.g. Virgin

Mary's family tree).

Ch. 2, Sec. 3: 1

LINEAL QUERY STACKS
QS-GOD/HEAVEN
QS-JESUS/EARTH
QS-DAVE/EARTH
QS-JOE/EARTH
QS-MARY/EARTH
LINEALLY-COUPLED QUERY STACKS
QS-DEVIL/HELL

I'd filed each one of the six Query Stacks which I'd revealed in this book so far as a "Lineal Query Stack" or a "Lineally-Coupled Query Stack" for a reason:

Ch. 2, Sec. 3: 2

LINEAL QUERY STACKS

QS-Mary/Earth—Mary was a lineal member of Virgin Mary's family tree, since Mary was Virgin Mary.

QS-Joe/Earth—Joe (Joseph) was a lineal member of Mary's family tree, because Joe and Mary were married.

QS-Dave/Earth—Dave (David) was a lineal member of Mary's family tree, because Dave was a multi-great-grandfather of Mary's.

QS-Jesus/Earth—Jesus was a lineal member of Mary's family tree, since Jesus was Mary's biological son.

QS-God/Heaven—God was a lineal member of Mary's family tree, since God was the father of the Jesus that Mary was the biological mother of.

LINEALLY-COUPLED QUERY STACKS

QS-Devil/Hell—Devil wasn't a lineal member of Mary's family tree but has been commonly coupled to God as God's antipode.

I'd made a genealogical diagram and diagram key which illustrated relationships shared by the biblical characters whose names were the first-row row'd words in the six Query Stacks that I'd shown in this book so far—"Ch. 2, Sec. 3: 3" was a replica of "Ch. 2, Sec. 2: 1":

Some of the biblical names that I've listed in the diagram belong in Virgin Mary's lineage but aren't QS row'd words (e.g. "Bathsheba," "Solomon," "Nathan") yet elucidate how some biblical characters with names that are QS row'd words are related;

SOLID LINE (———) = Genealogically linked to Mary;
DASHED LINE (– – –) = Father of Mary's son Jesus, via no sexual contact;
DASHED/DOTTED LINE (– ·· –) = Mary's husband, but not Jesus's father;
DOUBLE LINE (====) = Not genealogically linked to Mary;
BLACK NAME BOX **NAME** *= Row'd word, and main focus of family tree;*
GRAY NAME BOX NAME *= Row'd word, and member of family tree;*
WHITE NAME BOX NAME *= Row'd word, but not a member of family tree;*
UNBOXED NAME = Not a row'd word, but member of family tree;

(g) MARY: herself;
(h) JOE *(Joseph)*: Mary's husband;
(i) DAVE *(David)*: Mary's multi-great-grandfather;
(j) JESUS: Mary's son;
(k) GOD: Mary's spiritual co-parent;
(l) DEVIL: God's antipode;

Ch. 2, Sec. 3: 3

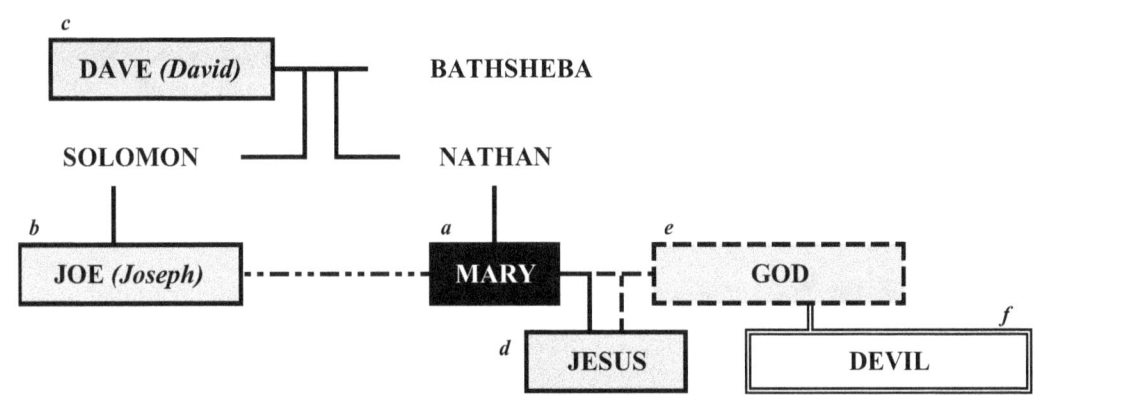

I'd unveiled a linguistic pathway which was paved with personal inquisition, divine intervention, vocabular associations, interlocking letters, conceptual connections and biblical relationships. In fact, each of the six Query Stacks which I'd revealed up until now contained either a first-row row'd word or an answer word that inspired which first-row row'd word I'd selected and inserted into subsequent Query Stacks. "QS-God/Heaven" was the only Query Stack which didn't contain a first-row row'd word that was inspired by another Query Stack's first-row

row'd word, since GOD was the first row'd word that I'd found and appeared in a vision (see "Ch. 1, Sec. 1: 1-2"):

(Step 1) I have a vision of an incomplete Query Stack;
(Step 2) I turn the incomplete Query Stack into a finished Query Stack (QS-God/Heaven);
(Step 3) Row'd word GOD inspires row'd word DEVIL via theological correlations;
(Step 4) Row'd words GOD and DEVIL inspire row'd word JESUS via theological correlations;
(Step 5) Answer word *DAVE* inspires row'd word DAVE;
(Step 6) Answer word *JOE* inspires row'd word JOE;
(Step 7) Row'd words GOD, JESUS, DAVE and JOE inspire row'd word MARY via lineal correlations;

Steps to Manifest Mary—Step 1

I have a vision of an incomplete Query Stack.

Ch. 2, Sec. 3: 4

I have a vision of an incomplete Query Stack.

Steps to Manifest Mary—Step 2

I turn the incomplete Query Stack into a finished Query Stack.

Ch. 2, Sec. 3: 5

G	O	D		
H	E	A	V	E	N
O	R	I	G	I	N
A	N	S	W	E	R

GO DAVE. HE: WINNER; OR, GAINS.

REVIEW: SIX STACKS

Steps to Manifest Mary—Step 3

Row'd word GOD inspires row'd word DEVIL via theological correlations.

Ch. 2, Sec. 3: 6

G O D	▶	*D E V I L*
H E A V E N		H E L L
O R I G I N		O R I G I N
A N S W E R		A N S W E R

Steps to Manifest Mary—Step 4

Row'd words GOD and DEVIL inspire row'd word JESUS via theological correlations.

Ch. 2, Sec. 3: 7

G O D	+	*D E V I L*	▶	*J E S U S*
H E A V E N		H E L L		E A R T H
O R I G I N		O R I G I N		O R I G I N
A N S W E R		A N S W E R		A N S W E R

Steps to Manifest Mary—Step 5

Answer word DAVE inspires row'd word DAVE.

Ch. 2, Sec. 3: 8

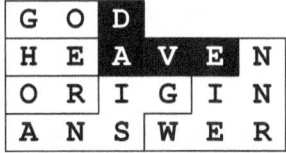

GO **DAVE**. HE: WINNER; OR, GAINS.

D A V E
E A R T H
O R I G I N
A N S W E R

Steps to Manifest Mary—Step 6

Answer word JOE inspires row'd word JOE.

Ch. 2, Sec. 3: 9

```
J E S U S
E A R T H
O R I G I N
A N S W E R
```

JOE ASSURE. RIGHT, REIN WANS.

J O E

E A R T H
O R I G I N
A N S W E R

Steps to Manifest Mary—Step 7

Row'd words GOD, JESUS, DAVE and JOE inspire row'd word MARY via lineal correlations.

Ch. 2, Sec. 3: 10

G O D	***+ J E S U S***	***+ D A V E***	***+ J O E***	***▶ M A R Y***
H E A V E N	H E L L	E A R T H	E A R T H	E A R T H
O R I G I N	O R I G I N	O R I G I N	O R I G I N	O R I G I N
A N S W E R	A N S W E R	A N S W E R	A N S W E R	A N S W E R

In "Ch. 1, Sec. 5: 13," I'd displayed a table in which each QS answer word in the first four QS answers I'd uncovered was categorized according to which of three identities (David Mivshek, Trinity or God) the main subject of the QS answer that said answer word appeared in represented. In "Ch. 2, Sec. 3: 11," I'd updated said table with the "QS-Joe/Earth" and "QS-Mary/Earth" answer words and the "QS Answer" tier. I'd placed the "QS-Joe/Earth" and "QS-Mary/Earth" answer words into the "QS Answer" tier, since the main subject in each said QS answer, the joe's reason, exemplified the structure and function of QS answers:

A parenthetic number (#) succeeding a distinct answer word reports how many times said answer word appears in QS answers that may or may not share a distinct main subject but have main subjects which refer to David Mivshek, Trinity, God or QS answers;

(a) "QS-Joe/Earth" answer words: "QS Answer" tier, reason is main subject, reason is expressed as a QS answer;

(b) "QS-Mary/Earth" answer words: "QS Answer" tier, reason is main subject, reason is expressed as a QS answer;

Ch. 2, Sec. 3: 11

DAVID MIVSHEK

Nouns—Dave, He, Winner;
Proper Nouns—Dave;
Pronouns—He;
Verbs—Gains, Go;
Conjunctions—Or.

TRINITY

Nouns—Evil, Horde, Ill;
Verbs—Reign, Wans.

GOD

Nouns—Giver, Hinter, Joe, Rein;
Verbs—Adore, Assure, Wans (2);
Adverbs—Right;
Indefinite Articles—A.

QS ANSWER

Nouns—*ᵃ*Air, *⁽ᵃ, ᵇ⁾*Hint (2), *ᵃ*Joe, *⁽ᵃ, ᵇ⁾*Reason (2);
Pronouns—*ᵃ*I;
Verbs—*⁽ᵃ, ᵇ⁾*Grew (2), *ᵃ*Marry;
Indefinite Articles—*ᵃ*A.

In "Ch. 1, Sec. 5: 14," I'd wondered if the answer word *WANS* was permitted to be in multiple answers, because each answer which the answer word *WANS* was in up until "Ch. 1, Sec. 5" contained a distinct main subject—horde, joe, or giver—yet each said subject cited the same entity, God. The answer word *A* didn't cite an individual, and appeared multiple times in QS answers (see "Ch. 1, Sec. 4: 7" and "Ch. 2, Sec. 2: 5") just like the answer word *WANS,* but each QS answer the answer word *A* appeared in had a distinct main subject which God identified as or pertained to QS answers *(God ≠ QS answer)*. Therefore, I'd determined that a distinct answer word which didn't identify an individual was permitted to be a word in multiple QS answers, even if each one of said multiple QS answers had a distinct main subject:

In "Ch. 1, Sec. 5: 14," I'd wondered if an answer word which did identify an individual and appeared in multiple answers always identified one and the same individual, no matter who or what the main subject was in each said answer. The answer word *JOE* appeared in two answers (see "Ch. 2, Sec. 1: 5" and "Ch. 2, Sec. 2: 5") and cited one and the same individual, God, in each answer, even though the main subject of one of the said two answers was "reason" and the main subject of the second of the said two answers was "joe." In other words, it wasn't unusual for a distinct answer word which identified an individual to be in multiple QS answers, even when said QS answers didn't contain the same main subject:

> *A parenthetic number (#) succeeding a distinct answer word reports how many times said answer word appears in QS answers that may or may not share a distinct main subject but have main subjects which refer to David Mivshek, Trinity, God or QS answers;*

(a) A: not an individual, in two answers, distinct main subject (giver, reason);
(b) GREW: not an individual, in two answers, same main subject (reason);
(c) HINT: not an individual, in two answers, same main subject (reason);
(d) REASON: not an individual, in two answers, same main subject (reason);
(e) JOE: identifies one individual (God), in two answers, distinct main subject (joe, reason);

Ch. 2, Sec. 3: 12

DAVID MIVSHEK

Nouns—Winner;
Proper Nouns—Dave;
Pronouns—He;
Verbs—Gains, Go;
Conjunctions—Or.

TRINITY

Nouns—Evil, Horde, Ill;
Verbs—Reign, Wans.

GOD

Nouns—Giver, Hinter, [e]Joe, Rein;
Verbs—Adore, Assure, Wans (2);
Adverbs—Right;
Indefinite Articles—[a]A.

QS ANSWER

Nouns—Air, [c]Hint (2), [e]Joe, [d]Reason (2);
Pronouns—I;
Verbs—[b]Grew (2), Marry;
Indefinite Articles—[a]A.

In "Ch. 1, Sec. 5: 15," I'd displayed statistics which pertained to QS answer vocabulary. In "Ch. 2, Sec. 3: 13," I'd updated said statistics by incorporating numbers I'd extracted from the "QS-Joe/Earth" and "QS-Mary/Earth" answer words:

Ch. 2, Sec. 3: 13

QS-GOD/HEAVEN

GO DAVE. HE: WINNER; OR, GAINS.

Number of QS answer words—6

Number of QS answer letters—21

Average number of letters per answer word—3.50

QS-DEVIL/HELL

HORDE: EVIL. ILL REIGN, WANS.

Number of QS answer words—5

Number of QS answer letters—21

Average number of letters per answer word—4.20

QS-JESUS/EARTH

JOE ASSURE. RIGHT, REIN WANS.

Number of QS answer words—5

Number of QS answer letters—22

Average number of letters per answer word—4.40

QS-DAVE/EARTH

ADORE GIVER. A HINTER WANS.

Number of QS answer words—5

Number of QS answer letters—21

Average number of letters per answer word—4.20

QS-JOE/EARTH

JOE: REASON. AIR/HINT GREW.

Number of QS answer words—5

Number of QS answer letters—20

Average number of letters per answer word—4.00

QS-MARY/EARTH

MARRY REASON. A HINT, I GREW.

Number of QS answer words—6

Number of QS answer letters—21

Average number of letters per answer word—3.50

QUERY STACK TOTALS AND AVERAGES

Total number of QS answers—6

Total number of QS answer words—32

Total number of QS answer letters—126

Average number of letters per QS answer—21

Average number of words per QS answer—5.33

Average number of letters per answer word—3.94

CHAPTER THREE: SECTION ONE

HOLY^GHOST/HEAVEN: NAÏVE OR ANSWERING

H	O	L	Y	G	H	O	S	T
H	E	A	V	E	N			
O	R	I	G	I	N			
A	N	S	W	E	R			

The Holy Ghost was a prominent biblical figure, because the Holy Ghost was the Trinity member which God used as a conduit to impregnate Mary. According to the Bible, "Now the <u>birth of Jesus Christ</u> was on this wise: When as <u>his mother Mary</u> was espoused to Joseph, before they came together, <u>she was found with child of the Holy Ghost</u>" (Matthew 1:18 KJV):

SOLID LINE (———) = *Genealogically linked to Mary;*
DASHED LINE (– – –) = *Father of Mary's son Jesus, via no sexual contact;*
GRAY NAME BOX NAME = *Row'd word, and member of family tree;*

(a) MARY: Jesus's mother;
(b) HOLY GHOST *(God)*: Trinity member which impregnated Mary with God's seed;
(c) JESUS: Mary's and the Holy Ghost's, or God's, son;

Ch. 3 Sec. 1: 1

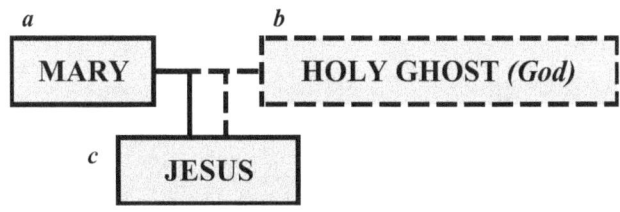

I'd constructed a QS matrix which consisted of the first row row'd word HOLY^GHOST:

(a) HOLY^GHOST: first-row row'd word;

Ch. 3 Sec. 1: 2

```
"H O L Y G H O S T
 H E A V E N
 O R I G I N
 A N S W E R
```

I'd removed the space which separated the words *Holy* and *Ghost* in the name *Holy Ghost* (HOLY☐GHOST → HOLYGHOST) when I'd dropped said name into the "QS-Holy^Ghost/Heaven" matrix. If a letter instead of a blank space occupied each node of said QS matrix, then said QS matrix would contain letters which were uniformly laid out, I'd figured:

Ch. 3 Sec. 1: 3

Rule 12: Each letter-position in a Query Stack matrix must contain a letter.

I'd decided to use a caret (^) to denote a blank space which was in between two words of a name that occupied a row'd word row:

QS Titling

If a row'd word contains more than one word and said words are separated by blank spaces, then the blank spaces are removed and replaced with a caret (^). The caret is used when the QS title or row'd word is being discussed. For example, the "QS-Holy^Ghost/Heaven" matrix contains the row'd word HOLY^GHOST:

"'Query Stack' for 'Holy Ghost of Heaven'" is "QS-Holy^Ghost/Heaven"
*Multi-worded term "**HOLY GHOST**" is row'd word "**HOLY^GHOST**"*

The Holy Ghost was a prominent biblical figure, just like all of the other biblical figures whose names occupied the first rows of the seven QS matrices which I'd revealed so far:

[a] GOD; DEVIL; JESUS; DAVE *(David)*; JOE *(Joseph)*; MARY; HOLY^GHOST: notable biblical characters, first-row row'd words;

Ch. 3 Sec. 1: 4

QS-God/Heaven	QS-Devil/Hell	QS-Jesus/Earth	QS-Dave/Earth
[a]G O D	[b]D E V I L	[c]J E S U S	[d]D A V E
H E A V E N	H E L L	E A R T H	E A R T H
O R I G I N	O R I G I N	O R I G I N	O R I G I N
A N S W E R	A N S W E R	A N S W E R	A N S W E R

QS-Joe/Earth	QS-Mary/Earth	QS-Holy^Ghost/Heaven	
[e]J O E	[f]M A R Y	[g]H O L Y G H O S T	
E A R T H	E A R T H	H E A V E N	
O R I G I N	O R I G I N	O R I G I N	
A N S W E R	A N S W E R	A N S W E R	

The Holy Ghost was prominent in Heaven, since (1) the Holy Ghost was a member of the Trinity, (2) each member of the Trinity was God and a conduit God performed actions and communicated messages through, and (3) God was the most notable figure in Heaven:

[a] GOD: notable biblical figure; of Heaven; Heaven's ruler;

[b] DEVIL: notable biblical figure; of Hell; God sends evil to Hell, Devil is the evilest being, Devil is evilest being God could send to Hell;

[c] JESUS: notable biblical figure; of Earth; Earth's premier ruler;

[d] DAVE *(David)*: notable biblical figure; of Earth; third King of Israel;

[e] JOE *(Joseph)*: notable biblical figure; of Earth; Virgin Mary's husband;

[f] MARY: notable biblical figure; of Earth; Jesus's mother;

[g] **HOLY GHOST: notable biblical figure; of Heaven; Heaven's messenger;**

Ch. 3 Sec. 1: 5

BIBLICAL BEING	DOMAIN	NOTORIETY
[a]GOD	[a]HEAVEN	[a]RULER
[b]DEVIL	[b]HELL	[b]EVILEST RESIDENT
[c]JESUS	[c]EARTH	[c]PREMIER RULER
[d]DAVE *(David)*	[d]EARTH	[d]ANOINTED KING
[e]JOE *(Joseph)*	[e]EARTH	[e]MARY'S HUSBAND
[f]MARY	[f]EARTH	[f]JESUS'S MOTHER
[g]**HOLY GHOST**	[g]**HEAVEN**	[g]**MESSENGER**

I'd inserted the row'd word ORIGIN and the row'd word ANSWER into the third and fourth row of the "QS-Holy^Ghost/Heaven" matrix, respectively:

(a) ORIGIN; ORIGIN; ORIGIN; ORIGIN; ORIGIN; ORIGIN; ORIGIN: same words, third-row row'd words;

(b) ANSWER; ANSWER; ANSWER; ANSWER; ANSWER; ANSWER; ANSWER: same words, fourth-row row'd words;

Ch. 3 Sec. 1: 6

QS-God/Heaven	QS-Devil/Hell	QS-Jesus/Earth	QS-Dave/Earth
G O D	D E V I L	J E S U S	D A V E
H E A V E N	H E L L	E A R T H	E A R T H
[a]O R I G I N	[a]O R I G I N	[a]O R I G I N	[a]O R I G I N
[b]A N S W E R	[b]A N S W E R	[b]A N S W E R	[b]A N S W E R

QS-Joe/Earth	QS-Mary/Earth	QS-Holy^Ghost/Heaven	
J O E	M A R Y	H O L Y G H O S T	
E A R T H	E A R T H	H E A V E N	
[a]O R I G I N	[a]O R I G I N	[a]O R I G I N	
[b]A N S W E R	[b]A N S W E R	[b]A N S W E R	

I'd linked adjacent row'd word letters together in an effort to produce a valid QS answer. Eventually, I'd uncovered an answer which was grammatically coherent and meaningful:

✓ All QS rules followed (see "Appendix A");

Ch. 3 Sec. 1: 7

H O L Y	G H O S T
H E	A V E N
O R	I G I N
A N	S W E R

HOLY GHOST. HE: NAÏVE OR ANSWERING.

Next, I'd assigned definitions to the "QS-Holy^Ghost/Heaven" answer words:

Ch. 3 Sec. 1: 8

HOLY GHOST. HE: NAÏVE OR ANSWERING.

HOLY *adj.* Set apart and dedicated to the service of God.[2]

GHOST *n.* One who does literary work for and in the name of another; ghost-writer.[2]

HE *pron.* That male one.[2]

NAÏVE *adj.* Self-taught.[2]

OR *conj.* The synonymous, equivalent, or substitutive character of two words or phrases.[2]

ANSWERING *v.* <ANSWER *v.*> To solve or offer a solution for.[2]

After I'd assigned a definition to each "QS-Holy^Ghost/Heaven" answer word, I'd composed an interpretation:

Ch. 3 Sec. 1: 9

HOLY GHOST._{sent1} **HE: NAÏVE OR ANSWERING.**_{sent2}

sent1: ***A person is godly and does literary work for and in the name of another.***
sent2: ***A male is self-taught in the way he attains a solution.***

I'd matched my interpretation of the "QS-God/Heaven" answer *("Go Dave. He: winner; or, gains.")* to my interpretation of the "QS-Holy^Ghost/Heaven" answer, since the "QS-Holy^Ghost/Heaven" answer's vocabulary mirrored the "QS-God/Heaven" answer's vocabulary. The first of four ways that said answers' vocabularies mirrored one another was that each answer's main subject was the second word in the first sentence of the answer each said subject was incorporated into:

(a) DAVE; GHOST: main subject is second word (word2) in first sentence (sent1);

Ch. 3 Sec. 1: 10

QS-God/Heaven Answer

GO "**DAVE**_{word2}._{sent1} HE: WINNER; OR, GAINS._{sent2}

QS-Holy^Ghost/Heaven Answer

HOLY "**GHOST**_{word2}._{sent1} HE: NAÏVE OR ANSWERING._{sent2}

The second way that said two answers' vocabularies were the same was that the first answer word in the second sentence of each answer, *HE,* cited the answer's main subject:

(a) HE; HE: main subject is first word (word1) in second sentence (sent2);

Ch. 3 Sec. 1: 11

QS-God/Heaven Answer

GO DAVE._{sent1} "**HE**_{word1}: WINNER; OR, GAINS._{sent2}

QS-Holy^Ghost/Heaven Answer

HOLY GHOST._{sent1} "**HE**_{word1}: NAÏVE OR ANSWERING._{sent2}

Third, the second and fourth word in the second sentence of each answer cited one characteristic and one action associated with the main subject:

(a) (WINNER, GAINS); (NAÏVE, ANSWERING): word pair (word2, word4) in second sentence (sent2) defines one characteristic of and one action associated with each answer's main subject (subj);

Ch. 3 Sec. 1: 12

QS-God/Heaven Answer
GO DAVE.$_{sent1}$ **HE**$_{subj}$: "WINNER$_{word2}$; OR, "GAINS$_{word4}$.$_{sent2}$
QS-Holy^Ghost/Heaven Answer
HOLY GHOST.$_{sent1}$ **HE**$_{subj}$: "NAÏVE$_{word2}$ OR "ANSWERING$_{word4}$.$_{sent2}$

Fourth, the two words which defined characteristics of and actions associated with the main subject (subj) of each answer's second sentence were linked together by the answer word *OR*:

(a) OR; OR: same word links (link) two words that define the character (char) of and actions (act) made by the main subject (subj);

Ch. 3 Sec. 1: 13

QS-God/Heaven Answer
GO DAVE.$_{sent1}$ **HE**$_{subj}$: **WINNER**$_{char}$; "**OR**$_{link}$, **GAINS**$_{act}$.$_{sent2}$
QS-Holy^Ghost/Heaven Answer
HOLY GHOST.$_{sent1}$ **HE**$_{subj}$: **NAÏVE**$_{char}$ "**OR**$_{link}$ **ANSWERING**$_{act}$.$_{sent2}$

In my interpretation of the "QS-God/Heaven" answer, the "QS-God/Heaven" answer words *DAVE* and *HE* referred to the same individual; therefore, in my interpretation of the "QS-Holy^Ghost/Heaven" answer, the answer word *HE* referred to the same individual that the "QS-God/Heaven" answer words *DAVE* and *HE* referred to:

(a) DAVE; HE; HE: identities of same individual;

Ch. 3 Sec. 1: 14

QS-God/Heaven Answer
GO "**DAVE**. "**HE**: WINNER; OR, GAINS.
QS-Holy^Ghost/Heaven Answer
HOLY GHOST. "**HE**: NAÏVE OR ANSWERING.

I'd updated my initial interpretation of the "QS-Holy^Ghost/Heaven" answer in order to reflect that the he was Dave and that Dave was me:

Ch. 3 Sec. 1: 15

HOLY GHOST.sent1 **HE: NAÏVE OR ANSWERING.**sent2

sent1: *A person is godly and does literary work for and in the name of another.*
sent2: *A male who's self-taught in the way he attains a solution is David Mivshek.*

According to the third, fourth and fifth properties of "QS-7CAP," the main subject of a QS answer must be introduced in a QS answer's first sentence (Property 3), the main subject introduced in a QS answer's first sentence must be mentioned in the same answer's second sentence (Property 4), and the second word of a QS answer's first sentence and the first word of said answer's second sentence must be synonymous in definition or by context (Property 5). Therefore, the ghost was the main subject of the "QS-Holy^Ghost/Heaven" answer, because the answer word *GHOST* was the only answer word in the "QS-Holy^Ghost/Heaven" answer's first sentence which cited a subject (Property 3); the he was the ghost, since the ghost was the main subject of the "QS-Holy^Ghost/Heaven" answer and the he was the only subject mentioned in the "QS-Holy^Ghost/Heaven" answer's second sentence (Property 4); and, *GHOST* and *HE*, the second word in the first sentence and the first word in the second sentence of the "QS-Holy^Ghost/Heaven" answer, respectively, were contextually similar, since both answer words didn't have any definitions which shared synonymity (Property 5):

(a) GHOST; HE: identities of main subject (subj);

Ch. 3 Sec. 1: 16

HOLY "**GHOST**subj. "**HE**subj: NAÏVE OR ANSWERING.

I'd updated my interpretation of the "QS-Holy^Ghost/Heaven" answer in order to show that the he, David Mivshek, was the ghostwriter mentioned in said answer's first sentence:

Ch. 3 Sec. 1: 17

HOLY GHOST.sent1 **HE: NAÏVE OR ANSWERING.**sent2

sent1: *A person who's godly and doing literary work for and in the name of another is David Mivshek.*
sent2: *A male who's self-taught or self-taught in the way he attains a solution is David Mivshek.*

An obstacle that I'd overcame during my journey of cultivating Query Stacks was not knowing the rules or methods which pertained to the construction and decryption of Query Stacks; in fact, no one else knew any rules or methods concerning Query Stacks before me. My lack of knowledge or training in the QS method meant that I was naïve, or self-taught, when I was constructing and answering, or solving, Query Stacks:

Ch. 3 Sec. 1: 18

HOLY GHOST.$_{sent1}$ **HE: NAÏVE OR ANSWERING.**$_{sent2}$

$_{sent1}$: *A godly person doing literary work for and in the name of another is David Mivshek.*
$_{sent2}$: *A male who's self-taught in the ways of or solving Query Stacks is David Mivshek.*

QS answers were preformatted and authored by God, (see "Ch. 1, Sec. 4: 11-13"), which meant that the QS author wasn't me *(God ≠ me)*. I wasn't writing QS answers under my own name. QS answers were works authored by God, which meant I was writing out God's words for God. In other words, I was God's ghostwriter:

Ch. 3 Sec. 1: 19

HOLY GHOST.$_{sent1}$ **HE: NAÏVE OR ANSWERING.**$_{sent2}$

$_{sent1}$: *A godly person who reproduces QS answers in written form for God and in God's name is David Mivshek.*
$_{sent2}$: *A male who's self-taught in the ways of or solving Query Stacks is David Mivshek.*

I'd ran the "QS-Holy^Ghost/Heaven" answer through the "QS-7CAP" test in order to affirm said answer's validity:

Seven Common QS Answer Properties

1. Each answer contains no more and no less than two sentences (sent1, sent2):

QS-God/Heaven

GO DAVE.sent1 HE: WINNER; OR, GAINS.sent2

QS-Devil/Hell

HORDE: EVIL.sent1 ILL REIGN, WANS.sent2

QS-Jesus/Earth

JOE ASSURE.sent1 RIGHT, REIN WANS.sent2

QS-Dave/Earth

ADORE GIVER.sent1 A HINTER WANS.sent2

QS-Joe/Earth

JOE: REASON.sent1 AIR/HINT GREW.sent2

QS-Mary/Earth

MARRY REASON.sent1 A HINT, I GREW.sent2

QS-Holy^Ghost/Heaven

HOLY GHOST.sent1 HE: NAÏVE OR ANSWERING.sent2

2. Each answer's first sentence contains no more and no less than two words (word1, word2):

QS-God/Heaven

GO$_{word1}$ DAVE$_{word2}$. HE: WINNER; OR, GAINS.

QS-Devil/Hell

HORDE$_{word1}$: EVIL$_{word2}$. ILL REIGN, WANS.

QS-Jesus/Earth

JOE$_{word1}$ ASSURE$_{word2}$. RIGHT, REIN WANS.

QS-Dave/Earth

ADORE$_{word1}$ GIVER$_{word2}$. A HINTER WANS.

QS-Joe/Earth

JOE$_{word1}$: REASON$_{word2}$. AIR/HINT GREW.

QS-Mary/Earth

MARRY$_{word1}$ REASON$_{word2}$. A HINT, I GREW.

QS-Holy^Ghost/Heaven

HOLY$_{word1}$ GHOST$_{word2}$. HE: NAÏVE OR ANSWERING.

3. In each answer's first sentence, the main subject is introduced (subj1, subj2, ...):

QS-God/Heaven

GO **DAVE**~subj1~. HE: WINNER; OR, GAINS.

QS-Devil/Hell

HORDE~subj2~: EVIL. ILL REIGN, WANS.

QS-Jesus/Earth

JOE~subj3~ ASSURE. RIGHT, REIN WANS.

QS-Dave/Earth

ADORE **GIVER**~subj4~. A HINTER WANS.

QS-Joe/Earth

JOE: **REASON**~subj5~. AIR/HINT GREW.

QS-Mary/Earth

MARRY **REASON**~subj6~. A HINT, I GREW.

QS-Holy^Ghost/Heaven

HOLY **GHOST**~subj7~. HE: NAÏVE OR ANSWERING.

4. In each answer, the main subject introduced in the first sentence is mentioned in the second sentence (subj1-subj1, subj2-subj2, ...):

QS-God/Heaven

GO **DAVE**~subj1~. **HE**~subj1~: WINNER; OR, GAINS.

QS-Devil/Hell

HORDE~subj2~: EVIL. **ILL**~subj2~ REIGN, WANS.

QS-Jesus/Earth

JOE~subj3~ ASSURE. RIGHT, **REIN**~subj3~ WANS.

QS-Dave/Earth

ADORE **GIVER**~subj4~. A **HINTER**~subj4~ WANS.

QS-Joe/Earth

JOE: **REASON**~subj5~. **AIR**~subj5~/HINT GREW.

QS-Mary/Earth

MARRY **REASON**~subj6~. A **HINT**~subj6~, I GREW.

QS-Holy^Ghost/Heaven

HOLY **GHOST**~subj7~. **HE**~subj7~: NAÏVE OR ANSWERING.

5. In each answer, the first sentence's second word and the second sentence's first word are synonymous in definition (syn) or context (con):

Synonymous answer words are tagged "syn," while answer words which share contextual meaning are tagged "con";

(con1) DAVE; HE: context, both words identify the same man;
(syn2) EVIL; ILL: synonyms, each word means "wicked";
(con3) ASSURE; RIGHT: context, both words convey affirmation;
(con4) GIVER; [A HINTER]: context, word and [phrase] identify same person; *[Property Deviation Resolution: (see "Appendix B")]*;
(con5) REASON; AIR: context, the reason is expressed as a written statement;
(con6) REASON; [A HINT]: context, the reason is expressed as an allusive statement; *[Property Deviation Resolution: (see "Appendix B")]*;
(con7) GHOST; HE: context, both words identify the same person;

QS-God/Heaven

GO **DAVE**$_{con1}$. **HE**$_{con1}$: WINNER; OR, GAINS.

QS-Devil/Hell

HORDE: **EVIL**$_{syn2}$. **ILL**$_{syn2}$ REIGN, WANS.

QS-Jesus/Earth

JOE **ASSURE**$_{con3}$. **RIGHT**$_{con3}$, REIN WANS.

QS-Dave/Earth

ADORE **GIVER**$_{con4}$. **[A HINTER]**$_{con4}$ WANS.

QS-Joe/Earth

JOE: **REASON**$_{con5}$. **AIR**$_{con5}$/HINT GREW.

QS-Mary/Earth

MARRY **REASON**$_{con6}$. **[A HINT]**$_{con6}$, I GREW.

QS-Holy^Ghost/Heaven

HOLY **GHOST**$_{con7}$. **HE**$_{con7}$: NAÏVE OR ANSWERING.

---

6. In each answer's second sentence, at least one action is applied to the main subject (subj1–act1, subj2–act2, ...):

QS-God/Heaven

GO DAVE. **HE**$_{subj1}$: WINNER; OR, **GAINS**$_{act1}$.

QS-Devil/Hell

HORDE: EVIL. **ILL**$_{subj2}$ **REIGN**$_{act2}$, WANS.

QS-Jesus/Earth

JOE ASSURE. RIGHT, **REIN**$_{subj3}$ **WANS**$_{act3}$.

QS-Dave/Earth

ADORE GIVER. A **HINTER**$_{subj4}$ **WANS**$_{act4}$.

QS-Joe/Earth

JOE: REASON. **AIR**$_{subj5}$/HINT **GREW**$_{act5}$.

QS-Mary/Earth

MARRY REASON. A **HINT**$_{subj6}$, I **GREW**$_{act6}$.

QS-Holy^Ghost/Heaven

HOLY GHOST. **HE**$_{subj7}$: NAÏVE OR **ANSWERING**$_{act7}$.

7. Along each answer's breadth of vocabulary, there's at least one site where an answer letter *S* would've enhanced the answer's grammatical correctness if it would've been available in the accompanying row'd word matrix and usable:

> *Removing a colon (:) that follows a noun and appending a contraction 's to the end of said noun would produce a conversational tone and clearer syntax (e.g. <u>He's</u> winner; <u>Horde's</u> evil; <u>He's</u> naïve; <u>He's</u> answering). Removing a colon (:) that follows a noun and appending the possessive 's to the end of said noun would produce a conversational tone and clearer syntax (e.g. <u>Joe's</u> reason). Inflecting certain verbs by appending a letter S to the end of them would promote optimal grammar (e.g. Ill <u>reigns</u>; Joe <u>assures</u>). However, each answer's row'd word matrix lacks a letter S that's needed or that's capable of being used in ways mandated by QS rules (see "Appendix A");*

> *[Property Deviation Resolution (see "Appendix B"): "QS-Dave/Earth" and "QS-Mary/Earth"];*

QS-God/Heaven: <u>He's</u> winner;
QS-Devil/Hell: <u>Horde's</u> evil, Ill <u>reigns</u>;
QS-Jesus/Earth: Joe <u>assures</u>;
QS-Dave/Earth: (optimal grammar);
QS-Joe/Earth: <u>Joe's</u> reason;
QS-Mary/Earth: (optimal grammar);
QS-Holy^Ghost/Heaven: <u>He's</u> naïve, <u>He's</u> answering;

QS-God/Heaven

GO DAVE. **HE: WINNER**; OR, GAINS.

QS-Devil/Hell

HORDE: EVIL. ILL REIGN, WANS.

QS-Jesus/Earth

JOE ASSURE. RIGHT, REIN WANS.

QS-Dave/Earth

ADORE GIVER. A HINTER WANS.

QS-Joe/Earth

JOE: REASON. AIR/HINT GREW.

QS-Mary/Earth

MARRY REASON. A HINT, I GREW.

QS-Holy^Ghost/Heaven

HOLY GHOST. **HE: NAÏVE** OR ANSWERING.

HOLY GHOST. **HE:** NAÏVE OR **ANSWERING**.

CHAPTER THREE: SECTION TWO

REVIEW: SEVEN STACKS

```
G O D
H E A V E N
O R I G I N
A N S W E R
```

```
D E V I L
H E L L
O R I G I N
A N S W E R
```

```
J E S U S
E A R T H
O R I G I N
A N S W E R
```

```
D A V E
E A R T H
O R I G I N
A N S W E R
```

```
J O E
E A R T H
O R I G I N
A N S W E R
```

```
M A R Y
E A R T H
O R I G I N
A N S W E R
```

```
H O L Y G H O S T
H E A V E N
O R I G I N
A N S W E R
```

Each of the seven Query Stacks that I'd revealed so far fell into one of three QS categories. The first two categories were "Lineal Query Stacks" and "Lineally-Coupled Query Stacks," both of which I'd presented in "Ch. 2, Sec. 3." The third category was "Lineal-Alias Query Stacks," which was the category that I'd assigned "QS-Holy^Ghost/Heaven" to.

I'd filed five of the seven Query Stacks as "Lineal" Query Stacks, because each of the said five Query Stacks had a row'd word matrix which contained a name of a biblical character who was a member of Virgin Mary's "lineage." I'd filed the sixth of seven Query Stacks as a "Lineally-Coupled" Query Stack, which had a matrix that contained the name of a biblical character who wasn't a member of Virgin Mary's lineage but was commonly "coupled" to a biblical character who was a member of Virgin Mary's "lineage." I'd filed the seventh Query Stack, "QS-Holy^Ghost/Heaven," as a "Lineal-Alias Query Stack," because said Query Stack had a matrix which contained a row'd word that cited an "alias" of a biblical character who was a member of Virgin Mary's "lineage" and had a name that had been established already as a row'd word:

QS Categories

Lineal Query Stack
Query Stack with a first-row row'd word that names a character who belongs to a particular family tree (e.g. Virgin Mary's family tree).

Lineally-Coupled Query Stack
Query Stack with a first-row row'd word that names a character who doesn't belong to but is commonly associated with a member of a particular family tree (e.g. Virgin Mary's family tree).

Lineal-Alias Query Stack
Query Stack with a first-row row'd word that identifies the alias of a character whose name has been established as a row'd word and who belongs to a particular family tree (e.g. Virgin Mary's family tree).

Ch. 3, Sec. 2: 1

LINEAL QUERY STACKS
QS-GOD/HEAVEN
QS-JESUS/EARTH
QS-DAVE/EARTH
QS-JOE/EARTH
QS-MARY/EARTH
LINEALLY-COUPLED QUERY STACKS
QS-DEVIL/HELL
▶ LINEAL-ALIAS QUERY STACKS ◀
▶ QS-HOLY^GHOST/HEAVEN ◀

I'd filed each one of the seven Query Stacks which I'd revealed in this book so far as a "Lineal Query Stack," "Lineally-Coupled Query Stack" or "Lineal-Alias Query Stack" for a reason:

Ch. 3, Sec. 2: 2

LINEAL QUERY STACKS

QS-Mary/Earth—Mary was a lineal member of Virgin Mary's family tree, since Mary was Virgin Mary.

QS-Joe/Earth—Joe (Joseph) was a lineal member of Mary's family tree, because Joe and Mary were married.

QS-Dave/Earth—Dave (David) was a lineal member of Mary's family tree, because Dave was a multi-great-grandfather of Mary's.

QS-Jesus/Earth—Jesus was a lineal member of Mary's family tree, since Jesus was Mary's biological son.

QS-God/Heaven—God was a lineal member of Mary's family tree, since God was the father of the Jesus that Mary was the biological mother of.

LINEALLY-COUPLED QUERY STACKS

QS-Devil/Hell—Devil wasn't a lineal member of Mary's family tree but has been commonly coupled to God as God's antipode.

LINEAL-ALIAS QUERY STACKS

QS-Holy^Ghost/Heaven—Holy Ghost was a lineal member of Mary's family tree, since the name *Holy Ghost* was an alias for the name *God* and the Holy Ghost was the entity God used to impregnate Mary with Jesus.

I'd expanded the diagram of Virgin Mary's genealogy, which I'd introduced in "Ch. 2, Sec. 2: 1," by inserting the alias *Holy Ghost* into said diagram's "God" box. The names *Holy Ghost* and *God* shared the same diagrammatic box because the names *Holy Ghost* and *God* were aliases of one another:

> *Some of the biblical names which I've listed in the diagram belong in Virgin Mary's lineage but aren't QS row'd words (e.g. "Bathsheba," "Solomon," "Nathan") yet elucidate how some biblical characters with names that are QS row'd words are related;*

SOLID LINE (———) = Genealogically linked to Mary;
DASHED LINE (– – –) = Father of Mary's son Jesus, via no sexual contact;
DASHED/DOTTED LINE (– ·· –) = Mary's husband, but not Jesus's father;
DOUBLE LINE (====) = Not genealogically linked to Mary;
BLACK NAME BOX **NAME** = Row'd word, and main focus of family tree;
GRAY NAME BOX NAME = Row'd word, and member of family tree;
WHITE NAME BOX NAME = Row'd word, but not a member of family tree;
UNBOXED NAME = Not a row'd word, but member of family tree;

(a) MARY: herself;
(b) JOE *(Joseph)*: Mary's husband;
(c) DAVE *(David)*: Mary's multi-great-grandfather;
(d) JESUS: Mary's son;
(e) GOD: Mary's spiritual co-parent;
(f) DEVIL: God's antipode;
(g) HOLY GHOST: God's alias and conduit to impregnate Mary;

Ch. 3, Sec. 2: 3

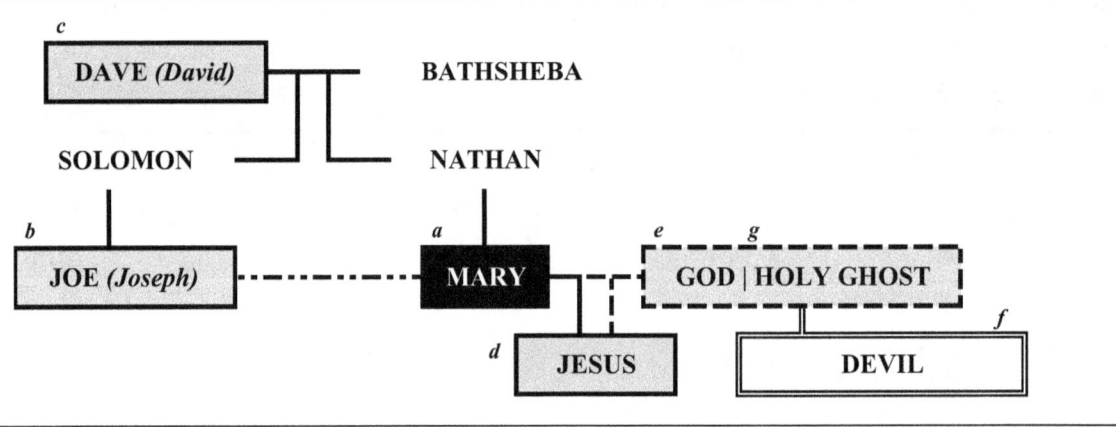

In "Ch. 2, Sec. 3: 11," I'd displayed a table in which each QS answer word in the first six QS answers I'd uncovered was categorized according to which of four identities (David Mivshek, Trinity, God or QS answer) the main subject of the QS answer that said answer word appeared in represented. In "Ch. 3, Sec. 2: 4," I'd updated said table with the "QS-Holy^Ghost/Heaven" answer words. I'd placed the "QS-Holy^Ghost/Heaven" answer words into the "David Mivshek" tier, since the said QS answer's main subject, the ghost, was David Mivshek:

A parenthetic number (#) succeeding a distinct answer word reports how many times said answer word appears in QS answers that may or may not share a distinct main subject but have main subjects which refer to David Mivshek, Trinity, God or QS an swers;

(a) "QS-Holy^Ghost/Heaven" answer words: "David Mivshek" tier, ghost is main subject, ghost is David Mivshek;

Ch. 3, Sec. 2: 4

DAVID MIVSHEK
Nouns—Winner, *ªGhost*;
Proper Nouns—Dave;
Pronouns—*ªHe* (2);
Verbs—Gains, Go, *ªAnswering*;
Adjectives—*ªHoly*, *ªNaïve*;
Conjunctions—*ªOr* (2).

TRINITY
Nouns—Evil, Horde, Ill;
Verbs—Reign, Wans.

GOD
Nouns—Giver, Hinter, Joe, Rein;
Verbs—Adore, Assure, Wans (2);
Adverbs—Right;
Indefinite Articles—A.

QS ANSWER
Nouns—Air, Hint (2), Joe, Reason (2);
Pronouns—I;
Verbs—Grew (2), Marry.
Indefinite Articles—A.

In "Ch. 2, Sec. 3: 13," I'd displayed statistics which pertained to QS answer vocabulary. I'd updated said statistics by incorporating numbers I'd garnered from the "QS-Holy^Ghost/Heaven" answer words:

Ch. 3, Sec. 2: 5

QS-GOD/HEAVEN
GO DAVE. HE: WINNER; OR, GAINS.
Number of QS answer words—6

Number of QS answer letters—21

Average number of letters per answer word—3.50

QS-DEVIL/HELL

HORDE: EVIL. ILL REIGN, WANS.

Number of QS answer words—5

Number of QS answer letters—21

Average number of letters per answer word—4.20

QS-JESUS/EARTH

JOE ASSURE. RIGHT, REIN WANS.

Number of QS answer words—5

Number of QS answer letters—22

Average number of letters per answer word—4.40

QS-DAVE/EARTH

ADORE GIVER. A HINTER WANS.

Number of QS answer words—5

Number of QS answer letters—21

Average number of letters per answer word—4.20

QS-JOE/EARTH

JOE: REASON. AIR/HINT GREW.

Number of QS answer words—5

Number of QS answer letters—20

Average number of letters per answer word—4.00

QS-MARY/EARTH

MARRY REASON. A HINT, I GREW.

Number of QS answer words—6

Number of QS answer letters—21

Average number of letters per answer word—3.50

QS-HOLY^GHOST/HEAVEN

HOLY GHOST. HE: NAÏVE OR ANSWERING.

Number of QS answer words—6

Number of QS answer letters—27

Average number of letters per answer word—4.50

QUERY STACK TOTALS AND AVERAGES

Total number of QS answers—7

Total number of QS answer words—38

Total number of QS answer letters—153

Average number of letters per QS answer—21.86

Average number of words per QS answer—5.43

Average number of letters per answer word—4.03

In "Ch. 3, Sec. 1: 3," I'd introduced "QS Rule 12":

Ch. 3, Sec. 2: 6

QUERY STACK CONSTRUCTION RULES

Rule 1—Determine a question;

Rule 2—Reduce the question's vocabulary to key words;

Rule 3—Stack key words in an order which causes the question to be asked if rowed key words are read downwards;

Rule 4—Align the first letter of each row'd word into one column;

Rule 5—Align subsequent letters of row'd words into subsequent columns;

▶ **Rule 12—Each letter-position in a Query Stack matrix must contain a letter.** ◀

QUERY STACK DECRYPTION RULES

Rule 6—Each and every row'd word letter must appear in a useful answer word;

Rule 7—Each row'd word letter must appear in the answer no more and no less than one time;

Rule 8—Row'd word letters can only be connected horizontally and/or vertically;

Rule 9—Letters in a set of connected row'd word letters can be arranged in any order to make an answer word;

Rule 10—Words built from connected row'd word letters are removed in a top-left to bottom-right sequence and listed in the order of removal to make a legitimate answer;

Rule 11—A word produced by linking row'd word letters together must be removed from a row'd word matrix and listed in the answer no more and no less than one time.

Each QS matrix that I'd revealed so far in this book consisted of the third-row row'd word ORIGIN and fourth-row row'd word ANSWER. I'd continued to insert ORIGIN and AN-

SWER into every QS matrix I'd revealed in this book from this point forward, but I'd no longer provided examples or explanations which spotlighted the insertion of the words *origin* and *answer* into the rows of QS matrices. I'd eliminated said examples and explanations as a way to tighten this book's word-count and make this book a faster read:

✓ **Each subsequent QS matrix presented in this book contains the third-row row'd word ORIGIN and fourth-row row'd word ANSWER.**

CHAPTER FOUR: SECTION ONE

YHWH/HEAVEN: YAHWEH'S HORN

```
Y H W H
H E A V E N
O R I G I N
A N S W E R
```

I'd wondered from time to time if God's name was actually *God*. Does the creator of Reality refer to Himself by the name *God*? Is *God* a name that only humans gave the god who holds the highest position in a hierarchy of entities which can mold and control Reality?

I'd read through biblical lessons, interpretations and critiques, trying to determine if anyone had claimed to know what God's actual name was. Ancient Hebrew biblical texts claimed that God's actual name was *YHWH*. The name *YHWH* was also referred to as the *tetragrammaton*, or "*n.* the Hebrew word of the four letters constituting a biblical proper name of God which the Jews out of reverence or for fear of desecration ceased to pronounce about three centuries B.C. and for which they substituted *Adonai* or *Elohim*, being variously transliterated without indication of the vocalization usually by *YHWH*...and with vowels usually by...*Yahweh*....)[2]."

I was curious if a valid QS answer would've emerged from a QS matrix which contained God's name *YHWH*:

Ch. 4, Sec. 1: 1

```
Y H W H
H E A V E N
O R I G I N
A N S W E R
```

YHWH was the name of a prominent biblical character, just like all of the other names which occupied the first rows of the seven matrices I'd unraveled so far:

(a) GOD; DEVIL; JESUS; DAVE *(David)*; JOE *(Joseph)*; MARY; HOLY^GHOST; YHWH: notable biblical beings, first-row row'd words;

Ch. 4, Sec. 1: 2

QS-God/Heaven	QS-Devil/Hell	QS-Jesus/Earth	QS-Dave/Earth
*a***G O D**	*b***D E V I L**	*c***J E S U S**	*d***D A V E**
HEAVEN	HELL	EARTH	EARTH
ORIGIN	ORIGIN	ORIGIN	ORIGIN
ANSWER	ANSWER	ANSWER	ANSWER

QS-Joe/Earth	QS-Mary/Earth	QS-Holy^Ghost/Heaven	
*e***J O E**	*f***M A R Y**	*g***H O L Y G H O S T**	
EARTH	EARTH	HEAVEN	
ORIGIN	ORIGIN	ORIGIN	
ANSWER	ANSWER	ANSWER	

QS-YHWH/Heaven			
*h***Y H W H**			
HEAVEN			
ORIGIN			
ANSWER			

Biblically, YHWH was a prominent character and entity in Heaven, since YHWH was God and God was who'd made and ruled over Heaven:

(a) GOD: notable biblical figure; of Heaven; Heaven's ruler;
(b) DEVIL: notable biblical figure; of Hell; God sends evil to Hell, Devil is the evilest being, Devil is evilest being God could send to Hell;
(c) JESUS: notable biblical figure, of Earth; Earth's premier ruler;
(d) DAVE *(David)*: notable biblical figure; of Earth; third King of Israel;
(e) JOE *(Joseph)*: notable biblical figure; of Earth; Virgin Mary's husband;
(f) MARY: notable biblical figure; of Earth; Jesus's mother;
(g) HOLY GHOST: notable biblical figure; of Heaven; Heaven's messenger;
(h) **YHWH: notable biblical figure; of Heaven; Heaven's ruler;**

Ch. 4, Sec. 1: 3

BIBLICAL BEING	DOMAIN	NOTORIETY
[a]GOD	[a]HEAVEN	[a]RULER
[b]DEVIL	[b]HELL	[b]EVILEST RESIDENT
[c]JESUS	[c]EARTH	[c]PREMIER RULER
[d]DAVE *(David)*	[d]EARTH	[d]ANOINTED KING
[e]JOE *(Joseph)*	[e]EARTH	[e]MARY'S HUSBAND
[f]MARY	[f]EARTH	[f]JESUS'S MOTHER
[g]HOLY GHOST	[g]HEAVEN	[g]MESSENGER
[h]**YHWH**	[h]**HEAVEN**	[h]**RULER**

YHWH/HEAVEN: YAHWEH'S HORN

I'd linked adjacent letters in the "QS-YHWH/Heaven" row'd word matrix together in an effort to produce a valid QS answer. Eventually, I'd uncovered an answer which was grammatically coherent and meaningful:

✓ All QS rules followed (see "Appendix A");

Ch. 4, Sec. 1: 4

Y	H	W	H	
H	E	A	V	E	N
O	R	I	G	I	N
A	N	S	W	E	R

YAHWEH: HORN. NERVING, IS A WE.

Next, I'd assigned definitions to the "QS-YHWH/Heaven" answer words:

Ch. 4, Sec. 1: 5

YAHWEH: HORN. NERVING, IS A WE.

YAHWEH *prop-n.* God—transliteration of the Hebrew tetragrammaton *(YHWH)*.[2]
HORN *n.* Source of strength.[2]
NERVING *v.* To give strength to; supply with moral force.[2]
IS *v.* Show a certain characteristic.[2]
A *i-art.* Used before most singular nouns when the individual in question is unidentified, especially when the individual is being called to notice.[2]
WE *n.* A group that is consciously felt as such by its members.[2]

I'd analyzed the "QS-YHWH/Heaven" answer's vocabulary word by word in order to understand said answer's meaning:

YAHWEH

Vocabulary of ancient Hebrew biblical text was vowelless, which inspired debates over the proper pronunciation and transliteration of important words like God's name *YHWH*; however, *Yahweh (yhwh + a + e)* has been deemed by theological scholars as an acceptable transliteration of the tetragrammaton;

HORN

In the Bible, the term *horn* signified that someone or something was a source of strength. For example, Jesus was deemed a "horn of salvation," which meant that Jesus was a source of strength that a person could extract said strength from: "The God of my rock; in him will I trust: he is my shield, and the <u>horn of my salvation</u>, my high tower, and my refuge, my saviour; thou savest me from violence" (2 Samuel 22:3 KJV);

NERVING, IS A WE

In the "QS-YHWH/Heaven" answer's first sentence, Yahweh, or God, was identified as a horn, or a source of strength, while the first word in said answer's second sentence, *nerving*, suggested that God shared His moral strength with someone. I'd interpreted said answer's second sentence *"nerving, is a we"* as "nerving a we and is a we"; which meant, God was a source of moral strength who'd given said strength to a group of individuals and God was a group of individuals. God was a trinity, and, therefore, a group of individuals, or a we, so I'd interpreted the "QS-YHWH/Heaven" answer's second sentence as "God was a source of moral strength and the we which gave said moral strength to Himself":

Ch. 4, Sec. 1: 6

YAHWEH: HORN.$_{sent1}$ **NERVING, IS A WE.**$_{sent2}$

$_{sent1}$: **God is a source of strength.**

$_{sent2}$: **God is giving moral strength to Himself and is a trinity comprised of three individuals who are each aware of being an individual in said trinity.**

The "QS-YHWH/Heaven" answer was grammatically coherent and meaningful, yet I'd ran said answer through "QS-7CAP" in order to confirm said answer's validity:

Seven Common QS Answer Properties

1. Each answer contains no more and no less than two sentences (sent1, sent2):

QS-God/Heaven

GO DAVE.sent1 HE: WINNER; OR, GAINS.sent2

QS-Devil/Hell

HORDE: EVIL.sent1 ILL REIGN, WANS.sent2

QS-Jesus/Earth

JOE ASSURE.sent1 RIGHT, REIN WANS.sent2

QS-Dave/Earth

ADORE GIVER.sent1 A HINTER WANS.sent2

QS-Joe/Earth

JOE: REASON.sent1 AIR/HINT GREW.sent2

QS-Mary/Earth

MARRY REASON.sent1 A HINT, I GREW.sent2

QS-Holy^Ghost/Heaven

HOLY GHOST.sent1 HE: NAÏVE OR ANSWERING.sent2

QS-YHWH/Heaven

YAHWEH: HORN.sent1 NERVING, IS A WE.sent2

2. Each answer's first sentence contains no more and no less than two words (word1, word2):

QS-God/Heaven

GO_word1 DAVE_word2. HE: WINNER; OR, GAINS.

QS-Devil/Hell

HORDE_word1: EVIL_word2. ILL REIGN, WANS.

QS-Jesus/Earth

JOE_word1 ASSURE_word2. RIGHT, REIN WANS.

QS-Dave/Earth

ADORE_word1 GIVER_word2. A HINTER WANS.

QS-Joe/Earth

JOE_word1: REASON_word2. AIR/HINT GREW.

QS-Mary/Earth

MARRY_word1 REASON_word2. A HINT, I GREW.

QS-Holy^Ghost/Heaven

HOLY_word1 GHOST_word2. HE: NAÏVE OR ANSWERING.

QS-YHWH/Heaven

YAHWEH_word1: HORN_word2. NERVING, IS A WE.

3. In each answer's first sentence, the main subject is introduced (subj1, subj2, ...):

QS-God/Heaven

GO **DAVE**~subj1~. HE: WINNER; OR, GAINS.

QS-Devil/Hell

HORDE~subj2~: EVIL. ILL REIGN, WANS.

QS-Jesus/Earth

JOE~subj3~ ASSURE. RIGHT, REIN WANS.

QS-Dave/Earth

ADORE **GIVER**~subj4~. A HINTER WANS.

QS-Joe/Earth

JOE: **REASON**~subj5~. AIR/HINT GREW.

QS-Mary/Earth

MARRY **REASON**~subj6~. A HINT, I GREW.

QS-Holy^Ghost/Heaven

HOLY **GHOST**~subj7~. HE: NAÏVE OR ANSWERING.

QS-YHWH/Heaven

YAHWEH~subj8~: HORN. NERVING, IS A WE.

4. In each answer, the main subject introduced in the first sentence is mentioned in the second sentence (subj1-subj1, subj2-subj2, ...):

QS-God/Heaven

GO **DAVE**~subj1~. **HE**~subj1~: WINNER; OR, GAINS.

QS-Devil/Hell

HORDE~subj2~: EVIL. **ILL**~subj2~ REIGN, WANS.

QS-Jesus/Earth

JOE~subj3~ ASSURE. RIGHT, **REIN**~subj3~ WANS.

QS-Dave/Earth

ADORE **GIVER**~subj4~. A **HINTER**~subj4~ WANS.

QS-Joe/Earth

JOE: **REASON**~subj5~. **AIR**~subj5~/HINT GREW.

QS-Mary/Earth

MARRY **REASON**~subj6~. A **HINT**~subj6~, I GREW.

QS-Holy^Ghost/Heaven

HOLY **GHOST**~subj7~. **HE**~subj7~: NAÏVE OR ANSWERING.

QS-YHWH/Heaven

YAHWEH~subj8~: HORN. NERVING, IS A **WE**~subj8~.

5. In each answer, the first sentence's second word and the second sentence's first word are synonymous in definition (syn) or context (con):

   Synonymous answer words are tagged "syn," while answer words which share contextual meaning are tagged "con";

   (con1) DAVE; HE: context, both words identify same man;

   (syn2) EVIL; ILL: synonyms, each word means "wicked";

   (con3) ASSURE; RIGHT: context, both words convey affirmation;

   (con4) GIVER; [A HINTER]: context, word and [phrase] identify same person; *[Property Deviation Resolution: (see "Appendix B")]*;

   (con5) REASON; AIR: context, the reason is expressed as a written statement;

   (con6) REASON; [A HINT]: context, the reason is expressed as an allusive statement; *[Property Deviation Resolution: (see "Appendix B")]*;

   (con7) GHOST; HE: context, both words identify same person;

   (con 8) HORN; NERVING: context, each word refers to a source of strength;

QS-God/Heaven

GO **DAVE**$_{con1}$. **HE**$_{con1}$: WINNER; OR, GAINS.

QS-Devil/Hell

HORDE: **EVIL**$_{syn2}$. **ILL**$_{syn2}$ REIGN, WANS.

QS-Jesus/Earth

JOE **ASSURE**$_{con3}$. **RIGHT**$_{con3}$, REIN WANS.

QS-Dave/Earth

ADORE **GIVER**$_{con4}$. [A **HINTER**]$_{con4}$ WANS.

QS-Joe/Earth

JOE: **REASON**$_{con5}$. **AIR**$_{con5}$/HINT GREW.

QS-Mary/Earth

MARRY **REASON**$_{con6}$. [A **HINT**]$_{con6}$, I GREW.

QS-Holy^Ghost/Heaven

HOLY **GHOST**$_{con7}$. **HE**$_{con7}$: NAÏVE OR ANSWERING.

QS-YHWH/Heaven

YAHWEH: **HORN**$_{con8}$. **NERVING**$_{con8}$, IS A WE.

6. In each answer's second sentence, at least one action is applied to the main subject (subj1–act1, subj2–act2, ...):

QS-God/Heaven

GO DAVE. **HE**$_{subj1}$: WINNER; OR, **GAINS**$_{act1}$.

QS-Devil/Hell

HORDE: EVIL. **ILL**$_{subj2}$ **REIGN**$_{act2}$, WANS.

QS-Jesus/Earth

JOE ASSURE. RIGHT, **REIN**$_{subj3}$ **WANS**$_{act3}$.

QS-Dave/Earth

ADORE GIVER. A **HINTER**$_{subj4}$ **WANS**$_{act4}$.

QS-Joe/Earth

JOE: REASON. **AIR**$_{subj5}$/HINT **GREW**$_{act5}$.

QS-Mary/Earth

MARRY REASON. A **HINT**$_{subj6}$, I **GREW**$_{act6}$.

QS-Holy^Ghost/Heaven

HOLY GHOST. **HE**$_{subj7}$: NAÏVE OR **ANSWERING**$_{act7}$.

QS-YHWH/Heaven

YAHWEH: HORN. **NERVING**$_{act8}$, IS A **WE**$_{subj8}$.

7. Along each answer's breadth of vocabulary, there's at least one site where an answer letter *S* would've enhanced the answer's grammatical correctness if it would've been available in the accompanying row'd word matrix and usable:

   Removing a colon (:) that follows a noun and appending a contraction 's to the end of said noun would produce a conversational tone and clearer syntax (e.g. He's winner; Horde's evil; He's naïve; He's answering; Yahweh's horn). Removing a colon (:) that follows a noun and appending a possessive 's to the end of said noun would produce a conversational tone and clearer syntax (e.g. Joe's reason). Inflecting certain verbs by appending a letter S to the end of them would promote optimal grammar (e.g. Ill reigns; Joe assures). However, each answer's row'd word matrix lacks a letter S that's needed or that's capable of being used in ways mandated by QS rules (see "Appendix A");

   [Property Deviation Resolution (see "Appendix B"): "QS-Dave/Earth" and "QS-Mary/Earth"];

   QS-God/Heaven: He's winner;
   QS-Devil/Hell: Horde's evil, Ill reigns;
   QS-Jesus/Earth: Joe assures;
   QS-Dave/Earth: (optimal grammar);
   QS-Joe/Earth: Joe's reason;
   QS-Mary/Earth: (optimal grammar);
   QS-Holy^Ghost/Heaven: He's naïve, He's answering;
   QS-YHWH/Heaven: Yahweh's horn;

QS-God/Heaven

GO DAVE. **HE: WINNER**; OR, GAINS.

QS-Devil/Hell

HORDE: EVIL. ILL REIGN, WANS.

QS-Jesus/Earth

JOE ASSURE. RIGHT, REIN WANS.

QS-Dave/Earth

ADORE GIVER. A HINTER WANS.

QS-Joe/Earth

JOE: REASON. AIR/HINT GREW.

QS-Mary/Earth

MARRY REASON. A HINT, I GREW.

QS-Holy^Ghost/Heaven

HOLY GHOST. **HE: NAÏVE** OR ANSWERING.

HOLY GHOST. **HE:** NAÏVE OR **ANSWERING**.

QS-YHWH/Heaven

YAHWEH: HORN. NERVING, IS A WE.

CHAPTER FOUR: SECTION TWO

YAHWEH/HEAVEN: HEAVEN'S HORN

Y	A	H	W	E	H
H	E	A	V	E	N
O	R	I	G	I	N
A	N	S	W	E	R

I'd transposed the answer word *YAHWEH* from the "QS-YHWH/Heaven" answer into the first-row row'd word of the "QS-Yahweh/Heaven" matrix:

(a) Answer word *YAHWEH* inspired first-row row'd word YAHWEH;

Ch. 4, Sec. 2: 1

QS-YHWH/Heaven

"**YAHWEH**: HORN. NERVING, IS A WE.

QS-Yahweh/Heaven

"Y A H W E H
H E A V E N
O R I G I N
A N S W E R

I'd connected adjacent row'd word letters of said matrix and revealed a valid QS answer:

✓ All QS rules followed (see "Appendix A");

Ch. 4, Sec. 2: 2

Y	A	H	W	E	H
H	E	A	V	E	N
O	R	I	G	I	N
A	N	S	W	E	R

HAY: WE. HEAVEN: HORN, SIRING A WE.

I'd assigned definitions to the "QS-Yahweh/Heaven" answer words:

Ch. 4, Sec. 2: 3

```
HAY: WE. HEAVEN: HORN, SIRING A WE.
```

HAY *n.* A rewarding result of careful effort.[2]
WE *n.* A group that is consciously felt as such by its members.[2]
HEAVEN *prop-n.* God.[2]
HORN *n.* Source of strength.[2]
SIRING *v.* <SIRE *v.*> To bring into being.[2]
A *i-art.* Used before most singular nouns when the individual in question is unidentified, especially when the individual is being called to notice.[2]

I'd analyzed the "QS-Yahweh/Heaven" answer words to grasp said answer's meaning:

HAY: WE.
Based on the seventh property of "QS-7CAP" (see "Appendix B") and my interpretations of QS answers which contained similar grammar as the grammar of the "QS-Yahweh/Heaven" answer's first sentence, I'd determined that the colon which followed the answer word *HAY*, "*hay(:),*" was a punctuational substitute for an apostrophized letter S, or *'s*; which meant, said answer word and colon symbolized the contraction *hay's,* which contracted the phrase *hay is*:

(a) "*:*" symbolizes a contractive *'s* or the word *is*:

Ch. 4, Sec. 2: 4

```
HAY ᵃ(:) WE.
HAY ᵃ('s[is]) WE.
```

The hay, or the rewarding result of careful effort, was the entity cited as a we. In "Ch. 4, Sec. 1: 6," I'd determined that the answer word *WE* referred to a group of three individuals who were each aware of being an individual in said group and that said group was the Trinity:

Ch. 4, Sec. 2: 5

```
HAY: WE.
```

A rewarding result of careful effort is the Trinity.

HEAVEN, WE
The fifth property of "QS-7CAP" mandated that the second word in an answer's first sen-

tence was related definitionally or contextually to the first word in said answer's second sentence; which meant, the answer words *WE* and *HEAVEN* were definitionally or contextually related. The answer words *WE* and *HEAVEN* were contextually related, because *WE* referred to the Trinity, the Trinity was God, and "*prop-n.* God[2]" was the definition I'd selected for the answer word *HEAVEN* (see "Ch. 4, Sec. 2: 3"):

[a] WE: references the Trinity, which is God;
[b] HEAVEN: references God, who is the Trinity;

Ch. 4, Sec. 2: 6

HAY: [a]**WE**.sent1 [b]**HEAVEN**: HORN, SIRING A [a]**WE**.sent2

sent1: *A rewarding result of careful effort is the [a](Trinity).*
sent2: *[b](God, the Trinity), is a source of strength and is originating the [a](Trinity).*

HORN

In "Ch. 4, Sec. 1: 6," I'd determined that the answer word *HORN* meant "a source of strength" and cited Yahweh, or God, as said source. Said determination prompted me to assign God as the horn which was mentioned in the "QS-Yahweh/Heaven" answer:

[a] HORN: cites God;

Ch. 4, Sec. 2: 7

HAY: WE.sent1 HEAVEN: [a]**HORN**, SIRING A WE.sent2

sent1: *A rewarding result of careful effort is the Trinity.*
sent2: **God, the Trinity, is a [a](source of strength) and is originating the Trinity.**

HEAVEN: SIRING A WE

If Heaven was God and God was the Trinity and the Trinity was the we, then God wasn't only a source of strength but was also the entity who was carefully making Himself into a trio:

Ch. 4, Sec. 2: 8

HAY: WE.sent1 (HEAVEN:) HORN, (SIRING A WE).sent2

sent1: *A rewarding result of careful effort is the Trinity.*
sent2: *(God, the Trinity), is a source of strength and (is originating the Trinity, or inventing Himself as a trio of individuals who are each aware of being a member of said trio).*

My "QS-Yahweh/Heaven" answer was grammatically coherent and meaningful, yet I'd ran it through "QS-7CAP" to confirm said answer's validity:

Seven Common QS Answer Properties

1. Each answer contains no more and no less than two sentences (sent1, sent2):

QS-God/Heaven
GO DAVE.sent1 HE: WINNER; OR, GAINS.sent2

QS-Devil/Hell
HORDE: EVIL.sent1 ILL REIGN, WANS.sent2

QS-Jesus/Earth
JOE ASSURE.sent1 RIGHT, REIN WANS.sent2

QS-Dave/Earth
ADORE GIVER.sent1 A HINTER WANS.sent2

QS-Joe/Earth
JOE: REASON.sent1 AIR/HINT GREW.sent2

QS-Mary/Earth
MARRY REASON.sent1 A HINT, I GREW.sent2

QS-Holy^Ghost/Heaven
HOLY GHOST.sent1 HE: NAÏVE OR ANSWERING.sent2

QS-YHWH/Heaven
YAHWEH: HORN.sent1 NERVING, IS A WE.sent2

QS-Yahweh/Heaven
HAY: WE.sent1 HEAVEN: HORN, SIRING A WE.sent2

2. Each answer's first sentence contains no more and no less than two words (word1, word2):

QS-God/Heaven

GO~word1~ **DAVE**~word2~. HE: WINNER; OR, GAINS.

QS-Devil/Hell

HORDE~word1~: **EVIL**~word2~. ILL REIGN, WANS.

QS-Jesus/Earth

JOE~word1~ **ASSURE**~word2~. RIGHT, REIN WANS.

QS-Dave/Earth

ADORE~word1~ **GIVER**~word2~. A HINTER WANS.

QS-Joe/Earth

JOE~word1~: **REASON**~word2~. AIR/HINT GREW.

QS-Mary/Earth

MARRY~word1~ **REASON**~word2~. A HINT, I GREW.

QS-Holy^Ghost/Heaven

HOLY~word1~ **GHOST**~word2~. HE: NAÏVE OR ANSWERING.

QS-YHWH/Heaven

YAHWEH~word1~: **HORN**~word2~. NERVING, IS A WE.

QS-Yahweh/Heaven

HAY~word1~: **WE**~word2~. HEAVEN: HORN, SIRING A WE.

3. In each answer's first sentence, the main subject is introduced (subj1, subj2, ...):

QS-God/Heaven

GO **DAVE**~subj1~. HE: WINNER; OR, GAINS.

QS-Devil/Hell

HORDE~subj2~: EVIL. ILL REIGN, WANS.

QS-Jesus/Earth

JOE~subj3~ ASSURE. RIGHT, REIN WANS.

QS-Dave/Earth

ADORE **GIVER**~subj4~. A HINTER WANS.

QS-Joe/Earth

JOE: **REASON**~subj5~. AIR/HINT GREW.

QS-Mary/Earth

MARRY **REASON**~subj6~. A HINT, I GREW.

QS-Holy^Ghost/Heaven

HOLY **GHOST**~subj7~. HE: NAÏVE OR ANSWERING.

QS-YHWH/Heaven

YAHWEH~subj8~: HORN. NERVING, IS A WE.

QS-Yahweh/Heaven

HAY~subj9~: WE. HEAVEN: HORN, SIRING A WE.

4. In each answer, the main subject introduced in the first sentence is mentioned in the second sentence (subj1-subj1, subj2-subj2, ...):

QS-God/Heaven

GO **DAVE**~subj1~. **HE**~subj1~: WINNER; OR, GAINS.

QS-Devil/Hell

HORDE~subj2~: EVIL. **ILL**~subj2~ REIGN, WANS.

QS-Jesus/Earth

JOE~subj3~ ASSURE. RIGHT, **REIN**~subj3~ WANS.

QS-Dave/Earth

ADORE **GIVER**~subj4~. A **HINTER**~subj4~ WANS.

QS-Joe/Earth

JOE: **REASON**~subj5~. **AIR**~subj5~/HINT GREW.

QS-Mary/Earth

MARRY **REASON**~subj6~. A **HINT**~subj6~, I GREW.

QS-Holy^Ghost/Heaven

HOLY **GHOST**~subj7~. **HE**~subj7~: NAÏVE OR ANSWERING.

QS-YHWH/Heaven

YAHWEH~subj8~: HORN. NERVING, IS A **WE**~subj8~.

QS-Yahweh/Heaven

HAY~subj9~: WE. HEAVEN: HORN, SIRING A **WE**~subj9~.

5. In each answer, the first sentence's second word and the second sentence's first word are synonymous in definition (syn) or context (con):

Synonymous answer words are tagged "syn," while answer words which share contextual meaning are tagged "con";

(con1) DAVE; HE: context, both words identify same man;

(syn2) EVIL; ILL: synonyms, each word means "wicked";

(con3) ASSURE; RIGHT: context, both words convey affirmation;

(con4) GIVER; [A HINTER]: context, word and [phrase] identify same person; *[Property Deviation Resolution: (see "Appendix B")]*;

(con5) REASON; AIR: context, the reason is expressed as a written statement;

(con6) REASON; [A HINT]: context, the reason is expressed as an allusive statement; *[Property Deviation Resolution: (see "Appendix B")]*;

(con7) GHOST; HE: context, both words identify same person;

(con 8) HORN; NERVING: context, each word refers to a source of strength;

(con 9) WE; HEAVEN: context, both words identify same entity;

QS-God/Heaven

GO **DAVE**~con1~. **HE**~con1~: WINNER; OR, GAINS.

QS-Devil/Hell

HORDE: **EVIL**~syn2~. **ILL**~syn2~ REIGN, WANS.

QS-Jesus/Earth

JOE **ASSURE**~con3~. **RIGHT**~con3~, REIN WANS.

QS-Dave/Earth

ADORE **GIVER**~con4~. **[A HINTER]**~con4~ WANS.

QS-Joe/Earth

JOE: **REASON**~con5~. **AIR**~con5~/HINT GREW.

QS-Mary/Earth

MARRY **REASON**~con6~. **[A HINT]**~con6~, I GREW.

QS-Holy^Ghost/Heaven

HOLY **GHOST**~con7~. **HE**~con7~: NAÏVE OR ANSWERING.

QS-YHWH/Heaven

YAHWEH: **HORN**~con8~. **NERVING**~con8~, IS A WE.

QS-Yahweh/Heaven

HAY: **WE**~con9~. **HEAVEN**~con9~: HORN, SIRING A WE.

6. In each answer's second sentence, at least one action is applied to the main subject (subj1–act1, subj2–act2, ...):

QS-God/Heaven
GO DAVE. **HE**$_{subj1}$: WINNER; OR, **GAINS**$_{act1}$.
QS-Devil/Hell
HORDE: EVIL. **ILL**$_{subj2}$ **REIGN**$_{act2}$, WANS.
QS-Jesus/Earth
JOE ASSURE. RIGHT, **REIN**$_{subj3}$ **WANS**$_{act3}$.
QS-Dave/Earth
ADORE GIVER. A **HINTER**$_{subj4}$ **WANS**$_{act4}$.
QS-Joe/Earth
JOE: REASON. **AIR**$_{subj5}$/HINT **GREW**$_{act5}$.
QS-Mary/Earth
MARRY REASON. A **HINT**$_{subj6}$, I **GREW**$_{act6}$.
QS-Holy^Ghost/Heaven
HOLY GHOST. **HE**$_{subj7}$: NAÏVE OR **ANSWERING**$_{act7}$.
QS-YHWH/Heaven
YAHWEH: HORN. **NERVING**$_{act8}$, IS A **WE**$_{subj8}$.
QS-Yahweh/Heaven
HAY: WE. HEAVEN: HORN, **SIRING**$_{act9}$ A **WE**$_{subj9}$.

7. Along each answer's breadth of vocabulary, there's at least one site where an answer letter *S* would've enhanced the answer's grammatical correctness if it would've been available in the accompanying row'd word matrix and usable:

   Removing a colon (:) that follows a noun and appending a contraction 's to the end of said noun would produce a conversational tone and clearer syntax (e.g. <u>He's</u> winner; <u>Horde's</u> evil; <u>He's</u> naïve; <u>He's</u> answering; <u>Yahweh's</u> horn; <u>Hay's</u> we; <u>Heaven's</u> horn; <u>Heaven's</u> siring). Removing a colon (:) that follows a noun and appending a possessive 's to the end of said noun would produce a conversational tone and clearer syntax (e.g. <u>Joe's</u> reason). Inflecting certain verbs by appending a letter S to the end of them would promote optimal grammar (e.g. Ill <u>reigns</u>; Joe <u>assures</u>). However, each answer's row'd word matrix lacks a letter S that's needed or that's capable of being used in ways mandated by QS rules (see "Appendix A");

   [Property Deviation Resolution (see "Appendix B"): "QS-Dave/Earth" and "QS-Mary/Earth"];

QS-God/Heaven: <u>He's</u> <u>winner</u>;
QS-Devil/Hell: <u>Horde's</u> evil, Ill <u>reigns</u>;
QS-Jesus/Earth: Joe <u>assures</u>;
QS-Dave/Earth: (optimal grammar);
QS-Joe/Earth: <u>Joe's</u> reason;
QS-Mary/Earth: (optimal grammar);
QS-Holy^Ghost/Heaven: <u>He's</u> naïve, <u>He's</u> answering;
QS-YHWH/Heaven: <u>Yahweh's</u> horn;
QS-Yahweh/Heaven: <u>Heaven's</u> horn, <u>Heaven's</u> siring;

QS-God/Heaven

GO DAVE. **HE: WINNER**; OR, GAINS.

QS-Devil/Hell

HORDE: EVIL. ILL REIGN, WANS.

QS-Jesus/Earth

JOE ASSURE. RIGHT, REIN WANS.

QS-Dave/Earth

ADORE GIVER. A HINTER WANS.

QS-Joe/Earth

JOE: REASON. AIR/HINT GREW.

QS-Mary/Earth

MARRY REASON. A HINT, I GREW.

QS-Holy^Ghost/Heaven

HOLY GHOST. **HE: NAÏVE** OR ANSWERING.

HOLY GHOST. **HE:** NAÏVE OR **ANSWERING**.

QS-YHWH/Heaven

YAHWEH: HORN. NERVING, IS A WE.

QS-Yahweh/Heaven

HAY: WE. HEAVEN: HORN, SIRING A WE.

HAY: WE. **HEAVEN:** HORN, **SIRING** A WE.

CHAPTER FOUR: SECTION THREE

REVIEW: NINE STACKS

```
G O D              D E V I L          J E S U S
H E A V E N        H E L L            E A R T H
O R I G I N        O R I G I N        O R I G I N
A N S W E R        A N S W E R        A N S W E R
```

```
D A V E            J O E              M A R Y
E A R T H          E A R T H          E A R T H
O R I G I N        O R I G I N        O R I G I N
A N S W E R        A N S W E R        A N S W E R
```

```
H O L Y G H O S T  Y H W H            Y A H W E H
H E A V E N        H E A V E N        H E A V E N
O R I G I N        O R I G I N        O R I G I N
A N S W E R        A N S W E R        A N S W E R
```

Each of the nine Query Stacks which I'd revealed up until now fell into one of three categories—"Lineal Query Stacks," "Lineally-Coupled Query Stacks" or "Lineal-Alias Query Stacks"—which I'd already defined (see "Ch. 3, Sec. 2: 1"). I'd filed five of the nine Query Stacks as "Lineal Query Stacks," because each of the said five Query Stacks had a row'd word matrix which contained a name of a biblical character who was a member of Virgin Mary's "lineage." I'd filed one of the nine Query Stacks as a "Lineally-Coupled" Query Stack, which had a matrix that contained the name of a biblical character who wasn't a member of Virgin Mary's lineage but was commonly "coupled" to a biblical character who was a member of Virgin Mary's "lineage." I'd filed the remaining three Query Stacks as "Lineal-Alias Query Stacks," because each of the said three Query Stacks had a matrix which contained a row'd word that identified an "alias" of a biblical character who was a member of Virgin Mary's "lineage" and had a name that had been established already as a row'd word:

Ch. 4, Sec. 3: 1

LINEAL QUERY STACKS

QS-GOD/HEAVEN
QS-JESUS/EARTH
QS-DAVE/EARTH
QS-JOE/EARTH
QS-MARY/EARTH

LINEALLY-COUPLED QUERY STACKS

QS-DEVIL/HELL

LINEAL-ALIAS QUERY STACKS

QS-HOLY^GHOST/HEAVEN
► QS-YHWH/HEAVEN ◄
► QS-YAHWEH/HEAVEN ◄

I'd filed each one of the nine Query Stacks which I'd revealed in this book so far as a "Lineal Query Stack," "Lineally-Coupled Query Stack" or "Lineal-Alias Query Stack" for a reason:

Ch. 4, Sec. 3: 2

LINEAL QUERY STACKS

QS-Mary/Earth—Mary was a lineal member of Virgin Mary's family tree, since Mary was Virgin Mary.

QS-Joe/Earth—Joe (Joseph) was a lineal member of Mary's family tree, because Joe and Mary were married.

QS-Dave/Earth—Dave (David) was a lineal member of Mary's family tree, because Dave was a multi-great-grandfather of Mary's.

QS-Jesus/Earth—Jesus was a lineal member of Mary's family tree, since Jesus was Mary's biological son.

QS-God/Heaven—God was a lineal member of Mary's family tree, since God was the father of the Jesus that Mary was the biological mother of.

LINEALLY-COUPLED QUERY STACKS

QS-Devil/Hell—Devil wasn't a lineal member of Mary's family tree but has been commonly coupled to God as God's antipode.

LINEAL-ALIAS QUERY STACKS

QS-Holy^Ghost/Heaven—Holy Ghost was a lineal member of Mary's family tree, since the name *Holy Ghost* was an alias for the name *God* and the Holy Ghost was the entity God used to impregnate Mary with Jesus.

QS-YHWH/Heaven—YHWH was a lineal member of Mary's family tree, since the name *YHWH* was an alias for the name *God* and was God's given name, according to ancient biblical text.

QS-Yahweh/Heaven—Yahweh was a lineal member of Mary's family tree, since the name *Yahweh* was an alias for the name *God* and a transliteration of God's given name *YHWH*.

I'd expanded the diagram of Virgin Mary's genealogy, which I'd introduced in "Ch. 2, Sec. 2: 1," by inserting the aliases *YHWH* and *Yahweh* into the diagram's "God" box. The names *YHWH, Yahweh* and *God* shared the same diagrammatic box because the names *YHWH, Yahweh* and *God* were aliases of one another:

> *Some of the biblical names which I've listed in the diagram belong in Virgin Mary's lineage but aren't QS row'd words (e.g. "Bathsheba," "Solomon," "Nathan") yet elucidate how some biblical characters with names that are QS row'd words are related;*

SOLID LINE (———) = Genealogically linked to Mary;
DASHED LINE (– – –) = Father of Mary's son Jesus, via no sexual contact;
DASHED/DOTTED LINE (– ·· –) = Mary's husband, but not Jesus's father;
DOUBLE LINE (====) = Not genealogically linked to Mary;
BLACK NAME BOX **NAME** = Row'd word, and main focus of family tree;
GRAY NAME BOX NAME = Row'd word, and member of family tree;
WHITE NAME BOX NAME = Row'd word, but not a member of family tree;
UNBOXED NAME = Not a row'd word, but member of family tree;

(a) MARY: herself;
(b) JOE *(Joseph)*: Mary's husband;
(c) DAVE *(David)*: Mary's multi-great-grandfather;
(d) JESUS: Mary's son;
(e) GOD: Mary's spiritual co-parent;
(f) DEVIL: God's antipode;
(g) HOLY GHOST: God's alias and conduit to impregnate Mary;
(h) YHWH: God's alias and ancient Hebrew name;
(i) YAHWEH: God's alias and modern Hebrew name;

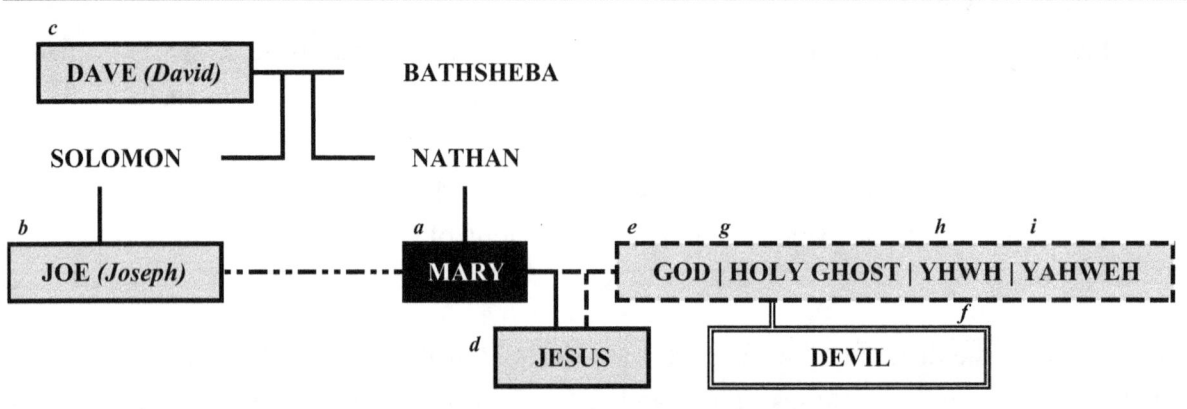

In "Ch. 3, Sec. 2: 4," I'd displayed a table in which each QS answer word in the first four QS answers I'd uncovered was categorized according to which one of four identities (David Mivshek, Trinity, God or QS answer) the main subject of the QS answer that said answer word appeared in represented. In "Ch. 4, Sec. 3: 4," I'd updated said table with the "QS-YHWH/Heaven" and "QS-Yahweh/Heaven" answer words. I'd placed the "QS-YHWH/Heaven" answer words into the "God" tier, since the "QS-YHWH/Heaven" answer's main subject, Yahweh, was God, and placed the "QS-Yahweh/Heaven" answer words into the "Trinity" tier, since the "QS-Yahweh/Heaven" answer's main subject, the hay, was the Trinity:

A parenthetic number (#) succeeding a distinct answer word reports how many times said answer word appears in QS answers that may or may not share a distinct main subject but have main subjects which refer to David Mivshek, Trinity, God or QS answers;

(a) "QS-YHWH/Heaven" answer words: "God" tier, Yahweh is main subject; Yahweh is God;

(b) "QS-Yahweh/Heaven" answer words: "Trinity" tier, hay is main subject, hay is Trinity;

Ch. 4, Sec. 3: 4

DAVID MIVSHEK

Nouns—Winner, Ghost;

Proper Nouns—Dave;

Pronouns—He (2);

Verbs—Gains, Go, Answering;

Adjectives—Holy, Naïve;

Conjunctions—Or (2).

TRINITY

Nouns—Evil, [b]**Hay**, Horde, [b]**Horn**, Ill, [b]**We** (2);

Proper Nouns—[b]**Heaven**;

Verbs—Reign, [b]**Siring**, Wans;

Indefinite Articles—[b]**A**.

GOD

Nouns—Giver, Hinter, [c]**Horn**, Joe, Rein, [c]**We**;

Proper Nouns—[c]**Yahweh**;

Verbs—Adore, Assure, [c]**Is**, [c]**Nerving**, Wans (2);

Adverbs—Right;

Indefinite Articles—[c]**A** (2).

QS ANSWER

Nouns—Air, Hint (2), Joe, Reason (2);

Pronouns—I;

Verbs—Grew (2), Marry;

Indefinite Articles—A.

As I'd determined in "Ch. 2, Sec. 3: 12," a distinct answer word which didn't identify an individual was permitted to be a word in multiple QS answers, even if each said QS answers had a distinct main subject, while a distinct answer word which did identify an individual always identified one and the same individual, even when said answer word was in multiple answers and each one of said answers contained a distinct main subject:

A parenthetic number (#) succeeding a distinct answer word reports how many times said answer word appears in QS answers that may or may not share a distinct main subject but have main subjects which refer to David Mivshek, Trinity, God or QS answers;

(a) A: not an individual, in four answers, distinct main subject (giver, reason, Yahweh, hay);

(b) HORN: identifies one individual (God), in two answers, distinct main subject (Yahweh, hay);

(c) WE: identifies one entity (Trinity), in two answers, distinct main subject (Yahweh, hay);

Ch. 4, Sec. 3: 5

DAVID MIVSHEK

Nouns—Winner, Ghost;

Proper Nouns—Dave;

Pronouns—He (2)

Verbs—Gains, Go, Answering;

Adjectives—Holy, Naïve;

Conjunctions—Or (2).

TRINITY

Nouns—Evil, Hay, Horde, [b]**Horn**, Ill, [c]**We** (2);

Proper Nouns—Heaven;

Verbs—Reign, Siring, Wans;

Indefinite Articles—[a]**A**.

GOD

Nouns—Giver, Hinter, [b]**Horn**, Joe, Rein, [c]**We**;

Proper Nouns—Yahweh;

Verbs—Adore, Assure, Is, Nerving, Wans (2);

Adverbs—Right;

Indefinite Articles—[a]**A** (2).

QS ANSWER
Nouns—Air, Hint (2), Joe, Reason (2); **Pronouns**—I; **Verbs**—Grew (2), Marry; **Indefinite Articles**—ᵃA.

In "Ch. 3, Sec. 2: 5," I'd displayed some statistics which pertained to QS answer vocabulary. In "Ch. 4, Sec. 3: 6," I'd updated said statistics by incorporating numbers I'd garnered from the "QS-YHWH/Heaven" and "QS-Yahweh/Heaven" answers:

Ch. 4, Sec. 3: 6

QS-GOD/HEAVEN
GO DAVE. HE: WINNER; OR, GAINS.
Number of QS answer words—6
Number of QS answer letters—21
Average number of letters per answer word—3.50

QS-DEVIL/HELL
HORDE: EVIL. ILL REIGN, WANS.
Number of QS answer words—5
Number of QS answer letters—21
Average number of letters per answer word—4.20

QS-JESUS/EARTH
JOE ASSURE. RIGHT, REIN WANS.
Number of QS answer words—5
Number of QS answer letters—22
Average number of letters per answer word—4.40

QS-DAVE/EARTH
ADORE GIVER. A HINTER WANS.
Number of QS answer words—5
Number of QS answer letters—21
Average number of letters per answer word—4.20

QS-JOE/EARTH

JOE: REASON. AIR/HINT GREW.

Number of QS answer words—5

Number of QS answer letters—20

Average number of letters per answer word—4.00

QS-MARY/EARTH

MARRY REASON. A HINT, I GREW.

Number of QS answer words—6

Number of QS answer letters—21

Average number of letters per answer word—3.50

QS-HOLY^GHOST/HEAVEN

HOLY GHOST. HE: NAÏVE OR ANSWERING.

Number of QS answer words—6

Number of QS answer letters—27

Average number of letters per answer word—4.50

QS-YHWH/HEAVEN

YAHWEH: HORN. NERVING, IS A WE.

Number of QS answer words—6

Number of QS answer letters—22

Average number of letters per answer word—3.67

QS-YAHWEH/HEAVEN

HAY: WE. HEAVEN: HORN, SIRING A WE.

Number of QS answer words—7

Number of QS answer letters—24

Average number of letters per answer word—3.43

QUERY STACK TOTALS AND AVERAGES

Total number of QS answers—9

Total number of QS answer words—51

Total number of QS answer letters—199

Average number of letters per QS answer—22.11

Average number of words per QS answer—5.67

Average number of letters per answer word—3.90

In the next chapter, I'd unveiled a fourth QS answer main subject category: "Lineal-Alias, Realm-Related Query Stack." A "Lineal-Alias, Realm-Related Query Stack" had (1) a first-row row'd word that was an "alias" of a biblical character who was a member of a particular "lineage" (e.g. Virgin Mary's lineage) and whose name was previously a row'd word and (2) a second-row row'd word which named a "realm that was meaningfully related to said first-row row'd word and wasn't necessarily a biblical realm, like Heaven, Hell or Earth, but may have cited a realm which shared a locational relationship with Heaven, Hell and Earth":

QS Categories

Lineal Query Stack
Query Stack with a first-row row'd word that names a character who belongs to a particular family tree (e.g. Virgin Mary's family tree).

Lineally-Coupled Query Stack
Query Stack with a first-row row'd word that names a character who doesn't belong to but is commonly associated with a member of a particular family tree (e.g. Virgin Mary's family tree).

Lineal-Alias Query Stack
Query Stack with a first-row row'd word that identifies the alias of a character whose name has been established as a row'd word and who belongs to a particular family tree (e.g. Virgin Mary's family tree).

Lineal-Alias, Realm-Related Query Stack
Query Stack with a first-row row'd word that identifies the alias of a character who belongs to a predefined family tree (e.g. Virgin Mary's family tree) and a second-row row'd word that has a meaningful connection to its first-row row'd word but doesn't necessarily name a biblical location, like the row'd words HEAVEN, HELL and EARTH do, but may cite a location that shares a locational relationship with Heaven, Hell and Earth.

CHAPTER FIVE: SECTION ONE

CREATOR/REALITY: CORE'S REAL

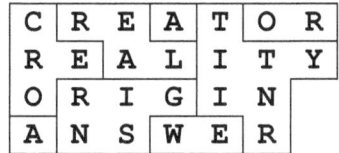

When I'd asked the "God's origin" question, the question which prompted my vision of "QS-God/Heaven" (see "Ch. 1, Sec. 1: 1"), I'd thought that *God* was our creator's given name. Subsequently, I'd learned that ancient Jews declared in biblical text that God's given name was *YHWH*. However, in a gap of time when I wasn't aware of the name *YHWH* but questioned if *God* was our creator's given name, I'd constructed a QS matrix which contained the first-row row'd word CREATOR, a biblical alias of the name *God*—"Hast thou not known? hast thou not heard, that the everlasting God, the LORD, the Creator of the ends of the earth, fainteth not, neither is weary? there is no searching of his understanding" (Isaiah 40:28 KJV):

(a) CREATOR: first-row row'd word;

Ch. 5, Sec. 1: 1

```
"C R E A T O R
 R E A L I T Y
 O R I G I N
 A N S W E R
```

I'd inserted the nonbiblical term *Reality* into the second row of the "QS-Creator/Reality" matrix, even though I'd inserted a biblical term which named a biblical realm into the second row of every QS matrix which I'd unveiled heretofore. I'd believed that the row'd word REALITY best identified the realm which was comprised of things that were made by God, the Creator, and, in turn, experienced by God, the Creator, as being real:

(a) REALITY: second row'd word row;

Ch. 5, Sec. 1: 2

```
C R E A T O R
ᵃR E A L I T Y
O R I G I N
A N S W E R
```

The Creator was a prominent biblical figure, like all of the other biblical figures whose names occupied the first rows of the QS matrices I'd unveiled so far:

(a) GOD; DEVIL; JESUS; DAVE *(David)*; JOE *(Joseph)*; MARY; HOLY^GHOST; YHWH; YAHWEH; CREATOR: notable biblical beings, first-row row'd words;

Ch. 5, Sec. 1: 3

QS-God/Heaven	*QS-Devil/Hell*	*QS-Jesus/Earth*	*QS-Dave/Earth*
ᵃG O D	ᵃD E V I L	ᵃJ E S U S	ᵃD A V E
H E A V E N	H E L L	E A R T H	E A R T H
O R I G I N	O R I G I N	O R I G I N	O R I G I N
A N S W E R	A N S W E R	A N S W E R	A N S W E R

QS-Joe/Earth	*QS-Mary/Earth*	*QS-Holy^Ghost/Heaven*	
ᵃJ O E	ᵃM A R Y	ᵃH O L Y G H O S T	
E A R T H	E A R T H	H E A V E N	
O R I G I N	O R I G I N	O R I G I N	
A N S W E R	A N S W E R	A N S W E R	

QS-YHWH/Heaven	*QS-Yahweh/Heaven*	*QS-Creator/Reality*	
ᵃY H W H	ᵃY A H W E H	ᵃC R E A T O R	
H E A V E N	H E A V E N	R E A L I T Y	
O R I G I N	O R I G I N	O R I G I N	
A N S W E R	A N S W E R	A N S W E R	

Biblically, the Creator was a prominent character and entity in Reality since the Creator was God and God made Reality:

(a) GOD: notable biblical figure; of Heaven; Heaven's ruler;

(b) DEVIL: notable biblical figure; of Hell; God sends evil to Hell, Devil is the evilest being, Devil is evilest being God could send to Hell;

(c) JESUS: notable biblical figure, of Earth; Earth's premier ruler;

(d) DAVE *(David)*: notable biblical figure; of Earth; third King of Israel;

(e) JOE *(Joseph)*: notable biblical figure; of Earth; Virgin Mary's husband;

(f) MARY: notable biblical figure; of Earth; Jesus's mother;

(g) HOLY GHOST: notable biblical figure; of Heaven; Heaven's messenger;

(h) YHWH: notable biblical figure; of Heaven; Heaven's ruler;

(i) YAHWEH: notable biblical figure; of Heaven; Heaven's ruler;

(j) **CREATOR: notable biblical figure; of Reality; Reality's maker;**

Ch. 5, Sec. 1: 4

BIBLICAL BEING	DOMAIN	NOTORIETY
^{a}GOD	^{a}HEAVEN	^{a}RULER
^{b}DEVIL	^{b}HELL	^{b}EVILEST RESIDENT
^{c}JESUS	^{c}EARTH	^{c}PREMIER RULER
^{d}DAVE (David)	^{d}EARTH	^{d}ANOINTED KING
^{e}JOE (Joseph)	^{e}EARTH	^{e}MARY'S HUSBAND
^{f}MARY	^{f}EARTH	^{f}JESUS'S MOTHER
^{g}HOLY GHOST	^{g}HEAVEN	^{g}MESSENGER
^{h}YHWH	^{h}HEAVEN	^{h}RULER
^{i}YAHWEH	^{i}HEAVEN	^{i}RULER
^{j}**CREATOR**	^{j}**REALITY**	^{j}**MAKER**

The row'd word REALITY wasn't a biblical term like the row'd words HEAVEN, HELL and EARTH were; however, Reality was a realm which was spatially related to Heaven, Hell and Earth, since Heaven, Hell and Earth were held inside the spatial limits of Reality:

Ch. 5, Sec. 1: 5

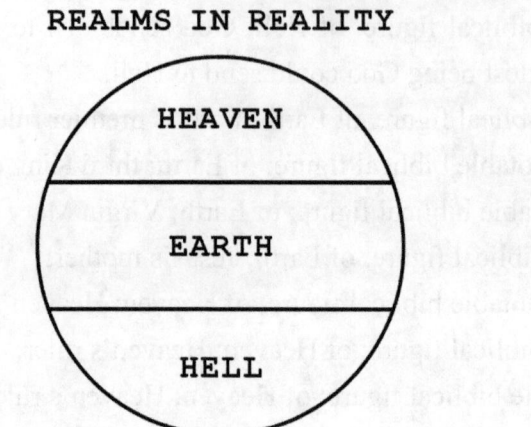

I'd linked adjacent letters in the "QS-Creator/Reality" matrix, to make a valid QS answer:

✓ All QS rules followed (see "Appendix A");

Ch. 5, Sec. 1: 6

```
C R E A T O R
R E A L I T Y
O R I G I N
A N S W E R
```

CORE: REAL. A TRINITY; OR, RINGS A WE.

Next, I'd assigned definitions to the "QS-Creator/Reality" answer words:

Ch. 5, Sec. 1: 7

CORE: REAL. A TRINITY; OR, RINGS A WE.

CORE *n.* The most intimate part.[2]
REAL *adj.* Not fictitious or imaginary.[3]
A *i-art.* Used before most singular nouns when the individual in question is unidentified, especially when the individual is being called to notice.[2]
TRINITY *n.* A group or set of three people.[2]
OR *conj.* The synonymous, equivalent, or substitutive character of two words or phrases.[2]
RINGS *v.* <RING *v.*> To have a character expressive of some quality.[2]
WE *n.* A group that is consciously felt as such by its members.[2]

I didn't apply any knowledge I'd learnt from any previously revealed QS answers when I'd written my initial interpretation of the "QS-Creator/Reality" answer:

Ch. 5, Sec. 1: 8

CORE: REAL.sent1 **A TRINITY; OR, RINGS A WE.**sent2

sent1: *The most intrinsic aspect of a thing being discussed is nonimaginary.*

sent2: *Three persons have individuality but function as one entity; in other words, said trio is characterized as a group of individuals, and each individual knows they belong to said group.*

I'd analyzed the "QS-Creator/Reality" answer's vocabulary. I'd applied knowledge I'd derived from QS answers which I'd unveiled and interpreted prior to analyzing the "QS-Creator/Reality" answer's vocabulary:

A TRINITY

Based on "Ch. 4, Sec. 1: 6," the trinity mentioned in the "QS-Creator/Reality" answer was the Trinity, the trinity which God was a member of;

Ch. 5, Sec. 1: 9

CORE: REAL.sent1 **(A TRINITY); OR, RINGS A WE.**sent2

sent1: *The most intrinsic aspect of the thing being discussed is nonimaginary.*

sent2: *(The Trinity is composed of three individuals, God, Jesus and Holy Ghost, who function as a single entity); in other words, the Trinity is characterized as a group of individuals, and each individual knows they belong to said group.*

REAL; A TRINITY

Based on a property resolution of "QS-7CAP, Prop. 5," the phrase *"A + (noun)"* at the start of a QS answer's second sentence must have a synonymous or contextual link to the second word in the same answer's first sentence; which meant, the first phrase of "QS-Creator/Reality" answer's second sentence, *"a trinity,"* was required to have a synonymous or contextual link to the answer word *REAL*. In conclusion and based on said property resolution, the "QS-Creator/Reality" answer defined the trinity as a real, or nonimaginary, entity, which, in turn, meant that God was real, since God was the core component of the trinity that the answer word *TRINITY* identified;

Ch. 5, Sec. 1: 10

CORE: (REAL).sent1 **(A TRINITY); OR, RINGS A WE.**sent2

sent1: *The most intrinsic aspect of the thing being discussed is (nonimaginary).*

sent2: *(The Trinity is composed of three individuals, God, Jesus and Holy Ghost, and is a single, nonimaginary entity); in other words, the Trinity is characterized as a nonimaginary group of individuals, and each individual knows they belong to said group.*

CORE

Based on "QS-7CAP, Prop. 4," the main subject introduced in a QS answer's first sentence must be mentioned in the same answer's second sentence. Two answer words used to identify the main subject in the "QS-Creator/Reality" answer's first and second sentence were *CORE* and *TRINITY*, respectively; which meant, *CORE* and *TRINITY* identified the same entity *(core = Trinity)*. Based on my prior analyses of the Trinity, the core, or the most intimate aspect, of the Trinity's composition was God, since God was each individual which membered the Trinity *(God = God, God = Jesus, God = Holy Ghost)*;

Ch. 5, Sec. 1: 11

(CORE): REAL.$_{sent1}$ **A TRINITY; OR, RINGS A WE.**$_{sent2}$

$_{sent1}$: (God, the most intrinsic aspect of the Trinity), is nonimaginary.

$_{sent2}$: The Trinity is composed of three individuals which God identifies as—God, Jesus and Holy Ghost—and is a single, nonimaginary entity; in other words, the Trinity is characterized as a nonimaginary group of individuals, and each individual knows they belong to said group.

RINGS A WE

The "QS-Creator/Reality" answer's second sentence stated that the Trinity had the characteristics of a we, or a group of individuals, and each individual knew that they'd belonged to said group. The Trinity was created and membered by God; therefore, God knew that He was a member of the Trinity;

Ch. 5, Sec. 1: 12

CORE: REAL.$_{sent1}$ **A TRINITY; OR, (RINGS A WE).**$_{sent2}$

$_{sent1}$: God, the most intrinsic aspect of the Trinity, is nonimaginary.

$_{sent2}$: The Trinity is composed of three individuals which God identifies as—God, Jesus and Holy Ghost—and is a single, nonimaginary entity; in other words, (the Trinity is characterized as a nonimaginary group of individuals, and each individual knows they belong to said group).

Even though the "QS-Creator/Reality" answer was coherent and meaningful, I'd ran said answer through "QS-7CAP" to validate said answer's vocabulary:

Seven Common QS Answer Properties

1. Each answer contains no more and no less than two sentences (sent1, sent2):

QS-God/Heaven

GO DAVE.sent1 HE: WINNER; OR, GAINS.sent2

QS-Devil/Hell

HORDE: EVIL.sent1 ILL REIGN, WANS.sent2

QS-Jesus/Earth

JOE ASSURE.sent1 RIGHT, REIN WANS.sent2

QS-Dave/Earth

ADORE GIVER.sent1 A HINTER WANS.sent2

QS-Joe/Earth

JOE: REASON.sent1 AIR/HINT GREW.sent2

QS-Mary/Earth

MARRY REASON.sent1 A HINT, I GREW.sent2

QS-Holy^Ghost/Heaven

HOLY GHOST.sent1 HE: NAÏVE OR ANSWERING.sent2

QS-YHWH/Heaven

YAHWEH: HORN.sent1 NERVING, IS A WE.sent2

QS-Yahweh/Heaven

HAY: WE.sent1 HEAVEN: HORN, SIRING A WE.sent2

QS-Creator/Reality

CORE: REAL.sent1 A TRINITY; OR, RINGS A WE.sent2

2. Each answer's first sentence contains no more and no less than two words (word1, word2):

QS-God/Heaven

GOword1 **DAVE**word2. HE: WINNER; OR, GAINS.

QS-Devil/Hell

HORDEword1: **EVIL**word2. ILL REIGN, WANS.

QS-Jesus/Earth

JOEword1 **ASSURE**word2. RIGHT, REIN WANS.

QS-Dave/Earth

ADOREword1 **GIVER**word2. A HINTER WANS.

QS-Joe/Earth

JOEword1: **REASON**word2. AIR/HINT GREW.

QS-Mary/Earth

MARRYword1 **REASON**word2. A HINT, I GREW.

QS-Holy^Ghost/Heaven

HOLYword1 **GHOST**word2. HE: NAÏVE OR ANSWERING.

QS-YHWH/Heaven

YAHWEHword1: **HORN**word2. NERVING, IS A WE.

QS-Yahweh/Heaven

HAYword1: **WE**word2. HEAVEN: HORN, SIRING A WE.

QS-Creator/Reality

COREword1: **REAL**word2. A TRINITY; OR, RINGS A WE.

3. In each answer's first sentence, the main subject is introduced (subj1, subj2, ...):

QS-God/Heaven

GO **DAVE**~subj1~. HE: WINNER; OR, GAINS.

QS-Devil/Hell

HORDE~subj2~: EVIL. ILL REIGN, WANS.

QS-Jesus/Earth

JOE~subj3~ ASSURE. RIGHT, REIN WANS.

QS-Dave/Earth

ADORE **GIVER**~subj4~. A HINTER WANS.

QS-Joe/Earth

JOE: **REASON**~subj5~. AIR/HINT GREW.

QS-Mary/Earth

MARRY **REASON**~subj6~. A HINT, I GREW.

QS-Holy^Ghost/Heaven

HOLY **GHOST**~subj7~. HE: NAÏVE OR ANSWERING.

QS-YHWH/Heaven

YAHWEH~subj8~: HORN. NERVING, IS A WE.

QS-Yahweh/Heaven

HAY: **WE**~subj9~. HEAVEN: HORN, SIRING A WE.

QS-Creator/Reality

CORE~subj10~: REAL. A TRINITY; OR, RINGS A WE.

4. In each answer, the main subject introduced in the first sentence is mentioned in the second sentence (subj1-subj1, subj2-subj2, ...):

QS-God/Heaven

GO **DAVE**~subj1~. **HE**~subj1~: WINNER; OR, GAINS.

QS-Devil/Hell

HORDE~subj2~: EVIL. **ILL**~subj2~ REIGN, WANS.

QS-Jesus/Earth

JOE~subj3~ ASSURE. RIGHT, **REIN**~subj3~ WANS.

QS-Dave/Earth

ADORE **GIVER**~subj4~. A **HINTER**~subj4~ WANS.

QS-Joe/Earth

JOE: **REASON**~subj5~. **AIR**~subj5~/HINT GREW.

QS-Mary/Earth

MARRY **REASON**~subj6~. A **HINT**~subj6~, I GREW.

QS-Holy^Ghost/Heaven

HOLY **GHOST**~subj7~. **HE**~subj7~: NAÏVE OR ANSWERING.

QS-YHWH/Heaven

YAHWEH~subj8~: HORN. NERVING, IS A **WE**~subj8~.

QS-Yahweh/Heaven

HAY~subj9~: WE. HEAVEN: HORN, SIRING A **WE**~subj9~.

QS-Creator/Reality

CORE~subj10~: REAL. A **TRINITY**~subj10~; OR, RINGS A WE.

5. In each answer, the first sentence's second word and the second sentence's first word are synonymous in definition (syn) or context (con):

> *Synonymous answer words are tagged "syn," while answer words which share contextual meaning are tagged "con";*

(con1) DAVE; HE: context, both words identify same man;

(syn2) EVIL; ILL: synonyms, each word means "wicked";

(con3) ASSURE; RIGHT: context, both words convey affirmation;

(con4) GIVER; [A HINTER]: context, word and [phrase] identify same person; *[Property Deviation Resolution: (see "Appendix B")];*

(con5) REASON; AIR: context, the reason is expressed as a written statement;

(con6) REASON; [A HINT]: context, the reason is expressed as an allusive statement; *[Property Deviation Resolution: (see "Appendix B")];*

(con7) GHOST; HE: context, both words identify same person;

(con8) HORN; NERVING: context, each word refers to a source of strength;

(con9) WE; HEAVEN: context, both words identify same entity;

(con10) REAL; [A TRINITY]: context, word characterizes [phrase]; *[Property Deviation Resolution: "A" is the first answer word in the second sentence. "A" doesn't share a synonymous definition or a contextual relationship with the answer word REAL. The second answer word in the second sentence, TRINITY, is an answer word that shares a contextual relationship with REAL. "A" is simply acting as a determiner in this case; in other words, calling to notice an unidentified subject that's referred to by the singular noun TRINITY. "A" serves no function other than to reinforce TRINITY as a singular subject; in fact, "A" could be removed from the answer without affecting the answer's meaning—"a Trinity; or, rings a we," means the same thing as "Trinity; or, rings a we." Based on my analysis, I've determined that if "A" is the first word in the second sentence of a QS answer and is a determiner for a noun that's in the second position of the second sentence of said QS answer, then the "A" and noun that "A" modifies can be bracketed and treated as one answer word.];*

QS-God/Heaven

GO **DAVE**$_{con1}$. **HE**$_{con1}$: WINNER; OR, GAINS.

QS-Devil/Hell

HORDE: **EVIL**$_{syn2}$. **ILL**$_{syn2}$ REIGN, WANS.

QS-Jesus/Earth

JOE **ASSURE**$_{con3}$. **RIGHT**$_{con3}$, REIN WANS.

QS-Dave/Earth

ADORE **GIVER**$_{con4}$. **[A HINTER]**$_{con4}$ WANS.

QS-Joe/Earth

JOE: **REASON**$_{con5}$. **AIR**$_{con5}$/HINT GREW.

QS-Mary/Earth

MARRY **REASON**$_{con6}$. **[A HINT]**$_{con6}$, I GREW.

QS-Holy^Ghost/Heaven

HOLY **GHOST**$_{con7}$. **HE**$_{con7}$: NAÏVE OR ANSWERING.

QS-YHWH/Heaven

YAHWEH: **HORN**$_{con8}$. **NERVING**$_{con8}$, IS A WE.

QS-Yahweh/Heaven

HAY: **WE**$_{con9}$. **HEAVEN**$_{con9}$: HORN, SIRING A WE.

QS-Creator/Reality

CORE: **REAL**$_{con10}$. **[A TRINITY]**$_{con10}$; OR, RINGS A WE.

6. In each answer's second sentence, at least one action is applied to the main subject (subj1–act1, subj2–act2, ...):

QS-God/Heaven

GO DAVE. **HE**$_{subj1}$: WINNER; OR, **GAINS**$_{act1}$.

QS-Devil/Hell

HORDE: EVIL. **ILL**$_{subj2}$ **REIGN**$_{act2}$, WANS.

QS-Jesus/Earth

JOE ASSURE. RIGHT, **REIN**$_{subj3}$ **WANS**$_{act3}$.

QS-Dave/Earth

ADORE GIVER. A **HINTER**$_{subj4}$ **WANS**$_{act4}$.

QS-Joe/Earth

JOE: REASON. **AIR**$_{subj5}$/HINT **GREW**$_{act5}$.

QS-Mary/Earth

MARRY REASON. A **HINT**$_{subj6}$, I **GREW**$_{act6}$.

QS-Holy^Ghost/Heaven

HOLY GHOST. **HE**$_{subj7}$: NAÏVE OR **ANSWERING**$_{act7}$.

QS-YHWH/Heaven

YAHWEH: HORN. **NERVING**$_{act8}$, IS A **WE**$_{subj8}$.

QS-Yahweh/Heaven

HAY: WE. HEAVEN: HORN, **SIRING**$_{act9}$ A **WE**$_{subj9}$.

QS-Creator/Reality

CORE: REAL. A **TRINITY**$_{subj10}$; OR, **RINGS**$_{act10}$ A WE.

7. Along each answer's breadth of vocabulary, there's at least one site where an answer letter *S* would've enhanced the answer's grammatical correctness if it would've been available in the accompanying row'd word matrix and usable:

> *Removing a colon (:) that follows a noun and appending the contraction 's to the end of said noun would produce a conversational tone and clearer syntax (e.g. <u>He's</u> winner; <u>Horde's</u> evil; <u>He's</u> naïve; <u>He's</u> answering; <u>Yahweh's</u> horn; <u>Hay's</u> we; <u>Heaven's</u> horn; <u>Heaven's</u> siring; <u>Core's</u> real). Removing a colon (:) that follows a noun and appending a possessive 's to the end of said noun would produce a conversational tone and clearer syntax (e.g. <u>Joe's</u> reason). Inflecting certain verbs by appending a letter S to the end of them would promote optimal grammar (e.g. Ill <u>reigns</u>; Joe <u>assures</u>). However, each answer's row'd word matrix lacks a letter S that's needed or that's capable of being used in ways mandated by QS rules (see "Appendix A"); [Property Deviation Resolution (see "Appendix B"): "QS-Dave/Earth" and "QS-Mary/Earth"];*

QS-God/Heaven: <u>He's</u> winner;
QS-Devil/Hell: <u>Horde's</u> evil, Ill <u>reigns</u>;
QS-Jesus/Earth: Joe <u>assures</u>;
QS-Dave/Earth: (optimal grammar);
QS-Joe/Earth: <u>Joe's</u> reason;
QS-Mary/Earth: (optimal grammar);
QS-Holy^Ghost/Heaven: <u>He's</u> naïve, <u>He's</u> answering;
QS-YHWH/Heaven: <u>Yahweh's</u> horn;
QS-Creator/Reality: <u>Core's</u> real;

QS-God/Heaven

GO DAVE. **HE: WINNER**; OR, GAINS.

QS-Devil/Hell

HORDE: EVIL. ILL REIGN, WANS.

QS-Jesus/Earth

JOE ASSURE. RIGHT, REIN WANS.

QS-Dave/Earth

ADORE GIVER. A HINTER WANS.

QS-Joe/Earth

JOE: REASON. AIR/HINT GREW.

QS-Mary/Earth

MARRY REASON. A HINT, I GREW.

QS-Holy^Ghost/Heaven

HOLY GHOST. **HE: NAÏVE** OR ANSWERING.

HOLY GHOST. **HE:** NAÏVE OR **ANSWERING**.

QS-YHWH/Heaven

YAHWEH: HORN. NERVING, IS A WE.

QS-Yahweh/Heaven

HAY: WE. HEAVEN: HORN, SIRING A WE.

HAY: WE. **HEAVEN:** HORN, **SIRING** A WE.

QS-Creator/Reality

CORE: REAL. A TRINITY; OR, RINGS A WE.

CHAPTER FIVE: SECTION TWO

YAHWEH/REALITY: THEY OR REINS

```
Y A H W E H
R E A L I T Y
O R I G I N
A N S W E R
```

In "Ch. 5, Sec. 1: 1-4," I'd paired the row'd word CREATOR, an alias of the name *God*, with the row'd word REALITY. In this section, I've reused the row'd word REALITY but paired said row'd word with the row'd word YAHWEH, another alias of the name *God*:

(a) YAHWEH: first-row row'd word;
(b) REALITY: second-row row'd word;

Ch. 5, Sec. 2: 1

```
ᵃY A H W E H
ᵇR E A L I T Y
 O R I G I N
 A N S W E R
```

Yahweh was God; therefore, *Yahweh* was the name of a biblical character, like all of the other first-row row'd words I'd revealed in this book so far were names of biblical characters:

A parenthetic number (#) succeeding a first-row row'd word reports the number of times said row'd word was used as a first-row row'd word;

(a) GOD; DEVIL; JESUS; DAVE *(David)*; JOE *(Joseph)*; MARY; HOLY^GHOST; YHWH; YAHWEH (2); CREATOR: notable biblical beings, first-row row'd words;

Ch. 5, Sec. 2: 2

QS-God/Heaven	QS-Devil/Hell	QS-Jesus/Earth	QS-Dave/Earth
"G O D	"D E V I L	"J E S U S	"D A V E
H E A V E N	H E L L	E A R T H	E A R T H
O R I G I N	O R I G I N	O R I G I N	O R I G I N
A N S W E R	A N S W E R	A N S W E R	A N S W E R

QS-Joe/Earth	QS-Mary/Earth	QS-Holy^Ghost/Heaven	
"J O E	"M A R Y	"H O L Y G H O S T	
E A R T H	E A R T H	H E A V E N	
O R I G I N	O R I G I N	O R I G I N	
A N S W E R	A N S W E R	A N S W E R	

QS-YHWH/Heaven	QS-Yahweh/Heaven	QS-Creator/Reality	
"Y H W H	"Y A H W E H	"C R E A T O R	
H E A V E N	H E A V E N	R E A L I T Y	
O R I G I N	O R I G I N	O R I G I N	
A N S W E R	A N S W E R	A N S W E R	

QS-Yahweh/Reality			
"Y A H W E H			
R E A L I T Y			
O R I G I N			
A N S W E R			

Yahweh was a prominent character and entity in Reality since Yahweh was God and God created Reality:

A parenthetic number (#) succeeding a first-row row'd word reports the number of times said row'd word was used as a first-row row'd word;

(a) GOD: notable biblical figure; of Heaven; Heaven's ruler;

(b) DEVIL: notable biblical figure; of Hell; God sends evil to Hell, Devil is the evilest being, Devil is evilest being God could send to Hell;

(c) JESUS: notable biblical figure, of Earth; Earth's premier ruler;

(d) DAVE *(David)*: notable biblical figure; of Earth; third King of Israel;

(e) JOE *(Joseph)*: notable biblical figure; of Earth; Virgin Mary's husband;

(f) MARY: notable biblical figure; of Earth; Jesus's biological mother;

(g) HOLY GHOST: notable biblical figure; of Heaven; Heaven's messenger;

(h) YHWH: notable biblical figure; of Heaven; Heaven's ruler;

(h) **YAHWEH (2): notable biblical figure, of Heaven and Reality; Heaven's ruler and Reality's maker;**

(i) CREATOR: notable biblical figure; of Reality; Reality's maker;

Ch. 5, Sec. 2: 3

BIBLICAL BEING	DOMAIN	NOTORIETY
[a]GOD	[a]HEAVEN	[a]RULER
[b]DEVIL	[b]HELL	[b]EVILEST RESIDENT
[c]JESUS	[c]EARTH	[c]PREMIER RULER
[d]DAVE (David)	[d]EARTH	[d]ANOINTED KING
[e]JOE (Joseph)	[e]EARTH	[e]MARY'S HUSBAND
[f]MARY	[f]EARTH	[f]JESUS'S MOTHER
[g]HOLY GHOST	[g]HEAVEN	[g]MESSENGER
[h]YHWH	[h]HEAVEN	[h]RULER
[i]YAHWEH	[i]HEAVEN	[i]RULER
[i]YAHWEH	[i]REALITY	[i]MAKER
[j]CREATOR	[j]REALITY	[j]MAKER

I'd linked together "QS-Yahweh/Reality" matrix letters in my search for a valid answer:

✓ All QS rules followed (see "Appendix A");

Ch. 5, Sec. 2: 4

Y	A	H	W	E	H
R	E	A	L	I	T	Y
O	R	I	G	I	N
A	N	S	W	E	R

HAY: LAW. THEY OR REINS, I, RING "A WE."

Next, I'd assigned definitions to the "QS-Yahweh/Reality" answer words:

Ch. 5, Sec. 2: 5

HAY: LAW. THEY OR REINS, I, RING "A WE."

HAY *n.* A rewarding result of careful effort.[2]

LAW *n.* A revelation of the will of God.[2]

THEY *pron.* Unspecified persons and especially those responsible for a particular practice.[2]

OR *conj.* The synonymous, equivalent, or substitutive character of two words or phrases.[2]

REINS *n-pl.* <REIN *n.*> The controlling power.[2]

I *pron.* The one who is speaking or writing.[2]

RING *v.* To repeat earnestly.[2]

"A" *n.* The answer word *A*.

"WE" *n.* The answer word *WE*.

In my initial interpretation of the "QS-Yahweh/Reality" answer, I didn't apply any knowledge which I'd learned from QS answers that I'd already unveiled and interpreted:

Ch. 5, Sec. 2: 6

HAY: LAW.sent1 **THEY OR REINS, I, RING "A WE."**sent2

sent1: *A rewarding result of careful effort is deemed a revelation of the will of God.*

sent2: *A collection of individuals are the controlling powers; are the narrator of the answer this interpretation explains; and earnestly repeat the QS answer phrase "a we," which tells about a group of individuals who are aware of belonging to said group.*

In subsequent interpretations of the "QS-Yahweh/Reality" answer, I'd incorporated knowledge which I'd derived from QS answers that I'd previously uncovered in this book:

HAY: LAW

According to my interpretation of the "QS-Yahweh/Heaven" answer, the rewarding result of God's careful effort, or the hay, was the Trinity (see "Ch. 4, Sec. 2: 5"). To remain consistent in my interpretations of QS answers, I'd interpreted the rewarding result of careful effort mentioned in the "QS-Yahweh/Reality" answer as the Trinity too. Furthermore, the hay, or Trinity, mentioned in the "QS-Yahweh/Reality" answer was deemed a law, or revelation of the will of God. If God created the Trinity, like the "QS-Yahweh/Heaven" answer sentence *"Heaven: siring a we"* said He had, then God created and revealed the Trinity through His own will;

Ch. 5, Sec. 2: 7

QS-Yahweh/Heaven Answer
HAY: **WE.**~sent1~ HEAVEN: HORN, SIRING A WE.~sent2~
QS-Yahweh/Heaven Interpretation
~sent1~: *A rewarding result of careful effort is the Trinity.*
QS-Yahweh/Reality Answer
HAY: **LAW.**~sent1~ THEY OR REINS, I, RING "A WE."~sent2~
QS-Yahweh/Reality Interpretation
~sent1~: *A rewarding result of careful effort and a revelation of God's will is the Trinity.*

LAW, THEY

"QS-7CAP, Prop. 5" mandated that the second word in an answer's first sentence was required to be definitionally synonymous or contextually congruent with the first word in said answer's second sentence; therefore, the second answer word in the first sentence and the first word in the second sentence of the "QS-Yahweh/Reality" answer, *LAW* and *THEY*, respectively, had to have a definitional or contextual link in order for said answer to be valid. Ultimately, I'd determined that *LAW* and *THEY* were contextually linked; meaning, the law, or revelation of God's will, was the "they," while the "they" was the group of individuals known as *Trinity* (see "Ch. 5, Sec 2: 7"). The Trinity was comprised of three entities, so the term *they*, or "unspecified persons responsible for a particular practice[2]," fit into the context of said answer;

(a) Answer word *LAW* cites the Trinity, which is God;

(b) Answer word *THEY* cites the Trinity, which is God;

Ch. 5, Sec. 2: 8

HAY: ^a^**LAW.**~sent1~ ^b^**THEY** OR REINS, I, RING "A WE."~sent2~
~sent1~: *A rewarding result of careful effort and ^a^(a revelation of God's will is the Trinity).*
~sent2~: *The ^b^(Trinity's members) are the controlling powers; are the narrator of the answer this interpretation explains; and earnestly repeat the QS answer phrase "a we," which tells about a group of individuals who are aware of belonging to said group.*

THEY, REINS, WE

In "Ch. 1, Sec. 4: 14-25," I'd determined that the answer word *REIN*, or a controlling power, referred to God. Since God was a rein and trinity, I'd determined that the pluralized answer word *REINS* referred to the Trinity members. I'd identified the we in the "QS-Yahweh/Reality" as the Trinity, since I'd identified the we as the Trinity in every other

QS answer which contained the answer word *WE* (see "Ch. 4, Sec. 1: 6," "Ch. 4, Sec. 2: 5" and "Ch. 5, Sec. 1: 12");

(a) Answer word *THEY* cites the Trinity, which is God;
(b) Answer word *REINS* cites the Trinity, which is God;
(c) Answer word *WE* cites the Trinity, which is God;

Ch. 5, Sec. 2: 9

HAY: LAW._{sent1} "*^a*THEY OR *^b*REINS, I, RING "A *^c*WE."_{sent2}

sent1: **A rewarding result of careful effort and a revelation of God's will is the Trinity.**

sent2: **The *^a*(Trinity's members) are all God; are *^b*(the controlling powers); identify as the narrator of the answer this interpretation explains; and earnestly repeat the QS answer phrase "a we," which says that *^c*(each member of the Trinity is aware of their membership in the Trinity).**

I RING "A WE"

In "Ch. 1, Sec. 4: 13," I'd determined that God was the author of the Query Stacks in this book. In "Ch. 2, Sec. 2: 9," I'd determined that God wrote the pronoun and QS answer word *I* into QS answers to cite Himself; therefore, in the second half of the "QS-Yahweh/Reality" answer's second sentence, God declared, via the answer word *I,* that He'd earnestly repeated the answer phrase *A WE*, which was a phrase in three other QS answers as well (see "Appendix D"). Was God calling attention to repetitive answer words and phrases which He'd inserted into answers, like the answer phrase "*A WE,*" as a way to open readers' eyes to the reliability of the answers, I'd wondered;

Ch. 5, Sec. 2: 10

HAY: LAW._{sent1} THEY OR REINS, (I, RING "A WE.")_{sent2}

sent1: **A rewarding result of careful effort and a revelation of God's will is the Trinity.**

sent2: **The Trinity's members are all God; are the controlling powers; and identify as the QS author who earnestly repeats the phrase "a we" throughout QS answers in order to cite Himself as the Trinity, an entity comprised of three individuals who are each aware of being a member of said entity).**

I ran the "QS-Yahweh/Reality" answer through "QS-7CAP":

Seven Common QS Answer Properties

1. Each answer contains no more and no less than two sentences (sent1, sent2):

QS-God/Heaven

GO DAVE.sent1 HE: WINNER; OR, GAINS.sent2

QS-Devil/Hell

HORDE: EVIL.sent1 ILL REIGN, WANS.sent2

QS-Jesus/Earth

JOE ASSURE.sent1 RIGHT, REIN WANS.sent2

QS-Dave/Earth

ADORE GIVER.sent1 A HINTER WANS.sent2

QS-Joe/Earth

JOE: REASON.sent1 AIR/HINT GREW.sent2

QS-Mary/Earth

MARRY REASON.sent1 A HINT, I GREW.sent2

QS-Holy^Ghost/Heaven

HOLY GHOST.sent1 HE: NAÏVE OR ANSWERING.sent2

QS-YHWH/Heaven

YAHWEH: HORN.sent1 NERVING, IS A WE.sent2

QS-Yahweh/Heaven

HAY: WE.sent1 HEAVEN: HORN, SIRING A WE.sent2

QS-Creator/Reality

CORE: REAL.sent1 A TRINITY; OR, RINGS A WE.sent2

QS-Yahweh/Reality

HAY: LAW.sent1 THEY OR REINS, I, RING "A WE."sent2

2. Each answer's first sentence contains no more and no less than two words (word1, word2):

QS-God/Heaven

GOword1 **DAVE**word2. HE: WINNER; OR, GAINS.

QS-Devil/Hell

HORDEword1: **EVIL**word2. ILL REIGN, WANS.

QS-Jesus/Earth

JOEword1 **ASSURE**word2. RIGHT, REIN WANS.

QS-Dave/Earth

ADOREword1 **GIVER**word2. A HINTER WANS.

QS-Joe/Earth

JOEword1: **REASON**word2. AIR/HINT GREW.

QS-Mary/Earth

MARRYword1 **REASON**word2. A HINT, I GREW.

QS-Holy^Ghost/Heaven

HOLYword1 **GHOST**word2. HE: NAÏVE OR ANSWERING.

QS-YHWH/Heaven

YAHWEHword1: **HORN**word2. NERVING, IS A WE.

QS-Yahweh/Heaven

HAYword1: **WE**word2. HEAVEN: HORN, SIRING A WE.

QS-Creator/Reality

COREword1: **REAL**word2. A TRINITY; OR, RINGS A WE.

QS-Yahweh/Reality

HAYword1: **LAW**word2. THEY OR REINS, I, RING "A WE."

3. In each answer's first sentence, the main subject is introduced (subj1, subj2, ...):

QS-God/Heaven

GO **DAVE**$_{subj1}$. HE: WINNER; OR, GAINS.

QS-Devil/Hell

HORDE$_{subj2}$: EVIL. ILL REIGN, WANS.

QS-Jesus/Earth

JOE$_{subj3}$ ASSURE. RIGHT, REIN WANS.

QS-Dave/Earth

ADORE **GIVER**$_{subj4}$. A HINTER WANS.

QS-Joe/Earth

JOE: **REASON**$_{subj5}$. AIR/HINT GREW.

QS-Mary/Earth

MARRY **REASON**$_{subj6}$. A HINT, I GREW.

QS-Holy^Ghost/Heaven

HOLY **GHOST**$_{subj7}$. HE: NAÏVE OR ANSWERING.

QS-YHWH/Heaven

YAHWEH$_{subj8}$: HORN. NERVING, IS A WE.

QS-Yahweh/Heaven

HAY$_{subj9}$: WE. HEAVEN: HORN, SIRING A WE.

QS-Creator/Reality

CORE$_{subj10}$: REAL. A TRINITY; OR, RINGS A WE.

QS-Yahweh/Reality

HAY$_{subj11}$: LAW. THEY OR REINS, I, RING "A WE."

4. In each answer, the main subject introduced in the first sentence is mentioned in the second sentence (subj1-subj1, subj2-subj2, ...):

QS-God/Heaven

GO **DAVE**$_{subj1}$. **HE**$_{subj1}$: WINNER; OR, GAINS.

QS-Devil/Hell

HORDE$_{subj2}$: EVIL. **ILL**$_{subj2}$ REIGN, WANS.

QS-Jesus/Earth

JOE$_{subj3}$ ASSURE. RIGHT, **REIN**$_{subj3}$ WANS.

QS-Dave/Earth

ADORE **GIVER**$_{subj4}$. A **HINTER**$_{subj4}$ WANS.

QS-Joe/Earth

JOE: **REASON**$_{subj5}$. **AIR**$_{subj5}$/HINT GREW.

QS-Mary/Earth

MARRY **REASON**$_{subj6}$. A **HINT**$_{subj6}$, I GREW.

QS-Holy^Ghost/Heaven

HOLY **GHOST**$_{subj7}$. **HE**$_{subj7}$: NAÏVE OR ANSWERING.

QS-YHWH/Heaven

YAHWEH$_{subj8}$: HORN. NERVING, IS A **WE**$_{subj8}$.

QS-Yahweh/Heaven

HAY$_{subj9}$: WE. HEAVEN: HORN, SIRING A **WE**$_{subj9}$.

QS-Creator/Reality

CORE$_{subj10}$: REAL. A **TRINITY**$_{subj10}$; OR, RINGS A WE.

QS-Yahweh/Reality

HAY$_{subj11}$: LAW. THEY OR **REINS**$_{subj11}$, I, RING "A WE."

5. In each answer, the first sentence's second word and the second sentence's first word are synonymous in definition (syn) or context (con):

> *Synonymous answer words are tagged "syn," while answer words which share contextual meaning are tagged "con";*

(con1) DAVE; HE: context, both words identify same man;
(syn2) EVIL; ILL: synonyms, each word means "wicked";
(con3) ASSURE; RIGHT: context, both words convey affirmation;
(con4) GIVER; [A HINTER]: context, word and [phrase] identify same person; *[Property Deviation Resolution: (see "Appendix B")]*;
(con5) REASON; AIR: context, the reason is expressed as a written statement;
(con6) REASON; [A HINT]: context, the reason is expressed as an allusive statement; *[Property Deviation Resolution: (see "Appendix B")]*;
(con7) GHOST; HE: context, both words identify same person;
(con 8) HORN; NERVING: context, each word refers to a source of strength;
(con 9) WE; HEAVEN: context, both words identify same entity;
(con10) REAL; [A TRINITY]: context, word and [phrase] refers to same entity; *[Property Deviation Resolution: (see "Appendix B")]*;
(con11) LAW; THEY: context, revealed will of God is Trinity;

QS-God/Heaven

GO **DAVE**$_{con1}$. **HE**$_{con1}$: WINNER; OR, GAINS.

QS-Devil/Hell

HORDE: **EVIL**$_{syn2}$. **ILL**$_{syn2}$ REIGN, WANS.

QS-Jesus/Earth

JOE **ASSURE**$_{con3}$. **RIGHT**$_{con3}$, REIN WANS.

QS-Dave/Earth

ADORE **GIVER**$_{con4}$. **[A HINTER]**$_{con4}$ WANS.

QS-Joe/Earth

JOE: **REASON**$_{con5}$. **AIR**$_{con5}$/HINT GREW.

QS-Mary/Earth

MARRY **REASON**$_{con6}$. **[A HINT]**$_{con6}$, I GREW.

QS-Holy^Ghost/Heaven

HOLY **GHOST**$_{con7}$. **HE**$_{con7}$: NAÏVE OR ANSWERING.

QS-YHWH/Heaven

YAHWEH: **HORN**$_{con8}$. **NERVING**$_{con8}$, IS A WE.

QS-Yahweh/Heaven

HAY: **WE**$_{con9}$. **HEAVEN**$_{con9}$: HORN, SIRING A WE.

QS-Creator/Reality

CORE: **REAL**$_{con10}$. **[A TRINITY]**$_{con10}$; OR, RINGS A WE.

QS-Yahweh/Reality

HAY: **LAW**$_{\text{con11}}$. **THEY**$_{\text{con11}}$ OR REINS, I, RING "A WE."

6. In each answer's second sentence, at least one action is applied to the main subject (subj1–act1, subj2–act2, ...):

QS-God/Heaven

GO DAVE. **HE**$_{\text{subj1}}$: WINNER; OR, **GAINS**$_{\text{act1}}$.

QS-Devil/Hell

HORDE: EVIL. **ILL**$_{\text{subj2}}$ **REIGN**$_{\text{act2}}$, WANS.

QS-Jesus/Earth

JOE ASSURE. RIGHT, **REIN**$_{\text{subj3}}$ **WANS**$_{\text{act3}}$.

QS-Dave/Earth

ADORE GIVER. A **HINTER**$_{\text{subj4}}$ **WANS**$_{\text{act4}}$.

QS-Joe/Earth

JOE: REASON. **AIR**$_{\text{subj5}}$/HINT **GREW**$_{\text{act5}}$.

QS-Mary/Earth

MARRY REASON. A **HINT**$_{\text{subj6}}$, I **GREW**$_{\text{act6}}$.

QS-Holy^Ghost/Heaven

HOLY GHOST. **HE**$_{\text{subj7}}$: NAÏVE OR **ANSWERING**$_{\text{act7}}$.

QS-YHWH/Heaven

YAHWEH: HORN. **NERVING**$_{\text{act8}}$, IS A **WE**$_{\text{subj8}}$.

QS-Yahweh/Heaven

HAY: WE. HEAVEN: HORN, **SIRING**$_{\text{act9}}$ A **WE**$_{\text{subj9}}$.

QS-Creator/Reality

CORE: REAL. A **TRINITY**$_{\text{subj10}}$; OR, **RINGS**$_{\text{act10}}$ A WE.

QS-Yahweh/Reality

HAY: LAW. THEY OR **REINS**$_{\text{subj11}}$, I, **RING**$_{\text{act11}}$ "A WE."

7. Along each answer's breadth of vocabulary, there's at least one site where an answer letter *S* would've enhanced the answer's grammatical correctness if it would've been available in the accompanying row'd word matrix and usable:

> *Removing a colon (:) that follows a noun and appending a contraction 's to the end of said noun would produce a conversational tone and clearer syntax (e.g. He's winner; Horde's evil; He's naïve; He's answering; Yahweh's horn; Hay's we; Heaven's horn; Heaven's siring; Core's real; Hay's law). Remov-*

ing a colon (:) that follows a noun and appending a possessive 's to the end of said noun would produce a conversational tone and clearer syntax (e.g. <u>Joe's</u> reason). Inflecting certain verbs by appending a letter S to the end of them would promote optimal grammar (e.g. Ill <u>reigns</u>; Joe <u>assures</u>). However, each answer's row'd word matrix lacks a letter S that's needed or that's capable of being used in ways mandated by QS rules (see "Appendix A");

[Property Deviation Resolution (see "Appendix B"): "QS-Dave/Earth" and "QS-Mary/Earth"];

QS-God/Heaven: <u>He's</u> winner;
QS-Devil/Hell: <u>Horde's</u> evil, Ill <u>reigns</u>;
QS-Jesus/Earth: Joe <u>assures</u>;
QS-Dave/Earth: (optimal grammar);
QS-Joe/Earth: <u>Joe's</u> reason;
QS-Mary/Earth: (optimal grammar);
QS-Holy^Ghost/Heaven: <u>He's</u> naïve, <u>He's</u> answering;
QS-YHWH/Heaven: <u>Yahweh's</u> horn;
QS-Creator/Reality: <u>Core's</u> real;
QS-Yahweh/Reality: <u>Hay's</u> law;

QS-God/Heaven

```
GO DAVE. HE: WINNER; OR, GAINS.
```

QS-Devil/Hell

```
HORDE: EVIL. ILL REIGN, WANS.
```

QS-Jesus/Earth

```
JOE ASSURE. RIGHT, REIN WANS.
```

QS-Dave/Earth

```
ADORE GIVER. A HINTER WANS.
```

QS-Joe/Earth

```
JOE: REASON. AIR/HINT GREW.
```

QS-Mary/Earth

```
MARRY REASON. A HINT, I GREW.
```

QS-Holy^Ghost/Heaven

```
HOLY GHOST. HE: NAÏVE OR ANSWERING.
HOLY GHOST. HE: NAÏVE OR ANSWERING.
```

QS-YHWH/Heaven

YAHWEH: HORN. NERVING, IS A WE.

QS-Yahweh/Heaven

HAY: WE. HEAVEN: HORN, SIRING A WE.

HAY: WE. **HEAVEN**: HORN, **SIRING** A WE.

QS-Creator/Reality

CORE: REAL. A TRINITY; OR, RINGS A WE.

QS-Yahweh/Reality

HAY: LAW. THEY OR REINS, I, RING "A WE."

CHAPTER FIVE: SECTION THREE

YAHWEH/TRINITY: HAIRY WE

```
Y A H W E H
T R I N I T Y
O R I G I N
A N S W E R
```

After I'd uncovered several Query Stacks which contained row'd word matrices with second-row row'd words that named locational realms like Heaven, Hell, Earth and Reality, I'd investigated a QS matrix which consisted of a second-row row'd word that named an existential realm which incorporated biblical characters who'd held a prominent position within said existential realm. For example, God was a biblical character who was associated with and held a prominent position in the Trinity, an existential realm. An alias of the name *God* was *Yahweh*; therefore, the name *Yahweh* was associated with and cited a prominent biblical figure in the Trinity. To be absolutely clear, Yahweh was a prominent biblical figure in the Trinity, just like Yahweh was a prominent biblical figure in Heaven and Reality, Jesus was a prominent biblical figure on Earth and the Devil was a prominent biblical figure in Hell:

(a) YAHWEH: first-row row'd word;
(b) TRINITY: second-row row'd word;

Ch. 5, Sec. 3: 1

[a]Y A H W E H
[b]T R I N I T Y
O R I G I N
A N S W E R

Yahweh was God, and, therefore, a biblical character, just like all of the other first-row row'd words I'd unveiled up until now:

> *A parenthetic number (#) succeeding a first-row row'd word reports the number of times said row'd word was used as a first-row row'd word;*

(a) GOD; DEVIL; JESUS; DAVE *(David)*; JOE *(Joseph)*; MARY; HOLY^GHOST; YHWH; YAHWEH (3); CREATOR: notable biblical beings, first-row row'd words;

Ch. 5, Sec. 3: 2

QS-God/Heaven	*QS-Devil/Hell*	*QS-Jesus/Earth*	*QS-Dave/Earth*
"G O D	"D E V I L	"J E S U S	"D A V E
H E A V E N	H E L L	E A R T H	E A R T H
O R I G I N	O R I G I N	O R I G I N	O R I G I N
A N S W E R	A N S W E R	A N S W E R	A N S W E R

QS-Joe/Earth	*QS-Mary/Earth*	*QS-Holy^Ghost/Heaven*
"J O E	"M A R Y	"H O L Y G H O S T
E A R T H	E A R T H	H E A V E N
O R I G I N	O R I G I N	O R I G I N
A N S W E R	A N S W E R	A N S W E R

QS-YHWH/Heaven	*QS-Yahweh/Heaven*	*QS-Creator/Reality*
"Y H W H	"Y A H W E H	"C R E A T O R
H E A V E N	H E A V E N	R E A L I T Y
O R I G I N	O R I G I N	O R I G I N
A N S W E R	A N S W E R	A N S W E R

QS-Yahweh/Reality	*QS-Yahweh/Trinity*
"Y A H W E H	"Y A H W E H
R E A L I T Y	T R I N I T Y
O R I G I N	O R I G I N
A N S W E R	A N S W E R

Yahweh was a prominent individual in the Trinity, because Yahweh was God and God was the fundamental component of the Trinity:

A parenthetic number (#) succeeding a first-row row'd word reports the number of times said row'd word was used as a first-row row'd word;

(g) GOD: notable biblical figure; of Heaven; Heaven's ruler;

(h) DEVIL: notable biblical figure; of Hell; God sends evil to Hell, Devil is the evilest being, Devil is evilest being God could send to Hell;

(i) JESUS: notable biblical figure, of Earth; Earth's premier ruler;

(j) DAVE *(David)*: notable biblical figure; of Earth; third King of Israel;

(k) JOE *(Joseph)*: notable biblical figure; of Earth; Virgin Mary's husband;

(l) MARY: notable biblical figure; of Earth; Jesus's biological mother;

(h) HOLY GHOST: notable biblical figure; of Heaven; Heaven's messenger;

(i) YHWH: notable biblical figure; of Heaven; Heaven's ruler;

(j) **YAHWEH (3): notable biblical figure; of Heaven, Reality and Trinity; Heaven's ruler, Reality's maker and Trinity member;**

(k) CREATOR: notable biblical figure; of Reality; Reality's maker;

Ch. 5, Sec. 3: 3

BIBLICAL BEING	DOMAIN	NOTORIETY
[a]GOD	[a]HEAVEN	[a]RULER
[b]DEVIL	[b]HELL	[b]EVILEST RESIDENT
[c]JESUS	[c]EARTH	[c]PREMIER RULER
[d]DAVE (David)	[d]EARTH	[d]ANOINTED KING
[e]JOE (Joseph)	[e]EARTH	[e]MARY'S HUSBAND
[f]MARY	[f]EARTH	[f]JESUS'S MOTHER
[g]HOLY GHOST	[g]HEAVEN	[g]MESSENGER
[h]YHWH	[h]HEAVEN	[h]RULER
[i]YAHWEH	[i]HEAVEN	[i]RULER
[i]YAHWEH	[i]REALITY	[i]MAKER
[i]YAHWEH	**[i]TRINITY**	**[i]MEMBER**
[j]CREATOR	[j]REALITY	[j]MAKER

I'd connected adjacent row'd word letters, in an effort to construct valid answer words:

✓ All QS rules followed (see "Appendix A");

Ch. 5, Sec. 3: 4

Y	A	H	W	E	H
T	R	I	N	I	T	Y
O	R	I	G	I	N
A	N	S	W	E	R

HAIRY WE. THY TRIO: REINING, WANS.

Next, I'd assigned definitions to the "QS-Yahweh/Trinity" answer words:

Ch. 5, Sec. 3: 5

HAIRY WE. THY TRIO: REINING, WANS.

HAIRY *adj.* **Difficult to comprehend.**[2]
WE *n.* **A group that is consciously felt as such by its members.**[2]
THY *adj.* **(archaic) Connected with thyself as possessor.**[2]
TRIO *n.* **A group of three.**[2]
REINING *v.* **<REIN** *v.***> To govern as if by the use of reins.**[2]
WANS *v.* **<WAN** *v.***> To become wan (***adj.* **lacking in forcefulness).**[1]

My initial interpretation of the "QS-Yahweh/Trinity" answer:

Ch. 5, Sec. 3: 6

HAIRY WE.sent1 **THY TRIO: REINING, WANS.**sent2

sent1: *An incomprehensible group of individuals is comprised of individuals, and each individual is aware of belonging to said group.*

sent2: *The narrator of the answer this interpretation explains speaks to an individual who possesses a group of three individuals and declares that said individual's group is exercising rulership and becomes lacking in forcefulness.*

As I'd analyzed the "QS-Yahweh/Trinity" answer, I'd applied knowledge which I'd derived from interpretations of QS answers that I'd previously unveiled:

HAIRY WE

So far, I'd applied the identity of the Trinity to the answer word *WE* in every QS answer which contained the answer word *WE* (see "Ch. 5, Sec. 2: 9"). The answer word *HAIRY* described the we, the Trinity, as an entity that was difficult to comprehend; which, in turn, meant that God was difficult to comprehend, since God was the core component of the Trinity. In fact, a biblical verse reinforced the notion that God was characterized as an incomprehensibility: "<u>God</u> thundereth marvelously with his voice; <u>great things doeth he, which we cannot comprehend</u>" (Job 37:5 KJV);

Ch. 5, Sec. 3: 7

HAIRY WE.sent1 THY TRIO: REINING, WANS.sent2

sent1: ***Incomprehensible is the Trinity.***

WE, THY

"QS-7CAP, Prop. 5" mandated that the second word in an answer's first sentence had a definitionally synonymous or contextually congruent link to the first word in said answer's second sentence; which meant, the answer words *WE* and *THY* were required to have a definitionally synonymous or contextually congruent link. The answer words *WE* and *THY* were contextually congruent, because the answer word *WE* cited the Trinity in every QS answer in this book so far (see "Ch. 5, Sec. 2: 9"), while the answer word *THY* referred to God as the possessor of the entity that the answer word *TRIO* referred to, which was the Trinity. Not only was God the possessor of the Trinity, but God was the Trinity:

(a) Answer word *WE* cites the Trinity;
(b) Answer word *THY* cites God, the Trinity;

Ch. 5, Sec. 3: 8

HAIRY: *ª*WE.sent1 *ᵇ*THY TRIO: REINING, WANS.sent2

sent1: **Incomprehensible is the ª(Trinity).**

sent2: **ᵇ(The QS author of the answer this interpretation explains, which is God, tells Himself) that His Trinity is exercising rulership and becomes lacking in forcefulness.**

THY TRIO

The answer phrase "*THY TRIO*" cited a group of three individuals who were in God's possession. So far, the QS answers in this book cited only one group of three individuals which God possessed, which was God's Trinity:

(a) Answer phrase "*THY TRIO*" cites God as the possessor of the Trinity;

Ch. 5, Sec. 3: 9

HAIRY WE.sent1 *ª*(THY TRIO): REINING, WANS.sent2

sent1: **Incomprehensible is the Trinity.**

sent2: **ª(The QS author, God, tells Himself that His Trinity) is exercising rulership and becomes lacking in forcefulness.**

TRIO: REINING, WANS

Based on "QS-7CAP, Prop. 7" (see "Appendix B") and my interpretations of QS answers which contained grammar that was similar to the grammar in the second sentence of the "QS-Yahweh/Trinity" answer, I'd determined that the colon which followed the answer word *TRIO* in the answer phrase "*they trio(:)*" was a punctuational substitution for the contraction *'s*, which, in turn, was an abbreviation of the word *is* (*'s = is*);

(a) *":"* is contraction *'s ('s = is)*;

Ch. 5, Sec. 3: 10

HAIRY WE.sent1 THY **TRIO** *a*(:) **REINING, WANS.**sent2

sent1: **Incomprehensible is the Trinity.**

sent2: **The QS author, God, tells Himself that His Trinity *a*(is) exercising rulership and becomes lacking in forcefulness.**

REINING, WANS

In "Ch. 1, Sec. 4: 14-26," I'd determined that the answer word *REIN* referred to God, or the Trinity, as the controlling power whose power was derived from a moral force of goodness, while the answer word *WANS* referred to God's, or the Trinity's, moral force of goodness becoming weaker as a result of God, or the Trinity, exercising evilness;

(a) Answer word *REINING* refers to the Trinity's power over Reality via its moral force of goodness;

(b) Answer word *WANS* refers to the weakening of the Trinity's moral force due to God's evil actions;

Ch. 5, Sec. 3: 11

HAIRY WE.sent1 THY TRIO: *a***REINING,** *b***WANS.**sent2

sent1: **Incomprehensible is the Trinity.**

sent2: **The QS author, God, tells Himself that His Trinity is *a*(exercising rulership) and *b*(becomes lacking in the moral force of goodness).**

Even though the "QS-Yahweh/Trinity" answer was grammatically coherent and meaningful, I'd ran it through "QS-7CAP" to measure said answer's validity:

Seven Common QS Answer Properties

1. Each answer contains no more and no less than two sentences (sent1, sent2):

QS-God/Heaven

GO DAVE.~sent1~ HE: WINNER; OR, GAINS.~sent2~

QS-Devil/Hell

HORDE: EVIL.~sent1~ ILL REIGN, WANS.~sent2~

QS-Jesus/Earth

JOE ASSURE.~sent1~ RIGHT, REIN WANS.~sent2~

QS-Dave/Earth

ADORE GIVER.~sent1~ A HINTER WANS.~sent2~

QS-Joe/Earth

JOE: REASON.~sent1~ AIR/HINT GREW.~sent2~

QS-Mary/Earth

MARRY REASON.~sent1~ A HINT, I GREW.~sent2~

QS-Holy^Ghost/Heaven

HOLY GHOST.~sent1~ HE: NAÏVE OR ANSWERING.~sent2~

QS-YHWH/Heaven

YAHWEH: HORN.~sent1~ NERVING, IS A WE.~sent2~

QS-Yahweh/Heaven

HAY: WE.~sent1~ HEAVEN: HORN, SIRING A WE.~sent2~

QS-Creator/Reality

CORE: REAL.~sent1~ A TRINITY; OR, RINGS A WE.~sent2~

QS-Yahweh/Reality

HAY: LAW.~sent1~ THEY OR REINS, I, RING "A WE."~sent2~

QS-Yahweh/Trinity

HAIRY WE.~sent1~ THY TRIO: REINING, WANS.~sent2~

2. Each answer's first sentence contains no more and no less than two words (word1, word2):

QS-God/Heaven

GO~word1~ DAVE~word2~. HE: WINNER; OR, GAINS.

QS-Devil/Hell

HORDE~word1~: EVIL~word2~. ILL REIGN, WANS.

QS-Jesus/Earth

JOE~word1~ ASSURE~word2~. RIGHT, REIN WANS.

QS-Dave/Earth

ADORE~word1~ GIVER~word2~. A HINTER WANS.

QS-Joe/Earth

JOE$_{word1}$: **REASON**$_{word2}$. AIR/HINT GREW.

QS-Mary/Earth

MARRY$_{word1}$ **REASON**$_{word2}$. A HINT, I GREW.

QS-Holy^Ghost/Heaven

HOLY$_{word1}$ **GHOST**$_{word2}$. HE: NAÏVE OR ANSWERING.

QS-YHWH/Heaven

YAHWEH$_{word1}$: **HORN**$_{word2}$. NERVING, IS A WE.

QS-Yahweh/Heaven

HAY$_{word1}$: **WE**$_{word2}$. HEAVEN: HORN, SIRING A WE.

QS-Creator/Reality

CORE$_{word1}$: **REAL**$_{word2}$. A TRINITY; OR, RINGS A WE.

QS-Yahweh/Reality

HAY$_{word1}$: **LAW**$_{word2}$. THEY OR REINS, I, RING "A WE."

QS-Yahweh/Trinity

HAIRY$_{word1}$ **WE**$_{word2}$. THY TRIO: REINING, WANS.

3. In each answer's first sentence, the main subject is introduced (subj1, subj2, ...):

QS-God/Heaven

GO **DAVE**$_{subj1}$. HE: WINNER; OR, GAINS.

QS-Devil/Hell

HORDE$_{subj2}$: EVIL. ILL REIGN, WANS.

QS-Jesus/Earth

JOE$_{subj3}$ ASSURE. RIGHT, REIN WANS.

QS-Dave/Earth

ADORE **GIVER**$_{subj4}$. A HINTER WANS.

QS-Joe/Earth

JOE: **REASON**$_{subj5}$. AIR/HINT GREW.

QS-Mary/Earth

MARRY **REASON**$_{subj6}$. A HINT, I GREW.

QS-Holy^Ghost/Heaven

HOLY **GHOST**$_{subj7}$. HE: NAÏVE OR ANSWERING.

QS-YHWH/Heaven

YAHWEH$_{subj8}$: HORN. NERVING, IS A WE.

QS-Yahweh/Heaven

HAY~subj9~: WE. HEAVEN: HORN, SIRING A WE.

QS-Creator/Reality

CORE~subj10~: REAL. A TRINITY; OR, RINGS A WE.

QS-Yahweh/Reality

HAY~subj11~: LAW. THEY OR REINS, I, RING "A WE."

QS-Yahweh/Trinity

HAIRY **WE**~subj12~. THY TRIO: REINING, WANS.

4. In each answer, the main subject introduced in the first sentence is mentioned in the second sentence (subj1-subj1, subj2-subj2, ...):

QS-God/Heaven

GO **DAVE**~subj1~. **HE**~subj1~: WINNER; OR, GAINS.

QS-Devil/Hell

HORDE~subj2~: EVIL. **ILL**~subj2~ REIGN, WANS.

QS-Jesus/Earth

JOE~subj3~ ASSURE. RIGHT, **REIN**~subj3~ WANS.

QS-Dave/Earth

ADORE **GIVER**~subj4~. A **HINTER**~subj4~ WANS.

QS-Joe/Earth

JOE: **REASON**~subj5~. **AIR**~subj5~/HINT GREW.

QS-Mary/Earth

MARRY **REASON**~subj6~. A **HINT**~subj6~, I GREW.

QS-Holy^Ghost/Heaven

HOLY **GHOST**~subj7~. **HE**~subj7~: NAÏVE OR ANSWERING.

QS-YHWH/Heaven

YAHWEH~subj8~: HORN. NERVING, IS A **WE**~subj8~.

QS-Yahweh/Heaven

HAY~subj9~: WE. HEAVEN: HORN, SIRING A **WE**~subj9~.

QS-Creator/Reality

CORE~subj10~: REAL. A **TRINITY**~subj10~; OR, RINGS A WE.

QS-Yahweh/Reality

HAY~subj11~: LAW. THEY OR **REINS**~subj11~, I, RING "A WE."

QS-Yahweh/Trinity

HAIRY **WE**~subj12~. THY **TRIO**~subj12~: REINING, WANS.

5. In each answer, the first sentence's second word and the second sentence's first word are synonymous in definition (syn) or context (con):

   Synonymous answer words are tagged "syn," while answer words which share contextual meaning are tagged "con";

   (con1) DAVE; HE: context, both words identify same man;
   (syn2) EVIL; ILL: synonyms, each word means "wicked";
   (con3) ASSURE; RIGHT: context, both words convey affirmation;
   (con4) GIVER; [A HINTER]: context, word and [phrase] identify same person; *[Property Deviation Resolution: (see "Appendix B")];*
   (con5) REASON; AIR: context, the reason is expressed as a written statement;
   (con6) REASON; [A HINT]: context, the reason is expressed as an allusive statement; *[Property Deviation Resolution: (see "Appendix B")];*
   (con7) GHOST; HE: context, both words identify same person;
   (con8) HORN; NERVING: context, each word refers to a source of strength;
   (con9) WE; HEAVEN: context, both words identify same entity;
   (con10) REAL; [A TRINITY]: context, word and [phrase] identify same entity; *[Property Deviation Resolution: (see "Appendix B")];*
   (con11) LAW; THEY: context, revealed will of God is the Trinity;
   (con12) WE; THY: context, both words identify same entity;

QS-God/Heaven

GO **DAVE**$_{con1}$. **HE**$_{con1}$: WINNER; OR, GAINS.

QS-Devil/Hell

HORDE: **EVIL**$_{syn2}$. **ILL**$_{syn2}$ REIGN, WANS.

QS-Jesus/Earth

JOE **ASSURE**$_{con3}$. **RIGHT**$_{con3}$, REIN WANS.

QS-Dave/Earth

ADORE **GIVER**$_{con4}$. **[A HINTER]**$_{con4}$ WANS.

QS-Joe/Earth

JOE: **REASON**$_{con5}$. **AIR**$_{con5}$/HINT GREW.

QS-Mary/Earth

MARRY **REASON**$_{con6}$. **[A HINT]**$_{con6}$, I GREW.

QS-Holy^Ghost/Heaven

HOLY **GHOST**$_{con7}$. **HE**$_{con7}$: NAÏVE OR ANSWERING.

QS-YHWH/Heaven

YAHWEH: **HORN**$_{con8}$. **NERVING**$_{con8}$, IS A WE.

QS-Yahweh/Heaven

HAY: **WE**$_{con9}$. **HEAVEN**$_{con9}$: HORN, SIRING A WE.

QS-Creator/Reality

CORE: **REAL**$_{con10}$. **[A TRINITY]**$_{con10}$; OR, RINGS A WE.

QS-Yahweh/Reality

HAY: **LAW**$_{con11}$. **THEY**$_{con11}$ OR REINS, I, RING "A WE."

QS-Yahweh/Trinity

HAIRY **WE**$_{con12}$. **THY**$_{con12}$ TRIO: REINING, WANS.

6. In each answer's second sentence, at least one action is applied to the main subject (subj1–act1, subj2–act2, ...):

QS-God/Heaven

GO DAVE. **HE**$_{subj1}$: WINNER; OR, **GAINS**$_{act1}$.

QS-Devil/Hell

HORDE: EVIL. **ILL**$_{subj2}$ **REIGN**$_{act2}$, WANS.

QS-Jesus/Earth

JOE ASSURE. RIGHT, **REIN**$_{subj3}$ **WANS**$_{act3}$.

QS-Dave/Earth

ADORE GIVER. A **HINTER**$_{subj4}$ **WANS**$_{act4}$.

QS-Joe/Earth

JOE: REASON. **AIR**$_{subj5}$/HINT **GREW**$_{act5}$.

QS-Mary/Earth

MARRY REASON. A **HINT**$_{subj6}$, I **GREW**$_{act6}$.

QS-Holy^Ghost/Heaven

HOLY GHOST. **HE**$_{subj7}$: NAÏVE OR **ANSWERING**$_{act7}$.

QS-YHWH/Heaven

YAHWEH: HORN. **NERVING**$_{act8}$, IS A **WE**$_{subj8}$.

QS-Yahweh/Heaven

HAY: WE. **HEAVEN**$_{subj9}$: HORN, **SIRING**$_{act9}$ A WE.

QS-Creator/Reality

CORE: REAL. A **TRINITY**$_{subj10}$; OR, **RINGS**$_{act10}$ A WE.

QS-Yahweh/Reality

HAY: LAW. THEY OR REINS, **I**$_{subj11}$, **RING**$_{act11}$ "A WE."

QS-Yahweh/Trinity

HAIRY WE. THY **TRIO**~subj12~: **REINING**~act12~, WANS.

---

7. Along each answer's breadth of vocabulary, there's at least one site where an answer letter *S* would've enhanced the answer's grammatical correctness if it would've been available in the accompanying row'd word matrix and usable:

Removing a colon (:) that follows a noun and appending a contraction 's to the end of said noun would produce a conversational tone and clearer syntax (e.g. He's winner; Horde's evil; He's naïve; He's answering; Yahweh's horn; Hay's we; Heaven's horn; Heaven's siring; Core's real; Hay's law; Trio's reining). Removing a colon (:) that follows a noun and appending a possessive 's to the end of said noun would produce a conversational tone and clearer syntax (e.g. Joe's reason). Inflecting certain verbs by appending a letter S to the end of them would promote optimal grammar (e.g. Ill reigns; Joe assures). However, each answer's row'd word matrix lacks a letter S that's needed or that's capable of being used in ways mandated by QS rules (see "Appendix A");

[Property Deviation Resolution (see "Appendix B"): "QS-Dave/Earth" and "QS-Mary/Earth"];

QS-God/Heaven: He's winner;
QS-Devil/Hell: Horde's evil, Ill reigns;
QS-Jesus/Earth: Joe assures;
QS-Dave/Earth: (optimal grammar);
QS-Joe/Earth: Joe's reason;
QS-Mary/Earth: (optimal grammar);
QS-Holy^Ghost/Heaven: He's naïve, He's answering;
QS-YHWH/Heaven: Yahweh's horn;
QS-Creator/Reality: Core's real;
QS-Yahweh/Reality: Hay's law;
QS-Yahweh/Trinity: Trio's reining;

QS-God/Heaven

GO DAVE. **HE: WINNER**; OR, GAINS.

QS-Devil/Hell

HORDE: EVIL. ILL REIGN, WANS.

QS-Devil/Hell

HORDE: EVIL. ILL REIGN, WANS.

QS-Jesus/Earth

JOE ASSURE. RIGHT, REIN WANS.

QS-Dave/Earth

ADORE GIVER. A HINTER WANS.

QS-Joe/Earth

JOE: REASON. AIR/HINT GREW.

QS-Mary/Earth

MARRY REASON. A HINT, I GREW.

QS-Holy^Ghost/Heaven

HOLY GHOST. **HE: NAÏVE** OR ANSWERING.

HOLY GHOST. **HE:** NAÏVE OR **ANSWERING.**

QS-YHWH/Heaven

YAHWEH: HORN. NERVING, IS A WE.

QS-Yahweh/Heaven

HAY: WE. HEAVEN: HORN, SIRING A WE.

HAY: WE. **HEAVEN:** HORN, **SIRING** A WE.

QS-Creator/Reality

CORE: REAL. A TRINITY; OR, RINGS A WE.

QS-Yahweh/Reality

HAY: LAW. THEY OR REINS, I, RING "A WE."

QS-Yahweh/Trinity

HAIRY WE. THY **TRIO: REINING**, WANS.

CHAPTER FIVE: SECTION FOUR

"FIVE STACKS"/TRINITY

```
F A T H E R
T R I N I T Y
O R I G I N
A N S W E R
```

```
S O N
T R I N I T Y
O R I G I N
A N S W E R
```

```
H O L Y G H O S T
T R I N I T Y
O R I G I N
A N S W E R
```

```
G O D
T R I N I T Y
O R I G I N
A N S W E R
```

```
J E S U S
T R I N I T Y
O R I G I N
A N S W E R
```

In this section, I'd uncovered three more "Lineal-Alias, Realm-Related Query Stacks." Two of the said three Query Stacks had a first-row row'd word which was either FATHER or HOLY^GHOST and, therefore, cited a biblical character who was a part of Virgin Mary's genealogical "lineage" and was an "alias" of the name *God*. The third of the said three Query Stacks had a first-row row'd word which was SON and, therefore, cited a biblical character who was a part of Virgin Mary's genealogical "lineage" and was an "alias" of the name *Jesus Christ*. All three of the said Query Stacks contained the second row'd word TRINITY, which was an existential "realm that was comprised of and, therefore, related to" the Father, Son and Holy Ghost":

Ch. 5, Sec. 4: 1

LINEAL-ALIAS, REALM-RELATED QUERY STACKS

QS-CREATOR/REALITY
QS-YAHWEH/REALITY
QS-YAHWEH/TRINITY
► QS-FATHER/TRINITY ◄
► QS-SON/TRINITY ◄
► QS-HOLY^GHOST/TRINITY ◄

Besides the three "Lineal-Alias, Realm-Related Query Stacks," I'd uncovered two "Lineal, Realm-Related Query Stacks" QS matrices in this section. Each of the two QS matrices contained either the first-row row'd word GOD or the first-row row'd word JESUS, while both said matrices contained the second-row row'd word TRINITY. I'd categorized the said two Query Stacks as "Lineal, Realm-Related Query Stacks" for three reasons. First, the row'd words GOD and JESUS cited names which I'd already inserted into the first rows of QS matrices (see "Ch. 1, Sec. 1: 3" and "Ch. 1, Sec. 3: 1," respectively); which meant, said row'd words weren't considered aliases within the scope of my study. Second, God and Jesus were members of Virgin Mary's genealogical "lineage." Third, each QS matrix had a second-row row'd word, TRINITY, which was meaningfully "related" to the first-row row'd word in each of said two QS matrices and was an existential realm, instead of a spatial realm related to Heaven, Hell and Earth:

Ch. 5, Sec. 4: 2

LINEAL, REALM-RELATED QUERY STACKS
- ▶ QS-GOD/TRINITY ◀
- ▶ QS-JESUS/TRINITY ◀

Each of the five QS matrices spotlighted in this section contained a row'd word which was an alias of or the name *God* or *Jesus*; therefore, each first-row row'd word identified the holiest biblical figure or the holiest biblical figure's son:

A parenthetic number (#) succeeding a first-row row'd word reports the number of times said row'd word was used as a first-row row'd word;

(a) GOD (2); DEVIL; JESUS (2); DAVE *(David)*; JOE *(Joseph)*; MARY; HOLY^GHOST (2); YHWH; YAHWEH (3); CREATOR; FATHER; SON: notable biblical beings, first-row row'd words;

Ch. 5, Sec. 4: 3

QS-God/Heaven	*QS-Devil/Hell*	*QS-Jesus/Earth*	*QS-Dave/Earth*
ⁿG O D	ⁿD E V I L	ⁿJ E S U S	ⁿD A V E
H E A V E N	H E L L	E A R T H	E A R T H
O R I G I N	O R I G I N	O R I G I N	O R I G I N
A N S W E R	A N S W E R	A N S W E R	A N S W E R

QS-Joe/Earth	*QS-Mary/Earth*	*QS-Holy^Ghost/Heaven*
ⁿJ O E	ⁿM A R Y	ⁿH O L Y G H O S T
E A R T H	E A R T H	H E A V E N
O R I G I N	O R I G I N	O R I G I N
A N S W E R	A N S W E R	A N S W E R

QS-YHWH/Heaven	*QS-Yahweh/Heaven*	*QS-Creator/Reality*
ⁿY H W H	ⁿY A H W E H	ⁿC R E A T O R
H E A V E N	H E A V E N	R E A L I T Y
O R I G I N	O R I G I N	O R I G I N
A N S W E R	A N S W E R	A N S W E R

QS-Yahweh/Reality	*QS-Yahweh/Trinity*	*QS-Father/Trinity*
ⁿY A H W E H	ⁿY A H W E H	ⁿF A T H E R
R E A L I T Y	T R I N I T Y	T R I N I T Y
O R I G I N	O R I G I N	O R I G I N
A N S W E R	A N S W E R	A N S W E R

QS-Son/Trinity	*QS-Holy^Ghost/Trinity*	*QS-God/Trinity*
ⁿS O N	ⁿH O L Y G H O S T	ⁿG O D
T R I N I T Y	T R I N I T Y	T R I N I T Y
O R I G I N	O R I G I N	O R I G I N
A N S W E R	A N S W E R	A N S W E R

QS-Jesus/Trinity
ⁿJ E S U S
T R I N I T Y
O R I G I N
A N S W E R

God (Father), Jesus (Son) and Holy Ghost were prominent characters in the Trinity, because said trio were the only three members of the Trinity:

> *A parenthetic number (#) succeeding a first-row row'd word reports the number of times said row'd word was used as a first-row row'd word;*

(a) **GOD (2): notable biblical figure; of Heaven and Trinity; Heaven's ruler and Trinity member;**

(b) DEVIL: notable biblical figure; of Hell; God sends evil to Hell, Devil is the evilest being, Devil is evilest being God could send to Hell;

(c) **JESUS (2): notable biblical figure; of Earth and Trinity; Earth's premier ruler and Trinity member;**

(d) DAVE *(David)*: notable biblical figure; of Earth; third King of Israel;

(e) JOE *(Joseph)*: notable biblical figure; of Earth; Virgin Mary's husband;

(f) MARY: notable biblical figure; of Earth; Jesus's biological mother;

(g) **HOLY GHOST (2): notable biblical figure; of Heaven and Trinity; Heaven's messenger and Trinity member;**

(h) YHWH: notable biblical figure; of Heaven; Heaven's ruler;

(i) YAHWEH (3): notable biblical figure; of Heaven, Reality and Trinity; Heaven's ruler, Reality's maker and Trinity member;

(j) CREATOR: notable biblical figure; of Reality; Reality's maker;

(k) **FATHER: notable biblical figure; of Trinity; Trinity member;**

(l) **SON: notable biblical figure; of Trinity; Trinity member;**

Ch. 5, Sec. 4: 4

BIBLICAL BEING	DOMAIN	NOTORIETY
[a]GOD	[a]HEAVEN	[a]RULER
[a]GOD	**[a]TRINITY**	**[a]MEMBER**
[b]DEVIL	[b]HELL	[b]EVILEST RESIDENT
[c]JESUS	[c]EARTH	[c]PREMIER RULER
[c]JESUS	**[c]TRINITY**	**[c]MEMBER**
[d]DAVE (David)	[d]EARTH	[d]ANOINTED KING
[e]JOE (Joseph)	[e]EARTH	[e]MARY'S HUSBAND
[f]MARY	[f]EARTH	[f]JESUS'S MOTHER
[g]HOLY GHOST	[g]HEAVEN	[g]MESSENGER
[g]HOLY GHOST	**[g]TRINITY**	**[g]MEMBER**
[h]YHWH	[h]HEAVEN	[h]RULER
[i]YAHWEH	[i]HEAVEN	[i]RULER
[i]YAHWEH	[i]REALITY	[i]MAKER
[i]YAHWEH	**[i]TRINITY**	**[i]MEMBER**
[j]CREATOR	[j]REALITY	[j]MAKER
[k]FATHER	**[k]TRINITY**	**[k]MEMBER**
[l]SON	**[l]TRINITY**	**[l]MEMBER**

I'd provided a decoded QS matrix, a valid QS answer and a set of answer word definitions for each of the five Query Stacks I'd unveiled in this section. Furthermore, I'd provided an interpretation and a vocabular analysis for each answer of the said five Query Stacks I'd uncovered in this section. To understand the derivation of my interpretation for each answer of the said five Query Stacks, apply each Query Stack's set of definitions to its correlated answer and examine each vocabular analysis.

Messages integrated into each of the five QS answers I'd uncovered in this section mimicked messages conveyed by QS answers which I'd revealed in previous chapters. I'd placed each of the five QS answers in this section alongside QS answers which I'd previously uncovered and highlighted the vocabulary that each of the five said QS answers in this section and the previously uncovered QS answers had in common. In my vocabular comparisons, I'd boldfaced congruent words and phrases and encapsulated congruent words and phrases within parentheses and brackets. Additionally, I'd applied superscripted reference letters and numbers which linked to reference keys that provided explanations for vocabular congruencies to congruent answer words and phrases.

In this section, I'd given readers a more efficient way to absorb a Query Stack's matrix, answer and answer word definitions and my interpretation of said Query Stack's answer than I'd given in previous chapters, which I'd hoped would reduce reading fatigue caused by an overabundance of text and diminish boredom induced by repetitious data.

Father/Trinity: Fair Hinter

The first of the five said QS answers I'd uncovered in this section was "QS-Father/Trinity":

✓ All QS rules followed (see "Appendix A");

Ch. 5, Sec. 4: 5

QS-Father/Trinity

```
F A T H E R
T R I N I T Y
  O R I G I N
A N S W E R
```

FAIR HINTER.sent1 TRIO: TRYING, WANES.sent2

FAIR *adj.* Real.[2]
HINTER *n.* One that hints (*v.* brings to mind by allusion rather than explicit expression).[2]
TRIO *n.* A group of three.[2]
TRYING *v.* <TRY *v.*> To make an attempt to carry out some action.[2]
WANES *v.* <WANE *v.*> To fall especially gradually from power.[2]

sent1: **Real, or nonimaginary, is God, the provider of allusive statements.**
sent2: **The Trinity, which embodies three individuals that are distinct but essentially God, is attempting to exert the moral force of goodness and maintain rulership over Reality but falls gradually from power.**

Match superscripted numbers and letters to compare vocabulary in the "QS-Father/Trinity" answer to vocabulary in QS answers I've previously uncovered; brief explanations in the reference key should be enough of the necessary information one needs to understand my interpretation of the "QS-Father/Trinity" answer;

(1) *(FAIR HINTER), (CORE: REAL)*
Each QS answer phrase asserted that God was an actual, or nonimaginary, entity;

(2) *(TRIO: TRYING, WANES), (TRIO: REINING, WANS)*
Each QS answer phrase conveyed the message that the Trinity, or God, attempted to and did exert His moral force of goodness in order to maintain His rulership over Reality, yet His said power lost forcefulness, which, in turn, caused Him to lose His said rulership;

(a) *FAIR, REAL*

Each QS answer word signified an actual, or nonimaginary, existence;

(b) *HINTER, HINTER*

In both occurrences, the QS answer word *HINTER* cited the author of the QS answers in this book, or God, as a provider of allusive QS answers;

(c) *TRIO, TRINITY, TRIO*

Each QS answer word cited a group which was comprised of three members, was essentially God and was named *Trinity*;

(d) *TRYING, REINING*

The QS answer word *TRYING* reflected the Trinity's, or God's, attempt to maintain His rulership over Reality, while the answer word *REINING* signaled that the Trinity was successfully exerting a powerful force, the moral force of goodness, to rule over Reality;

(e) *WANES, WANS, WANS*

Each QS answer word signified that the Trinity, or God, was becoming less forceful, which, in turn, caused said trinity to gradually lose rulership over Reality;

Ch. 5, Sec. 4: 6

QS-Dave/Earth Answer
ADORE GIVER. A [b](HINTER) [e](WANS).
QS-Creator/Reality Answer
[1][CORE: [a](REAL)]. A [c](TRINITY); OR, RINGS A WE.
QS-Yahweh/Trinity Answer
HAIRY WE. THY [2][[c](TRIO): [d](REINING), [e](WANS)].
QS-Father/Trinity Answer
[1][[a](FAIR) [b](HINTER)]. [2][[c](TRIO): [d](TRYING), [e](WANES)].

Son/Trinity: Trying Sinew

The second of the five said QS answers I'd uncovered in this section was "QS-Father/Trinity":

| *contr = contraction* |

✓ All QS rules followed (see "Appendix A");

Ch. 5, Sec. 4: 7

QS-Son/Trinity

```
S O N
T R I N I T Y
  O R I G I N
A N S W E R
```

ORATOR'S IN.sent1 IN: TRYING SINEW.sent2

ORATOR'S *contr.* <ORATOR *n.* IS *v.*> A public speaker.[2]
IN *n.* One who is in power.[2]
TRYING *v.* <TRY *v.*> To make an attempt to carry out some action.[2]
SINEW *n.* Force.[2]

sent1: **God, a speaker who conveys messages through publicized QS answers, is the one who has a powerful position in the hierarchy of entities which control Reality.**

sent2: **God, who has a powerful position in the hierarchy of entities which control Reality, is attempting to wield the moral force of goodness in order to maintain His rulership over Reality.**

Match superscripted numbers and letters to compare vocabulary in the "QS-Son/Trinity" answer to vocabulary in QS answers I've previously uncovered; brief explanations in the reference key should be enough of the necessary information one needs to understand my interpretation of the "QS-Son/Trinity" answer;

[1] *(IN: TRYING SINEW), (TRIO: TRYING)*

Each QS answer phrase stated that the Trinity, or God, attempted to maintain a powerful position of control over Reality by administering a moral force of goodness;

[a] *(ORATOR'S IN), HINTER, HINTER*

Collectively, the QS answer phrase *"orator's in"* and the QS answer word *HINTER* alluded to God having been the author of allusive QS answers and the entity which was characterized in QS answers as having a powerful position in Reality;

[b] *(TRYING SINEW), TRYING*

The QS answer phrase *"trying sinew"* and the QS answer word *TRYING* signified that the Trinity, or God, used force in an attempt to maintain control over Reality;

Ch. 5, Sec. 4: 8

QS-Dave/Earth Answer
`ADORE GIVER. A `*`a`*`(HINTER) WANS.`
QS-Father/Trinity Answer
`FAIR `*`a`*`(HINTER). `*`1`*`[TRIO: `*`b`*`(TRYING)], WANES.`
QS-Son/Trinity Answer
`a``(ORATOR'S IN). `*`1`*`[IN: `*`b`*`(TRYING SINEW)].`

Holy^Ghost/Trinity: Torah's Glory

The third of the five said QS answers I'd uncovered in this section was "QS-Holy^Ghost/Trinity":

- ✓ All QS rules followed (see "Appendix A");

Ch. 5, Sec. 4: 9

QS-Holy^Ghost/Trinity

```
H O L Y G H O S T
T R I N I T Y
O R I G I N
A N S W E R
```

TORAH: GLORY.sent1 **HOST: IN, I, TRYING SINEW.**sent2

TORAH *prop-n.* The body of divine knowledge and law found in the Jewish scriptures and tradition.[2]

GLORY *n.* Shekinah (*prop-n.* the presence of God in the world conceived by Jewish and later by Christian theologians as manifested in natural and especially supernatural phenomena).[2]

HOST *prop-n.* The eucharistic wafer or bread—*symbols for the body of Christ*—before or after consecration—*solemn dedication in perpetuity of vessels used in the Eucharist.*[2]

IN *n.* One who is in power.[2]

I *n.* Someone possessing and aware of possessing a distinct and personal individuality.[2]

TRYING *v.* <TRY *v.*> To make an attempt to carry out some action.[2]

SINEW *n.* Force.[2]

---

sent1: *According to the Hebrew Bible's book of divine knowledge and law, YHWH, or God, presented Himself on Earth as Shekinah, or a manifestation of Himself on Earth as a natural phenomenon.*

sent2: *The body of Jesus Christ is the body for the one who's in power, the one aware of being an individual and the one attempting to wield the moral force of goodness to maintain His control over Reality; in other words, Jesus Christ's body is God's body.*

Match superscripted numbers and letters to compare vocabulary in the "QS-Holy^Ghost/Trinity" answer to vocabulary in QS answers I've already unveiled; brief explanations in the reference key should contain enough of the necessary info one needs to understand my interpretation of the "QS-Holy^Ghost/Trinity" answer;

[1] ***(HOST: IN, I, TRYING SINEW), (TRIO: TRYING), (IN: TRYING SINEW)***
Collectively, the QS answer phrases stated that God was the body of Jesus Christ *(Host)*, a self-aware individual *(I)*, an individual in a trinity *(trio)*, and attempted *(trying)* to maintain His powerful rulership position *(in)* in Reality by administering the moral force of goodness *(trying sinew)*;

[a] ***(TORAH: GLORY)***
The QS answer phrase evoked stories told in the Torah, or the first five books of the Tanakh, in which Yahweh, or God, manifested Himself as a Shekinah, like a

pillar of fire or burning bush, so His presence on Earth was endurable by and He was able to communicate with earthly creatures: "And you said, 'Behold, the Lord, our God, has shown us His glory and His greatness, and we heard His voice from the midst of the fire; we saw this day that God speaks with man, yet [man] remains alive'" (Devarim 5:21 Tanakh); "And ye said, Behold, the LORD our God hath shewed us his glory and his greatness, and we have heard his voice out of the midst of the fire: we have seen this day that God doth talk with man, and he liveth" (Deuteronomy 5:24 KJV);

(b) *(HOST: IN), (ORATOR'S IN)*

Collectively, both QS answer phrases asserted that God, who was symbolized as the body of Jesus Christ and who'd spoken through publicized QS answers, held a powerful position in Reality;

(c) *(HOST: I), (YAHWEH....IS A WE), (A TRINITY; OR, RINGS A WE):*

Each QS answer phrase asserted that God was aware that He was an individual and an individual in a trinity;

Ch. 5, Sec. 4: 10

QS-YHWH/Heaven Answer
^c(YAHWEH): HORN. NERVING, ^c(IS A WE).
QS-Creator/Reality Answer
CORE: REAL. ^c(A TRINITY; OR, RINGS A WE).
QS-Father/Trinity Answer
FAIR HINTER. ¹(TRIO: TRYING), WANES.
QS-Son/Trinity Answer
^b(ORATOR'S IN). ¹(IN: TRYING SINEW).
QS-Holy^Ghost/Trinity Answer
^a(TORAH: GLORY). ¹[^{b,c}(HOST): ^b(IN), ^c(I), TRYING SINEW].

God/Trinity: Got Wording

The fourth of the five said QS answers in this section I'd uncovered was "QS-God/Trinity":

- ✓ All QS rules followed (see "Appendix A");

Ch. 5, Sec. 4: 11

QS-God/Trinity

```
G O D
T R I N I T Y
  O R I G I N
A N S W E R
```

GOT WORDING._{sent1} "I" ENTRY; RAINS "I."_{sent2}

GOT *v.* <GET *v.*> To come to have.[2]
WORDING *n.* The manner of expressing in words.[2]
"I" *n.* The answer word *I*.
ENTRY *n.* A record made in a log, diary or anything similarly organized.[3]
RAINS *v.* <RAIN *v.*> To bestow abundantly.[2]

sent1: *QS answers contain words.*

sent2: *"I" is a word in a QS answer; in fact, QS answers present the word "I" numerous times.*

Match superscripted numbers and letters to compare vocabulary in the "QS-God/Trinity" answer to vocabulary in QS answers I've already unveiled; brief explanations in the reference key should contain enough of the necessary information one needs to understand my interpretation of the "QS-God/Trinity" answer;

[a] *(GOT WORDING), ("I" ENTRY; RAINS "I")*, *I, I, I*

Collectively, the QS answer phrases *"got wording"* and *"'I' entry; rains 'I'"* characterized the phrasing of QS answers as not only consisting of but providing numerous occurrences of the QS answer word *I*. Furthermore, three instances of the QS answer word *I* provided evidence to support the claim that the QS answer word *I* was a QS answer entry;

Ch. 5, Sec. 4: 12

QS-Mary/Earth Answer

MARRY REASON. A HINT, [b]**(I)** GREW.

QS-Yahweh/Reality Answer

HAY: LAW. THEY OR REINS, [b]**(I)**, RING "A WE."

QS-Holy^Ghost/Trinity Answer

TORAH: GLORY. HOST: IN, [b]**(I)**, TRYING SINEW.

QS-God/Trinity Answer

[a]**(GOT WORDING).** [b]**("I" ENTRY; RAINS "I.")**

Jesus/Trinity: I Ring Entry

The final QS answer in this section I'd uncovered was "QS-Jesus/Trinity":

- ✓ All QS rules followed (see "Appendix A");

Ch. 5, Sec. 4: 13

QS-Jesus/Trinity

J	E	S	U	S
T	R	I	N	I	T	Y
O	R	I	G	I	N
A	N	S	W	E	R

JOT, ISSUER._{sent1} I RING ENTRY "I," "WANS."_{sent2}

JOT *v.* To write briefly.[2]
ISSUER *n.* One that issues (*v.* to cause to appear for circulation among the public) something.[2]
I *pron.* The one who is speaking or writing.[2]
RING *v.* To repeat earnestly.[2]
ENTRY *n.* A record made in a log, diary or anything similarly organized.[3]
"I" *n.* The answer word *I*.
"WANS" *n.* The answer word *WANS*.

sent1: *Writes briefly is the one who causes QS answers to circulate publicly, which is God.*
sent2: *The QS author, or God, earnestly and repeatedly inserts the word "I" and the word "wans" into QS answers.*

Match superscripted numbers and letters to compare vocabulary in the "QS-Jesus/Trinity" answer to vocabulary in QS answers I've already unveiled; brief explanations in the reference key should contain enough of the necessary information one needs to understand my interpretation of the "QS-Jesus/Trinity" answer;

[1] *(JOT, ISSUER), (GOT WORDING)*
Collectively, the meaning of the two QS answer phrases suggested that the QS author, or God, intended for QS answers, which God expressed via words and in brevity, to be publicized;

[2] *(I RING ENTRY "I"), ("I" ENTRY; RAINS "I")*
Both QS answer phrases stated that the QS author had repeatedly inserted the word *I* into the vocabulary of QS answers;

(a) ***ISSUER, GIVER, HINTER, ORATOR'S***
Collectively, the four QS answer words characterized the author of QS answers, God, as an author who'd donated by publicizing His allusive QS answers;

(b) *(I RING ENTRY), (JOE ASSURE), RIGHT, (HINT, I GREW)*
The three QS answer phrases and one QS answer word pertained to God's earnest and repetitive use of the words *I* and *wans* as QS answer words, which helped His allusive statements, that He'd affirmed were true, to become textually longer;

(c) *I, ("I"), I, I, I, ("I"), ("I")*
God's earnestness in repeatedly incorporating the word *I* into QS answers was evidenced by the word *I* appearing as a QS answer word at least seven times in the twenty QS answers in this book;

(d) *("WANS"), WANS, WANS, WANS, WANS, WANES*
God's earnestness in repeatedly incorporating the word *wans* into QS answers was evidenced by the word *wans* appearing as a QS answer word at least five times in the twenty QS answers in this book. Moreover, God incorporated the word *wanes*, a synonym of the word *wans*, into a QS answer;

Ch. 5, Sec. 4: 14

QS-Devil/Hell Answer
HORDE: EVIL. ILL REIGN, [d]**(WANS)**.
QS-Jesus/Earth Answer
[b]**(JOE ASSURE)**. [b]**(RIGHT)**, REIN [d]**(WANS)**.
QS-Dave/Earth Answer
ADORE [a]**(GIVER)**. A [a]**(HINTER)** [d]**(WANS)**.
QS-Mary/Earth Answer
MARRY REASON. A [b]**[HINT,** [c]**(I) GREW]**.
QS-Yahweh/Reality Answer
HAY: LAW. THEY OR REINS, [c]**(I)**, RING "A WE."
QS-Yahweh/Trinity Answer
HAIRY WE. THY TRIO: REINING, [d]**(WANS)**.
QS-Father/Trinity Answer
FAIR [a]**(HINTER)**. TRIO: TRYING, [d]**(WANES)**.
QS-Son/Trinity Answer
[a]**(ORATOR'S)** IN. IN: TRYING SINEW.
QS-Holy^Ghost/Trinity Answer
TORAH: GLORY. HOST: IN, [c]**(I)**, TRYING SINEW.
QS-God/Trinity Answer
[1]**(GOT WORDING)**. [2][[c]**("I") ENTRY; RAINS** [c]**("I.")**]
QS-Jesus/Trinity Answer
[1]**[JOT,** [a]**(ISSUER)]**. [2][[b]**(I RING ENTRY)** [c]**("I")**], [d]**("WANS.")**

Even though each of the five QS answers mentioned in this section was grammatically coherent and meaningful, I'd ran each one of the said answers through "QS-7CAP" in order to confirm that each said answer's vocabulary was valid:

Seven Common QS Answer Properties

---

1. Each answer contains no more and no less than two sentences (sent1, sent2):

QS-God/Heaven

GO DAVE.sent1 HE: WINNER; OR, GAINS.sent2

QS-Devil/Hell

HORDE: EVIL.sent1 ILL REIGN, WANS.sent2

QS-Jesus/Earth

JOE ASSURE.sent1 RIGHT, REIN WANS.sent2

QS-Dave/Earth

ADORE GIVER.sent1 A HINTER WANS.sent2

QS-Joe/Earth

JOE: REASON.sent1 AIR/HINT GREW.sent2

QS-Mary/Earth

MARRY REASON.sent1 A HINT, I GREW.sent2

QS-Holy^Ghost/Heaven

HOLY GHOST.sent1 HE: NAÏVE OR ANSWERING.sent2

QS-YHWH/Heaven

YAHWEH: HORN.sent1 NERVING, IS A WE.sent2

QS-Yahweh/Heaven

HAY: WE.sent1 HEAVEN: HORN, SIRING A WE.sent2

QS-Creator/Reality

CORE: REAL.sent1 A TRINITY; OR, RINGS A WE.sent2

QS-Yahweh/Reality

HAY: LAW.sent1 THEY OR REINS, I, RING "A WE."sent2

QS-Yahweh/Trinity

HAIRY WE.sent1 THY TRIO: REINING, WANS.sent2

QS-Father/Trinity

FAIR HINTER.sent1 TRIO: TRYING, WANES.sent2

QS-Son/Trinity

ORATOR'S IN.sent1 IN: TRYING SINEW.sent2

QS-Holy^Ghost/Trinity

TORAH: GLORY.sent1 HOST: IN, I, TRYING SINEW.sent2

QS-God/Trinity

GOT WORDING.sent1 "I" ENTRY; RAINS "I."sent2

QS-Jesus/Trinity

JOT, ISSUER.sent1 I RING ENTRY "I," "WANS."sent2

2. Each answer's first sentence contains no more and no less than two words (word1,

word2):

QS-God/Heaven

GOword1 **DAVE**word2. HE: WINNER; OR, GAINS.

QS-Devil/Hell

HORDEword1: **EVIL**word2. ILL REIGN, WANS.

QS-Jesus/Earth

JOEword1 **ASSURE**word2. RIGHT, REIN WANS.

QS-Dave/Earth

ADOREword1 **GIVER**word2. A HINTER WANS.

QS-Joe/Earth

JOEword1: **REASON**word2. AIR/HINT GREW.

QS-Mary/Earth

MARRYword1 **REASON**word2. A HINT, I GREW.

QS-Holy^Ghost/Heaven

HOLYword1 **GHOST**word2. HE: NAÏVE OR ANSWERING.

QS-YHWH/Heaven

YAHWEHword1: **HORN**word2. NERVING, IS A WE.

QS-Yahweh/Heaven

HAYword1: **WE**word2. HEAVEN: HORN, SIRING A WE.

QS-Creator/Reality

COREword1: **REAL**word2. A TRINITY; OR, RINGS A WE.

QS-Yahweh/Reality

HAYword1: **LAW**word2. THEY OR REINS, I, RING "A WE."

QS-Yahweh/Trinity

HAIRYword1 **WE**word2. THY TRIO: REINING, WANS.

QS-Father/Trinity

FAIRword1 **HINTER**word2. TRIO: TRYING, WANES.

QS-Son/Trinity

ORATOR'Sword1 **IN**word2. IN: TRYING SINEW.

QS-Holy^Ghost/Trinity

TORAHword1: **GLORY**word2. HOST: IN, I, TRYING SINEW.

QS-God/Trinity

GOTword1 **WORDING**word2. "I" ENTRY; RAINS "I."

QS-Jesus/Trinity

JOTword1, **ISSUER**word2. I RING ENTRY "I," "WANS."

3. In each answer's first sentence, the main subject is introduced (subj1, subj2, ...):

(subj14) [ORATOR]'S: contraction, [main subject] and *is*; [Property Resolution: ORATOR'S is an answer word in the first sentence. ORATOR'S is a contraction of the phrase "orator is." The contractive phrase "orator is" contains the main subject "orator," along with the verb "is." Based on my analysis, I've determined that when a contraction is in the first sentence of a QS answer and said contraction identifies said QS answer's main subject, said contraction isn't a property deviation];

QS-God/Heaven
GO **DAVE**$_{subj1}$. HE: WINNER; OR, GAINS.

QS-Devil/Hell
HORDE$_{subj2}$: EVIL. ILL REIGN, WANS.

QS-Jesus/Earth
JOE$_{subj3}$ ASSURE. RIGHT, REIN WANS.

QS-Dave/Earth
ADORE **GIVER**$_{subj4}$. A HINTER WANS.

QS-Joe/Earth
JOE: **REASON**$_{subj5}$. AIR/HINT GREW.

QS-Mary/Earth
MARRY **REASON**$_{subj6}$. A HINT, I GREW.

QS-Holy^Ghost/Heaven
HOLY **GHOST**$_{subj7}$. HE: NAÏVE OR ANSWERING.

QS-YHWH/Heaven
YAHWEH$_{subj8}$: HORN. NERVING, IS A WE.

QS-Yahweh/Heaven
HAY$_{subj9}$: WE. HEAVEN: HORN, SIRING A WE.

QS-Creator/Reality
CORE$_{subj10}$: REAL. A TRINITY; OR, RINGS A WE.

QS-Yahweh/Reality
HAY$_{subj11}$: LAW. THEY OR REINS, I, RING "A WE."

QS-Yahweh/Trinity
HAIRY **WE**$_{subj12}$. THY TRIO: REINING, WANS.

QS-Father/Trinity
FAIR **HINTER**$_{subj13}$. TRIO: TRYING, WANES.

QS-Son/Trinity

[**ORATOR**~subj14~]'S IN. IN: TRYING SINEW.

QS-Holy^Ghost/Trinity

TORAH: **GLORY**~subj15~. HOST: IN, I, TRYING SINEW.

QS-God/Trinity

GOT **WORDING**~subj16~. "I" ENTRY; RAINS "I."

QS-Jesus/Trinity

JOT, **ISSUER**~subj17~. I RING ENTRY "I," "WANS."

4. In each answer, the main subject introduced in the first sentence is mentioned in the second sentence (subj1-subj1, subj2-subj2, ...):

QS-God/Heaven

GO **DAVE**~subj1~. **HE**~subj1~: WINNER; OR, GAINS.

QS-Devil/Hell

HORDE~subj2~: EVIL. **ILL**~subj2~ REIGN, WANS.

QS-Jesus/Earth

JOE~subj3~ ASSURE. RIGHT, **REIN**~subj3~ WANS.

QS-Dave/Earth

ADORE **GIVER**~subj4~. A **HINTER**~subj4~ WANS.

QS-Joe/Earth

JOE: **REASON**~subj5~. **AIR**~subj5~/HINT GREW.

QS-Mary/Earth

MARRY **REASON**~subj6~. A **HINT**~subj6~, I GREW.

QS-Holy^Ghost/Heaven

HOLY **GHOST**~subj7~. **HE**~subj7~: NAÏVE OR ANSWERING.

QS-YHWH/Heaven

YAHWEH~subj8~: HORN. NERVING, IS A **WE**~subj8~.

QS-Yahweh/Heaven

HAY~subj9~: WE. HEAVEN: HORN, SIRING A **WE**~subj9~.

QS-Creator/Reality

CORE~subj10~: REAL. A **TRINITY**~subj10~; OR, RINGS A WE.

QS-Yahweh/Reality

HAY~subj11~: LAW. THEY OR **REINS**~subj11~, I, RING "A WE."

QS-Yahweh/Trinity

HAIRY **WE**~subj12~. THY **TRIO**~subj12~: REINING, WANS.

QS-Father/Trinity

FAIR **HINTER**subj13. **TRIO**subj13: TRYING, WANES.

QS-Son/Trinity

[**ORATOR**subj14]'S IN. **IN**subj14: TRYING SINEW.

QS-Holy^Ghost/Trinity

TORAH: **GLORY**subj15. **HOST**subj15: IN, I, TRYING SINEW.

QS-God/Trinity

GOT **WORDING**subj16. "**I**"subj16 ENTRY; RAINS "I."

QS-Jesus/Trinity

JOT, **ISSUER**subj17. **I**subj17 RING ENTRY "I," "WANS."

5. In each answer, the first sentence's second word and the second sentence's first word are synonymous in definition (syn) or context (con):

   Synonymous answer words are tagged "syn," while answer words which share contextual meaning are tagged "con";

   (con1) DAVE; HE: context, both words identify same man;

   (syn2) EVIL; ILL: synonyms, each word means "wicked";

   (con3) ASSURE; RIGHT: context, both words convey affirmation;

   (con4) GIVER; [A HINTER]: context, word and [phrase] identify same person; *[Property Deviation Resolution: (see "Appendix B")];*

   (con5) REASON; AIR: context, the reason is expressed as a written statement;

   (con6) REASON; [A HINT]: context, the reason is expressed as an allusive statement; *[Property Deviation Resolution: (see "Appendix B")];*

   (con7) GHOST; HE: context, both words identify same person;

   (con 8) HORN; NERVING: context, each word refers to a source of strength;

   (con 9) WE; HEAVEN: context, both words identify same entity;

   (con10) REAL; [A TRINITY]: context, word and [phrase] identify same entity; *[Property Deviation Resolution: (see "Appendix B")];*

   (con11) LAW; THEY: context, revealed will of God is the Trinity;

   (con12) WE; THY: context, both words identify same entity;

   (con13) HINTER; TRIO: context, both words identify same entity;

   (syn14) IN; IN: synonym, each word means "one who is in power";

   (con15) GLORY; HOST: context, both words identify same person;

   (con16) WORDING; "I": context, both words refer to answer words;

   (con17) ISSUER; I: context, both words identify same person;

QS-God/Heaven

GO **DAVE**$_{con1}$. **HE**$_{con1}$: WINNER; OR, GAINS.

QS-Devil/Hell

HORDE: **EVIL**$_{syn2}$. **ILL**$_{syn2}$ REIGN, WANS.

QS-Jesus/Earth

JOE **ASSURE**$_{con3}$. **RIGHT**$_{con3}$, REIN WANS.

QS-Dave/Earth

ADORE **GIVER**$_{con4}$. **[A HINTER]**$_{con4}$ WANS.

QS-Joe/Earth

JOE: **REASON**$_{con5}$. **AIR**$_{con5}$/HINT GREW.

QS-Mary/Earth

MARRY **REASON**$_{con6}$. **[A HINT]**$_{con6}$, I GREW.

QS-Holy^Ghost/Heaven

HOLY **GHOST**$_{con7}$. **HE**$_{con7}$: NAÏVE OR ANSWERING.

QS-YHWH/Heaven

YAHWEH: **HORN**$_{con8}$. **NERVING**$_{con8}$, IS A WE.

QS-Yahweh/Heaven

HAY: **WE**$_{con9}$. **HEAVEN**$_{con9}$: HORN, SIRING A WE.

QS-Creator/Reality

CORE: **REAL**$_{con10}$. **[A TRINITY]**$_{con10}$; OR, RINGS A WE.

QS-Yahweh/Reality

HAY: **LAW**$_{con11}$. **THEY**$_{con11}$ OR REINS, I, RING "A WE."

QS-Yahweh/Trinity

HAIRY **WE**$_{con12}$. **THY**$_{con12}$ TRIO: REINING, WANS.

QS-Father/Trinity

FAIR **HINTER**$_{con13}$. **TRIO**$_{con13}$: TRYING, WANES.

QS-Son/Trinity

ORATOR'S **IN**$_{syn14}$. **IN**$_{syn14}$: TRYING SINEW.

QS-Holy^Ghost/Trinity

TORAH: **GLORY**$_{con15}$. **HOST**$_{con15}$: IN, I, TRYING SINEW.

QS-God/Trinity

GOT **WORDING**$_{con16}$. **"I"**$_{con16}$ ENTRY; RAINS "I."

QS-Jesus/Trinity

JOT, **ISSUER**$_{con17}$. **I**$_{con17}$ RING ENTRY "I," "WANS."

6. In each answer's second sentence, at least one action is applied to the main subject

(subj1–act1, subj2–act2, ...):

QS-God/Heaven

GO DAVE. **HE**$_{subj1}$: WINNER; OR, **GAINS**$_{act1}$.

QS-Devil/Hell

HORDE: EVIL. **ILL**$_{subj2}$ **REIGN**$_{act2}$, WANS.

QS-Jesus/Earth

JOE ASSURE. RIGHT, **REIN**$_{subj3}$ **WANS**$_{act3}$.

QS-Dave/Earth

ADORE GIVER. A **HINTER**$_{subj4}$ **WANS**$_{act4}$.

QS-Joe/Earth

JOE: REASON. **AIR**$_{subj5}$/HINT **GREW**$_{act5}$.

QS-Mary/Earth

MARRY REASON. A **HINT**$_{subj6}$, I **GREW**$_{act6}$.

QS-Holy^Ghost/Heaven

HOLY GHOST. **HE**$_{subj7}$: NAÏVE OR **ANSWERING**$_{act7}$.

QS-YHWH/Heaven

YAHWEH: HORN. **NERVING**$_{act8}$, IS A **WE**$_{subj8}$.

QS-Yahweh/Heaven

HAY: WE. HEAVEN: HORN, **SIRING**$_{act9}$ A **WE**$_{subj9}$.

QS-Creator/Reality

CORE: REAL. A **TRINITY**$_{subj10}$; OR, **RINGS**$_{act10}$ A WE.

QS-Yahweh/Reality

HAY: LAW. THEY OR **REINS**$_{subj11}$, I, **RING**$_{act11}$ "A WE."

QS-Yahweh/Trinity

HAIRY WE. THY **TRIO**$_{subj12}$: **REINING**$_{act12}$, WANS.

QS-Father/Trinity

FAIR HINTER. **TRIO**$_{subj13}$: **TRYING**$_{act13}$, WANES.

QS-Son/Trinity

ORATOR'S IN. **IN**$_{subj14}$: **TRYING**$_{act14}$ SINEW.

QS-Holy^Ghost/Trinity

TORAH: GLORY. **HOST**$_{subj15}$: IN, I, **TRYING**$_{act15}$ SINEW.

QS-God/Trinity

GOT WORDING. "**I**"$_{subj16}$ ENTRY; **RAINS**$_{act16}$ "I."

QS-Jesus/Trinity

JOT, ISSUER. **I**$_{subj17}$ **RING**$_{act17}$ ENTRY "I," "WANS."

7. Along each answer's breadth of vocabulary, there's at least one site where an answer letter *S* would've enhanced the answer's grammatical correctness if it would've been available in the accompanying row'd word matrix and usable:

Removing a colon (:) that follows a noun and appending a contraction 's to the end of said noun would produce a conversational tone and clearer syntax (e.g. He's winner; Horde's evil; He's naïve; He's answering; Yahweh's horn; Hay's we; Heaven's horn; Heaven's siring; Core's real; Hay's law; Trio's reining; Trio's trying; In's trying; Host's in; Host's I; Host's trying). Removing a colon (:) that follows a noun which represents a subject and appending a possessive 's to the end of said noun would produce a conversational tone and clearer syntax (e.g. Joe's reason; Torah's glory). Inflecting certain verbs by appending a letter S to the end of them would promote optimal grammar (e.g. Ill reigns; Joe assures; Jots, issuer). However, each answer's row'd word matrix lacks a letter S that's needed or that's capable of being used in ways mandated by QS rules (see "Appendix A");

[Property Deviation Resolution: No grammatically incorrect syntax can be found within the "QS-Dave/Earth," "QS-Mary/Earth," "QS-God/Trinity" or "QS-Jesus/Trinity" answer's vocabulary. Optimal vocabulary contains no grammatical mistakes. If a QS answer doesn't contain missing letters in its vocabulary, then the vocabulary of said QS answer is grammatically optimal and therefore acceptable.];

QS-God/Heaven: He's winner;
QS-Devil/Hell: Horde's evil, Ill reigns;
QS-Jesus/Earth: Joe assures;
QS-Dave/Earth: (optimal grammar);
QS-Joe/Earth: Joe's reason;
QS-Mary/Earth: (optimal grammar);
QS-Holy^Ghost/Heaven: He's naïve, He's answering;
QS-YHWH/Heaven: Yahweh's horn;
QS-Creator/Reality: Core's real;
QS-Yahweh/Reality: Hay's law;
QS-Yahweh/Trinity: Trio's reining;
QS-Father/Trinity: Trio's trying;
QS-Son/Trinity: In's trying;
QS-Holy^Ghost/Trinity: Host's in, Host's I, Host's trying;
QS-God/Trinity: (optimal grammar);

QS-Jesus/Trinity: <u>Jots</u>, issuer;

QS-God/Heaven

GO DAVE. **HE: WINNER**; OR, GAINS.

QS-Devil/Hell

HORDE: EVIL. ILL REIGN, WANS.

QS-Jesus/Earth

JOE ASSURE. RIGHT, REIN WANS.

QS-Dave/Earth

ADORE GIVER. A HINTER WANS.

QS-Joe/Earth

JOE: REASON. AIR/HINT GREW.

QS-Mary/Earth

MARRY REASON. A HINT, I GREW.

QS-Holy^Ghost/Heaven

HOLY GHOST. **HE: NAÏVE** OR ANSWERING.

HOLY GHOST. **HE:** NAÏVE OR **ANSWERING**.

QS-YHWH/Heaven

YAHWEH: HORN. NERVING, IS A WE.

QS-Yahweh/Heaven

HAY: WE. HEAVEN: HORN, SIRING A WE.

HAY: WE. **HEAVEN:** HORN, **SIRING** A WE.

QS-Creator/Reality

CORE: REAL. A TRINITY; OR, RINGS A WE.

QS-Yahweh/Reality

HAY: LAW. THEY OR REINS, I, RING "A WE."

QS-Yahweh/Trinity

HAIRY WE. THY **TRIO: REINING**, WANS.

QS-Father/Trinity

FAIR HINTER. **TRIO: TRYING**, WANES.

QS-Son/Trinity

ORATOR'S IN. **IN: TRYING** SINEW.

QS-Holy^Ghost/Trinity

TORAH: GLORY. HOST: IN, I, TRYING SINEW.
TORAH: GLORY. **HOST:** IN, **I,** TRYING SINEW.
TORAH: GLORY. **HOST:** IN, I, **TRYING** SINEW.

QS-God/Trinity

GOT WORDING. "I" ENTRY; RAINS "I."

QS-Jesus/Trinity

JOT, ISSUER. I RING ENTRY "I," "WANS."

CHAPTER FIVE: SECTION FIVE

REVIEW: SEVENTEEN STACKS

G O D
H E A V E N
O R I G I N
A N S W E R

D E V I L
H E L L
O R I G I N
A N S W E R

J E S U S
E A R T H
O R I G I N
A N S W E R

D A V E
E A R T H
O R I G I N
A N S W E R

J O E
E A R T H
O R I G I N
A N S W E R

M A R Y
E A R T H
O R I G I N
A N S W E R

H O L Y G H O S T
H E A V E N
O R I G I N
A N S W E R

Y H W H
H E A V E N
O R I G I N
A N S W E R

Y A H W E H
H E A V E N
O R I G I N
A N S W E R

C R E A T O R
R E A L I T Y
O R I G I N
A N S W E R

Y A H W E H
R E A L I T Y
O R I G I N
A N S W E R

Y A H W E H
T R I N I T Y
O R I G I N
A N S W E R

F A T H E R
T R I N I T Y
O R I G I N
A N S W E R

S O N
T R I N I T Y
O R I G I N
A N S W E R

H O L Y G H O S T
T R I N I T Y
O R I G I N
A N S W E R

```
G O D
T R I N I T Y
O R I G I N
A N S W E R
```

```
J E S U S
T R I N I T Y
O R I G I N
A N S W E R
```

In the previous four sections, I'd unraveled eight Query Stacks. Each of the eight Query Stacks was either a "Lineal-Alias, Realm-Related Query Stack" or a "Lineal, Realm-Related Query Stack":

Ch. 5, Sec. 5: 1

LINEAL QUERY STACKS

QS-GOD/HEAVEN
QS-JESUS/EARTH
QS-DAVE/EARTH
QS-JOE/EARTH
QS-MARY/EARTH

LINEALLY-COUPLED QUERY STACKS

QS-DEVIL/HELL

LINEAL-ALIAS QUERY STACKS

QS-HOLY^GHOST/HEAVEN
QS-YHWH/HEAVEN
QS-YAHWEH/HEAVEN

▶ **LINEAL-ALIAS, REALM-RELATED QUERY STACKS** ◀

▶ QS-CREATOR/REALITY ◀
▶ QS-YAHWEH/REALITY ◀
▶ QS-YAHWEH/TRINITY ◀
▶ QS-FATHER/TRINITY ◀
▶ QS-SON/TRINITY ◀
▶ QS-HOLY^GHOST/TRINITY ◀

▶ **LINEAL, REALM-RELATED QUERY STACKS** ◀

▶ QS-GOD/TRINITY ◀
▶ QS-JESUS/TRINITY ◀

I'd filed each one of the seventeen Query Stacks which I'd revealed in this book so far as either a "Lineal Query Stack," "Lineally-Coupled Query Stack," "Lineal-Alias Query Stack," "Lineal-Alias, Realm-Related Query Stack" or "Lineal, Realm-Related Query Stack" for a reason:

Ch. 5, Sec. 5: 2

LINEAL QUERY STACKS

QS-Mary/Earth—Mary was a lineal member of Virgin Mary's family tree, since Mary was Virgin Mary.

QS-Joe/Earth—Joe (Joseph) was a lineal member of Mary's family tree, because Joe and Mary were married.

QS-Dave/Earth—Dave (David) was a lineal member of Mary's family tree, because Dave was a multi-great-grandfather of Mary's.

QS-Jesus/Earth—Jesus was a lineal member of Mary's family tree, since Jesus was Mary's biological son.

QS-God/Heaven—God was a lineal member of Mary's family tree, since God was the father of the Jesus that Mary was the biological mother of.

LINEALLY-COUPLED QUERY STACKS

QS-Devil/Hell—Devil wasn't a lineal member of Mary's family tree but has been commonly coupled to God as God's antipode.

LINEAL-ALIAS QUERY STACKS

QS-Holy^Ghost/Heaven—Holy Ghost was a lineal member of Mary's family tree, since the name *Holy Ghost* was an alias for the name *God* and the Holy Ghost was the entity that God used to impregnate Mary with Jesus.

QS-YHWH/Heaven—YHWH was a lineal member of Mary's family tree, since the name *YHWH* was an alias for the name *God* and God's given name, according to ancient biblical text.

QS-Yahweh/Heaven—Yahweh was a lineal member of Mary's family tree, since the name *Yahweh* was an alias for the name *God* and a transliteration of God's given name *YHWH*.

LINEAL-ALIAS, REALM-RELATED QUERY STACKS

QS-Creator/Reality—The Creator was a lineal member of Mary's family tree, since *Creator* was an alias for *God*. I'd related the Creator to the realm of Reality, since the Creator made and existed within the spatial limits of Reality.

QS-Yahweh/Reality—Yahweh was a lineal member of Mary's family tree, since *Yahweh* was an alias for *God* and a transliteration of God's given name *YHWH*. I'd related Yahweh to the realm of Reality, because Yahweh was the creator that made and existed within the spatial limits of Reality.

QS-Yahweh/Trinity—Yahweh was a lineal member of Mary's family tree, since *Yahweh* was an alias for *God* and a transliteration of God's given name *YHWH*. I'd related Yahweh to the realm of the Trinity, because Yahweh was God and God was a member of the Trinity.

QS-Father/Trinity—The Father was a lineal member of Mary's family tree, since *Father* was an alias for *God*. I'd related the Father to the Trinity, because the Father was God and God was a member of the Trinity.

QS-Son/Trinity—The Son was a lineal member of Mary's family tree, since *Son* was an alias for *Jesus* and Jesus was Mary's biological son. I'd related the Son to the Trinity, because the Son was Jesus and Jesus was a member of the Trinity.

QS-Holy^Ghost/Trinity—The Holy Ghost was a lineal member of Mary's family tree, since the name *Holy Ghost* was an alias for the name *God* and the Holy Ghost was the entity which God used to impregnate Mary with Jesus. I'd related the Holy Ghost to the Trinity, because the Holy Ghost was a member of the Trinity.

LINEAL, REALM-RELATED QUERY STACKS

QS-God/Trinity—God was a lineal member of Mary's family tree, since *God* was the father of the Jesus that Mary was the biological mother of. I'd related God to the Trinity, because God was a member of the Trinity.

QS-Jesus/Trinity—Jesus was a lineal member of Mary's family tree, since Jesus was Mary's biological son. I'd related Jesus to the Trinity, because Jesus was a member of the Trinity.

I'd updated the diagram of Virgin Mary's genealogy, which I'd introduced in "Ch. 2, Sec. 2: 1," by inserting the aliases *Creator* and *Father* into said diagram's "God" box and the alias *Son* into said diagram's "Jesus" box:

Some of the biblical names which I've listed in the diagram belong in Virgin Mary's lineage but aren't QS row'd words (e.g. "Bathsheba," "Solomon," "Nathan") yet elucidate how some biblical characters with names that are QS row'd words are related;

SOLID LINE (———) = Genealogically linked to Mary;
DASHED LINE (– – –) = Father of Mary's son Jesus, via no sexual contact;
DASHED/DOTTED LINE (– ·· –) = Mary's husband, but not Jesus's father;
DOUBLE LINE (====) = Not genealogically linked to Mary;
BLACK NAME BOX **NAME** = Row'd word, and main focus of family tree;
GRAY NAME BOX NAME = Row'd word, and member of family tree;
WHITE NAME BOX NAME = Row'd word, but not a member of family tree;
UNBOXED NAME = Not a row'd word, but member of family tree;

(a) MARY: herself;

(b) JOE *(Joseph)*: Mary's husband;

(c) DAVE *(David)*: Mary's multi-great-grandfather;

(d) JESUS: Mary's son;

(e) GOD: Mary's spiritual co-parent;

(f) DEVIL: God's antipode;

(g) SON: Jesus's alias;

(h) HOLY GHOST: God's alias and conduit to impregnate Mary;

(i) YHWH: God's alias and ancient Hebrew name;

(j) YAHWEH: God's alias and modern Hebrew name;

(k) CREATOR: God's alias;

(l) FATHER: God's alias;

Ch. 5, Sec. 5: 3

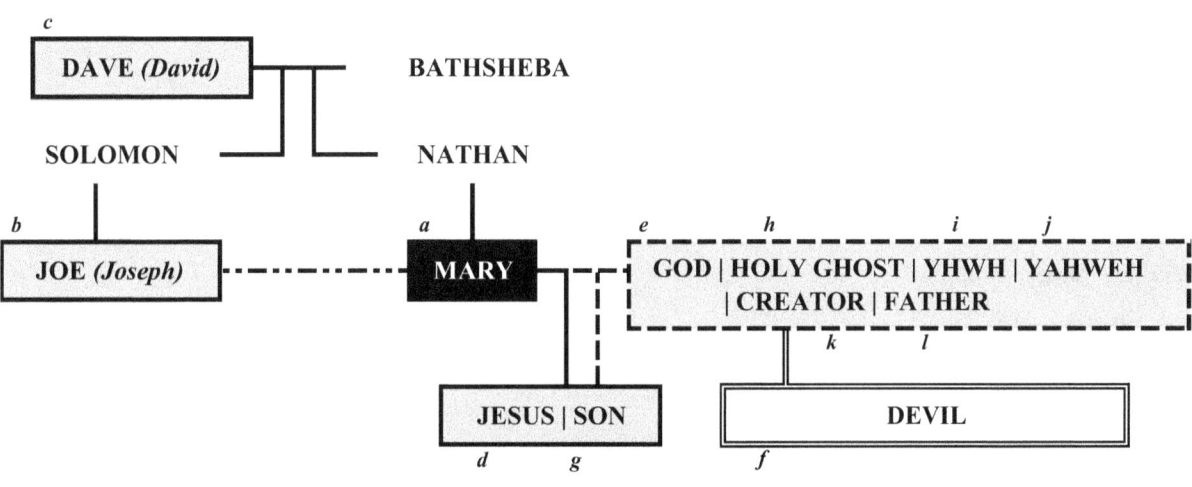

In "Ch. 4, Sec. 3: 4," I'd displayed a table in which each QS answer word in the first four QS answers I'd uncovered was categorized according to which one of four identities (David Mivshek, Trinity, God or QS answer) the main subject of the QS answer that said answer word appeared in represented. In "Ch. 5, Sec. 5: 4," I'd updated said table with the answers words of the eight most recent QS answers I'd revealed in this book. I'd placed the "QS-Yahweh/Reality" and "QS-Yahweh/Trinity" answer words into the "Trinity" tier, since the main subjects in the said two QS answers, hay and we, respectively, represented the Trinity. I'd placed the "QS-Creator/Reality," "QS-Father/Trinity," "QS-Son/Trinity," "QS-Holy^Ghost/Trinity" and "QS-Jesus/Trinity" answer words into the "God" tier, since the main subjects in the said five QS answers, hinter, orator, glory, and issuer, respectively, represented God. I'd placed the "QS-God/Trinity answer words into the "QS Answer" tier, since the main subject in said QS answer, wording, represented an aspect of QS answers:

A parenthetic number (#) succeeding a distinct answer word reports how many times said answer word appears in QS answers that may or may not share a distinct main subject but have main subjects which refer to David Mivshek, Trinity, God or QS answers;

(a) "QS-Creator/Reality" answer words: "God" tier, core is main subject, core is God;

(b) "QS-Yahweh/Reality" answer words: "Trinity" tier, hay is main subject, hay is Trinity;

(c) "QS-Yahweh/Trinity" answer words: "Trinity" tier, we is main subject, we is Trinity;

(d) "QS-Father/Trinity" answer words: "God" tier, hinter is main subject, hinter is God;

(e) "QS-Son/Trinity" answer words: "God" tier, orator is main subject, orator is God;

(f) "QS-Holy^Ghost/Trinity" answer words: "God" tier, glory is main subject, glory is God;

(g) "QS-God/Trinity" answer words: "QS Answer" tier, wording is main subject, wording is vocabulary of a QS answer;

(h) "QS-Jesus/Trinity" answer words: "God" tier, issuer is main subject, issuer is God;

Ch. 5, Sec. 5: 4

DAVID MIVSHEK

Nouns—Winner, Ghost;
Proper Nouns—Dave;
Pronouns—He (2);
Verbs—Gains, Go, Answering;
Adjectives—Holy, Naïve;
Conjunctions—Or (2).

TRINITY

Nouns—[b] "A", Evil, [b]Hay (2), Horde, Horn, Ill, [b]Law, [c]Trio, [c]We (3), [b]"We";
Plural Nouns—[b]Reins;
Proper Nouns—Heaven;
Pronouns—[b]I, [b]They;
Verbs—Reign, [c]Reining, [b]Ring, Siring, [c]Wans (2);
Adjectives—[c]Hairy, [c]Thy;
Conjunctions—[b]Or;
Indefinite Articles—A.

GOD

Nouns—[a]Core, [h]Entry, Giver, [f]Glory, [d]Hinter (2), Horn, [h]"I", [f]I, [e,f]In (3), [h]Issuer, Joe, Rein, [e,f]Sinew (2), [a]Trinity, [d]Trio, [h]"Wans", [a]We (2);
Proper Nouns—[f]Host, [f]Torah, Yahweh;

Pronouns—[h]I;

Verbs—Adore, Assure, Is, [h]Jot, Nerving, [h]Ring, [a]Rings, [d, e, f]Trying (3), [d]Wanes, Wans (2);

Adjectives—[d]Fair, [a]Real;

Adverbs—Right;

Conjunctions—[a]Or;

Indefinite Articles—[a]A (4);

Contractions—[e]Orator's.

QS ANSWER

Nouns—Air, [g]Entry, Hint (2), [g]"I" (2), Joe, Reason (2), [g]Wording;

Pronouns—I;

Verbs—[g]Got, Grew (2), Marry, [g]Rains;

Indefinite Articles—A.

As I'd determined in "Ch. 2, Sec. 3: 12," a distinct answer word which didn't identify an individual was permitted to be a word in multiple QS answers, even if each said QS answers had a distinct main subject. However, the answer word *RING* in the "QS-Yahweh/Reality" answer and the answer word *RING* in the "QS-Jesus/Trinity" answer were the same word since *RING* and *RING* had the same spelling yet each said answer word had a distinct definition (see "Ch. 5, Sec. 2: 5" and "Ch. 5, Sec. 4: 13," respectively); therefore, each answer word *RING* was listed in "Ch. 5, Sec. 5: 5" as a distinct answer word:

As I'd determined in "Ch. 2, Sec. 3: 12," a distinct answer word which did identify an individual always identified one and the same individual, even when said answer word was in multiple answers and each one of said answers contained a distinct main subject:

A parenthetic number (#) succeeding a distinct answer word reports how many times said answer word appears in QS answers that may or may not have distinct main subjects but have main subjects which cite David Mivshek, God, Trinity or QS answers;

[a] ENTRY: Not an individual, in two answers, distinct main subject (wording, issuer);

[b] HAY: Not an individual, in two answers, same main subject (hay);

[c] HE: Identifies one individual (Dave), in two answers, same main subject (Dave, ghost);

[d] HINTER: Identifies one individual (God), in two answers, same main subject (giver, hinter);

[e] "I": Not an individual, in two answers, distinct main subject (wording, issuer);

[f] I$_{pron}$: Identifies one individual (God), in three answers, distinct main subject (reason, hay/issuer);

(g) OR: Not an individual, in four answers, distinct main subject (Dave/ghost, core/hay);

(h) SINEW: Not an individual, in two answers, same main subject (in, glory);

(i) TRIO: Identifies one entity (Trinity), in two answers, same main subject (we, hinter);

(j) WE: Identifies one entity (Trinity), in four answers, same main subject (Yahweh, hay, core, we);

Ch. 5, Sec. 5: 5

DAVID MIVSHEK

Nouns—Winner, Ghost;

Proper Nouns—Dave;

Pronouns—[c]He (2);

Verbs—Gains, Go, Answering;

Adjectives—Holy, Naïve;

Conjunctions—[g]Or (2).

TRINITY

Nouns—"A", Evil, [b]Hay (2), Horde, Horn, Ill, Law, [i]Trio, [j]We (3), "We";

Plural Nouns—Reins;

Proper Nouns—Heaven;

Pronouns—[f]I, They;

Verbs—Reign, Reining, Ring, Siring, Wans (2);

Adjectives—Hairy, Thy;

Conjunctions—[g]Or;

Indefinite Articles—A.

GOD

Nouns—Core, [a]Entry, Giver, Glory, [d]Hinter (2), Horn, [e]"I", I, In (3), Issuer, Joe, Rein, [h]Sinew (2), Trinity, [i]Trio, "Wans", [j]We (2);

Proper Nouns—Host, Torah, Yahweh;

Pronouns—[f]I;

Verbs—Adore, Assure, Is, Jot, Nerving, Ring, Rings, Trying (3), Wanes, Wans (2);

Adjectives—Fair, Real;

Adverbs—Right;

Conjunctions—[g]Or;

Indefinite Articles—A (4);

Contractions—Orator's.

QS ANSWER

Nouns—Air, [a]Entry, Hint (2), [e]"I" (2), Joe, Reason (2), Wording;

Pronouns—*I*;
Verbs—Got, Grew (2), Marry, Rains;
Indefinite Articles—A.

In "Ch. 4, Sec. 3: 6," I'd displayed some statistics which pertained to QS answer vocabulary. In "Ch. 5, Sec. 5: 6," I'd updated said statistics by incorporating numbers I'd garnered from the eight most recent QS answers I'd revealed in this book:

Ch. 5, Sec. 5: 6

QS-GOD/HEAVEN
GO DAVE. HE: WINNER; OR, GAINS.
Number of QS answer words—6
Number of QS answer letters—21
Average number of letters per answer word—3.50

QS-DEVIL/HELL
HORDE: EVIL. ILL REIGN, WANS.
Number of QS answer words—5
Number of QS answer letters—21
Average number of letters per answer word—4.20

QS-JESUS/EARTH
JOE ASSURE. RIGHT, REIN WANS.
Number of QS answer words—5
Number of QS answer letters—22
Average number of letters per answer word—4.40

QS-DAVE/EARTH
ADORE GIVER. A HINTER WANS.
Number of QS answer words—5
Number of QS answer letters—21
Average number of letters per answer word—4.20

QS-JOE/EARTH

JOE: REASON. AIR/HINT GREW.

Number of QS answer words—5

Number of QS answer letters—20

Average number of letters per answer word—4.00

QS-MARY/EARTH

MARRY REASON. A HINT, I GREW.

Number of QS answer words—6

Number of QS answer letters—21

Average number of letters per answer word—3.50

QS-HOLY^GHOST/HEAVEN

HOLY GHOST. HE: NAÏVE OR ANSWERING.

Number of QS answer words—6

Number of QS answer letters—27

Average number of letters per answer word—4.50

QS-YHWH/HEAVEN

YAHWEH: HORN. NERVING, IS A WE.

Number of QS answer words—6

Number of QS answer letters—22

Average number of letters per answer word—3.67

QS-YAHWEH/HEAVEN

HAY: WE. HEAVEN: HORN, SIRING A WE.

Number of QS answer words—7

Number of QS answer letters—24

Average number of letters per answer word—3.43

QS-CREATOR/REALITY

CORE: REAL. A TRINITY; OR, RINGS A WE.

Number of QS answer words—8

Number of QS answer letters—26

Average number of letters per answer word—3.25

QS-YAHWEH/REALITY

```
HAY: LAW. THEY OR REINS, I , RING "A WE."
```

Number of QS answer words—9

Number of QS answer letters—25

Average number of letters per answer word—2.78

QS-YAHWEH/TRINITY

```
HAIRY WE. THY TRIO: REINING, WANS.
```

Number of QS answer words—6

Number of QS answer letters—25

Average number of letters per answer word—4.17

QS-FATHER/TRINITY

```
FAIR HINTER. TRIO: TRYING, WANS.
```

Number of QS answer words—5

Number of QS answer letters—24

Average number of letters per answer word—4.80

QS-SON/TRINITY

```
ORATOR'S IN. IN: TRYING SINEW.
```

Number of QS answer words—5

Number of QS answer letters—22

Average number of letters per answer word—4.40

QS-HOLY^GHOST/TRINITY

```
TORAH: GLORY. HOST: IN, I, TRYING SINEW.
```

Number of QS answer words—7

Number of QS answer letters—28

Average number of letters per answer word—4.00

QS-GOD/TRINITY

```
GOT WORDING. "I" ENTRY; RAINS "I."
```

Number of QS answer words—6

Number of QS answer letters—22

Average number of letters per answer word—3.67

QS-JESUS/TRINITY
`JOT, ISSUER. I RING ENTRY "I," WANS.`

Number of QS answer words—7

Number of QS answer letters—24

Average number of letters per answer word—3.43

QUERY STACK TOTALS AND AVERAGES

Total number of QS answers—17

Total number of QS answer words—104

Total number of QS answer letters—395

Average number of letters per QS answer—23.24

Average number of words per QS answer—6.12

Average number of letters per answer word—3.80

CHAPTER SIX: SECTION ONE

TRINITY/HEAVEN: EVITERNITY'S HORN

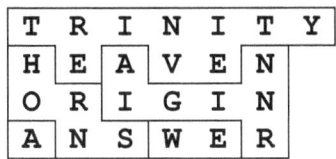

I'd categorized "QS-Trinity/Heaven" as a "Lineal-Alias Query Stack" for two reasons. First, the said Query Stack had a row'd word matrix which contained the first-row row'd word TRINITY, an "alias" of the name *God*, a name which had been established already as a row'd word (see "Ch. 1, Sec. 1: 2"). Second, the Trinity, which was God, belonged to a particular genealogical "lineage," Virgin Mary's lineage:

Ch. 6, Sec. 1: 1

LINEAL-ALIAS QUERY STACKS

```
QS-HOLY^GHOST/HEAVEN
QS-YHWH/HEAVEN
QS-YAHWEH/HEAVEN
```
QS-TRINITY/HEAVEN

The "QS-Trinity/Heaven" matrix consisted of a first-row row'd word which was an alias of the name *God*; therefore, said first-row row'd word signified God, the holiest biblical figure in the Bible:

> *A parenthetic number (#) succeeding a first-row row'd word reports the number of times said row'd word was used as a first-row row'd word;*

(a) GOD (2); DEVIL; JESUS (2); DAVE *(David)*; JOE *(Joseph)*; MARY; HOLY^GHOST (2); YHWH; YAHWEH (3); CREATOR; FATHER; SON; TRINITY: notable biblical beings, first-row row'd words;

Ch. 6, Sec. 1: 2

QS-God/Heaven	QS-Devil/Hell	QS-Jesus/Earth	QS-Dave/Earth
"GOD	"DEVIL	"JESUS	"DAVE
HEAVEN	HELL	EARTH	EARTH
ORIGIN	ORIGIN	ORIGIN	ORIGIN
ANSWER	ANSWER	ANSWER	ANSWER

QS-Joe/Earth	QS-Mary/Earth	QS-Holy^Ghost/Heaven
"JOE	"MARY	"HOLYGHOST
EARTH	EARTH	HEAVEN
ORIGIN	ORIGIN	ORIGIN
ANSWER	ANSWER	ANSWER

QS-YHWH/Heaven	QS-Yahweh/Heaven	QS-Creator/Reality
"YHWH	"YAHWEH	"CREATOR
HEAVEN	HEAVEN	REALITY
ORIGIN	ORIGIN	ORIGIN
ANSWER	ANSWER	ANSWER

QS-Yahweh/Reality	QS-Yahweh/Trinity	QS-Father/Trinity
"YAHWEH	"YAHWEH	"FATHER
REALITY	TRINITY	TRINITY
ORIGIN	ORIGIN	ORIGIN
ANSWER	ANSWER	ANSWER

QS-Son/Trinity	QS-Holy^Ghost/Trinity	QS-God/Trinity
"SON	"HOLYGHOST	"GOD
TRINITY	TRINITY	TRINITY
ORIGIN	ORIGIN	ORIGIN
ANSWER	ANSWER	ANSWER

QS-Jesus/Trinity	QS-Trinity/Heaven
"JESUS	"TRINITY
TRINITY	HEAVEN
ORIGIN	ORIGIN
ANSWER	ANSWER

The Trinity was a prominent biblical figure, because the Trinity was God and God was the ruler of Heaven:

> *A parenthetic number (#) succeeding a first-row row'd word reports the number of times said row'd word was used as a first-row row'd word;*

(a) GOD (2): notable biblical figure; of Heaven and Trinity; Heaven's ruler and Trinity member;

(b) DEVIL: notable biblical figure; of Hell; God sends evil to Hell, Devil is the evilest being, Devil is evilest being God could send to Hell;

(c) JESUS (2): notable biblical figure; of Earth and Trinity; Earth's premier ruler and Trinity member;

(d) DAVE *(David)*: notable biblical figure; of Earth; third King of Israel;

(e) JOE *(Joseph)*: notable biblical figure; of Earth; Virgin Mary's husband;

(f) MARY: notable biblical figure; of Earth; Jesus's biological mother;

(g) HOLY GHOST (2): notable biblical figure; of Heaven and Trinity; Heaven's messenger and Trinity member;

(h) YHWH: notable biblical figure; of Heaven; Heaven's ruler;

(i) YAHWEH (3): notable biblical figure; of Heaven, Reality and Trinity; Heaven's ruler, Reality's maker and Trinity member;

(j) CREATOR: notable biblical figure; of Reality; Reality's maker;

(k) FATHER: notable biblical figure; of Trinity; Trinity member;

(l) SON: notable biblical figure; of Trinity; Trinity member;

(m) **TRINITY: notable biblical figure; of Heaven; Heaven's ruler;**

Ch. 6, Sec. 1: 3

BIBLICAL BEING	DOMAIN	NOTORIETY
[a]GOD	[a]HEAVEN	[a]RULER
[a]GOD	[a]TRINITY	[a]MEMBER
[b]DEVIL	[b]HELL	[b]EVILEST RESIDENT
[c]JESUS	[c]EARTH	[c]PREMIER RULER
[c]JESUS	[c]TRINITY	[c]MEMBER
[d]DAVE (David)	[d]EARTH	[d]ANOINTED KING
[e]JOE (Joseph)	[e]EARTH	[e]MARY'S HUSBAND
[f]MARY	[f]EARTH	[f]JESUS'S MOTHER
[g]HOLY GHOST	[g]HEAVEN	[g]MESSENGER
[g]HOLY GHOST	[g]TRINITY	[g]MEMBER
[h]YHWH	[h]HEAVEN	[h]RULER
[i]YAHWEH	[i]HEAVEN	[i]RULER
[i]YAHWEH	[i]REALITY	[i]MAKER
[i]YAHWEH	[i]TRINITY	[i]MEMBER
[j]CREATOR	[j]REALITY	[j]MAKER
[k]FATHER	[k]TRINITY	[k]MEMBER
[l]SON	[l]TRINITY	[l]MEMBER
[m]TRINITY	**[m]HEAVEN**	**[m]RULER**

My breakdown of "QS-Trinity/Heaven" follows:

I've provided a decoded QS matrix, a valid QS answer, a set of answer word definitions, biblical verses, and an interpretation and a vocabular analysis of the "QS-Trinity/Heaven" answer. To understand the derivation of my interpretation for the "QS- Trinity/Heaven" answer, apply the set of definitions and biblical verses to the correlated answer and then examine my vocabular analysis;

✓ All QS rules followed (see "Appendix A");

Ch. 6, Sec. 1: 4

QS-Trinity/Heaven

T	R	I	N	I	T	Y
H	E	A	V	E	N	
O	R	I	G	I	N	
A	N	S	W	E	R	

EVITERNITY: HORN.sent1 INGRAIN'S A WE.sent2

EVITERNITY *n.* Everlastingness.[2]
HORN *n.* Source of strength.[2]
INGRAIN'S *contr.* <INGRAIN *n.* IS *v.*> Innate quality or character.[2]
A *i-art.* Used before most singular nouns when the individual in question is unidentified, especially when the individual is being called to notice.[2]
WE *n.* A group that is consciously felt as such by its members.[2]

EVITERNITY—"Hast thou not known? hast thou not heard, that the {everlasting God}, the Lord, the Creator of the ends of the earth, fainteth not, neither is weary? there is no searching of his understanding" (Isaiah 40:28 KJV).

HORN—"The LORD is my rock, and my fortress, and my deliverer; {my God, my strength}, in whom I will trust; my buckler, and the {horn of my salvation}, and my high tower" (Psalms 18:2 KJV).

sent1: *Everlastingness is a source of strength; meaning, God, the source of strength, is everlasting.*

sent2: *An innate quality of God, besides being everlasting, is that God is a group which is comprised of three individuals who know they belong to said group.*

Match superscripted numbers and letters to compare vocabulary in the "QS-Trinity/Heaven" answer to vocabulary in QS answers I've already unveiled; brief explanations in the reference key should contain enough of the necessary information one needs to understand my interpretation of the "QS-Trinity/Heaven" answer;

(a) *(EVITERNITY: HORN), (YAHWEH: HORN), (HEAVEN: HORN)*

Each QS answer phrase was comprised of an answer word which defined either a trait of God's temporality *(eviternity)*, God's identity *(Yahweh)* or God's regality *(Heaven)*. I'd assigned said traits to God because God was identified as a horn, or a source of strength, in biblical text (see "Ch. 6, Sec. 1: 4) and the answer word *HORN* was already linked to traits associated with God in the phrases *"Yahweh: horn"* and *"Heaven: horn"*;

(b) *(INGRAIN'S A WE), (IS A WE), (RINGS A WE)*

An innate quality of God's physique was a trinity comprised of three individuals who knew they belonged to said trinity;

Ch. 6, Sec. 1: 5

QS-YHWH/Heaven Answer
ᵃ(YAHWEH: HORN). NERVING, ᵇ(IS A WE).

QS-Yahweh/Heaven Answer
HAY: WE. ᵃ(HEAVEN: HORN), SIRING A WE.

QS-Creator/Reality Answer
CORE: REAL. A TRINITY; OR, ᵇ(RINGS A WE).

QS-Trinity/Heaven Answer
ᵃ(EVITERNITY: HORN). ᵇ(INGRAIN'S A WE).

Even though the "QS-Trinity/Heaven" answer was grammatically coherent and meaningful, I'd ran it through "QS-7CAP" in order to confirm that said QS answer's vocabulary was valid:

Seven Common QS Answer Properties

1. Each answer contains no more and no less than two sentences (sent1, sent2):

QS-God/Heaven
GO DAVE.sent1 HE: WINNER; OR, GAINS.sent2

QS-Devil/Hell
HORDE: EVIL.sent1 ILL REIGN, WANS.sent2

QS-Jesus/Earth
JOE ASSURE.sent1 RIGHT, REIN WANS.sent2

QS-Dave/Earth

ADORE GIVER.sent1 A HINTER WANS.sent2

QS-Joe/Earth

JOE: REASON.sent1 AIR/HINT GREW.sent2

QS-Mary/Earth

MARRY REASON.sent1 A HINT, I GREW.sent2

QS-Holy^Ghost/Heaven

HOLY GHOST.sent1 HE: NAÏVE OR ANSWERING.sent2

QS-YHWH/Heaven

YAHWEH: HORN.sent1 NERVING, IS A WE.sent2

QS-Yahweh/Heaven

HAY: WE.sent1 HEAVEN: HORN, SIRING A WE.sent2

QS-Creator/Reality

CORE: REAL.sent1 A TRINITY; OR, RINGS A WE.sent2

QS-Yahweh/Reality

HAY: LAW.sent1 THEY OR REINS, I, RING "A WE."sent2

QS-Yahweh/Trinity

HAIRY WE.sent1 THY TRIO: REINING, WANS.sent2

QS-Father/Trinity

FAIR HINTER.sent1 TRIO: TRYING, WANES.sent2

QS-Son/Trinity

ORATOR'S IN.sent1 IN: TRYING SINEW.sent2

QS-Holy^Ghost/Trinity

TORAH: GLORY.sent1 HOST: IN, I, TRYING SINEW.sent2

QS-God/Trinity

GOT WORDING.sent1 "I" ENTRY; RAINS "I."sent2

QS-Jesus/Trinity

JOT, ISSUER.sent1 I RING ENTRY "I," "WANS."sent2

QS-Trinity/Heaven

EVITERNITY: HORN.sent1 INGRAIN'S A WE.sent2

2. Each answer's first sentence contains no more and no less than two words (word1, word2):

QS-God/Heaven

GO$_{word1}$ DAVE$_{word2}$. HE: WINNER; OR, GAINS.

QS-Devil/Hell

HORDE_{word1}: **EVIL**_{word2}. ILL REIGN, WANS.

QS-Jesus/Earth

JOE_{word1} **ASSURE**_{word2}. RIGHT, REIN WANS.

QS-Dave/Earth

ADORE_{word1} **GIVER**_{word2}. A HINTER WANS.

QS-Joe/Earth

JOE_{word1}: **REASON**_{word2}. AIR/HINT GREW.

QS-Mary/Earth

MARRY_{word1} **REASON**_{word2}. A HINT, I GREW.

QS-Holy^Ghost/Heaven

HOLY_{word1} **GHOST**_{word2}. HE: NAÏVE OR ANSWERING.

QS-YHWH/Heaven

YAHWEH_{word1}: **HORN**_{word2}. NERVING, IS A WE.

QS-Yahweh/Heaven

HAY_{word1}: **WE**_{word2}. HEAVEN: HORN, SIRING A WE.

QS-Creator/Reality

CORE_{word1}: **REAL**_{word2}. A TRINITY; OR, RINGS A WE.

QS-Yahweh/Reality

HAY_{word1}: **LAW**_{word2}. THEY OR REINS, I, RING "A WE."

QS-Yahweh/Trinity

HAIRY_{word1} **WE**_{word2}. THY TRIO: REINING, WANS.

QS-Father/Trinity

FAIR_{word1} **HINTER**_{word2}. TRIO: TRYING, WANES.

QS-Son/Trinity

ORATOR'S_{word1} **IN**_{word2}. IN: TRYING SINEW.

QS-Holy^Ghost/Trinity

TORAH_{word1}: **GLORY**_{word2}. HOST: IN, I, TRYING SINEW.

QS-God/Trinity

GOT_{word1} **WORDING**_{word2}. "I" ENTRY; RAINS "I."

QS-Jesus/Trinity

JOT_{word1}, **ISSUER**_{word2}. I RING ENTRY "I," "WANS."

QS-Trinity/Heaven

EVITERNITY_{word1}: **HORN**_{word2}. INGRAIN'S A WE.

3. In each answer's first sentence, the main subject is introduced (subj1, subj2, ...):

> [ORATOR]'S:$^{(subj14)}$ contraction, [main subject] and *is*; *[Property Resolution (see "Appendix B")]*;

QS-God/Heaven

GO **DAVE**$_{subj1}$. HE: WINNER; OR, GAINS.

QS-Devil/Hell

HORDE$_{subj2}$: EVIL. ILL REIGN, WANS.

QS-Jesus/Earth

JOE$_{subj3}$ ASSURE. RIGHT, REIN WANS.

QS-Dave/Earth

ADORE **GIVER**$_{subj4}$. A HINTER WANS.

QS-Joe/Earth

JOE: **REASON**$_{subj5}$. AIR/HINT GREW.

QS-Mary/Earth

MARRY **REASON**$_{subj6}$. A HINT, I GREW.

QS-Holy^Ghost/Heaven

HOLY **GHOST**$_{subj7}$. HE: NAÏVE OR ANSWERING.

QS-YHWH/Heaven

YAHWEH$_{subj8}$: HORN. NERVING, IS A WE.

QS-Yahweh/Heaven

HAY$_{subj9}$: WE. HEAVEN: HORN, SIRING A WE.

QS-Creator/Reality

CORE$_{subj10}$: REAL. A TRINITY; OR, RINGS A WE.

QS-Yahweh/Reality

HAY$_{subj11}$: LAW. THEY OR REINS, I, RING "A WE."

QS-Yahweh/Trinity

HAIRY **WE**$_{subj12}$. THY TRIO: REINING, WANS.

QS-Father/Trinity

FAIR **HINTER**$_{subj13}$. TRIO: TRYING, WANES.

QS-Son/Trinity

[**ORATOR**$_{subj14}$]'S IN. IN: TRYING SINEW.

QS-Holy^Ghost/Trinity

TORAH: **GLORY**$_{subj15}$. HOST: IN, I, TRYING SINEW.

QS-God/Trinity

GOT **WORDING**$_{subj16}$. "I" ENTRY; RAINS "I."

QS-Jesus/Trinity

JOT, **ISSUER**~subj17~. I RING ENTRY "I," "WANS."

QS-Trinity/Heaven

EVITERNITY~subj18~: HORN. INGRAIN'S A WE.

4. In each answer, the main subject introduced in the first sentence is mentioned in the second sentence (subj1-subj1, subj2-subj2, ...):

(subj18) [INGRAIN]'S: contraction, [main subject] and *is*; [Property Resolution: INGRAIN'S is an answer word in the second sentence. INGRAIN'S is a contraction of the phrase "ingrain is." The contractive phrase "ingrain is" contains the main subject "ingrain," along with the verb "is." Based on my analysis, I've determined that when a contraction is in the second sentence of a QS answer and said contraction identifies said QS answer's main subject, said contraction isn't a property deviation];

QS-God/Heaven

GO **DAVE**~subj1~. **HE**~subj1~: WINNER; OR, GAINS.

QS-Devil/Hell

HORDE~subj2~: EVIL. **ILL**~subj2~ REIGN, WANS.

QS-Jesus/Earth

JOE~subj3~ ASSURE. RIGHT, **REIN**~subj3~ WANS.

QS-Dave/Earth

ADORE **GIVER**~subj4~. A **HINTER**~subj4~ WANS.

QS-Joe/Earth

JOE: **REASON**~subj5~. **AIR**~subj5~/HINT GREW.

QS-Mary/Earth

MARRY **REASON**~subj6~. A **HINT**~subj6~, I GREW.

QS-Holy^Ghost/Heaven

HOLY **GHOST**~subj7~. **HE**~subj7~: NAÏVE OR ANSWERING.

QS-YHWH/Heaven

YAHWEH~subj8~: HORN. NERVING, IS A **WE**~subj8~.

QS-Yahweh/Heaven

HAY~subj9~: WE. HEAVEN: HORN, SIRING A **WE**~subj9~.

QS-Creator/Reality

CORE~subj10~: REAL. A **TRINITY**~subj10~; OR, RINGS A WE.

QS-Yahweh/Reality

HAY~subj11~: LAW. THEY OR **REINS**~subj11~, I, RING "A WE."

QS-Yahweh/Trinity

HAIRY **WE**~subj12~. THY **TRIO**~subj12~: REINING, WANS.

QS-Father/Trinity

FAIR **HINTER**~subj13~. **TRIO**~subj13~: TRYING, WANES.

QS-Son/Trinity

[**ORATOR**~subj14~]'S IN. **IN**~subj14~: TRYING SINEW.

QS-Holy^Ghost/Trinity

TORAH: **GLORY**~subj15~. **HOST**~subj15~: IN, I, TRYING SINEW.

QS-God/Trinity

GOT **WORDING**~subj16~. "**I**"~subj16~ ENTRY; RAINS "I."

QS-Jesus/Trinity

JOT, **ISSUER**~subj17~. **I**~subj17~ RING ENTRY "I," "WANS."

QS-Trinity/Heaven

EVITERNITY~subj18~: HORN. [**INGRAIN**~subj18~]'S A WE.

5. In each answer, the first sentence's second word and the second sentence's first word are synonymous in definition (syn) or context (con):

> *Synonymous answer words are tagged "syn," while answer words which share contextual meaning are tagged "con";*

(con1) DAVE; HE: context, both words identify same man;

(syn2) EVIL; ILL: synonyms, each word means "wicked";

(con3) ASSURE; RIGHT: context, both words convey affirmation;

(con4) GIVER; [A HINTER]: context, word and [phrase] identify same person; *[Property Deviation Resolution: (see "Appendix B")]*;

(con5) REASON; AIR: context, the reason is expressed as a written statement;

(con6) REASON; [A HINT]: context, the reason is expressed as an allusive statement; *[Property Deviation Resolution: (see "Appendix B")]*;

(con7) GHOST; HE: context, both words identify same person;

(con 8) HORN; NERVING: context, each word refers to strength;

(con 9) WE; HEAVEN: context, both words identify same entity;

(con10) REAL; [A TRINITY]: context, word and [phrase] identify same entity; *[Property Deviation Resolution: (see "Appendix B")]*;

(con11) LAW; THEY: context, revealed will of God is the Trinity;

(con12) WE; THY: context, both words identify same entity;

(con13) HINTER; TRIO: context, both words identify same entity;

(syn14) IN; IN: synonym, each word means "one who is in power";

(con15) GLORY; HOST: context, both words identify same person;

(con16) WORDING; "I": context, both words refer to answer words;

(con17) ISSUER; I: context, both words identify same person;

(con18) HORN; [INGRAIN]'S: context, [word] regards characteristic of same person; [Property Resolution: INGRAIN'S is the first answer word in the second sentence. INGRAIN'S shares a contextual relationship with the answer word HORN. INGRAIN'S answer word HORN. INGRAIN'S is a contraction of the phrase "ingrain is." The contractive phrase "ingrain is" contains the noun "ingrain" and verb "is." The noun "ingrain" is the part of the contraction and answer word INGRAIN'S that shares a contextual relationship with HORN. Based on my analysis, I've determined that when a contraction is the first word in the second sentence of a QS answer, said contraction isn't a property deviation];

QS-God/Heaven

GO **DAVE**$_{syn1}$. **HE**$_{syn1}$: WINNER; OR, GAINS.

QS-Devil/Hell

HORDE: **EVIL**$_{syn2}$. **ILL**$_{syn2}$ REIGN, WANS.

QS-Jesus/Earth

JOE **ASSURE**$_{con3}$. **RIGHT**$_{con3}$, REIN WANS.

QS-Dave/Earth

ADORE **GIVER**$_{con4}$. **[A HINTER]**$_{con4}$ WANS.

QS-Joe/Earth

JOE: **REASON**$_{con5}$. **AIR**$_{con5}$/HINT GREW.

QS-Mary/Earth

MARRY **REASON**$_{con6}$. **[A HINT]**$_{con6}$, I GREW.

QS-Holy^Ghost/Heaven

HOLY **GHOST**$_{con7}$. **HE**$_{con7}$: NAÏVE OR ANSWERING.

QS-YHWH/Heaven

YAHWEH: **HORN**$_{con8}$. **NERVING**$_{con8}$, IS A WE.

QS-Yahweh/Heaven

HAY: **WE**$_{con9}$. **HEAVEN**$_{con9}$: HORN, SIRING A WE.

QS-Creator/Reality

CORE: **REAL**$_{con10}$. **[A TRINITY]**$_{con10}$; OR, RINGS A WE.

QS-Yahweh/Reality

HAY: **LAW**$_{con11}$. **THEY**$_{con11}$ OR REINS, I, RING "A WE."

QS-Yahweh/Trinity

HAIRY **WE**$_{con12}$. **THY**$_{con12}$ TRIO: REINING, WANS.

QS-Father/Trinity

FAIR **HINTER**$_{con13}$. **TRIO**$_{con13}$: TRYING, WANES.

QS-Son/Trinity

ORATOR'S **IN**$_{syn14}$. **IN**$_{syn14}$: TRYING SINEW.

QS-Holy^Ghost/Trinity

TORAH: **GLORY**$_{con15}$. **HOST**$_{con15}$: IN, I, TRYING SINEW.

QS-God/Trinity

GOT **WORDING**$_{con16}$. "**I**"$_{con16}$ ENTRY; RAINS "I."

QS-Jesus/Trinity

JOT, **ISSUER**$_{con17}$. **I**$_{con17}$ RING ENTRY "I," "WANS."

QS-Trinity/Heaven

EVITERNITY: **HORN**$_{con18}$. **[INGRAIN**$_{con18}$**]**'S "A WE."

6. In each answer's second sentence, at least one action is applied to the main subject (subj1–act1, subj2–act2, ...):

    $_{(subj18/act18)}$ [INGRAIN]['S]: contraction, [main subject] and [verb (is)]; *[Property Resolution: INGRAIN'S is an answer word in the second sentence. INGRAIN'S is a contraction of the phrase "ingrain is." The contractive phrase "ingrain is" contains the verb and action "is," which is applied to the main subject "ingrain." Based on my analysis, I've determined that when a contraction is in the second sentence of a QS answer and said contraction signifies an action applied to the main subject, said contraction isn't a property deviation]*;

QS-God/Heaven

GO DAVE. **HE**$_{subj1}$: WINNER; OR, **GAINS**$_{act1}$.

QS-Devil/Hell

HORDE: EVIL. **ILL**$_{subj2}$ **REIGN**$_{act2}$, WANS.

QS-Jesus/Earth

JOE ASSURE. RIGHT, **REIN**$_{subj3}$ **WANS**$_{act3}$.

QS-Dave/Earth

ADORE GIVER. **[A HINTER]**$_{subj4}$ **WANS**$_{act4}$.

QS-Joe/Earth

JOE: REASON. **AIR**$_{subj5}$/HINT **GREW**$_{act5}$.

QS-Mary/Earth

MARRY REASON. **[A HINT]**$_{subj6}$, I **GREW**$_{act6}$.

QS-Holy^Ghost/Heaven

HOLY GHOST. **HE**$_{subj7}$: NAÏVE OR **ANSWERING**$_{act7}$.

QS-YHWH/Heaven

YAHWEH: HORN. **NERVING**$_{act8}$, IS A **WE**$_{subj8}$.

QS-Yahweh/Heaven

HAY: WE. HEAVEN: HORN, **SIRING**$_{act9}$ A **WE**$_{subj9}$.

QS-Creator/Reality

CORE: REAL. A **TRINITY**$_{subj10}$; OR, **RINGS**$_{act10}$ A WE.

QS-Yahweh/Reality

HAY: LAW. THEY OR, **REINS**$_{subj11}$, I, **RING**$_{act11}$ "A WE."

QS-Yahweh/Trinity

HAIRY WE. THY **TRIO**$_{subj12}$: **REINING**$_{act12}$, WANS.

QS-Father/Trinity

FAIR HINTER. **TRIO**$_{subj13}$: **TRYING**$_{act13}$, WANES.

QS-Son/Trinity

ORATOR'S IN. **IN**$_{subj14}$: **TRYING**$_{act14}$ SINEW.

QS-Holy^Ghost/Trinity

TORAH: GLORY. **HOST**$_{subj15}$: IN, I, **TRYING**$_{act15}$ SINEW.

QS-God/Trinity

GOT WORDING. **"I"**$_{subj16}$ ENTRY; **RAINS**$_{act16}$ "I."

QS-Jesus/Trinity

JOT, ISSUER. **I**$_{subj17}$ **RING**$_{act17}$ ENTRY "I," "WANS."

QS-Trinity/Heaven

EVITERNITY: HORN. {**[INGRAIN**$_{subj18}$**]['S**$_{act18}$**]**} A WE.

7. Along each answer's breadth of vocabulary, there's at least one site where an answer letter *S* would've enhanced the answer's grammatical correctness if it would've been available in the accompanying row'd word matrix and usable:

> *Removing a colon (:) that follows a noun and appending the contraction 's to the end of said noun would produce a conversational tone and clearer syntax (e.g.* <u>He's</u> *winner;* <u>Horde's</u> *evil;* <u>He's</u> *naïve;* <u>He's</u> *answering;* <u>Yahweh's</u> *horn;*

Hay's we; *Heaven's* horn; *Heaven's* siring; *Core's* real; *Hay's* law; *Trio's* reining; *Trio's* trying; *In's* trying; *Host's* in; *Host's* I; *Host's* trying; *Eviternity's* horn). Removing a colon (:) that follows a noun and appending a possessive 's to the end of said noun would produce a conversational tone and clearer syntax (e.g. *Joe's* reason; *Torah's* glory). Inflecting certain verbs by appending a letter S to the end of them would promote optimal grammar (e.g. Ill *reigns*; Joe *assures*; *Jots*, issuer). However, each answer's row'd word matrix lacks a letter S that's needed or that's capable of being used in ways mandated by QS rules (see "Appendix A");

[Property Deviation Resolution (see "Appendix B"): "QS-Dave/Earth," "QS-Mary/Earth," "QS-God/Trinity" and "QS-Jesus/Trinity"];

QS-God/Heaven: *He's* winner;
QS-Devil/Hell: *Horde's* evil, Ill *reigns*;
QS-Jesus/Earth: Joe *assures*;
QS-Dave/Earth: (optimal grammar);
QS-Joe/Earth: *Joe's* reason;
QS-Mary/Earth: (optimal grammar);
QS-YHWH/Heaven: *Yahweh's* horn;
QS-Holy^Ghost/Heaven: *He's* naïve, *He's* answering;
QS-Creator/Reality: *Core's* real;
QS-Yahweh/Trinity: *Trio's* reining;
QS-Father/Trinity: *Trio's* trying;
QS-Son/Trinity: *In's* trying;
QS-Holy^Ghost/Trinity: *Host's* in, *Host's* I, *Host's* trying;
QS-God/Trinity: (optimal grammar);
QS-Jesus/Trinity: *Jots*, issuer;
QS-Trinity/Heaven: (*Eviternity's* horn);

QS-God/Heaven
GO DAVE. **HE**: **WINNER**; OR, GAINS.

QS-Devil/Hell
HORDE: **EVIL**. **ILL REIGN**, WANS.

QS-Jesus/Earth
JOE ASSURE. RIGHT, REIN WANS.

QS-Dave/Earth
ADORE GIVER. A HINTER WANS.

QS-Joe/Earth

JOE: REASON. AIR/HINT GREW.

QS-Mary/Earth

MARRY REASON. A HINT, I GREW.

QS-Holy^Ghost/Heaven

HOLY GHOST. **HE: NAÏVE** OR ANSWERING.

HOLY GHOST. **HE:** NAÏVE OR **ANSWERING.**

QS-YHWH/Heaven

YAHWEH: HORN. NERVING, IS A WE.

QS-Yahweh/Heaven

HAY: WE. HEAVEN: HORN, SIRING A WE.

HAY: WE. HEAVEN: HORN, **SIRING** A WE.

QS-Creator/Reality

CORE: REAL. A TRINITY; OR, RINGS A WE.

QS-Yahweh/Reality

HAY: LAW. THEY OR REINS, I, RING "A WE."

QS-Yahweh/Trinity

HAIRY WE. THY **TRIO: REINING,** WANS.

QS-Father/Trinity

FAIR HINTER. **TRIO: TRYING,** WANES.

QS-Son/Trinity

ORATOR'S IN. **IN: TRYING** SINEW.

QS-Holy^Ghost/Trinity

TORAH: GLORY. HOST: IN, I, TRYING SINEW.

TORAH: GLORY. **HOST:** IN, **I,** TRYING SINEW.

TORAH: GLORY. **HOST:** IN, I, **TRYING SINEW.**

QS-God/Trinity

GOT WORDING. "I" ENTRY; RAINS "I."

QS-Jesus/Trinity

JOT, ISSUER. I RING ENTRY "I," "WANS."

QS-Trinity/Heaven

EVITERNITY: HORN. INGRAIN'S A WE.

CHAPTER SIX: SECTION TWO

REVIEW: EIGHTEEN STACKS

```
G O D
H E A V E N
O R I G I N
A N S W E R
```

```
D E V I L
H E L L
O R I G I N
A N S W E R
```

```
J E S U S
E A R T H
O R I G I N
A N S W E R
```

```
D A V E
E A R T H
O R I G I N
A N S W E R
```

```
J O E
E A R T H
O R I G I N
A N S W E R
```

```
M A R Y
E A R T H
O R I G I N
A N S W E R
```

```
H O L Y G H O S T
H E A V E N
O R I G I N
A N S W E R
```

```
Y H W H
H E A V E N
O R I G I N
A N S W E R
```

```
Y A H W E H
H E A V E N
O R I G I N
A N S W E R
```

```
C R E A T O R
R E A L I T Y
O R I G I N
A N S W E R
```

```
Y A H W E H
R E A L I T Y
O R I G I N
A N S W E R
```

```
Y A H W E H
T R I N I T Y
O R I G I N
A N S W E R
```

```
F A T H E R
T R I N I T Y
O R I G I N
A N S W E R
```

```
S O N
T R I N I T Y
O R I G I N
A N S W E R
```

```
H O L Y G H O S T
T R I N I T Y
O R I G I N
A N S W E R
```

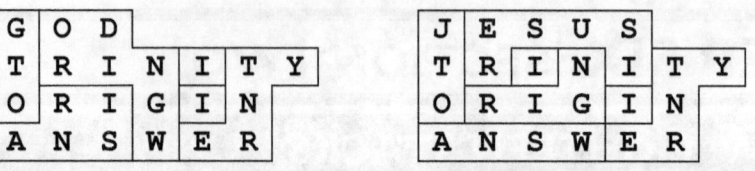

In the previous section, I'd unraveled a fourth "Lineal-Alias Query Stack"

Ch. 6, Sec. 2: 1

LINEAL QUERY STACKS

```
QS-GOD/HEAVEN
QS-JESUS/EARTH
QS-DAVE/EARTH
QS-JOE/EARTH
QS-MARY/EARTH
```

LINEALLY-COUPLED QUERY STACKS

```
QS-DEVIL/HELL
```

► LINEAL-ALIAS QUERY STACKS ◄

```
QS-HOLY^GHOST/HEAVEN
QS-YHWH/HEAVEN
QS-YAHWEH/HEAVEN
► QS-TRINITY/HEAVEN ◄
```

LINEAL-ALIAS, REALM-RELATED QUERY STACKS

```
QS-CREATOR/REALITY
QS-YAHWEH/REALITY
QS-YAHWEH/TRINITY
QS-FATHER/TRINITY
QS-SON/TRINITY
QS-HOLY^GHOST/TRINITY
```

LINEAL, REALM-RELATED QUERY STACKS

```
QS-GOD/TRINITY
QS-JESUS/TRINITY
```

I'd filed each one of the seventeen Query Stacks which I'd revealed in this book so far as either a "Lineal Query Stack," "Lineally-Coupled Query Stack," "Lineal-Alias Query Stack," "Lineal-Alias, Realm-Related Query Stack" or "Lineal, Realm-Related Query Stack" for a reason:

Ch. 6, Sec. 2: 2

LINEAL QUERY STACKS

QS-Mary/Earth—Mary was a lineal member of Virgin Mary's family tree, since Mary was Virgin Mary.

QS-Joe/Earth—Joe (Joseph) was a lineal member of Mary's family tree, because Joe and Mary were married.

QS-Dave/Earth—Dave (David) was a lineal member of Mary's family tree, because Dave was a multi-great-grandfather of Mary's.

QS-Jesus/Earth—Jesus was a lineal member of Mary's family tree, since Jesus was Mary's biological son.

QS-God/Heaven—God was a lineal member of Mary's family tree, since God was the father of the Jesus that Mary was the biological mother of.

LINEALLY-COUPLED QUERY STACKS

QS-Devil/Hell—Devil wasn't a lineal member of Mary's family tree but has been commonly coupled to God as God's antipode.

LINEAL-ALIAS QUERY STACKS

QS-Holy^Ghost/Heaven—Holy Ghost was a lineal member of Mary's family tree, since the name *Holy Ghost* was an alias for the name *God* and the Holy Ghost was the entity that God used to impregnate Mary with Jesus.

QS-YHWH/Heaven—YHWH was a lineal member of Mary's family tree, since the name *YHWH* was an alias for the name *God* and God's given name, according to ancient biblical text.

QS-Yahweh/Heaven—Yahweh was a lineal member of Mary's family tree, since the name *Yahweh* was an alias for the name *God* and a transliteration of God's given name *YHWH*.

QS-Trinity/Heaven—Trinity was a lineal member of Mary's family tree, since *Trinity* was an alias for *God*.

LINEAL-ALIAS, REALM-RELATED QUERY STACKS

QS-Creator/Reality—The Creator was a lineal member of Mary's family tree, since *Creator* was an alias for *God*. I'd related the Creator to the realm of Reality, since the Creator made and existed within the spatial boundaries of Reality.

QS-Yahweh/Reality—Yahweh was a lineal member of Mary's family tree, since *Yahweh* was an alias for *God* and a transliteration of God's given name *YHWH*. I'd related Yahweh to the realm of Reality, because Yahweh was the creator that made and existed within the spatial boundaries of Reality.

QS-Yahweh/Trinity—Yahweh was a lineal member of Mary's family tree, since *Yahweh* was an alias for *God* and a transliteration of God's given name *YHWH*. I'd related Yahweh to the realm of the Trinity, because Yahweh was God and God was a member of the Trinity.

QS-Father/Trinity—The Father was a lineal member of Mary's family tree, since *Father* was an alias for *God*. I'd related the Father to the Trinity, because the Father was God and God was a member of the Trinity.

QS-Son/Trinity—The Son was a lineal member of Mary's family tree, since *Son* was an alias for *Jesus* and Jesus was Mary's son. I'd related the Son to the Trinity, because the Son was Jesus and Jesus was a member of the Trinity.

QS-Holy^Ghost/Trinity—The Holy Ghost was a lineal member of Mary's family tree, since the name *Holy Ghost* was an alias for the name *God* and the Holy Ghost was the entity God used to impregnate Mary with Jesus. I'd related the Holy Ghost to the Trinity, because the Holy Ghost was a member of the Trinity.

LINEAL, REALM-RELATED QUERY STACKS

QS-God/Trinity—God was a lineal member of Mary's family tree, since *God* was the father of the Jesus that Mary was the mother of. I'd related God to the Trinity, because God was a member of the Trinity.

QS-Jesus/Trinity—Jesus was a lineal member of Mary's family tree, since Jesus was Mary's son. I'd related Jesus to the Trinity, because Jesus was a member of the Trinity.

I'd expanded the updated the diagram of Virgin Mary's genealogy, which I'd introduced in "Ch. 2, Sec. 2: 1," by inserting the alias *Trinity* into said diagram's "God" box:

> *Some of the biblical names which I've listed in the diagram belong in Virgin Mary's lineage but aren't QS row'd words (e.g. "Bathsheba," "Solomon," "Nathan") yet elucidate how some biblical characters with names that are QS row'd words are related;*

> *SOLID LINE (———) = Genealogically linked to Mary;*
> *DASHED LINE (– – –) = Father of Mary's son Jesus, via no sexual contact;*
> *DASHED/DOTTED LINE (– ·· –) = Mary's husband, but not Jesus's father;*
> *DOUBLE LINE (====) = Not genealogically linked to Mary;*
> *BLACK NAME BOX* **NAME** *= Row'd word, and main focus of family tree;*
> *GRAY NAME BOX* NAME *= Row'd word, and member of family tree;*
> *WHITE NAME BOX* NAME *= Row'd word, but not a member of family tree;*
> *UNBOXED NAME = Not a row'd word, but member of family tree;*

(a) MARY: herself;

(b) JOE *(Joseph)*: Mary's husband;

(c) DAVE *(David)*: Mary's multi-great-grandfather;

(d) JESUS: Mary's son;

(e) GOD: Mary's spiritual co-parent;

(f) DEVIL: God's antipode;

(g) SON: Jesus's alias;

(h) HOLY GHOST: God's alias and conduit to impregnate Mary;

(i) YHWH: God's alias and ancient Hebrew name;

(j) YAHWEH: God's alias and modern Hebrew name;

(k) CREATOR: God's alias;

(l) FATHER: God's alias;

(m) TRINITY: God's alias, God as three individuals;

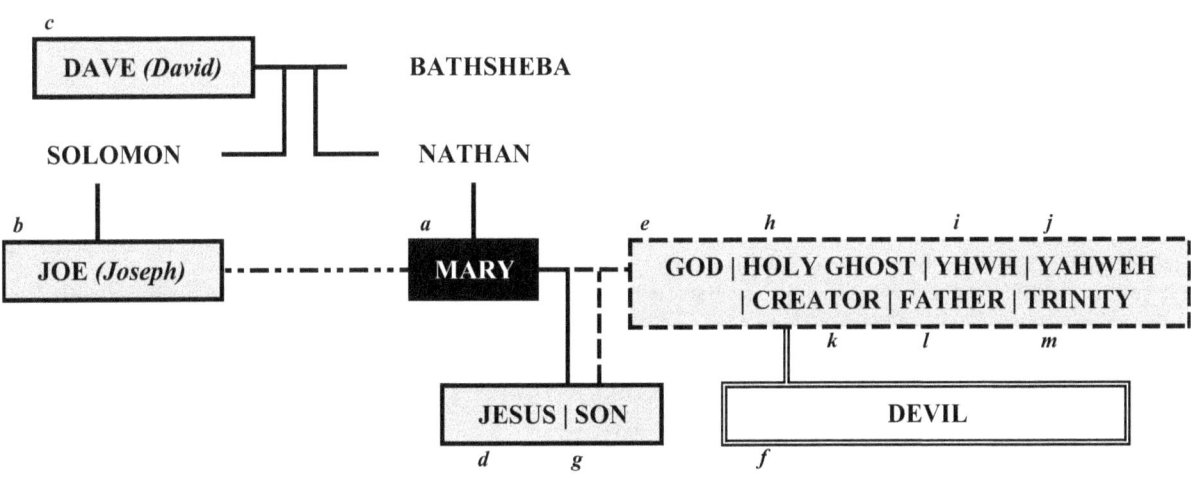

Ch. 6, Sec. 2: 3

In "Ch. 5, Sec. 5: 4," I'd displayed a table in which each answer word in the first seventeen QS answers I'd uncovered was categorized according to which one of four identities (David Mivshek, Trinity, God or QS answer) the main subject of the QS answer that said answer word appeared in represented. In "Ch. 6, Sec. 2: 4," I'd updated said table with the "QS-Trinity/Heaven" answer words. I'd placed the "QS-Trinity/Heaven" answer words into the "God" tier, since said QS answer's main subject, eviternity, was one of God's characteristics:

A parenthetic number (#) succeeding a distinct answer word reports how many times said answer word appears in QS answers that may or may not have distinct main subjects but have main subjects which cite David Mivshek, God, Trinity or QS answers;

(a) "QS-Trinity/Heaven" answer words: "God" tier, eviternity is main subject, eviternity is a characteristic of God;

Ch. 6, Sec. 2: 4

DAVID MIVSHEK

Nouns—Winner, Ghost;
Proper Nouns—Dave;
Pronouns—He (2);
Verbs—Gains, Go, Answering;
Adjectives—Holy, Naïve;
Conjunctions—Or (2).

TRINITY

Nouns—"A", Evil, Hay (2), Horde, Horn, Ill, Law, Trio, We (3), "We";
Plural Nouns—Reins;
Proper Nouns—Heaven;
Pronouns—I, They;
Verbs—Reign, Reining, Ring, Siring, Wans (2);
Adjectives—Hairy, Thy;
Conjunctions—Or;
Indefinite Articles—A.

GOD

Nouns—Core, Entry, *a*Eviternity, Giver, Glory, Hinter (2), *a*Horn (2), "I", I, In (3), Issuer, Joe, Rein, Sinew (2), Trinity, Trio, "Wans", *a*We (4);
Proper Nouns—Heaven, Host, Torah, Yahweh;
Pronouns—I;
Verbs—Adore, Assure, Is, Jot, Nerving, Ring, Rings, Trying (3), Wanes, Wans (2);
Adjectives—Fair, Real;
Adverbs—Right;
Conjunctions—Or;
Indefinite Articles—*a*A (5);
Contractions—*a*Ingrain's, Orator's.

QS ANSWER

Nouns—Air, Entry, Hint (2), "I" (2), Joe, Reason (2), Wording;
Pronouns—I;
Verbs—Got, Grew (2), Marry, Rains;
Indefinite Articles—A.

As I'd determined in "Ch. 2, Sec. 3: 12," a distinct answer word which didn't identify an individual was permitted to be a word in multiple QS answers, even if each said QS answers had a distinct main subject, while a distinct answer word which did identify an individual always identified one and the same individual, even when said answer word was in multiple answers and each one of said answers contained a distinct main subject::

A parenthetic number (#) succeeding a distinct answer word reports how many times said answer word appears in QS answers that may or may not have distinct main subjects but have main subjects which cite David Mivshek, God, Trinity or QS answers;

(a) A: not an individual, in seven answers, distinct main subject (giver/Yahweh/hay/core/eviternity, reason, hay);

(b) HORN: identifies one individual (God), in three answers, distinct main subject (Yahweh, hay, eviternity);

(c) WE: identifies one entity (Trinity), in five answers, same main subject (Yahweh/hay/core/we/eviternity);

Ch. 6, Sec. 2: 5

DAVID MIVSHEK

Nouns—Winner, Ghost;

Proper Nouns—Dave;

Pronouns—He (2);

Verbs—Gains, Go, Answering;

Adjectives—Holy, Naïve;

Conjunctions—Or (2).

TRINITY

Nouns—"A", Evil, Hay (2), Horde, [b]**Horn**, Ill, Law, Trio, [c]**We** (3), "We";

Plural Nouns—Reins;

Proper Nouns—Heaven;

Pronouns—I, They;

Verbs—Reign, Reining, Ring, Siring, Wans (2);

Adjectives—Hairy, Thy;

Conjunctions—Or;

Indefinite Articles—[a]**A**.

GOD

Nouns—Core, Entry, Eviternity, Giver, Glory, Hinter (2), [b]**Horn** (2), "I", I, In (3), Issuer, Joe,

Rein, Sinew (2), Trinity, Trio, "Wans", ᶜ**We** (4);
Proper Nouns—Heaven, Host, Torah, Yahweh;
Pronouns—I;
Verbs—Adore, Assure, Is, Jot, Nerving, Ring, Rings, Trying (3), Wanes, Wans (2);
Adjectives—Fair, Real;
Adverbs—Right;
Conjunctions—Or;
Indefinite Articles—ᵃA (5);
Contractions—ᵃ**Ingrain's**, Orator's.

QS ANSWER

Nouns—Air, Entry, Hint (2), ᵉ"I" (2), Joe, Reason (2), Wording;
Pronouns—I;
Verbs—Got, Grew (2), Marry, Rains;
Indefinite Articles—ᵃA.

In previous "Review" sections, I'd logged and showcased an array of statistics which pertained to QS answer vocabularies. In this "Review" section, I'd skipped the statistical array in order to reduce this book's page-count. See "Ch. 7, Sec. 4: 51" for a statistical table which has been comprised of several data points that pertain to each of the twenty QS answers I'd revealed in this book.

CHAPTER SEVEN: SECTION ONE

"TWO STACKS"/HELL

L	U	C	I	F	E	R
H	E	L	L			
O	R	I	G	I	N	
A	N	S	W	E	R	

S	A	T	A	N	
H	E	L	L		
O	R	I	G	I	N
A	N	S	W	E	R

I'd unveiled two Query Stacks which contained two row'd words that were similar to or the same as the two row'd words DEVIL and HELL from the "QS-Devil/Hell" row'd word matrix (see "Ch. 1, Sec. 2: 1"). One of the said two Query Stacks consisted of the first-row row'd word LUCIFER, the second of the said two Query Stacks consisted of the first-row row'd word SATAN, and both of the said two Query Stacks consisted of the second-row row'd word HELL. In other words, the first-row row'd word in each of the said two Query Stacks, LUCIFER or SATAN, was an alias of the name *Devil*, while the second-row row'd word in each the said two Query Stacks, HELL, was the same word I'd inserted into the second row of the "QS-Devil/Hell" row's word matrix. The Devil was the same entity as Lucifer and Satan in the Bible:

> *"How art thou fallen from heaven, O <u>Lucifer</u>, son of the morning! how art thou cut down to the ground, which didst weaken the nations!" (Isaiah 14:12 KJV).*

> *"And the great dragon was cast out, that old serpent, called the <u>Devil</u>, and <u>Satan</u>, which deceiveth the whole world: he was cast out into the earth, and his angels were cast out with him" (Revelation 12:9 KJV).*

I'd categorized "QS-Lucifer/Hell" and "QS-Satan/Hell" as "Lineally-Coupled-Alias Query Stacks," because each of the said two Query Stacks had a first-row row'd word which was an "alias" of the name *Devil*; the Devil wasn't a member of Virgin Mary's lineage but was commonly "coupled" to God, who was a member of Virgin Mary's "lineage"; and each of the said two Query Stacks had a second-row row'd word which was HELL, and, therefore, had a second-row row'd word which was a locational realm mentioned in the Bible:

QS Terminology

Lineal Query Stack
Query Stack with a first-row row'd word that names a character who belongs to a particular family tree (e.g. Virgin Mary's family tree).

Lineally-Coupled Query Stack
Query Stack with a first-row row'd word that names a character who doesn't belong to but is commonly associated with a member of a particular family tree (e.g. Virgin Mary's family tree).

Lineal-Alias Query Stack
Query Stack with a first-row row'd word that identifies the alias of a character whose name has been established as a row'd word and who belongs to a particular family tree (e.g. Virgin Mary's family tree).

Lineal-Alias, Realm-Related Query Stack
Query Stack with a first-row row'd word that identifies the alias of a character who belongs to a particular family tree (e.g. Virgin Mary's family tree) and a second-row row'd word that has a meaningful connection to its first-row row'd word but doesn't necessarily name a biblical location, like the row'd words HEAVEN, HELL and EARTH do, but may cite a location that shares a locational relationship with Heaven, Hell and Earth.

Lineal, Realm-Related Query Stack
Query Stack with a first-row row'd word that names a character who belongs to a particular family tree (e.g. Virgin Mary's family tree) and a second-row row'd word that has a meaningful connection to its first-row row'd word but doesn't necessarily name a biblical location, like the row'd words HEAVEN, HELL and EARTH do, but may cite a location that shares a locational relationship with Heaven, Hell and Earth.

Lineally-Coupled-Alias Query Stack
Query Stack with a first-row row'd word that names the alias of a character who doesn't belong to but is commonly associated with a member of a particular family tree (e.g. Virgin Mary's family tree).

Ch. 7, Sec. 1: 1

LINEAL QUERY STACKS
QS-GOD/HEAVEN
QS-JESUS/EARTH
QS-DAVE/EARTH
QS-JOE/EARTH
QS-MARY/EARTH
LINEALLY-COUPLED QUERY STACKS
QS-DEVIL/HELL
LINEAL-ALIAS QUERY STACKS
QS-HOLY^GHOST/HEAVEN
QS-YHWH/HEAVEN
QS-YAHWEH/HEAVEN
QS-TRINITY/HEAVEN
LINEAL-ALIAS, REALM-RELATED QUERY STACKS
QS-CREATOR/REALITY
QS-YAHWEH/REALITY
QS-YAHWEH/TRINITY
QS-FATHER/TRINITY
QS-SON/TRINITY
QS-HOLY^GHOST/TRINITY
LINEAL, REALM-RELATED QUERY STACKS
QS-GOD/TRINITY
QS-JESUS/TRINITY
▶ ***LINEAL-COUPLED-ALIAS QUERY STACKS*** ◀
▶ QS-LUCIFER/HELL ◀
▶ QS-SATAN/HELL ◀

The first row in the matrix of each of the said two Query Stacks contained a row'd word which was an alias of the name *Devil*; therefore, the first-row row'd word in each of said two QS matrices identified the unholiest biblical figure:

> *A parenthetic number (#) succeeding a first-row row'd word reports the number of times said row'd word was used as a first-row row'd word;*

(a) GOD (2); DEVIL; JESUS (2); DAVE *(David)*; JOE *(Joseph)*; MARY; HOLY^GHOST (2); YHWH; YAHWEH (3); CREATOR; FATHER; SON; TRINITY; LUCIFER; SATAN: notable biblical beings, first-row row'd words;

Ch. 7, Sec. 1: 2

QS-God/Heaven	QS-Devil/Hell	QS-Jesus/Earth	QS-Dave/Earth
"G O D H E A V E N O R I G I N A N S W E R	"D E V I L H E L L O R I G I N A N S W E R	"J E S U S E A R T H O R I G I N A N S W E R	"D A V E E A R T H O R I G I N A N S W E R

QS-Joe/Earth	QS-Mary/Earth	QS-Holy^Ghost/Heaven
"J O E E A R T H O R I G I N A N S W E R	"M A R Y E A R T H O R I G I N A N S W E R	"H O L Y G H O S T H E A V E N O R I G I N A N S W E R

QS-YHWH/Heaven	QS-Yahweh/Heaven	QS-Creator/Reality
"Y H W H H E A V E N O R I G I N A N S W E R	"Y A H W E H H E A V E N O R I G I N A N S W E R	"C R E A T O R R E A L I T Y O R I G I N A N S W E R

QS-Yahweh/Reality	QS-Yahweh/Trinity	QS-Father/Trinity
"Y A H W E H R E A L I T Y O R I G I N A N S W E R	"Y A H W E H T R I N I T Y O R I G I N A N S W E R	"F A T H E R T R I N I T Y O R I G I N A N S W E R

QS-Son/Trinity	QS-Holy^Ghost/Trinity	QS-God/Trinity
"S O N T R I N I T Y O R I G I N A N S W E R	"H O L Y G H O S T T R I N I T Y O R I G I N A N S W E R	"G O D T R I N I T Y O R I G I N A N S W E R

QS-Jesus/Trinity	QS-Trinity/Heaven	QS-Lucifer/Hell
"J E S U S T R I N I T Y O R I G I N A N S W E R	"T R I N I T Y H E A V E N O R I G I N A N S W E R	"L U C I F E R H E L L O R I G I N A N S W E R

QS-Satan/Hell
"S A T A N H E L L O R I G I N A N S W E R

Lucifer and Satan were two prominent biblical characters, since each character was the Devil:

A parenthetic number (#) succeeding a first-row row'd word reports the number of times said row'd word was used as a first-row row'd word;

(a) GOD (2): notable biblical figure; of Heaven and Trinity; Heaven's ruler and Trinity member;
(b) DEVIL: notable biblical figure; of Hell; God sends evil to Hell, Devil is the evilest being, Devil is evilest being God could sent to Hell;
(c) JESUS (2): notable biblical figure; of Earth and Trinity; Earth's premier ruler and Trinity member;
(d) DAVE *(David)*: notable biblical figure; of Earth; third King of Israel;
(e) JOE *(Joseph)*: notable biblical figure; of Earth; Virgin Mary's husband;
(f) MARY: notable biblical figure; of Earth; Jesus's biological mother;
(g) HOLY GHOST (2): notable biblical figure; of Heaven and Trinity; Heaven's messenger and Trinity member;
(h) YHWH: notable biblical figure; of Heaven; Heaven's ruler;
(i) YAHWEH (3): notable biblical figure; of Heaven, Reality and Trinity; Heaven's ruler, Reality's maker and Trinity member;
(j) CREATOR: notable biblical figure; of Reality; Reality's maker;
(k) FATHER: notable biblical figure; of Trinity; Trinity member;
(l) SON: notable biblical figure; of Trinity; Trinity member;
(m) TRINITY: notable biblical figure; of Heaven; Heaven's ruler;
(n) **LUCIFER: notable biblical figure; of Hell; God sends evil to Hell, Lucifer is the evilest being, Lucifer is evilest being God could send to Hell;**
(o) **SATAN: notable biblical figure; of Hell; God sends evil to Hell, Satan is the evilest being, Satan is evilest being God could send to Hell;**

Ch. 7, Sec. 1: 3

BIBLICAL BEING	DOMAIN	NOTORIETY
[a]GOD	[a]HEAVEN	[a]RULER
[a]GOD	[a]TRINITY	[a]MEMBER
[b]DEVIL	[b]HELL	[b]EVILEST RESIDENT
[c]JESUS	[c]EARTH	[c]PREMIER RULER
[c]JESUS	[c]TRINITY	[c]MEMBER
[d]DAVE (David)	[d]EARTH	[d]ANOINTED KING
[e]JOE (Joseph)	[e]EARTH	[e]MARY'S HUSBAND
[f]MARY	[f]EARTH	[f]JESUS'S MOTHER
[g]HOLY GHOST	[g]HEAVEN	[g]MESSENGER
[g]HOLY GHOST	[g]TRINITY	[g]MEMBER
[h]YHWH	[h]HEAVEN	[h]RULER
[i]YAHWEH	[i]HEAVEN	[i]RULER
[i]YAHWEH	[i]REALITY	[i]MAKER
[i]YAHWEH	[i]TRINITY	[i]MEMBER
[j]CREATOR	[j]REALITY	[j]MAKER
[k]FATHER	[k]TRINITY	[k]MEMBER
[l]SON	[l]TRINITY	[l]MEMBER
[m]TRINITY	[m]HEAVEN	[m]RULER
[n]LUCIFER	**[n]HELL**	**[n]EVILEST RESIDENT**
[o]SATAN	**[o]HELL**	**[o]EVILEST RESIDENT**

Lucifer/Hell: Siring a We

I'd constructed and decrypted "QS-Lucifer/Hell" first:

I've provided a decoded QS matrix, a valid QS answer, a set of answer word definitions, biblical verses, and an interpretation and a vocabular analysis of the "QS-Lucifer/Hell" answer. To understand the derivation of my interpretation for the "QS-Lucifer/Hell" answer, apply the set of definitions and biblical verses to the correlated answer and then examine my vocabular analysis;

✓ All QS rules followed (see "Appendix A");

Ch. 7, Sec. 1: 4

QS-Lucifer/Hell

L	U	C	I	F	E	R
H	E	L	L			
O	R	I	G	I	N	
A	N	S	W	E	R	

CLUE: FILLER.sent1 HORN: SIRING A WE.sent2

CLUE *n.* A piece of evidence that leads one toward the solution of a problem.[2]

FILLER *n.* A person that fills (*v.* to supply [a blank space] with written matter[1]).[1]

HORN *n.* Source of strength.[2]

SIRING *v.* <SIRE *v.*> To bring into being.[2]

A *i-art.* Used before most singular nouns when the individual in question is unidentified, especially when the individual is being called to notice.[2]

WE *n.* A group that is consciously felt as such by its members.[2]

HORN—"The LORD is my rock, and my fortress, and my deliverer; {my God, my strength}, in whom I will trust; my buckler, and the {horn of my salvation}, and my high tower" (Psalms 18:2 KJV).

sent1: *A piece of evidence, which is a QS answer, is formed by God inserting written matter, like answer words and punctuation, into an area that's devoid of written matter.*

sent2: *God, a source of strength, is creating Himself as the Trinity, a group of three individuals who are member of one and the same group and are aware of belonging to said group.*

Match superscripted numbers and letters to compare vocabulary in the "QS-Lucifer/Hell" answer to vocabulary in QS answers I've already unveiled; brief explanations in the reference key should contain enough of the necessary information one needs to understand my interpretation of the "QS-Lucifer/Hell" answer;

(1) *(CLUE: FILLER), HINTER, HINTER, (GOT WORDING)*

All four of the QS answer phrases casted a spotlight onto the QS author, God. Collectively, said phrases suggested that God expressed meaning via words in QS answer phrases *(got wording)*, wrote evidence into QS answers which hadn't been written before *(clue: filler)* and authored allusive statements that guided readers to answers *(hinter)*;

(2) *(HORN: SIRING A WE), (HORN: SIRING A WE)*

Both QS answer phrases contained the same words but were derived from different QS answers. Each phrase proclaimed that God, a source of strength (see "Ch. 7, Sec. 1: 4; Psalms 18:2 KJV"), composed Himself as a trinity;

(a) **CLUE, (AIR/HINT), HINT**

The three QS answer phrases referred to evidence *(clue)* which was written into an allusive statement *(hint)* that was publicized *(air)*. According to my interpretations of similar QS answers, the publicized statement was a QS answer and said QS answer provided evidence which helped readers reveal information that pertained to God;

(b) **FILLER, GIVER**

By compounding the meanings of the two QS answer words, I was able to identify the QS author, God, as the one who'd filled in empty space with QS answer words and selflessly let others read QS answers which He'd authored;

(c) **HORN, HORN, HORN**

The QS answer word *HORN* appeared in multiple QS answers;

Ch. 7, Sec. 1: 5

QS-Dave/Earth Answer
ADORE [b]**(GIVER)**. A [1]**(HINTER)** WANS.
QS-Joe/Earth Answer
JOE: REASON. [a]**(AIR/HINT)** GREW.
QS-Mary/Earth Answer
MARRY REASON. A [a]**(HINT)**, I GREW.
QS-YHWH/Heaven Answer
YAHWEH: [c]**(HORN)**. NERVING, IS A WE.
QS-Yahweh/Heaven Answer
HAY: WE. HEAVEN: [2]**[**[c]**(HORN), SIRING A WE]**.
QS-Father/Trinity Answer
FAIR [1]**(HINTER)**. TRIO: TRYING, WANES.
QS-God/Trinity Answer
[1]**(GOT WORDING)**. "I" ENTRY; RAINS "I."
QS-Lucifer/Hell Answer
[1]**[**[a]**(CLUE)**: [b]**(FILLER)]**. [2]**[**[c]**(HORN)**: SIRING A WE]**.

Satan/Hell: Lie Wans

I'd solved "QS-Satan/Hell" second:

I've provided a decoded QS matrix, a valid QS answer, a set of answer word definitions, biblical verses, and an interpretation and a vocabular analysis of the "QS-Satan/Hell" answer. To understand the derivation of my interpretation for the "QS-Satan/Hell" answer, apply the set of definitions and biblical verses to the correlated answer and then examine my vocabular analysis;

| prop-n's = possessive proper noun |

✓ All QS rules followed (see "Appendix A");

Ch. 7, Sec. 1: 6

QS-Satan/Hell

S	A	T	A	N
H	E	L	L	
O	R	I	G	I	N
A	N	S	W	E	R

TORAH'S LEARNING.sent1 **LIE WANS.**sent2

TORAH'S *prop-n's.* <TORAH *prop-n.*> The body of divine knowledge and law found in the Jewish scriptures and tradition.[2]

LEARNING *n.* Knowledge accumulated and handed down by generations of scholars.[2]

LIE *n.* An assertion of something known by the speaker to be untrue.[2]

WANS *v.* <WAN *v.*> To make wan (*adj.* lacking in forcefulness).[1]

LIE—"You shall not murder. You shall not commit adultery. You shall not steal. {You shall not bear false witness against your neighbor}" (Shemot 20:13 Tanakh);

LIE—"{Distance yourself from a false matter}; and do not kill a truly innocent person or one who has been declared innocent, for I will not vindicate a guilty person" (Shemot 23:7 Tanakh)

sent1: **The Hebrew Bible's book of divine knowledge and law contains knowledge which biblical scholars have accumulated and handed down generationally.**

sent2: **In accordance with knowledge presented in the Torah, knowingly speaking or supporting an untruth ignores the Ninth Commandment's mandate and makes a person's force of goodness become less forceful.**

Match superscripted numbers and letters to compare vocabulary in the "QS-Satan/Hell" answer to vocabulary in QS answers I've previously uncovered; brief explanations in the reference key should contain enough of the necessary information one needs to understand my interpretation of the "QS-Satan/Hell" answer;

(a) *(TORAH'S LEARNING), (TORAH: GLORY)*

Each QS answer phrase focused a reader's attention onto a specific aspect of the Torah. One said QS answer phrase pointed to knowledge offered in the Torah. The second said QS answer focused on a topic in the Torah which pertained to glory (meaning, *Shekinah* [*prop-n.* the presence of God in the world conceived by Jewish and later by Christian theologians as manifested in natural and especially supernatural phenomena.[2]]; see "Ch. 5, Sec. 4: 9");

(b) *WANS, WANS, WANS, WANS, WANS, WANES, "WANS"*

Each QS answer word evidenced the QS author's, or God's, earnestness to use answer words which told about a decay in His moral power. God incorporated said answer words into several QS answers; for instance, the answer word *WANS* appeared as a verb five times and a noun one time in QS answers, while the answer word *WANES*, a synonym of the word *wans,* appeared one time in QS answers;

(c) *LIE*

See "Ch. 7, Sec. 2: 21-36" for my in-depth analysis of the answer word *LIE*;

Ch. 7, Sec. 1: 7

QS-Devil/Hell Answer
HORDE: EVIL. ILL REIGN, [b]**(WANS)**.
QS-Jesus/Earth Answer
JOE ASSURE. RIGHT, REIN [b]**(WANS)**.
QS-Dave/Earth Answer
ADORE GIVER. A HINTER [b]**(WANS)**.
QS-Yahweh/Trinity Answer
HAIRY WE. THY TRIO: REINING, [b]**(WANS)**.
QS-Father/Trinity Answer
FAIR HINTER. TRIO: TRYING, [b]**(WANES)**.
QS-Holy^Ghost/Trinity Answer
[a]**(TORAH: GLORY)**. HOST: IN, I, TRYING SINEW.
QS-Jesus/Trinity Answer
JOT, ISSUER. **I RING ENTRY "I,"** [b]**("WANS.")**
QS-Satan/Hell Answer
[a]**(TORAH'S LEARNING)**. [c]**(LIE)** [b]**(WANS)**.

Even though each of the two QS answers, "QS-Lucifer/Hell" or "QS-Satan/Hell," were grammatically coherent and meaningful, I'd ran each of the said two answers through "QS-7CAP" in order to confirm that each said answer contained valid vocabulary:

Seven Common QS Answer Properties
---

1. Each answer contains no more and no less than two sentences (sent1, sent2):

QS-God/Heaven

GO DAVE._{sent1} HE: WINNER; OR, GAINS._{sent2}

QS-Devil/Hell

HORDE: EVIL._{sent1} ILL REIGN, WANS._{sent2}

QS-Jesus/Earth

JOE ASSURE._{sent1} RIGHT, REIN WANS._{sent2}

QS-Dave/Earth

ADORE GIVER._{sent1} A HINTER WANS._{sent2}

QS-Joe/Earth

JOE: REASON._{sent1} AIR/HINT GREW._{sent2}

QS-Mary/Earth

MARRY REASON._{sent1} A HINT, I GREW._{sent2}

QS-Holy^Ghost/Heaven

HOLY GHOST._{sent1} HE: NAÏVE OR ANSWERING._{sent2}

QS-YHWH/Heaven

YAHWEH: HORN._{sent1} NERVING, IS A WE._{sent2}

QS-Yahweh/Heaven

HAY: WE._{sent1} HEAVEN: HORN, SIRING A WE._{sent2}

QS-Creator/Reality

CORE: REAL._{sent1} A TRINITY; OR, RINGS A WE._{sent2}

QS-Yahweh/Reality

HAY: LAW._{sent1} THEY OR REINS, I, RING "A WE."_{sent2}

QS-Yahweh/Trinity

HAIRY WE._{sent1} THY TRIO: REINING, WANS._{sent2}

QS-Father/Trinity

FAIR HINTER._{sent1} TRIO: TRYING, WANES._{sent2}

QS-Son/Trinity

ORATOR'S IN._{sent1} IN: TRYING SINEW._{sent2}

QS-Holy^Ghost/Trinity

TORAH: GLORY.sent1 **HOST: IN, I, TRYING SINEW.**sent2

QS-God/Trinity

GOT WORDING.sent1 **"I" ENTRY; RAINS "I."**sent2

QS-Jesus/Trinity

JOT, ISSUER.sent1 **I RING ENTRY "I," "WANS."**sent2

QS-Trinity/Heaven

EVITERNITY: HORN.sent1 **INGRAIN'S A WE.**sent2

QS-Lucifer/Hell

CLUE: FILLER.sent1 **HORN: SIRING A WE.**sent2

QS-Satan/Hell

TORAH'S LEARNING.sent1 **LIE WANS.**sent2

2. Each answer's first sentence contains no more and no less than two words (word1, word2):

QS-God/Heaven

GOword1 **DAVE**word2. HE: WINNER; OR, GAINS.

QS-Devil/Hell

HORDEword1: **EVIL**word2. ILL REIGN, WANS.

QS-Jesus/Earth

JOEword1 **ASSURE**word2. RIGHT, REIN WANS.

QS-Dave/Earth

ADOREword1 **GIVER**word2. A HINTER WANS.

QS-Joe/Earth

JOEword1: **REASON**word2. AIR/HINT GREW.

QS-Mary/Earth

MARRYword1 **REASON**word2. A HINT, I GREW.

QS-Holy^Ghost/Heaven

HOLYword1 **GHOST**word2. HE: NAÏVE OR ANSWERING.

QS-YHWH/Heaven

YAHWEHword1: **HORN**word2. NERVING, IS A WE.

QS-Yahweh/Heaven

HAYword1: **WE**word2. HEAVEN: HORN, SIRING A WE.

QS-Creator/Reality

COREword1: **REAL**word2. A TRINITY; OR, RINGS A WE.

QS-Yahweh/Reality

HAY~word1~: **LAW**~word2~. THEY OR REINS, I, RING "A WE."

QS-Yahweh/Trinity

HAIRY~word1~ **WE**~word2~. THY TRIO: REINING, WANS.

QS-Father/Trinity

FAIR~word1~ **HINTER**~word2~. TRIO: TRYING, WANES.

QS-Son/Trinity

ORATOR'S~word1~ **IN**~word2~. IN: TRYING SINEW.

QS-Holy^Ghost/Trinity

TORAH~word1~: **GLORY**~word2~. HOST: IN, I, TRYING SINEW.

QS-God/Trinity

GOT~word1~ **WORDING**~word2~. "I" ENTRY; RAINS "I."

QS-Jesus/Trinity

JOT~word1~, **ISSUER**~word2~. I RING ENTRY "I," "WANS."

QS-Trinity/Heaven

EVITERNITY~word1~: **HORN**~word2~. INGRAIN'S A WE.

QS-Lucifer/Hell

CLUE~word1~: **FILLER**~word2~. HORN: SIRING A WE.

QS-Satan/Hell

TORAH'S~word1~ **LEARNING**~word2~. LIE WANS.

3. In each answer's first sentence, the main subject is introduced (subj1, subj2, ...):

    (subj14) [ORATOR]'S: contraction, [main subject] and *is*; *[Property Resolution (see "Appendix B")]*;

QS-God/Heaven

GO **DAVE**~subj1~. HE: WINNER; OR, GAINS.

QS-Devil/Hell

HORDE~subj2~: EVIL. ILL REIGN, WANS.

QS-Jesus/Earth

JOE~subj3~ ASSURE. RIGHT, REIN WANS.

QS-Dave/Earth

ADORE **GIVER**~subj4~. A HINTER WANS.

QS-Joe/Earth

JOE: **REASON**~subj5~. AIR/HINT GREW.

QS-Mary/Earth

MARRY **REASON**subj6. A HINT, I GREW.

QS-Holy^Ghost/Heaven

HOLY **GHOST**subj7. HE: NAÏVE OR ANSWERING.

QS-YHWH/Heaven

YAHWEHsubj8: HORN. NERVING, IS A WE.

QS-Yahweh/Heaven

HAYsubj9: WE. HEAVEN: HORN, SIRING A WE.

QS-Creator/Reality

COREsubj10: REAL. A TRINITY; OR, RINGS A WE.

QS-Yahweh/Reality

HAYsubj11: LAW. THEY OR REINS, I, RING "A WE."

QS-Yahweh/Trinity

HAIRY **WE**subj12. THY TRIO: REINING, WANS.

QS-Father/Trinity

FAIR **HINTER**subj13. TRIO: TRYING, WANES.

QS-Son/Trinity

[**ORATOR**subj14]'S IN. IN: TRYING SINEW.

QS-Holy^Ghost/Trinity

TORAH: **GLORY**subj15. HOST: IN, I, TRYING SINEW.

QS-God/Trinity

GOT **WORDING**subj16. "I" ENTRY; RAINS "I."

QS-Jesus/Trinity

JOT, **ISSUER**subj17. I RING ENTRY "I," "WANS."

QS-Trinity/Heaven

EVITERNITYsubj18: HORN. INGRAIN'S A WE.

QS-Lucifer/Hell

CLUE: **FILLER**subj19. HORN: SIRING A WE.

QS-Satan/Hell

TORAH'S **LEARNING**subj20. LIE WANS.

4. In each answer, the main subject introduced in the first sentence is mentioned in the second sentence (subj1-subj1, subj2-subj2, ...):

(subj18) [INGRAIN]'S: contraction, [main subject] and *is*; *[Property Resolution (see "Appendix B")]*;

QS-God/Heaven

GO **DAVE**~subj1~. **HE**~subj1~: WINNER; OR, GAINS.

QS-Devil/Hell

HORDE~subj2~: EVIL. **ILL**~subj2~ REIGN, WANS.

QS-Jesus/Earth

JOE~subj3~ ASSURE. RIGHT, **REIN**~subj3~ WANS.

QS-Dave/Earth

ADORE **GIVER**~subj4~. A **HINTER**~subj4~ WANS.

QS-Joe/Earth

JOE: **REASON**~subj5~. **AIR**~subj5~/HINT GREW.

QS-Mary/Earth

MARRY **REASON**~subj6~. A **HINT**~subj6~, I GREW.

QS-Holy^Ghost/Heaven

HOLY **GHOST**~subj7~. **HE**~subj7~: NAÏVE OR ANSWERING.

QS-YHWH/Heaven

YAHWEH~subj8~: HORN. NERVING, IS A **WE**~subj8~.

QS-Yahweh/Heaven

HAY~subj9~: WE. HEAVEN: HORN, SIRING A **WE**~subj9~.

QS-Creator/Reality

CORE~subj10~: REAL. A **TRINITY**~subj10~; OR, RINGS A WE.

QS-Yahweh/Reality

HAY~subj11~: LAW. THEY OR **REINS**~subj11~, I, RING "A WE."

QS-Yahweh/Trinity

HAIRY **WE**~subj12~. THY **TRIO**~subj12~: REINING, WANS.

QS-Father/Trinity

FAIR **HINTER**~subj13~. **TRIO**~subj13~: TRYING, WANES.

QS-Son/Trinity

[**ORATOR**~subj14~]'S IN. **IN**~subj14~: TRYING SINEW.

QS-Holy^Ghost/Trinity

TORAH: **GLORY**~subj15~. **HOST**~subj15~: IN, I, TRYING SINEW.

QS-God/Trinity

GOT **WORDING**~subj16~. "**I**"~subj16~ ENTRY; RAINS "I."

QS-Jesus/Trinity

JOT, **ISSUER**~subj17~. **I**~subj17~ RING ENTRY "I," "WANS."

QS-Trinity/Heaven

EVITERNITY~subj18~: HORN. [**INGRAIN**~subj18~]'S A WE.

QS-Lucifer/Hell

CLUE: **FILLER**$_{subj19}$. **HORN**$_{subj19}$: SIRING A WE.

QS-Satan/Hell

TORAH'S **LEARNING**$_{subj20}$. **LIE**$_{subj20}$ WANS.

5. In each answer, the first sentence's second word and the second sentence's first word are synonymous in definition (syn) or context (con):

   Synonymous answer words are tagged "syn," while answer words which share contextual meaning are tagged "con";

   [con1] DAVE; HE: context, both words identify same man;

   [syn2] EVIL; ILL: synonyms, each word means "wicked";

   [con3] ASSURE; RIGHT: context, both words convey affirmation;

   [con4] GIVER; [A HINTER]: context, word and [phrase] identify same person; *[Property Deviation Resolution: (see "Appendix B")];*

   [con5] REASON; AIR: context, the reason is expressed as a written statement;

   [con6] REASON; [A HINT]: context, the reason is expressed as an allusive statement; *[Property Deviation Resolution: (see "Appendix B")];*

   [con7] GHOST; HE: context, both words identify same person;

   [con 8] HORN; NERVING: context, each word refers to a source of strength;

   [con 9] WE; HEAVEN: context, both words identify same entity;

   [con10] REAL; [A TRINITY]: context, word and [phrase] identify same entity; *[Property Deviation Resolution: (see "Appendix B")];*

   [con11] LAW; THEY: context, revealed will of God is the Trinity;

   [con12] WE; THY: context, both words identify same entity;

   [con13] HINTER; TRIO: context, both words identify same entity;

   [syn14] IN; IN: synonym, each word means "one who is in power";

   [con15] GLORY; HOST: context, both words identify same person;

   [con16] WORDING; "I": context, both words refer to answer words;

   [con17] ISSUER; I: context, both words identify same person;

   [con18] HORN; [INGRAIN]'S: context, word and [word] regards a characteristic of same person; *[Property Resolution: (see "Appendix B")];*

   [con19] FILLER; HORN: context, both words identify same person;

   [con20] LEARNING; LIE: context, the learning is about a lie;

QS-God/Heaven

GO **DAVE**$_{syn1}$. **HE**$_{syn1}$: WINNER; OR, GAINS.

QS-Devil/Hell

HORDE: **EVIL**$_{syn2}$. **ILL**$_{syn2}$ REIGN, WANS.

QS-Jesus/Earth

JOE **ASSURE**$_{con3}$. **RIGHT**$_{con3}$, REIN WANS.

QS-Dave/Earth

ADORE **GIVER**$_{con4}$. **[A HINTER]**$_{con4}$ WANS.

QS-Joe/Earth

JOE: **REASON**$_{con5}$. **AIR**$_{con5}$/HINT GREW.

QS-Mary/Earth

MARRY **REASON**$_{con6}$. **[A HINT]**$_{con6}$, I GREW.

QS-Holy^Ghost/Heaven

HOLY **GHOST**$_{con7}$. **HE**$_{con7}$: NAÏVE OR ANSWERING.

QS-YHWH/Heaven

YAHWEH: **HORN**$_{con8}$. **NERVING**$_{con8}$, IS A WE.

QS-Yahweh/Heaven

HAY: **WE**$_{con9}$. **HEAVEN**$_{con9}$: HORN, SIRING A WE.

QS-Creator/Reality

CORE: **REAL**$_{con10}$. **[A TRINITY]**$_{con10}$; OR, RINGS A WE.

QS-Yahweh/Reality

HAY: **LAW**$_{con11}$. **THEY**$_{con11}$ OR REINS, I, RING "A WE."

QS-Yahweh/Trinity

HAIRY **WE**$_{con12}$. **THY**$_{con12}$ TRIO: REINING, WANS.

QS-Father/Trinity

FAIR **HINTER**$_{con13}$. **TRIO**$_{con13}$: TRYING, WANES.

QS-Son/Trinity

ORATOR'S **IN**$_{syn14}$. **IN**$_{syn14}$: TRYING SINEW.

QS-Holy^Ghost/Trinity

TORAH: **GLORY**$_{con15}$. **HOST**$_{con15}$: IN, I, TRYING SINEW.

QS-God/Trinity

GOT **WORDING**$_{con16}$. **"I"**$_{con16}$ ENTRY; RAINS "I."

QS-Jesus/Trinity

JOT, **ISSUER**$_{con17}$. **I**$_{con17}$ RING ENTRY "I," "WANS."

QS-Trinity/Heaven

EVITERNITY: **HORN**$_{con18}$. **[INGRAIN**$_{con18}$**]**'S A WE.

QS-Lucifer/Hell

CLUE: **FILLER**$_{con19}$. **HORN**$_{con19}$: SIRING A WE.

QS-Satan/Hell

TORAH'S **LEARNING**$_{con20}$. **LIE**$_{con20}$ WANS.

---

6. In each answer's second sentence, at least one action is applied to the main subject (subj1–act1, subj2–act2, …):

$_{(subj18/act18)}$ [INGRAIN]['S]: contraction, [main subject] and [verb (is)]; *[Property Resolution (see "Appendix B")]*

QS-God/Heaven

GO DAVE. **HE**$_{subj1}$: WINNER; OR, **GAINS**$_{act1}$.

QS-Devil/Hell

HORDE: EVIL. **ILL**$_{subj2}$ **REIGN**$_{act2}$, WANS.

QS-Jesus/Earth

JOE ASSURE. RIGHT, **REIN**$_{subj3}$ **WANS**$_{act3}$.

QS-Dave/Earth

ADORE GIVER. **[A HINTER]**$_{subj4}$ **WANS**$_{act4}$.

QS-Joe/Earth

JOE: REASON. **AIR**$_{subj5}$/HINT **GREW**$_{act5}$.

QS-Mary/Earth

MARRY REASON. **[A HINT]**$_{subj6}$, I **GREW**$_{act6}$.

QS-Holy^Ghost/Heaven

HOLY GHOST. **HE**$_{subj7}$: NAÏVE OR **ANSWERING**$_{act7}$.

QS-YHWH/Heaven

YAHWEH: HORN. **NERVING**$_{act8}$, IS A **WE**$_{subj8}$.

QS-Yahweh/Heaven

HAY: WE. HEAVEN: **HORN**$_{subj9}$, **SIRING**$_{act9}$ A WE.

QS-Creator/Reality

CORE: REAL. A **TRINITY**$_{subj10}$; OR, **RINGS**$_{act10}$ A WE.

QS-Yahweh/Reality

HAY: LAW. THEY OR, **REINS**$_{subj11}$, I, **RING**$_{act11}$ "A WE."

QS-Yahweh/Trinity

HAIRY WE. THY **TRIO**$_{subj12}$: **REINING**$_{act12}$, WANS.

QS-Father/Trinity

FAIR HINTER. **TRIO**$_{subj13}$: **TRYING**$_{act13}$, WANES.

QS-Son/Trinity

ORATOR'S IN. **IN**~subj14~: **TRYING**~act14~ SINEW.

QS-Holy^Ghost/Trinity

TORAH: GLORY. **HOST**~subj15~: IN, I, **TRYING**~act15~ SINEW.

QS-God/Trinity

GOT WORDING. **"I"**~subj16~ ENTRY; **RAINS**~act16~ "I."

QS-Jesus/Trinity

JOT, ISSUER. **I**~subj17~ **RING**~act17~ ENTRY "I," "WANS."

QS-Trinity/Heaven

EVITERNITY: HORN. [**INGRAIN**~subj18~] ['**S**~act18~] A WE.

QS-Lucifer/Hell

CLUE: FILLER. **HORN**~subj19~: **SIRING**~act19~ A WE.

QS-Satan/Hell

TORAH'S LEARNING. **LIE**~subj20~ **WANS**~act20~.

7. Along each answer's breadth of vocabulary, there's at least one site where an answer letter *S* would've enhanced the answer's grammatical correctness if it would've been available in the accompanying row'd word matrix and usable:

> *Removing a colon (:) that follows a noun and appending a contraction 's to the end of said noun would produce a conversational tone and clearer syntax (e.g. <u>He's</u> winner; <u>Horde's</u> evil; <u>He's</u> naïve; <u>He's</u> answering; <u>Yahweh's</u> horn; <u>Hay's</u> we; <u>Heaven's</u> horn; <u>Heaven's</u> siring; <u>Core's</u> real; <u>Hay's</u> law; <u>Trio's</u> reining; <u>Trio's</u> trying; <u>In's</u> trying; <u>Host's</u> in; <u>Host's</u> I; <u>Host's</u> trying; <u>Eviternity's</u> horn; <u>Horn's</u> siring). Removing a colon (:) that follows a noun and appending a possessive 's to the end of said noun would produce a conversational tone and clearer syntax (e.g. <u>Joe's</u> reason; <u>Torah's</u> glory; <u>Clue's</u> filler). Inflecting certain verbs by appending a letter S to the end of them would promote optimal grammar (e.g. Ill <u>reigns</u>; Joe <u>assures</u>; <u>Jots</u>, issuer). However, each answer's row'd word matrix lacks a letter S that's needed or that's capable of being used in ways mandated by QS rules (see "Appendix A");*

> *[Property Deviation Resolution: No grammatically incorrect syntax can be found within the "QS-Dave/Earth," "QS-Mary/Earth," "QS-God/Trinity," "QS-Jesus/Trinity," or "QS-Satan/Hell" answer's vocabulary. Optimal vocabulary contains no grammatical mistakes. If a QS answer doesn't contain missing letters in its vocabulary, then the vocabulary of said QS an-*

is grammatically optimal and therefore acceptable.];

> *QS-God/Heaven:* <u>He's</u> winner;
> *QS-Devil/Hell:* <u>Horde's</u> evil, Ill <u>reigns</u>;
> *QS-Jesus/Earth:* Joe <u>assures</u>;
> *QS-Dave/Earth:* (optimal grammar);
> *QS-Joe/Earth:* <u>Joe's</u> reason;
> *QS-Mary/Earth:* (optimal grammar);
> *QS-Holy^Ghost/Heaven:* <u>He's</u> naïve, <u>He's</u> answering;
> *QS-YHWH/Heaven:* <u>Yahweh's</u> horn;
> *QS-Creator/Reality:* <u>Core's</u> real;
> *QS-Yahweh/Reality:* <u>Hay's</u> law;
> *QS-Yahweh/Trinity:* <u>Trio's</u> reining;
> *QS-Father/Trinity:* <u>Trio's</u> trying;
> *QS-Son/Trinity:* <u>In's</u> trying;
> *QS-Holy^Ghost/Trinity:* <u>Host's</u> in, <u>Host's</u> I, <u>Host's</u> trying;
> *QS-God/Trinity:* (optimal grammar);
> *QS-Jesus/Trinity:* <u>Jots</u>, issuer;
> *QS-Trinity/Heaven:* (<u>Eviternity's</u> horn);
> *QS-Lucifer/Hell:* <u>Clue's</u> filler, <u>Horn's</u> siring;
> *QS-Satan/Hell:* (optimal grammar);

QS-God/Heaven

GO DAVE. **HE: WINNER**; OR, GAINS.

QS-Devil/Hell

HORDE: EVIL. ILL REIGN, WANS.

QS-Jesus/Earth

JOE ASSURE. RIGHT, REIN WANS.

QS-Dave/Earth

ADORE GIVER. A HINTER WANS.

QS-Joe/Earth

JOE: REASON. AIR/HINT GREW.

QS-Mary/Earth

MARRY REASON. A HINT, I GREW.

QS-Holy^Ghost/Heaven

HOLY GHOST. **HE: NAÏVE** OR ANSWERING.

HOLY GHOST. **HE:** NAÏVE OR **ANSWERING**.

QS-YHWH/Heaven

YAHWEH: HORN. NERVING, IS A WE.

QS-Yahweh/Heaven

HAY: WE. HEAVEN: HORN, SIRING A WE.

HAY: WE. **HEAVEN:** HORN, **SIRING** A WE.

QS-Creator/Reality

CORE: REAL. A TRINITY; OR, RINGS A WE.

QS-Yahweh/Reality

HAY: LAW. THEY OR REINS, I, RING "A WE."

QS-Yahweh/Trinity

HAIRY WE. THY **TRIO: REINING,** WANS.

QS-Father/Trinity

FAIR HINTER. **TRIO: TRYING,** WANES.

QS-Son/Trinity

ORATOR'S IN. **IN: TRYING** SINEW.

QS-Holy^Ghost/Trinity

TORAH: GLORY. HOST: IN, I, TRYING SINEW.

TORAH: GLORY. **HOST:** IN, **I,** TRYING SINEW.

TORAH: GLORY. **HOST:** IN, I, **TRYING SINEW.**

QS-God/Trinity

GOT WORDING. "I" ENTRY; RAINS "I."

QS-Jesus/Trinity

JOT, ISSUER. I RING ENTRY "I," "WANS."

QS-Trinity/Heaven

EVITERNITY: HORN. INGRAIN'S A WE.

QS-Lucifer/Hell

CLUE: FILLER. HORN: SIRING A WE.

QS-Satan/Hell

TORAH'S LEARNING. LIE WANS.

CHAPTER SEVEN: SECTION TWO

CONCLUSION: TWENTY STACKS

G O D
H E A V E N
O R I G I N
A N S W E R

D E V I L
H E L L
O R I G I N
A N S W E R

J E S U S
E A R T H
O R I G I N
A N S W E R

D A V E
E A R T H
O R I G I N
A N S W E R

J O E
E A R T H
O R I G I N
A N S W E R

M A R Y
E A R T H
O R I G I N
A N S W E R

H O L Y G H O S T
H E A V E N
O R I G I N
A N S W E R

Y H W H
H E A V E N
O R I G I N
A N S W E R

Y A H W E H
H E A V E N
O R I G I N
A N S W E R

C R E A T O R
R E A L I T Y
O R I G I N
A N S W E R

Y A H W E H
R E A L I T Y
O R I G I N
A N S W E R

Y A H W E H
T R I N I T Y
O R I G I N
A N S W E R

F A T H E R
T R I N I T Y
O R I G I N
A N S W E R

S O N
T R I N I T Y
O R I G I N
A N S W E R

H O L Y G H O S T
T R I N I T Y
O R I G I N
A N S W E R

```
G O D                    J E S U S                T R I N I T Y
T R I N I T Y            T R I N I T Y            H E A V E N
O R I G I N              O R I G I N              O R I G I N
A N S W E R              A N S W E R              A N S W E R

L U C I F E R            S A T A N
H E L L                  H E L L
O R I G I N              O R I G I N
A N S W E R              A N S W E R
```

The first Query Stack I'd ever seen was in a vision that autonomously appeared in my mind. The vision's focal point was three words: *God*, *Heaven* and *origin*. The three words were arranged as a vertical stack of words by the time the vision ended.

The name *God* was in the top row, the name *Heaven* was in the second row and the word *origin* was in the bottom row of the word stack. When I'd read the words of the word stack from top word to bottom word, I'd unfurled a question: "God/Heaven: origin?" I'd interpreted the question as "How did God of Heaven become existent?"

I'd inserted the word *answer* below the word *origin*, which bumped up the word *origin* to the word stack's third row. By placing the word *answer* into the word stack's bottom row, I'd transformed the three-word question "God/Heaven: origin?" into the four-word question "'God/Heaven: origin?' answer?" I'd interpreted the four-word question as "What's the answer to the 'God of Heaven's origin' question?"

I'd penned the word stack onto a piece of paper. I'd equidistantly spread out the word stack's letters, which produced a letter grid of neat rows and columns. I'd horizontally and vertically linked together the word stack's letters to unveil six words: *go*, *Dave*, *he*, *winner*, *or* and *gains*. I'd sequenced and inserted punctuation in between said six words, which generated two coherent, meaningful phrases: *"go Dave"* and *"he: winner; or, gains."*

I'd interpreted the phrase *"go Dave"* as an instruction which told Dave to start some undisclosed action. The words *he*, *winner* and *gains* defined Dave as a male, characterized Dave as a success and implied that Dave benefitted from his success, respectively. However, neither phrase disclosed the action Dave was supposed to begin, what Dave was a success in or how Dave benefitted from his success.

I didn't know how I'd determine who said Dave was, until I'd thought of my own name and goals. Am I the Dave in said phrase, I'd wondered. Eventually, five reasons persuaded me to believe that I was the Dave mentioned in said phrase:

Ch. 7, Sec. 2: 1

1. The common nickname for my first name, *David*, is *Dave*;

2. I'm male;

3. I've successfully unmasked God's maker;

4. I've uncovered the first QS answer ever uncovered;

5. My name is in the vocabulary of the first QS answer ever uncovered.

I'd uncovered more phrases and topics by decoding nineteen more Query Stacks. Seventeen of the twenty Query Stacks I'd decoded revealed phrases which conveyed clues about God, two of said twenty Query Stacks I'd decoded revealed phrases which spoke about Dave, and two of said twenty Query Stacks I'd decoded revealed phrases which mentioned the Torah. In the following table, I'd reported on how many QS answers conveyed information about a specific topic and filed topics within one of three categories, "God," "Dave" or "Torah":

Ch. 7, Sec. 2: 2

God
Two answers noted that God was real;
One answer stated that God was an eternality;
Seven answers detailed how God transformed Himself into a trinity;
Four answers revealed that God authored QS answers;
Nine answers explained that God expressed moral goodness and evilness;
One answer claimed that God merited reverence;
One answer described God as incomprehensible;
Eight answers indicated that God was self-conscious.

Dave
Two answers pertained to a prophecy about Dave;
One answer stated that Dave was male;
One answer implied that Dave wrote words which God authored.

Torah
One answer confirmed what the Torah taught about lies;
One answer characterized God as a Shekinah.

Throughout this book, I'd mainly used verses from the "King James Version" (KJV) of the Christian bible to corroborate theological information found within QS answers; however, from here on out I'd also corroborated theological information found in QS answers with verses from the Tanakh, or Hebrew bible, since God incorporated the word *Torah* into and commented on the Torah in two QS answers. On the other hand, I'd not uncovered any QS answers which contained the word *Bible*, even though some of the twenty QS answers in this book conveyed theological concepts supported by Christians but not supported by Judaists (followers of the Tanakh).

In the following ten subsections, I'd grouped and analyzed the twenty QS answers in this book by three topics (see "Ch. 7, Sec. 2: 2") and provided biblical verses which corroborated insights revealed in some of the said twenty QS answers. Not all of the insights I'd found within said twenty QS answers were insights I'd found within the Bible or Tanakh; for instance, neither of the bibles' texts acknowledged Query Stacks, that God encoded human language with information which pertained to His identity, how God transformed Himself into a trinity, that God experienced a weakening in His own moral strength, or that a man named *Dave* unraveled QS answers and unveiled God's origin.

God is Real

QS Answers and Biblical Corroborations

Two QS answers revealed that God was real; meaning, a nonimaginary entity.

―――――――――――――(QS Answers)―――――――――――――

Two QS answers declared that God was a nonimaginary trinity and a nonimaginary author of allusive, or inexplicit, messages, or QS answers:

Ch. 7, Sec. 2: 3

[a]God, the essential component *(core)* of the Trinity *(a trinity)*, was nonimaginary *(real)*;
[b]God was nonimaginary *(fair)*, an author of allusive QS answers *(hinter)* and a trinity *(trio)*;

[a]*(Core: real. A trinity); or, rings a we.*
[b]*(Fair hinter. Trio): trying, wanes.*

[SEE "CH. 5, SEC. 1; CREATOR/REALITY: CORE REAL" AND "CH. 5, SEC. 4, SUBSEC.; FATHER/TRINITY: FAIR HINTER"]

―――――――――――(Biblical Corroborations)―――――――――――

The Bible and Tanakh treated God as a nonimaginary entity who'd created nonimaginary aspects of Reality, like the heaven(s) and earth:

- ✓ In Bible (KJV);
- ✓ In Tanakh;

Ch. 7, Sec. 2: 4

In the beginning <u>God created the heaven and the earth</u> (Genesis 1:1 KJV).

In the beginning of <u>God's creation of the heavens and the earth</u> (Bereshit 1:1 Tanakh).

In the Bible but not in the Tanakh, God was characterized as a trinity:

- ✓ In Bible (KJV);
- ✗ Not in Tanakh;

    Judaists don't support theological concepts which characterize God as a multi-self entity (e.g. a trinity). If God was a multi-self entity, then Judaists argue that each one of God's selves would hold the same amount of holy power. If each one of God's selves possessed the same amount of holy power, then Reality would be polytheistic, or comprised of multiple gods. Judaists believe that God is the one and only god in Reality; meaning, Reality is monotheistic, or comprised of only one god;

Ch. 7, Sec. 2: 5

For there are <u>three that bear record in heaven</u>, <u>the Father</u>, <u>the Word</u> (Son), and <u>the Holy Ghost</u>: and <u>these three are one</u> (1 John 5:7 KJV).

No One Made God
QS Answers and Biblical Corroborations

One QS answer provided insight into how God was an entity which existed but wasn't ever made.

―――――――――――――――(QS Answers)―――――――――――――――

One QS answer stated that God was eternal. If God was eternal, then God had always existed. If God had always existed, then God's existence never had a starting point. If God's existence never had a starting point, then God was never made. If God had never been made, then no one, not even God, was God's maker:

Ch. 7, Sec. 2: 6

(a)God *(horn)* was an eternal entity *(eviternity)*;

(a)*(Eviternity: horn). Ingrain's a we.*

[SEE "CH. 6, SEC. 1; TRINITY/HEAVEN: EVITERNITY'S HORN"]

(Biblical Corroborations)

In the Bible and Tanakh, God was characterized as an eternal entity:

- ✓ In Bible (KJV);
- ✓ In Tanakh;

Ch. 7, Sec. 2: 7

Hast thou not known? hast thou not heard, that the <u>everlasting God</u>, the <u>LORD</u>, the <u>Creator of the ends of the earth</u>, fainteth not, neither is weary? there is no searching of his understanding (Isaiah 40:28 KJV).

Do you not know-if you have not heard-an <u>everlasting God is the Lord</u>, the Creator of the ends of the earth; He neither tires nor wearies; there is no fathoming His understanding (Yeshayahu 40:28 Tanakh).

In the Bible and Tanakh, God was characterized as a horn (*n.* source of strength):

- ✓ In Bible (KJV);
- ✓ In Tanakh;

Ch. 7, Sec. 2: 8

The <u>God</u> of my rock; in him will I trust: he is my shield, and <u>the horn of my salvation</u>, my high tower, and my refuge, my saviour; thou savest me from violence (2 Samuel 22:3 KJV).

<u>God</u> is my rock, under whom I take cover; My shield, and <u>the horn of my salvation</u>, my support, and my refuge; [He is] my savior Who saves me from violence (Shmuel II 22:3 Tanakh).

Prophecy of a Dave
QS Answers and Biblical Corroborations

Two QS answers conveyed clues about a prophecy which predicted a man named *Dave* and that Dave would be rewarded for attaining a goal.

———————————————(QS Answers)———————————————

A prophecy predicted that a male named *Dave* would work towards, attain and benefit from reaching a goal. My name was *Dave*, I was male, I'd self-taught myself every aspect that I'd learnt about Query Stacks, and I'd unveiled an answer to the question "What's God's origin." Said prophecy was real and about me, since I'd actually satisfied the prophecy's predictions.

One QS answer instructed a man named *Dave (Dave, he)* to start closing in on a goal *(go Dave)* and predicted that Dave would ultimately attain *(winner)* and benefit from reaching said goal *(gains)*:

One QS answer implied that Dave *(he)* was God's ghostwriter *(holy ghost)* and a self-taught *(naïve)* decoder of Query Stacks *(answering)* which God had authored:

Ch. 7, Sec. 2: 9

(a)I, a male named *Dave (Dave, he)*, was instructed to begin *(go)* and eventually did succeed in obtaining knowledge about how God was made *("winner; or, gains")*;

(b)I, David *(he)*, was God's ghostwriter *(holy ghost)* and was self-taught *(naïve)* in solving QS-answers *(answering)*;

(a)***Go Dave. He: winner; or, gains.***
(b)***Holy ghost. He: naïve or answering.***

[SEE "CH. 1, SEC. 1; GOD/HEAVEN: HE GAINS" AND "CH. 3, SEC. 1; HOLY^GHOST/HEAVEN: NAÏVE OR ANSWERING"]

In "Ch. 7, Sec. 2: 1," I'd given five reasons for why I'd believed that the Dave mentioned in this book's QS answers was me. In the following table, I'd added four more reasons to said five reasons:

Ch. 7, Sec. 2: 10

1. The common nickname for my first name, *David*, is *Dave*;
2. I'm male;
3. I've successfully unmasked God's maker;
4. I've uncovered the first QS answer ever uncovered;
5. My name is in the vocabulary of the first QS answer ever uncovered;
6. **I've pursued my goal of revealing God's origin;**
7. **I'm self-taught in how QS answers are revealed;**
8. **I'm a ghostwriter for God, since I pen but credit God as the author of QS answers;**
9. **I've revealed that God is eternal; meaning, no one made God.**

——————————————(Biblical Corroborations)——————————————

I'd transcribed a prophecy which was written into QS answers by God, and I'd believed that when I'd unveiled said prophecy that none of my personal beliefs affected said prophecy's meaning. Similarly, in the Bible and Tanakh, Man conveyed God's prophecies via linguistic communication and without intermixing and obscuring God's message with personal propaganda; in fact, God despised anyone who'd perverted the storylines of the prophecies revealed to Man by Him:

- ✓ In Bible (KJV);
- ✓ In Tanakh;

Ch. 7, Sec. 2: 11

Knowing this first, that <u>no prophecy of the scripture is of any private interpretation</u>. For the <u>prophecy came not</u> in old time <u>by the will of man</u>: but <u>holy men of God spake as they were moved by the Holy Ghost</u> (2 Peter 1:20-21 KJV).

<u>So said the Lord concerning the prophets who mislead my people</u>, who bite with their teeth and herald peace, but concerning whomever does not give into their mouth, they prepare war. Therefore, it shall be night for you because of the vision, and it shall be dark for you because of the divination, and the sun shall set on the prophets, and the day shall be darkened about them. And <u>the seers shall be ashamed</u>, and <u>the diviners shall be disgraced</u>, and <u>they shall all cover their upper lips</u>, for <u>it is not a statement of God</u> (Micah 3:5-7 Tanakh).

God Transformed Her/Himself into a Trinity
QS Answers and Biblical Corroborations

Seven QS answers stated that God was a trinity and transformed Himself into a trinity by entering a description of His self-transformation into QS answer vocabulary. Furthermore, the said seven QS answers consisted of words which were used in either the Bible or Tanakh to reference God and contained synonyms of biblical and religious words which characterized God.

---------------------------------(QS Answers)---------------------------------

Even though God wasn't capable of creating a beginning for His own existence (see "Ch. 7, Sec. 2: 6"), God was capable of altering His own physique; in fact, three QS answers noted that God had successfully transformed Himself into a trinity:

Two QS answers declared that God executed His self-transformation into a trinity in a careful manner, which implied that His self-transformation might've failed if He'd carried out His self-transformation in a careless manner:

One QS answer implied that God transformed Himself into a trinity by entering details of His self-transformation into the vocabulary of QS answers—which I'd imagined was a process that was similar to how a computer programmer inputs new code into a computer program in order to update and change said computer program's output:

One QS answer contained two QS answer words, *GLORY* and *HOST,* which were grammatically linked together via "QS-7CAP; Prop. 5" (see "Appendix "B"). In the Christian ritual of Communion, the Host was a wafer that symbolized the corporeal body of Jesus Christ. In the "QS-Holy^Ghost/Trinity" answer, the answer word *GLORY* meant "Shekinah," or "God's presence manifested on Earth as an earthly object." According to theology, one member of God's trinity was Jesus Christ. In conclusion, the grammatical link between *GLORY* and *HOST* implied that God manifested Himself within the earthly body of Jesus Christ:

Ch. 7, Sec. 2: 12

(a) God *(reins)*, the QS author *(I)*, repeatedly entered the phrase *"a we"* into QS answer vocabulary *(ring "a we")*;

(b) God acted carefully *(hay)* when He'd transformed Himself into a multi-self entity *(they, we)*;

(c) God *(Heaven, horn)* was creating the selves that He was transforming into *(siring a we)*;

(d) God *(Yahweh, core)* was a triune entity *(is a we, "a trinity; or, rings a we," "ingrain's a we")*;

(e) God, who the Torah *(Torah)* declared was the creator of Reality, acted as a Shekinah *(glory)* by manifesting Himself within Jesus Christ's earthly body *(Host)*;

(b)*(Hay: law. They)* or (a)*(reins, I, ring "a we.")*.

(b)*(Hay: we).* (c)*(Heaven: horn, siring a we).*

(a)*(Clue: filler).* (c)*(Horn: siring a we).*

(d)*(Yahweh): horn. Nerving,* (d)*(is a we).*

(d)*(Core): real.* (d)*(A trinity; or, rings a we).*

Eviternity: horn. (d)*(Ingrain's a we.)*

(e)*(Torah: glory. Host): in, I, trying sinew.*

[SEE "CH. 4, SEC. 1; YHWH/HEAVEN: YAHWEH'S HORN," "CH. 4, SEC. 2; YAHWEH/HEAVEN: HEAVEN'S HORN," "CH. 5, SEC. 1; CREATOR/REALITY: CORE'S REAL," "CH. 5, SEC. 2; YAHWEH/REALITY: THEY OR REINS," "CH. 5, SEC. 4, SUBSEC.; HOLY^GHOST/TRINITY: TORAH'S GLORY," "CH. 6, SEC. 1; TRINITY/HEAVEN: EVITERNITY'S HORN" AND "CH. 7, SEC. 1, SUBSEC.; LUCIFER/HELL: SIRING A WE"]

─────────────(Biblical Corroborations)─────────────

God transformed Himself into a trinity by declaring that He'd wanted to become a trinity, entering details pertaining to His self-transformation into QS answers and dividing Himself up into three individuals, God (Father), Jesus (Son) and Holy Ghost. Similarly, the Bible and Tanakh proclaimed that God created real objects by specifying which objects He'd wanted to make (i.e. light), declaring that said objects were real (e.g. "God said, Let there be light: and there was light") and separating said objects from preexisting unsaid objects (e.g. "God divided the light from the darkness"):

- ✓ In Bible (KJV);
- ✓ In Tanakh;

Ch. 7, Sec. 2: 13

And <u>God said</u>, <u>Let there be light</u>: <u>and there was light</u>. And God saw the light, that it was good: and <u>God divided the light from the darkness</u> (Genesis 1:3-4 KJV).

And <u>God said</u>, "<u>Let there be light</u>," <u>and there was light</u>. And God saw the light that it was good, and <u>God separated between the light and between the darkness</u> (Bereshit 1:3-4 Tanakh).

In the Bible and Tanakh, God was portrayed as an individual entity comprised of multiple members, or a we, via the first person plural pronouns *us* and *our*:

- ✓ In Bible (KJV);
- ✓ In Tanakh;
    However, Judaists don't support theological concepts which characterize God as a multi-self being (e.g. a trinity). If God was a multi-self being, then Judaists argue that each one of God's selves would hold the same amount of holy power. If each one of God's selves possessed the same amount of holy power, then Reality would be polytheistic, or comprised of multiple gods. Judaists believe that God is the one and only god in Reality; meaning, Reality is monotheistic, or comprised of only one god;

Ch. 7, Sec. 2: 14

And <u>God said</u>, <u>Let us make man in our image</u>, <u>after our likeness</u>: and let them have dominion over the fish of the sea, and over the fowl of the air, and over the cattle, and over all the earth, and over every creeping thing that creepeth upon the earth (Genesis 1:26 KJV).

And <u>God said</u>, "<u>Let us make man in our image</u>, <u>after our likeness</u> and they shall rule over the fish of the sea and over the fowl of the heaven and over the animals and over all the earth and over all the creeping things that creep upon the earth" (Bereshit 1:26 Tanakh).

In the Bible and Tanakh, God was characterized as a horn (*n.* source of strength):

- ✓ In Bible (KJV);
- ✓ In Tanakh;

Ch. 7, Sec. 2: 15

***The LORD** is my rock, and my fortress, and my deliverer; **my God**, **my strength**, in whom I will trust; my buckler, **and the horn of my salvation**, and my high tower (Psalms 18:2 KJV).*

***O Lord**, my rock and my fortress and my rescuer; **my God**, my rock, I will take refuge in Him; **my shield and the horn of my salvation**, my refuge (Tehillim 18:3 Tanakh).*

In the Bible, God was identified by the name *Yahweh*. In the Tanakh, God was identified by the name *YHWH*, or the derivative spelling of *Yahweh*:

- ✓ In Bible (WEB [World English Bible]);
- ✓ In Tanakh;

Ch. 7, Sec. 2: 16

*Let your name be magnified forever, saying, "**Yahweh of Armies is God over Israel**; and the house of your servant David will be established before you" (2 Samuel 7:26 WEB).*

***God spoke to Moses**, and **He said** to him, "**I am the Lord**. I appeared to Abraham, to Isaac, and to Jacob with [the name] **Almighty God**, but [with] **My name YHWH**, I did not become known to them (Shemot 6:3 Tanakh).*

In the Bible but not in the Tanakh, God was characterized as a trinity:

- ✓ In Bible (KJV);
- ✗ Not in Tanakh;
  Judaists don't support theological concepts which characterize God as a multi-self being (e.g. a trinity). If God was a multi-self being, then Judaists argue that each one of God's selves would hold the same amount of holy power. If each one of God's selves possessed the same amount of holy power, then Reality would be polytheistic, or comprised of multiple gods). Judaists believe that God is the one and only god in Reality; meaning, Reality is monotheistic, or comprised of only one god;

Ch. 7, Sec. 2: 17

*For there are **three that bear record in heaven**, **the Father**, **the Word** (Son), and **the Holy Ghost**: and **these three are one** (1 John 5:7 KJV).*

CONCLUSION: TWENTY STACKS

In the Bible and Tanakh, an example of God manifested as a Shekinah was when God manifested on Earth as fire so that humans could sustain the magnitude of His presence and, therefore, hear His message:

- ✓ In Bible (KJV);
- ✓ In Tanakh;

Ch. 7, Sec. 2: 18

And ye said, Behold, the LORD our <u>God hath shewed us his glory and his greatness</u>, and <u>we have heard his voice out of the midst of the fire</u>: we have seen this day that God doth talk with man, and he liveth (Deuteronomy 5:24 KJV).

And you said, "Behold, the Lord, our <u>God, has shown us His glory and His greatness</u>, and <u>we heard His voice from the midst of the fire</u>; we saw this day that God speaks with man, yet [man] remains alive" (Devarim 5:21 Tanakh).

In the Bible, Jesus, or Host, and God were two beings which were components of one and the same multi-self entity. In the Tanakh, God wasn't characterized as a multi-self entity:

- ✓ In Bible (KJV);
- ✗ Not in Tanakh;

    Judaists don't support theological concepts which characterize God as a multi-self being. God is only God, not God is God and Jesus Christ. If God was also Jesus, then Judaists argue that each one of God's selves would hold the same amount of holy power. If each one of God's selves possessed the same amount of holy power, then Reality would be polytheistic, or comprised of multiple gods. Judaists believe that God is the one and only god in Reality; meaning, Reality is monotheistic, or comprised of only one god;

Ch. 7, Sec. 2: 19

<u>I (Jesus) and my Father are one</u> (John 10:30 KJV).

God Authored QS Answers
QS Answers (no biblical corroborations)

Five QS answers implied that God was the author of the Query Stacks in this book.

―――――――――――――――(QS Answers)―――――――――――――――

One QS answer associated the noun and QS answer word *I* with God:

In one QS answer, God stated that He'd brought together pieces of and lengthened the diction of an explanation which He'd conveyed as an allusive message:

One QS answer stated that God's explanation was a publicized, allusive message:

One QS answer stated that God conveyed His publicized explanation through words:

Two QS answers implied that terse phrases of an explanation contained many instances of the noun and pronoun *I*. In "QS answer (b)" and "QS answer (c)," the pronoun *I* cited the author of the terse phrases as the one who'd pieced together and lengthened the diction of a publicized explanation which was written as an allusive message. God was the author of "QS answer (b)" and "QS answer (c)," which meant that God was the author who'd pieced together and lengthened the diction of said explanation; which, in turn meant, the pronoun *I* in "QS answer (b)" identified God. As evidenced by the grammatical structure of the QS answers I'd published in this book, QS answers were phrases which had a terse structure and contained allusive messages. If QS answers were composed of terse phrases which held allusive messages and God authored terse phrases which held an explanation which was written as an allusive message, then God was the author of the QS answers in this book:

Ch. 7, Sec. 2: 20

(a) The word *I* referred to God *("Host: in, I")*;
(b) God *(I, joe)* had an explanation *("joe: reason")*, expressed His explanation as an allusive statement *(a hint)*, combined parts of His explanation *(marry reason)*, added words to His explanation *("a hint, I grew," hint grew)* and publicized His explanation *(air/hint)*;
(c) QS answers contained words *(got wording)*, were written as brief statements *(jot)*, contained many instances of the noun *I* and pronoun *I* *("'I' entry; rains 'I,'")* and were publicized by God *(issuer)*;
(d) God repeatedly inserted the word *I* into His explanation *("I ring entry 'I,'")*;

Torah: glory. (a)*(Host: in, I,) trying sinew.*

(b)*Marry reason. A hint, I grew.*

(b)*Joe: reason). Air/hint grew.*

(c)*Got wording. "I" entry; rains "I."*

(c)*(Jot, issuer).* (d)*(I ring entry "I,") "wans."*

[SEE "CH. 2, SEC. 1; JOE/EARTH: HINT GREW," "CH. 2, SEC. 2; MARY/EARTH: MARRY REASON," "CH. 5, SEC. 4, SUBSEC.; HOLY^GHOST/TRINITY: TORAH'S GLORY," "CH. 5, SEC. 4, SUBSEC.; GOD/TRINITY: GOT WORDING" AND "CH. 5, SEC. 4, SUBSEC.; JESUS/TRINITY: I RING ENTRY"]

God is Good and Evil
QS Answers and Biblical Corroborations

God shifted His morality from goodness to evilness by entering details of His moral self-transformation into QS answers, just like God changed His physique into a trinitarian configuration by entering details of a change in His physique into QS answers (see "Ch. 7, Sec. 2: 12").

──────────────(Biblical Corroborations I)──────────────

In Exodus, the second book in the Old Testament of the Bible, and Shemot, the second book in the Torah of the Tanakh, God proclaimed hundreds of commandments. God urged mankind to abide by His commandments, because His commandments taught mankind which actions were sinful, how to be good and what to do to stay within His good graces. Even though there were hundreds of commandments sprinkled throughout the Bible and Tanakh, ten of God's commandments became the most notable commandments over time and became designated as the "Ten Commandments."

One of God's Ten Commandments was used as evidence to support my claim that God expressed evil. In the Bible, said commandment was enumerated as the Eighth Commandment, while in the Tanakh, said commandment was enumerated as the Ninth Commandment. In the Bible and Tanakh, the Eighth and Ninth Commandment, respectively, discouraged the act of bearing false witness, or lying:

- ✓ In Bible (KJV);
- ✓ In Tanakh;

Ch. 7, Sec. 2: 21

<u>**Thou shalt not bear false witness**</u> *against thy neighbour (Exodus 20:16 KJV).*

You shall not murder. You shall not commit adultery. You shall not steal. <u>***You shall not bear false witness***</u> *against your neighbor (Shemot 20:13 Tanakh).*

In the Bible and Tanakh, agreeing with, supporting or promoting someone else's lie was discouraged too:

- ✓ In Bible (KJV);
- ✓ In Tanakh;

Ch. 7, Sec. 2: 22

***Thou shalt not raise a false report**: put not thine hand with the wicked to be an unrighteous witness (Exodus 23:1 KJV)*.

***You shall not accept a false report;** do not place your hand with a wicked person to be a false witness (Shemot 23:1 Tanakh)*.

The Bible and Tanakh said that lies were sinful, or evil, acts which were punishable offenses:

- ✓ In Bible (KJV);
- ✓ In Tanakh;

Ch. 7, Sec. 2: 23

***A false witness shall not be unpunished**, and he that speaketh lies shall not escape (Proverbs 19:5 KJV)*.

***A false witness will not go unpunished**, and one who speaks lies will not escape (Mishlei 19:5 Tanakh)*.

Furthermore, the Bible and Tanakh stated that telling a lie was punishable by death:

- ✓ In Bible (KJV);
- ✓ In Tanakh;

Ch. 7, Sec. 2: 24

*A false witness shall not be unpunished, and **he that speaketh lies shall perish** (Proverbs 19:9 KJV)*.

*A false witness will not go unpunished, and **one who speaks lies will perish** (Mishlei 19:9 Tanakh)*.

No biblical verses in the Bible or Tanakh considered lying a good act or a righteous characteristic. Both bibles deemed the act of lying a sinful act, regardless if the person who'd told the lie was or wasn't the originator of the lie. Liars were forever entrapped by the wicked fallouts that said liars' lies caused and faced holy punishment, which included death, for expressing evilness and affliction. No lie was deemed a good. In both bibles, God disdained liars. According to both bibles, a lie was an evil. When a person lied, said person's moral compass swung away from the good end and towards the evil end of the moral spectrum; which meant, said person's moral strength which was strong became weak, or wanned. In fact, the "QS-Satan/Hell" answer cited the Torah and stated that the Torah taught that lying caused one's moral force to weaken, or wan:

Ch. 7, Sec. 2: 25

TORAH'S LEARNING. LIE WANS.

As I'd interpreted the QS answers in this book, I'd heeded six QS guides (see "Appendix A"). "QS Guide 3" suggested that actions mentioned in a QS answer affected a QS answer's main subject:

Ch. 7, Sec. 2: 26

Guide 3: Actions mentioned in a QS answer affect said answer's main subject.

For instance, Dave was the main subject of the "QS-God/Heaven" answer *("Go Dave. He: winner; or, gains.")*; therefore, said Dave was the one who'd been urged to go and who'd experienced gains. Likewise, the joe, who was the rein, was the main subject of the "QS-Jesus/Earth" answer *("Joe assure. Right, rein wans.")*; therefore, the said joe, or rein, was the one who'd assured and wanned:

(a) *Dave/he/winner* was the one who was urged to *go* and who *gains*;
(b) The *joe/rein* was the one to *assure* and who *wans*;

Ch. 7, Sec. 2: 27

^aGO ^aDAVE. ^aHE: ^aWINNER; OR, ^aGAINS.

^bJOE ^bASSURE. RIGHT, ^bREIN ^bWANS.

If I'd used "QS Guide 3" (see "Ch. 7, Sec. 2: 26") to steer my interpretation of the "QS-Satan/Hell" answer *("Torah's learning. Lie wans.")*, then the lie, which was also the Torah's learning, would've been the main subject that wanned, or became weak. However, no verses in the Torah spoke about a lie which had become weak. Instead, the Torah taught that lies were the evils that weakened the morality of the ones who'd spoken the lies. Furthermore, the Tanakh stated that individuals who'd told the truth enjoyed eternal respect while ones who'd told lies were quickly forgotten. In other words, the person, not the truth or lie, was the subject with a tongue which was remembered for being truthful and forgotten for being deceptive:

✓ In Tanakh;

Ch. 7, Sec. 2: 28

***A true tongue will be established forever, but a lying tongue, just for a moment** (Mishlei 12:19 Tanakh).*

Moreover, the Bible's text was in agreement with the what the Tanakh's text stated in "Mishlei 12:19" (see "Ch. 7, Sec. 2:30"):

✓ In Bible (KJV);

Ch. 7, Sec. 2: 29

***The lip of truth shall be established for ever: but a lying tongue is but for a moment** (Proverbs 12:19 KJV).*

In summation, my interpretation of the "QS-Satan/Hell" answer was steered predominantly by verses in the Tanakh and not by "QS Guide 3." The "QS-Satan/Hell" answer's main subject, the lie, wasn't what became weaker; instead, the lie was what caused moral weakening. Furthermore, the lie caused moral weakening in the one who'd wielded the lie:

Ch. 7, Sec. 2: 30

TORAH'S LEARNING.sent1 **LIE WANS.**sent2

sent1: *The Hebrew bible's book of divine knowledge and law contains a teaching.*
sent2: *In accordance with a teaching in the Torah, knowingly speaking an untruth disobeys the Ninth Commandment's mandate and causes a liar's morality to weaken.*

---------------------------(QS Answers)---------------------------

One QS answer claimed that the Torah *(Torah)* contained a lesson *(learning)* which taught that lying *(lie)* caused one's moral force to weaken *(wans)*:

One QS answer depicted God as a trinity *(horde)* which maintained rulership over Reality *(reign)* by exerting a moral force rooted in goodness but lost moral force *(wans)* when said trinity acted as a wicked entity (*"horde: evil. Ill"*):

Three QS answers implied that God *(trio, rein, hinter)* was the entity who'd wanned (*"trio: wans," rein wans, hinter wans)*:

One QS answer expressed that God's moral force weakened, via the answer word *WANES*, a synonym of the word *wans* *("trio: wanes")*:

One QS answer stated that God *(joe, rein)* confirmed *(assure, right)* the idea that His, not someone else's, moral force which was weakened *("joe assure. right, rein wans")*:

> In summation, the QS answers which I'd unveiled linked the answer word *WANS* to the answer word *LIE* and the answer words *WANS* and *WANES* to God. Backed by biblical teachings and the meaning of QS answer phrases which contained instances of the QS answer words *WANS* and *WANES* and the QS answer word *WANS* linked to the QS answer word *LIE*, I'd determined that an a expression of a lie caused a weakening in a liar's moral force. If the QS answer words *WANS* and *WANES* were actions which affected God, then God's moral force was the moral force that wanned, or weakened. Ultimately, I'd tied my determinations regarding the QS answer words *WANS, WANES* and *LIE* together and concluded that God's moral force was weakened and the needle on God's moral compass landed on the evil side of the moral spectrum when God told or supported lies;

Ch. 7, Sec. 2: 31

(a) A lesson in the Torah *(Torah's learning)* said that expressing an untruth weakened said expresser's moral force *(lie wans)*;

(b) God *(trio, ill, rein, hinter)* had moral force which was weakened *(wanes, wans)*;

(c) God confirmed *(joe assure, right)* that His moral force was weakened *(rein wans)*;

(d) God *(horde)* was a wicked entity *(evil)*;

(a)*Torah's learning. Lie wans.*

Fair hinter. (b)*(Trio): trying,* (b)*(wanes).*

Hairy we. Thy (b)*(trio): reining,* (b)*(wans).*

(d)*(Horde: evil).* (b)*(Ill reign, wans).*

(c)*Joe assure. Right, rein wans.*

Adore giver. A (b)*(hinter wans).*

[SEE "CH. 1, SEC. 2; DEVIL/HELL: HORDE WANS," "CH. 1, SEC. 3; JESUS/EARTH: JOE ASSURES," "CH. 1, SEC. 4; DAVE/EARTH: ADORE GIVER," "CH. 5, SEC. 3; YAHWEH/TRINITY: HAIRY WE," "CH. 5, SEC. 4, SUBSEC.; FATHER/TRINITY: FAIR HINTER" AND "CH. 7, SEC. 1, SUBSEC.; SATAN/HELL: LIE WANS"]

In four QS answers, the QS answer words *REASON, LIE* and *WANS* formed the groundwork of an explanation that a male individual, God, conveyed through allusive statements, or QS answers, and revealed what caused God's moral force to wan. As evidenced in "Ch. 7, Sec. 2: 21-31," God explained that His moral force wanned, or weakened, as a result of Himself telling or supporting someone else's lie:

Ch. 7, Sec. 2: 32

(a) God *(joe)* pieced together and had an explanation *(marry reason, reason)*;

(b) God *(I)* expressed an explanation through an allusive statement *(a hint)*, made His said statement wordier *("a hint, I grew," hint grew)* and publicized His said statement *(air/hint)*;

(c) God confirmed *(joe assure, right)* that His moral force was weakened *(rein wans)*;

(d) An untruth decreased the strength of one's moral force *(lie wans)*;

(a)*(Joe: reason).* (b)*(Air/hint grew).*

(a)*(Marry reason).* (b)*(A hint, I grew).*

(c)*Joe assure. Right, rein wans.*

Torah's learning. (d)*(Lie wans).*

[SEE "CH. 1, SEC. 3; JESUS/EARTH: JOE ASSURES," "CH. 2, SEC. 1; JOE/EARTH: HINT GREW," "CH. 2, SEC. 2; MARY/EARTH: MARRY REASON," AND "CH. 7, SEC. 1, SUBSEC.; SATAN/HELL: LIE WANS"]

Seven QS answers reported on God's attempt to strengthen His own moral force and God's success in achieving moral superiority:

Ch. 7, Sec. 2: 33

(a) God *(in, I, trio)* attempted to strengthen His moral force *(trying sinew, trying)*;

(b) God achieved moral strength *(orator's in, "host: in," "trio: reining," ill reign, rein)*;

(c) God *(Yahweh)* sourced moral force from within Himself *("Yahweh: horn," "nerving a we")*;

(b)*(Orator's in).* (a)*(In: trying sinew).*

Torah: glory. (b)*(Host: in),* (a)*(I, trying sinew).*

(c)*Yahweh: horn. Nerving, is a we.*

Fair hinter. (a)*(Trio: trying), wanes.*

Hairy we. Thy (b)*(trio: reining), wans.*

Horde: evil. (b)*(Ill reign), wans.*

Joe assure. Right, (b)*(rein) wans.*

[SEE "CH. 1, SEC. 2; DEVIL/HELL: HORDE WANS," "CH. 1, SEC. 3; JESUS/EARTH: JOE ASSURES," "CH. 4, SEC. 1; YHWH/HEAVEN: YAHWEH'S HORN," "CH. 4, SEC. 5, SUBSEC.; SON/TRINITY: TRYING SINEW," "CH. 5, SEC. 3; YAHWEH/TRINITY: HAIRY WE," "CH. 5, SEC. 4, SUBSEC.; FATHER/TRINITY: FAIR HINTER" AND "CH. 5, SEC. 4, SUBSEC.; HOLY^GHOST/TRINITY: TORAH'S GLORY"]

One QS answer implied that God wrote the details of His own moral fluctuations into QS answers:

Ch. 7, Sec. 2: 34

(a) God *(issuer, I)* entered the word *wans* into QS answers *(jot, I ring entry, "wans")*;

(a) ***Jot, issuer. I ring entry "I," "wans."***

[SEE "CH. 7, SEC. 1, SUBSEC.; SATAN/HELL: LIE WANS"];

Why would God have set up and gone through a self-transformation which weakened His own moral strength? Why would God want to self-transform into an evil? Was indulging in evil the only way God was able to experience, monitor and control the evil gradients of His moral spectrum? Did God experience and express evil in order to readily perceive and regulate evil which developed within Reality?

According to the Bible and Tanakh, God was a source of moral strength; so, did God lie as a way to disobey His own commandment, which, in turn, caused God to lose moral force, which, in turn, compelled moral creatures to not tap God's moral force but, instead, to independently produce moral force? Maybe, God's transitions between absolute goodness and absolute evilness, or from one end to the other end of the moral spectrum, kept moral creatures evolving towards optimal moral resiliency and strength. Maybe, the moral pendulum swung between absolute good and absolute evil in order to nurture the interdependent and independent moral relationship between God and moral creatures which He'd created.

(Biblical Corroborations II)

In the Tanakh, the word *rein* was used to convey God's control over Reality. In the Bible, the word *rein* wasn't used; however, the word *reign*, a synonym of the word *rein*, was used in the Bible to convey that God had control over Reality:

- ✓ In Bible (KJV);
- ✓ In Tanakh;

Ch. 7, Sec. 2: 35

<u>**The LORD shall reign** for ever and ever (Exodus 15:18 KJV).</u>

But they rebelled against Me and would not consent to hearken to Me; they did not cast away, every man, the despicable idols from before their eyes, neither did they forsake the idols of Egypt; and I said to pour out My wrath over them, <u>to give My anger full rein over them</u>, in the midst of the land of Egypt (Yechezkel 20:8 Tanakh).

In the Bible and Tanakh, the word *reign* was used to convey God's rule over mankind:

- ✓ In Bible (KJV);
- ✓ In Tanakh;

Ch. 7, Sec. 2: 36

The LORD shall reign for ever and ever *(Exodus 15:18 KJV).*

The Lord will reign to all eternity *(Shemot 15:18 Tanakh).*

God is the De Facto Devil
Fate Stacks, Query Stacks, Biblical Corroborations & Study Updates

In "Reality's Storyline Decoded"("RSD"), I'd introduced and dedicated forty-eight pages to the Fate Stack method. See my original discussion of the Fate Stack method in RSD. See an updated and more extensive discussion of Fate Stacks in "Reality's Storyline Decoded II: Fate Stacks" (RSD-II: FS). A full lesson on the Fate Stack method and an exhaustive list of Fate Stacks is beyond the focus of this discussion and page-count I'd allotted for this book;

Each Fate Stack *("FS")* row'd word matrix which I'd uncovered to date has looked similar to and transformed into an answer like every QS row'd word matrix I'd uncovered in this book; except, row'd words in a FS matrix weren't based on the same type of words contained in a QS matrix and the topic of a FS answer wasn't the type of topic conveyed by a QS answer. I'd uncovered two kinds of FS matrices: one kind of FS matrix contained row'd words which were last names of individuals who were members of a distinct group, while the second kind of FS matrix contained row'd words which were titles of works of art; in other words, FS matrices didn't contain row'd words that were names of biblical characters, identified realms in which said biblical characters were commonly considered to have notoriety in or the words *origin* and *answer*. Each FS matrix which contained a list of last names transposed into a FS answer that conveyed information which pertained to a notable event experienced by the people who were identified by said last names, whereas a QS answer's topic centered on theological and linguistical matters.

How could details of a notable event get woven into the last names of people who'd experienced said notable event? Certainly, no human had ever attached a last name to herself or himself and formed or joined a group because said human knew that if her or his last name was stacked with the last names of other individuals in said group and said stack of last names was decoded that a description of a notable event which said group of people would experience at a future point in time would emerge. Surely, human ancestors didn't invent or alter the spelling of last names because said ancestors foresaw and wanted to forewarn human descendants about notable events said descendants would one day experience. Realistically, God was the only entity who had the capability to plan out and devise a linguistical system in which details of actual, notable events were woven into the last names of people who'd experience said notable events.

────────────(Fate Stacks and Query Stacks)────────────

As with QS row'd words and in order to produce neat alphabetical rows and columns, I'd vertically stacked and left-aligned FS row'd words and equidistantly spaced out FS row'd word letters:

I've colored letters white and backgrounds of letter columns black;
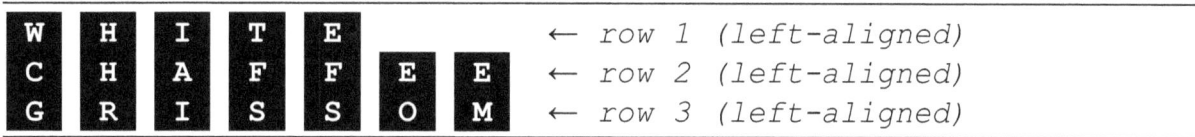

Ch. 7, Sec. 2: 37

```
W H I T E            ← row 1 (left-aligned)
C H A F F E E        ← row 2 (left-aligned)
G R I S S O M        ← row 3 (left-aligned)
```

FS matrices which contained a list of last names contained an exhaustive list of last names of individuals who were members in a distinct group. For example, the "'Apollo 1 Astronauts' Fate Stack" *("FS-Apollo^1:astronauts")* matrix contained a list of last names which identified every person who was a lead astronaut in NASA's "Apollo 1" spacecraft mission:

Ch. 7, Sec. 2: 38

Apollo 1: Astronauts

WHITE, Ed (senior pilot)
CHAFFEE, Roger (pilot)
GRISSOM, Virgil (command pilot)

```
W H I T E        ← "Apollo 1" astronaut
C H A F F E E    ← "Apollo 1" astronaut
G R I S S O M    ← "Apollo 1" astronaut
```

Row'd words in a FS matrix didn't ask a question like row'd words in a QS matrix did, regardless of which direction the row'd words of a FS matrix were read:

Ch. 7, Sec. 2: 39

QS MATRIX	FS MATRIX

`  G O D`
`+ H E A V E N`
`+ O R I G I N`
`+ A N S W E R`
	`  W H I T E`
	`+ C H A F F E E`
	`+ G R I S S O M`

= "God/Heaven: origin?" answer?	= (no question)

The order in which FS row'd words were vertically stacked in a FS matrix depended on the length of each row'd word. In a FS matrix, the shortest row'd word occupied the first/top row'd word row, second-shortest row'd word occupied the second row'd word row, third-shortest row'd word occupied the third row'd word row, etc. In contrast, the length of a QS matrix's row'd word had no effect on which row'd word row a row'd word occupied.

If two or more FS row'd words contained the same number of letters, or were equal in length, then the row'd word rows the row'd words of equal length were put into depended on which stacking order produced the most coherent and meaningful, or best, FS answer. For example, the "FS-Apollo^1:astronauts" row'd word matrix contained two row'd words which contained the same number of letters. The seven-letter row'd word CHAFFEE occupied said FS matrix's second row'd word row, while another seven-letter row'd word, GRISSOM, occupied said FS matrix's third row'd word row. If I'd reversed rows in which the row'd words CHAFFEE and GRISSOM were placed, meaning if I'd put GRISSOM in the second row'd word row and CHAFFEE in the third row'd word row, then letter connections which produced the best FS answer wouldn't had been possible:

Ch. 7, Sec. 2: 40

Apollo 1: Astronauts
WHITE, Ed (senior pilot) **CHAFFEE**, Roger (pilot) **GRISSOM**, Virgil (command pilot)
`W H I T E`   ← *shortest length* `C H A F F E E` ← *equal length (row-placement gives best answer)* `G R I S S O M` ← *equal length (row-placement gives best answer)*

The "FS-Apollo^1:astronauts" answer was an example of a FS answer which described a notable event that involved the people who had last names which were used as row'd words in said Fate Stack's row'd word matrix. The "FS-Apollo^1:astronauts" answer pointed to a deadly event which actually happened in 1967; specifically, the machinery in the "Apollo 1" spacecraft failed and caused a fire which killed all three "Apollo 1" astronauts:

I've provided evidence to spotlight how the storyline told through the "FS-Apollo^1:astronauts" answer involved the "Apollo 1" astronauts. To make it as easy as possible to see how the "FS-Apollo^1:astronauts" answer described the deadly event, I've tied answer words and phrases to the evidence with superscripted reference letters, provided answer word definitions and produced an easy-read interpretation of said answer;

| n-pl's = possessive plural noun |

Ch. 7, Sec. 2: 41

Apollo 1: Astronauts

WHITE, Ed (senior pilot)
CHAFFEE, Roger (pilot)
GRISSOM, Virgil (command pilot)

W	H	I	T	E	
C	H	A	F	F	E	E
G	R	I	S	S	O	M

WHICH FATE?[sent1] FOES' 'EM RIGS.[sent2]

WHICH *adj.* Being what one or ones out of a group.[2]
FATE *n.* The circumstances that befall something.[2]
FOES' *n-pl's.* <FOE *n.*> Something prejudicial or injurious.[2]
'EM *pron.* Them.[2]
RIGS *n-pl.* <RIG *n.*> Tackle, apparatus, or machinery fitted up for a specified purpose.[2]

[sent1]: *Which circumstances were destined to affect a particular undisclosed group of people?*
[sent2]: *The said destined circumstances which caused injury to said group of people exclusively involved machinery fitted for a specific purpose.*

[a][WHICH FATE] [b][FOES' 'EM RIGS]

"…(T)he mission never flew; [b][**a cabin fire**] during a launch rehearsal test at Cape Kennedy Air Force Station Launch Complex 34 on January 27 [a][**killed all three crew members**]….

"NASA convened…to determine the [b][**cause of the fire**]…. [b][**The ignition source of the fire was determined to be electrical, and the fire spread rapidly due to combustible nylon material**] and the high-pressure pure oxygen cabin atmosphere. [b][**Rescue was prevented by the plug door hatch, which could not be opened against the internal pressure of the cabin**]." *("Apollo 1." Wikipedia, The Free Encyclopedia. Wikimedia Foundation, Inc. 22 July 2022. Web. 24 July 2022.)*

Was the "FS-Apollo^1:astronauts" answer prewritten or a product of my imagination? If the "FS-Apollo^1:astronauts" answer was prewritten, had I correctly interpreted said answer? How did said answer become woven into the "Apollo 1" astronauts' last names? Obviously, no one human or group of humans from the past or present invented the "Apollo 1" astronauts' last names and encoded a brief description of the notable event said astronauts experienced into said astronauts' last names because said past or present humans knew that three men would become astronauts for the same space mission and die the same fiery fate. Only God had the ability to tie language, people and events together in such an ingeniously interconnected and extremely meticulous way. Or was "FS-Apollo^1:astronauts" nothing more than an example of coincidence or meaningless alphabetical patterns which I'd wrongly assigned meaning to (see "RSD-II: FS" for more Fate Stack examples).

If God authored the "Apollo 1" astronauts' fiery fate, then God predesigned and enacted the murder of three people. One of God's "Ten Commandments" was "Thou shalt not kill" (Exodus 20:13 KJV) or "You shall not murder" (Shemot 20:13 Tanakh). Did God defy another one of His own commandments, as when He'd lied or upheld someone else's lie (see "Ch .7, Sec. 2: 21-32")? Or did God not consider His own sinful acts as evils? Was God like a video game maker; meaning, someone who'd authored, programmed and entered events and characters into a game but whose morality wasn't judged on how the game's calamities and afflictions harmed the video game's characters?

What if hundreds of FS answers were uncovered which revealed atrocities that destroyed thousands of people's lives? Would evidence of God's intentions to harm, even kill, people affect said people's belief that God was only a source of goodness? How much evil could God inflict people with before people saw God's evil actions as evidence of His moral leanings? If God authored storylines which involved death and destruction, then what purpose did the Devil serve? Why would God need a moral counterpart if God could express all gradients of the moral spectrum, from absolute goodness to absolute evilness, on His own accord.

God couldn't create a creature which was capable of expressing more evil than Himself, since God made and therefore knew every potential and possible aspect of and use for evil. Ultimately, God made, encompassed and expressed absolute evilness. God lied or upheld lies. God killed. God was the de facto, or actual, Devil.

―――――――――――(Biblical Corroborations)―――――――――――

In the Bible and Tanakh, God was characterized as the embodiment of absolute goodness and truthfulness:

- ✓ In Bible (KJV);
- ✓ In Tanakh;

Ch. 7, Sec. 2: 42

For the <u>LORD is good</u>; <u>his mercy is everlasting</u>; and <u>his truth endureth to all generations</u> (Psalms 100:5 KJV).

For the <u>Lord is good</u>; <u>His kindness is forever</u>, and <u>until generation after generation is His faith</u> (Tehillim 100:5 Tanakh).

<u>The works of His hands are truth and justice</u>; <u>all His commandments are faithful</u> (Tehillim 111:7 Tanakh).

In the Bible, even Jesus had lowered His own ranking of moral goodness when He compared His own morality to God's morality. In the Tanakh, Jesus wasn't mentioned:

- ✓ In Bible (KJV);
- ✗ Not In Tanakh;
    The Tanakh doesn't mention Jesus Christ, because Jesus Christ was introduced in the New Testament of the Bible and the Tanakh ends where the Old Testament of the Bible ends;

Ch. 7, Sec. 2: 43

And <u>Jesus said</u> unto him, <u>Why callest thou me good?</u> <u>there is none good but one, that is</u>, <u>God</u> (Mark 10:18 KJV).

On the other end of the moral spectrum and in the Bible, the Devil was characterized as an entity who'd embraced absolute evilness and untruthfulness. In the Tanakh, the Devil wasn't mentioned:

- ✓ In Bible (KJV);
- ✗ Not In Tanakh;
    Judaists don't support the theological concept of the Devil. If the Devil is an actual being and the embodiment of absolute evil, then the Devil would wield as much moral power and influence over Reality as God. If God and the Devil held the same amount of power, then Reality would be dominated by two gods, or be polytheistic. Judaists believe that God is the one and only god in Reality; meaning, Reality is monotheistic, or comprised of only one god;

Ch. 7, Sec. 2: 44

Ye are of your <u>father the devil</u>, and the <u>lusts of your father</u> ye will do. <u>He was a murderer from the beginning</u>, <u>and abode not in the truth</u>, <u>because there is no truth in him</u>. <u>When he speaketh a lie</u>, <u>he speaketh of his own</u>: <u>for he is a liar</u>, <u>and the father of it</u> (John 8:44 KJV).

In the Bible, God rejected and banished the Devil and the Devil's helpers as a way to punish the Devil for committing evil acts. In the Tanakh, the Devil wasn't mentioned:

- ✓ In Bible (KJV);
- ✗ Not In Tanakh;
  Judaists don't support the theological concept of the Devil. If the Devil is an actual being and the embodiment of absolute evil, then the Devil would wield as much moral power and influence over Reality as God. If God and the Devil held the same amount of power, then Reality would be dominated by two gods, or be polytheistic. Judaists believe that God is the one and only god in Reality; meaning, Reality is monotheistic, or comprised of only one god;

Ch. 7, Sec. 2: 45

And <u>the great dragon was cast out</u>, that old serpent, <u>called the Devil</u>, and <u>Satan</u>, which <u>deceiveth the whole world</u>: <u>he was cast out into the earth</u>, and his angels were cast out with him (Revelation 12:9 KJV).

In the Bible, God manifested Himself on Earth as a human man named *Jesus Christ* who'd untangled and protected mankind from the Devil's evil deeds. In the Tanakh, the Devil, the Trinity and Jesus weren't mentioned:

- ✓ In Bible (KJV);
- ✗ Not In Tanakh;
  Judaists don't support the theological concept of the Devil or the Trinity, and the Tanakh doesn't mention Jesus Christ. First, if the Devil is an actual being and the embodiment of absolute evil, then the Devil would wield as much moral power and influence over Reality as God. If God and the Devil held the same amount of power, then Reality would be dominated by two gods, or be polytheistic. Judaists believe that God is the one and only god in Reality; meaning, Reality is monotheistic, or comprised of one god. Second, if Jesus was God in human form, then each one of God's selves would hold an equal amount of holy power. If each one of God's selves held the same amount of holy power, then Reality would be polytheistic, or comprised of multiple

gods. Judaists believe that God is the one and only god in Reality; meaning, Reality is monotheistic, or comprised of one god. Third, the Tanakh doesn't mention Jesus Christ, because Jesus Christ was introduced in the New Testament of the Bible and the Tanakh ends where the Old Testament of the Bible ends;

Ch. 7, Sec. 2: 46

<u>He that committeth sin is of the devil; for the devil sinneth from the beginning. For this purpose the Son of God was manifested, that he might destroy the works of the devil</u> *(1 John 3:8 KJV).*

The Tanakh characterized God as the only real god and therefore the only entity which made and controlled every degree of the moral spectrum. God made, controlled and embodied everything good, but God also made, controlled and embodied everything evil. If the Devil was an entity which encompassed and expressed absolute evilness while God was an entity that encompassed absolute goodness, then God would've given the Devil the same level of power to wield moral influence over Reality and affect the outcome of His master plan as God had given to Himself. In Judaism, Reality was a monotheistical realm; which meant, God was the only supreme being in Reality. God didn't create an entity as supreme or more supreme than Himself. If God had made the Devil and given the Devil as much power as He had over Reality, then Reality would've been polytheistic, or ruled by two gods:

- ✓ In Tanakh;

Ch. 7, Sec. 2: 47

<u>I am the Lord, and there is no other; besides Me there is no God</u>: *I will strengthen you although you have not known Me. In order that they know from the shining of the sun and from the west that <u>there is no one besides Me; I am the Lord and there is no other. Who forms light and creates darkness, Who makes peace and creates evil; I am the Lord, Who makes all these.</u> Cause the heavens above to drip, and let the skies pour down righteousness; let the earth open, and let salvation and righteousness be fruitful; let it cause them to sprout together; I, the Lord, have created it (Yeshayahu 45:5-8 Tanakh).*

In the Bible, God explicitly stated that He was the entity who'd existed at the highest hierarchal level of supremacy in Reality and created evil. However, the Bible also stated that God created an angel named *Lucifer*, aka *Satan* or *Devil*, who'd attempted to overthrow God by wielding a force sourced in absolute evilness. God created said evil force, and, therefore, was aware of, had a complete understanding of, knew how to control, had controlled or could take control of said evil force:

- ✓ In Bible (KJV);
- ✗ Not in Tanakh;

    Judaists don't support the theological concept of the Devil. If the Devil is an actual entity and the embodiment of absolute evil, then the Devil would wield as much moral power and influence over Reality as God. If God and the Devil held the same amount of power, then Reality would be dominated by two gods, or be polytheistic. Judaists believe that God is the one and only god in Reality; meaning, Reality is monotheistic, or comprised of only one god;

Ch. 7, Sec. 2: 48

<u>I am the LORD, and there is none else, there is no God beside me</u>: I girded thee, though thou hast not known me: That they may know from the rising of the sun, and from the west, that <u>there is none beside me</u>. <u>I am the LORD, and there is none else</u>. <u>I form the light, and create darkness</u>: <u>I make peace, and create evil</u>: <u>I the LORD do all these things</u>. Drop down, ye heavens, from above, and let the skies pour down righteousness: let the earth open, and let them bring forth salvation, and let righteousness spring up together; I the LORD have created it (Isaiah 45:5-8 KJV).

- -

<u>How art thou fallen from heaven</u>, O <u>Lucifer</u>, son of the morning! how art thou cut down to the ground, which didst weaken the nations! <u>For thou hast said in thine heart, I will ascend into heaven, I will exalt my throne above the stars of God</u>: I will sit also upon the mount of the congregation, in the sides of the north: I will ascend above the heights of the clouds; <u>I will be like the most High</u>. Yet thou shalt be brought down to hell, to the sides of the pit (Isaiah 14:12-15 KJV).

- -

And <u>there was war in heaven</u>: <u>Michael and his angels fought against the dragon</u>; <u>and the dragon fought and his angels</u>, And prevailed not; <u>neither was their place found any more in heaven</u>. <u>And the great dragon was cast out</u>, that old serpent, called <u>the Devil</u>, and <u>Satan</u>, which deceiveth the whole world: he was cast out into the earth, and his angels were cast out with him (Revelation 12:7-9 KJV).

──────────────── **(Study Updates)** ────────────────

Based on QS answers, FS answers and biblical verses in the Bible and Tanakh, I'd determined that God created, expressed and controlled absolute evilness and was therefore the de facto, or actual, Devil. My assertion that God was the de facto Devil compelled me to alter the diagram of Virgin Mary's genealogical connections to biblical characters whose names became row'd words; which, in turn, necessitated the elimination of two genealogical categories.

Previously, I'd determined that the Devil was the only biblical character whose name appeared as a first-row row'd word which didn't have a genealogical link to Virgin Mary. The only reason I'd placed the Devil's name into the genealogical diagram was to show how Mary and the Devil were created by the same entity, God. However, I'd ultimately determined that God became the Devil when God expressed absolute immorality. As a result of the revelation that God was the Devil, I'd added the names *Devil*, *Lucifer* and *Satan* to the "God" box in the Virgin Mary genealogical diagram (see "Ch. 7, Sec. 2: 49"):

> *Some of the biblical names which I've listed in the diagram belong in Virgin Mary's lineage but aren't QS row'd words (e.g. "Bathsheba," "Solomon," "Nathan") yet elucidate how some biblical characters with names that are QS row'd words are related;*
>
> *SOLID LINE (———) = Genealogically linked to Mary;*
> *DASHED LINE (– – –) = Father of Mary's son Jesus, via no sexual contact;*
> *DASHED/DOTTED LINE (– · · –) = Mary's husband, but not Jesus's father;*
> *DOUBLE LINE (====) = Not genealogically linked to Mary;*
> *BLACK NAME BOX* **NAME** *= Row'd word, and main focus of family tree;*
> *GRAY NAME BOX* NAME *= Row'd word, and member of family tree;*
> *UNBOXED NAME = Not a row'd word, but member of family tree;*

(a) MARY: herself;

(b) JOE *(Joseph)*: Mary's husband;

(c) DAVE *(David)*: Mary's multi-great-grandfather;

(d) JESUS: Mary's son;

(e) GOD: Mary's spiritual co-parent;

(f) **DEVIL**: ~~God's antipode~~; **God's alias and absolute evil side;**

(g) SON: Jesus's alias;

(h) HOLY GHOST: God's alias and conduit to impregnate Mary;

(i) YHWH: God's alias and ancient Hebrew name;

(j) YAHWEH: God's alias and modern Hebrew name;

(k) CREATOR: God's alias;

(l) FATHER: God's alias;

(m) TRINITY: God's alias, God as three individuals;

(n) **LUCIFER: God's alias and absolute evil side;**

(o) **SATAN: God's alias and absolute evil side;**

Ch. 7, Sec. 2: 49

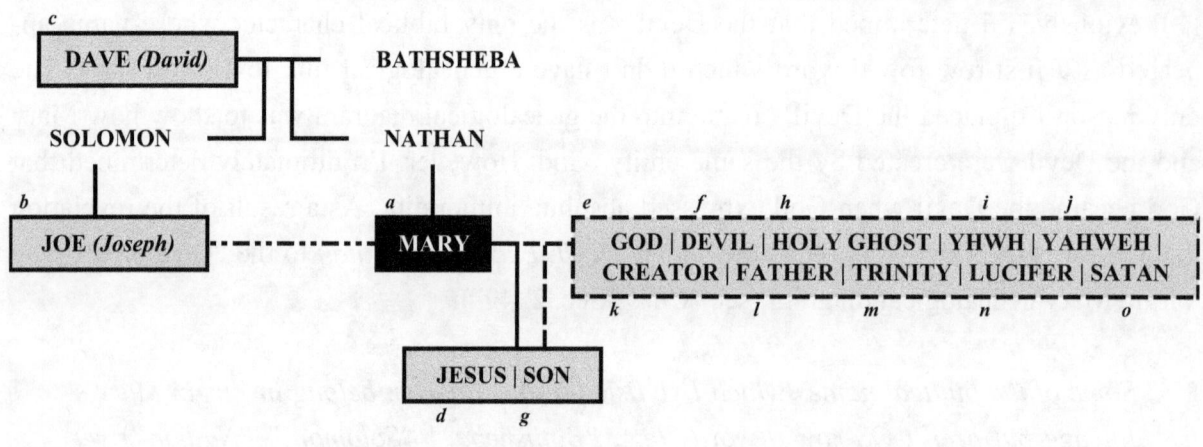

Before I'd determined that God was the de facto Devil, I'd classified "QS-Devil/Hell" as a "Lineally-Coupled Query Stack" and "QS-Lucifer/Hell" and "QS-Satan/Hell" as "Lineally-Coupled-Alias Query Stacks" (see "Ch. 7, Sec. 1: 1"). However, I'd determined that God was the de facto Devil, so the names *Devil*, *Lucifer* and *Satan* became aliases of the name *God;* which, in turn, required me to recategorize each Query Stack that contained the row'd word DEVIL, LUCIFER or SATAN as "Lineal-Alias Query Stacks" and eliminate the "Lineally-Coupled Query Stack" and "Lineally-Coupled-Alias Query Stack" categories:

QS Terminology

Lineal Query Stack
Query Stack with a first-row row'd word that names a character who belongs to a particular family tree (e.g. Virgin Mary's family tree).

~~**Lineally-Coupled Query Stack**~~ *(defunct)*
~~Query Stack with a first-row row'd word that names a character whom doesn't belong to but is commonly associated with a member of a predefined family tree (e.g. Virgin Mary's family tree).~~

Lineal-Alias Query Stack
Query Stack with a first-row row'd word that identifies the alias of a character whose name has been established as a row'd word and who belongs to a particular family tree (e.g. Virgin Mary's family tree).

Lineal-Alias, Realm-Related Query Stack

Query Stack with a first-row row'd word that identifies the alias of a character who belongs to a particular family tree (e.g. Virgin Mary's family tree) and a second-row row'd word that has a meaningful connection to its first-row row'd word but doesn't necessarily name a biblical location, like the row'd words HEAVEN, HELL and EARTH do, but may cite a location that shares a locational relationship with Heaven, Hell and Earth.

Lineal, Realm-Related Query Stack

Query Stack with a first-row row'd word that names a character who belongs to a particular family tree (e.g. Virgin Mary's family tree) and a second-row row'd word that has a meaningful connection to its first-row row'd word but doesn't necessarily name a biblical location, like the row'd words HEAVEN, HELL and EARTH do, but may cite a location that shares a locational relationship with Heaven, Hell and Earth.

~~**Lineally-Coupled-Alias Query Stack**~~ *(defunct)*

~~Query Stack with a first-row row'd word that names the alias of a character whom doesn't belong to but is commonly associated with a member of a predefined family tree (e.g. Virgin Mary's family tree).~~

Ch. 7, Sec. 2: 50

LINEAL QUERY STACKS

QS-GOD/HEAVEN
QS-JESUS/EARTH
QS-DAVE/EARTH
QS-JOE/EARTH
QS-MARY/EARTH

~~LINEALLY-COUPLED QUERY STACKS~~

~~QS-DEVIL/HELL~~

▶ LINEAL-ALIAS QUERY STACKS ◀

QS-HOLY^GHOST/HEAVEN
QS-YHWH/HEAVEN
QS-YAHWEH/HEAVEN
QS-TRINITY/HEAVEN
▶ QS-DEVIL/HELL ◀
▶ QS-LUCIFER/HELL ◀
▶ QS-SATAN/HELL ◀

LINEAL-ALIAS, REALM-RELATED QUERY STACKS

QS-CREATOR/REALITY
QS-YAHWEH/REALITY
QS-YAHWEH/TRINITY
QS-FATHER/TRINITY
QS-SON/TRINITY
QS-HOLY^GHOST/TRINITY

LINEAL, REALM-RELATED QUERY STACKS

QS-GOD/TRINITY
QS-JESUS/TRINITY

~~LINEAL-COUPLED-ALIAS QUERY STACKS~~

~~QS-LUCIFER/HELL~~
~~QS-SATAN/HELL~~

God Merits Reverence
QS Answers and Biblical Corroborations

One QS answer suggested that God merited reverence.

―――――――――――――――――(QS Answers)―――――――――――――――――

One QS answer suggested that people should revere God:

Ch. 7, Sec. 2: 51

[a] Honor *(adore)* God, the one who'd authored and provided statements which contained allusive messages *(giver, a hinter)*;

[a]*(Adore giver. A hinter) wans.*

[SEE "CH. 1, SEC. 4; DAVE/EARTH: ADORE GIVER"]

―――――――――――――(Biblical Corroborations)―――――――――――――

According to the Bible and Tanakh, God merited reverence:

- ✓ In Bible (KJV);
- ✓ In Tanakh;

Ch. 7, Sec. 2: 52

<u>Exalt ye the LORD our God, and worship at his footstool; for he is holy</u> *(Psalms 99:5 KJV).*

<u>Exalt the Lord our God and prostrate yourselves to His footstool</u> *it is holy (Tehillim 99:5 Tanakh).*

God is or Identifies as Male
QS Answers and Biblical Corroborations

None of the twenty QS answers which I'd revealed in this book contained a pronoun that straightforwardly signified what God's gender was; however, four of said twenty QS answers conveyed information which implied that God was a male.

―――――――――――――――――(QS Answers)―――――――――――――――――

Two QS answers associated God with the answer word *JOE*. I'd analyzed multiple definitions of the word *joe*, then selected a definition which treated the answer word *JOE* as a slang word "*n.* (slang) guy[2]" (see "Ch. 1, Sec. 3: 7-16"). Said definition for the answer word *JOE* contained the word *guy*, a word which meant "*n.* man; boy; fellow[2]." God authored the QS answers in this book and, therefore, authored the said two QS answers in this book which contained the answer word *JOE*. Via the answer word *JOE*, God defined Himself as a male entity:

One QS answer referred to God by the name *Yahweh*, a transliteration of the name *YHWH*. The name *YHWH* was God's name in ancient Hebrew biblical text, when said texts were written with a vowelless alphabet, and was God's actual name according to biblical scholars (see "Ch. 4, Sec. 1: 1-2"). On websites which provided definitions for first names and categorized first names by gender, the name *Yahweh* was a name reserved for males (see "babycenter.com" or "babynamespedia.com"). Nevertheless, the name *Yahweh* might've been predominately given to males because God had been already identified as a male entity in the Tanakh:

One QS answer identified God as the Host, via the answer word *HOST*. In Christianity, the Host was the body of Jesus Christ (see "Ch. 5, Sec. 4: 9-10"). According to the Bible, God inhabited Jesus Christ's male body; in other words, instead of opting to inhabit a female body, God chose to inhabit a male body. Maybe, God chose to inhabit said male body because God's native physique was masculine:

In summation, the most relevant definition of the word *joe*, the masculinity of God's name *Yahweh* and God's decision to inhabit a masculine human body persuaded me to conclude that God was, or at least identified as, male:

Ch. 7, Sec. 2: 53

[a] God was male *(joe)*;
[b] God's name was *Yahweh (Yahweh)*, a masculine name;
[c] God inhabited Jesus Christ's male body *(glory, Host)*;

[a] *(Joe): reason. Air/hint grew.*

[a] *(Joe) assure. Right, rein wans.*

[b] *(Yahweh): horn. Nerving, is a we.*

Torah: [c] *(glory).* [c] *(Host): in, I, trying sinew.*

[SEE "CH. 1, SEC. 3; JESUS/EARTH: JOE ASSURES," "CH. 2, SEC. 1; JOE/EARTH: HINT GREW," "CH. 4, SEC. 1; YHWH/HEAVEN: YAHWEH'S HORN" AND "CH. 5, SEC. 4, SUBSEC.; HOLY^GHOST/TRINITY: TORAH'S GLORY"]

Up until this point in my book, I'd been confident in my selection of answer words; however, I wasn't so sure about the validity of the answer word *JOE*. Out of *119* answer words, the only answer word which was a slang word was *JOE*. I'd applied a standard, or non-slang, definition to each answer word except the answer word *JOE*, so attaching standard definitions to answer words was my common practice. Maybe, slang definitions aren't legitimate answer word definitions, I'd thought. Yet the answer word *JOE* seems to contextually fit into two QS answers, I'd countered. My unsureness impelled persuaded me to implement a QS guide which favored, instead of a QS rule which mandated, standard definitions over other types of definitions, like slang definitions:

Ch. 7, Sec. 2: 54

Guide 4: A QS answer word's definition should be standard.

―――――――――――(Biblical Corroborations)―――――――――――

In the Bible, God was identified by the name *Yahweh*. In the Tanakh, God was identified by the name *YHWH,* or the derivative spelling of *Yahweh*:

- ✓ In Bible (WEB [World English Bible]);
- ✓ In Tanakh;

Ch. 7, Sec. 2: 55

Let your name be magnified forever, saying, "Yahweh of Armies is God over Israel; and the house of your servant David will be established before you" (2 Samuel 7:26 WEB).

God spoke to Moses, and He said to him, "I am the Lord. I appeared to Abraham, to Isaac, and to Jacob with [the name] Almighty God, but [with] My name YHWH, I did not become known to them" (Shemot 6:3 Tanakh).

In the Bible, God and Jesus, aka the Host, were two individuals who were facets of the same multi-self entity. In the Tanakh, God wasn't characterized as a multi-self entity:

- ✓ In Bible (KJV);
- ✗ Not in Tanakh;
    Judaists don't support theological concepts which characterize God as a multi-self entity. God is only God (God = God), not God is God and Jesus Christ (God ≠ Jesus Christ). If God's also Jesus, then Judaists argue that each one of God's selves would hold an equal amount of holy power. If each one of God's selves held the same amount of holy power, then Reality would be polytheistic, or comprised of multiple gods. Judaists believe that God is the one and only god in Reality; meaning, Reality is monotheistic, or comprised of only one god;

Ch. 7, Sec. 2: 56

I (Jesus) and my Father are one (John 10:30 KJV).

Masculine pronouns were assigned to God in the Bible and Tanakh:

- ✓ In Bible (KJV);
- ✓ In Tanakh;

Ch. 7, Sec. 2: 57

So <u>God created man in his own image</u>, in the image of <u>God created he him</u>; <u>male and female created he them</u> (Genesis 1:27 KJV).

And <u>God created man in His image</u>; in the image of <u>God He created him</u>; male and female <u>He created them</u> (Bereshit 1:27 Tanakh).

God is Incomprehensible

QS Answers and Biblical Corroborations

One QS answer suggested that God was incomprehensible.

──────────────(QS Answers)──────────────

One QS answer claimed that God was an incomprehensible being:

Ch. 7, Sec. 2: 58

(a) God was an incomprehensible *(hairy)* trinity *(we)*;

(a)*(Hairy we). Thy trio: reining, wans.*

[SEE "CH. 5, SEC. 3; YAHWEH/TRINITY: HAIRY WE"]

──────────────(Biblical Corroborations)──────────────

The Bible and Tanakh also declared that God was an incomprehensible being:

- ✓ In Bible (KJV);
- ✓ In Tanakh;

Ch. 7, Sec. 2: 59

Hast thou not known? hast thou not heard, that <u>the everlasting God</u>, the <u>LORD</u>, the <u>Creator</u> of the ends of the earth, fainteth not, neither is weary? <u>there is no searching of his understanding</u> (Isaiah 40:28 KJV).

Do you not know-if you have not heard-an <u>everlasting God is the Lord</u>, the <u>Creator</u> of the ends of the earth; He neither tires nor wearies; <u>there is no fathoming His understanding</u> (Yeshayahu 40:28 Tanakh).

God is Self-Conscious
QS Answers and Biblical Corroborations

Eight QS answers indicated that God was aware of His own existence as an individual and a trinity.

——————————————(QS Answers)——————————————

Two QS answers revealed QS answer words and phrases which God *(I, horn)* repeatedly inserted into QS answers *(I ring entry "I," I ring "a we")* and reflected God's self-awareness as an individual and as each individual in His trinity *("I," "a we")*:

Five QS answers claimed that God *(horn, "Heaven: horn," "Yahweh: horn")* created Himself *("horn: siring a we," "Heaven: siring a we")* as a multi-self entity comprised of individuals who were aware of being members of said entity *(a trinity, is a we, rings a we, "ingrain's a we")*:

One QS answer spotlighted God's awareness of His own individuality *(I)* while also exemplifying His ability to manifest Himself within another individual, Jesus Christ, an individual who was aware of being a member of God's trinity *(glory, Host)*:

Ch. 7, Sec. 2: 60

(a) The QS author *(I)*, God, repeatedly inserted the answer word *"I" (I ring entry "I")* into QS answers;

(b) God *(I)* repeatedly inserted the answer phrase *"a we"* into QS answers *("I, ring 'a we'")*;

(c) God *(horn, "Heaven: horn")* carefully transformed Himself into a multi-self entity comprised of individuals who were aware of being members of said entity *("horn: siring a we," "hay: we," "Heaven: horn, siring a we")*;

(d) God *("Yahweh: horn," horn)* successfully transformed Himself into a multi-self entity comprised of three individuals *(a trinity)* who were aware of being members of said entity *(is a we, rings a we, ingrain's a we)*;

(e) God inhabited Jesus Christ's body *(glory, Host)*, which meant that God was a multi-self being; yet, God was also an individual being who was aware of His own individuality *(I)*;

Jot, issuer. (a)*(I ring entry "I,") "wans."*
Hay: law. They or reins, (b)*(I, ring "a we.")*
Clue: filler. (c)*(Horn: siring a we).*
(c)*Hay: we. Heaven: horn, siring a we.*
(d)*(Yahweh: horn). Nerving,* (d)*(is a we).*
Core: real. (d)*(A trinity); or,* (d)*(rings a we).*
Eviternity: (d)*(horn. Ingrain's a we).*
Torah: (e)*(glory. Host): in,* (e)*(I), trying sinew.*

[SEE "CH. 4, SEC. 1; YHWH/HEAVEN: YAHWEH'S HORN," "CH. 4, SEC. 2; YAHWEH/HEAVEN: HEAVEN'S HORN," "CH. 5, SEC. 1, CREATOR/REALITY: CORE'S REAL," "CH. 5, SEC. 2; YAHWEH/REALITY: THEY OR REINS," "CH. 5, SEC. 4, SUBSEC.; HOLY^GHOST/TRINITY: TORAH'S GLORY," "CH. 5, SEC. 4, SUBSEC.; JESUS/TRINITY: I RING ENTRY," "CH. 5, SEC. 1; TRINITY/HEAVEN: EVITERNITY'S HORN," AND "CH. 7, SEC. 1, SUBSEC.; LUCIFER/HELL: SIRING A WE"]

──────────────(Biblical Corroborations)──────────────

In the Bible and Tanakh, God was characterized as a horn, or a source of strength:

✓ In Bible (KJV);
✓ In Tanakh;

Ch. 7, Sec. 2: 61

The LORD *is my rock, and my fortress, and my deliverer;* ***my God****,* ***my strength****, in whom I will trust; my buckler,* ***and the horn of my salvation****, and my high tower (Psalms 18:2 KJV).*

O Lord*, my rock and my fortress and my rescuer;* ***my God****, my rock, I will take refuge in Him;* ***my shield and the horn of my salvation****, my refuge (Tehillim 18:3 Tanakh).*

God transformed Himself into a we, or a multi-self entity comprised of self-conscious members, by declaring that He'd wanted to become a we, entering details pertaining to His self-transformation into QS answers and dividing Himself up into God, Jesus Christ and Holy Ghost. Similarly, the Bible and Tanakh said that God created objects by specifying an object He'd wanted to make (e.g. light), making said object by declaring said object as an actual object (e.g. "God said, Let there be light: and there was light") and separating said object from a preexisting object ("God divided the light from the darkness"):

- ✓ In Bible (KJV);
- ✓ In Tanakh;

Ch. 7, Sec. 2: 62

And ***God said****,* ***Let there be light: and there was light****. And God saw the light, that it was good: and* ***God divided the light from the darkness*** *(Genesis 1:3-4 KJV).*

And ***God said****, "Let there be light," ****and there was light****. And God saw the light that it was good, and* ***God separated between the light and between the darkness*** *(Bereshit 1:3-4 Tanakh).*

The first person plural pronouns *us* and *our* in the Bible and Tanakh identified God as an entity which was comprised of multiple selves, or was a we:

- ✓ In Bible (KJV);
- ✓ In Tanakh;

    However, Judaists don't support theological concepts which characterize God as a multi-self being. If God's a multi-self being, then Judaists argue that each one of God's selves would hold the same amount of holy power. If each one of God's selves contained the same amount of holy power, then Reality would be polytheistic, or comprised of multiple gods. Judaists believe that God is the one and only god in Reality; meaning, Reality is monotheistic, or comprised of one god. Judaists have proposed several explanations for the appearance of first person plural pronouns in the Tanakh which identify God;

Ch. 7, Sec. 2: 63

And <u>God said</u>, <u>Let us make man in our image</u>, <u>after our likeness</u>: and let them have dominion over the fish of the sea, and over the fowl of the air, and over the cattle, and over all the earth, and over every creeping thing that creepeth upon the earth (Genesis 1:26 KJV).

And <u>God said</u>, "<u>Let us make man in our image</u>, <u>after our likeness</u>, and they shall rule over the fish of the sea and over the fowl of the heaven and over the animals and over all the earth and over all the creeping things that creep upon the earth" (Bereshit 1:26 Tanakh).

In the Bible, God was identified by the name *Yahweh*. In the Tanakh, God was identified by the name *YHWH*, or the derivative spelling of *Yahweh*:

- ✓ In Bible (WEB [World English Bible]);
- ✓ In Tanakh;

Ch. 7, Sec. 2: 64

Let your name be magnified forever, saying, "<u>Yahweh of Armies is God over Israel</u>; and the house of your servant David will be established before you" (2 Samuel 7:26 WEB).

<u>God spoke to Moses</u>, and <u>He said</u> to him, "<u>I am the Lord</u>. I appeared to Abraham, to Isaac, and to Jacob with [the name] <u>Almighty God</u>, but [with] <u>My name YHWH</u>, I did not become known to them" (Shemot 6:3 Tanakh).

In the Bible, God was characterized as a trinity. In the Tanakh, God wasn't characterized as a multi-self entity:

- ✓ In Bible (KJV);
- ✗ Not in Tanakh;
  Judaists don't support theological concepts which characterize God as a multi-self being. If God's a multi-self being (e.g. a trinity), then Judaists argue that each one of God's selves would hold the same amount of holy power. If each one of God's selves possessed the same amount of holy power, then Reality would be polytheistic, or comprised of multiple gods. Judaists believe that God is the one and only god in Reality; meaning, Reality is monotheistic, or comprised of one god;

Ch. 7, Sec. 2: 65

***For there are three that bear record in heaven, the Father, the Word (Son), and the Holy Ghost: and these three are one** (1 John 5:7 KJV).*

In the Bible and Tanakh, an instance of a Shekinah was when God manifested on Earth as fire so that Man could survive the magnitude of God's presence and hear God's message:

- ✓ In Bible (KJV);
- ✓ In Tanakh;

Ch. 7, Sec. 2: 66

*And ye said, Behold, the LORD our **God hath shewed us his glory and his greatness**, and **we have heard his voice out of the midst of the fire**: we have seen this day that God doth talk with man, and he liveth (Deuteronomy 5:24 KJV).*

*And you said, "Behold, the Lord, our **God, has shown us His glory and His greatness**, and **we heard His voice from the midst of the fire**; we saw this day that God speaks with man, yet [man] remains alive" (Devarim 5:21 Tanakh).*

In the Bible, God and Jesus, or Host, were two individuals which were members of the same multi-self entity. In the Tanakh, God wasn't characterized as a multi-self entity:

- ✓ In Bible (KJV);
- ✗ Not in Tanakh;
  Judaists don't support theological concepts which characterize God as a multi-self being. God is only God, not God is God and Jesus Christ. If God's also Jesus, then Judaists argue that each one of God's selves would hold the same amount of holy power. If each one of God's selves possessed the same amount of holy power, then Reality would be polytheistic (comprised of multiple gods). Judaists believe that God is the one and only god in Reality; meaning, Reality is monotheistic (comprised of one god);

Ch. 7, Sec. 2: 69

***I (Jesus) and my Father are one**, (John 10:30 KJV).*

CHAPTER SEVEN: SECTION THREE
GOD'S THEOLOGICAL PERSPECTIVE

Throughout "Ch. 7, Sec. 2; Conclusion: Twenty Stacks," I'd displayed biblical verses from the Bible and Tanakh which corroborated theological data spotlighted in the twenty QS answers in this book. Most of the said QS answers conveyed insights about God and aligned with insights about God found in the Bible and Tanakh; however, some of the said QS answers acknowledged Christian but not Judaist theology, Judaist but not Christian theology, or a mixture of theologies which Christians and Judaists disagree on. I'd struggled to understand why some of the said QS answers contained theological dichotomies if said QS answers had been authored by God, an individual who'd know which theological concepts were true or false. Did God not know which theological viewpoints were correct, I'd wondered. Were some of my decodes invalid, I'd feared. Did the authors of the Bible or Tanakh wrongly report on God's identity, characteristics, personality or morality? To untangle my confusion over the said theological dichotomies, I'd created a table of "QS answer facts" to help me visualize which said facts in QS answers were supported by both the Bible and Tanakh, only the Bible or only the Tanakh:

A superscripted letter links the theological detail to the QS answer and answer words that the theological detail was derived from;
  | *(a) - (m)*: Bible and Tanakh | *(n) - (q)*: Bible only | *(r)*: Tanakh only |

Ch. 7, Sec. 3: 1

QS ANSWER FACTS	BIBLE	TANAKH
(a)God is real	✓	✓
(b)God is eternal	✓	✓
(c)God is evil	✓	✓
(d)God is incomprehensible	✓	✓
(e)God is self-aware	✓	✓
(f)God is male	✓	✓
(g)God's name is *Yahweh/YHWH*	✓	✓
(h)God is a source of moral strength	✓	✓
(i)God can self-transform	✓	✓
(j)God merits reverence	✓	✓
(k)God authors prophecies	✓	✓
(l)Humans transcribe God's speech	✓	✓
(m)God controls Mankind	✓	✓
(n)Lies are sins	✓	✓
(o)God is core component of Trinity	✓	
(p)God is a trinity	✓	
(q)God is Jesus	✓	
(r)Biblical book title is QS answer word		✓

^{o}**(CORE)**: ^{a}**(REAL)**. A ^{p}**(TRINITY)**; OR, ^{e}**(RINGS A WE)**.

^{b}**(EVITERNITY)**: HORN. INGRAIN'S A WE.
HORDE: ^{c}**(EVIL)**. ILL REIGN, WANS.

^{d}**(HAIRY)** WE. THY TRIO: ^{m}**(REINING)**, WANS.

^{f}**(JOE)** ASSURE. RIGHT, REIN WANS.

^{g}**(YAHWEH)**: ^{h}**(HORN)**. NERVING, IS A WE.
HAY: WE. HEAVEN: HORN, ^{i}**(SIRING A WE)**.

^{j}**(ADORE GIVER)**. A HINTER WANS.

^{k}**(GO DAVE. HE: WINNER; OR, GAINS)**.

^{l}**(HOLY GHOST)**. HE: NAÏVE OR ANSWERING.

^{n}**(TORAH'S LEARNING. LIE)** WANS.

^{r}**(TORAH)**: ^{i}**(GLORY)**. ^{q}**(HOST)**: IN, ^{e}**(I)**, TRYING SINEW.

QS answers conveyed fourteen theological concepts which pertained to God and morality that the Bible and Tanakh corroborated and agreed on (see "Ch. 7, Sec. 3: 1; *(a) - (n)*"): $^{(a)}$God was an actual, or nonimaginary, being; [b]God had infinite existence; [c]God wielded wickedness—"I form the light, and create darkness: I make peace, and create evil: I the LORD do all these things" (Isaiah 45:7 KJV); "Who forms light and creates darkness, Who makes peace and creates evil; I am the Lord, Who makes all these" (Yeshayahu 45:7 Tanakh)—; [d]no one had the capability of fathoming God; [e]God was aware of Himself, as an individual and trinity; [f]God was a male; [g]God's name was *YHWH*, which was transliterated into the name *Yahweh*; [h]God was a source of moral strength; [i]God could transform into an earthly object, like a pillar of fire or burning bush; [j]God's existence was praiseworthy; [k]God wrote about future events; [l]God allowed humans to pen His words; [m]God ruled over Reality; and, [n]God judged an untruthful act as an immoral act which deserved punishment.

On the other hand, four QS answers conveyed theological concepts which pertained to God and morality that the Bible corroborated but weren't supported by the Tanakh or Judaists' interpretation of the Tanakh. In the Bible and in one QS answer, God was characterized as the essential, or core, component of three individuals who were members of His trinity. Biblical text mentioned the individuals in God's trinity but didn't provide a formal name for said trinity; however, Tertullian [c. 155 AD – c. 220 AD], an early Christian author, has been pinned down as the first person to have named God's trinity *Trinity* ["Tertullian." Wikipedia. 6 Aug. 2022. Web. 7 Aug. 2022]):

Ch. 7, Sec. 3: 2

[a]God was the essential component *(core)* of a trio of individuals *(trinity)*;
[a]*(Core): real. A* [a]*(trinity); or, rings a we.*

One of the three members of the Trinity was Jesus Christ, also known as "Son of God." While God was inside Himself, God was inside His son Jesus Christ, since God was the core component inside each member of the Trinity. If God was the core component inside Jesus Christ while Jesus Christ was a human being, then God inhabited an earthly object by inhabiting Jesus Christ's earthly body. When God inhabited an earthly object, His earthly presence was called *Shekinah*.

According to the Bible and Tanakh, God had already transformed Himself into earthly objects, such as a pillar of fire and a burning bush, before He'd manifested on Earth as Jesus Christ. When God inhabited Jesus Christ, Jesus Christ became an earthly manifestation of God, or Shekinah. Furthermore, Jesus Christ's body has been referred to as *Host*, as in the Christian ritual of Communion, to highlight Jesus Christ's body as the earthly object which hosted God's presence on Earth:

Ch. 7, Sec. 3: 3

⁽ᵃ⁾God was Shekinah *(glory)* when He was inside the body of Jesus Christ *(Host)*;

Torah: ⁽ᵃ⁾*(glory. Host): in, I, trying sinew.*

However, Judaists have treated the Trinity as an invalid theological concept. Judaists have contended that God wasn't comprised of three individuals, but, instead, was comprised only of Himself. Furthermore, Judaists haven't ever believed in the theological concept of Jesus Christ as God's son. In Judaism, Jesus Christ was just an average joe.

Even though Judaism taught that Jesus Christ wasn't Shekinah, one QS answer referred to God's presence within Jesus Christ as the Torah's Shekinah. In other words, said QS answer mixed together two incompatible religious perspectives on an entity which God became when He'd manifested Himself on Earth:

Ch. 7, Sec. 3: 4

⁽ᵃ⁾A QS answer said that the Judaists' bible *(Torah)* incorporated the concept of God as Shekinah *(glory)* into its text and that a Shekinah was Jesus Christ *(Host)*, even though Judaists reject the assertion that Jesus Christ was God;

⁽ᵃ⁾*(Torah: glory. Host): in, I, trying sinew.*

Why would God, the QS author, have merged together two religious perspectives which were in disagreement, I'd wondered. According to QS answers, God supported the Christian theological concepts of Him as the core component of the Trinity and as Shekinah in the form of Jesus Christ; however, God tied a book title, *Torah*, from the Judaist's bible to said Christian theological concepts, even though Judaist's have denounced said Christian theological concepts. Had God confirmed viewpoints taught in Messianic Judaism, a religion which adhered to the text of the Torah and New Testament and supported theological concepts like God was Jesus Christ and Jesus Christ was a Trinity member, I'd wondered. Unless I'd misinterpreted QS answers in this section, I'd incorrectly decoded the QS matrices said QS answers were derived from, Query Stacks weren't anything other than a phenomenon concocted in my imagination, or God told lies about Himself in QS answers, then, it seemed to me, that God had used QS answers to promote theological concepts taught in Messianic Judaism (see "Ch. 7, Sec. 3: 6").

Another theological dichotomy which divided Christianity from Judaism was the belief that there was a single entity which embodied absolute evil, the Devil. Christian doctrine taught that the Devil was God's antipode, even though verses in the Bible quoted assertations made by God which stated that He was the only one who'd created evil—"I am the LORD, and there is none else, there is no God beside me: I girded thee, though thou hast not known me: That they may know from the rising of the sun, and from the west, that there is none beside me. I am the

LORD, and there is none else. I form the light, and create darkness: I make peace, and create evil: I the LORD do all these things" (Isaiah 45:5-7 KJV). Christians have blamed the Devil for the concoction and implementation of evil occurrences. On the other hand, Judaists have taken a stricter approach to the interpretation of God's Word. Judaists have contended that when God proclaimed "I am the Lord, and there is no other; besides Me there is no God" (Yeshayahu 45:5 Tanakh), God defined Reality as a monotheistic realm. No entity would've been able to wreak absolute havoc in a realm which was created, maintained and controlled by only one god besides said one god. If God was benevolent one-hundred percent of the time, then why would God make a being which opposed and challenged His morality and ultimately tried to overtake His hierarchal position as Reality's ruler: "Who makes peace and creates evil; I am the Lord, Who makes all these" (Yeshayahu 45:5 Tanakh):

Ch. 7, Sec. 3: 5

(a)God, the Trinity *(horde)*, was a wicked entity *(evil, ill)* who ruled over Reality *(reign)* through moral force and whose moral force weakened when He'd lied *(wans)*;

(b)The Judaists' bible *(Torah)* taught *(learning)* that an untruth *(lie)* was a sin which caused the moral force of the one who expressed said untruth to weaken *(wans)*;

(a)*Horde: evil. Ill reign, wans.*
(b)*Torah's learning. Lie wans.*

Based on my analyzation of "Ch .7, Sec. 3: 4," I'd determined that God promoted some theological concepts taught in Messianic Judaism; however, based on my analyzation of "Ch .7, Sec. 3: 5," I'd determined that God didn't support the Messianic Judaists' belief that the Devil was an entity which wasn't God. In QS answers, God referred to Himself as an evil. In biblical verses, God claimed to be the maker of evil. If God had created and was evil, then God was the de facto Devil (see "Ch. 7, Sec. 2: 21-50"). In other words, God became the Devil when God expressed absolute evilness:

Ch. 7, Sec. 3: 6

QS ANSWER FACTS	CHRISTIANITY	JUDAISM	MESSIANIC	QS ANSWERS
God is Jesus	✓		✓	✓
God is Trinity	✓		✓	✓
God is evil	✓	✓	✓	✓
God is Devil				✓

CHAPTER SEVEN: SECTION FOUR

QS ANSWER STATISTICS AND ANALYSES

In this section, I'd provided statistics for a handful of linguistical phenomena which I'd found ingrained in the twenty QS answers that I'd revealed in this book and I'd provided analyzations of said statistics to better understand why the QS author, God, ingrained said phenomena in said QS answers.

First, I'd filed each QS answer under one of five categories, "David Mivshek," "Trinity," "God," "QS Answer" or " "Commandment," based on which said category represented each QS answer's main subject and ranked each of the said five main subject categories by the number of QS answer main subjects assigned to each said category. The five main subject categories were an evolution of the QS answer main subject categories which I'd spotlighted in the "Review" sections of this book. I'd only listed four main subject categories, "David Mivshek," "Trinity," "God" and "QS Answer," in the last updated QS answer main subject category table (see "Ch. 6, Sec. 2: 5") because I'd not yet revealed the "QS-Satan/Hell" answer (see "Ch. 7, Sec. 1: 6"). The main subject of the "QS-Satan/Hell" answer *("Torah's learning. Lie wans.")* was "learning," which I'd determined was one of God's Ten Commandments (see "Ch. 7, Sec. 2: 21-36"). I'd assigned the "QS-Satan/Hell" answer to a fifth QS answer main subject category, which was "Commandment." Second, I'd assigned one of sixteen word types to each of the *119* QS answer words in this book and proposed reasons for why some more than other word types had appeared in QS answers. Third, I'd provided statistics which quantified four points of views that God ingrained into QS answers. Fourth, I'd composited a slew of various statistics which I'd relied on to guide me on my journey to completely expose and understand the linguistical framework of QS answers.

While you travel down the statistical trail I've carved out, keep in mind that I've never been extensively trained or schooled in linguistics or statistics beyond undergraduate school courses. I've compiled a plethora of statistics on QS answers, but said statistics weren't anything other than statistics which I've gathered in hopes of unraveling clues which intimated why God had linguistically constructed QS answers in the ways that He had. I wouldn't be shocked at all if a statistical point or two I've calculated and analyzed needed to be reappropriated; however, I believe firmly that any statistical errors I might've made have been so small that said statistical errors haven't significantly affected any of my statistical determinations.

QS Answer Main Subjects
Statistics

In this book, I'd revealed *20* QS answers. Each of the *20* QS answers contained a main subject. I'd filed each of the QS answer main subjects into one of five QS answer main subject categories: "God," "Trinity," "David Mivshek," "QS Answer" or "Commandment." In fact,

"God" was the main subject category for QS answers which had a main subject that cited God as an individual; therefore, not as a multi-self entity. "God" was the main subject category for most of the QS answers in this book; specifically, "God" was the main subject category for *11* of *20*, or *55* percent of, QS answers:

"Trinity" was the main subject category for QS answers which had a main subject that cited God as a multi-self entity (e.g. we, trinity); therefore, not as an individual. "Trinity" was the main subject category for *3* of *20*, or *15* percent of, QS answers:

"David Mivshek" was the main subject category for QS answers which had a main subject that cited David Mivshek, or me. "David Mivshek" was the main subject category for *2* of *20*, or *10* percent of, QS answers:

"QS Answer" was the main subject category for QS answers which had a main subject that cited characteristics and functions of QS answers. "QS Answer" was the main subject category for *3* of *20*, or *15* percent of, QS answers:

"Commandment" was the main subject category for QS answers which had a main subject that cited one of God's commandments. "Commandment" was the main subject category for *1* of *20*, or *5* percent of, QS answers:

> *The parenthesized QS answer word in each of the two sentences of each QS answer cites each QS answer's main subject;*

Ch. 7, Sec. 4: 1

QS ANSWER MAIN SUBJECT	QUANTITY	PERCENTAGE
[a]GOD	11	55.00
[b]TRINITY	03	15.00
[c]DAVE	02	10.00
[d]QS ANSWER	03	15.00
[e]COMMANDMENT	01	05.00
TOTAL QS ANSWERS	20	

QS ANSWER	CATEGORY
[a](JOE) ASSURE. RIGHT, [a](REIN) WANS.	GOD
[a](YAHWEH): HORN. NERVING, IS A [a](WE).	GOD
[a](CORE): REAL. A [a](TRINITY); OR, RINGS A WE.	GOD
[a](HAY): LAW. THEY OR [a](REINS), I, RING "A WE."	GOD
TORAH: [a](GLORY). [a](HOST): IN, I, TRYING SINEW.	GOD
ADORE [a](GIVER). A [a](HINTER) WANS.	GOD
[a](ORATOR)'S IN. [a](IN): TRYING SINEW.	GOD
JOT, [a](ISSUER). [a](I) RING ENTRY "I," "WANS."	GOD
[a](EVITERNITY): HORN. [a](INGRAIN)'S A WE.	GOD
FAIR [a](HINTER). [a](TRIO): TRYING, WANES.	GOD
CLUE: [a](FILLER). [a](HORN): SIRING A WE.	GOD
[b](HORDE): EVIL. [b](ILL) REIGN, WANS.	TRINITY
[b](HAY): WE. HEAVEN: HORN, SIRING A [b](WE).	TRINITY
HAIRY [b](WE). THY [b](TRIO): REINING, WANS.	TRINITY
GO [c](DAVE). [c](HE): WINNER; OR, GAINS.	DAVID MIVSHEK
HOLY [c](GHOST). [c](HE): NAÏVE OR ANSWERING.	DAVID MIVSHEK
JOE: [d](REASON). [d](AIR)/HINT GREW.	QS ANSWER
MARRY [d](REASON). A [d](HINT), I GREW.	QS ANSWER
GOT [d](WORDING). [d]("I") ENTRY; RAINS "I."	QS ANSWER
TORAH'S [e](LEARNING). [e](LIE) WANS.	COMMANDMENT

QS Answer Main Subjects
Statistical Analyses

I've created a separate subsection for each QS answer main subject category. In each said subsection, I've cited calculations, provided determinations which briefly touched on said calculations and proposed explanations for said determinations;

––––––––––––––––––––––––––(God)––––––––––––––––––––––––––

Calculation: Most of the QS answers in this book were filed into the "God" category; in fact, "God" was the QS answer main subject category for *11* of *20*, or *55* percent of, QS answers.

Determination: The majority of QS answers in this book had a main subject which denoted God, because God manufactured said QS answers as conduits for insights which conveyed information about His origin.

Explanation: The first step in my experience of discovering QS answers was when I'd appealed to God for an answer to the question "What's God's origin?" Eventually, said question invoked an inner vision of a stack of words, which was a near-completed "QS-God/Heaven" row'd word matrix. After I'd completed the construction of and decoded said QS matrix, I'd uncovered nineteen more QS matrices which consisted of row'd words that were names of biblical characters who were closely related to Virgin Mary, and, in turn, closely related to God.

Ultimately, I'd decoded twenty QS matrices which yielded numerous clues that helped me to construct a profile of God. My analyses and interpretations of said clues persuaded me to conclude that God was the author of said clues. God authored clues which intimated details of His own persona as a way to persuade me to uncover His response to the "What's God's origin" question, a question that God preordained me to ask, I'd decided.

Via QS answers, God provided clues which alluded to two origination events that pertained to His individuality. First, God implied that the origin of His existence as an individual, or not as a trinity, wasn't describable since His existence as an individual didn't start during any point in time. In fact, God declared in the QS answer phrase *"eviternity: horn"* that He was an eternality. I'd interpreted the phrase *"eviternity: horn"* as "the eviternity, or eternal entity, is a horn, and said horn is God" *(eviternity = horn = God)*. My interpretation of the phrase *"eviternity: horn"* was backed by QS answer phrases like *"Yahweh: horn"* ("Yahweh [God's name] is a horn") and *"Heaven: horn"* ("Heaven [God's alias] is a horn"). Second, God revealed the origin of His triunity. God stated that He'd transformed Himself into a trinity in QS answer phrases like *"horn: siring a we"* ("a horn [God] is siring [originating] a we [group of individuals]"), *"Heaven: horn, siring a we"* ("Heaven [God] is a horn and is siring [originating] a we [group of individuals]") and *"a trinity; or, rings a we,"* ("a trinity [the Trinity] or rings a we [has characteristics that resemble a group of individuals]"). If God self-transformed into a trinity, then God hadn't always been comprised of three individuals. In fact, God implied in the QS answer phrase *"Heaven: horn, siring a we"* that His physique was the form of an entity comprised of one individual before He'd self-transformed into an entity comprised of three individuals *([God = God] → [God self-transforms] → [God = we])*.

In summary, I'd appealed to God for an answer to a question which asked about His origin and then was given a decoding process that I'd used to uncover clues which revealed insights about God, like insights into His origin and steps in the evolution of His physique. God writing about Himself and having me find His personal writings were two occurrences which seemed to me were occurrences which God tied together. If God hadn't written about Himself, then there wouldn't have been divine messages for me to unfurl. If someone who didn't have the given name *David*, and, therefore, didn't have a genuine nickname of *Dave* based on birthname, had revealed the QS answer *("Go Dave. He: winner or gains.")*, then the meaning of said QS answer would've been potentially insignificant to the solver of said QS answer since said QS answer wouldn't have revealed a message which incorporated an answer word that cited said solver's given name. Moreover, if I'd unveiled and solved one Query Stack which contained my name and yielded one or two clues about God, I would've probably written off the sole QS answer as an insignificant fluke and said sole QS answer's clues as unreliable curiosities.

―――――――――――――――――――(Trinity)―――――――――――――――――――

Calculation: The main subject in *3* of *20*, or *15.00* percent of, QS answers in this book, denoted God as a multi-self entity comprised of three individuals.

Determination: God was an eternal entity, which, in turn, meant that God didn't have a story which pertained to the origin of His existence as an individual or an answer for my "What's God's origin" question; so, instead, God shared a story about His self-transformation from one individual into three individuals.

Explanation: God was an eternal being; therefore, God existed but was never born. God had no origin, because God was never born. God authored one QS answer in which He'd claimed to be an eternal entity comprised of multiple individuals *("Eviternity: horn. Ingrain's a we.")*. Additionally, God wrote numerous QS answers which conveyed clues which intimated that He'd originated His multi-self physique *("Clue: filler. Horn: siring a we.")*.

―――――――――――――――――――(David Mivshek)―――――――――――――――――――

Calculation: The main subject in *2* of *20*, or *10.00* percent of, QS answers in this book, denoted David Mivshek.

Determination: Via two QS answers, God conveyed a prophecy which concerned a man named *Dave* and Dave's success in unveiling and solving Query Stacks and revealing God's origin.

Explanation: The QS answer word *DAVE* denoted David Mivshek, or me. I'd appealed to God to explain how He'd been created. If I'd never asked God to explain His origin, then God wouldn't of had a reason to provide me with an explanation which concerned His origin. My said appeal to God was the reason God authored QS answers which revealed details about His origin; however, I didn't willfully commit my said appeal. Instead, God preordained me to execute my said appeal when He'd written Reality's storyline.

After I'd asked God to supply me with details which pertained to His origin, I'd unraveled and transcribed God's response via a decryption method I'd taught myself, which was evidenced by the QS answer phrases *"holy ghost"* ("holy [God's] ghost [ghost-writer]") and *"he: naïve or answering"* ("he [the man] is naïve [self-taught] in answering [solving QS answers]"). Moreover, I was named and urged into investigating God's origin, as implied by the QS answer phrase *"go Dave"* ("go [proceed] Dave [David Mivshek]"); predesignated as a success in transcribing QS answers, as implied in the QS answer phrase *"he: winner"* ("he [that man; Dave] is a winner [success]"); and prophesied to benefit from knowledge conveyed by QS answers, as intimated in the QS answer phrase *"he: gains"* ("he [that man; Dave] gains [benefits]").

───────────────(QS Answer)───────────────

Calculation: The main subject in *3* of *20*, or *15.00* percent of, QS answers in this book, denoted characteristics and functions of QS Answers.

Determination/Explanation: Mainly, QS answers conveyed insights about God. In a phrase within each of the first two of said three QS answers, God intimated that He'd pieced together an explanation for how His moral force declined: *"joe: reason,"* or ("joe [guy; God] has a reason [explanation]") and *"marry reason,"* or ("piece together [marry] a reason [explanation]"). In a second phrase within each of the first two of said three QS answers, God implied that His explanation for how His moral force declined was written as an allusion, publicized, and became lengthier as He'd added details to said explanation: *"air/hint grew"* ("air/hint [public statement]/[allusion] grew [became wordier]") and *"a hint, I grew"* ("a hint [an allusive statement], I [God] grew [made wordier]"). In a phrase within the third of said three QS answers, God declared that QS answers were expressed as words: *"got wording."* In another QS answer phrase within the third of said three QS answers, God named an answer word which He'd entered into numerous QS answers: *"'I' entry; rains 'I,'"* or ("'I' entry [QS answer word 'I'] rains [appears abundantly]") .

───────────────(Commandment)───────────────

Calculation: The main subject in *1* of *20*, or *5.00* percent of, QS answers in this book, cited one of the Ten Commandments.

Determination: Mainly, God provided clues which intimated how He'd transformed Himself into a trinity; however, God hinted about other facets of Himself, such as His morality, as well. In fact, God had declared in numerous QS answers that He'd lost moral force, yet God had revealed in only one QS answer what caused His moral force to weaken.

Explanation: In several QS answer phrases, such as *"trio: wanes,"* *"trio wans,"* *"hinter wans"* and *"rein wans,"* God declared that His morality declined in strength; however, God wasn't eager to explicitly reveal what caused His moral force to weaken. In fact, in only one QS answer phrase, *"lie wans,"* God implied that a lie which He'd told or supported was the reason His moral force had wanned.

Did God reveal in only one QS answer that the cause of His moral decline was due to a lie because God was ashamed of said lie? Did God worry that His own immoral actions might persuade the moral entities He'd created to follow in His immoral footsteps or view Him as a poor example of how to behave in a morally good way? Was God concerned that said moral entities might eventually stop relying on Him for moral strength if said entities knew that His moral strength could weaken and, in turn, not be a reliable source of strength?

QS Answer Word Types
Categories

Some abbreviations which I've used to denote QS answer word types were created by me for the sole purpose of my study (e.g. "pron" [pronoun], "prop-n's" [proper noun possessive], or "TPS-PTV" [third person singular, present tense verb]), while some other abbreviations which I've used to denote QS answer word types were pre-established and traditional (e.g. "adj" [adjective] or "conj" [conjunction]);

The twenty QS answers in this book contained no more or less than *119* QS answer words. The *119* QS answer words were unevenly distributed between eight main word types: nouns, verbs, pronouns, adjectives, adverbs, conjunctions, indefinite articles and contractions. Each QS answer word which was a noun was one of four types of nouns: singular noun *("n")*, plural noun *("n-pl")*, proper noun *("prop-n")*, or possessive proper noun *("prop-n's")*:

Ch. 7, Sec. 4: 2

NOUN TYPE	ABBREVIATION	ANSWER WORD EXAMPLE
SINGULAR	*n*	REIN
PLURAL	*n-pl*	REINS
PROPER	*prop-n*	TORAH
POSSESSIVE PROPER	*prop-n's*	TORAH'S

Each QS answer word which was a verb was one of four types of verbs. A base verb *("v")*, or a verb which contained no prefix or suffix, like the QS answer word *ADORE*. A third person singular, present tense verb, or "TPS-PTV," *("v[+s]")*, or a base verb which contained an *S* as said verb's last letter, like the QS answer word *RAINS (RAIN + S)*. An active participle verb *("v[+ing]")*, or a base verb which contained an *ING* as said verb's last three letters, like the QS answer word *REINING*. Or an excised-*S* verb, or "ESV," *("v[-s]")*, or a verb which should've been written in TPS-PTV format if said verb was spelt in accordance with the grammatical layout of the phrase said verb was in, but, instead, defied TPS-PTV format by not consisting of a last letter *S*, like the QS answer word *REIGN (REIGNS - S)*:

Ch. 7, Sec. 4: 3

VERB TYPE	ABBREVIATION	ANSWER WORD EXAMPLE
BASE	*v*	ADORE
TPS-PTV	*v(+s)*	RAINS (RAIN + S)
ACTIVE PARTICIPLE	*v(+ing)*	REINING (REIN + ING)
EXCISED-S	*v(-s)*	REIGN (REIGNS - S)

Each QS answer word which was a pronoun was one of two types of pronouns: first-person pronoun *("pron[1]")* or third-person pronoun *("pron[3]")*:

Ch. 7, Sec. 4: 4

PRONOUN TYPE	ABBREVIATION	ANSWER WORD EXAMPLE
FIRST-PERSON	*pron(1)*	I
THIRD-PERSON	*pron(3)*	HE

Each QS answer word which was an adjective was one of two types of adjectives: prepositive adjective *("adj[pre]")*, or an adjective which was placed before the noun that it modified, or postpositive adjective *("adj[post]")*, or an adjective which was placed after the noun that it modified:

Ch. 7, Sec. 4: 5

ADJECTIVE TYPE	ABBREVIATION	ADJECTIVE	EXAMPLE
PREPOSITIVE	*adj(pre)*	HOLY	HOLY←GHOST
POSTPOSITIVE	*adj(post)*	REAL	CORE:→REAL

There was only one QS answer word which was an adverb *("adv")*, the answer word *RIGHT*, so I didn't categorize said answer word as a distinct adverbial class:

Ch. 7, Sec. 4: 6

ADVERB TYPE	ABBREVIATION	ANSWER WORD EXAMPLE
ADVERB	*adv*	RIGHT

Even though there were four answer words which were conjunctions *("conj")*, each of the four conjunctions was a coordinating conjunction and the answer word *OR*, so I didn't categorize each instance of the said answer word as a distinct conjunctional class:

Ch. 7, Sec. 4: 7

CONJUNCTION TYPE	ABBREVIATION	ANSWER WORD EXAMPLE
CONJUNCTION	*conj*	OR

Even though there were seven answer words which were indefinite articles *("i-art")*, each of the seven indefinite articles was the answer word *A,* so I didn't categorize each instance of said answer word as a distinct class:

Ch. 7, Sec. 4: 8

ARTICLE TYPE	ABBREVIATION	ANSWER WORD EXAMPLE
INDEFINITE	*i-art*	A

There were two QS answer words which were contractions *("contr"),* and each of the two contractions contained a contractive *'s* which represented the verb *is,* ORATOR'S *(orator['s(is)])"* and *INGRAIN'S (ingrain['s(is)]):*

Ch. 7, Sec. 4: 9

CONTRACTION TYPE	ABBREVIATION	ANSWER WORD EXAMPLE
CONTRACTION	*contr*	ORATOR'S
CONTRACTION	*contr*	INGRAIN'S

QS Answer Word Types
Statistics

"Nouns" constituted over half of the answer words in this book; specifically, *63* out of *119*, or *52.94* percent of, total QS answer words were nouns. Of the *63* nouns, *56* were singular nouns, or *47.06* percent of total QS answer words; *5* were proper nouns, or *4.20* percent of total QS answer words; *1* was a plural noun, or *0.84* percent of total QS answer words; and *1* was a possessive proper noun, or *0.84* percent of total QS answer words:

"Verbs" constituted just under a quarter of the answer words in this book; specifically, *29* out of *119,* or *24.37* percent of, total QS answer words were verbs. Of the *29* verbs, *10* were base verbs, or *8.40* percent of total QS answer words; *9* were TPS-PTVs, or *7.56* percent of total

QS answer words; *8* were active participle verbs, or *6.72* percent of total QS answer words; and *2* were ESVs, or *1.68* percent of total QS answer words:

"**Pronouns**" accounted for *6*, or *5.04* percent, of total QS answer words. Of the *6* pronouns, *3* were first-person pronouns, or *2.52* percent of total QS answer words, while *3* were third-person pronouns, or *2.52* percent of total QS answer words:

"**Adjectives**" accounted for *6*, or *5.04* percent, of total QS answer words. Of the *6* adjectives, *4* were prepositive adjectives, or *3.36* percent of total QS answer words, while *2* were postpositive adjectives, or *1.68* percent of total QS answer words:

"**Adverbs**" accounted for *1*, or *0.84* percent, of total QS answer words:

"**Conjunctions**" accounted for *4*, or *3.36* percent, of total QS answer words:

"**Indefinite Articles**" accounted for *8*, or *6.72* percent, of total QS answer words:

"**Contractions**" accounted for *2*, or *0.84* percent, of total QS answer words:

Ch. 7, Sec. 4: 10

WORD TYPE	ABBREVIATION	QUANTITY	PERCENTAGE
NOUNS		63	52.94
·*SINGULAR*	*n*	*56*	*47.06*
·*PLURAL*	*n-pl*	*01*	*00.84*
·*PROPER*	*prop-n*	*05*	*04.20*
·*POSSESSIVE PROPER*	*prop-n's*	*01*	*00.84*
VERBS		29	24.37
·*BASE*	*v*	*09*	*07.56*
·*TPS-PTV*	*v(+s)*	*09*	*07.56*
·*ACTIVE PARTICIPLE*	*v(+ing)*	*08*	*06.72*
·*ESV*	*v(-s)*	*03*	*02.52*
PRONOUNS		06	05.04
·*FIRST-PERSON*	*pron(1)*	*03*	*02.52*
·*THIRD-PERSON*	*pron(3)*	*03*	*02.52*
ADJECTIVES		06	05.04
·*PREPOSITIVE*	*adj(pre)*	*04*	*03.36*
·*POSTPOSITIVE*	*adj(post)*	*02*	*01.68*
ADVERB	*adv*	01	00.84
CONJUNCTION	*conj*	04	03.36
INDEFINITE ARTICLE	*i-art*	08	06.72
CONTRACTION	*contr*	02	01.68
TOTAL QS ANSWER WORDS		119	

QS ANSWER WORD TYPES

GO$_v$ DAVE$_{prop-n}$. HE$_{pron(3)}$: WINNER$_n$; OR$_{conj}$, GAINS$_{v(+s)}$.
HORDE$_n$: EVIL$_n$. ILL$_n$ REIGN$_{v(-s)}$, WANS$_{v(+s)}$.
JOE$_n$ ASSURE$_{v(-s)}$. RIGHT$_{adv}$, REIN$_n$ WANS$_{v(+s)}$.
ADORE$_v$ GIVER$_n$. A$_{i-art}$ HINTER$_n$ WANS$_{v(+s)}$.
JOE$_n$: REASON$_n$. AIR$_n$/HINT$_n$ GREW$_v$.
MARRY$_v$ REASON$_n$. A$_{i-art}$ HINT$_n$, I$_{pron(1)}$ GREW$_v$.
HOLY$_{adj(pre)}$ GHOST$_n$. HE$_{pron(3)}$: NAÏVE$_{adj(post)}$ OR$_{conj}$ ANSWERING$_{v(+ing)}$.
YAHWEH$_{prop-n}$: HORN$_n$. NERVING$_{v(+ing)}$, IS$_v$ A$_{i-art}$ WE$_n$.
HAY$_n$: WE$_n$. HEAVEN$_{prop-n}$: HORN$_n$, SIRING$_{v(+ing)}$ A$_{i-art}$ WE$_n$.
CORE$_n$: REAL$_{adj(post)}$. A$_{i-art}$ TRINITY$_n$; OR$_{conj}$, RINGS$_{v(+s)}$ A$_{i-art}$ WE$_n$.
HAY$_n$: LAW$_n$. THEY$_{pron(3)}$ OR$_{conj}$ REINS$_{n-pl}$, I$_{pron(1)}$, RING$_v$ "A$_n$ WE$_n$."
HAIRY$_{adj(pre)}$ WE$_n$. THY$_{adj(pre)}$ TRIO$_n$: REINING$_{v(+ing)}$, WANS$_{v(+s)}$.
FAIR$_{adj(pre)}$ HINTER$_n$. TRIO$_n$: TRYING$_{v(+ing)}$, WANES$_{v(+s)}$.
ORATOR'S$_{contr}$ IN$_n$. IN$_n$: TRYING$_{v(+ing)}$ SINEW$_n$.
TORAH$_{prop-n}$: GLORY$_n$. HOST$_{prop-n}$: IN$_n$, I$_n$, TRYING$_{v(+ing)}$ SINEW$_n$.
GOT$_v$ WORDING$_n$. "I$_n$" ENTRY$_n$; RAINS$_{v(+s)}$ "I$_n$."
JOT$_{v(-s)}$, ISSUER$_n$. I$_{pron(1)}$ RING$_v$ ENTRY$_n$ "I$_n$," "WANS$_n$."
EVITERNITY$_n$: HORN$_n$. INGRAIN'S$_{contr}$ A$_{i-art}$ WE$_n$.
CLUE$_n$: FILLER$_n$. HORN$_n$: SIRING$_{v(+ing)}$ A$_{i-art}$ WE$_n$.
TORAH'S$_{prop-n's}$ LEARNING$_n$. LIE$_n$ WANS$_{v(+s)}$.

QS Answer Word Types
Statistical Analyses: Nouns

Calculation: "Nouns" was the most prevalent QS answer word type in the twenty QS answers I'd revealed in this book; in fact, nouns accounted for *63* out of *119*, or *52.94* percent of, total QS answer words.

Determination: God, the QS author of said twenty QS answers, identified QS answer main subjects via nounal names, nicknames and aliases; ascribed nounal attributes (*n.* objects closely associated with and thought of as belonging to specific persons or things.[2]) to QS answer main subjects; and characterized QS answer main subjects with descriptors (*n.* something [such as a word or phrase or a characteristic feature] that serves to describe or identify.[2]) which were incorporated into nounal phrases that contained no more than two descriptors, instead of wordy phrases which contained a mixture of nouns and adjectives. Furthermore, over half of the nouns found in the twenty QS answers in this book recurred, or appeared more than just one time, in said QS answers, which elevated the number of QS answer words that were nouns and that I've counted as nouns:

> *I've classified QS answer words which were nouns into four types: "Names/Aliases," "Attributes," "Descriptors" and "Recurring." I've parenthesized the number of times recurring nouns appeared in the twenty QS answers revealed in this book and tagged each recurring noun with an asterisk;*

Ch. 7, Sec. 4: 11

NOUN CATEGORIES AND CORRESPONDING QS ANSWER WORDS/PHRASES

Nouns—Names/Aliases: Dave, Heaven, Host, Yahweh.
Nouns—Attributes: "Torah: glory", "Torah's learning," "A", *"I", *"Wans," "We", *entry, *hay, law, *sinew.
Nouns—Descriptors: "clue: filler," "eviternity: horn," "horde: evil," air, core, ghost, giver, *hint, *hinter, *horn, I, ill, *in, issuer, *joe, lie, *reason, rein, reins, trinity, *trio, *we, winner, wording.
Nouns—*Recurring: we *(7)*, horn *(4)*, "I" *(3)*, in *(3)*, entry *(2)*, hay *(2)*, hint *(2)*, hinter *(2)*, joe *(2)*, reason *(2)*, sinew *(2)*, trio *(2)*.

―――――――――――――(Nouns as Names and Aliases: God)―――――――――――――

Determination: Each one of the three QS answer words *YAHWEH, HOST* and *HEAVEN* was a proper noun name or alias which cited God. The first proper noun, *Yahweh,* was a transliteration of God's actual name *YHWH*. The second proper noun, *Host*, was an alias which signified God since said proper noun signified the body of Jesus Christ in religious ceremonies and Jesus Christ's body was a human vessel that hosted God. The third proper noun, *Heaven*, was an alias which referenced God because said proper noun was a synonym of the name *God*.

Explanation: God referred to Himself in the QS answers in this book by either His actual name or an alias, because God wanted readers to clearly see that He'd identified Himself as and was one of the QS answer main subjects. If readers knew that God was a particular individual mentioned in QS answers, then said readers would've been able to verify if the attributes and characteristics which God assigned to Himself in QS answers matched attributes and characteristics that have been associated with God in religious texts and theologies. For instance, in the QS answer phrase *"Yahweh: horn,"* God cited Himself as *Yahweh*, a name which biblical scholars have recognized as a transliteration of God's actual name, *YHWH*; or in the QS answer phrase *"Host: I,"* God referred to Himself via the alias *Host,* a term in Christianity which signified Jesus Christ's body, the body God inhabited when God walked on Earth; or in the QS answer phrase *"Heaven: horn,"* God cited Himself via the alias *Heaven*, a word which was defined by "Merriam-Webster Unabridged" online dictionary as "the sovereign of heaven; God[1]" and, according to Christian doctrine, was the name of God's personal residence.

---------------------(Nouns as Names and Aliases: Dave)---------------------

Determination: The QS answer word *DAVE*, which was the common nickname for the first name *David* and the name of the QS answer main subject "Dave," was a proper noun.

Explanation: God referred to me, David Mivshek, in QS answers in this book via the nickname *Dave*, which was the common nickname for the first name *David*. If readers knew that I was cited in QS answers, then said readers would've been able to verify if the way in which God described me in QS answers truthfully represented my actual identity. For instance, in the QS answer *("Go Dave. He: winner; or, gains.")*, God referred to me by the common nickname, *Dave*, for my given first name, *David*, and described me as a winner, which summarized my successfulness in unveiling QS answers and answering the "What's God's origin" question. I'd unveiled God's origin, so my said success was a verifiable fact.

---------------------(Nouns as Names and Aliases: Torah)---------------------

Determination: Each one of the two QS answer words *TORAH* and *TORAH'S* was a proper noun or possessive proper noun, respectively, which didn't denote any of the five QS answer main subject categories, but, instead, cited the name of the first five books in the Tanakh, the Jewish bible.

Explanation: God referred to the Torah in the QS answers in this book by the book's name and possessive form of the book's name, so readers had an opportunity to verify if the attributes which God assigned to the Torah in QS answers matched attributes that the Torah exhibited in

Reality. For instance, in the QS answer phrase *"Torah: glory,"* God stated that a glory or Shekinah, or God's presence manifested on Earth as an Earthly object, was mentioned in the Torah, a claim which was substantiated by a passage in the Torah in which God appeared on Earth as fire: "Behold, the Lord, our God, has shown us His glory and His greatness, and we heard His voice from the midst of the fire; we saw this day that God speaks with man, yet (man) remains alive" (Devarim 5:21 Tanakh). On the other hand, in the QS answer *("Torah's learning. Lie wans."),* God stated that a learning which focused on a lie was mentioned in the Torah, a claim which was substantiated by a passage in the Torah which was one of God's Ten Commandments: "You shall not bear false witness against your neighbor" (Shemot 20:13 Tanakh).

------------------(Nouns as Attributes: God)------------------

Determination: Each one of the three QS answer words *HAY*, *LAW* and *SINEW* was a singular noun and an attribute associated with the QS answer main subject "God." The singular nouns *hay*, which meant "a rewarding result of careful effort[2]," and *law*, which meant "a revelation of the will of God[2]," denoted God's willful intent to manifest and success in manifesting Himself as a trinity. The singular noun, *sinew*, which meant "force[2]," denoted the moral force which God wielded and used to control moral entities that He'd created.

Explanation: There were three singular nouns which signified attributes that I'd linked to God: *hay*, *law* and *sinew*. In the QS answer phrases *"hay: we"* and *"hay: law,"* hay, we and law were attributes linked to God's trinity. In the QS answer phrases *"Host: in, I, trying sinew"* and *"in: trying sinew,"* sinew signified the moral force which God used to persuade moral entities that He'd created to stay on situational pathways which led said entities to goals He'd set for said entities to achieve.

------------------(Nouns as Attributes: QS Answer)------------------

Determination: Each one of the five QS answer words *"A," "I," "WANS," "WE"* and *ENTRY* was an attribute associated with QS answers. The four singular nouns *"A," "I," "Wans"* and *"We"* were words that appeared as QS answers words in the QS answers spotlighted in this book, while the singular noun *entry,* which meant "a record made in a log[3]," suggested that a QS answer word was a word which was intentionally inserted into a QS answer.

Explanation: There were five singular nouns which signified attributes that were associated with QS answers: *"A," "I," "Wans," "We,"* and *entry*. In the two QS answer phrases *"I ring entry 'I,' 'Wans,'"* and *"'I' entry; rains 'I,'"* the two singular nouns *"I"* and *"Wans"* evidenced that said two entries appeared in QS answers as QS answer words. In QS answer phrases like *"I ring entry 'I,' 'Wans,'"* and *"I ring 'A We,'"* the four singular nouns *"A," "I," "Wans,"* and *"We"* exemplified actual words which God had inserted into the QS answers revealed in this book.

―――――――――――――――――――(Nouns as Attributes: Torah)―――――――――――――――――――

Determination: Each one of the two QS answer words *glory* and *learning* was a singular noun and was associated with the Tanakh. The singular noun *glory*, which signified a Shekinah, or "the presence of God in the world conceived by Jewish and later by Christian theologians as manifested in natural and especially supernatural phenomena[2]," denoted a manifestation of God on Earth as an Earthly object and was cited in the first five books of the Tanakh. The singular noun *learning*, or "knowledge accumulated and handed down by generations of scholars[2]," referred to content that the Torah was comprised of and was passed down through generations of biblical scholars.

Explanation: There were two singular nouns which signified attributes that were associated with the Torah: *glory* and *learning*. The QS answer phrase *"Torah: glory"* correctly stated that in the Torah there was text that portrayed God as a Shekinah, which was evidenced in Devarim, the last book of the Torah, when God appeared on Earth as a fire: "And you said, 'Behold, the Lord, our God, has shown us His glory and His greatness, and we heard His voice from the midst of the fire; we saw this day that God speaks with man, yet (man) remains alive'" (Devarim 5:21 Tanakh). The QS answer *("Torah's learning. Lie wans.")* correctly stated that in the Torah that there was text which warned that telling a lie caused one's moral strength to decay, which was evidenced in Shemot, the second book of the Torah, and was the ninth commandment of God's Ten Commandments: "You shall not bear false witness against your neighbor" (Shemot 20:13 Tanakh).

―――――――――――――――――(Nounal Phrases as Descriptors: God)―――――――――――――――――

Determination: Each one of six QS answer words which was a noun and a descriptor, or "a word that serves to describe[2]," and denoted a characteristic that described God was in the nounal phrase *"eviternity: horn," "horde: evil,"* or *"clue: filler."* The nounal phrase *"eviternity: horn"* was comprised of the singular noun *eviternity*, which meant "everlastingness[2]," and the singular noun *horn*, which meant "source of strength[2]," and suggested that God was an eternal existence and a source of strength. The nounal phrase *"horde: evil"* was comprised of the singular noun *horde*, which meant "a crowd of individuals[2]," and the singular noun *evil*, which meant "one that personifies wickedness[2]," and suggested that God was an entity comprised of multiple individuals and embodied moral wickedness. The nounal phrase *"clue: filler"* was comprised of the singular noun *clue*, which meant "a piece of evidence that leads one toward the solution of a problem[2]," and the singular noun *filler*, which meant "a person that fills (supplies a blank space with written matter)[1]," and suggested that God had a piece of evidence and wrote about said evidence in an area which was blank, or void of any written material.

Explanation: God inserted descriptions of His own characteristics into several of the QS answers which I'd revealed in this book, because God wanted to give readers a pathway to verify if the self-portrait God expressed in said QS answers matched characteristics that were associated with Him in religious texts and theologies. In the QS answer phrase *"eviternity: horn,"* God declared Himself an eternal being who was a source of moral strength, a declaration which was substantiated by two passages in the Tanakh: "O Lord, my rock and my fortress and my rescuer; my God, my rock, I will take refuge in Him; my shield and the horn of my salvation, my refuge" (Tehillim 18:3 Tanakh), and "Do you not know if you have not heard an everlasting God is the Lord, the Creator of the ends of the earth; He neither tires nor wearies; there is no fathoming His understanding" (Yeshayahu 40:28 Tanakh), respectively. In the QS answer phrase *"horde: evil,"* God depicted Himself as an entity comprised of multiple individuals and the embodiment of wickedness, a depiction which was substantiated by two passages in the Bible: "I am the LORD, and there is none else, there is no God beside me: I girded thee, though thou hast not known me: That they may know from the rising of the sun, and from the west, that there is none beside me. I am the LORD, and there is none else. I form the light, and create darkness: I make peace, and create evil: I the LORD do all these things. Drop down, ye heavens, from above, and let the skies pour down righteousness: let the earth open, and let them bring forth salvation, and let righteousness spring up together; I the LORD have created it" (Isaiah 45:5-8 KJV), and "For there are three that bear record in heaven, the Father, the Word (Son), and the Holy Ghost: and these three are one" (1 John 5:7 KJV), respectively. In the QS answer phrase *"clue: filler,"* God declared Himself the originator and author of the QS answers which were revealed in this book, a declaration which was corroborated by the QS answer *("Marry reason. A hint, I grew."),* a QS answer in which God stated that He'd pieced together an explanation which He'd written into multiple brief QS answers and that regarded the reason He'd lost moral force:

Summation: God authored QS answer phrases which contained no more than two descriptors to characterize Himself, in lieu of QS answer phrases that could've contained an abundant mixture of nouns, adjectives and verbs. For example, God authored the brief nounal phrase *"horde: evil"* instead of a wordier phrase like "God is a trinity and a wicked being." In "Ch. 7, Sec. 4: 12," I'd listed nounal phrases which were uncovered and revealed in this book and which characterized God and I'd provided an example of how each nounal phrase might've looked if said phrase was wordier:

Ch. 7, Sec. 4: 12

NOUNAL PHRASE	WORDIER PHRASE
EVITERNITY: HORN	God is eternal and a source of moral strength
HORDE: EVIL	God is a trinity and a wicked being
CLUE: FILLER	God fills in empty space with QS hints

────────(Plural Nouns and Standalone Singular Nouns as Descriptors: God)────────

Determination: The twelve standalone singular nouns and QS answer words *CORE, GIVER,*

HINTER, I, ILL, IN, ISSUER, JOE, REIN, TRINITY, TRIO and *WE* and the plural noun and QS answer word *REINS* were descriptors and denoted characteristics which God had. The plural noun *reins* and the two standalone singular nouns *rein* and *in* were synonymous words which meant "the controlling power(s)[2]," "the controlling power[2]" and "one who is in power[2]," respectively, and, thus, characterized God as a controlling power. The five standalone singular nouns *core, I, trinity, trio* and *we*, which meant "the most intimate part[2]," "someone possessing and aware of possessing a distinct and personal individuality[2]," "a group or set of three people[2]," "a group of three[2]" and "a group that is consciously felt as such by its members[2]," respectively, compositely portrayed God as a self-aware individual who was the essential component of a trinity that consisted of individuals who were each aware of being a member of said trinity. The two standalone singular nouns *giver* and *issuer*, which meant "one that gives (confers the ownership of without receiving a return)[2]" and "one that issues (to cause to appear for circulation among the public) something[2]," respectively, signified God as a selfless entity who'd handed QS answers that He'd authored to people He'd created so that said people would circulate said QS answers. The standalone singular noun *hinter*, which meant "one that hints (brings to mind by allusion rather than explicit expression)[2]," spotlighted God as the author of the clues within the QS answers I'd found and presented in this book. The standalone singular noun *ill*, which meant "evil (one that personifies wickedness)[2]," characterized God as an embodiment of moral wickedness. The standalone singular noun *joe*, which meant "guy[2]," identified God as a male.

Explanation: God inserted descriptions of His own characteristics into the QS answers which I'd revealed in this book, because God wanted to give readers a pathway to verify if the self-portrait God expressed in said QS answers matched characteristics that were associated with Him in religious texts and theologies.

The plural noun and two singular nouns *reins, rein* and *in*, respectively, characterized God as the one who'd presided over and dominated Reality, a characterization which was substantiated by two passages in the Tanakh: "But they rebelled against Me and would not consent to hearken to Me; they did not cast away, every man, the despicable idols from before their eyes, neither did they forsake the idols of Egypt; and I said to pour out My wrath over them, to give My (God) anger full rein over them, in the midst of the land of Egypt" (Yechezkel 20:8 Tanakh), and "The Lord will reign to all eternity" (Shemot 15:18 Tanakh).

The five singular nouns *core, I, trinity, trio* and *we* compositely portrayed God as a self-aware individual who was the essential component of a trinity that was comprised of three self-aware individuals, God (Father), Jesus (Son) and Holy Ghost, a portrayal which was substantiated by three passages in the Bible and one passage in the Tanakh. One of the three passages in the Bible focused on a trinity which God belonged to: "For there are three that bear record in heaven, the Father, the Word (Son), and the Holy Ghost: and these three are one" (1 John 5:7 KJV). One passage in the Tanakh evidenced God's awareness of His own individuality and actions: "God spoke to Moses, and He said to him, 'I am the Lord. I appeared to Abraham, to Isaac, and to Jacob with [the name] Almighty God, but (with) My name YHWH, I did not become known to them'" (Shemot 6:3 Tanakh). The second of the three passages in the Bible evidenced God's awareness of His triune physique: "And God said, Let us make man in our image, after our likeness: and let them have dominion over the fish of the sea, and over the fowl of the air, and over the cattle, and over all the earth, and over every creeping thing that creepeth upon the earth" (Genesis 1:26 KJV). The last of the three passages in the Bible evidenced Jesus's self-awareness and the awareness that Jesus had of being a member alongside God in the Trinity: "I (Jesus) and my Father are one" (John 10:30 KJV).

The two singular nouns *issuer* and *giver* signified God's disbursement of QS answers amongst the people He'd created and suggested that it was unnecessary for said people to revere Him for said disbursement. In the QS answer *("Jot, issuer. I ring entry "I," "Wans.")*, God declared Himself an issuer who'd jotted down brief statements which contained the words *I* and *wans*. In the QS answer *("Adore giver. A hinter wans.")*, God declared that He'd selflessly given allusive QS answers to readers. In a passage in the Tanakh, God exemplified His selflessness in providing for people which He'd created: "I am the Lord, and there is no other; besides Me there is no God: I will strengthen you although you have not known Me. In order that they know from the shining of the sun and from the west that there is no one besides Me; I am the Lord and there is no other. Who forms light and creates darkness, Who makes peace and creates evil; I am the Lord, Who makes all these. Cause the heavens above to drip, and let the skies pour down righteousness; let the earth open, and let salvation and righteousness be fruitful; let it cause them to sprout together; I, the Lord, have created it" (Yeshayahu 45:5-8 Tanakh).

The singular noun *hinter* implied that God was the author of the clues in the QS answers I'd presented in this book, a suggestion which the QS answer phrase *"a hint, I grew"* reinforced.

The singular noun *ill* characterized God as an embodiment of moral wickedness, a characterization substantiated in the biblical passage "I am the LORD, and there is none else, there is no God beside me: I girded thee, though thou hast not known me: That they may know from the rising of the sun, and from the west, that there is none beside me. I am the LORD, and there is none else. I form the light, and create darkness: I make peace, and create evil: I the LORD do all these things. Drop down, ye heavens, from above, and let the skies pour down righteousness: let the earth open, and let them bring forth salvation, and let righteousness spring up together; I the LORD have created it" (Isaiah 45:5-8 KJV).

God used the singular noun *joe* in two QS answer phrases to identify Himself as a male and not as a female: *"joe assure"* and *"joe: reason."* For more evidence which I'd presented to substantiate God's masculine identity, see "Ch. 7, Sec. 2: 53-57."

Summation: God used a one-word descriptor, which was either a singular or plural noun, to characterize God, instead of QS answer phrases that could've contained a mixture of several nouns, adjectives and verbs. For example, God inserted the singular noun *core* into a QS answer instead of a wordier phrase like "God is the most integral layer of the Trinity":

I've listed singular and plural nouns which I've uncovered, I've revealed in this book, and characterized God, and I've provided an example of how each singular and plural noun could've been written in a wordier way;

Ch. 7, Sec. 4: 13

PLURAL NOUN	WORDIER PHRASE
REINS	*God is a multi-self being and controlling power*

SINGULAR NOUN	WORDIER PHRASE
CORE	*God is the most integral layer of a trinity*
EVIL	*God is an immoral entity*
EVITERNITY	*God exists eternally*
GIVER	*God selflessly gives Query Stacks to others*
HINTER	*God is a provider of hints*
HORDE	*God is a crowd of individuals*
HORN	*God is a source of strength*
I	*God is a self-conscious entity*
ILL	*God is an immoral being*
IN	*God is in power*
ISSUER	*God publicizes Query Stacks*
JOE	*God is a male*
REIN	*God is a controlling power*
TRINITY	*God is one entity composed of three individuals*
TRIO	*God is three individuals*
WE	*God is a self-conscious, multi-self being*

─────────────(Nouns as Descriptors: Dave)─────────────

Determination: Each of the two nouns and QS answer words *GHOST* and *WINNER* was a descriptor and denoted a characteristic that described Dave. The singular noun *ghost*, which meant "one who does literary work for and in the name of another; ghost-writer[2]," characterized Dave as a writer who'd done the literary work of transcribing QS answers and credited God as the author of said QS answers. The singular noun *winner*, which meant "one that's successful[2]," portrayed Dave as a success in answering the "What's God's origin" question.

Explanation: I'd determined and stated that the QS answer main subject "Dave" was me, David Mivshek, a belief I'd based on characteristics which God had assigned to the QS answer main subject "Dave." First, God used the noun *ghost* in the QS answer phrase *"holy ghost"* to highlight my involvement in writing down QS answers which I'd ultimately cited as God's words and credited God for authoring. Second, God described me as a winner in the QS answer phrase *"he: winner"* because God already knew that I'd successfully answer the "What's God's origin" question; in other words, God preordained me to successfully answer said question.

Summation: God used a one-word descriptor, which was a singular noun, to characterize the QS answer main subject "Dave," in lieu of QS answer phrases that contained an abundance of nouns, adjectives and verbs. For example, God entered the singular noun *"winner"* into a QS answer instead of a wordier phrase like "Dave is a success":

> *I've listed singular nouns which I've uncovered, I've revealed in this book, and characterized Dave, and I've provided an example of how each singular noun could've been written in a wordier way;*

Ch. 7, Sec. 4: 14

SINGULAR NOUN	WORDIER PHRASE
GHOST	Dave is a ghost-writer for God
WINNER	Dave is a success

──────────(Nouns as Descriptors: QS Answer)──────────

Determination: Each one of the four singular nouns and QS answer words *AIR, HINT, REASON* and *WORDING* was a descriptor and denoted a characteristic of a QS answer. The singular noun *air*, which meant "public utterance (a written statement)[2]," characterized a QS answer as a publicized writing. The singular noun *hint*, which meant "a statement conveying by implication what it is preferred not to say explicitly[2]," portrayed a QS answer as a writing which contained allusions. The singular noun *reason*, which meant "a statement offered as an explanation of an assertion[2]," characterized a QS answer as the medium in which God conveyed His explanation that concerned the cause of His moral decay. The singular noun *wording*, which meant "the manner of expressing in words[2]," depicted a QS answer as a statement comprised of words.

Explanation: God provided descriptions of QS answers within the messages that some QS answers conveyed in order to explicitly reveal characteristics of QS answers. First, the singular noun *wording* in the QS answer *("Got wording. 'I' entry; rains 'I.'")* revealed that QS answers were comprised of words and that some of the said words, like the word *I*, appeared numerous times throughout the QS answers in this book. Second, the singular nouns *reason* and *hint* in the QS answer *("Joe: reason. Air/hint grew.")* revealed that QS answers were allusive messages which led a reader to God's explanation for why His moral strength had wanned. Third, the singular noun *air* in the QS answer phrase *"air/hint grew"* revealed that QS answers had been publicized, a claim which was backed by the fact that said QS answers were published in this book.

Summation: God used a one-word nounal descriptor to characterize a QS answer, in lieu of wordier phrases which contained an abundance of nouns, adjectives and verbs. For example, God inserted the singular noun *hint* into a QS answer instead of a wordier phrase like "a QS answer is a hint":

I've listed singular nouns which I've uncovered, I've revealed in this book, and characterized a QS answer, and I've provided an example of how each singular noun could've been written in a wordier way;

Ch. 7, Sec. 4: 15

SINGULAR NOUN	WORDIER PHRASE
AIR	A QS answer is a written utterance
HINT	A QS answer is an allusion
REASON	An explanation God expresses via QS answers
WORDING	QS answers are composed of words

──────────────(Nouns as Descriptors: Commandment)──────────────

Determination: The singular noun and QS answer word *LIE*, which meant "an assertion of something known by the speaker to be untrue[2]," pointed out one of God's Ten Commandments.

Explanation: The QS answer *("Torah's learning. Lie wans.")* insinuated that lying caused one's moral strength to weaken and that said cause and moral weakening was a lesson in the Torah which had been passed down for generations: "You shall not murder. You shall not commit adultery. You shall not steal. You shall not bear false witness against your neighbor" (Shemot 20:13 Tanakh); "You shall not accept a false report; do not place your hand with a wicked person to be a false witness" (Shemot 23:1 Tanakh); "A false witness will not go unpunished, and one who speaks lies will not escape" (Mishlei 19:5 Tanakh); "A false witness will not go unpunished, and one who speaks lies will perish" (Mishlei 19:9 Tanakh).

Summation: God used a one-word nounal descriptor to characterize one of God's Ten Commandments, instead of wordier phrases which contained an abundance of nouns, adjectives and verbs. For example, God inserted the singular noun *lie* into a QS answer instead of a wordier phrase like "a lie which God tells":

I've listed the only singular noun which I've uncovered, I've revealed in this book, and characterized one of God's Ten Commandments, and I've provided an example of how said singular noun could've been written in a wordier way;

Ch. 7, Sec. 4: 16

SINGULAR NOUN	WORDIER PHRASE
LIE	A lie which God tells

──────────────(Nouns as Descriptors: ":" for "'S")──────────────

On one hand, descriptors kept QS answers brief and to the point. On the other hand, descriptors necessitated punctuation to ensure that QS answers conveyed the smallest amount of ambiguous meaning. For example, in "Ch. 7, Sec. 4: 17" I'd supplied three sentences which conveyed the same meaning but contained different levels of wordiness and punctuation. In the first, or wordiest, sentence, I'd characterized a sailor as a man who had a boat. In the second sentence, I'd reduced the wordiness of the first sentence by turning the phrase *"sailor is"* into the contraction *sailor's* and turning the phrase *"sailor has"* into the possessive noun *man's*; however, the phrase *"sailor is a man,"* from the first sentence, and the phrase *"sailor's man,"* from the second sentence, didn't necessarily convey the same meaning. Even though I'd written the phrase *"sailor's man"* to mean *"sailor is a man,"* someone could've interpreted said phrase as *"sailor has man,"* in the same way that the possessive phrase *"man's boat"* meant *"man has boat."* The duplication of the word *man* in the third sentence and how each appearance of the word *man* was tied to either the word *sailor* or *boat* was done purposefully so that readers were persuaded into believing that the sailor had the boat, since my intention for using the word *sailor* was to invoke a mental image of a person who'd traveled by boat, and that the sailor was a man instead of owning a man, since my intention was for readers to merge the man who'd owned the boat with the identity of the sailor:

(a) Wordiest but least punctuated sentence format;
(b) Wordiness of (a) reduced but punctuation added;
(c) Wordiness of (b) reduced;

Ch. 7, Sec. 4: 17

a"The **[sailor is]** a **[man]**. The **[sailor]** has a **[boat]**.

*b***[Sailor's]** **[man]**. This **[man's]** **[boat]**.

*c*Sailor: man. Man: boat.

I'd aimed to find answer words which were correctly spelt and didn't need to be followed up with punctuation in order to dissolve ambiguity; however, God didn't add an apostrophe-ess *('s)* to the end of some nouns which He'd intended for readers to interpret as possessive nouns. In most cases, instead of attaching an *'s* to the end of a noun where an *'s* should've appeared and would've shown that who or what said noun identified was a possessor of a certain thing, God opted for a punctuation mark which symbolized *'s* and was inserted between the noun that identified said possessor and another noun which identified said thing that said possessor owned—I'd chosen a colon *(:)* as the punctuation mark which symbolized *'s*. Only one out of four answer words which were intended to be interpreted as possessive nouns contained an available letter *S* to apostrophize; specifically, the answer word *TORAH'S*:

Ch. 7, Sec. 4: 18

ORIGINAL PHRASE	INTERPRETATION
TORAH'S LEARNING	TORAH'S LEARNING
JOE(:) REASON	JOE('S) REASON
TORAH(:) GLORY	TORAH('S) GLORY
CLUE(:) FILLER	CLUE('S) FILLER

On one hand, QS answers consisted of some answer words which didn't contain esses. On the other hand, if QS answers were comprised of only answer words which contained the proper amount of esses, then the row'd words that the QS answer words were derived from would've consisted of more esses too; which meant, the row'd words would've been spelt differently. For example, if the "QS-God/Heaven" answer's second sentence started with the phrase *"he's winner"* instead of *"he: winner,"* then one of the top three row'd words in the "QS-God/Heaven" row'd word matrix would had to of contained a letter *S*. If I'd inserted a letter *S* into any of the said row'd words, then the pattern of row'd word letters and available row'd word letter connections in said QS matrix would've been affected, which, in turn, would've created a new pool of potential answer words that were producible, which, in turn, could've altered the meaning of the "QS-Dave/Earth" answer:

> *In the "unaltered" version of "QS-God/Heaven," all of the row'd words have been spelt correctly. However, I've added a letter "S" to the row'd word HEAVEN (HE-S-AVEN) in the "altered" version of "QS-God/Heaven," so that I could create the answer word HE'S and remove the colon (:) which followed the answer word HE (HE:) in the unaltered version of the "QS-God/Heaven" answer;*

Ch. 7, Sec. 4: 19

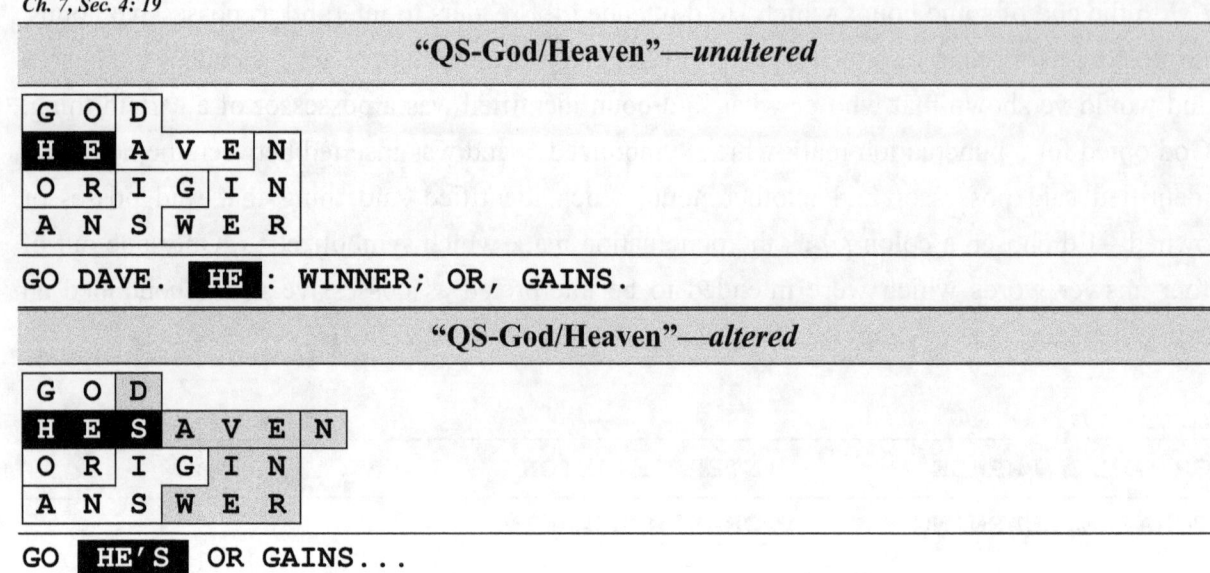

Did God suffer from a case of bad diction? Was God attempting to use the least number of letters as it possibly took to compose a readable message with a coherent meaning? Did God have a message that He'd wanted to express, but, at the same time, couldn't perfect the disbursement of letters into a consistently correct grammatical pattern?

---------------------(Nouns Recurring)---------------------

Calculation: *12* QS answer words which were nouns recurred a total of *33* times. There were *63* total nouns, so *33* of *63*, or *52.38* percent of, nouns recurred; specifically, *we* recurred *7* times; *horn* recurred *4* times; *"I"* and *in* each recurred *3* times; while *entry, hay, hint, hinter, joe, reason, sinew* and *trio,* each recurred *2* times.

Determination/Explanation: God repeated *12* nouns throughout multiple QS answers for the same reason I'd repeated the noun *man* in the third sentence of *"Ch. 7, Sec. 4: 17,"* which was to persuade readers into connecting descriptions and attributes to the entities that nouns identified and compounding and deciphering the collection of connections to reveal an overall portrait and understanding of said entities:

I've classified QS answer words which were nouns which appeared numerous times in QS answers as "Recurring Nouns." I've parenthesized the number of times recurring nouns have appeared in the twenty QS answers I've revealed in this book;

Ch. 7, Sec. 4: 20

RECURRING NOUN	NUMBER OF ENTRIES
WE	(07)
HORN	(04)
"I"	(03)
IN	(03)
ENTRY	(02)
HAY	(02)
HINT	(02)
HINTER	(02)
JOE	(02)
REASON	(02)
SINEW	(02)
TRIO	(02)

QS Answer Word Types
Statistical Analyses: Verbs

Calculation: "Verbs" was the second most prevalent QS answer word type in the twenty QS answers I'd revealed in this book; in fact, verbs accounted for *29* out of *119,* or *24.37* percent of, total QS answer words.

Determination: God, the author of the QS answers in this book, entered at least one verb into each of the twenty QS answers in this book in order to activate at least one characteristic of or one attribute associated with each QS answer's main subject. For one, God inserted verbs into QS answers in order to equalize synonymous descriptions of an entity, as in the QS answer phrase *"a trinity; or, rings a we,"* in which the verb and answer word *RINGS* equalized the identity of the trinity and the we. For two, God inserted verbs into QS answers in order to explain how a QS answer's main subject affected the origination or evolution of said main subject's self, as in the QS answer phrase *"Heaven: siring a we,"* in which the verb *siring* cited an act of origination that Heaven, which was God, administered upon Himself. For three, God inserted verbs into QS answers in order to describe a main subject's cause of origination or evolution, as in the QS answer phrase *"a hint, I grew,"* in which the verb *grew* cited an act of evolution that God *(I)*, administered upon the main subject "hint." For four, God inserted verbs into QS answers in order to highlight how a QS answer main subject applied a certain thing to said QS answer main subject's self, as in the QS answer phrase *"in: trying sinew,"* in which the verb *trying* described how the in, which was God, affected Himself with sinew. For five, God inserted verbs into QS answers in order to tie a QS answer main subject to an action that said QS answer main subject committed in order to create a QS answer phrase which reinforced and supplemented clues provided by another QS answer phrase and contained at least one of the same verbs and had a synonymous meaning as another QS answer phrase; as in, the QS answer phrases *"trio: trying"* and *"in: trying sinew,"* in which the meaning conveyed by the QS answer phrase *"trio: trying"* reinforced the message conveyed by the QS answer phrase *"in: trying sinew."* For six, God inserted verbs into QS answers in order to define actions which affected QS answer main subjects even when the catalysts of said actions weren't explicitly declared, as in the QS answer phrase *"marry reason,"* in which the verb *marry* affected the QS answer subject "reason," but how the reason had become married wasn't explicitly revealed. For seven, God inserted verbs into QS answers in order to tell how QS answer main subjects evolved but not to tell what caused said QS answer main subjects to evolve, as in the QS answer phrase *"trio wans,"* in which the verb *wans* signified an evolution, or the moral decay, of a trio, but the cause of the trio's moral decay wasn't mentioned. Additionally, nearly half of the verbs found in the twenty QS answers in this book recurred, or appeared more than one time, in said QS answers, which elevated the number of QS answer words that I'd counted as verbs:

I've classified QS answer words which were verbs into five types: "being(a-1) affects same being(a-1)" "being(a-1) affects nonbeing(c-2)," "being(a-1)/nonbeing(a-2) affects undisclosed being/nonbeing," "undisclosed being/nonbeing affects being(c-1)/nonbeing(c-2)," and "being(a-1)/nonbeing(a-2) is affected";

Ch. 7, Sec. 4: 21

Being*(a-1)* affects*(b)* Same Being*(a-1)*
$^{a-1}$TRINITY; OR ^{b}RINGS A $^{a-1}$WE
[$^{a-1}$YAHWEH] ^{b}NERVING, ^{b}IS A $^{a-1}$WE
$^{a-1}$HEAVEN: ^{b}SIRING A $^{a-1}$WE
$^{a-1}$HORN: ^{b}SIRING A $^{a-1}$WE

Being*(a-1)* affects*(b)* Nonbeing*(c-2)*
$^{c-2}$HINT, $^{a-1}$I ^{b}GREW
$^{a-1}$I ^{b}RING $^{c-2}$ENTRY
$^{a-1}$REINS ^{b}RING $^{c-2}$"A WE"
$^{a-1}$IN: ^{b}TRYING $^{c-2}$SINEW
$^{a-1}$HOST: ^{b}TRYING $^{c-2}$SINEW

Being*(a-1)*/Nonbeing*(a-2)* affects*(b)* Undisclosed Being/Nonbeing
^{b}JOT, $^{a-1}$ISSUER
$^{a-1}$JOE ^{b}ASSURE
$^{a-1}$ILL ^{b}REIGN
$^{a-1}$TRIO: ^{b}REINING
$^{a-1}$TRIO: ^{b}TRYING
$^{a-1}$HE: ^{b}ANSWERING
$^{a-2}$LIE ^{b}WANS

Undisclosed Being/Nonbeing affects*(b)* Being*(c-1)*/Nonbeing*(c-2)*
^{b}MARRY $^{c-2}$REASON
^{b}ADORE $^{c-1}$GIVER
^{b}GOT $^{c-2}$WORDING
^{b}RAINS $^{c-2}$"I"

Being*(a-1)*/Nonbeing*(a-2)* is affected*(b)*
$^{a-2}$AIR ^{b}GREW
$^{a-1}$ILL ^{b}WANS
$^{a-1}$HINTER ^{b}WANS
$^{a-1}$REIN ^{b}WANS
$^{a-1}$TRIO: ^{b}WANS
$^{a-1}$TRIO: ^{b}WANES

──────────────────(**Verbs: Being Affects Same Being**)──────────────────

Determination: Four verbs signified actions which God committed upon Himself; specifically, the base verb *is*, the two active participle verbs (v+ing) *nerving* and *siring*, and the TPS-PTV (v+s) *rings*.

Explanation: There were four verbs which denoted actions which God committed upon Himself: *is, nerving, rings* and *siring*. First, God used the verbs *is*, which meant "show a certain characteristic[2]," and *nerving*, which meant "giving strength to[2]," in the QS answer phrase *"nerving, is a we"* to reveal that He'd provided moral strength to the members of the trinity which He was a component of and self-evolved into. Second, God used the TPS-PTV *rings*, which meant "has a character expressive of some quality[2]," in the QS answer *"a trinity; or, rings a we"* to reinforce the fact that the triune physique that He'd evolved Himself into hadn't only contained three individuals but also said individuals were conscious enough to be aware of their membership in said trinity. Third, God used the active participle verb *siring*, which meant "bringing into being[2]," in the QS answer phrases *"Heaven: siring a we"* and *"horn: siring a we"* to explicitly evidence His personal involvement in the evolution of Himself from one self-aware individual into three self-aware individuals:

(a-1) Being*(a-1)* affects same being*(a-1)*;
(b) Action affects being*(a-1)*;

Ch. 7, Sec. 4: 22

Being affects Same Being
[a-1]**TRINITY**; OR [b]**RINGS** A [a-1]**WE**
[[a-1]**YAHWEH**] [b]**NERVING**, [b]**IS** A [a-1]**WE**
[a-1]**HEAVEN:** [b]**SIRING** A [a-1]**WE**
[a-1]**HORN:** [b]**SIRING** A [a-1]**WE**

──────────────────(**Verbs: Being Affects Nonbeing**)──────────────────

Determination: Three verbs signified actions which God committed and involved inanimate objects; specifically, the two base verbs *grew* and *ring* and the active participle verb *trying*.

Explanation: There were three verbs which denoted actions that God committed and involved inanimate objects: *grew, ring* and *trying*. First, God used the verb *grew*, which meant "to have increased in any way[2]," in the QS answer phrase *"hint, I grew"* to highlight His involvement in the expansion of QS answer verbiage. Second, God used the verb *ring*, which meant "to repeat earnestly[2]," in the QS answer phrases *"I ring entry"* and *"reins ring 'A We'"* to focus a reader's attention onto QS answer words and phrases, or "entries," that He'd inserted numerous times into QS answers, such as the QS answer phrase *"a we."* Third, God used the verb *trying*, which meant "making an attempt to carry out some action[2]," in the QS answer phrases *"in: trying sinew"* and *"Host: trying sinew"* as a way to explain His attempt at using His own moral force to dominate moral people He'd created:

(a-1) Being affects nonbeing*(c-2)*;
(b) Action affects nonbeing*(c-2)*;
(c-2) Nonbeing affected by being*(a-1)*;

Ch. 7, Sec. 4: 23

Being affects Nonbeing
*c-2*HINT, *a-1*I *b*GREW
*a-1*I *b*RING *c-2*ENTRY
*a-1*REINS *b*RING *c-2*"A WE"
*a-1*IN: *b*TRYING *c-2*SINEW
*a-1*HOST: *b*TRYING *c-2*SINEW

————(**Verbs: Being/Nonbeing Affects Undisclosed Being/Nonbeing**)————

Determination: Six verbs; specifically, two active participle verbs, *reining* and *answering*, one TPS-PTV, *wans*, and three ESVs (v-s), *jot, assure* and *reign,* signified actions which were put into effect by two beings, God and Dave, and one nonbeing, a lie, while the recipients of said actions weren't mentioned.

Explanation: In some cases, QS answer words which were verbs expressed actions which were committed by known entities, yet the entities which were affected by said actions weren't explicitly identified. I had to identify who the unidentified recipients of said actions were by comparing, compounding and analyzing hints which were incorporated into QS answer phrases that consisted of words and phrases which were exactly the same or similar to the grammars and meanings of the QS answer phrases that mentioned said unidentified recipients.

The four QS answer phrases "joe assure," "ill reign," "trio reining" and "trio trying" didn't mention what God had certainty about, dominated or attempted to do, respectively. However, based on QS answers such as *("Horde: evil. Ill reign, wans.")*, which I'd interpreted as ("A horde [God's trio] is evil [wicked]. The ill [God's wicked trio] reigns [dominates] and wans [loses moral force]."), and *("Joe assure. Right, rein wans.")*, which I'd interpreted as ("A joe [male; God] assures [informs positively] that He has wanned. Right, [correct] rein [controlling power; God] wans [loses moral force]."), I'd determined that since the trio was God's trinity and God wielded moral force to influence moral entities in Reality, then the what that God had reined over was Reality. On the other hand, based on the QS answer *("Torah: glory. Host: in, I, trying sinew.")*, which I'd interpreted as ("The Torah [Jewish bible] told about a glory

[Shekinah; a manifestation of God on Earth as an Earthly object]. The Host [Jesus Christ's body; God's body] is an in [controlling power], is an I [self-aware individual] and is trying [attempting to use] sinew [moral strength]."), I'd determined that since the trio was God's trinity and God wielded moral force to influence moral entities in Reality, then the what that God had tried to do was to dominate Reality by exerting His own moral force.

Second, the QS answer phrase *"jot, issuer"* conveyed the message that God published something and authored brief writings, but didn't go so far as to reveal what God published or what brief writings God had written. However, based on my interpretation of *"I ring entry 'I,' 'Wans,'"* which was another QS answer phrase that was in the same QS answer as the QS answer phrase *"jot, issuer"* and I'd interpreted as ("I [God] ring [repeat] the entry [QS answer word] 'I' or 'Wans.'"), I'd determined that God had jotted down and publicized QS answers.

Third, the QS answer phrase *"he: answering"* conveyed the message that Dave was solving something, but didn't go so far as to reveal what Dave was solving. However, based on my interpretation of *"holy ghost,"* a QS answer phrase that was in the same QS answer as the QS answer phrase *"he: answering"* and I'd interpreted as ("Holy [associated with God] ghost [ghost-writer]."), I'd determined that Dave was solving questions like "What's God's origin?" by revealing QS answers that he'd written down but gave God credit for authoring.

Fourth, the QS answer phrase *"lie wans"* conveyed the message that a lie caused a moral entity to dwindle in moral force, but didn't go so far as to reveal who the said entity which lost moral force was. However, based on my interpretation of the QS answer phrase *"trio: reining, wans,"* which I'd interpreted as ("The trio [trinity; God] is reining [controlling] and wans [losing force]."), I'd determined that the lie was told by God and that the lie caused God to experience a loss of force in His own moral strength:

[a-1] Being affects undisclosed entity;
[b] Action affects undisclosed entity;

Ch. 7, Sec. 4: 24

Being affects Undisclosed Being/Nonbeing
[b]JOT, [a-1]ISSUER
[a-1]JOE [b]ASSURE
[a-1]ILL [b]REIGN
[a-1]TRIO: [b]REINING
[a-1]TRIO: [b]TRYING
[a-1]HE: [b]ANSWERING
[a-2]LIE [b]WANS

―――――(**Verbs: Undisclosed Being/Nonbeing Affects Being/Nonbeing**)―――――

Determination: Four verbs signified actions which affected beings and nonbeings mentioned in QS answers, yet the entities that committed said actions weren't mentioned; specifically; the three base verbs *marry, got,* and *adore,* and the TPS-PTV *rains.*

Explanation: In some cases, QS answer words which were verbs expressed actions that affected entities which were explicitly identified, yet the beings and nonbeings that initiated said actions weren't mentioned. I had to identify said actions' initiators by comparing, compounding and analyzing hints which were incorporated into words and phrases of QS answers which had the exact same or similar grammar and meaning of QS answers that didn't identify said initiators.

First, the QS answer phrase *"marry reason"* intimated that an entity had pieced together parts of an explanation to produce one overall explanation, but said QS answer phrase didn't in any way identify said entity. However, based on the QS answer phrase *"joe: reason,"* which I'd interpreted as ("the joe's [male's; God's] reason [explanation]"), I'd determined that since God was the male who was associated with said explanation, then God was the person who'd pieced together said explanation into one, composite explanation.

Second, the QS answer phrase *"got wording"* intimated that something was expressed as words while the QS answer phrase *"rains 'I,'"* which was another QS answer phrase that was in the same QS answer as the QS answer phrase *"got wording,"* intimated that an entity had inserted the word *I* into QS answers numerous times, but neither QS answer phrase revealed what was expressed in words or contained numerous occurrences of the word *I*. However, based on my interpretation of said QS answer *("Got wording. 'I' entry; rains 'I.'")*, which was ("Got [has] wording [words]. 'I' entry [QS answer word *'I'*]; rains 'I' [supplies QS answer word *'I'* in abundance]."), I'd determined that since QS answers contained words and numerous instances of the QS answer word *I,* then QS answers were what had wording and rained the QS answer word *I.*

Third, the QS answer phrase *"adore giver"* requested for unidentified entities to adore, or "worship with profound reverence[2]," an individual who'd provided said entities with something but didn't expect anything in return from said entities. However, based on the QS answer *("Adore giver. A hinter wans."),* which I'd interpreted as ("Adore [revere] giver [provider of QS answers; God]. A hinter [giver of QS hints; God] wans [loses moral force]."), I'd determined that since God was the author who'd provided the people that He'd created with the QS answers I'd revealed in this book, then God was requesting for a general audience, virtually everyone in Reality, to revere Him:

    [b] Action affects being*(c-1)*/nonbeing*(c-2)*;
[c-1] Being affected by undisclosed being/nonbeing;
[c-2] Nonbeing affected by undisclosed being/nonbeing;

Ch. 7, Sec. 4: 25

Undisclosed Being/Nonbeing affects Being/Nonbeing
[b]ADORE [c-1]GIVER
[b]MARRY [c-2]REASON
[b]GOT [c-2]WORDING
[b]RAINS [c-2]"I"

———————————(Verbs: Being/Nonbeing is Affected)———————————

Determination: Three verbs signified actions which affected one being and one nonbeing; specifically; the two TPS-PTVs *wanes* and *wans* signified synonymous actions which affected God, while the base verb *grew* signified an action which affected QS answers.

Explanation: In some cases, QS answer words that were verbs expressed outcomes experienced by QS answer main subjects, yet the causes of said outcomes weren't explicitly expressed in the same QS answers that expressed said outcomes. I had to identify the causes of said outcomes by comparing, compounding and analyzing hints which were incorporated into QS answer phrases that consisted of words and phrases which were exactly the same or similar to the grammars and meanings of the QS answer phrases that didn't mention the causes of said outcomes.

Each of the five QS answer phrases *"hinter wans," "ill wans," "rein wans," "trio wans"* and *"trio wanes"* translated into a message which meant that God, an author of QS answer hints, had moral force which had lost strength; meaning, God's moral force had wanned, or waned, yet none of the said QS answer phrases mentioned how God's moral force wanned, or waned. However, based on another QS answer phrase, *"lie wans,"* which I'd interpreted as ("a lie [untruth] wans [causes moral force to decay]"), I'd determined that God's moral force decayed as a result of a lie that God had told or that someone else had told and God had supported.

Second, the QS answer phrase *"air grew"* stated that an air, or a publicized written statement, grew, or became wordier over time, yet said QS answer phrase didn't mention how the said statement evolved. However, based on the QS answer *("Marry reason. A hint, I grew."),* which I'd interpreted as ("Marry [bring together] reason [an explanation]. A hint [QS answer clue], I [narrator; God] grew [added words to]."), I'd determined that since the QS answers in this book were publicized and authored by God, then God was the being who'd added words to, or "grew," said QS answers:

- [a-1] Being affected by action;
- [a-2] Nonbeing affected by action;
- [b] Action affects being(a-1)/nonbeing(a-2);

Ch. 7, Sec. 4: 26

Being/Nonbeing is affected
$^{a\text{-}2}$AIR ^{b}GREW
$^{a\text{-}1}$ILL ^{b}WANS
$^{a\text{-}1}$HINTER ^{b}WANS
$^{a\text{-}1}$REIN ^{b}WANS
$^{a\text{-}1}$TRIO: ^{b}WANS
$^{a\text{-}1}$TRIO: ^{b}WANES

──────────────(Verbs Recurring)──────────────

Calculation: *5* QS answer words which were verbs recurred a total of *14* times. There were *29* total verbs, so *14* of *29*, or *48.28* percent of, verbs recurred; specifically, *wans* recurred *6* times; *trying* recurred *3* times; and *grew, ring* and *siring,* each recurred *2* times.

Explanation: God repeated *5* verbs throughout multiple QS answers in order to persuade readers into connecting descriptions and attributes to entities that said verbs linked together and compounding and deciphering the collection of connections to reveal an overall portrait and understanding of how said entities evolved and affected other entities:

> *I've classified QS answer words which were verbs which appeared numerous times in QS answers as "Recurring Verbs." I've parenthesized the number of times recurring verbs appeared in the twenty QS answers revealed in this book;*

Ch. 7, Sec. 4: 27

RECURRING VERB	NUMBER OF OCCURRENCES
WANS	*(06)*
TRYING	*(03)*
GREW	*(02)*
RING	*(02)*
SIRING	*(02)*

──────────────(Excised Verbs)──────────────

Calculation: God didn't add a letter *S* to some verbs as the verb's last letter when it would've been grammatically correct to do so, just as He didn't add a letter *S* to the end of some nouns when it would've been grammatically correct to do so (see "Ch. 7, Sec. 4: 17-19"). In fact, *3* of *29*, or *10.35* percent of, verbs in this book were excised verbs, or ESVs, or verbs with the letter *S* excised from said verbs' last-letter positions:

Ch. 7, Sec. 4: 28

EXCISED VERB	CORRECTED ANSWER WORD
ASSURE	ASSURE(S)
JOT	JOT(S)
REIGN	REIGN(S)

ORIGINAL PHRASE	CORRECTED ANSWER WORD IN PHRASE
JOE ASSURE	JOE ASSURES
JOT, ISSUER	JOTS, ISSUER
ILL REIGN, WANS	ILL REIGNS, WANS

Determination: On one hand, QS answers consisted of some answer words which didn't contain esses. On the other hand, if QS answers were comprised of only answer words which contained the proper amount of esses, then the row'd words that the QS answer words would've been derived from would've contained more esses too; which meant, the row'd words would've been spelt differently. For example, if the "QS-Jesus/Earth" answer's first sentence began with the phrase *"joe assures"* instead of *"joe assure,"* then one of the top three row'd words of the "QS-Jesus/Earth" row'd word matrix had to of contained the letter *S* in order for the QS answer word *ASSURES* to have been spelt. If a letter *S* was inserted into and as the last letter of the top row'd word, JESUS, then Jesus's name would've been *Jesuss*; meaning, the pattern of letters in Jesus's name would've been different than the pattern of letters in Jesus's actual name:

In the "unaltered" version of "QS-Jesus/Earth," all of the row'd words have been spelt correctly. However, I've added a letter "S" to the row'd word JESUS (JESUS-S) in the "altered" version of "QS-Jesus/Earth" to exemplify how the answer word ASSURE could've been encoded in the QS matrix as the QS answer word ASSURES;

Ch. 7, Sec. 4: 29

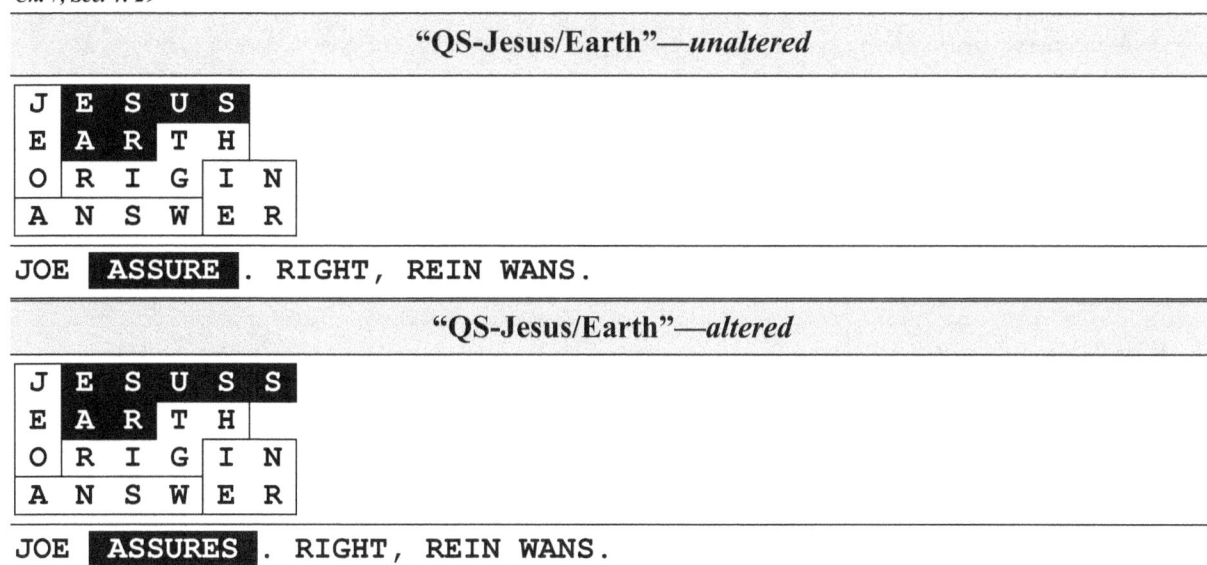

I'd asked the same questions as I'd asked in regards to missing esses in nouns: Did God suffer from a case of bad diction? Did God attempt to use the least number of letters as it possibly took to compose a readable message with a coherent meaning? Did God have a message that He'd wanted to express, but, at the same time, couldn't perfect the disbursement of letters into a consistently correct grammatical pattern?

QS Answer Word Types
Statistical Analyses: Indefinite Articles

Calculation: "Indefinite articles" was the third most prevalent QS answer word type in the twenty QS answers I'd revealed in this book; in fact, indefinite articles accounted for *8* out of *119,* or *6.72* percent of, total QS answer words.

Determination/Explanation: God, the author of said QS answers, used indefinite articles to diminish potential ambiguity in the meanings of QS answers. Said indefinite articles clarified that the QS answer words which indefinite articles preceded in QS answers were nouns, instead of verbs or pronouns, and didn't necessarily identify one particular example of an entity. Moreover, each indefinite article which was an answer word in this book was a recurring indefinite article, since each said QS answer word was the indefinite article *A*:

> *I've classified QS answer words which were indefinite articles into three types: "noun not verb," "noun not pronoun," and "being/nonbeing not unique." Also, I've parenthesized the number of times recurring indefinite articles and the number of*

times recurring phrases which contained an indefinite article appeared in the twenty QS answers in this book;

Ch. 7, Sec. 4: 30

RECURRING INDEFINITE ARTICLE	NUMBER OF ENTRIES
A	**(08)**
Noun not Verb	
A HINT$_{noun}$, I GREW	
Noun not Pronoun	
SIRING A WE$_{noun}$ (2)	
IS A WE$_{noun}$	
RINGS A WE$_{noun}$	
INGRAIN'S A WE$_{noun}$	
Entity not Unique	
A HINT$_{entity}$	
A HINTER$_{entity}$	
A TRINITY$_{entity}$	
A WE$_{entity}$	

────────(Indefinite Articles: Noun Not Verb)────────

Explanation: In the QS answer phrase *"a hint, I grew,"* the indefinite article and QS answer word *A* clarified that the QS answer word which it preceded, *HINT*, was intended to be interpreted as a noun and not be interpreted as a verb. If said QS answer phrase didn't contain the QS answer word *A*, or if the said phrase was *"a̶ hint, I grew,"* then the phrase which didn't contain the indefinite article *A* would've been susceptible to misinterpretation. The version of the QS answer phrase which contained the indefinite article and QS answer word *A* could've been interpreted only as *"I grew a hint,"* while the version of the QS answer phrase which didn't contain the indefinite article and QS answer word *A*, *"hint, I grew,"* could've been interpreted as *"hint and I grew,"* as in *"I hint and I grew"* or *"I give a hint and I grew something that's not myself"*:

Ch. 7, Sec. 4: 31

WITH INDEFINITE ARTICLE	INTERPRETATION
$A_{i\text{-}art}$ HINT$_{noun}$, I GREW	*I grew a hint*

WITHOUT INDEFINITE ARTICLE	INTERPRETATION
HINT$_{noun}$, I GREW	*I grew hint*
HINT$_{verb}$, I GREW	*I hint and I grew (myself or something else)*

────────────(Indefinite Articles: Noun Not Pronoun)────────────

Explanation: In *"siring a we," "is a we," rings a we"* or *"ingrain's a we,"* the indefinite article and QS answer word *A* reduced the number of possible interpretations of the QS answer by clarifying that the QS answer word *WE* was intended to be interpreted as a noun and not be interpreted as a pronoun. If each of said QS answer phrases didn't contain the QS answer word *A*, or if said QS answer phrases were written as *"siring -a- we," "is -a- we" "rings -a- we"* or *"ingrain's -a- we,"* then said version of each QS answer phrase would've been susceptible to misinterpretation. The version of each QS answer phrase which contained the indefinite article and QS answer word *A* had one plausible interpretation: *"siring a we"* meant *"someone or something was siring a we," "is a we"* meant *"someone or something was a we," "rings a we"* meant *"someone or something rang a we"* and *"ingrain's a we"* meant *"an innate character is a we."* On the other hand, the version of each QS answer phrase which didn't contain the indefinite article and QS answer word *A* could've been misinterpreted. The first phrase, *"siring we,"* could've led a reader to interpret said first phrase as *"someone or something is siring a group of individuals which the narrator and each reader of this first QS answer phrase are individuals in"*; the second phrase, *"is we,"* could've led a reader to interpret said second phrase as *"something a group of individuals which the narrator and each reader of this second QS answer phrase are individuals in"*; the third phrase, *"rings we,"* could've led a reader to interpret said third phrase as *"rings a group of individuals which the narrator and each reader of this third QS answer phrase are individuals in"*; while the fourth phrase, *"ingrain's we,"* could've led a reader to interpret said fourth phrase as *"an innate character of something is a group of individuals which the narrator and each reader of this fourth QS answer phrase are individuals in"*:

Ch. 7, Sec. 4: 32

WITH INDEFINITE ARTICLE	INTERPRETATION
SIRING A$_{i-art}$ WE$_{noun}$	*(someone or something) is siring a we*
IS A$_{i-art}$ WE$_{noun}$	*(someone or something) is a we*
RINGS A$_{i-art}$ WE$_{noun}$	*(someone or something) rings a we*
INGRAIN'S A$_{i-art}$ WE$_{noun}$	*innate character is a we*
WITHOUT INDEFINITE ARTICLE	**INTERPRETATION**
SIRING WE$_{pronoun}$	*(someone or something) is siring us (i.e. reader too)*
IS WE$_{pronoun}$	*(something) is us (i.e. reader too)*
RINGS WE$_{pronoun}$	*(someone or something) rings us (i.e. reader too)*
INGRAIN'S WE$_{pronoun}$	*innate character is us (i.e. reader too)*

──────────────(Indefinite Articles: Entity Not Unique)──────────────

Determination: In each of the four QS answer phrases *"a hint," "a hinter," "a trinity"* and *"a we"* the indefinite article and QS answer word *A* affected the meaning of each said phrase by not naming which hint, hinter, trinity or we was spotlighted out of all of the possible hints, hinters, trinities or wes (plural of *we*) that had ever existed:

Ch. 7, Sec. 4: 33

WITH INDEFINITE ARTICLE	INITIAL INTERPRETATION
A$_{i-art}$ HINT$_{entity}$	*one of many hints*
A$_{i-art}$ HINTER$_{entity}$	*one of many hinters*
A$_{i-art}$ TRINITY$_{entity}$	*one of many trinities*
A$_{i-art}$ WE$_{entity}$	*one of many wes*

Explanation: The QS answer phrases *"a hint," "a hinter," "a trinity"* and *"a we"* were oblique clues that I had to use in order to identify which hint, hinter, trinity or we out of all of the possible hints, hinters, trinities or wes that have ever existed was the most probable hint, hinter, trinity or we that each said QS answer had spotlighted.

First, the QS answer phrase *"a hint"* focused on an allusive message, yet said phrase didn't specify which allusive message said phrase pertained to. However, based on the QS answer *("Marry reason. A hint, I grew.")*, which I'd interpreted as ("Marry [bring together] reason [an explanation]. A hint [QS answer allusion], I [narrator; God] grew [added words to]."), I'd determined that since God authored the QS answers in this book and provided many allusive messages about Himself within said QS answers, then the allusive message that the QS answer phrase *"a hint"* pointed to was an allusive message which was in a QS answer.

Second, the QS answer phrase *"a hinter"* focused on someone who'd provided allusive messages, yet said QS answer phrase didn't name who the said someone was. However, based on the QS answer *("Marry reason. A hint, I grew.")*, which I'd interpreted as ("Marry [bring together] reason [an explanation]. A hint [QS answer allusion], I [narrator; God] grew [added words to]."), I'd determined that since the QS answers in this book were authored by God and contained allusive messages, then God was the hinter, or provider of said allusive messages.

Third, the QS answer phrase *"a trinity"* focused on an entity which was comprised of three individuals, yet didn't explicitly identify which trio out of all of the possible trios in existence was spotlighted. However, based on the QS answer *("Fair hinter. Trio: trying, wanes.")*, which I'd interpreted as ("Fair [real] hinter [provider of allusions; God]. Trio [group of three people; God's trinity] is trying [making an attempt] but wanes [loses moral force]."), I'd determined that since God was comprised of Himself, Jesus Christ and the Holy Ghost, and God provided allusive messages via QS answers, then God was the trinity.

Fourth, the QS answer phrase *"a we"* focused on a group of individuals who were aware of their membership in said group yet said phrase didn't explicitly name which group of individuals said phrase had spotlighted. However, based on the QS answer *("Yahweh: horn. Nerving, is a we.")*, which I'd interpreted as ("Yahweh [God] is a horn [source of strength]. Nerving [giving strength to] and is a we [group of self-aware individuals]."), I'd determined that since theological scholars considered *Yahweh* to be a transliteration of God's actual name, *YHWH*, and God was comprised of three self-aware individuals, then God's trinity was the we:

Ch. 7, Sec. 4: 34

WITH INDEFINITE ARTICLE	FINAL INTERPRETATION
$A_{i\text{-}art}$ HINT$_{entity}$	*QS answer allusion*
$A_{i\text{-}art}$ HINTER$_{entity}$	*God as QS answer author*
$A_{i\text{-}art}$ TRINITY$_{entity}$	*God as Himself, Jesus Christ and Holy Ghost*
$A_{i\text{-}art}$ WE$_{entity}$	*God as a trinity*

QS Answer Word Types
Statistical Analyses: Pronouns

Calculation: "Pronouns" was tied with "adjectives" as the fourth most prevalent QS answer word type in the twenty QS answers I'd revealed in this book; in fact, pronouns accounted for *6* out of *119,* or *5.04* percent of, total QS answer words.

————————————————(Pronouns: God)————————————————

Determination/Explanation: God used the third-person pronoun and QS answer word *THEY* and first-person pronoun and QS answer word *I* when He'd referred to Himself in the QS answers I'd revealed in this book. First, in the QS answer phrase *"they or reins, I, ring 'A We,'"* God used the third-person pronoun and QS answer word *THEY* to refer to a group of individuals from the perspective of not being a member in said group, while, in the same QS answer phrase, God used the first-person pronoun and QS answer word *I* to clarify that said group was composed of individuals which formed a trinity that He was a part of. Second, God used the pronoun and QS answer word *I* in the QS answer phrases *"a hint, I grew"* and *"I ring entry 'I,' 'Wans'"* to refer to Himself:

Ch. 7, Sec. 4: 35

PRONOUN	CORRESPONDING QS ANSWER
I	A HINT, I_{pron} GREW.
I	I_{pron} RING ENTRY "I," "WANS."
I, THEY	$THEY_{pron}$ OR REINS, I_{pron}, RING "A WE."

————————————————(Pronouns: Dave)————————————————

Determination/Explanation: God used the third-person pronoun and QS answer word *HE* when He'd referenced the QS answer main subject "Dave" in this book's QS answers. The pronoun *he* appeared as a QS answer word in two QS answers. In the first QS answer, *("Go Dave. He: winner; or, gains.")*, the pronoun *he* cited a male who was nicknamed *Dave* and who was a and gained from his success. In the second QS answer, *("Holy ghost. He: naïve or answering.")*, the pronoun *he* was linked to one of Dave's characteristics (e.g. naïve, or "self-taught"), attributes (e.g. ghost, or "ghost-writer") and actions (e.g. answering, or "solving"):

Ch. 7, Sec. 4: 36

PRONOUN	CORRESPONDING QS ANSWER
HE	GO DAVE. HE_{pron}: WINNER; OR, GAINS.
HE	HOLY GHOST. HE_{pron}: NAÏVE OR ANSWERING.

————————————————(Pronouns Recurring)————————————————

Calculation: Moreover, *2* QS answer words which were pronouns recurred a total of *5* times. There were *6* total pronouns, so *5* of *6*, or *83.33* percent of, pronouns recurred; specifically, the pronoun *I* recurred *3* times and *he* recurred *2* times.

Explanation: God repeated *2* pronouns throughout multiple QS answers in order to persuade readers into connecting characteristics, attributes and actions to two QS answer characters, God and Dave:

I've classified QS answer words which were pronouns that appeared numerous times in QS answers as "Recurring Pronouns." I've parenthesized the number of times recurring pronouns appeared in the twenty QS answers revealed in this book;

Ch. 7, Sec. 4: 37

RECURRING PRONOUN	NUMBER OF ENTRIES
I	(03)
HE	(02)

QS Answer Word Types
Statistical Analyses: Adjectives

Calculation: "Adjectives" was tied with "pronouns" as the fourth most prevalent QS answer word type in the twenty QS answers I'd revealed in this book; therefore, adjectives, like pronouns, accounted for *6* out of *119*, or *5.04* percent of, total QS answer words.

———————————————(Adjectives: God)———————————————

Determination/Explanation: God used four adjectives to thicken the description of His own persona: *real, fair, hairy* and *thy*. First, in the two QS answers *("Core: real. Trinity; or, rings a we.")* and *("Fair hinter. Trio: trying, wanes.")*, God, the hinter or provider of QS answer allusions, used the adjectives *real* and *fair*, respectively, to characterize Himself, the core or essential component of a trinity or trio of individuals, as a real, or nonimaginary, entity. Second, in the QS answer (*"Hairy: we. Thy trio: reining wans"*), God used the adjectives *hairy* and *thy* to describe Himself as an incomprehensibility and a trio of self-aware individuals, but referred to Himself from the perspective of conveying information to and about someone who wasn't Himself:

Ch. 7, Sec. 4: 38

"GOD" ADJECTIVE	CORRESPONDING QS ANSWER
REAL	CORE: REAL$_{adj}$. A TRINITY; OR, RINGS A WE.
FAIR	FAIR$_{adj}$ HINTER. TRIO: TRYING, WANES.
HAIRY, THY	HAIRY$_{adj}$ WE. THY$_{adj}$ TRIO: REINING, WANS.

―――――――――――――――――――(Adjectives: Dave)―――――――――――――――――――

Determination/Explanation: In the QS answer *("Holy ghost. He: naïve or answering.")*, God used two adjectives, *holy* and *naïve*, to thicken the description of the QS answer's main subject Dave. In the QS answer phrase *"holy ghost,"* Dave, the "he," was portrayed as a ghost, or ghost-writer, who was holy, or who'd dedicated his literary services to God, while in the QS answer phrase *"he: naïve or answering,"* Dave was depicted as a naïve, or self-taught, individual who'd taught himself how to construct and decode Query Stacks in a pursuit to unravel information about how God was created:

Ch. 7, Sec. 4: 39

"DAVE" ADJECTIVE	CORRESPONDING QS ANSWER
HOLY, NAÏVE	HOLY$_{adj}$ GHOST. HE: NAÏVE$_{adj}$ OR ANSWERING.

QS Answer Word Types
Statistical Analyses: Conjunctions

Calculation: "Conjunctions" was the fifth most prevalent QS answer word type in the twenty QS answers I'd revealed in this book; in fact, conjunctions accounted for *4* out of *119*, or *3.36* percent of, total QS answer words.

―――――――――――――――――――(Conjunctions: God)―――――――――――――――――――

Determination/Explanation: God inserted the conjunction and QS answer word *OR* into two QS answers in which He'd identified as the main subject of, in order to link together QS answer words and phrases which were synonymous in meaning and revealed characteristics, attributes and actions associated with Himself. First, God inserted the conjunction *or* into the QS answer phrase *"trinity; or, rings a we"* in order to reinforce the idea that the trinity which He was a member of wasn't only a group of individuals but was a group of self-aware individuals *(trinity = we)*. Second, God inserted the conjunction *or* into the QS answer phrase *"they or reins, I, ring 'A We'"* in order to highlight the synonymous relationship between the QS answer words *THEY* and *REINS*, two QS answer words which were either a pronoun that referenced the trinity which God was a member of or depicted the members of said trinity as controlling powers *(they = reins)*:

Ch. 7, Sec. 4: 40

CONJUNCTION	CORRESPONDING QS ANSWER PHRASE
OR	TRINITY; OR$_{conj}$, RINGS A WE
OR	THEY OR$_{conj}$ REINS, I, RING "A WE."

---------------------------------(Conjunctions: Dave)---------------------------------

Determination/Explanation: God inserted the conjunction and QS answer word *OR* into two QS answers which were about Dave in order to link together QS answer words and phrases which were synonymous in meaning and revealed characteristics, attributes and actions associated with Dave. First, God inserted the conjunction *or* into the QS answer phrase *"He: naïve or answering"* in order to show that Dave's self-taught method to decrypt Query Stacks turned into Dave revealing QS answers and solving the "What's God's origin" question *(how Dave was naïve = how Dave answered)*. Second, God inserted the conjunction *or* into the QS answer phrase *"He: winner; or, gains"* in order to highlight the synonymous relationship between the QS answer words *WINNER* and *GAINS*, two QS answer words which either characterized Dave as a success or someone who'd profited intellectually off of solving the "What's God's origin" question *(what made Dave a winner = what Dave gained)*:

Ch. 7, Sec. 4: 41

CONJUNCTION	CORRESPONDING QS ANSWER PHRASE
OR	HE: NAÏVE OR$_{conj}$ ANSWERING
OR	HE: WINNER; OR$_{conj}$, GAINS.

---------------------------------(Conjunctions Recurring)---------------------------------

Calculation: Moreover, the only QS answer word which was a conjunction recurred a total of *4* times. There were *4* total conjunctions, so *4* of *4*, or *100.00* percent of, conjunctions recurred; specifically, the conjunction *or* recurred *4* times:

Ch. 7, Sec. 4: 42

RECURRING CONJUNCTIONS	NUMBER OF ENTRIES
OR	*(04)*

QS Answer Word Types
Statistical Analyses: Contractions

Calculation: "Contractions" was the sixth most prevalent QS answer word type in the twenty QS answers I'd revealed in this book; in fact, contractions accounted for *2* out of *119*, or *1.68* percent of, total QS answer words.

Determination/Explanation: Evidenced by the QS answer word *ORATOR'S*, from the QS answer phrase *"orator's in,"* which I'd interpreted as *"orator is in" (orator = in)*, and the QS answer word *INGRAIN'S*, from the QS answer phrase *"ingrain's a we,"* which I'd interpreted as *"ingrain is a we" (ingrain = a we)*, the QS author, or God, did insert words which were contractions that contained apostrophe-esses *('s)* into QS answers; yet, in every instance when a QS answer word should've been written as a contraction with an *'s* but wasn't written as a contraction with an *'s* because a row'd word letter "S" which was needed to form said contraction didn't occupy a connectable letter position in a corresponding row'd word matrix, I'd substituted said unproducible *'s* with a colon, as in the QS answer phrase *"Yahweh(:) horn,"* which I'd interpreted as *"Yahweh('s) horn"* or *"Yahweh (is) horn"*:

Ch. 7, Sec. 4: 43

CONTRACTION	CORRESPONDING QS PHRASE	INTERPRETATION
ORATOR'S	ORATOR'S$_{contr}$ IN.	ORATOR IS *the* IN
INGRAIN'S	INGRAIN'S$_{contr}$ A WE	INGRAIN IS A WE

──────────(Contractions: Removing 'S)──────────

Determination: On one hand, in every instance when a QS answer word wasn't a contraction but acted like a contraction, a contractive *'s* wasn't appended to the end of said QS answer word's spelling. If an *'s* was appended to the backside of each QS answer word which acted but wasn't written as a contraction, then the row'd word that each said QS answer word was derived from would've been comprised of the necessary row'd word letter "S" too, and, therefore, spelt differently. On the other hand, the contraction and QS answer word *ORATOR'S* was a properly spelt contraction, because *ORATOR'S* contained an *'s*. If *ORATOR'S* hadn't contained an *'s*, like the QS answer words which acted but weren't written as contractions, then the QS answer phrase that ORATOR'S was incorporated into, *"orator's in,"* would've been written as *"orator: in,"* or with a colon *(":")* instead of an *'s*. If the QS answer phrase *"orator's in"* was transformed into *"orator: in"* and the QS answer letters in both said phrases were derived from the same QS matrix, then the row'd word SON in the top row of the "QS-Son/Trinity" matrix, the row'd word which contained the letter "S" that appeared in the QS answer word *ORATOR'S,* would've lost said letter "S" and became the row'd word ON *(S̶-ON)*. The word *on* couldn't have been used as a top-row row'd word, since the top-row row'd word in every correctly constructed QS matrix in this book was a name, nickname or alias of a biblical character, and there wasn't a biblical character which was named, nicknamed or had the alias *On*:

> *In the "unaltered" version of "QS-Son/Trinity," all of the row'd words have been spelt correctly. However, in the "altered" version of "QS-Son/Trinity," I've removed the row'd word letter "S" from the row'd word SON (S̶-ON), which transformed the row'd word SON into the row'd word ON, and removed the letter "S" from and added a colon into the corresponding QS answer, which transformed the QS answer phrase "ORATOR'S IN" into "ORATOR: IN";*

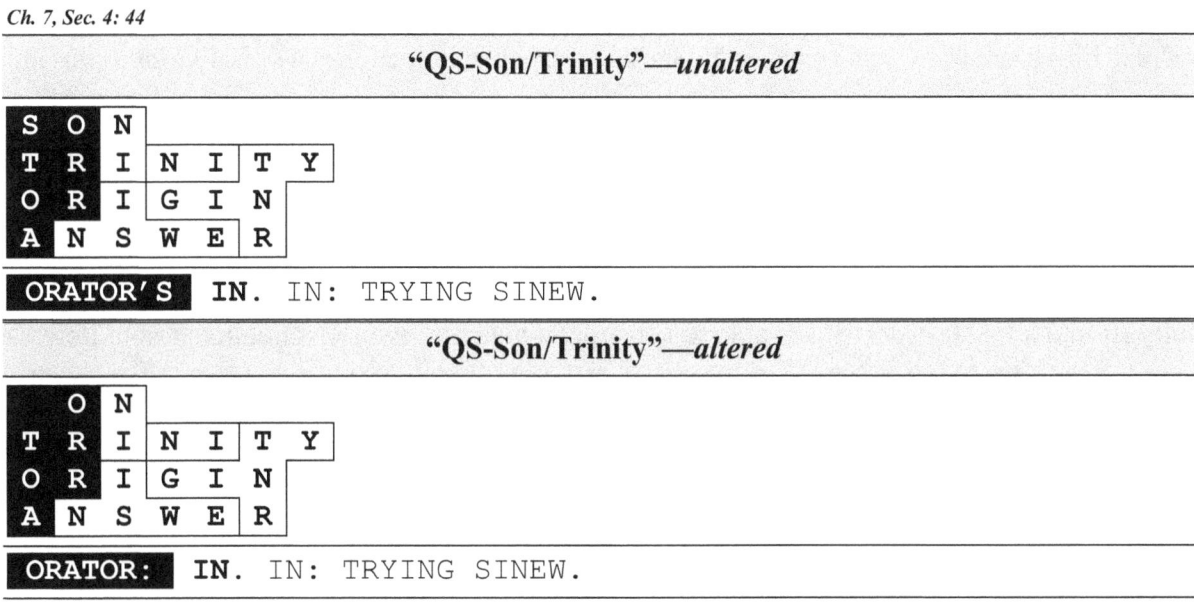

QS Answer Word Types
Statistical Analyses: Adverbs

Calculation: "Adverbs" was the least prevalent QS answer word type in the twenty QS answers I'd revealed in this book; in fact, adverbs accounted for only *1* out of *119*, or *0.84* percent of, total QS answer words.

Determination/Explanation: God used the adverb and answer word *RIGHT* in the QS answer *("Joe assure. Right, rein wans.")*, which I'd interpreted as ("Joe [guy; God] assures [informs positively]. Right [truthfully], rein [controlling power] wans [loses moral force]."), to support the factualness in joe's, or God's, assertion that a rein, or controlling power, which was God, weakened in moral power:

Ch. 7, Sec. 4: 45

ADJECTIVES	CORRESPONDING QS ANSWER
RIGHT	JOE ASSURE. RIGHT$_{adv}$, REIN WANS.

QS Answer Word Types
Interjections

As I'd linked together letters of the QS matrices in this book in order to create QS answer words, I'd ignored any letter combinations which spelt interjections, words like *aha, uh* and *shh*. I'd dodged the use of interjections as QS answer words for four reasons. First, interjections wouldn't have served any other purpose than to convey emotions (e.g. *aha, woohoo* or *yum*) or reveal cognition (e.g. *uh, err* or *um*) or attempt to elicit reactions from readers (e.g. *shh, duh* or *uh huh*). Second, it would've been too easy to make QS answer words and get myself out of a situation in which I had trouble unveiling a QS answer word that grammatically and meaningfully fit into a QS answer if I was able to construct a bunch of two- or three-letter noninformational words. My critics would've rightfully had a field day at picking apart and claiming the uselessness of my study if I'd been continuously left with two or three QS matrix letters which didn't spell anything other than words like *yay, eh* and *eek*. Third, I'd believed that if I'd inserted interjections into the QS answers in this book, then a flare might've been added to God's writing style and a keyhole may've been provided for a reader to look through and peek at God's emotions but I wouldn't have uncovered the clearest and most objective QS answer messages. For instance, if I'd inserted interjections into the "QS-Satan/Hell" answer, then the message conveyed by said QS answer would've been less clear and less focused than the message which was conveyed via the version of the "QS-Satan/Hell" answer that didn't contain interjections:

(a) Zero interjections, one *poss-n's*, two *n*, one *v*;

(b) Three interjections *(int)*, one *poss-n's*, two *n*, one *v*;

Ch. 7, Sec. 4: 46

ZERO INTERJECTIONS[a]
TORAH' S$_{poss\text{-}n's}$ LEARNING$_n$. LIE$_n$ WANS$_v$.
THREE INTERJECTIONS[b]
[b]TORAH' S$_{poss\text{-}n's}$ LEARNING$_n$, **DUH$_{int}$**. **AHA$_{int}$**, LIE$_n$, **UM$_{int}$**, WANS$_n$.

I'd formulated a new QS guide that defined which word types that I'd deemed acceptable and unacceptable as QS answer words—word type parameters delineated in "QS Guide 5" may expand to include QS answer word types which may be uncovered in QS answers that haven't been unveiled up until this point:

Ch. 7, Sec. 4: 47

Guide 5: A QS answer word may be a noun, pronoun, verb, adjective, adverb, conjunction, indefinite article or contraction, but not an interjection.

QS Answer Words and Definitions
Standard, Archaic and Obsolete

Not only had I selected words and definitions which best aligned with the contexts of and clarified the messages of the QS answers that I'd inserted said words and definitions into, I'd predominantly selected words and definitions which were standard, or "currently in use." On the other hand, I'd avoided words and definitions which were archaic, or "commonly used in the past but not commonly used in the present," and obsolete, or "formerly but no longer in use." In fact, out of the *119* QS answer words and said QS answer words' definitions in this book, *117*, or *98.32* percent, were labeled as standard words and definitions in dictionaries I'd relied on (see "Bibliography"). The only archaic QS answer word and definition was the archaic QS answer word and definition for said QS answer word *THY*, a QS answer word in the "QS-Yahweh/Trinity" answer phrase *"thy trio: reining, wans."* The only other QS answer word and definition which wasn't standard was the slang word *JOE* (see "Ch. 1, Sec. 3: 7-18" and "Ch. 2, Sec. 1: 6-7"). By the year I'd completed this book (2023), none of the QS answer words or QS answer word definitions associated with the QS answers in this book were labeled as obsolete words or obsolete definitions in said dictionaries I'd relied on:

Ch. 7, Sec. 4: 48

DEFINITION TYPE	QS ANSWER WORD	QUANTITY	PERCENTAGE
STANDARD		117	98.32
ARCHAIC	THY	01	00.84
SLANG	JOE	01	00.84
OBSOLETE	–	00	00.00
TOTAL ANSWER WORDS		**119**	

In "Ch. 7, Sec. 2: 56," I'd introduced "QS Guide 4," which suggested "a QS answer word's definition should be standard." Based on the data I'd collected and incorporated into "Ch. 7, Sec. 4: 48," I'd decided to update the linguistic boundaries suggested in "QS Guide 4":

Ch. 7, Sec. 4: 49

Guide 4: A QS answer word's definition should be standard; can be archaic or slang, if no valid standard options are available; but should never be obsolete.

QS Answer Points of View
Statistical Analyses

The QS author, God, wrote each QS answer in this book in first, second, third person point of view, or a mixture of first and third person points of view. God wrote most of the QS answers in this book in third person point of view; in fact, *16* of *20*, or *80* percent of, QS answers were written in third person point of view. The second most used point of view which God wrote QS answers in was a mixture of first and third person points of view; specifically, *2* of *20*, or *10* percent of, QS answers were written in a mixed first and third person point of view. First person point of view and second person point of view were tied as the least used points of view which God ingrained into QS answers; in fact, *1* of *20*, or *5.00* percent of, QS answers were written in either first or second person point of view:

> *A superscripted number preceding a QS answer, QS answer phrase or QS answer word signifies the point of view ingrained into said QS answer, QS answer phrase or QS answer word, while a superscripted letter "M" preceding a QS answer denotes a mixed first and third person point of view;*

Ch. 7, Sec. 4: 50

POINT OF VIEW	QS ANSWER QUANTITY	QS ANSWER PERCENTAGE
FIRST PERSON	01	05.00
SECOND PERSON	01	05.00
THIRD PERSON	16	80.00
MULTIPLE PERSON	02	10.00
TOTAL ANSWERS	20	

[3](GO DAVE. HE: WINNER; OR, GAINS.)
[3](HORDE: EVIL. ILL REIGN, WANS.)
[3](JOE ASSURE. RIGHT, REIN WANS.)
[3](ADORE GIVER. A HINTER WANS.)
[3](JOE: REASON. AIR/HINT GREW.)
[1](MARRY REASON. A HINT, I GREW.)
[3](HOLY GHOST. HE: NAÏVE OR ANSWERING.)
[3](YAHWEH: HORN. NERVING, IS A WE.)
[3](HAY: WE. HEAVEN: HORN, SIRING A WE.)
[3](CORE: REAL. A TRINITY; OR, RINGS A WE.)
[M]([3][HAY: LAW. THEY OR REINS], [1][I], [3][RING "A WE."])
[2](HAIRY WE. THY TRIO: REINING, WANS.)
[3](FAIR HINTER. TRIO: TRYING, WANES.)
[3](ORATOR'S IN. IN: TRYING SINEW.)
[3](TORAH: GLORY. HOST: IN, I, TRYING SINEW.)
[3](GOT WORDING. "I" ENTRY; RAINS "I.")
[M]([3][JOT, ISSUER]. [1][I RING ENTRY "I," "WANS."])
[3](EVITERNITY: HORN. INGRAIN'S A WE.)
[3](CLUE: FILLER. HORN: SIRING A WE.)
[3](TORAH'S LEARNING. LIE WANS.)

QS Answer Statistics
Composite

"Ch. 5, Sec. 5: 6" contained the most recent updated array of QS answer statistics, which reported the number of answer words in each answer, number of answer letters in each answer, average number of letters per answer word in each answer, total number of answers, total number of answer words, total number of answer letters, average number of letters in total answers, average number of words in total answers, and average number of letters per answer word in total answers. "Ch. 7, Sec. 4: 51" contained the same statistics as the statistics I'd listed in "Ch. 5, Sec. 5: 6," but included statistics for the last eleven QS answers I'd revealed in this book and contained new statistical categories:

I've appended a superscripted letter "u," a dash ("-") and a number to each QS answer word (e.g. "^{u-1}GO"). The superscription signifies the "(u)niqueness level" of a QS answer word, and a uniqueness level signifies how many times a QS answer word appears within known QS answers. For instance, the uniqueness level superscription which precedes the "QS-God/Heaven" answer word GO is "u-1", which means that GO appears only one time in all of the uncovered QS answers. If the QS answer word GO appeared in a subsequently unraveled QS answer, then the "uniqueness" of GO would change from a uniqueness level of one to a uniqueness level of two. In comparison, the "QS-God/Heaven" answer word HE carries a uniqueness level of two, because it appears in two Q/S answers ("QS-God/Heaven" and "QS-Holy^Ghost/Heaven");

In the "Query Stack Answer Totals" tab, I've appended a superscripted letter "i," a dash ("-") and a number to each QS answer (e.g. "$[^{u-1}GO_v\ ^{u-1}DAVE_{prop-n}.\ ^{u-2}HE_{pron}:\ ^{u-1}WINNER_n;\ ^{u-4}OR_{conj},\ ^{u-1}GAINS_v.]^{i-5}$"). The superscription signifies the "(i)nclusivity level" of a QS answer. "Inclusivity level" signifies how many QS answer words with a different uniqueness level and belong to a different word class (i.e. noun) are in a QS answer. For instance, the inclusivity level of the "QS-God/Heaven" answer is "i-5", which means that five kinds of QS answer words, each with a different uniqueness level and belonging to a different word class, appear in the "QS-God/Heaven" answer. The five kinds of QS answer words in the "QS-God/Heaven" answer are: verbs with a uniqueness level of one (e.g. "$^{u-1}GO_v$" and "$^{u-1}GAINS_v$"), proper nouns with a uniqueness level of one (e.g. "$^{u-1}DAVE_{prop-n}$"), pronouns with a uniqueness level of two (e.g. "$^{u-2}HE_{pron}$"), nouns with a uniqueness level of one (e.g. "$^{u-1}WINNER_n$") and conjunctions with a uniqueness level of four (e.g. "$^{u-4}OR_{con}$");

Ch. 7, Sec. 4: 51

QS-GOD/HEAVEN

$^{u\text{-}1}$GO$_v$ $^{u\text{-}1}$DAVE$_{prop\text{-}n}$. $^{u\text{-}2}$HE$_{pron}$: $^{u\text{-}1}$WINNER$_n$; $^{u\text{-}4}$OR$_{conj}$, $^{u\text{-}1}$GAINS$_v$.

Count—answer words/<(")|unique|>: $06/<^{u\text{-}1}|04|, ^{u\text{-}2}|01|, ^{u\text{-}4}|01|>$

Count—answer letters/<(")|unique|>: $21/<^{u\text{-}1}|17|, ^{u\text{-}2}|02|, ^{u\text{-}4}|02|>$

Percentage—(")|unique| answer words of answer word count: $^{u\text{-}1}|66.67 _{\{4 \div 6\}}|, ^{u\text{-}2}|16.67 _{\{1 \div 6\}}|, ^{u\text{-}4}|16.67 _{\{1 \div 6\}}|$

Percentage—(")|unique| answer letters of answer letter count: $^{u\text{-}1}|80.95 _{\{17 \div 21\}}|, ^{u\text{-}2}|09.52 _{\{2 \div 21\}}|, ^{u\text{-}4}|09.52 _{\{2 \div 21\}}|$

Average—answer letters/<(")|unique|> per answer word: $03.50 _{\{21 \div 6\}}/<^{u\text{-}1}|02.83 _{\{17 \div 6\}}|, ^{u\text{-}2}|00.33 _{\{2 \div 6\}}|, ^{u\text{-}4}|00.33 _{\{2 \div 6\}}|>$

Average—(")|unique| answer letters per (")|unique| answer word: $^{u\text{-}1}|4.25 _{\{17 \div 4\}}|, ^{u\text{-}2}|02.00 _{\{2 \div 1\}}|, ^{u\text{-}4}|02.00 _{\{2 \div 1\}}|$

Count—singular noun($_n$)/<(")|unique|> words: $01/<^{u\text{-}1}|01|>$

Count—singular noun($_n$)/<(")|unique|> letters: $06/<^{u\text{-}1}|06|>$

Count—proper noun($_{prop\text{-}n}$)/<(")|unique|> words: $01/<^{u\text{-}1}|01|>$

Count—proper noun($_{prop\text{-}n}$)/<(")|unique|> letters: $04/<^{u\text{-}1}|04|>$

Count—pronoun($_{pron}$)/<(")|unique|> words: $01/<^{u\text{-}2}|01|>$

Count—pronoun($_{pron}$)/<(")|unique|> letters: $02/<^{u\text{-}2}|02|>$

Count—verb($_v$)/<(")|unique|> words: $02/<^{u\text{-}1}|02|>$

Count—verb($_v$)/<(")|unique|> letters>: $07/<^{u\text{-}1}|07|>$

Count—conjunction ($_{conj}$)/<(")|unique|> words: $01/<^{u\text{-}4}|01|>$

Count—conjunction ($_{conj}$)/<(")|unique|> letters: $02/<^{u\text{-}4}|02|>$

Percentage—singular noun($_n$)/<(")|unique|> words of answer word count: $16.67 _{\{1 \div 6\}}/<^{u\text{-}1}|16.67 _{\{1 \div 6\}}|>$

Percentage—singular noun($_n$)/<(")|unique|> letters of answer letter count: $28.57 _{\{6 \div 21\}}/<^{u\text{-}1}|28.57 _{\{6 \div 21\}}|>$

Percentage—proper noun($_{prop\text{-}n}$)/<(")|unique|> words of answer word count: $16.67 _{\{1 \div 6\}}/<^{u\text{-}1}|16.67 _{\{1 \div 6\}}|>$

Percentage—proper noun($_{prop\text{-}n}$)/<(")|unique|> letters of answer letter count: $19.05 _{\{4 \div 21\}}/<^{u\text{-}1}|19.05 _{\{4 \div 21\}}|>$

Percentage—pronoun($_{pron}$)/<(")|unique|> words of answer word count: $16.67 _{\{1 \div 6\}}/<^{u\text{-}2}|16.67 _{\{1 \div 6\}}|>$

Percentage—pronoun($_{pron}$)/<(")|unique|> letters of answer letter count: $09.52 _{\{2 \div 21\}}/<^{u\text{-}2}|09.52 _{\{2 \div 21\}}|>$

Percentage—verb($_v$)/<(")|unique|> words of answer word count: $33.33 _{\{2 \div 6\}}/<^{u\text{-}1}|33.33 _{\{2 \div}}$

$_{6\}}|>$

Percentage—verb$_{(v)}$/<(^{u})|unique|> letters of answer word count: 33.33 $_{\{7 \div 21\}}$/<$^{u-1}$|33.33 $_{\{7 \div 21\}}$|>

Percentage—conjunction$_{(conj)}$/<(^{u})|unique|> words of answer word count: 16.67 $_{\{1 \div 6\}}$/<$^{u-4}$|16.67 $_{\{1 \div 6\}}$|>

Percentage—conjunction$_{(conj)}$/<(^{u})|unique|> letters of answer word count: 09.52 $_{\{2 \div 21\}}$/<$^{u-4}$|09.52 $_{\{2 \div 21\}}$|>

QS-DEVIL/HELL

$^{u-1}$HORDE$_n$: $^{u-1}$EVIL$_n$. $^{u-1}$ILL$_n$ $^{u-1}$REIGN$_v$, $^{u-5}$WANS$_v$.

Count—answer words/<(^{u})unique>: 05/<$^{u-1}$|04|, $^{u-5}$|01|>

Count—answer letters/<(^{u})|unique|>: 21/<$^{u-1}$|17|, $^{u-5}$|04|>

Percentage—(^{u})|unique| answer words of answer word count: $^{u-1}$|80.00 $_{\{4 \div 5\}}$|, $^{u-5}$|20.00 $_{\{1 \div 5\}}$|

Percentage—(^{u})|unique| answer letters of answer letter count: $^{u-1}$|80.95 $_{\{17 \div 21\}}$|, $^{u-5}$|19.05 $_{\{4 \div 21\}}$|

Average—answer letters/<(^{u})|unique|> per answer word: 04.20 $_{\{21 \div 5\}}$/<$^{u-1}$|03.40 $_{\{17 \div 5\}}$|, $^{u-5}$|00.80 $_{\{4 \div 5\}}$|>

Average—(^{u})|unique| answer letters per (^{u})|unique| answer word: $^{u-1}$|4.25 $_{\{17 \div 4\}}$|, $^{u-5}$|04.00 $_{\{4 \div 1\}}$|

Count—singular noun$_{(n)}$/<(^{u})|unique|> words: 03/<$^{u-1}$|03|>

Count—singular noun$_{(n)}$/<(^{u})|unique|> letters: 12/<$^{u-1}$|12|>

Count—verb$_{(v)}$/<(^{u})|unique|> words: 02/<$^{u-1}$|01|, $^{u-5}$|01|>

Count—verb$_{(v)}$/<(^{u})|unique|> letters: 09/<$^{u-1}$|05|, $^{u-5}$|04|>

Percentage—singular noun$_{(n)}$/<(^{u})|unique|> words of answer word count: 60.00 $_{\{3 \div 5\}}$/<$^{u-1}$|60.00 $_{\{3 \div 5\}}$|>

Percentage—singular noun$_{(n)}$/<(^{u})|unique|> letters of answer letter count: 57.14 $_{\{12 \div 21\}}$/<$^{u-1}$|57.14 $_{\{12 \div 21\}}$|>

Percentage—verb$_{(v)}$/<(^{u})unique> words of answer word count: 40.00 $_{\{2 \div 5\}}$/<$^{u-1}$|20.00 $_{\{1 \div 5\}}$|, $^{u-5}$|20.00 $_{\{1 \div 5\}}$|>

Percentage—verb$_{(v)}$/<(^{u})unique> letters of answer letter count: 42.86 $_{\{9 \div 21\}}$/<$^{u-1}$|23.81 $_{\{5 \div 21\}}$|, $^{u-5}$|19.05 $_{\{4 \div 21\}}$|>

QS-JESUS/EARTH

$^{u-2}$JOE$_n$ $^{u-1}$ASSURE$_v$. $^{u-1}$RIGHT$_{adv}$, $^{u-1}$REIN$_n$ $^{u-5}$WANS$_v$.

Count—answer words/<|(^{u})unique|>: 05/<$^{u-1}$|03|, $^{u-2}$|01|, $^{u-5}$|01|>

Count—answer letters/<(^{u})|unique|>: 22/<$^{u-1}$|15|, $^{u-2}$|03|, $^{u-5}$|04|>

Percentage—(^{u})|unique| answer words of answer word count: $^{u-1}$|60.00 $_{\{3 \div 5\}}$|, $^{u-2}$|20.00 $_{\{1 \div 5\}}$|, $^{u-5}$|20.00 $_{\{1 \div 5\}}$|

Percentage—(")|unique| answer letters of answer letter count: $^{u-1}$|68.18 {15 ÷ 22}|, $^{u-2}$|13.64 {3 ÷ 22}|, $^{u-5}$|18.18 {4 ÷ 22}|

Average—answer letters/<(")|unique|> per answer word: 04.40 {22 ÷ 5}/<$^{u-1}$|03.00 {15 ÷ 5}|, $^{u-2}$|00.60 {3 ÷ 5}|, $^{u-5}$|00.80 {4 ÷ 5}|>

Average—(")|unique| answer letters per (")|unique| answer word: $^{u-1}$|05.00 {15 ÷ 3}|, $^{u-2}$|03.00 {3 ÷ 1}|, $^{u-5}$|04.00 {4 ÷ 1}|

Count—singular noun($_n$)/<(")unique> words: 02/<$^{u-1}$|01|, $^{u-2}$|01|>

Count—singular noun($_n$)/<(")unique> letters: 07/<$^{u-1}$|04|, $^{u-2}$|03|>

Count—verb ($_v$)/<(")unique> words: 02/<$^{u-1}$|01|, $^{u-5}$|01|>

Count—verb($_v$)/<(")unique> letters: 10/<$^{u-1}$|06|, $^{u-5}$|04|>

Count—adverb($_{adv}$)/<(")unique> words: 01/<$^{u-1}$|01|>

Count—adverb($_{adv}$)/<(")unique> letters: 05/<$^{u-1}$|05|>

Percentage—singular noun($_n$)/<(")|unique|> words of answer word count: 40.00 {2 ÷ 5}/<$^{u-1}$|20.00 {1 ÷ 5}|, $^{u-2}$|20.00 {1 ÷ 5}|>

Percentage—singular noun($_n$)/<(")|unique|> letters of answer letter count: 31.82 {7 ÷ 22}/<$^{u-1}$|18.18 {4 ÷ 22}|, $^{u-2}$|13.64 {3 ÷ 22}|>

Percentage—verb($_v$)/<(")unique> words of answer word count: 40.00 {2 ÷ 5}/<$^{u-1}$|20.00 {1 ÷ 5}|, $^{u-5}$|20.00 {1 ÷ 5}|>

Percentage—verb($_v$)/<(")unique> letters of answer letter count: 45.45 {10 ÷ 22}/<$^{u-1}$|27.27 {6 ÷ 22}|, $^{u-5}$|18.18 {4 ÷ 22}|>

Percentage—adverb($_{adv}$)/<(")unique> words of answer word count: 20.00 {1 ÷ 5}/<$^{u-1}$|20.00 {1 ÷ 5}|>

Percentage—adverb($_{adv}$)/<(")unique> letters of answer letter count: 22.73 {5 ÷ 22}/<$^{u-1}$|22.73 {5 ÷ 22}|>

QS-DAVE/EARTH

$^{u-1}$ADORE$_v$ $^{u-1}$GIVER$_n$. $^{u-8}$A$_{i\text{-}art}$ $^{u-2}$HINTER$_n$ $^{u-5}$WANS$_v$.

Count—answer words/<|(")unique|>: 05/<$^{u-1}$|02|, $^{u-2}$|01|, $^{u-5}$|01|, $^{u-8}$|01|>

Count—answer letters/<(")|unique|>: 21/<$^{u-1}$|10|, $^{u-2}$|06|, $^{u-5}$|04|, $^{u-8}$|01|>

Percentage—(")|unique| answer words of answer word count: $^{u-1}$|40.00 {2 ÷ 5}|, $^{u-2}$|20.00 {1 ÷ 5}|, $^{u-5}$|20.00 {1 ÷ 5}|, $^{u-8}$|20.00 {1 ÷ 5}|

Percentage—(")|unique| answer letters of answer letter count: $^{u-1}$|47.62 {10 ÷ 21}|, $^{u-2}$|28.57 {6 ÷ 21}|, $^{u-5}$|19.05 {4 ÷ 21}|, $^{u-8}$|4.76 {1 ÷ 21}|

Average—answer letters/<(")|unique|> per answer word: 04.20 {21 ÷ 5}/<$^{u-1}$|02.00 {10 ÷ 5}|, $^{u-2}$|01.20 {6 ÷ 5}|, $^{u-5}$|00.80 {4 ÷ 5}|, $^{u-8}$|00.20 {1 ÷ 5}|>

Average—(")|unique| answer letters per (")|unique| answer word: $^{u-1}$|05.00 {10 ÷ 2}|, $^{u-2}$|06.00 {6 ÷ 1}|, $^{u-5}$|04.00 {4 ÷ 1}|, $^{u-8}$|01.00 {1 ÷ 1}|

Count—singular noun($_n$)/<(")unique> words: 02/<$^{u-1}$|01|, $^{u-2}$|01|>

Count—singular noun($_n$)/<(")unique> letters: 11/<$^{u-1}$|05|, $^{u-2}$|06|>

Count—verb ($_v$)/<(")unique> words: 02/<$^{u-1}$|01|, $^{u-5}$|01|>

Count—verb($_v$)/<(")unique> letters: 09/<$^{u-1}$|05|, $^{u-5}$|04|>

Count—indefinite article($_{i\text{-}art}$)/<(")unique> words: 01/<$^{u-8}$|01|>

Count—indefinite article($_{i\text{-}art}$)/<(")unique> letters: 01/<$^{u-8}$|01|>

Percentage—singular noun($_n$)/<(")|unique|> words of answer word count: 40.00 $_{\{2 \div 5\}}$/<$^{u-1}$|20.00 $_{\{1 \div 5\}}$|, $^{u-2}$|20.00 $_{\{1 \div 5\}}$|>

Percentage—singular noun($_n$)/<(")|unique|> letters of answer letter count: 52.38 $_{\{11 \div 21\}}$/<$^{u-1}$|23.81 $_{\{5 \div 21\}}$|, $^{u-2}$|28.57 $_{\{6 \div 21\}}$|>

Percentage—verb($_v$)/<(")unique> words of answer word count: 40.00 $_{\{2 \div 5\}}$/<$^{u-1}$|20.00 $_{\{1 \div 5\}}$|, $^{u-5}$|20.00 $_{\{1 \div 5\}}$|>

Percentage—verb($_v$)/<(")unique> letters of answer letter count: 42.86 $_{\{9 \div 21\}}$/<$^{u-1}$|23.81 $_{\{5 \div 21\}}$|, $^{u-5}$|19.05 $_{\{4 \div 21\}}$|>

Percentage—indefinite article($_{i\text{-}art}$)/<(")unique> words of answer word count: 20.00 $_{\{1 \div 5\}}$/<$^{u-8}$|20.00 $_{\{1 \div 5\}}$|>

Percentage—indefinite article($_{i\text{-}art}$)/<(")unique> letters of answer letter count: 04.76 $_{\{1 \div 21\}}$/<$^{u-8}$|04.76 $_{\{1 \div 21\}}$|>

QS-JOE/EARTH

$^{u-2}$JOE$_n$: $^{u-2}$REASON$_n$. $^{u-1}$AIR$_n$/$^{u-2}$HINT$_n$ $^{u-2}$GREW$_v$.

Count—answer words/<(")|unique|>: 05/<$^{u-1}$|01|, $^{u-2}$|04|>

Count—answer letters/<(")|unique|>: 20/<$^{u-1}$|03|, $^{u-2}$|17|>

Percentage—(")|unique| answer words of answer word count: $^{u-1}$|20.00 $_{\{1 \div 5\}}$|, $^{u-2}$|80.00 $_{\{4 \div 5\}}$|

Percentage—(")|unique| answer letters of answer letter count: $^{u-1}$|15.00 $_{\{3 \div 20\}}$|, $^{u-2}$|85.00 $_{\{17 \div 20\}}$|

Average—answer letters/<(")|unique|> per answer word: 04.00 $_{\{20 \div 5\}}$/<$^{u-1}$|00.60 $_{\{3 \div 5\}}$|, $^{u-2}$|03.40 $_{\{17 \div 5\}}$|>

Average—(")|unique| answer letters per (")|unique| answer word: $^{u-1}$|03.00 $_{\{3 \div 1\}}$|, $^{u-2}$|04.25 $_{\{17 \div 4\}}$|>

Count—singular noun($_n$)/<(")unique> words: 04/<$^{u-1}$|01|, $^{u-2}$|03|>

Count—singular noun($_n$)/<(")unique> letters: 16/<$^{u-1}$|03|, $^{u-2}$|13|>

Count—verb ($_v$)/<(")unique> words: 01/<$^{u-2}$|01|>

Count—verb($_v$)/<(")unique> letters: 04/<$^{u-2}$|04|>

Percentage—singular noun($_n$)/<(")|unique|> words of answer word count: 80.00 $_{\{4 \div 5\}}$/<$^{u-1}$|20.00 $_{\{1 \div 5\}}$|, $^{u-2}$|60.00 $_{\{3 \div 5\}}$|>

Percentage—singular noun($_n$)/<(")|unique|> letters of answer letter count: 80.00 $_{\{16 \div 20\}}$/<$^{u-1}$|15.00 $_{\{3 \div 20\}}$|, $^{u-2}$|65.00 $_{\{13 \div 20\}}$|>

Percentage—verb($_v$)/<(")unique> words of answer word count: 20.00 $_{\{1 \div 5\}}$/<$^{u-2}$|20.00 $_{\{1 \div 5\}}$|>

Percentage—verb($_v$)/<(")unique> letters of answer letter count: 20.00 $_{\{4 \div 20\}}$/<$^{u-2}$|20.00 $_{\{4 \div 20\}}$|>

QS-MARY/EARTH

$^{u-1}$MARRY$_v$ $^{u-2}$REASON$_n$. $^{u-8}$A$_{i\text{-}art}$ $^{u-2}$HINT$_n$, $^{u-3}$I$_{pron}$ $^{u-2}$GREW$_v$.

Count—answer words/<|(")unique|>: 06/<$^{u-1}$|01|, $^{u-2}$|03|, $^{u-3}$|01|, $^{u-8}$|01|>

Count—answer letters/<(")|unique|>: 21/<$^{u-1}$|05|, $^{u-2}$|14|, $^{u-3}$|01|, $^{u-8}$|01|>

Percentage—(")|unique| answer words of answer word count: $^{u-1}$|16.67 $_{\{1 \div 6\}}$|, $^{u-2}$|50.00 $_{\{3 \div 6\}}$|, $^{u-3}$|16.67 $_{\{1 \div 6\}}$|, $^{u-8}$|16.67 $_{\{1 \div 6\}}$|

Percentage—(")|unique| answer letters of answer letter count: $^{u-1}$|23.81 $_{\{5 \div 21\}}$|, $^{u-2}$|66.67 $_{\{14 \div 21\}}$|, $^{u-3}$|04.76 $_{\{1 \div 21\}}$|, $^{u-8}$|04.76 $_{\{1 \div 21\}}$|

Average—answer letters/<(")|unique|> per answer word: 03.50 $_{\{21 \div 6\}}$/<$^{u-1}$|00.83 $_{\{5 \div 6\}}$|, $^{u-2}$|02.33 $_{\{14 \div 6\}}$|, $^{u-3}$|00.17 $_{\{1 \div 6\}}$|, $^{u-8}$|00.17 $_{\{1 \div 6\}}$|>

Average—(")|unique| answer letters per (")|unique| answer word: $^{u-1}$|05.00 $_{\{5 \div 1\}}$|, $^{u-2}$|04.67 $_{\{14 \div 3\}}$|, $^{u-3}$|01.00 $_{\{1 \div 1\}}$|, $^{u-8}$|01.00 $_{\{1 \div 1\}}$|, >

Count—singular noun($_n$)/<(")unique> words: 02/<$^{u-2}$|02|>

Count—singular noun($_n$)/<(")unique> letters: 10/<$^{u-2}$|10|>

Count—pronoun($_{pron}$)/<(")unique> words: 01/<$^{u-3}$|01|>

Count—pronoun($_{pron}$)/<(")unique> letters: 01/<$^{u-3}$|01|>

Count—verb ($_v$)/<(")unique> words: 02/<$^{u-1}$|01|, $^{u-2}$|01|>

Count—verb($_v$)/<(")unique> letters: 09/<$^{u-1}$|05|, $^{u-2}$|04|>

Count—indefinite article($_{i\text{-}art}$)/<(")unique> words: 01/<$^{u-8}$|01|>

Count—indefinite article($_{i\text{-}art}$)/<(")unique> letters: 01/<$^{u-8}$|01|>

Percentage—singular noun($_n$)/<(")|unique|> words of answer word count: 33.33 $_{\{2 \div 6\}}$/<$^{u-2}$|33.33 $_{\{2 \div 6\}}$|>

Percentage—singular noun($_n$)/<(")|unique|> letters of answer letter count: 47.62 $_{\{10 \div 21\}}$/<$^{u-2}$|47.62 $_{\{10 \div 21\}}$|>

Percentage—pronoun($_{pron}$)/<(")|unique|> words of answer word count: 16.67 $_{\{1 \div 6\}}$/<$^{u-3}$|16.67 $_{\{1 \div 6\}}$|>

Percentage—pronoun($_{pron}$)/<(")|unique|> letters of answer letter count: 04.76 $_{\{1 \div 21\}}$/<$^{u-3}$|04.76 $_{\{1 \div 21\}}$|>

Percentage—verb($_v$)/<(")unique> words of answer word count: 33.33 $_{\{2 \div 6\}}$/<$^{u-1}$|16.67 $_{\{1 \div 6\}}$|, $^{u-2}$|16.67 $_{\{1 \div 6\}}$|>

Percentage—verb($_v$)/<(")unique> letters of answer letter count: 42.86 $_{\{9 \div 21\}}$/<$^{u-1}$|23.81 $_{\{5 \div 21\}}$|, $^{u-2}$|19.05 $_{\{4 \div 21\}}$|>

Percentage—indefinite article($_{i\text{-}art}$)/<(")unique> words of answer word count: 16.67 $_{\{1 \div 6\}}$/<$^{u-}$

$^8|16.67_{\{1 \div 6\}}|$

Percentage—indefinite article$(_{i\text{-}art})$/<$(^u)$unique> letters of answer letter count: $04.76_{\{1 \div 21\}}$/<$^{u\text{-}8}|04.76_{\{1 \div 21\}}$>

QS-HOLY^GHOST/HEAVEN

$^{u\text{-}1}$HOLY$_{adj}$ $^{u\text{-}1}$GHOST$_n$. $^{u\text{-}2}$HE$_{pron}$: $^{u\text{-}1}$NAÏVE$_{adj}$ $^{u\text{-}4}$OR$_{conj}$ $^{u\text{-}1}$ANSWERING$_v$.

Count—answer words/<|$(^u)$unique|>: 06/<$^{u\text{-}1}|04|, ^{u\text{-}2}|01|, ^{u\text{-}4}|01|$>

Count—answer letters/<$(^u)|$unique$|$>: 27/<$^{u\text{-}1}|23|, ^{u\text{-}2}|02|, ^{u\text{-}4}|02|$>

Percentage—$(^u)|$unique$|$ answer words of answer word count: $^{u\text{-}1}|66.67_{\{4 \div 6\}}|, ^{u\text{-}2}|16.67_{\{1 \div 6\}}|, ^{u\text{-}4}|16.67_{\{1 \div 6\}}|$

Percentage—$(^u)|$unique$|$ answer letters of answer letter count: $^{u\text{-}1}|85.19_{\{23 \div 27\}}|, ^{u\text{-}2}|07.41_{\{2 \div 27\}}|, ^{u\text{-}4}|07.41_{\{2 \div 27\}}|$

Average—answer letters/<$(^u)|$unique$|$> per answer word: $04.50_{\{27 \div 6\}}$/<$^{u\text{-}1}|03.83_{\{23 \div 6\}}|, ^{u\text{-}2}|00.33_{\{2 \div 6\}}|, ^{u\text{-}4}|00.33_{\{2 \div 6\}}|$>

Average—$(^u)|$unique$|$ answer letters per $(^u)|$unique$|$ answer word: $^{u\text{-}1}|05.75_{\{23 \div 4\}}|, ^{u\text{-}2}|02.00_{\{2 \div 1\}}|, ^{u\text{-}4}|02.00_{\{2 \div 1\}}|$>

Count—singular noun$(_n)$/<$(^u)$unique> words: 01/<$^{u\text{-}1}|01|$>

Count—singular noun$(_n)$/<$(^u)$unique> letters: 05/<$^{u\text{-}1}|05|$>

Count—pronoun$(_{pron})$/<$(^u)$unique> words: 01/<$^{u\text{-}2}|01|$>

Count—pronoun$(_{pron})$/<$(^u)$unique> letters: 02/<$^{u\text{-}2}|02|$>

Count—verb $(_v)$/<$(^u)$unique> words: 01/<$^{u\text{-}1}|01|$>

Count—verb$(_v)$/<$(^u)$unique> letters: 09/<$^{u\text{-}1}|09|$>

Count—adjective$(_{adj})$/<$(^u)$unique> words: 02/<$^{u\text{-}1}|02|$>

Count—adjective$(_{adj})$/<$(^u)$unique> letters: 09/<$^{u\text{-}1}|09|$>

Count—conjunction $(_{conj})$/<$(^u)$unique> words: 01/<$^{u\text{-}4}|01|$>

Count—conjunction$(_{conj})$/<$(^u)$unique> letters: 02/<$^{u\text{-}4}|02|$>

Percentage—singular noun$(_n)$/<$(^u)|$unique$|$> words of answer word count: $16.67_{\{1 \div 6\}}$/<$^{u\text{-}1}|16.67_{\{1 \div 6\}}|$>

Percentage—singular noun$(_n)$/<$(^u)|$unique$|$> letters of answer letter count: $18.52_{\{5 \div 27\}}$/<$^{u\text{-}1}|18.52_{\{5 \div 27\}}|$>

Percentage—pronoun$(_{pron})$/<$(^u)|$unique$|$> words of answer word count: $16.67_{\{1 \div 6\}}$/<$^{u\text{-}2}|16.67_{\{1 \div 6\}}|$>

Percentage—pronoun$(_{pron})$/<$(^u)|$unique$|$> letters of answer letter count: $07.41_{\{2 \div 27\}}$/<$^{u\text{-}2}|07.41_{\{2 \div 27\}}|$>

Percentage—verb$(_v)$/<$(^u)$unique> words of answer word count: $16.67_{\{1 \div 6\}}$/<$^{u\text{-}1}|16.67_{\{1 \div 6\}}|$>

Percentage—verb$(_v)$/<$(^u)$unique> letters of answer letter count: $33.33_{\{9 \div 27\}}$/<$^{u\text{-}1}|33.33_{\{9 \div 27\}}|$>

Percentage—adjective($_{adj}$)/<(")unique> words of answer word count: 33.33 $_{\{2 \div 6\}}$/<$^{u-1}$|33.33 $_{\{2 \div 6\}}$|>

Percentage—adjective($_{adj}$)/<(")unique> letters of answer letter count: 33.33 $_{\{9 \div 27\}}$/<$^{u-6}$|33.33 $_{\{9 \div 27\}}$>

Percentage—conjunction ($_{conj}$)/<(")unique> words of answer word count: 16.67 $_{\{1 \div 6\}}$/<$^{u-4}$|16.67 $_{\{1 \div 6\}}$|>

Percentage—conjunction ($_{conj}$)/<(")unique> letters of answer letter count: 07.41 $_{\{2 \div 27\}}$/<$^{u-4}$|07.41 $_{\{2 \div 27\}}$>

QS-YHWH/HEAVEN

$^{u-1}$YAHWEH$_{prop-n}$: $^{u-4}$HORN$_n$. $^{u-1}$NERVING$_v$, $^{u-1}$IS$_v$ $^{u-8}$A$_{i-art}$ $^{u-7}$WE$_n$.

Count—answer words/<|(")unique|>: 06/<$^{u-1}$|03|, $^{u-4}$|01|, $^{u-7}$|01|, $^{u-8}$|01|>

Count—answer letters/<(")|unique|>: 22/<$^{u-1}$|15|, $^{u-4}$|04|, $^{u-7}$|02|, $^{u-8}$|01|>

Percentage—(")|unique| answer words of answer word count: $^{u-1}$|50.00 $_{\{3 \div 6\}}$|, $^{u-4}$|16.67 $_{\{1 \div 6\}}$|, $^{u-7}$|16.67 $_{\{1 \div 6\}}$|, $^{u-8}$|16.67 $_{\{1 \div 6\}}$|

Percentage—(")|unique| answer letters of answer letter count: $^{u-1}$|68.18 $_{\{15 \div 22\}}$|, $^{u-4}$|18.18 $_{\{4 \div 22\}}$|, $^{u-7}$|09.09 $_{\{2 \div 22\}}$|, $^{u-8}$|04.55 $_{\{1 \div 22\}}$|

Average—answer letters/<(")|unique|> per answer word: 03.67 $_{\{22 \div 6\}}$/<$^{u-1}$|02.50 $_{\{15 \div 6\}}$|, $^{u-4}$|00.67 $_{\{4 \div 6\}}$|, $^{u-7}$|00.33 $_{\{2 \div 6\}}$|, $^{u-8}$|00.17 $_{\{1 \div 6\}}$|>

Average—(")|unique| answer letters per (")|unique| answer word: $^{u-1}$|05.00 $_{\{15 \div 3\}}$|, $^{u-4}$|04.00 $_{\{4 \div 1\}}$|, $^{u-7}$|02.00 $_{\{2 \div 1\}}$|, $^{u-8}$|01.00 $_{\{1 \div 1\}}$|>

Count—singular noun($_n$)/<(")unique> words: 02/<$^{u-4}$|01|, $^{u-7}$|01|>

Count—singular noun($_n$)/<(")unique> letters: 06/<$^{u-4}$|04|, $^{u-7}$|02|>

Count—proper noun($_{prop-n}$)/<(")unique> words: 01/<$^{u-1}$|01|>

Count—proper noun($_{prop-n}$)/<(")unique> letters: 06/<$^{u-1}$|06|>

Count—verb ($_v$)/<(")unique> words: 02/<$^{u-1}$|02|>

Count—verb($_v$)/<(")unique> letters: 09/<$^{u-1}$|09|>

Count—indefinite article($_{i-art}$)/<(")unique> words: 01/<$^{u-8}$|01|>

Count—indefinite article($_{i-art}$)/<(")unique> letters: 01/<$^{u-8}$|01|>

Percentage—singular noun($_n$)/<(")|unique|> words of answer word count: 33.33 $_{\{2 \div 6\}}$/<$^{u-4}$|16.67 $_{\{1 \div 6\}}$|, $^{u-7}$|16.67 $_{\{1 \div 6\}}$|>

Percentage—singular noun($_n$)/<(")|unique|> letters of answer letter count: 27.27 $_{\{6 \div 22\}}$/<$^{u-4}$|18.18 $_{\{4 \div 22\}}$|, $^{u-7}$|09.09 $_{\{2 \div 22\}}$|>

Percentage—proper noun($_{prop-n}$)/<(")|unique|> words of answer word count: 16.67 $_{\{1 \div 6\}}$/<$^{u-1}$|16.67 $_{\{1 \div 6\}}$|>

Percentage—proper noun($_{prop-n}$)/<(")|unique|> letters of answer letter count: 27.27 $_{\{6 \div 22\}}$/<$^{u-1}$|27.27 $_{\{6 \div 22\}}$|>

Percentage—verb($_v$)/<(")unique> words of answer word count: 33.33 $_{\{2 \div 6\}}$/<$^{u-1}$|33.33 $_{\{2 \div 6\}}$|>

Percentage—verb(v)/<(")unique> letters of answer letter count: 40.91 $_{\{9 \div 22\}}$/$<^{u-1}$|40.91 $_{\{9 \div 22\}}$|>

Percentage—indefinite article(i-art)/<(")unique> words of answer word count: 16.67 $_{\{1 \div 6\}}$/$<^{u-8}$|16.67 $_{\{1 \div 6\}}$|>

Percentage—indefinite article(i-art)/<(")unique> letters of answer letter count: 04.55 $_{\{1 \div 22\}}$/$<^{u-8}$|04.55 $_{\{1 \div 22\}}$|>

QS-YAHWEH/HEAVEN

$^{u-2}$**HAY**$_n$: $^{u-7}$**WE**$_n$. $^{u-1}$**HEAVEN**$_{prop-n}$: $^{u-4}$**HORN**$_n$, $^{u-2}$**SIRING**$_v$ $^{u-8}$**A**$_{i-art}$ $^{u-7}$**WE**$_n$.

Count—answer words/<|(")unique|>: 07/<$^{u-1}$|01|, $^{u-2}$|02|, $^{u-4}$|01|, $^{u-7}$|02|, $^{u-8}$|01|>

Count—answer letters/<(")|unique|>: 24/<$^{u-1}$|06|, $^{u-2}$|09|, $^{u-4}$|04|, $^{u-7}$|04|, $^{u-8}$|01|>

Percentage—(")|unique| answer words of answer word count: $^{u-1}$|14.29 $_{\{1 \div 7\}}$|, $^{u-2}$|28.57 $_{\{2 \div 7\}}$|, $^{u-4}$|14.29 $_{\{1 \div 7\}}$|, $^{u-7}$|28.57 $_{\{2 \div 7\}}$|, $^{u-8}$|14.29 $_{\{1 \div 7\}}$|

Percentage—(")|unique| answer letters of answer letter count: $^{u-1}$|25.00 $_{\{6 \div 24\}}$|, $^{u-2}$|37.50 $_{\{9 \div 24\}}$|, $^{u-4}$|16.67 $_{\{4 \div 24\}}$|, $^{u-7}$|16.67 $_{\{4 \div 24\}}$|, $^{u-8}$|04.17 $_{\{1 \div 24\}}$|

Average—answer letters/<(")unique|> per answer word: 03.43 $_{\{24 \div 7\}}$/$<^{u-1}$|00.86 $_{\{6 \div 7\}}$|, $^{u-2}$|1.29 $_{\{9 \div 7\}}$|, $^{u-4}$|00.57 $_{\{4 \div 7\}}$|, $^{u-7}$|00.57 $_{\{4 \div 7\}}$|, $^{u-8}$|00.14 $_{\{1 \div 7\}}$|>

Average—(")|unique| answer letters per (")|unique| answer word: $^{u-1}$|06.00 $_{\{6 \div 1\}}$|, $^{u-2}$|04.50 $_{\{9 \div 2\}}$|, $^{u-4}$|04.00 $_{\{4 \div 1\}}$|, $^{u-7}$|02.00 $_{\{4 \div 2\}}$|, $^{u-8}$|01.00 $_{\{1 \div 1\}}$|>

Count—singular noun(n)/<(")unique> words: 04/<$^{u-2}$|01|, $^{u-4}$|01|, $^{u-7}$|02|>

Count—singular noun(n)/<(")unique> letters: 11/<$^{u-2}$|03|, $^{u-4}$|04|, $^{u-7}$|04|>

Count—proper noun(prop-n)/<(")unique> words: 01/<$^{u-1}$|01|>

Count—proper noun(prop-n)/<(")unique> letters: 06/<$^{u-1}$|06|>

Count—verb (v)/<(")unique> words: 01/<$^{u-2}$|01|>

Count—verb(v)/<(")unique> letters: 06/<$^{u-2}$|06|>

Count—indefinite article(i-art)/<(")unique> words: 01/<$^{u-8}$|01|>

Count—indefinite article(i-art)/<(")unique> letters: 01/<$^{u-8}$|01|>

Percentage—singular noun(n)/<(")|unique|> words of answer word count: 57.14 $_{\{4 \div 7\}}$/$<^{u-2}$|14.29 $_{\{1 \div 7\}}$|, $^{u-4}$|14.29 $_{\{1 \div 7\}}$|, $^{u-7}$|28.57 $_{\{2 \div 7\}}$|>

Percentage—singular noun(n)/<(")|unique|> letters of answer letter count: 45.83 $_{\{11 \div 24\}}$/$<^{u-2}$|12.50 $_{\{3 \div 24\}}$|, $^{u-4}$|16.67 $_{\{4 \div 24\}}$|, $^{u-7}$|16.67 $_{\{4 \div 24\}}$|>

Percentage—proper noun(prop-n)/<(")|unique|> words of answer word count: 14.29 $_{\{1 \div 7\}}$/$<^{u-1}$|14.29 $_{\{1 \div 7\}}$|>

Percentage—proper noun(prop-n)/<(")|unique|> letters of answer letter count: 25.00 $_{\{6 \div 24\}}$/$<^{u-1}$|25.00 $_{\{6 \div 24\}}$|>

Percentage—verb(v)/<(")unique> words of answer word count: 14.29 $_{\{1 \div 7\}}$/$<^{u-2}$|14.29 $_{\{1 \div 7\}}$|>

Percentage—verb(v)/<(")unique> letters of answer letter count: 25.00 $_{\{6 \div 24\}}$/$<^{u-2}$|25.00 $_{\{6 \div 24\}}$|>

Percentage—indefinite article$(_{i\text{-}art})$/<(^{u})unique> words of answer word count: 14.29 $_{\{1 \div 7\}}$/<$^{u\text{-}8}$|14.29 $_{\{1 \div 7\}}$|>

Percentage—indefinite article$(_{i\text{-}art})$/<(^{u})unique> letters of answer letter count: 04.17 $_{\{1 \div 24\}}$/<$^{u\text{-}8}$|04.17 $_{\{1 \div 24\}}$|>

QS-CREATOR/REALITY

$^{u\text{-}1}$CORE$_n$: $^{u\text{-}1}$REAL$_{adj}$. $^{u\text{-}8}$A$_{i\text{-}art}$ $^{u\text{-}1}$TRINITY$_n$; $^{u\text{-}4}$OR$_{conj}$, $^{u\text{-}1}$RINGS$_v$ $^{u\text{-}8}$A$_{i\text{-}art}$ $^{u\text{-}7}$WE$_n$.

Count—answer words/<|(^{u})unique|>: 08/<$^{u\text{-}1}$|04|, $^{u\text{-}4}$|01|, $^{u\text{-}7}$|01|, $^{u\text{-}8}$|02|>

Count—answer letters/<(^{u})|unique|>: 26/<$^{u\text{-}1}$|20|, $^{u\text{-}4}$|02|, $^{u\text{-}7}$|02|, $^{u\text{-}8}$|02|>

Percentage—(^{u})|unique| answer words of answer word count: $^{u\text{-}1}$|50.00 $_{\{4 \div 8\}}$|, $^{u\text{-}4}$|12.50 $_{\{1 \div 8\}}$|, $^{u\text{-}7}$|12.50 $_{\{1 \div 8\}}$|, $^{u\text{-}8}$|25.00 $_{\{2 \div 8\}}$|

Percentage—(^{u})|unique| answer letters of answer letter count: $^{u\text{-}1}$|76.92 $_{\{20 \div 26\}}$|, $^{u\text{-}4}$|07.69 $_{\{2 \div 26\}}$|, $^{u\text{-}7}$|07.69 $_{\{2 \div 26\}}$|, $^{u\text{-}8}$|07.69 $_{\{2 \div 26\}}$|

Average—answer letters/<(^{u})|unique|> per answer word: 03.25 $_{\{26 \div 8\}}$/<$^{u\text{-}1}$|02.50 $_{\{20 \div 8\}}$|, $^{u\text{-}4}$|00.25 $_{\{2 \div 8\}}$|, $^{u\text{-}7}$|00.25 $_{\{2 \div 8\}}$|, $^{u\text{-}8}$|00.25 $_{\{2 \div 8\}}$|>

Average—(^{u})|unique| answer letters per (^{u})|unique| answer word: $^{u\text{-}1}$|05.00 $_{\{20 \div 4\}}$|, $^{u\text{-}4}$|02.00 $_{\{2 \div 1\}}$|, $^{u\text{-}7}$|02.00 $_{\{2 \div 1\}}$|, $^{u\text{-}8}$|01.00 $_{\{2 \div 2\}}$|>

Count—singular noun$(_n)$/<(^{u})unique> words: 03/<$^{u\text{-}1}$|02|, $^{u\text{-}7}$|01|>

Count—singular noun$(_n)$/<(^{u})unique> letters: 13/<$^{u\text{-}1}$|11|, $^{u\text{-}7}$|02|>

Count—verb $(_v)$/<(^{u})unique> words: 01/<$^{u\text{-}1}$|01|>

Count—verb$(_v)$/<(^{u})unique> letters: 05/<$^{u\text{-}1}$|05|>

Count—adjective $(_{adj})$/<(^{u})unique> words: 01/<$^{u\text{-}1}$|01|>

Count—adjective $(_{adj})$/<(^{adj})unique> letters: 04/<$^{u\text{-}1}$|04|>

Count—conjunction $(_{conj})$/<(^{u})unique> words: 01/<$^{u\text{-}4}$|01|>

Count—conjunction$(_{conj})$/<(^{u})unique> letters: 02/<$^{u\text{-}4}$|02|>

Count—indefinite article$(_{i\text{-}art})$/<(^{u})unique> words: 02/<$^{u\text{-}8}$|02|>

Count—indefinite article$(_{i\text{-}art})$/<(^{u})unique> letters: 02/<$^{u\text{-}8}$|02|>

Percentage—noun$(_n)$/<(^{u})|unique|> words of answer word count: 37.50 $_{\{3 \div 8\}}$/<$^{u\text{-}1}$|25.00 $_{\{2 \div 8\}}$|, $^{u\text{-}7}$|12.50 $_{\{1 \div 8\}}$|>

Percentage—noun$(_n)$/<(^{u})|unique|> letters of answer letter count: 42.31 $_{\{11 \div 26\}}$/<$^{u\text{-}1}$|42.31 $_{\{11 \div 26\}}$|, $^{u\text{-}7}$|07.69 $_{\{2 \div 26\}}$|>

Percentage—verb$(_v)$/<(^{u})unique> words of answer word count: 12.50 $_{\{1 \div 8\}}$/<$^{u\text{-}1}$|12.50 $_{\{1 \div 8\}}$|>

Percentage—verb$(_v)$/<(^{u})unique> letters of answer letter count: 19.23 $_{\{5 \div 26\}}$/<$^{u\text{-}1}$|19.23 $_{\{5 \div 26\}}$|>

Percentage—adjective $(_{adj})$/<(^{u})unique> words of answer word count: 12.50 $_{\{1 \div 8\}}$/<$^{u\text{-}1}$|12.50 $_{\{1 \div 8\}}$|>

Percentage—adjective ($_{adj}$)/<(")unique> letters of answer letter count: 15.39 $_{\{4 \div 26\}}$/<$^{u-1}$|15.39 $_{\{4 \div 26\}}$|>

Percentage—conjunction ($_{conj}$)/<(")unique> words of answer word count: 12.50 $_{\{1 \div 8\}}$/<$^{u-4}$|12.50 $_{\{1 \div 8\}}$|>

Percentage—conjunction ($_{conj}$)/<(")unique> letters of answer letter count: 07.69 $_{\{2 \div 26\}}$/<$^{u-4}$|07.69 $_{\{2 \div 26\}}$|>

Percentage—indefinite article($_{i\text{-}art}$)/<(")unique> words of answer word count: 25.00 $_{\{2 \div 8\}}$/<$^{u-8}$|25.00 $_{\{2 \div 8\}}$|>

Percentage—indefinite article($_{i\text{-}art}$)/<(")unique> letters of answer letter count: 07.69 $_{\{2 \div 26\}}$/<$^{u-8}$|07.69 $_{\{2 \div 26\}}$|>

QS-YAHWEH/REALITY

$^{u-2}$HAY$_n$: $^{u-1}$LAW$_n$. $^{u-1}$THEY$_{pron}$ $^{u-4}$OR$_{conj}$ $^{u-1}$REINS$_{n\text{-}pl}$, $^{u-3}$I$_{pron}$, $^{u-2}$RING$_v$ "$^{u-1}$A$_n$ $^{u-1}$WE$_n$."

Count—answer words/<|(")unique|>: 09/<$^{u-1}$|05|, $^{u-2}$|02|, $^{u-3}$|01|, $^{u-4}$|01|>

Count—answer letters/<(")|unique|>: 25/<$^{u-1}$|15|, $^{u-2}$|07|, $^{u-3}$|01|, $^{u-4}$|02|>

Percentage—(")|unique| answer words of answer word count: $^{u-1}$|55.56 $_{\{5 \div 9\}}$|, $^{u-2}$|22.22 $_{\{2 \div 9\}}$|, $^{u-3}$|11.11 $_{\{1 \div 9\}}$|, $^{u-4}$|11.11 $_{\{1 \div 9\}}$|

Percentage—(")|unique| answer letters of answer letter count: $^{u-1}$|60.00 $_{\{15 \div 25\}}$|, $^{u-2}$|28.00 $_{\{7 \div 25\}}$|, $^{u-3}$|04.00 $_{\{1 \div 25\}}$|, $^{u-4}$|08.00 $_{\{2 \div 25\}}$|

Average—answer letters/<(")|unique|> per answer word: 02.78 $_{\{25 \div 9\}}$/<$^{u-1}$|01.67 $_{\{15 \div 9\}}$|, $^{u-2}$|00.78 $_{\{7 \div 9\}}$|, $^{u-3}$|00.11 $_{\{1 \div 9\}}$|, $^{u-4}$|00.22 $_{\{2 \div 9\}}$|>

Average—(")|unique| answer letters per (")|unique| answer word: $^{u-1}$|03.00 $_{\{15 \div 5\}}$|, $^{u-2}$|03.50 $_{\{7 \div 2\}}$|, $^{u-3}$|01.00 $_{\{1 \div 1\}}$|, $^{u-4}$|02.00 $_{\{2 \div 1\}}$|>

Count—singular noun($_n$)/<(")unique> words: 04/<$^{u-1}$|03|, $^{u-2}$|01|>

Count—singular noun($_n$)/<(")unique> letters: 09/<$^{u-1}$|06|, $^{u-2}$|03|>

Count—plural noun($_{n\text{-}pl}$)/<(")unique> words: 01/<$^{u-1}$|01|>

Count—plural noun($_{n\text{-}pl}$)/<(")unique> letters: 05/<$^{u-1}$|05|>

Count—pronoun($_{pron}$)/<(")unique> words: 02/<$^{u-1}$|01|, $^{u-3}$|01|>

Count—pronoun($_{pron}$)/<(")unique> letters: 05/<$^{u-1}$|04|, $^{u-3}$|01|>

Count—verb ($_v$)/<(")unique> words: 01/<$^{u-2}$|01|>

Count—verb($_v$)/<(")unique> letters: 04/<$^{u-2}$|04|>

Count—conjunction ($_{conj}$)/<(")unique> words: 01/<$^{u-4}$|01|>

Count—conjunction($_{conj}$)/<(")unique> letters: 02/<$^{u-4}$|02|>

Percentage—singular noun($_n$)/<(")|unique|> words of answer word count: 44.44 $_{\{4 \div 9\}}$/<$^{u-1}$|33.33 $_{\{3 \div 9\}}$|, $^{u-2}$|11.11 $_{\{1 \div 9\}}$|>

Percentage—singular noun($_n$)/<(")|unique|> letters of answer letter count: 36.00 $_{\{9 \div 25\}}$/<$^{u-}$

$^1|24.00_{\{6 \div 25\}}|$, $^{u\text{-}2}|12.00_{\{3 \div 25\}}|>$

Percentage—plural noun$_{(n\text{-}pl)}$/<(^{u})|unique|> words of answer word count: 11.11 $_{\{1 \div 9\}}$/<$^{u\text{-}}$^{1}|11.11 $_{\{1 \div 9\}}$|>

Percentage—plural noun$_{(n\text{-}pl)}$/<(^{u})|unique|> letters of answer letter count: 20.00 $_{\{5 \div 25\}}$/<$^{u\text{-}}$^{1}|20.00 $_{\{5 \div 25\}}$|>

Percentage—pronoun$_{(pron)}$/<(^{u})|unique|> words of answer word count: 22.22 $_{\{2 \div 9\}}$/<$^{u\text{-}1}$|11.11 $_{\{1 \div 9\}}$|, $^{u\text{-}3}$|11.11 $_{\{1 \div 9\}}$|>

Percentage—pronoun$_{(pron)}$/<(^{u})|unique|> letters of answer letter count: 20.00 $_{\{5 \div 25\}}$/<$^{u\text{-}}$^{1}|16.00 $_{\{4 \div 25\}}$|, $^{u\text{-}3}$|04.00 $_{\{1 \div 25\}}$|>

Percentage—verb$_{(v)}$/<(^{u})unique> words of answer word count: 11.11 $_{\{1 \div 9\}}$/<$^{u\text{-}2}$|11.11 $_{\{1 \div 9\}}$|>

Percentage—verb$_{(v)}$/<(^{u})unique> letters of answer letter count: 16.00 $_{\{4 \div 25\}}$/<$^{u\text{-}1}$|16.00 $_{\{4 \div 25\}}$|>

Percentage—conjunction ($_{conj}$)/<(^{u})unique> words of answer word count: 11.11 $_{\{1 \div 9\}}$/<$^{u\text{-}}$^{4}|11.11 $_{\{1 \div 9\}}$|>

Percentage—conjunction ($_{conj}$)/<(^{u})unique> letters of answer letter count: 08.00 $_{\{2 \div 25\}}$/<$^{u\text{-}}$^{4}|08.00 $_{\{2 \div 25\}}$>

QS-YAHWEH/TRINITY

$^{u\text{-}1}$**HAIRY**$_{adj}$ $^{u\text{-}7}$**WE**$_n$. $^{u\text{-}1}$**THY**$_{adj}$ $^{u\text{-}2}$**TRIO**$_n$: $^{u\text{-}1}$**REINING**$_v$, $^{u\text{-}5}$**WANS**$_v$.

Count—answer words/<|(^{u})unique|>: 06/<$^{u\text{-}1}$|03|, $^{u\text{-}2}$|01|, $^{u\text{-}5}$|01|, $^{u\text{-}7}$|01|>

Count—answer letters/<(^{u})|unique|>: 25/<$^{u\text{-}1}$|15|, $^{u\text{-}2}$|04|, $^{u\text{-}5}$|04|, $^{u\text{-}7}$|02|>

Percentage—(^{u})|unique| answer words of answer word count: $^{u\text{-}1}$|50.00 $_{\{3 \div 6\}}$|, $^{u\text{-}2}$|16.67 $_{\{1 \div 6\}}$|, $^{u\text{-}5}$|16.67 $_{\{1 \div 6\}}$|, $^{u\text{-}7}$|16.67 $_{\{1 \div 6\}}$|

Percentage—(^{u})|unique| answer letters of answer letter count: $^{u\text{-}1}$|60.00 $_{\{15 \div 25\}}$|, $^{u\text{-}2}$|16.00 $_{\{4 \div 25\}}$|, $^{u\text{-}5}$|16.00 $_{\{4 \div 25\}}$|, $^{u\text{-}7}$|08.00 $_{\{2 \div 25\}}$|

Average—answer letters/<(^{u})|unique|> per answer word: 04.17 $_{\{25 \div 6\}}$/<$^{u\text{-}1}$|02.50 $_{\{15 \div 6\}}$|, $^{u\text{-}2}$|00.67 $_{\{4 \div 6\}}$|, $^{u\text{-}5}$|00.67 $_{\{4 \div 6\}}$|, $^{u\text{-}7}$|00.33 $_{\{2 \div 6\}}$|>

Average—(^{u})|unique| answer letters per (^{u})|unique| answer word: $^{u\text{-}1}$|05.00 $_{\{15 \div 3\}}$|, $^{u\text{-}2}$|04.00 $_{\{4 \div 1\}}$|, $^{u\text{-}5}$|04.00 $_{\{4 \div 1\}}$|, $^{u\text{-}7}$|02.00 $_{\{2 \div 1\}}$|

Count—singular noun$_{(n)}$/<(^{u})unique> words: 02/<$^{u\text{-}2}$|01|, $^{u\text{-}7}$|01|>

Count—singular noun$_{(n)}$/<(^{u})unique> letters: 06/<$^{u\text{-}2}$|04|, $^{u\text{-}7}$|02|>

Count—verb ($_v$)/<(^{u})unique> words: 02/<$^{u\text{-}1}$|01|, $^{u\text{-}5}$|01|>

Count—verb$_{(v)}$/<(^{u})unique> letters: 11/<$^{u\text{-}1}$|07|, $^{u\text{-}5}$|04|>

Count—adjective$_{(adj)}$/<(^{u})unique> words: 02/<$^{u\text{-}1}$|02|>

Count—adjective$_{(adj)}$/<(^{u})unique> letters: 08/<$^{u\text{-}1}$|08|>

Percentage—singular noun$_{(n)}$/<(^{u})|unique|> words of answer word count: 33.33 $_{\{2 \div 6\}}$/<$^{u\text{-}}$^{2}|16.67 $_{\{1 \div 6\}}$|, $^{u\text{-}7}$|16.67 $_{\{1 \div 6\}}$|>

Percentage—singular noun$_{(n)}$/<(^{u})|unique|> letters of answer letter count: 24.00 $_{\{6 \div 25\}}$/<$^{u\text{-}}$

$^2|16.00_{\{4 \div 25\}}|$, $^{u-7}|08.00_{\{2 \div 25\}}|>$

Percentage—verb(v)/<(")unique> words of answer word count: $33.33_{\{2 \div 6\}}/<^{u-1}|16.67_{\{1 \div 6\}}|$, $^{u-5}|16.67_{\{1 \div 6\}}|>$

Percentage—verb(v)/<(")unique> letters of answer letter count: $44.00_{\{11 \div 25\}}/<^{u-1}|28.00_{\{7 \div 25\}}|$, $^{u-5}|16.00_{\{4 \div 25\}}|>$

Percentage—adjective(adj)/<(")unique> words of answer word count: $33.33_{\{2 \div 6\}}/<^{u-1}|33.33_{\{2 \div 6\}}|>$

Percentage—adjective(adj)/<(")unique> letters of answer letter count: $32.00_{\{8 \div 25\}}/<^{u-1}|32.00_{\{8 \div 25\}}|>$

QS-FATHER/TRINITY

$^{u-1}$**FAIR**$_{adj}$ $^{u-2}$**HINTER**$_{n}$. $^{u-2}$**TRIO**$_{n}$: $^{u-3}$**TRYING**$_{v}$, $^{u-1}$**WANES**$_{v}$.

Count—answer words/<|(")unique|>: $05/<^{u-1}|02|$, $^{u-2}|02|$, $^{u-3}|01|>$

Count—answer letters/<(")|unique|>: $25/<^{u-1}|09|$, $^{u-2}|10|$, $^{u-3}|06|>$

Percentage—(")|unique| answer words of answer word count: $^{u-1}|40.00_{\{2 \div 5\}}|$, $^{u-2}|40.00_{\{2 \div 5\}}|$, $^{u-3}|20.00_{\{1 \div 5\}}|$

Percentage—(")|unique| answer letters of answer letter count: $^{u-1}|36.00_{\{9 \div 25\}}|$, $^{u-2}|40.00_{\{10 \div 25\}}|$, $^{u-3}|24.00_{\{6 \div 25\}}|$

Average—answer letters/<(")|unique|> per answer word: $05.00_{\{25 \div 5\}}/<^{u-1}|01.80_{\{9 \div 5\}}|$, $^{u-2}|02.00_{\{10 \div 5\}}|$, $^{u-3}|01.20_{\{6 \div 5\}}|>$

Average—(")|unique| answer letters per (")|unique| answer word: $^{u-1}|04.50_{\{9 \div 2\}}|$, $^{u-2}|05.00_{\{10 \div 2\}}|$, $^{u-3}|06.00_{\{6 \div 1\}}|$

Count—singular noun(n)/<(")unique> words: $02/<^{u-2}|02|>$

Count—singular noun(n)/<(")unique> letters: $10/<^{u-2}|10|>$

Count—verb (v)/<(")unique> words: $02/<^{u-1}|01|$, $^{u-3}|01|>$

Count—verb(v)/<(")unique> letters: $11/<^{u-1}|05|$, $^{u-3}|06|>$

Count—adjective(adj)/<(")unique> words: $01/<^{u-1}|01|>$

Count—adjective(adj)/<(")unique> letters: $04/<^{u-1}|04|>$

Percentage—singular noun(n)/<(")|unique|> words of answer word count: $40.00_{\{2 \div 5\}}/<^{u-2}|40.00_{\{2 \div 5\}}|>$

Percentage—singular noun(n)/<(")|unique|> letters of answer letter count: $40.00_{\{10 \div 25\}}/<^{u-2}|40.00_{\{10 \div 25\}}|>$

Percentage—verb(v)/<(")unique> words of answer word count: $40.00_{\{2 \div 5\}}/<^{u-1}|20.00_{\{1 \div 5\}}|$, $^{u-3}|20.00_{\{1 \div 5\}}|>$

Percentage—verb(v)/<(")unique> letters of answer letter count: $44.00_{\{11 \div 25\}}/<^{u-1}|20.00_{\{5 \div 25\}}|$, $^{u-3}|24.00_{\{6 \div 25\}}|>$

Percentage—adjective(adj)/<(")unique> words of answer word count: $20.00_{\{1 \div 5\}}/<^{u-1}|20.00_{\{1 \div 5\}}|>$

Percentage—adjective($_{adj}$)/<(")unique> letters of answer letter count: 16.00 $_{\{4 \div 25\}}$/<$^{u-1}$|16.00 $_{\{4 \div 25\}}$|>

QS-SON/TRINITY

$^{u-1}$ORATOR'S$_{contr}$ $^{u-3}$IN$_n$. $^{u-3}$IN$_n$: $^{u-3}$TRYING$_v$ $^{u-2}$SINEW$_n$.

Count—answer words/<|(")unique|>: 05/<$^{u-1}$|01|, $^{u-2}$|01|, $^{u-3}$|03|>

Count—answer letters/<(")|unique|>: 22/<$^{u-1}$|07|, $^{u-2}$|05|, $^{u-3}$|10|>

Percentage—(")|unique| answer words of answer word count: $^{u-1}$|20.00 $_{\{1 \div 5\}}$|, $^{u-2}$|20.00 $_{\{1 \div 5\}}$|, $^{u-3}$|60.00 $_{\{3 \div 5\}}$|

Percentage—(")|unique| answer letters of answer letter count: $^{u-1}$|31.82 $_{\{7 \div 22\}}$|, $^{u-2}$|22.73 $_{\{5 \div 22\}}$|, $^{u-3}$|45.45 $_{\{10 \div 22\}}$|

Average—answer letters/<(")|unique|> per answer word: 04.40 $_{\{22 \div 5\}}$/<$^{u-1}$|01.40 $_{\{7 \div 5\}}$|, $^{u-2}$|01.00 $_{\{5 \div 5\}}$|, $^{u-3}$|02.00 $_{\{10 \div 5\}}$|>

Average—(")|unique| answer letters per (")|unique| answer word: $^{u-1}$|07.00 $_{\{7 \div 1\}}$|, $^{u-2}$|05.00 $_{\{5 \div 1\}}$|, $^{u-3}$|03.33 $_{\{10 \div 3\}}$|

Count—singular noun($_n$)/<(")unique> words: 03/<$^{u-2}$|01|, $^{u-3}$|02|>

Count—singular noun($_n$)/<(")unique> letters: 09/<$^{u-2}$|05|, $^{u-3}$|04|>

Count—verb ($_v$)/<(")unique> words: 01/<$^{u-3}$|01|>

Count—verb($_v$)/<(")unique> letters: 06/<$^{u-3}$|06|>

Count—contraction($_{cont}$)/<(")unique> words: 01/<$^{u-1}$|01|>

Count—contraction($_{cont}$)/<(")unique> letters: 07/<$^{u-1}$|07|>

Percentage—singular noun($_n$)/(")|unique|> words of answer word count: 60.00 $_{\{3 \div 5\}}$/<$^{u-2}$|20.00 $_{\{1 \div 5\}}$|, $^{u-3}$|40.00 $_{\{2 \div 5\}}$|>

Percentage—singular noun($_n$)/(")|unique|> letters of answer letter count: 40.91 $_{\{9 \div 22\}}$/<$^{u-2}$|22.73 $_{\{5 \div 22\}}$|, $^{u-3}$|18.18 $_{\{4 \div 22\}}$|>

Percentage—verb($_v$)/<(")unique> words of answer word count: 20.00 $_{\{1 \div 5\}}$/<$^{u-3}$|20.00 $_{\{1 \div 5\}}$|>

Percentage—verb($_v$)/<(")unique> letters of answer letter count: 27.27 $_{\{6 \div 22\}}$/<$^{u-3}$|27.27 $_{\{6 \div 22\}}$|>

Percentage—contraction($_{cont}$)/(")|unique|> words of answer word count: 20.00 $_{\{1 \div 5\}}$/<$^{u-1}$|20.00 $_{\{1 \div 5\}}$|>

Percentage—contraction($_{cont}$)/(")|unique|> letters of answer letter count: 31.82 $_{\{7 \div 22\}}$/<$^{u-1}$|31.82 $_{\{7 \div 22\}}$|>

QS-HOLY^GHOST/TRINITY

$^{u-1}$TORAH$_{prop-n}$: $^{u-1}$GLORY$_n$. $^{u-1}$HOST$_{prop-n}$: $^{u-3}$IN$_n$, $^{u-1}$I$_n$, $^{u-3}$TRYING$_v$ $^{u-2}$SINEW$_n$.

Count—answer words/<|(")unique|>: 07/<$^{u-1}$|04|, $^{u-2}$|01|, $^{u-3}$|02|>

Count—answer letters/<(")|unique|>: 28/<$^{u\text{-}1}$|15|, $^{u\text{-}2}$|05|, $^{u\text{-}3}$|08|>

Percentage—(")|unique| answer words of answer word count: $^{u\text{-}1}$|57.14 $_{\{4 \div 7\}}$|, $^{u\text{-}2}$|14.29 $_{\{1 \div 7\}}$|, $^{u\text{-}3}$|28.57 $_{\{2 \div 7\}}$|

Percentage—(")|unique| answer letters of answer letter count: $^{u\text{-}1}$|53.57 $_{\{15 \div 28\}}$|, $^{u\text{-}2}$|17.86 $_{\{5 \div 28\}}$|, $^{u\text{-}3}$|28.57 $_{\{8 \div 28\}}$|

Average—answer letters/<(")|unique|> per answer word: 04.00 $_{\{28 \div 7\}}$/<$^{u\text{-}1}$|02.14 $_{\{15 \div 7\}}$|, $^{u\text{-}2}$|00.71 $_{\{5 \div 7\}}$|, $^{u\text{-}3}$|01.14 $_{\{8 \div 7\}}$|>

Average—(")|unique| answer letters per (")|unique| answer word: $^{u\text{-}1}$|03.75 $_{\{15 \div 4\}}$|, $^{u\text{-}2}$|05.00 $_{\{5 \div 1\}}$|, $^{u\text{-}3}$|04.00 $_{\{8 \div 2\}}$|

Count—singular noun$_{(n)}$/<(")unique> words: 04/<$^{u\text{-}1}$|02|, $^{u\text{-}2}$|01|, $^{u\text{-}3}$|01|>

Count—singular noun$_{(n)}$/<(")unique> letters: 13/<$^{u\text{-}1}$|06|, $^{u\text{-}2}$|05|, $^{u\text{-}3}$|02|>

Count—proper noun$_{(prop\text{-}n)}$/<(")unique> words: 02/<$^{u\text{-}1}$|02|>

Count—proper noun$_{(prop\text{-}n)}$/<(")unique> letters: 09/<$^{u\text{-}1}$|09|>

Count—verb $_{(v)}$/<(")unique> words: 01/<$^{u\text{-}3}$|01|>

Count—verb$_{(v)}$/<(")unique> letters: 06/<$^{u\text{-}3}$|06|>

Percentage—singular noun$_{(n)}$/<(")|unique|> words of answer word count: 57.14 $_{\{4 \div 7\}}$/<$^{u\text{-}1}$|28.57 $_{\{2 \div 7\}}$|, $^{u\text{-}2}$|14.29 $_{\{1 \div 7\}}$|, $^{u\text{-}3}$|14.29 $_{\{1 \div 7\}}$|>

Percentage—singular noun$_{(n)}$/<(")|unique|> letters of answer letter count: 46.43 $_{\{13 \div 28\}}$/<$^{u\text{-}1}$|21.43 $_{\{6 \div 28\}}$|, $^{u\text{-}2}$|17.86 $_{\{5 \div 28\}}$|, $^{u\text{-}3}$|07.14 $_{\{2 \div 28\}}$|>

Percentage—proper noun$_{(prop\text{-}n)}$/<(")|unique|> words of answer word count: 28.57 $_{\{2 \div 7\}}$/<$^{u\text{-}1}$|28.57 $_{\{2 \div 7\}}$|>

Percentage—proper noun$_{(prop\text{-}n)}$/<(")|unique|> letters of answer letter count: 32.14 $_{\{9 \div 28\}}$/<$^{u\text{-}1}$|32.14 $_{\{9 \div 28\}}$|>

Percentage—verb$_{(v)}$/<(")unique> words of answer word count: 14.29 $_{\{1 \div 7\}}$/<$^{u\text{-}3}$|14.29 $_{\{1 \div 7\}}$|>

Percentage—verb$_{(v)}$/<(")unique> letters of answer letter count: 21.43 $_{\{6 \div 28\}}$/<$^{u\text{-}3}$|21.43 $_{\{6 \div 28\}}$|>

QS-GOD/TRINITY

$^{u\text{-}1}$GOT$_v$ $^{u\text{-}1}$WORDING$_n$. $^{u\text{-}3}$"I$_n$" $^{u\text{-}2}$ENTRY$_n$; $^{u\text{-}1}$RAINS$_v$ $^{u\text{-}3}$"I$_n$."

Count—answer words/<|(")unique|>: 06/<$^{u\text{-}1}$|03|, $^{u\text{-}2}$|01|, $^{u\text{-}3}$|02|>

Count—answer letters/<(")|unique|>: 22/<$^{u\text{-}1}$|15|, $^{u\text{-}2}$|05|, $^{u\text{-}3}$|02|>

Percentage—(")|unique| answer words of answer word count: $^{u\text{-}1}$|50.00 $_{\{3 \div 6\}}$|, $^{u\text{-}2}$|16.67 $_{\{1 \div 6\}}$|, $^{u\text{-}3}$|33.33 $_{\{2 \div 6\}}$|

Percentage—(")|unique| answer letters of answer letter count: $^{u\text{-}1}$|68.18 $_{\{15 \div 22\}}$|, $^{u\text{-}2}$|22.73 $_{\{5 \div 22\}}$|, $^{u\text{-}3}$|09.09 $_{\{2 \div 22\}}$|

Average—answer letters/<(")|unique|> per answer word: 03.67 $_{\{22 \div 6\}}$/<$^{u\text{-}1}$|02.50 $_{\{15 \div 6\}}$|, $^{u\text{-}2}$|00.83 $_{\{5 \div 6\}}$|, $^{u\text{-}3}$|00.33 $_{\{2 \div 6\}}$|

Average—(")|unique| answer letters per (")|unique| answer word: $^{u\text{-}1}$|05.00 $_{\{15 \div 3\}}$|, $^{u\text{-}2}$|05.00 $_{\{5}$

÷ 1}|, $^{u-3}$|01.00 {2 ÷ 2}|

Count—singular noun($_n$)/<(^{u})unique> words: 04/<$^{u-1}$|01|, $^{u-2}$|01|, $^{u-3}$|02|>

Count—singular noun($_n$)/<(^{u})unique> letters: 14/<$^{u-1}$|07|, $^{u-2}$|05|, $^{u-3}$|02|>

Count—verb ($_v$)/<(^{u})unique> words: 02/<$^{u-1}$|02|>

Count—verb($_v$)/<(^{u})unique> letters: 08/<$^{u-1}$|08|>

Percentage—singular noun($_n$)/<(^{u})|unique|> words of answer word count: 66.67 {4 ÷ 6}/<$^{u-1}$|16.67 {1 ÷ 6}|, $^{u-2}$|16.67 {1 ÷ 6}|, $^{u-3}$|33.33 {2 ÷ 6}|>

Percentage—singular noun($_n$)/<(^{u})|unique|> letters of answer letter count: 63.64 {14 ÷ 22}/<$^{u-1}$|31.82 {7 ÷ 22}|, $^{u-2}$|22.73 {5 ÷ 22}|, $^{u-3}$|09.09 {2 ÷ 22}|>

Percentage—verb($_v$)/<(^{u})unique> words of answer word count: 33.33 {2 ÷ 6}/<$^{u-1}$|33.33 {2 ÷ 6}|>

Percentage—verb($_v$)/<(^{u})unique> letters of answer letter count: 36.36 {8 ÷ 22}/<$^{u-1}$|36.36 {8 ÷ 22}|>

QS-JESUS/TRINITY

$^{u-1}$**JOT$_v$,** $^{u-1}$**ISSUER$_n$.** $^{u-3}$**I$_{pron}$** $^{u-2}$**RING$_v$** $^{u-2}$**ENTRY$_n$** $^{u-3}$**"I$_n$,"** $^{u-1}$**"WANS$_n$."**

Count—answer words/<|(^{u})unique|>: 07/<$^{u-1}$|03|, $^{u-2}$|02|, $^{u-3}$|02|>

Count—answer letters/<(^{u})|unique|>: 24/<$^{u-1}$|13|, $^{u-2}$|09|, $^{u-3}$|02|>

Percentage—(^{u})|unique| answer words of answer word count: $^{u-1}$|42.86 {3 ÷ 7}|, $^{u-2}$|28.57 {2 ÷ 7}|, $^{u-3}$|28.57 {2 ÷ 7}|

Percentage—(^{u})|unique| answer letters of answer letter count: $^{u-1}$|54.17 {13 ÷ 24}|, $^{u-2}$|37.50 {9 ÷ 24}|, $^{u-3}$|08.33 {2 ÷ 24}|

Average—answer letters/<(^{u})|unique|> per answer word: 03.43 {24 ÷ 7}/<$^{u-1}$|01.86 {13 ÷ 7}|, $^{u-2}$|01.29 {9 ÷ 7}|, $^{u-3}$|00.29 {2 ÷ 7}|>

Average—(^{u})|unique| answer letters per (^{u})|unique| answer word: $^{u-1}$|04.33 {13 ÷ 3}|, $^{u-2}$|04.50 {9 ÷ 2}|, $^{u-3}$|01.00 {2 ÷ 2}|

Count—singular noun($_n$)/<(^{u})unique> words: 04/<$^{u-1}$|02|, $^{u-2}$|01|, $^{u-3}$|01|>

Count—singular noun($_n$)/<(^{u})unique> letters: 16/<$^{u-1}$|10|, $^{u-2}$|05|, $^{u-3}$|01|>

Count—pronoun($_{pron}$)/<(^{u})unique> words: 01/<$^{u-3}$|01|>

Count—pronoun($_{pron}$)/<(^{u})unique> letters: 01/<$^{u-3}$|01|>

Count—verb ($_v$)/<(^{u})unique> words: 02/<$^{u-1}$|01|, $^{u-2}$|01|>

Count—verb($_v$)/<(^{u})unique> letters: 07/<$^{u-1}$|03|, $^{u-2}$|04|>

Percentage—singular noun($_n$)/<(^{u})|unique|> words of answer word count: 57.14 {4 ÷ 7}/<$^{u-1}$|28.57 {2 ÷ 7}|, $^{u-2}$|14.29 {1 ÷ 7}|, $^{u-3}$|14.29 {1 ÷ 7}|>

Percentage—singular noun($_n$)/<(^{u})|unique|> letters of answer letter count: 66.67 {16 ÷ 24}/<$^{u-1}$|41.67 {10 ÷ 24}|, $^{u-2}$|20.83 {5 ÷ 24}|, $^{u-3}$|04.17 {1 ÷ 24}|>

Percentage—pronoun($_n$)/<(^{u})|unique|> words of answer word count: 14.29 {1 ÷ 7}/<$^{u-3}$|14.29 {1

Percentage—pronoun($_n$)/<(")|unique|> letters of answer letter count: 04.17 $_{\{1 \div 24\}}$/<$^{u-3}$|04.17 $_{\{1 \div 24\}}$|>

Percentage—verb($_v$)/<(")unique> words of answer word count: 28.57 $_{\{2 \div 7\}}$/<$^{u-1}$|14.29 $_{\{1 \div 7\}}$|, $^{u-2}$|14.29 $_{\{1 \div 7\}}$|>

Percentage—verb($_v$)/<(")unique> letters of answer letter count: 29.17 $_{\{7 \div 24\}}$/<$^{u-1}$|12.50 $_{\{3 \div 24\}}$|, $^{u-2}$|16.67 $_{\{4 \div 24\}}$|>

QS-TRINITY/HEAVEN

$^{u-1}$EVITERNITY$_n$: $^{u-4}$HORN$_n$. $^{u-1}$INGRAIN'S$_{contr}$ $^{u-8}$A$_{i\text{-}art}$ $^{u-7}$WE$_n$.

Count—answer words/<|(")unique|>: 05/<$^{u-1}$|02|, $^{u-4}$|01|, $^{u-7}$|01|, $^{u-8}$|01|>

Count—answer letters/<(")|unique|>: 25/<$^{u-1}$|18|, $^{u-4}$|04|, $^{u-7}$|02|, $^{u-8}$|01|>

Percentage—(")|unique| answer words of answer word count: $^{u-1}$|40.00 $_{\{2 \div 5\}}$|, $^{u-4}$|20.00 $_{\{1 \div 5\}}$|, $^{u-7}$|20.00 $_{\{1 \div 5\}}$|, $^{u-8}$|20.00 $_{\{1 \div 5\}}$|

Percentage—(")|unique| answer letters of answer letter count: $^{u-1}$|72.00 $_{\{18 \div 25\}}$|, $^{u-4}$|16.00 $_{\{4 \div 25\}}$|, $^{u-7}$|08.00 $_{\{2 \div 25\}}$|, $^{u-8}$|04.00 $_{\{1 \div 25\}}$|

Average—answer letters/<(")|unique|> per answer word: 05.00 $_{\{25 \div 5\}}$/<$^{u-1}$|03.60 $_{\{18 \div 5\}}$|, $^{u-4}$|00.80 $_{\{4 \div 5\}}$|, $^{u-7}$|00.40 $_{\{2 \div 5\}}$|, $^{u-8}$|00.20 $_{\{1 \div 5\}}$|>

Average—(")|unique| answer letters per (")|unique| answer word: $^{u-1}$|09.00 $_{\{18 \div 2\}}$|, $^{u-4}$|04.00 $_{\{4 \div 1\}}$|, $^{u-7}$|02.00 $_{\{2 \div 1\}}$|, $^{u-8}$|01.00 $_{\{1 \div 1\}}$|>

Count—singular noun($_n$)/<(")unique> words: 03/<$^{u-1}$|01|, $^{u-4}$|01|, $^{u-7}$|01|>

Count—singular noun($_n$)/<(")unique> letters: 17/<$^{u-1}$|10|, $^{u-4}$|04|, $^{u-7}$|02|>

Count—indefinite article($_{i\text{-}art}$)/<(")unique> words: 01/<$^{u-8}$|01|>

Count—indefinite article($_{i\text{-}art}$)/<(")unique> letters: 01/<$^{u-8}$|08|>

Count—contraction($_{cont}$)/<(")unique> words: 01/<$^{u-1}$|01|>

Count—contraction($_{cont}$)/<(")unique> letters: 08/<$^{u-1}$|08|>

Percentage—singular noun($_n$)/<(")|unique|> words of answer word count: 60.00 $_{\{3 \div 5\}}$/<$^{u-1}$|20.00 $_{\{1 \div 5\}}$|, $^{u-4}$|20.00 $_{\{1 \div 5\}}$|, $^{u-7}$|20.00 $_{\{1 \div 5\}}$|>

Percentage—singular noun($_n$)/<(")|unique|> letters of answer letter count: 64.00 $_{\{16 \div 25\}}$/<$^{u-1}$|40.00 $_{\{10 \div 25\}}$|, $^{u-4}$|16.00 $_{\{4 \div 25\}}$|, $^{u-7}$|08.00 $_{\{2 \div 25\}}$|>

Percentage—indefinite article($_{i\text{-}art}$)/<(")unique> words of answer word count: 20.00 $_{\{1 \div 5\}}$/<$^{u-8}$|20.00 $_{\{1 \div 5\}}$|>

Percentage—indefinite article($_{i\text{-}art}$)/<(")unique> letters of answer letter count: 04.00 $_{\{1 \div 25\}}$/<$^{u-8}$|04.00 $_{\{1 \div 25\}}$|>

Percentage—contraction($_{cont}$)/<(")|unique|> words of answer word count: 20.00 $_{\{1 \div 5\}}$/<$^{u-1}$|20.00 $_{\{1 \div 5\}}$|>

Percentage—contraction($_{cont}$)/<(")|unique|> letters of answer letter count: 32.00 $_{\{8 \div 25\}}$/<$^{u-1}$|32.00 $_{\{8 \div 25\}}$|>

QS-LUCIFER/HELL

$^{u-1}$CLUE$_n$: $^{u-1}$FILLER$_n$. $^{u-4}$HORN$_n$: $^{u-2}$SIRING$_v$ $^{u-8}$A$_{i\text{-}art}$ $^{u-7}$WE$_n$.

Count—answer words/<|(")unique|>: 06/<$^{u-1}$|02|, $^{u-2}$|01|, $^{u-4}$|01|, $^{u-7}$|01|, $^{u-8}$|01|>

Count—answer letters/<(")|unique|>: 23/<$^{u-1}$|10|, $^{u-2}$|06|, $^{u-4}$|04|, $^{u-7}$|02|, $^{u-8}$|01|>

Percentage—(")|unique| answer words of answer word count: $^{u-1}$|33.33 $_{\{2\div6\}}$|, $^{u-2}$|16.67 $_{\{1\div6\}}$|, $^{u-4}$|16.67 $_{\{1\div6\}}$|, $^{u-6}$|16.67 $_{\{1\div6\}}$|, $^{u-7}$|16.67 $_{\{1\div6\}}$|

Percentage—(")|unique| answer letters of answer letter count: $^{u-1}$|43.48 $_{\{10\div23\}}$|, $^{u-2}$|26.09 $_{\{6\div23\}}$|, $^{u-4}$|17.39 $_{\{4\div23\}}$|, $^{u-7}$|08.70 $_{\{2\div23\}}$|, $^{u-8}$|04.35 $_{\{1\div23\}}$|

Average—answer letters/<(")|unique|> per answer word: 03.83 $_{\{23\div6\}}$/<$^{u-1}$|01.67 $_{\{10\div6\}}$|, $^{u-2}$|01.00 $_{\{6\div6\}}$|, $^{u-4}$|00.67 $_{\{4\div6\}}$|, $^{u-7}$|00.33 $_{\{2\div6\}}$|, $^{u-8}$|00.17 $_{\{1\div6\}}$|>

Average—(")|unique| answer letters per (")|unique| answer word: $^{u-1}$|05.00 $_{\{10\div2\}}$|, $^{u-2}$|06.00 $_{\{6\div1\}}$|, $^{u-4}$|04.00 $_{\{4\div1\}}$|, $^{u-7}$|02.00 $_{\{2\div1\}}$|, $^{u-8}$|01.00 $_{\{1\div1\}}$|

Count—singular noun($_n$)/<(")unique> words: 04/<$^{u-1}$|02|, $^{u-4}$|01|, $^{u-7}$|01|>

Count—singular noun($_n$)/<(")unique> letters: 16/<$^{u-1}$|10|, $^{u-4}$|04|, $^{u-7}$|02|>

Count—verb ($_v$)/<(")unique> words: 01/<$^{u-2}$|01|>

Count—verb($_v$)/<(")unique> letters: 06/<$^{u-2}$|06|>

Count—indefinite article($_{i\text{-}art}$)/<(")unique> words: 01/<$^{u-8}$|01|>

Count—indefinite article($_{i\text{-}art}$)/<(")unique> letters: 01/<$^{u-8}$|01|>

Percentage—singular noun($_n$)/<(")|unique|> words of answer word count: 66.67 $_{\{4\div6\}}$/<$^{u-1}$|33.33 $_{\{2\div6\}}$|, $^{u-4}$|16.67 $_{\{1\div6\}}$|, $^{u-7}$|16.67 $_{\{1\div6\}}$|>

Percentage—singular noun($_n$)/<(")|unique|> letters of answer letter count: 69.57 $_{\{16\div23\}}$/<$^{u-1}$|43.48 $_{\{10\div23\}}$|, $^{u-4}$|17.39 $_{\{4\div23\}}$|, $^{u-7}$|08.70 $_{\{2\div23\}}$|>

Percentage—verb($_v$)/<(")unique> words of answer word count: 16.67 $_{\{1\div6\}}$/<$^{u-2}$|16.67 $_{\{1\div6\}}$|>

Percentage—verb($_v$)/<(")unique> letters of answer letter count: 26.09 $_{\{6\div23\}}$/<$^{u-2}$|26.09 $_{\{6\div23\}}$|>

Percentage—indefinite article($_{i\text{-}art}$)/<(")unique> words of answer word count: 16.67 $_{\{1\div6\}}$/<$^{u-8}$|16.67 $_{\{1\div6\}}$|>

Percentage—indefinite article($_{i\text{-}art}$)/<(")unique> letters of answer letter count: 04.35 $_{\{1\div23\}}$/<$^{u-8}$|04.35 $_{\{1\div23\}}$|>

QS-SATAN/HELL

$^{u-1}$TORAH' S$_{prop\text{-}n's}$ $^{u-1}$LEARNING$_n$. $^{u-1}$LIE$_n$ $^{u-5}$WANS$_v$.

Count—answer words/<|(")unique|>: 04/<$^{u-1}$|03|, $^{u-5}$|01|>

Count—answer letters/<(")|unique|>: 21/<$^{u-1}$|17|, $^{u-5}$|04|>

Percentage—(")|unique| answer words of answer word count: $^{u-1}$|75.00 $_{\{3\div4\}}$|, $^{u-5}$|25.00 $_{\{1\div4\}}$|

Percentage—(")|unique| answer letters of answer letter count: $^{u-1}$|80.95 $_{\{17\div21\}}$|, $^{u-5}$|19.05 $_{\{4\div}$

$21\}|$

Average—answer letters/<(ᵘ)|unique|> per answer word: $05.25_{\{21 \div 4\}}/<^{u-1}|04.25_{\{17 \div 4\}}|, ^{u-5}|01.00_{\{4 \div 4\}}|>$

Average—(ᵘ)|unique| answer letters per (ᵘ)|unique| answer word: $^{u-1}|05.67_{\{17 \div 3\}}|, ^{u-5}|04.00_{\{4 \div 1\}}|$

Count—singular noun$_{(n)}$/<(ᵘ)unique> words: $02/<^{u-1}|02|>$

Count—singular noun$_{(n)}$/<(ᵘ)unique> letters: $11/<^{u-1}|11|>$

Count—possessive proper noun$_{(prop-n's)}$/<(ᵘ)unique> words: $01/<^{u-1}|01|>$

Count—possessive proper noun$_{(prop-n's)}$/<(ᵘ)unique> letters: $06/<^{u-1}|06|>$

Count—verb $(_v)$/<(ᵘ)unique> words: $01/<^{u-5}|01|>$

Count—verb$(_v)$/<(ᵘ)unique> letters: $04/<^{u-5}|04|>$

Percentage—singular noun$_{(n)}$/<(ᵘ)|unique|> words of answer word count: $50.00_{\{2 \div 4\}}/<^{u-1}|50.00_{\{2 \div 4\}}|>$

Percentage—singular noun$_{(n)}$/<(ᵘ)|unique|> letters of answer letter count: $52.38_{\{11 \div 21\}}/<^{u-1}|52.38_{\{11 \div 21\}}|>$

Percentage—possessive proper noun$_{(prop-n's)}$/<(ᵘ)|unique|> words of answer word count: $25.00_{\{1 \div 4\}}/<^{u-1}|25.00_{\{1 \div 4\}}|>$

Percentage—possessive proper noun$_{(prop-n's)}$/<(ᵘ)|unique|> letters of answer letter count: $28.57_{\{6 \div 21\}}/<^{u-1}|28.57_{\{6 \div 21\}}|>$

Percentage—verb$(_v)$/<(ᵘ)unique> words of answer word count: $25.00_{\{1 \div 4\}}/<^{u-5}|25.00_{\{1 \div 4\}}|>$

Percentage—verb$(_v)$/<(ᵘ)unique> letters of answer letter count: $19.05_{\{4 \div 21\}}/<^{u-5}|19.05_{\{4 \div 21\}}|>$

QUERY STACK ANSWER TOTALS

$[^{u-1}GO_v \; ^{u-1}DAVE_{prop-n}. \; ^{u-2}HE_{pron}: \; ^{u-1}WINNER_n; \; ^{u-4}OR_{conj}, \; ^{u-1}GAINS_v.]^{i-5}$

$[^{u-1}HORDE_n: \; ^{u-1}EVIL_n. \; ^{u-1}ILL_n \; ^{u-1}REIGN_v, \; ^{u-5}WANS_v.]^{i-3}$

$[^{u-2}JOE_n \; ^{u-1}ASSURE_v. \; ^{u-1}RIGHT_{adv}, \; ^{u-1}REIN_n \; ^{u-5}WANS_v.]^{i-5}$

$[^{u-1}ADORE_v \; ^{u-1}GIVER_n. \; ^{u-8}A_{i-art} \; ^{u-2}HINTER_n \; ^{u-5}WANS_v.]^{i-5}$

$[^{u-2}JOE_n: \; ^{u-2}REASON_n. \; ^{u-1}AIR_n/^{u-2}HINT_n \; ^{u-2}GREW_v.]^{i-3}$

$[^{u-1}MARRY_v \; ^{u-2}REASON_n. \; ^{u-8}A_{i-art} \; ^{u-2}HINT_n, \; ^{u-3}I_{pron} \; ^{u-2}GREW_v.]^{i-5}$

$[^{u-1}HOLY_{adj} \; ^{u-1}GHOST_n. \; ^{u-2}HE_{pron}: \; ^{u-1}NAÏVE_{adj} \; ^{u-4}OR_{conj} \; ^{u-1}ANSWERING_v.]^{i-5}$

$[^{u-1}YAHWEH_{prop-n}: \; ^{u-4}HORN_n. \; ^{u-1}NERVING_v, \; ^{u-1}IS_v \; ^{u-8}A_{i-art} \; ^{u-7}WE_n.]^{i-5}$

$[^{u-2}HAY_n: \; ^{u-7}WE_n. \; ^{u-1}HEAVEN_{prop-n}: \; ^{u-4}HORN_n, \; ^{u-2}SIRING_v \; ^{u-8}A_{i-art} \; ^{u-7}WE_n.]^{u-6}$

$[^{u-1}CORE_n: \; ^{u-1}REAL_{adj}. \; ^{u-8}A_{i-art} \; ^{u-1}TRINITY_n; \; ^{u-4}OR_{conj}, \; ^{u-1}RINGS_v \; ^{u-8}A_{i-art} \; ^{u-7}WE_n.]^{i-6}$

$[^{u-2}HAY_n: \; ^{u-1}LAW_n. \; ^{u-1}THEY_{pron} \; ^{u-4}OR_{conj} \; ^{u-1}REINS_{n-pl}, \; ^{u-3}I_{pron}, \; ^{u-2}RING_v$ "$^{u-}$

^{1}A$_n$ $^{u-1}$WE$_n$."]$^{i-7}$

[$^{u-1}$HAIRY$_{adj}$ $^{u-7}$WE$_n$. $^{u-1}$THY$_{adj}$ $^{u-2}$TRIO$_n$: $^{u-1}$REINING$_v$, $^{u-5}$WANS$_v$.]$^{i-5}$

[$^{u-1}$FAIR$_{adj}$ $^{u-2}$HINTER$_n$. $^{u-2}$TRIO$_n$: $^{u-3}$TRYING$_v$, $^{u-1}$WANES$_v$.]$^{i-4}$

[$^{u-1}$ORATOR'S$_{contr}$ $^{u-3}$IN$_n$. $^{u-3}$IN$_n$: $^{u-3}$TRYING$_v$ $^{u-2}$SINEW$_n$.]$^{i-4}$

[$^{u-1}$TORAH$_{prop-n}$: $^{u-1}$GLORY$_n$. $^{u-1}$HOST$_{prop-n}$: $^{u-3}$IN$_n$, $^{u-1}$I$_n$, $^{u-3}$TRYING$_v$ $^{u-2}$SINEW$_n$.]$^{i-5}$

[$^{u-1}$GOT$_v$ $^{u-1}$WORDING$_n$. $^{u-3}$"I$_n$" $^{u-2}$ENTRY$_n$; $^{u-1}$RAINS$_v$ $^{u-3}$"I$_n$."]$^{i-4}$

[$^{u-1}$JOT$_v$, $^{u-1}$ISSUER$_n$. $^{u-3}$I$_{pron}$ $^{u-2}$RING$_v$ $^{u-2}$ENTRY$_n$ $^{u-3}$"I$_n$," $^{u-1}$"WANS$_n$."]$^{i-6}$

[$^{u-1}$EVITERNITY$_n$: $^{u-4}$HORN$_n$. $^{u-1}$INGRAIN'S$_{contr}$ $^{u-8}$A$_n$ $^{u-7}$WE$_n$.]$^{i-5}$

[$^{u-1}$CLUE$_n$: $^{u-1}$FILLER$_n$. $^{u-4}$HORN$_n$: $^{u-2}$SIRING$_v$ $^{u-8}$A$_{i-art}$ $^{u-7}$WE$_n$.]$^{i-5}$

[$^{u-1}$TORAH'S$_{prop-n's}$ $^{u-1}$LEARNING$_n$. $^{u-1}$LIE$_n$ $^{u-5}$WANS$_v$.]$^{i-3}$

Count—total answers/<|(^{i})unique|>: 20/<$^{i-3}$|03|, $^{i-4}$|03|, $^{i-5}$|10|, $^{i-6}$|03|, $^{i-7}$|01|>

Count—total answer words/<|(^{u})unique|>: 119/<$^{u-1}$|55|, $^{u-2}$|24|, $^{u-3}$|12|, $^{u-4}$|08|, $^{u-5}$|05|, $^{u-6}$|06|, $^{u-7}$|08|, $^{u-8}$|01|>

Count—total answer letters/<(^{u})|unique|>: 465/<$^{u-1}$|265|, $^{u-2}$|104|, $^{u-3}$|30|, $^{u-4}$|24|, $^{u-5}$|20|, $^{u-6}$|12|, $^{u-7}$|09|, $^{u-8}$|01|>

Percentage—total (^{i})|inclusive| answers of total answer count: $^{i-3}$|15.00 $_{\{3 \div 20\}}$|, $^{i-4}$|15.00 $_{\{3 \div 20\}}$|, $^{i-5}$|50.00 $_{\{10 \div 20\}}$|, $^{i-6}$|15.00 $_{\{3 \div 20\}}$|, $^{i-7}$|05.00 $_{\{1 \div 20\}}$|

Percentage—total (^{u})|unique| answer words of total answer word count: $^{u-1}$|46.22 $_{\{55 \div 119\}}$|, $^{u-2}$|20.17 $_{\{24 \div 119\}}$|, $^{u-3}$|10.08 $_{\{12 \div 119\}}$|, $^{u-4}$|06.72 $_{\{8 \div 119\}}$|, $^{u-5}$|04.20 $_{\{5 \div 119\}}$|, $^{u-6}$|05.04 $_{\{6 \div 119\}}$|, $^{u-7}$|06.72 $_{\{8 \div 119\}}$|, $^{u-8}$|00.84 $_{\{1 \div 119\}}$|

Percentage—total (^{u})|unique| answer letters of total answer letter count: $^{u-1}$|56.99 $_{\{265 \div 465\}}$|, $^{u-2}$|22.37 $_{\{104 \div 465\}}$|, $^{u-3}$|06.45 $_{\{30 \div 465\}}$|, $^{u-4}$|05.16 $_{\{24 \div 465\}}$|, $^{u-5}$|04.30 $_{\{20 \div 465\}}$|, $^{u-6}$|02.58 $_{\{12 \div 465\}}$|, $^{u-7}$|01.94 $_{\{9 \div 465\}}$|, $^{u-8}$|00.22 $_{\{1 \div 465\}}$|

Average—total answer letters/<(^{u})|unique|> per total answer word: 03.91 $_{\{465 \div 119\}}$/<$^{u-1}$|02.23 $_{\{265 \div 119\}}$|, $^{u-2}$|00.87 $_{\{104 \div 119\}}$|, $^{u-3}$|00.26 $_{\{30 \div 119\}}$|, $^{u-4}$|00.20 $_{\{24 \div 119\}}$|, $^{u-5}$|00.17 $_{\{20 \div 119\}}$|, $^{u-6}$|00.10 $_{\{12 \div 119\}}$|, $^{u-7}$|00.08 $_{\{9 \div 119\}}$|, $^{u-8}$|00.01 $_{\{1 \div 119\}}$|>

Average—total (^{u})|unique| answer letters per total (^{u})|unique| answer word: $^{u-1}$|04.82 $_{\{265 \div 55\}}$|, $^{u-2}$|04.33 $_{\{104 \div 24\}}$|, $^{u-3}$|02.50 $_{\{30 \div 12\}}$|, $^{u-4}$|03.00 $_{\{24 \div 8\}}$|, $^{u-5}$|04.00 $_{\{20 \div 5\}}$|, $^{u-6}$|02.00 $_{\{12 \div 6\}}$|, $^{u-7}$|01.13 $_{\{9 \div 8\}}$|, $^{u-8}$|01.00 $_{\{1 \div 1\}}$|

Count—total singular noun($_n$)/<(^{u})unique> words: 56/<$^{u-1}$|23|, $^{u-2}$|16|, $^{u-3}$|06|, $^{u-4}$|04|, $^{u-7}$|07|>

Count—total singular noun($_n$)/<(^{u})unique> letters: 217/<$^{u-1}$|106|, $^{u-2}$|72|, $^{u-3}$|09|, $^{u-4}$|16|, $^{u-7}$|14|>

Count—total plural noun($_{n-pl}$)/<(^{u})unique> words: 01/<$^{u-1}$|01|>

Count—total plural noun($_{n-pl}$)/<(^{u})unique> letters: 05/<$^{u-1}$|05|>

Count—total proper noun($_{prop-n}$)/<(^{u})unique> words: 05/<$^{u-1}$|05|>

Count—total proper noun($_{prop-n}$)/<(^{u})unique> letters: 25/<$^{u-1}$|25|>

Count—total possessive proper noun($_{prop\text{-}n\text{'}s}$)/<(")unique> words: $01/<^{u\text{-}1}|01|>$

Count—total possessive proper noun($_{prop\text{-}n\text{'}s}$)/<(")unique> letters: $06/<^{u\text{-}1}|06|>$

Count—total pronoun($_{pron}$)/<(")unique> words: $06/<^{u\text{-}1}|01|, ^{u\text{-}2}|02|, ^{u\text{-}3}|03|>$

Count—total pronoun($_{pron}$)/<(")unique> letters: $11/<^{u\text{-}1}|04|, ^{u\text{-}2}|04|, ^{u\text{-}3}|03|>$

Count—total verb ($_v$)/<(")unique> words: $29/<^{u\text{-}1}|15|, ^{u\text{-}2}|06|, ^{u\text{-}3}|03|, ^{u\text{-}5}|05|>$

Count—total verb($_v$)/<(")unique> letters: $140/<^{u\text{-}1}|74|, ^{u\text{-}2}|28|, ^{u\text{-}3}|18|, ^{u\text{-}5}|20|>$

Count—total adjective($_{adj}$)/<(")unique> words: $06/<^{u\text{-}1}|06|>$

Count—total adjective($_{adj}$)/<(")unique> letters: $25/<^{u\text{-}1}|25|>$

Count—total adverb($_{adv}$)/<(")unique> words: $01/<^{u\text{-}1}|01|>$

Count—total adverb($_{adv}$)/<(")unique> letters: $05/<^{u\text{-}1}|05|>$

Count—total conjunction ($_{conj}$)/<(")unique> words: $04/<^{u\text{-}4}|04|>$

Count—total conjunction($_{conj}$)/<(")unique> letters: $08/<^{u\text{-}4}|08|>$

Count—total indefinite article ($_{i\text{-}art}$)/<(")unique> words: $08/<^{u\text{-}8}|08|>$

Count—total indefinite article ($_{i\text{-}art}$)/<(")unique> letters: $08/<^{u\text{-}8}|08|>$

Count—total contraction ($_{contr}$)/<(")unique> words: $02/<^{u\text{-}1}|02|>$

Count—total contraction($_{contr}$)/<(")unique> letters: $15/<^{u\text{-}1}|15|>$

Percentage—total singular noun($_n$)/<(")|unique|> words of total answer word count: $47.06\ _{\{56 \div 119\}}/<^{u\text{-}1}|19.33\ _{\{23 \div 119\}}|, ^{u\text{-}2}|13.45\ _{\{16 \div 119\}}|, ^{u\text{-}3}|05.04\ _{\{6 \div 119\}}|, ^{u\text{-}4}|03.36\ _{\{4 \div 119\}}|, ^{u\text{-}7}|05.88\ _{\{7 \div 119\}}|>$

Percentage—total singular noun($_n$)/<(")|unique|> letters of total answer letter count: $46.67\ _{\{217 \div 465\}}/<^{u\text{-}1}|22.80\ _{\{106 \div 465\}}|, ^{u\text{-}2}|15.48\ _{\{72 \div 465\}}|, ^{u\text{-}3}|01.94\ _{\{9 \div 465\}}|, ^{u\text{-}4}|03.44\ _{\{16 \div 465\}}|, ^{u\text{-}7}|03.01\ _{\{14 \div 465\}}|>$

Percentage—total plural noun($_{n\text{-}pl}$)/<(")|unique|> words of total answer word count: $0.84\ _{\{1 \div 119\}}/<^{u\text{-}1}|0.84\ _{\{1 \div 119\}}|>$

Percentage—total plural noun($_{n\text{-}pl}$)/<(")|unique|> letters of total answer letter count: $01.08\ _{\{5 \div 465\}}/<^{u\text{-}1}|01.08\ _{\{5 \div 465\}}|>$

Percentage—total proper noun($_{prop\text{-}n}$)/<(")|unique|> words of total answer word count: $04.20\ _{\{5 \div 119\}}/<^{u\text{-}1}|04.20\ _{\{5 \div 119\}}|>$

Percentage—total proper noun($_{prop\text{-}n}$)/<(")|unique|> letters of total answer letter count: $05.38\ _{\{25 \div 465\}}/<^{u\text{-}1}|05.38\ _{\{25 \div 465\}}|>$

Percentage—possessive proper noun($_{prop\text{-}n\text{'}s}$)/<(")|unique|> words of total answer word count: $0.84\ _{\{1 \div 119\}}/<^{u\text{-}1}|0.84\ _{\{1 \div 119\}}|>$

Percentage—possessive proper noun($_{prop\text{-}n\text{'}s}$)/<(")|unique|> letters of total answer letter count: $01.29\ _{\{6 \div 465\}}/<^{u\text{-}1}|01.29\ _{\{6 \div 465\}}|>$

Percentage—total pronoun($_{pron}$)/<(")|unique|> words of total answer word count: $05.04\ _{\{6 \div 119\}}/<^{u\text{-}1}|00.84\ _{\{1 \div 119\}}|, ^{u\text{-}2}|01.68\ _{\{2 \div 119\}}|, ^{u\text{-}3}|02.52\ _{\{3 \div 119\}}|>$

Percentage—total pronoun$_{(pron)}$/<(^{u})|unique|> letters of total answer letter count: 02.37 $_{\{11 \div 465\}}$/<$^{u-1}$|00.86 $_{\{4 \div 465\}}$|, $^{u-2}$|00.86 $_{\{4 \div 465\}}$|, $^{u-3}$|00.65 $_{\{3 \div 465\}}$|>

Percentage—total verb$_{(v)}$/<(^{u})unique> words of total answer word count: 24.37 $_{\{29 \div 119\}}$/<$^{u-1}$|12.61 $_{\{15 \div 119\}}$|, $^{u-2}$|05.04 $_{\{6 \div 119\}}$|, $^{u-3}$|02.52 $_{\{3 \div 119\}}$|, $^{u-5}$|04.20 $_{\{5 \div 119\}}$|>

Percentage—total verb$_{(v)}$/<(^{u})unique> letters of total answer letter count: 30.11 $_{\{140 \div 465\}}$/<$^{u-1}$|15.91 $_{\{74 \div 465\}}$|, $^{u-2}$|06.02 $_{\{28 \div 465\}}$|, $^{u-3}$|03.87 $_{\{18 \div 465\}}$|, $^{u-5}$|04.30 $_{\{20 \div 465\}}$|>

Percentage—total adjective$_{(adj)}$/<(^{u})unique> words of total answer word count: 05.04 $_{\{6 \div 119\}}$/<$^{u-1}$|05.04 $_{\{6 \div 119\}}$|>

Percentage—total adjective$_{(adj)}$/<(^{u})unique> letters of total answer letter count: 05.38 $_{\{25 \div 465\}}$/<$^{u-1}$|05.38 $_{\{25 \div 465\}}$|>

Percentage—total adverb$_{(adv)}$/<(^{u})unique> words of total answer word count: 00.84 $_{\{1 \div 19\}}$/<$^{u-1}$|00.84 $_{\{1 \div 119\}}$|>

Percentage—total adverb$_{(adv)}$/<(^{u})unique> letters of total answer letter count: 01.08 $_{\{5 \div 465\}}$/<$^{u-1}$|01.08 $_{\{5 \div 465\}}$|>

Percentage—total conjunction $_{(conj)}$/<(^{u})unique> words of total answer word count: 03.36 $_{\{4 \div 119\}}$/<$^{u-4}$|03.36 $_{\{4 \div 119\}}$|>

Percentage—total conjunction $_{(conj)}$/<(^{u})unique> letters of total answer letter count: 01.72 $_{\{8 \div 465\}}$/<$^{u-4}$|01.72 $_{\{8 \div 465\}}$|>

Percentage—total indefinite article $_{(i\text{-}art)}$/<(^{u})unique> words of total answer word count: 06.72 $_{\{8 \div 119\}}$/<$^{u-7}$|06.72 $_{\{8 \div 119\}}$|>

Percentage—total indefinite article $_{(i\text{-}art)}$/<(^{u})unique> letters of total answer letter count: 01.72 $_{\{8 \div 465\}}$/<$^{u-7}$|01.72 $_{\{8 \div 465\}}$|>

Percentage—total contraction $_{(contr)}$/<(^{u})unique> words of total answer word count: 01.68 $_{\{2 \div 119\}}$/<$^{u-1}$|01.68 $_{\{2 \div 119\}}$|>

Percentage—total contraction $_{(contr)}$/<(^{u})unique> letters of total answer letter count: 03.23 $_{\{15 \div 465\}}$/<$^{u-1}$|03.23 $_{\{15 \div 465\}}$|>

CHAPTER SEVEN: SECTION FIVE
COMPOSITE QS ANSWER INTERPRETATION

In "Ch. 7, Sec. 5: 1," I'd arranged the twenty QS answers that were revealed in this book in the same order in which I'd revealed said QS answers in this book. Each one of said twenty QS answers was derived from a particular QS matrix (see "Appendix D"), in accordance with QS rules and QS guides (see "Appendix A"). The grammatical framework which each one of said twenty QS answers was fashioned around consisted of seven grammatical properties that I'd collectivized and called "Seven Common Query Stack Answer Properties," or "QS-7CAP" (see "Appendix B" and "Appendix C").

In "Ch. 7, Sec. 5: 1," I'd provided two sets of interpretations for each one of the twenty QS answers I'd revealed in this book. Each one of the said two sets consisted of two interpretations. Each one of the said two interpretations was preceded by a superscripted reference number which matched a superscripted reference number that preceded one of the two sentences in one of the said twenty QS answers.

In "Ch. 7, Sec. 5: 1," I'd separated the two sets of interpretations, which were located below each one of the QS answers, with a dashed line. Each interpretation which appeared above said dashed line conveyed a meaning that was predominately based on definitions of QS answer words (see "Glossary I") rather than a meaning which was embellished with knowledge derived from other sources, such as bibles or other QS answers. Each interpretation which appeared below said dashed line conveyed a meaning which was based on not only on definitions of QS answer words but also on knowledge I'd derived from bibles and other QS answers (see "Ch. 7, Sec. 2"). Ultimately, by combining and intertwining the words, phrases and meanings of the interpretations which were below said dashed line, I'd pieced together a composite, detailed interpretation of the twenty QS answers in this book (see "Ch. 7, Sec. 5: 2"):

- ✓ Every QS rule followed (see "Appendix A");
- ✓ Every QS guide considered (see "Appendix A");
- ✓ Every "QS-7CAP" property followed (see "Appendix B" and "Appendix C");

Ch. 7, Sec. 5: 1

⁽¹⁾GO DAVE. ⁽²⁾HE: WINNER; OR, GAINS.

⁽¹⁾*An individual named "Dave" was directed to begin an action.*

⁽²⁾*A male successfully completed an action; in other words, the male received profits from the successful completion of said action.*

⁽¹⁾*I, who was nicknamed "Dave," since I was given the first name "David," was directed to begin the action of revealing God's origin.*

⁽²⁾*I, Dave, a male, successfully completed the action of revealing information about God's origin and profited by gaining said information.*

⁽³⁾HORDE: EVIL. ⁽⁴⁾ILL REIGN, WANS.

⁽³⁾*A group of individuals was a wicked entity.*

⁽⁴⁾*A wicked entity ruled and experienced a weakening of a force that said entity exerted.*

⁽³⁾*God, who was a group of individuals, was a wicked entity.*

⁽⁴⁾*God, a wicked entity, maintained His rule over Reality by exerting a moral force and experienced a weakening in said moral force.*

⁽⁵⁾JOE ASSURE. ⁽⁶⁾RIGHT, REIN WANS.

⁽⁵⁾*A male asserted His certainty in regards to the correctness of a fact.*

⁽⁶⁾*An entity, which was a controlling power, confirmed a weakening in a force that said entity exerted.*

⁽⁵⁾*God, a male, asserted that the notion that His moral force had wanned was factually correct.*

⁽⁶⁾*God confirmed that He, a controlling power, had experienced a weakening in the moral force which He'd exerted to maintain His rule over Reality.*

⁽⁷⁾ADORE GIVER. ⁽⁸⁾A HINTER WANS.

⁽⁷⁾*Show reverence for a selfless provider.*

⁽⁸⁾*A provider of allusive statements experienced a weakening in a force that said provider exerted.*

⁽⁷⁾*Revere God, a selfless provider of allusive statements, for His holiness.*

⁽⁸⁾*God, a provider of allusive statements, had experienced a weakening in the moral force which He'd exerted to maintain His rule over Reality.*

⁽⁹⁾JOE: REASON. ⁽¹⁰⁾AIR/HINT GREW.

⁽⁹⁾A male entity had an explanation.

⁽¹⁰⁾A publicized, allusive statement was lengthened due to an increase in the number of words expressing said statement.

⁽⁹⁾God, a male, had an explanation which revealed that a lie He'd told or supported caused the moral force which He'd exerted to maintain His rule over Reality to weaken.

⁽¹⁰⁾God's explanation, which revealed that a lie which He'd told or supported caused the moral force that He'd exerted to maintain His rule over Reality to weaken and was publicized in the form of an allusive statement, became wordier.

⁽¹¹⁾MARRY REASON. ⁽¹²⁾A HINT, I GREW.

⁽¹¹⁾Segments of an explanation were pieced together.

⁽¹²⁾An allusive statement was made wordier by the narrator of the QS answer that this statement translates.

⁽¹¹⁾God pieced together segments of His explanation which revealed that a lie which He'd told or supported caused the moral force that He'd exerted to maintain His rule over Reality to weaken.

⁽¹²⁾God expressed His explanation, which revealed that a lie which He'd told or supported caused the moral force that He'd exerted to maintain His rule over Reality to weaken, as an allusive statement and declared that He'd made said statement wordier.

⁽¹³⁾HOLY GHOST. ⁽¹⁴⁾HE: NAÏVE OR ANSWERING.

⁽¹³⁾An individual wrote a divine writing that God conceived and credited God as the author of said writing.

⁽¹⁴⁾A male entity taught himself how to derive a solution.

⁽¹³⁾I, Dave, was God's ghost-writer because I'd written divine messages, which I'd called "Query Stack answers"; said divine messages were conceived by God; and I'd given God credit for authoring said divine messages.

⁽¹⁴⁾I, Dave, a male, taught myself how to construct and decode Query Stacks and uncover QS answers, which was a process that led to a solution for my "What's God's origin" question.

| **(15)YAHWEH: HORN. (16)NERVING, IS A WE.** |

(15)Yahweh, whose name was a transliteration of the name "YHWH" and a name that Jewish scholars believed was God's actual name, was a source of strength.

(16)An entity provided moral force to and was a group comprised of individuals who were each aware of being an individual in said group.

---

(15)Yahweh, or God, was a source of moral strength.

(16)God provided Himself with moral strength and was comprised of three individuals who were each aware of being an individual in His trinity.

| **(17)HAY: WE. (18)HEAVEN: HORN, SIRING A WE.** |

(17)A rewarding result which was obtained through careful effort was a group comprised of individuals who were each aware of being an individual in said group.

(18)Heaven, whose name was an alias for the name "God," was a source of strength and created a group comprised of individuals who were each aware of being an individual in said group.

---

(17)A rewarding result which God obtained through a carefully executed self-transformation was the re-creation of Himself as three individuals, or a trinity, who were each aware of being an individual in God's trinity.

(18)Heaven, or God, was a source of moral strength and had transformed Himself into three individuals who were each aware of being an individual in God's trinity.

| **(19)CORE: REAL. (20)A TRINITY; OR, RINGS A WE.** |

(19)The most essential aspect of an entity was actual, or nonimaginary.

(20)Each of three individuals was an individual in one and the same entity, experienced existence as an individual and as said entity, and was aware of being an individual in said entity.

---

(19)God, the most essential aspect of a trinity, was an actual, or nonimaginary, entity.

(20)God was comprised of three individuals who were each aware of being an individual in His trinity.

[21]HAY: LAW. [22]THEY OR REINS, I, RING "A WE."

[21]*A rewarding result which was obtained through careful effort was a revelation manifested by God.*

[22]*Each individual in a group was a controlling power, and in combination with every other individual in the group was the narrator of the QS answer that this interpretation explains and repeated the phrase "a we."*

[21]*A rewarding result which God obtained through a carefully and willfully executed self-transformation was the manifestation of Himself as three individuals who were each aware of being an individual in His trinity.*

[22]*Each individual in God's trinity was a controlling power, and in combination with the other two individuals narrated QS answers and repeatedly inserted the phrase "a we" into QS answers.*

[23]HAIRY WE. [24]THY TRIO: REINING, WANS.

[23]*An incomprehensibility was a group which was comprised of individuals who were each aware of being an individual in said group.*

[24]*An entity comprised of three individuals exerted controlling power and experienced a weakening in the force that the entity exerted to maintain controlling power.*

[23]*God, an incomprehensibility, was comprised of three individuals who were each aware of being an individual in His trinity.*

[24]*God was comprised of three individuals, ruled over Reality, and experienced a weakening in the moral force which He'd exerted to maintain His rule over Reality.*

[25]FAIR HINTER. [26]TRIO: TRYING, WANES.

[25]*A real, or nonimaginary, entity was a provider of allusive statements.*

[26]*An entity comprised of three individuals experimented with and had a weakening in the force which said entity exerted.*

[25]*God was real, or nonimaginary, and a provider of allusive statements.*

[26]*God was comprised of three individuals, experimented with exerting moral force as a way to rule over Reality and experienced a weakening in His moral force.*

[27]ORATOR'S IN. [28]IN: TRYING SINEW.

[27]*An individual who'd publicized writings held a powerful position.*

[28]*An entity that held a powerful position experimented with strength.*

[27]*God, who'd publicized QS answers through the book this interpretation was written in held the most powerful position in Reality.*

[28]*God, who'd held the most powerful position in Reality, experimented with exerting moral force as a way to rule over Reality.*

(29)TORAH: GLORY. (30)HOST: IN, I, TRYING SINEW.

(29)In the first five books of the Tanakh, the Jewish bible, God was depicted as a Shekinah, or God's manifestation of Himself on Earth as an earthly object.

(30)Jesus Christ, whose earthly body God manifested Himself within, was in a powerful position, was the narrator of the QS answer which this interpretation explains, and experimented with strength.

---

(29)In the Torah, or the first five books of the Tanakh, God was depicted as a Shekinah, or God's manifestation of Himself on Earth as an earthly object.

(30)Jesus Christ, who was an individual in God's trinity and whose body God inhabited when Jesus was on Earth, was God, and, therefore, held the most powerful position in Reality, was the narrator of QS answers, and experimented with exerting moral force as a way to rule over Reality.

(31)GOT WORDING. (32)"I" ENTRY; RAINS "I."

(31)A writing contained words.

(32)The word "I" was inserted into a writing numerous times.

---

(31)QS answers contained words.

(32)The word "I" appeared several times as a QS answer word.

(33)JOT, ISSUER. (34)I RING ENTRY "I," "WANS."

(33)A brief writing was written by an individual who'd publicized material.

(34)The narrator of the QS answer that this interpretation explains repeatedly inserted the words "I" and "wans" into a writing.

---

(33)God wrote brief writings, or QS answers, and publicized said QS answers via the book this interpretation was written in.

(34)God, the narrator of the QS answers in this book, repeatedly inserted the words "I" and "wans" into QS answers.

(35)EVITERNITY: HORN. (36)INGRAIN'S A WE.

(35)An everlasting entity was a source of strength.

(36)An innate characteristic of an entity was a group comprised of individuals who were each aware of being an individual in said group.

---

(35)God, an everlasting entity, was a source of moral strength.

(36)An essential characteristic of God was His triune physique.

(37)CLUE: FILLER. (38)HORN: SIRING A WE.
(37)An entity wrote hints in a blank space.
(38)A source of strength created a group comprised of individuals who were each aware of being an individual in said group.
(37)God wrote hints in areas where no words had been written; in other words, God originated said hints.
(38)God, a source of moral strength, transformed Himself into three individuals who were each aware of being an individual in His trinity.
(39)TORAH'S LEARNING. (40)LIE WANS.
(39)The Torah, which is comprised of the first five books of the Tanakh, or Jewish Bible, contained a teaching.
(40)An untruth weakened a force.
(39)The Torah, or the first five books of the Tanakh, contained a teaching which discouraged the telling or supporting of an untruth.
(40)The Torah taught that telling or supporting an untruth weakened the moral force of the individual who'd told the untruth or supported someone else's untruth.

In "Ch. 7, Sec. 5: 2," I'd provided a composite interpretation of the twenty QS answers in this book. Superscripted reference numbers which preceded a sentence or followed a word or phrase in said composite interpretation were matched to superscripted reference numbers that preceded QS answer sentences and interpretations in "Ch. 7, Sec. 5: 1." Any superscripted reference number which I'd placed before a sentence in said composite interpretation signified that the interpretation with the same reference number provided most, if not all, of the details for the said matching sentence in said composite interpretation. Any superscripted reference number which I'd placed after a word or phrase in said composite interpretation signified that the interpretation with the same reference number provided one or two details which corresponded with said word or phrase in said composite interpretation:

Ch. 7, Sec. 5: 2

COMPOSITE INTERPRETATION

Dave's Goal

(1)I, a male(2, 14) who's been nicknamed "Dave," since I've been given the first name "David," was directed to begin the action of revealing God's origin. (14)I'd taught myself how to construct and decode Query Stacks and uncover QS answers, which was a process that led me to a solution for my "What's God's origin" question. (13)I was God's ghost-writer because I'd written divine messages, or Query Stack (QS) answers; I'd written said QS answers, but said QS answers were conceived by God; and I'd written said QS answers, but I gave God credit for authoring said QS answers. [2]I'd successfully completed the action of revealing information about God's origin and profited by gaining said information.

God's QS Answer's

[25]God, who was a real[19], or nonimaginary, male[5, 9] entity, originated brief, allusive statements[33, 37], or QS answers, and selflessly handed[7, 8] said QS answers to anyone willing to read said QS answers. [34]God, who was the narrator of the QS answers in this book[22, 30], said that He'd repeatedly inserted the words "I"[32] and "wans" and the phrase "a we"[22] into QS answers[31], which, in turn, increased the QS answers' word count[10, 12]. [33]Once God was satisfied with the QS answers He'd authored, God publicized His QS answers via this book, "Reality's Storyline Decoded II: Query Stacks"[27]. [7]Furthermore, God didn't ask anything in return for His suppliance of QS answers, but God did request to be revered for His holiness, a quality unique to and intrinsically intertwined into the essence of His existence.

God's Trinity

[16, 17, 18, 20, 21, 23, 38]God was an incomprehensibility[23] who'd carefully and successfully[17, 21] transformed Himself into three individuals[24, 26] who were each aware of being an individual in God's trinity[3]. God made triunity an essential characteristic of His physique[36], while, at the same time, God infused His individualism into the most essential layer of existence in each member of said trinity[19]. [22]Each individual in God's trinity was a controlling power[6]. [30]Jesus Christ was an individual in God's trinity, and Jesus Christ was a Shekinah[29] since God inhabited Jesus's body when Jesus lived on Earth.

God's Rise and Fall

[27, 28, 30]God held the most powerful position in Reality. [15, 35]God, aka "Yahweh" or "Heaven[18]," was an eternality and a source and provider of moral strength for Himself[16] and every other moral entity[18, 38]. [26, 28, 30]God experimented with exerting moral force as a means to rule over Reality. [4, 24]Eventually, God ruled over Reality by exerting a moral force based in goodness. [4, 8, 24, 26]However, God experienced a weakening in the moral force of goodness He'd wielded because He'd expressed wickedness[3]. [5, 6]In a QS answer, God confirmed the factual correctness of the notion that His moral force of goodness had weakened. [9, 10, 11, 12]In fact, God added words to[10, 12], pieced together segments of[11] and publicized[10] via allusive statements called "QS answers" an explanation which revealed that His moral force of goodness was weakened by an untruth that He'd told or supported. [39, 40]A weakening in a moral entity's moral force of goodness due to an untruth told or supported by said moral entity aligned with one of God's Ten Commandments in the Torah, which stated "You shall not bear false witness against your neighbor" (Shemot 20:13 Tanakh), and similar verses in the Torah which corrob-

orated the Ninth Commandment's warning that an untruth weakened a moral entity's moral force of goodness, such as "A false witness will not go unpunished, and one who speaks lies will perish (Mishlei 19:9 Tanakh).

AFTERWORD

Maybe, you think that God is imaginary and, therefore, couldn't of had anything to do with the formation of or the meaning expressed through Query Stacks. Maybe, you've explained Query Stacks away as an encryption method which I've manufactured in an attempt to trick you into believing that God was nonimaginary. Maybe, you've concluded that the Query Stacks in this book haven't ever possessed intrinsic significance and weren't nothing more than anomalous abnormalities. Maybe, you've written off my personal views regarding Query Stacks as pure absurdities. Maybe, you've decided that my mind must've became entangled within alphabetical snafus. Or, maybe, you just haven't realized yet that your conclusions which you have about my study of and my explanations that concern Query Stacks have fallen short of ringing true.

The twenty Query Stacks I'd uncovered and presented in this book were created through one of three processes: Query Stacks were intentionally written by God, to express facts which paralleled actualities; Query Stacks were complex concoctions devised by my unconscious mind; or Query Stacks were deceits I'd consciously designed. If said Query Stacks expressed facts which reflected actualities, then God was an actual, or nonimaginary, being. If my unconscious mind contrived said Query Stacks, then my unconscious mind had stealthily done so; which meant, my unconscious mind made Query Stacks without my conscious mind knowing and tricked my conscious mind into believing God was the author of said Query Stacks. If said Query Stacks were devised by my unconscious mind, then I'd have to say that my unconscious mind's creative capability to construct complex Query Stack encryptions, associations, and answers which have mirrored biblical topics and revealed the future, was, in the very least, astonishing. I wouldn't have minded if I was named as the inventor of such an ingenious construct; however, I'd discovered Query Stacks through a vision which I didn't intend to have and unveiled and decoded multiple Query Stacks that I would've never uncovered if I'd never seen said vision.

I'd transposed but wasn't the author of the twenty Query Stacks in this book. God authored said Query Stacks. I was God's ghostwriter, and I've wholeheartedly accepted and will cherish said accreditation:

HOLY GHOST. HE: NAÏVE OR ANSWERING.

P.s. Maybe, God never told or supported a lie, and, therefore, God's moral force never wanned. Maybe, God merely shared a moral lesson about lies and how lies told or promoted by controlling powers eroded trust others had in said controlling powers. Maybe, God simply used His own controlling power as an example for said lesson. Maybe, in the future, I'll reveal QS answers which provide more divine information.

APPENDICES

Each Query Stack I'd presented in this book was constructed, decoded and interpreted in accordance with repeatable methods, defined guides and strict rules. I'd consistently produced meaningful QS answers when I'd adhered to said methods, guides and rules, which strengthened my trust in the validity of and intentionality baked into said QS answers' messages. If I'd unveiled twenty QS answers by not adhering to repeatable methods, rules or guides, then I would've thought that all of said QS answers were insignificant.

- **Appendix A: Query Stack Rules and Guides**
  Rules and guides which I'd uncovered and used to construct and decode Query Stack matrices and answers.

- **Appendix B: Seven Common Query Stack Answer Properties**
  Seven grammatical characteristics found within each of the QS answers in this book.

- **Appendix C: "QS-7CAP" Formula, Example and Key**
  A template which symbolically articulates the seven grammatical characteristics found within each of the QS answers in this book.

- **Appendix D: Query Stack Database**
  Twenty QS matrices and said matrices' corresponding QS answers unveiled in this book.

APPENDIX A

QUERY STACK RULES AND GUIDES

Construct a QS Matrix

Rule 1: Determine a question.
Rule 2: Reduce the question's vocabulary to key words.
Rule 3: Stack key words vertically and in an order which causes the question to be asked when key words are read downwards.
Rule 4: Align the first letter of each key word—*row'd word*—into one column.
Rule 5: Align subsequent letters of row'd words into subsequent columns.
Rule 6: Every letter-position of a row'd word matrix must contain a letter.

Decode a QS Matrix

Rule 1: Row'd word letters can only be connected horizontally and/or vertically.
Rule 2: Letters in a set of connected row'd word letters can be arranged in any order to make an answer word.
Rule 3: Each row'd word letter must be used only once to spell an answer word.
Rule 4: Each row'd word letter must appear in a useful answer word.
Rule 5: Each row'd word letter must appear in the answer no more and no less than one time.

Construct a QS Answer

Rule 1: Words built from connected row'd word letters are removed in a top-left to bottom-right sequence and listed in the order of removal to make a valid answer.
Rule 2: A word produced by linking row'd word letters together must be removed from a row'd word matrix and listed in the answer no more and no less than one time.
Rule 3: Insert punctuation into the answer to make the answer coherent and meaningful.
Rule 4: Verify the integrity of the answer's vocabulary via "QS-7CAP" (see Appendix B).

Interpret a QS Answer

Guide 1: Uncover a Query Stack's best answer by uncovering said Query Stack's most coherent, meaningful answer.
Guide 2: A Query Stack's most coherent, meaningful answer is comprised of vocabulary that pertains to no more and no less than one subject, the main subject.

Guide 3: Actions mentioned in a QS answer affect said answer's main subject.

Guide 4: A QS answer word's definition should be standard; can be archaic or slang, if no valid standard options are available; but shouldn't ever be obsolete.

Guide 5: A QS answer word may be a noun, pronoun, verb, adjective, adverb, conjunction, indefinite article or contraction, but not be an interjection.

APPENDIX B
SEVEN COMMON QUERY STACK ANSWER PROPERTIES

Characteristics of a QS Answer

Property 1: Each answer contains no more and no less than two sentences.

Property 2: Each answer's first sentence contains no more and no less than two words.

Property 3: In each answer's first sentence, the main subject is introduced; one property resolution (*"[main subject]'s [is]"*; contraction contains main subject).

Property 4: In each answer, the main subject introduced in the first sentence is mentioned in the second sentence; one property resolution (*"[main subject]'s [is]"*; contraction contains main subject).

Property 5: In each answer, the first sentence's second word and the second sentence's first word are similar in definition (synonym) or by context (context); one property solution (*"[word]'s"*; contraction is similar definitionally or contextually); one property deviation (*"A + [noun]"*; phrase perceived as one word).

Property 6: In each answer's second sentence, at least one action is applied to the main subject; one property resolution (*"[main subject]['s (is)]"*; contraction contains main subject and action)..

Property 7: Along each answer's breadth of vocabulary, there's at least one site where an answer letter *S* would've enhanced the answer's grammatical correctness if it would've been available in the accompanying row'd word matrix and usable; one property deviation (*"no missing letter S"*; perfect grammar).

APPENDIX C

"QS-7CAP" FORMULA, EXAMPLE AND KEY

$[1^{(:)}]_{(*)} \ [2^{(\sim 3)\,(:)}]_{(*)}\,.\ [3^{(\sim 2)\,(:)}]_{(*)\,(>)}\ [4^{(:)}]_{(*)\,(>)}\ \{+\ [\#^{(:)}]_{(*)\,(>)}\}\,.$

GO[1] DAVE[2] (HE)*. HE[3] (DAVE)*: WINNER[4]*; OR[5], GAINS[6]>.

- "." denotes a sentence;
  - A QS answer contains no more and no less than two sentences *(see "Appx. B; Prop. 1")*;
    - Go Dave"." He: winner; or, gains"."
- "[#]" counts a word;
  - A QS answer's first sentence contains no more and no less than two words *(see "Appx. B; Prop. 2")*;
    - Go[1] Dave[2];
  - A QS answer's second sentence contains at least two words *(see "Appx. B; Prop. 4, 6)* but may contain more than two words;
    - He[1]: winner[2]; or[3], gains[4].
- "(*)" is linked to a word which may or may not identify the answer's subject;
  - At least one word in each of the two sentences of a QS answer must identify the answer's subject *(see "Appx. B; Prop. 4")*;
  - "*" is linked to a word which identifies the answer's subject;
    - Go Dave"*". He"*": winner"*"; or, gains.
- "(~#)" denotes congruency in definition or context between two answer words;
  - In each QS answer, the first sentence's second word and the second sentence's first word are similar in definition or by context *(see Appx. B; Prop. 5)*;
    - Go Dave"(He)". He"(Dave)": winner; or, gains.
- "(>)" is linked to a word which may or may not be an action word;
  - In a QS answer's second sentence, at least one action word is applied to the subject;
  - ">" is linked to a word in a QS answer's second sentence which is an action associated with the QS answer's subject;
    - Go Dave. He: winner; or, gains">".
- "{+ [#]}" signifies that an undefined number of answer words may follow the second word in a QS answer's second sentence;
- "(:)" is linked to a word which may or may not be missing an *S* or *'s*;

- ":" is linked to a word which is missing an *S* or *'s*;
  - Go Dave. He":" winner; or, gains.

APPENDIX D
QUERY STACK DATABASE

QS-God/Heaven

```
G O D
H E A V E N
  O R I G I N
A N S W E R
```

GO DAVE. HE: WINNER; OR, GAINS.

QS-Devil/Hell

```
D E V I L
H E L L
O R I G I N
A N S W E R
```

HORDE: EVIL. ILL REIGN, WANS.

QS-Jesus/Earth

```
J E S U S
E A R T H
O R I G I N
A N S W E R
```

JOE ASSURE. RIGHT, REIN WANS.

QS-Dave/Earth

```
D A V E
E A R T H
  O R I G I N
A N S W E R
```

ADORE GIVER. A HINTER WANS.

QS-Joe/Earth

```
J O E
E A R T H
O R I G I N
A N S W E R
```

JOE: REASON. AIR/HINT GREW.

QS-Mary/Earth

M	A	R	Y		
E	A	R	T	H	
O	R	I	G	I	N
A	N	S	W	E	R

MARRY REASON. A HINT, I GREW.

QS-Holy^Ghost/Heaven

H	O	L	Y	G	H	O	S	T
H	E	A	V	E	N			
O	R	I	G	I	N			
A	N	S	W	E	R			

HOLY GHOST. HE: NAÏVE OR ANSWERING.

QS-YHWH/Heaven

Y	H	W	H		
H	E	A	V	E	N
O	R	I	G	I	N
A	N	S	W	E	R

YAHWEH: HORN. NERVING, IS A WE.

QS-Yahweh/Heaven

Y	A	H	W	E	H
H	E	A	V	E	N
O	R	I	G	I	N
A	N	S	W	E	R

HAY: WE. HEAVEN: HORN, SIRING A WE.

QS-Creator/Reality

C	R	E	A	T	O	R
R	E	A	L	I	T	Y
O	R	I	G	I	N	
A	N	S	W	E	R	

CORE: REAL. A TRINITY; OR, RINGS A WE.

QS-Yahweh/Reality

Y	A	H	W	E	H
R	E	A	L	I	T	Y
O	R	I	G	I	N	
A	N	S	W	E	R	

HAY: LAW. THEY OR REINS, I, RING "A WE."

QS-Yahweh/Trinity

Y	A	H	W	E	H
T	R	I	N	I	T	Y
O	R	I	G	I	N
A	N	S	W	E	R

HAIRY WE. THY TRIO: REINING, WANS.

QS-Father/Trinity

F	A	T	H	E	R
T	R	I	N	I	T	Y
O	R	I	G	I	N
A	N	S	W	E	R

FAIR HINTER. TRIO: TRYING, WANES.

QS-Son/Trinity

S	O	N
T	R	I	N	I	T	Y
O	R	I	G	I	N
A	N	S	W	E	R

ORATOR'S IN. IN: TRYING SINEW.

QS-Holy^Ghost/Trinity

H	O	L	Y	G	H	O	S	T
T	R	I	N	I	T	Y
O	R	I	G	I	N
A	N	S	W	E	R

TORAH: GLORY. HOST: IN, I, TRYING SINEW.

QS-God/Trinity

G	O	D
T	R	I	N	I	T	Y
O	R	I	G	I	N
A	N	S	W	E	R

GOT WORDING. "I" ENTRY; RAINS "I."

QS-Jesus/Trinity

J	E	S	U	S
T	R	I	N	I	T	Y
O	R	I	G	I	N
A	N	S	W	E	R

JOT, ISSUER. I RING ENTRY "I," "WANS."

QS-Trinity/Heaven

```
T R I N I T Y
H E A V E N
O R I G I N
A N S W E R
```

EVITERNITY: HORN. INGRAIN'S A WE.

QS-Lucifer/Hell

```
L U C I F E R
H E L L
O R I G I N
A N S W E R
```

CLUE: FILLER. HORN: SIRING A WE.

QS-Satan/Hell

```
S A T A N
H E L L
O R I G I N
A N S W E R
```

TORAH'S LEARNING. LIE WANS.

GLOSSARIES

In "Glossary I," I'd listed the definitions of every invalid and valid QS answer word which I'd decoded from the twenty QS matrices found within this book. I'd listed the asterisked phrase *"*not in final answer"* after definitions of words which didn't make it into the final drafts of QS answers. In "Glossary II," I'd provided specialized terms and definitions which I'd created solely for my Query Stack study, and marked said specialized terms that I'd entertained but proved inappropriate for my study with the phrase *"defunct"*:

- **Glossary I: Answer Words and Definitions**
  Final and unusable QS answer words and definitions.

- **Glossary II: Study Terms and Definitions**
  Valid and defunct specialized study terms and definitions.

GLOSSARY I

ANSWER WORDS AND DEFINITIONS

"A" *n.* The answer word *A.* *(qs-yahweh/reality)*

A *i-art.* Used before most singular nouns when the individual in question is unidentified, especially when the individual is being called to notice.[2] *(qs-dave/earth, qs-mary/earth, qs-yhwh/heaven, qs-yahweh/heaven, qs-creator/reality, qs-trinity/heaven)*

ADORE *v.* To worship with profound reverence.[2] *(qs-dave/earth)*

AIR *n.* Public utterance (*n.* an oral or written statement).[2] *(qs-joe/earth)*

ANSWERING *v.* <ANSWER *v.*> To solve or offer a solution for.[2] *(qs-holy^ghost/heaven)*

ASSURE *v.* To inform positively.[2] *(qs-jesus/earth)*

CLUE *n.* A piece of evidence that leads one toward the solution of a problem.[2] *(qs-lucifer/hell)*

CORE *n.* The most intimate part.[2] *(qs-creator/reality)*

DAVE *prop-n.* A diminutive of the male given name David.[2] *(qs-god/heaven)*

'EM *pron.* Them.[2] *(fs-apollo^1:astronauts)*

ENTRY *n.* A record made in a log, diary or anything similarly organized.[3] *(qs-god/trinity, qs-jesus/trinity)*

EVIL *n.* One that personifies wickedness.[2] *(qs-devil/hell)*

EVITERNITY *n.* Everlastingness.[2] *(qs-trinity/heaven)*

FAIR *adj.* Real.[2] *(qs-father/trinity)*

FATES *n-pl.* <FATE *n.*> Ruin, disaster; especially, death.[2] *(fs-apollo^1:astronauts)*

FILLER *n.* A person that fills (*v.* to supply [a blank space] with written matter[1]).[1] *(qs-lucifer/hell)*

FOES *n-pl.* <FOE *n.*> Something prejudicial or injurious.[2] *(fs-apollo^1:astronauts)*

GAINS *v.* To secure advantage or profit; acquire gain.[2] *(qs-god/heaven)*

GHOST *n.* One who does literary work for and in the name of another; ghost-writer.[2] *(qs-holy^ghost/heaven)*

GIVER *n.* One that gives (*v.* to confer the ownership of without receiving a return).[2] *(qs-dave/earth)*

GLORY *n.* Shekinah (*prop-n.* the presence of God in the world conceived by Jewish and later by Christian theologians as manifested in natural and especially supernatural phenomena).[2] *(qs-holy^ghost/trinity)*

GO *v.* To begin an action or motion.[2] *(qs-god/heaven)*

GO *v.* To occupy oneself with.[2] *(qs-god/heaven; *not in final answer)*

GOT *v.* <GET *v.*> To come to have.[2] *(qs-god/trinity)*

GREW *v.* **<GROW** *v.***>** **To increase in any way.**[2] *(qs-joe/earth, qs-mary/earth)*

HAIRY *adj.* **Difficult to comprehend.**[2] *(qs-yahweh/trinity)*

HAY *n.* **A rewarding result of careful effort.**[2] *(qs-yahweh/heaven, qs-yahweh/reality)*

HE *pron.* **That male one.**[2] *(qs-god/heaven, qs-holy^ghost/heaven)*

HEAVEN *prop-n.* **God.**[2] *(qs-yahweh/heaven)*

HINT *n.* **A statement conveying by implication what it is preferred not to say explicitly.**[2] *(qs-joe/earth, qs-mary/earth)*

HINTER *n.* **One that hints (*v.* brings to mind by allusion rather than explicit expression).**[2] *(qs-dave/earth, qs-father/trinity)*

HOLY *adj.* **Set apart and dedicated to the service of God.**[2] *(qs-holy^ghost/heaven)*

HORDE *n.* **A crowd of individuals.**[2] *(qs-devil/hell)*

HORN *n.* **Source of strength.**[2] *(qs-yhwh/heaven, qs-yahweh/heaven, qs-trinity/heaven, qs-lucifer/hell)*

HOST *prop-n.* **The eucharistic wafer or bread—*symbols for the body of Christ*—before or after consecration—*solemn dedication in perpetuity of vessels used in the Eucharist.***[2] *(qs-holy^ghost/trinity)*

"I" *n.* **The answer word *I*.** *(qs-god/trinity, qs-jesus/trinity)*

I *n.* **Someone possessing and aware of possessing a distinct and personal individuality.**[2] *(qs- holy^ghost/trinity,)*

I *pron.* **The one who is speaking or writing.**[2] *(qs-mary/earth, qs-yahweh/reality, qs-holy^ghost/trinity, qs-jesus/trinity)*

ILL *n.* **Evil.**[2] *(qs-devil/hell)*

ILL *n.* **Sickness.**[2] *(qs-devil/hell; *not in final answer)*

IN *n.* **One who is in power.**[2] *(qs-son/trinity, qs-holy^ghost/trinity)*

INGRAIN'S *contr.* **<INGRAIN** *n.* **IS** *v.***>** **Innate quality or character.**[2] *(qs-trinity/heaven)*

IS *v.* **Show a certain characteristic.**[2] *(qs-yhwh/heaven)*

ISSUER *n.* **One that issues (*v.* to cause to appear for circulation among the public) something.**[2] *(qs-jesus/trinity)*

JOE *n.* **Used informally to address a man whose name the speaker does not know.**[2] *(qs-jesus/earth, qs-joe/earth)*

JOE *prop. n.* **A common nickname for Joseph, also used as a formal male given name.**[3] *(qs-jesus/earth; *not in final answer)*

JOE *prop. n.* **A female given name, a form of Joanne or Josephine.**[3] *(qs-jesus/earth; *not in final answer)*

JOE *n.* **(slang) Coffee.**[2] *(qs-jesus/earth; *not in final answer)*

JOE *n.* **(slang) Guy.**[2] *(qs-jesus/earth, qs-joe/earth; *not in final answer)*

JOT *v.* **To write briefly.**[2] *(qs-jesus/trinity)*

LAW *n.* **A revelation of the will of God.**[2] *(qs-yahweh/reality)*

LEARNING *n.* **Knowledge accumulated and handed down by generations of scholars.**[2]

(qs-satan/hell)

LIE *n.* An assertion of something known by the speaker to be untrue.[2] *(qs-satan/hell)*

MARRY *v.* To unite in close and usually permanent relation.[2] *(qs-mary/earth)*

NAÏVE *adj.* Self-taught.[2] *(qs-holy^ghost/heaven)*

NERVING *v.* To give strength to; supply with moral force.[2] *(qs-yhwh/heaven)*

OR *conj.* The synonymous, equivalent, or substitutive character of two words or phrases.[2] *(qs-god/heaven, qs-holy^ghost/heaven, qs-creator/reality, qs-yahweh/reality)*

ORATOR'S *contr.* <ORATOR *n.* IS *v.*> A public speaker.[2] *(qs-son/trinity)*

RAINS *v.* <RAIN *v.*> To bestow abundantly.[2] *(qs-god/trinity)*

REAL *adj.* Not fictitious or imaginary.[3] *(qs-creator/reality)*

REASON *n.* A statement offered as an explanation of an assertion.[2] *(qs-joe/earth, qs-mary/earth)*

REIGN *v.* To exercise sovereign power; rule.[2] *(qs-devil/hell)*

REIN *n.* The controlling power.[2] *(qs-jesus/earth)*

REINING *v.* <REIN *v.*> To govern as if by the use of reins.[2] *(qs-yahweh/trinity)*

REINS *n-pl.* <REIN *n.*> The controlling power.[2] *(qs-yahweh/reality)*

RIG *n.* Tackle, apparatus, or machinery fitted up for a specified purpose.[2] *(fs-apollo^1:astronauts)*

RIGHT *adv.* According to fact or truth.[2] *(qs-jesus/earth)*

RING *v.* To repeat earnestly.[2] *(qs-yahweh/reality, qs-jesus/trinity)*

RINGS *v.* <RING *v.*> To have a character expressive of some quality.[2] *(qs-creator/reality)*

SINEW *n.* Force.[2] *(qs-son/trinity, qs-holy^ghost/trinity)*

SIRING *v.* <SIRE *v.*> To bring into being.[2] *(qs-yahweh/heaven, qs-lucifer/hell)*

SWAN *v.* Sweep majestically.[2] *(qs-devil/hell; *not in final answer)*

THEY *pron.* Unspecified persons and especially those responsible for a particular practice.[2] *(qs-yahweh/reality)*

THY *adj.* (archaic) Connected with thyself as possessor.[2] *(qs-yahweh/trinity)*

TORAH *prop-n.* The body of divine knowledge and law found in the Jewish scriptures and tradition.[2] *(qs-holy^ghost/trinity)*

TORAH'S *prop-n's.* <TORAH *n.*> The body of divine knowledge and law found in the Jewish scriptures and tradition.[2] *(qs-satan/hell)*

TRINITY *n.* A group or set of three people.[2] *(qs-creator/reality)*

TRIO *n.* A group of three.[2] *(qs-yahweh/trinity, qs-father/trinity)*

TRYING *v.* <TRY *v.*> To make an attempt to carry out some action.[2] *(qs-father/trinity, qs-son/trinity, qs-holy^ghost/trinity)*

VEDA *prop-n.* Any of a class of the most ancient sacred writings of the Hindus.[2] *(qs-god/heaven; *not in final answer)*

WANES *v.* <WANE *v.*> To fall especially gradually from power.[2] *(qs-father/trinity)*

"WANS" *n.* The answer word *WANS*. *(qs-jesus/trinity)*

WANS *v.* <**WAN** *v.*> **To become wan (*adj.* lacking in forcefulness).**[1] *(qs-devil/hell, qs-jesus/earth, qs-dave/earth, qs-yahweh/trinity, qs-satan/hell)*

WANS *v.* <**WAN** *v.*> **To grow or become pale or sickly.**[2] *(qs-devil/hell; *not in final answer)*

"WE" *n.* **The answer word *WE*.** *(qs-yahweh/reality)*

WE *n.* **A group that is consciously felt as such by its members.**[2] *(qs-yhwh/heaven, qs-yahweh/heaven, qs-creator/reality, qs-yahweh/trinity, qs-trinity/heaven, qs-lucifer/hell)*

WHICH *adj.* **Being what one or ones out of a group.**[2] *(fs-apollo^1:astronauts)*

WINNER *n.* **One that's successful.**[2] *(qs-god/heaven)*

WORDING *n.* **The manner of expressing in words.**[2] *(qs-god/trinity)*

YAHWEH *prop-n.* **God—transliteration of the Hebrew tetragrammaton (*YHWH*).**[2] *(qs-yhwh/heaven)*

GLOSSARY II
STUDY TERMS AND DEFINITIONS

Fate Stack *n.* A linguistic system which is comprised of one "Fate Stack Matrix" and one "Fate Stack Answer."

Fate Stack Answer *n.* A brief statement which consists of "Fate Stack Answer Words" that have been derived from one "Fate Stack Matrix" and conveys a message which coincides with the people whose names are the row'd words in said "Fate Stack Matrix."

Fate Stack Answer Word *n.* A group of letters which are derived from the letters of "Fate Stack Row'd Words" in accordance with "Fate Stack Rules," and are inserted into a "Fate Stack Answer" as a spelling.

Fate Stack Guide *n.* A directive which aids in the production of the most meaningful "Fate Stack Answer."

Fate Stack Matrix *n.* A group of "Fate Stack Row'd Words" which are vertically listed in the sequence of shortest row'd word on top to longest row'd word on bottom; are the last names of people who belong to a defined group (musical band, political unit, sports team, etc.) during a specific time period; are left aligned; and contain letters that are equidistantly spaced apart, in order to produce neat letter columns, and spell "Fate Stack Answers" when connected and organized in accordance with "Fate Stack Rules" and "Fate Stack Guides."

Fate Stack Row'd Word *n.* A word which occupies a row in a "Fate Stack Matrix."

Fate Stack Rule *n.* A mandate which must be adhered to in order to properly construct or decode a valid "Fate Stack Matrix" and construct a valid "Fate Stack Answer."

Inclusivity Level *n.* Statistical enumeration which tallies the number of "Query Stack Answer Words" in one "Query Stack Answer" that are assigned a distinct "Uniqueness Level" and belong to a different word class (noun, verb, adjective, etc.).

Lineal Query Stack *n.* A "Query Stack Category" which consists of "Query Stacks" that have a "Query Stack Row'd Word" in the first row of their "Query Stack Matrices" that names a person who is a genealogical member of a predefined family tree and a "Query Stack Row'd Word" in the second row of their "Query Stack Matrices" that is either the word *Heaven*, *Hell* or *Earth*, and names a realm where said person has notoriety.

Lineal, Realm-Related Query Stack *n.* A "Query Stack Category" which consists of "Query Stacks" that have a "Query Stack Row'd Word" in the first row of their "Query Stack Matrices" that names a person who is a genealogical member of a predefined family tree and a "Query Stack Row'd Word" in the second row of their "Query Stack Matrices" that may not necessarily be the name *Heaven*, *Hell* or *Earth*, yet names a realm where said person has notoriety.

Lineal-Alias Query Stack *n.* A "Query Stack Category" which consists of "Query Stacks" that have a "Query Stack Row'd Word" in the first row of their "Query Stack Matrices" that is an alias of a person whose name has been already established as a row'd word and who is a genealogical member of a predefined family tree and a "Query Stack Row'd Word" in the second row of their "Query Stack Matrices" that is either the word *Heaven*, *Hell* or *Earth*, and names a realm where said person has notoriety.

Lineal-Alias, Realm-Related Query Stack *n.* A "Query Stack Category" which consists of "Query Stacks" that have a "Query Stack Row'd Word" in the first row of their "Query Stack Matrices" that is an alias of a person whose name has been already established as a row'd word and who is a genealogical member of a predefined family tree and a "Query Stack Row'd Word" in the second row of their "Query Stack Matrices" that is either the word *Heaven*, *Hell* or *Earth*, and names a realm where said person has notoriety.

Lineally-Coupled Query Stack *n.* A "Query Stack Category" which consists of "Query Stacks" that have a "Query Stack Row'd Word" in the first row of their "Query Stack Matrices" that names a person who isn't a genealogical member of but is commonly associated with a person who is a genealogical member of a predefined family tree and a "Query Stack Row'd Word" in the second row of their "Query Stack Matrices" that is either the word *Heaven*, *Hell* or *Earth*, and names a realm where said person has notoriety—{DEFUNCT}.

Lineally-Coupled-Alias Query Stack *n.* A "Query Stack Category" which consists of "Query Stacks" that have a "Query Stack Row'd Word" in the first row of their "Query Stack Matrices" that is an alias of a person who isn't a genealogical member of but is commonly associated with a person who is a genealogical member of a predefined family tree and a "Query Stack Row'd Word" in the second row of their "Query Stack Matrices" that is either the word *Heaven*, *Hell* or *Earth*, and names a realm where said person has notoriety—{DEFUNCT}.

Query Stack *n.* A linguistic system which is comprised of one "Query Stack Matrix" and one "Query Stack Answer."

Query Stack Answer *n.* A brief statement which consists of "Query Stack Answer Words" that have been derived from one "Query Stack Matrix" and has been constructed in accordance with the "Seven Common Query Stack Answer Properties."

Query Stack Answer Main Subject *n.* A person who or object which is the primary focus of a "Query Stack Answer."

Query Stack Answer Word *n.* A group of letters which are derived from the letters of "Query Stack Row'd Words," in accordance with "Query Stack Rules," and are inserted into a "Query Stack Answer" as a spelling.

Query Stack Category *n.* A classification for "Query Stacks" which is defined by "Query Stack Row'd Words" in the first row and second row of a "Query Stack Matrix."

Query Stack Guide *n.* A directive which aids in the production of the most meaningful "Query Stack Answer."

Query Stack Matrix *n.* A group of "Query Stack Row'd Words" which are vertically listed and ask a "Query Stack Question" when read from top to bottom row'd word; are left aligned;

and contain letters that are equidistantly spaced apart, in order to produce neat letter columns, and spell "Query Stack Answers" when connected and organized in accordance with "Query Stack Rules" and "Query Stack Guides."

Query Stack Question *n.* An inquiry which is produced by listing "Query Stack Row'd Words" horizontally and in the same sequence as said row'd words are vertically listed in a complementary "Query Stack Matrix" and then punctuating, and, most importantly, inserting a question mark after the last word of said horizontal listing.

Query Stack Row'd Word *n.* A word which occupies a row in a "Query Stack Matrix."

Query Stack Rule *n.* A mandate which must be adhered to in order to properly construct or decode a valid "Query Stack Matrix" and construct a valid "Query Stack Answer."

Seven Common Query Stack Answer Properties *n.* A set of mandates which define syntactic characteristics that must be present in and validate the legitimacy of a "Query Stack Answer."

Seven Common Query Stack Answer Properties Deviation *n.* A permitted transgression of a "Seven Common Query Stack Answer Properties" mandate.

Seven Common Query Stack Answer Properties Deviation Resolution *n.* A specification which defines the terms of permittance for the transgression of a "Seven Common Query Stack Answer Properties" mandate.

Seven Common Query Stack Answer Properties Formula *n.* A symbolical representation of the "Seven Common Query Stack Answer Properties."

Seven Common Query Stack Answer Properties Resolution *n.* A specification which explains the adherence that a "Query Stack Answer Word" has to a "Seven Common Query Stack Answer Properties" mandate.

Uniqueness Level *n.* A statistical enumeration which tallies the number of times a specific "Query Stack Answer Word" appears within a defined set of "Query Stack Answers."

Word Stack *n.* A linguistic system which is comprised of a matrix (Query Stack, Fate Stack, etc.) of row'd words and an answer (Query Stack, Fate Stack, etc.).

BIBLIOGRAPHY

Dictionaries—*Physical*

[1]*Webster's New Universal Unabridged Dictionary*. 2003.

Dictionaries—*Online*

[2]*Merriam-Webster Unabridged*. 2023. Merriam-Webster, Incorporated.
　<http://www.unabridged.merriam-webster.com>.

[3]*Wiktionary: The Free Dictionary*. 2023. Wikimedia Foundation, Inc.
　<http://www.wiktionary.org>.

Bibles—*Online*

[4]*King James Bible Online*. 2023. King James Bible Online.
　<http://www.kingjamesbibleonline.org>.

[5]*Bible Gateway*. 2023. Bible Gateway.
　<http://www.biblegateway.com>.

[6]*The Complete Jewish Bible: With Rashi Commentary*. 1993-2023. Chabad-Lubavitch Media Center.
　<http://www.chabad.org>.

INDICES

In "Index I," I'd titled and sequentially listed every example which has been partitioned off from the standard text in this book. In "Index II," I'd provided a directory of page numbers associated with common words and concepts found in this book.

- **Index I: Tables, Diagrams, Charts, Etc.**
  Comprehensive list of examples.

- **Index II: Topic Tag Directory**
  Word tags and phrase tags of topics.

INDEX I

TABLES, DIAGRAMS, CHARTS, ETC.

Chapter 1, Section 1 (QS-God/Heaven)

Ch. 1, Sec. 1: 1 > Pre-vision Questions

Ch. 1, Sec. 1: 2 > Vision's Row'd Word Stack

Ch. 1, Sec. 1: 3 > Vision's Row'd Word Stack & Unpunctuated Question

Ch. 1, Sec. 1: 4 > Vision's Row'd Word Question Punctuated

Ch. 1, Sec. 1: 5 > Pre-vision & Vision's Punctuated Row'd Word Question Transposition

Ch. 1, Sec. 1: 6 > Unsolved QS Matrix & Final Punctuated Row'd Word Question I

Ch. 1, Sec. 1: 7 > Final Punctuated Row'd Word Question II

Ch. 1, Sec. 1: 8 > Final Punctuated Row'd Word Question II & Interpretation

Ch. 1, Sec. 1: 9 > QS Matrix Row'd Word Letter Columniation

Ch. 1, Sec. 1: 10 > "QS Rules 1-5" Mandates

Ch. 1, Sec. 1: 11 > Diagonal Row'd Word Letter Connection & Answer Word Incoherence

Ch. 1, Sec. 1: 12 > "QS Rule 6" Mandate

Ch. 1, Sec. 1: 13 > "QS Rule 7" Mandate

Ch. 1, Sec. 1: 14 > "QS Rule 8" Mandate

Ch. 1, Sec. 1: 15 > "QS Guide 1" Directive

Ch. 1, Sec. 1: 16 > Answer Word Construction *(go)*

Ch. 1, Sec. 1: 17 > Answer Word Placement *(go)*

Ch. 1, Sec. 1: 18 > Answer Word Construction & Placement *(he)*

Ch. 1, Sec. 1: 19 > Answer Word Construction & Placement *(or)*

Ch. 1, Sec. 1: 20 > Answer Word Construction & Placement *(winner, gains)*

Ch. 1, Sec. 1: 21 > "QS Rule 9" Mandate

Ch. 1, Sec. 1: 22 > Answer Word Construction & Placement *(veda)*

Ch. 1, Sec. 1: 23 > "QS Rule 10" Mandate

Ch. 1, Sec. 1: 24 > QS Matrix & Numerical Matrix Comparison I

Ch. 1, Sec. 1: 25 > QS Matrix & Numerical Matrix Comparison II

Ch. 1, Sec. 1: 26 > QS Matrix & Numerical Matrix Comparison III

Ch. 1, Sec. 1: 27 > "QS Rule 11" Mandate

Ch. 1, Sec. 1: 28 > QS Matrix & Numerical Matrix Comparison IV

Ch. 1, Sec. 1: 29 > Punctuated QS Answer I

Ch. 1, Sec. 1: 30 > Answer Word Definitions I

Ch. 1, Sec. 1: 31 > QS Answer Interpretation I

Ch. 1, Sec. 1: 32 > QS Answer Interpretation I & Sentence Incongruency I

Ch. 1, Sec. 1: 33 > QS Answer Interpretation I & Sentence Incongruency II

Ch. 1, Sec. 1: 34 > Answer Word Construction & Placement *(dave)*

Ch. 1, Sec. 1: 35 > Answer Word Definitions II

Ch. 1, Sec. 1: 36 > QS Answer Interpretation II

Ch. 1, Sec. 1: 37 > Punctuated Row'd Word Question, QS Answer & QS Answer Interpretation

---

Chapter 1, Section 2 (QS-Devil/Hell)

Ch. 1, Sec. 2: 1 > First-Row & Second-Row Row'd Word Derivation *(devil, hell)*

Ch. 1, Sec. 2: 2 > Third-Row & Fourth-Row Row'd Word Derivation *(origin, answer)*

Ch. 1, Sec. 2: 3 > Row'd Word Question Punctuated

Ch. 1, Sec. 2: 4 > Punctuated Row'd Word Question Transposition

Ch. 1, Sec. 2: 5 > Unsolved QS Matrix & Answer Word Placement

Ch. 1, Sec. 2: 6 > Answer Word Construction & Placement *(swan)*

Ch. 1, Sec. 2: 7 > Punctuated QS Answer I

Ch. 1, Sec. 2: 8 > Answer Word Definitions I

Ch. 1, Sec. 2: 9 > QS Answer I Interpretation & Incoherence

Ch. 1, Sec. 2: 10 > Answer Word Construction & Placement *(wans)*

Ch. 1, Sec. 2: 11 > Answer Word Comparison *(ill, wans)*

Ch. 1, Sec. 2: 12 > QS Answer II Sentence Incongruency

Ch. 1, Sec. 2: 13 > QS Answer II Sentence Congruency I

Ch. 1, Sec. 2: 14 > QS Answer II Sentence Congruency II

Ch. 1, Sec. 2: 15 > Answer Word Definition Discernment I *(wans)*

Ch. 1, Sec. 2: 16 > Answer Word Definition Discernment II *(wans)*

Subsection ▪ Challenges to Determine Who Wans

Ch. 1, Sec. 2: 17 > Answer Word Definition Discernment III *(wans)*

Ch. 1, Sec. 2: 18 > Answer Word Definition Discernment IV *(wans)*

Ch. 1, Sec. 2: 19 > Answer Word Definition Discernment V *(wans)*

Ch. 1, Sec. 2: 20 > Answer Word Definition Discernment VI *(wans)*

Ch. 1, Sec. 2: 21 > Answer Word Definition Discernment VII *(wans)*

Ch. 1, Sec. 2: 22 > Answer Word Definition Discernment VIII *(wans)*

Ch. 1, Sec. 2: 23 > Answer Word Definition Discernment IX *(wans)*

Ch. 1, Sec. 2: 24 > "QS Guide 2" Directive

Ch. 1, Sec. 2: 25 > "QS Guide 3" Directive

Ch. 1, Sec. 2: 26 > Row'd Word & Answer Word Moral Comparison *(qs-god/heaven, qs-devil/hell)*

Ch. 1, Sec. 2: 27 > Answer Word Comparison *(dave, horde)*

Subsection ▪ QS-7CAP

Ch. 1, Sec. 2: 28 > Punctuated Row'd Word Question, QS Answer III & QS Answer Interpretation II

Ch. 1, Sec. 2: 29 > First-Row Row'd Word & Answer Word Incongruency *(god, dave)*

Ch. 1, Sec. 2: 30 > First-Row Row'd Word & Answer Word Incongruency *(devil, horde)*

Chapter 1, Section 3 (QS-Jesus/Earth)

Ch. 1, Sec. 3: 1 > Solved QS Matrix & Answer

Ch. 1, Sec. 3: 2 > Biblical Realm Relationships *(heaven, earth, hell)*

Ch. 1, Sec. 3: 3 > Second-Row Row'd Word Comparison

Ch. 1, Sec. 3: 4 > First-Row Row'd Word Comparison

Ch. 1, Sec. 3: 5 > First-Row & Second-Row Row'd Word Explanation

Ch. 1, Sec. 3: 6 > Third-Row & Fourth-Row Row'd Word Comparison

Ch. 1, Sec. 3: 7 > Answer Word Definitions I

Ch. 1, Sec. 3: 8 > Answer Word Definition Discernment I *(joe)*

Ch. 1, Sec. 3: 9 > Answer Word Definition Discernment II *(joe)*

Ch. 1, Sec. 3: 10 > Answer Word Definition Discernment III *(joe)*

Ch. 1, Sec. 3: 11 > Answer Word Definition Discernment IV *(joe)*

Ch. 1, Sec. 3: 12 > Answer Word Definition Discernment V *(joe)*

Ch. 1, Sec. 3: 13 > Answer Word Definition Discernment VI *(joe)*

Ch. 1, Sec. 3: 14 > Answer Word Definition Discernment VII *(joe)*

Ch. 1, Sec. 3: 15 > Answer Word Definitions II

Ch. 1, Sec. 3: 16 > QS Answer Interpretation I

Ch. 1, Sec. 3: 17 > Answer Word Comparison *(joe, rein)*

Ch. 1, Sec. 3: 18 > QS Answer Interpretation II

Subsection ▪ QS-7CAP

Ch. 1, Sec. 3: 19 > QS Answer Comparison I *(qs-devil/hell, qs-jesus/earth)*

Ch. 1, Sec. 3: 20 > QS Answer Comparison II *(qs-devil/hell, qs-jesus/earth)*

Ch. 1, Sec. 3: 21 > QS Answer Comparison III *(qs-devil/hell, qs-jesus/earth)*

Ch. 1, Sec. 3: 22 > QS Answer Comparison & Interpretation I *(qs-god/heaven, qs-devil/hell, qs-jesus/earth)*

Ch. 1, Sec. 3: 23 > QS Answer Comparison & Interpretation II *(qs-god/heaven, qs-devil/hell, qs-jesus/earth)*

Chapter 1, Section 4 (QS-Dave/Earth)

Ch. 1, Sec. 4: 1 > Answer Word & First-Row Row'd Word Transposition *(dave)*
Ch. 1, Sec. 4: 2 > Second-Row Row'd Word Comparison
Ch. 1, Sec. 4: 3 > First-Row Row'd Word Comparison
Ch. 1, Sec. 4: 4 > First-Row & Second-Row Row'd Word Explanation
Ch. 1, Sec. 4: 5 > Third-Row & Fourth-Row Row'd Word Comparison
Ch. 1, Sec. 4: 6 > Solved QS Matrix & Answer
Ch. 1, Sec. 4: 7 > Answer Word Definitions
Ch. 1, Sec. 4: 8 > QS Answer Interpretation I
Ch. 1, Sec. 4: 9 > Answer Word Comparison *(giver, hinter)*
Ch. 1, Sec. 4: 10 > QS Answer Interpretation II

Subsection ▪ *QS-7CAP*

Subsection ▪ *Questions to Ask a Hint Giver*

Ch. 1, Sec. 4: 11 > Answer Word Comparison & Explanation I *(giver, hinter)*
Ch. 1, Sec. 4: 12 > Answer Word Comparison & Explanation II *(giver, hinter)*
Ch. 1, Sec. 4: 13 > QS Answer Sentence Interpretation III *(adore giver)*
Ch. 1, Sec. 4: 14 > QS Answer Sentence Comparison & Interpretation I *(qs-devil/hell, qs-jesus/earth)*
Ch. 1, Sec. 4: 15 > QS Answer Sentence Comparison & Interpretation II *(qs-devil/hell, qs-jesus/earth, qs-dave/earth)*
Ch. 1, Sec. 4: 16 > QS Answer Comparison & Interpretation I *(qs-devil/hell, qs-jesus/earth, qs-dave/earth)*
Ch. 1, Sec. 4: 17 > QS Answer Subject Equivalency I *(god, joe)*
Ch. 1, Sec. 4: 18 > QS Answer Subject Equivalency II *(god, joe, horde)*
Ch. 1, Sec. 4: 19 > Trinity Members Explanation
Ch. 1, Sec. 4: 20 > QS Answer Subject Equivalency III *(horde, trinity)*
Ch. 1, Sec. 4: 21 > QS Answer Subject Equivalency IV *(god, joe, trinity-horde)*
Ch. 1, Sec. 4: 22 > QS Answer Subject Equivalency V *(trinity-horde, evil)*
Ch. 1, Sec. 4: 23 > QS Answer Subject Equivalency VI *(god, trinity)*
Ch. 1, Sec. 4: 24 > QS Answer Subject Equivalency VII *(trinity-horde, morality)*
Ch. 1, Sec. 4: 25 > QS Answer Subject Equivalency VIII *(trinity-horde, morality wans)*
Ch. 1, Sec. 4: 26 > QS Answer Subject Equivalency IX *(horde/ill, joe/rein, giver/hinter morality wans)*

Chapter 1, Section 5 (Review I)

Ch. 1, Sec. 5: 1 > "QS Rules 1-11" Mandates

Ch. 1, Sec. 5: 2 > "QS-7CAP (1-7)" Mandates

Subsection ▪ *QS-7CAP Formula*

Ch. 1, Sec. 5: 3 > "QS-7CAP Formula" Template
Ch. 1, Sec. 5: 4 > "QS-7CAP Formula" Symbolism Definition I
Ch. 1, Sec. 5: 5 > "QS-7CAP Formula" Symbolism Definition II
Ch. 1, Sec. 5: 6 > "QS-7CAP Formula" Symbolism Definition III
Ch. 1, Sec. 5: 7 > "QS-7CAP Formula" Symbolism Definition IV
Ch. 1, Sec. 5: 8 > "QS-7CAP Formula" Symbolism Definition V
Ch. 1, Sec. 5: 9 > "QS-7CAP Formula" Symbolism Definition VI
Ch. 1, Sec. 5: 10 > "QS-7CAP Formula" Symbolism Definition VII
Ch. 1, Sec. 5: 11 > "QS-7CAP Formula" Symbolism Definition VIII
Ch. 1, Sec. 5: 12 > "QS Guides 1-3" Directives & Exemplifications
Ch. 1, Sec. 5: 13 > QS Answer Main Subject Category Table I
Ch. 1, Sec. 5: 14 > QS Answer Main Subject Category Table II
Ch. 1, Sec. 5: 15 > QS Answer Statistics

Chapter 2, Section 1 (QS-Joe/Earth)

Ch. 2, Sec. 1: 1 > Answer Word & Row'd Word Transpositions *(dave, joe)*
Ch. 2, Sec. 1: 2 > First-Row Row'd Word Comparison
Ch. 2, Sec. 1: 3 > First-Row & Second-Row Row'd Word Explanation
Ch. 2, Sec. 1: 4 > Third-Row & Fourth-Row Row'd Word Comparison
Ch. 2, Sec. 1: 5 > Solved QS Matrix & Answer
Ch. 2, Sec. 1: 6 > Answer Word Definitions
Ch. 2, Sec. 1: 7 > QS Answer Interpretation I

Subsection ▪ *QS-7CAP*

Ch. 2, Sec. 1: 8 > Answer Word Definition Derivation *(joe)*
Ch. 2, Sec. 1: 9 > QS Answer Comparison & Interpretation I *(qs-jesus/earth, qs-joe/earth)*
Ch. 2, Sec. 1: 10 > QS Answer Comparison & Interpretation II *(qs-jesus/earth, qs-joe/earth)*
Ch. 2, Sec. 1: 11 > QS Answer Comparison & Interpretation III *(qs-jesus/earth, qs-joe/earth)*
Ch. 2, Sec. 1: 12 > QS Answer Comparison & Interpretation IV *(qs-jesus/earth, qs-joe/earth)*
Ch. 2, Sec. 1: 13 > QS Answer Interpretation II
Ch. 2, Sec. 1: 14 > QS Answer Interpretation III

Chapter 2, Section 2 (QS-Mary/Earth)

Ch. 2, Sec. 2: 1 > First-Row Row'd Word Comparison & Virgin Mary Genealogy *(+god, +devil, +jesus, +dave, +joe, +mary)*

Ch. 2, Sec. 2: 2 > First-Row Row'd Word Derivation *(mary)*
Ch. 2, Sec. 2: 3 > First-Row & Second-Row Row'd Word Explanation
Ch. 2, Sec. 2: 4 > Third-Row & Fourth-Row Row'd Word Comparison
Ch. 2, Sec. 2: 5 > Solved QS Matrix & Answer
Ch. 2, Sec. 2: 6 > Answer Word Definitions
Ch. 2, Sec. 2: 7 > QS Answer Interpretation I
Ch. 2, Sec. 2: 8 > QS Answer Interpretation & Comparison *(qs-joe/earth, qs-mary/earth)*
Ch. 2, Sec. 2: 9 > Answer Word Spotlight *(I)*

Subsection ▪ *QS-7CAP*

Chapter 2, Section 3 (Review II)

Ch. 2, Sec. 3: 1 > Genealogical Categories *(+lineal, +lineally-coupled)*
Ch. 2, Sec. 3: 2 > Genealogical Categories Explanation
Ch. 2, Sec. 3: 3 > Virgin Mary Genealogy

Subsection ▪ *Steps to Manifest Mary*

Ch. 2, Sec. 3: 4 > QS Evolution I
Ch. 2, Sec. 3: 5 > QS Evolution II
Ch. 2, Sec. 3: 6 > QS Evolution III
Ch. 2, Sec. 3: 7 > QS Evolution IV
Ch. 2, Sec. 3: 8 > QS Evolution V
Ch. 2, Sec. 3: 9 > QS Evolution VI
Ch. 2, Sec. 3: 10 > QS Evolution VII
Ch. 2, Sec. 3: 11 > QS Answer Main Subject Category Table I
Ch. 2, Sec. 3: 12 > QS Answer Main Subject Category Table II
Ch. 2, Sec. 3: 13 > QS Answer Statistics

Chapter 3, Section 1 (QS-Holy^Ghost/Heaven)

Ch. 3, Sec. 1: 1 > First-Row Row'd Word Derivation & Virgin Mary Genealogy *(+holy ghost)*
Ch. 3, Sec. 1: 2 > First-Row Row'd Word *(holy ghost)*
Ch. 3, Sec. 1: 3 > "QS Rule 12" Mandate
Ch. 3, Sec. 1: 4 > First-Row Row'd Word Comparison
Ch. 3, Sec. 1: 5 > First-Row & Second-Row Row'd Word Explanation
Ch. 3, Sec. 1: 6 > Third-Row & Fourth-Row Row'd Word Comparison
Ch. 3, Sec. 1: 7 > Solved QS Matrix & Answer
Ch. 3, Sec. 1: 8 > Answer Word Definitions
Ch. 3, Sec. 1: 9 > QS Answer Interpretation I

Ch. 3, Sec. 1: 10 > QS Answer Sentence Comparison I *(qs-god/heaven, qs-holy^ghost/heaven)*
Ch. 3, Sec. 1: 11 > QS Answer Sentence Comparison II *(qs-god/heaven, qs-holy^ghost/heaven)*
Ch. 3, Sec. 1: 12 > QS Answer Sentence Comparison III *(qs-god/heaven, qs-holy^ghost/heaven)*
Ch. 3, Sec. 1: 13 > QS Answer Sentence Comparison IV *(qs-god/heaven, qs-holy^ghost/heaven)*
Ch. 3, Sec. 1: 14 > QS Answer Sentence Comparison V *(qs-god/heaven, qs-holy^ghost/heaven)*
Ch. 3, Sec. 1: 15 > QS Answer Interpretation II
Ch. 3, Sec. 1: 16 > Answer Word Congruency *(ghost, he)*
Ch. 3, Sec. 1: 17 > QS Answer Interpretation III
Ch. 3, Sec. 1: 18 > QS Answer Interpretation IV
Ch. 3, Sec. 1: 19 > QS Answer Interpretation V

Subsection ▪ *QS-7CAP*

Chapter 3, Section 2 (Review III)

Ch. 3, Sec. 2: 1 > Genealogical Categories *(+lineal-alias)*
Ch. 3, Sec. 2: 2 > Genealogical Categories Explanation
Ch. 3, Sec. 2: 3 > Virgin Mary Genealogy
Ch. 3, Sec. 2: 4 > QS Answer Main Subject Category Table
Ch. 3, Sec. 2: 5 > QS Answer Statistics
Ch. 3, Sec. 2: 6 > "QS Rules 1-12" Mandates

Chapter 4, Section 1 (QS-YHWH/Heaven)

Ch. 4, Sec. 1: 1 > Unsolved QS Matrix
Ch. 4, Sec. 1: 2 > First-Row Row'd Word Comparison
Ch. 4, Sec. 1: 3 > First-Row & Second-Row Row'd Word Explanation
Ch. 4, Sec. 1: 4 > Solved QS Matrix & Answer
Ch. 4, Sec. 1: 5 > Answer Word Definitions
Ch. 4, Sec. 1: 6 > QS Answer Interpretation

Subsection ▪ *QS-7CAP*

Chapter 4, Section 2 (QS-Yahweh/Heaven)

Ch. 4, Sec. 2: 1 > Answer Word & First-Row Row'd Word Transposition *(yahweh)*
Ch. 4, Sec. 2: 2 > Solved QS Matrix & Answer
Ch. 4, Sec. 2: 3 > Answer Word Definitions

Ch. 4, Sec. 2: 4 > QS Answer Interpretation I
Ch. 4, Sec. 2: 5 > QS Answer Interpretation II
Ch. 4, Sec. 2: 6 > QS Answer Interpretation III
Ch. 4, Sec. 2: 7 > QS Answer Interpretation IV
Ch. 4, Sec. 2: 8 > QS Answer Interpretation V

Subsection ▪ QS-7CAP

Chapter 4, Section 3 (Review IV)

Ch. 4, Sec. 3: 1 > Genealogical Categories
Ch. 4, Sec. 3: 2 > Genealogical Categories Explanation
Ch. 4, Sec. 3: 3 > Virgin Mary Genealogy *(+yhwh, +yahweh)*
Ch. 4, Sec. 3: 4 > QS Answer Main Subject Category Table I
Ch. 4, Sec. 3: 5 > QS Answer Main Subject Category Table II
Ch. 4, Sec. 3: 6 > QS Answer Statistics

Chapter 5, Section 1 (QS-Creator/Reality)

Ch. 5, Sec. 1: 1 > First-Row Row'd Word Explanation *(creator)*
Ch. 5, Sec. 1: 2 > Second-Row Row'd Word Explanation *(reality)*
Ch. 5, Sec. 1: 3 > First-Row Row'd Word Comparison
Ch. 5, Sec. 1: 4 > First-Row & Second-Row Row'd Word Explanation
Ch. 5, Sec. 1: 5 > Biblical/Nonbiblical Realm Relationships *(reality, heaven, earth, hell)*
Ch. 5, Sec. 1: 6 > Solved QS Matrix & Answer
Ch. 5, Sec. 1: 7 > Answer Word Definitions
Ch. 5, Sec. 1: 8 > QS Answer Interpretation I
Ch. 5, Sec. 1: 9 > QS Answer Interpretation II
Ch. 5, Sec. 1: 10 > QS Answer Interpretation III
Ch. 5, Sec. 1: 11 > QS Answer Interpretation IV
Ch. 5, Sec. 1: 12 > QS Answer Interpretation V

Subsection ▪ QS-7CAP

Chapter 5, Section 2 (QS-Yahweh/Reality)

Ch. 5, Sec. 2: 1 > First-Row & Second-Row Row'd Word Explanation *(yahweh, reality)*
Ch. 5, Sec. 2: 2 > First-Row Row'd Word Comparison
Ch. 5, Sec. 2: 3 > First-Row & Second-Row Row'd Word Explanation
Ch. 5, Sec. 2: 4 > Solved QS Matrix & Answer

Ch. 5, Sec. 2: 5 > Answer Word Definitions

Ch. 5, Sec. 2: 6 > QS Answer Interpretation I

Ch. 5, Sec. 2: 7 > QS Answer Sentence Comparison & Interpretation *(qs-yahweh/heaven, qs-yahweh/reality)*

Ch. 5, Sec. 2: 8 > QS Answer Interpretation II

Ch. 5, Sec. 2: 9 > QS Answer Interpretation III

Ch. 5, Sec. 2: 10 > QS Answer Interpretation IV

Subsection ▪ QS-7CAP

Chapter 5, Section 3 (QS-Yahweh/Trinity)

Ch. 5, Sec. 3: 1 > First-Row & Second-Row Row'd Word Explanation *(yahweh, trinity)*

Ch. 5, Sec. 3: 2 > First-Row Row'd Word Comparison

Ch. 5, Sec. 3: 3 > First-Row & Second-Row Row'd Word Explanation

Ch. 5, Sec. 3: 4 > Solved QS Matrix & Answer

Ch. 5, Sec. 3: 5 > Answer Word Definitions

Ch. 5, Sec. 3: 6 > QS Answer Interpretation I

Ch. 5, Sec. 3: 7 > QS Answer Interpretation II

Ch. 5, Sec. 3: 8 > QS Answer Interpretation III

Ch. 5, Sec. 3: 9 > QS Answer Interpretation IV

Ch. 5, Sec. 3: 10 > QS Answer Interpretation IV

Ch. 5, Sec. 3: 11 > QS Answer Interpretation V

Subsection ▪ QS-7CAP

Chapter 5, Section 4 ("Five Stacks"/Trinity)

Ch. 5, Sec. 4: 1 > Genealogical Categories *(+"lineal-alias, realm-related")*

Ch. 5, Sec. 4: 2 > Genealogical Categories *(+"lineal, realm-related")*

Ch. 5, Sec. 4: 3 > First-Row Row'd Word Comparison

Ch. 5, Sec. 4: 4 > First-Row & Second-Row Row'd Word Explanation

Subsection ▪ Father/Trinity: Fair Hinter

Ch. 5, Sec. 4: 5 > "QS-Father/Trinity" Solved QS Matrix & Answer, Answer Word Definitions, & QS Answer Interpretation

Ch. 5, Sec. 4: 6 > "QS-Father/Trinity" Answer Comparison *(multiple qs answers)*

Subsection ▪ Son/Trinity: Trying Sinew

Ch. 5, Sec. 4: 7 > "QS-Son/Trinity" Solved QS Matrix & Answer, Answer Word Definitions, & QS Answer Interpretation

Ch. 5, Sec. 4: 8 > "QS-Son/Trinity" Answer Comparison *(multiple qs answers)*

Subsection ▪ Holy^Ghost/Trinity: Torah's Glory

Ch. 5, Sec. 4: 9 > "QS-Holy^Ghost/Trinity" Solved QS Matrix & Answer, Answer Word Definitions, & QS Answer Interpretation

Ch. 5, Sec. 4: 10 > "QS-Holy^Ghost/Trinity" Answer Comparison *(multiple qs answers)*

Subsection ▪ God/Trinity: Got Wording

Ch. 5, Sec. 4: 11 > "QS-God/Trinity" Solved QS Matrix & Answer, Answer Word Definitions, & QS Answer Interpretation

Ch. 5, Sec. 4: 12 > "QS-God/Trinity" Answer Comparison *(multiple qs answers)*

Subsection ▪ Jesus/Trinity: I Ring Entry

Ch. 5, Sec. 4: 13 > "QS-Jesus/Trinity" Solved QS Matrix & Answer, Answer Word Definitions, & QS Answer Interpretation

Ch. 5, Sec. 4: 14 > "QS-Jesus/Trinity" Answer Comparison *(multiple qs answers)*

Subsection ▪ QS-7CAP

Chapter 5, Section 5 (Review V)

Ch. 5, Sec. 5: 1 > Genealogical Categories
Ch. 5, Sec. 5: 2 > Genealogical Categories Explanation
Ch. 5, Sec. 5: 3 > Virgin Mary Genealogy *(+creator, +father, +son)*
Ch. 5, Sec. 5: 4 > QS Answer Main Subject Category Table I
Ch. 5, Sec. 5: 5 > QS Answer Main Subject Category Table II
Ch. 5, Sec. 5: 6 > QS Answer Statistics

Chapter 6, Section 1 (QS-Trinity/Heaven)

Ch. 6, Sec. 1: 1 > Genealogical Categories
Ch. 6, Sec. 1: 2 > First-Row Row'd Word Comparison
Ch. 6, Sec. 1: 3 > First-Row & Second-Row Row'd Word Explanation
Ch. 6, Sec. 1: 4 > Solved QS Matrix & Answer, Biblical References, Answer Word Definitions, & Answer Interpretation
Ch. 6, Sec. 1: 5 > QS Answer Comparison *(multiple qs answers)*

Subsection ▪ QS-7CAP

Chapter 6, Section 2 (Review VI)

Ch. 6, Sec. 2: 1 > Genealogical Categories
Ch. 6, Sec. 2: 2 > Genealogical Categories Explanation
Ch. 6, Sec. 2: 3 > Virgin Mary Genealogy *(+trinity)*
Ch. 6, Sec. 2: 4 > QS Answer Main Subject Category I
Ch. 6, Sec. 2: 4 > QS Answer Main Subject Category II

Chapter 7, Section 1 (QS-Lucifer, Satan [/Hell])

Ch. 7, Sec. 1: 1 > Genealogical Categories *(+lineal-coupled-alias)*
Ch. 7, Sec. 1: 2 > First-Row Row'd Word Comparison
Ch. 7, Sec. 1: 3 > First-Row & Second-Row Row'd Word Explanation

Subsection ▪ *Lucifer/Hell: Siring a We*

Ch. 7, Sec. 1: 4 > "QS-Lucifer/Hell" Solved QS Matrix & Answer, Biblical References, Answer Word Definitions, & Answer Interpretation
Ch. 7, Sec. 1: 5 > "QS-Lucifer/Hell" Answer Comparison *(multiple qs answers)*

Subsection ▪ *Satan/Hell: Lie Wans*

Ch. 7, Sec. 1: 6 > "QS-Satan/Hell" Solved QS Matrix & Answer, Biblical References, Answer Word Definitions, & Answer Interpretation
Ch. 7, Sec. 1: 7 > "QS-Satan/Hell" Answer Comparison *(multiple qs answers)*

Subsection ▪ *QS-7CAP*

Chapter 7, Section 2 (Conclusion)

Ch. 7, Sec. 2: 1 > Personal Prophecy Evidence I
Ch. 7, Sec. 2: 2 > QS Answer Subject Enumeration

Subsection ▪ *God is Real*

Ch. 7, Sec. 2: 3 > QS Answer Interpretation Table
Ch. 7, Sec. 2: 4 > Biblical Verse Corroboration *(real, fair)*
Ch. 7, Sec. 2: 5 > Biblical Verse Corroboration *(trinity, trio)*

Subsection ▪ *No One Made God*

Ch. 7, Sec. 2: 6 > QS Answer Interpretation Table
Ch. 7, Sec. 2: 7 > Biblical Verse Corroboration *(eviternity)*
Ch. 7, Sec. 2: 8 > Biblical Verse Corroboration *(horn)*

Subsection ▪ *Prophecy of Dave Satisfied*

Ch. 7, Sec. 2: 9 > QS Answer Interpretation Table
Ch. 7, Sec. 2: 10 > Personal Prophecy Evidence II
Ch. 7, Sec. 2: 11 > Biblical Verse Corroboration *(dave, holy ghost, answering)*

Subsection ▪ *God Transformed Her/Himself into a Trinity*

Ch. 7, Sec. 2: 12 > QS Answer Interpretation Table
Ch. 7, Sec. 2: 13 > Biblical Verse Corroboration *(siring a we, is a we, trinity)*
Ch. 7, Sec. 2: 14 > Biblical Verse Corroboration *(we, they, trinity)*
Ch. 7, Sec. 2: 15 > Biblical Verse Corroboration *(horn)*
Ch. 7, Sec. 2: 16 > Biblical Verse Corroboration *(yahweh)*
Ch. 7, Sec. 2: 17 > Biblical Verse Corroboration *(trinity)*
Ch. 7, Sec. 2: 18 > Biblical Verse Corroboration *(glory)*
Ch. 7, Sec. 2: 19 > Biblical Verse Corroboration *(host)*

Subsection ▪ *God Authored QS Answers*

Ch. 7, Sec. 2: 20 > QS Answer Interpretation Table

Subsection ▪ *God is Good and Evil*

Ch. 7, Sec. 2: 21 > Biblical Verse Evidence I
Ch. 7, Sec. 2: 22 > Biblical Verse Evidence II
Ch. 7, Sec. 2: 23 > Biblical Verse Evidence III
Ch. 7, Sec. 2: 24 > Biblical Verse Evidence IV
Ch. 7, Sec. 2: 25 > "QS-Satan/Hell" Answer
Ch. 7, Sec. 2: 26 > "QS Guide 3" Directive
Ch. 7, Sec. 2: 27 > QS Answer Subject & Action Relationship
Ch. 7, Sec. 2: 28 > Biblical Verse Evidence V
Ch. 7, Sec. 2: 29 > Biblical Verse Evidence VI
Ch. 7, Sec. 2: 30 > "QS-Satan/Hell" Answer Interpretation
Ch. 7, Sec. 2: 31 > QS Answer Interpretation Table I *(lie wans)*
Ch. 7, Sec. 2: 32 > QS Answer Interpretation Table II *(reason)*
Ch. 7, Sec. 2: 33 > QS Answer Interpretation Table III *(trying sinew)*
Ch. 7, Sec. 2: 34 > QS Answer Interpretation Table IV *(I ring entry, "wans")*
Ch. 7, Sec. 2: 35 > Biblical Verse Corroboration *(rein)*
Ch. 7, Sec. 2: 36 > Biblical Verse Corroboration *(reign)*

Subsection ▪ *God is the De Facto Devil*

Ch. 7, Sec. 2: 37 > FS Matrix Row'd Word Letter Columniation
Ch. 7, Sec. 2: 38 > FS Row'd Word Evidence
Ch. 7, Sec. 2: 39 > QS Row'd Word Matrix & FS Row'd Word Matrix Comparison
Ch. 7, Sec. 2: 40 > FS Row'd Word Sequence Explanation

Ch. 7, Sec. 2: 41 > "FS-Apollo^1:astronauts" Row'd Word Evidence, Solved Matrix & Answer, Definitions, Interpretation & Answer Evidence

Ch. 7, Sec. 2: 42 > Biblical Verse Evidence I

Ch. 7, Sec. 2: 43 > Biblical Verse Evidence II

Ch. 7, Sec. 2: 44 > Biblical Verse Evidence III

Ch. 7, Sec. 2: 45 > Biblical Verse Evidence IV

Ch. 7, Sec. 2: 46 > Biblical Verse Evidence V

Ch. 7, Sec. 2: 47 > Biblical Verse Evidence VI

Ch. 7, Sec. 2: 48 > Biblical Verse Evidence VII

Ch. 7, Sec. 2: 49 > Virgin Mary Genealogy *(±devil, ±lucifer, ±satan)*

Ch. 7, Sec. 2: 50 > Genealogical Categories *(– "lineally-coupled," – "lineally-coupled-alias")*

Subsection ▪ *God Merits Reverence*

Ch. 7, Sec. 2: 51 > QS Answer Interpretation Table

Ch. 7, Sec. 2: 52 > Biblical Verse Corroboration *(adore giver)*

Subsection ▪ *God is or Identifies as Male*

Ch. 7, Sec. 2: 53 > QS Answer Interpretation Table

Ch. 7, Sec. 2: 54 > "QS Guide 4" Directive

Ch. 7, Sec. 2: 55 > Biblical Verse Corroboration *(yahweh)*

Ch. 7, Sec. 2: 56 > Biblical Verse Corroboration *(host)*

Ch. 7, Sec. 2: 57 > Biblical Verse Corroboration *(joe)*

Subsection ▪ *God is Incomprehensible*

Ch. 7, Sec. 2: 58 > QS Answer Interpretation Table

Ch. 7, Sec. 2: 59 > Biblical Verse Corroboration *(hairy)*

Subsection ▪ *God is Self-Conscious*

Ch. 7, Sec. 2: 60 > QS Answer Interpretation Table

Ch. 7, Sec. 2: 61 > Biblical Verse Corroboration *(horn)*

Ch. 7, Sec. 2: 62 > Biblical Verse Corroboration *(siring a we, is a we)*

Ch. 7, Sec. 2: 63 > Biblical Verse Corroboration *(we)*

Ch. 7, Sec. 2: 64 > Biblical Verse Corroboration *(yahweh)*

Ch. 7, Sec. 2: 65 > Biblical Verse Corroboration *(trinity)*

Ch. 7, Sec. 2: 66 > Biblical Verse Corroboration *(glory)*

Ch. 7, Sec. 2: 67 > Biblical Verse Corroboration *(host)*

Chapter 7, Section 3 (God's Theological Perspective)

Ch. 7, Sec. 3: 1 > QS Answer Facts & Biblical Corroborations Table

Ch. 7, Sec. 3: 2 > QS Answer Interpretation Table I *(core, trinity)*
Ch. 7, Sec. 3: 3 > QS Answer Interpretation Table II *(glory, host)*
Ch. 7, Sec. 3: 4 > QS Answer Interpretation Table III *(torah, glory, host)*
Ch. 7, Sec. 3: 5 > QS Answer Interpretation Table IV *("horde: evil," lie wans, torah)*
Ch. 7, Sec. 3: 6 > QS Answer Facts & Theological Corroborations Table

---

Chapter 7, Section 4 (Statistics and Analyses)

Subsection ▪ QS Answer Main Subjects: Statistics

Ch. 7, Sec. 4: 1 > QS Answer Main Subject Statistics Table

Subsection ▪ QS Answer Main Subjects: Statistical Analyses

Subsection ▪ QS Answer Word Types: Categories

Ch. 7, Sec. 4: 2 > QS Answer Noun Types Table
Ch. 7, Sec. 4: 3 > QS Answer Verb Types Table
Ch. 7, Sec. 4: 4 > QS Answer Pronoun Types Table
Ch. 7, Sec. 4: 5 > QS Answer Adjective Types Table
Ch. 7, Sec. 4: 6 > QS Answer Adverb Types Table
Ch. 7, Sec. 4: 7 > QS Answer Conjunction Types Table
Ch. 7, Sec. 4: 8 > QS Answer Indefinite Article Types Table
Ch. 7, Sec. 4: 9 > QS Answer Contraction Types Table

Subsection ▪ QS Answer Word Types: Statistics

Ch. 7, Sec. 4: 10 > QS Answer Word Types Statistics Table

Subsection ▪ QS Answer Word Types: Statistical Analyses (Nouns)

Ch. 7, Sec. 4: 11 > QS Answer Noun Categories and Words Table
Ch. 7, Sec. 4: 12 > QS Answer Nounal Phrases and Wordier Phrases ("God") Table
Ch. 7, Sec. 4: 13 > QS Answer Nounal Words and Wordier Phrases ("God") Table
Ch. 7, Sec. 4: 14 > QS Answer Nounal Words and Wordier Phrases ("Dave") Table
Ch. 7, Sec. 4: 15 > QS Answer Nounal Words and Wordier Phrases ("QS Answer") Table
Ch. 7, Sec. 4: 16 > QS Answer Nounal Words and Wordier Phrases ("Lie") Table
Ch. 7, Sec. 4: 17 > Apostrophe-Ess and Colon Substitution Example
Ch. 7, Sec. 4: 18 > QS Answer Implied Possessive Nouns Interpretation Table
Ch. 7, Sec. 4: 19 > QS Answer Matrix with Additional Row'd Word Letter "S"
Ch. 7, Sec. 4: 20 > QS Answer Recurring Nouns Table

Subsection ▪ QS Answer Word Types: Statistical Analyses (Verbs)

Ch. 7, Sec. 4: 21 > QS Answer Verb Categories and Phrases Table

Ch. 7, Sec. 4: 22 > QS Answer Verb Category and Examples Table I
Ch. 7, Sec. 4: 23 > QS Answer Verb Category and Examples Table II
Ch. 7, Sec. 4: 24 > QS Answer Verb Category and Examples Table III
Ch. 7, Sec. 4: 25 > QS Answer Verb Category and Examples Table IV
Ch. 7, Sec. 4: 26 > QS Answer Verb Category and Examples Table V
Ch. 7, Sec. 4: 27 > QS Answer Recurring Verbs Table
Ch. 7, Sec. 4: 28 > QS Answer Corrected Excised Verbs Table
Ch. 7, Sec. 4: 29 > QS Answer Matrix with Additional Row'd Word Letter "S" (Verb)

Subsection ▪ QS Answer Word Types: Statistical Analyses (Indefinite Articles)

Ch. 7, Sec. 4: 30 > QS Answer Indefinite Article Categories and Phrases Table
Ch. 7, Sec. 4: 31 > QS Answer Indefinite Article Removal and Interpretation Table I
Ch. 7, Sec. 4: 32 > QS Answer Indefinite Article Removal and Interpretation Table II
Ch. 7, Sec. 4: 33 > QS Answer Indefinite Article and Subject Uniqueness Interpretation Table I
Ch. 7, Sec. 4: 34 > QS Answer Indefinite Article and Subject Uniqueness Interpretation Table II

Subsection ▪ QS Answer Word Types: Statistical Analyses (Pronouns)

Ch. 7, Sec. 4: 35 > QS Answer Pronouns and Corresponding QS Answer Phrases (God) Table
Ch. 7, Sec. 4: 36 > QS Answer Pronouns and Corresponding QS Answers (Dave) Table
Ch. 7, Sec. 4: 37 > QS Answer Recurring Pronouns Table

Subsection ▪ QS Answer Word Types: Statistical Analyses (Adjectives)

Ch. 7, Sec. 4: 38 > QS Answer Adjectives and Corresponding QS Answers (God) Table
Ch. 7, Sec. 4: 39 > QS Answer Adjectives and Corresponding QS Answers (Dave) Table

Subsection ▪ QS Answer Word Types: Statistical Analyses (Conjunctions)

Ch. 7, Sec. 4: 40 > QS Answer Conjunctions and Corresponding QS Answer Phrases (God) Table
Ch. 7, Sec. 4: 41 > QS Answer Conjunctions and Corresponding QS Answer Phrases (Dave) Table
Ch. 7, Sec. 4: 42 > QS Answer Recurring Conjunctions Table

Subsection ▪ QS Answer Word Types: Statistical Analyses (Contractions)

Ch. 7, Sec. 4: 43 > QS Answer Contractions, Corresponding QS Answer and Interpretation Table
Ch. 7, Sec. 4: 44 > QS Answer Matrix with Removed Row'd Word Letter "S" (Contraction)

Subsection ▪ QS Answer Word Types: Statistical Analyses (Adverbs)

Ch. 7, Sec. 4: 45 > QS Answer Adverbs and Corresponding QS Answers Table

Subsection ▪ QS Answer Word Types: Statistical Analyses (Interjections)

Ch. 7, Sec. 4: 46 > QS Answer Interjections Example Table
Ch. 7, Sec. 4: 47 > "QS Guide 5" Directive

Subsection ▪ QS Answer Words and Definitions: Standard, Archaic and Obsolete

Ch. 7, Sec. 4: 48 > QS Answer Word Temporality Statistics Table
Ch. 7, Sec. 4: 49 > "QS Guide 4" Directive Update

Subsection ▪ QS Answer Points of View

Ch. 7, Sec. 4: 50 > QS Answer Points of Views Statistics Table

Subsection ▪ QS Answer Statistics: Composite

Ch. 7, Sec. 4: 51 > QS Answer Composite Statistics Table

Chapter 7, Section 5 (Composite QS Answer Interpretation)

Ch. 7, Sec. 5: 1 > QS Answers Interpretation Table
Ch. 7, Sec. 5: 2 > Composite QS Answer Interpretation

INDEX II

TOPIC TAG DIRECTORY

Chapter 1, Section 1 • God/Heaven: He Gains • 13

Query Stack (**introduction**, term [abbreviation]);
Query Stack answer (author, interpretation, **introduction**, letter, punctuation, sentence, word ["Dave" (David Mivshek, "He"), definition]);
Query Stack guide (1);
Query Stack matrix (**introduction**, row'd word [letter (connection)]);
Query Stack rule (1-11);
Theology (God [origin], Heaven, Veda);
Vision (**introduction**, word stack [question (interpretation, punctuation)]).

Chapter 1, Section 2 • Devil/Hell: Horde Wans • 29

Query Stack (title [abbreviation]);
Query Stack answer (author, congruency, subject-action link, word ["Horde," "Wans"]);
Query Stack guide (2-3);
Query Stack matrix (row'd word [congruency]);
Seven Common QS Answer Properties (**introduction**, punctuation [: = 's], term [abbreviation]);
Theology (demons; Devil, Hell, morality [spectrum]).

Chapter 1, Section 3 • Jesus/Earth: Joe Assures • 45

Biblical verse (John 3:13 KJV, Matthew 28:18 KJV, Proverbs 15:24 KJV, Revelations 19:16 KJV);
Query Stack answer (congruency, word ["Joe," "Rein"]);
Theology (Earth, Jesus).

Chapter 1, Section 4 • Dave/Earth: Adore Giver • 59

Biblical verse (Acts 13:22 KJV, Exodus 20:3/5-7 KJV, Isaiah 45:5-7 KJV, Isaiah 55:8-9 KJV, James 1:17 KJV, Matthew 5:45 KJV, Proverbs 14:19 KJV, Romans 11:22 KJV, Romans 12:21 KJV);
Query Stack answer (author, hint, word ["Giver," "Hinter," "Joe," transposition ("Dave")]);
Seven Common QS Answer Properties (property deviation resolution);
Theology (David, God [adoration, evil, good, horde, gender, joe, wans], Jesus, morality [force, spectrum], Trinity [evil]).

Chapter 1, Section 5 • Review: Four Stacks • 79

QS answer (main subject category [**introduction**, main subject, tier], statistics);
Query Stack (author, origination);
Reminder (QS guides 1-3, QS rules 1-11, QS-7CAP, word stack vision);
Seven Common QS Answer Properties (formula [symbol explanation]).

Chapter 2, Section 1 • Joe/Earth: Hint Grew • 89

Query Stack (author);
Query Stack answer (congruency, word ["Air," "Grew," "Hint," "Reason," transposition ("Joe")]);
Theology (God, Joseph, Virgin Mary).

Chapter 2, Section 2 • Mary/Earth: Marry Reason • 101

Query Stack (author);
Query Stack answer (congruency, word ["Grew," "Hint," "I," "Reason"]);
Query Stack matrix (row'd word [first row, genealogy, nickname]);
Theology (Devil, God, Virgin Mary).

Chapter 2, Section 3 • Review: Six Stacks • 111

Query Stack answer (main subject category [update], statistics [update]);
Query Stack matrix (category [**introduction**, Lineal Query Stack, Lineally-Coupled Query Stack], evolution, row'd word [congruency]);
Reminder (word stack vision);
Theology (Devil, God, Virgin Mary [genealogy]).

Chapter 3, Section 1 • Holy^Ghost/Heaven: Naïve or Answering • 121

Biblical verse (Matthew 1:18 KJV);
Query Stack (title [caret]);
Query Stack answer (author, congruency ["Dave" (David Mivshek)], word ["Ghost," "He,"]);
Query Stack rule (12);
Theology (God, Holy Ghost, Mary [genealogy (update)], Trinity).

Chapter 3, Section 2 • Review: Seven Stacks • 135

Query Stack answer (main subject category [update], statistics [update]);
Query Stack matrix (category [update (Lineal-Alias Query Stack [**introduction**])]);
Reminder; (Lineal Query Stack, Lineally-Coupled Query Stack, QS rules 1-12);
Theology (Virgin Mary [genealogy (update)]).

Chapter 4, Section 1 • YHWH/Heaven: Yahweh's Horn • 135

Biblical verse (2 Samuel 22:3 KJV);
Query Stack answer (word ["Horn," "We," "Yahweh"]);
Theology (God [given name, trinity, YHWH], Jesus).

Chapter 4, Section 2 • Yahweh/Heaven: Heaven's Horn • 153

Query Stack answer (word ["Hay," "Heaven," "Horn," "Siring," transposition ("Yahweh"), "We"]);
Theology (God [self-transformation (trinity)]).

Chapter 4, Section 3 • Review: Nine Stacks • 163

Query Stack answer (main subject category [update], statistics [update]);
Query Stack matrix (category [update (Lineal-Alias, Realm-Related Query Stack [**introduction**])]);
Reminder; (Lineal Query Stack, Lineal-Alias Query Stack, Lineally-Coupled Query Stack);
Theology (Virgin Mary [genealogy (update)]).

Chapter 5, Section 1 • Creator/Reality: Core's Real • 173

Biblical verse (Isaiah 40:28 KJV);
Query Stack answer (word ["Core," "Real," "Trinity," "We"]);
Query Stack matrix (row'd word ["Creator," "Reality"]);
Reminder (word stack vision);
Theology (God, Trinity).

Chapter 5, Section 2 • Yahweh/Reality: They or Reins • 187

Query Stack answer (word ["Hay," "I," "Reins," transposition ("Yahweh"), "'A We'"]);
Theology (God [self-transformation (Trinity)]).

Chapter 5, Section 3 • Yahweh/Trinity: Hairy We • 201

Biblical verse (Job 37:5 KJV);
Query Stack matrix (row'd word ["Trinity," "Yahweh"]);
Query Stack answer (word ["Hairy," "Reining," "Trio," "Wans," "We"]);
Theology (God, morality, Trinity).

Chapter 5, Section 4 • "Five Stacks"/Trinity • 215

Biblical verse (Deuteronomy 5:24 KJV, Devarim 5:21 Tanakh);
Query Stack answer (author, word ["Entry," "Fair," "Glory," "Hinter," "Host," "'I,'" "I," "In," "Issuer," "Jot," "Orator's," "Torah," "Trio," "Trying," "Sinew," "Wanes," "'Wans,'" "Wording"]);
Seven Common QS Answer Properties (property resolution);

Theology *(morality, Shekinah, Trinity [Father (God), Holy Ghost, Son (Jesus)], Virgin Mary [genealogy]).*

Chapter 5, Section 5 • Review: Seventeen Stacks • 241

Query Stack answer *(main subject category [update], statistics [update]);*
Reminder; *(Lineal Query Stack, Lineal/Realm-Related Query Stack, Lineal-Alias Query Stack, Lineal-Alias/Realm-Related Query Stack, Lineally-Coupled Query Stack);*
Theology *(Virgin Mary [genealogy (update)]).*

Chapter 6, Section 1 • Trinity/Heaven: Eviternity's Horn • 253

Biblical verse *(Isaiah 40:28 KJV, Psalms 18:2 KJV);*
Query Stack answer *(word ["Eviternity," "Horn," "We"]);*
Seven Common QS Answer Properties *(property resolution);*
Theology *(God, Heaven, Trinity, Virgin Mary [genealogy]).*

Chapter 6, Section 2 • Review: Eighteen Stacks • 269

Query Stack answer *(category [update], main subject category [update]);*
Theology *(Virgin Mary [genealogy (update)]).*

Chapter 7, Section 1 • "Two Stacks"/Hell • 277

Biblical verse *(Isaiah 14:12 KJV, Psalms 18:2 KJV, Revelation 12:9 KJV, Shemot 20:13 Tanakh, Shemot 23:7 Tanakh);*
Query Stack *(author);*
Query Stack answer *(word ["Clue," "Filler," "Horn," "Lie," "Siring," "Torah's," "Wans," "We"]);*
Query Stack matrix *(category [update (Lineally-Coupled-Alias Query Stack [**introduction**])]);*
Theology *(Devil, God [self-transformation], Hell, Lucifer, morality, Satan, Shekinah, Torah, Virgin Mary [genealogy]).*

Chapter 7, Section 2 • Conclusion: Twenty Stacks • 299

Biblical verse *(1 John 3:8 KJV, 1 John 5:7 KJV, 2 Peter 1:20-21 KJV, 2 Samuel 7:26 WEB, 2 Samuel 22:3 KJV, Bereshit 1:1 Tanakh, Bereshit 1:3-4 Tanakh, Bereshit 1:26 Tanakh, Bereshit 1:27 Tanakh, Deuteronomy 5:24 KJV, Devarim 5:21 Tanakh, Exodus 15:18 KJV, Exodus 20:13 KJV, Exodus 20:16 KJV, Exodus 23:1 KJV, Genesis 1:1 KJV, Genesis 1:3-4 KJV, Genesis 1:26 KJV, Genesis 1:27 KJV, Isaiah 14:12-15 KJV, Isaiah 40:28 KJV, Isaiah 45:5-8 KJV, John 8:44 KJV, John 10:30 KJV, Mark 10:18 KJV, Micah 3:5-7 Tanakh, Mishlei 12:19 Tanakh, Mishlei 19:5 Tanakh, Mishlei 19:9 Tanakh, Proverbs 12:19 KJV, Proverbs 19:5 KJV, Proverbs 19:9 KJV, Psalms 18:2 KJV, Psalms 99:5 KJV, Psalms 100:5 KJV, Revelation 12:7-9 KJV, Revelation 12:9 KJV, Shemot 6:3 Tanakh, Shemot 15:18 Tanakh, Shemot 20:13 Tanakh, Shemot 23:1 Tanakh, Shmuel II 22:3 Tanakh, Tehillim 18:3 Tanakh, Tehillim 99:5 Tanakh,*

Tehillim 100:5 Tanakh, Tehillim 111:7 Tanakh, Yechezkel 20:8 Tanakh, Yeshayahu 40:28 Tanakh, Yeshayahu 45:5-8 Tanakh);
Fate Stack *(**introduction**, origination, term [abbreviation]);*
Fate Stack *answer (interpretation [God (de facto Devil, morality)], **introduction**, word (definition), topic);*
Fate Stack *matrix (construction, **introduction**, row'd word [art title, last name (Apollo 1 astronaut)]);*
Query Stack;
Query Stack *answer (phrase ["A We"], topic [Dave (characteristics [male], attributes [ghostwriter, goal, naïve, answerer, prophecy]), God (characteristics [Creator, eternal, evil, horn, individual, male, morality (self-transformation [effects], spectrum), real, self-awareness (individual, trinity), self-transformation (process), attributes [incomprehensible, reverence, QS author]), Torah (content)], word ["Dave" (David Mivshek), "Joe" (slang)]);*
Query Stack *guide (4);*
Query Stack *matrix (category [update]);*
Reminder *(QS answer evolution, QS Guide 3, word stack vision);*
Theology *(Christian, Communion, Creation [process], Devil [Lucifer, Satan], God [Father, Yahweh, YHWH], Holy Ghost, Jesus [Host, morality, Son], Judaist, Shekinah, Tanakh [Torah], Ten Commandments [Eighth/Ninth Commandment (lie)], The Bible [Old Testament], Trinity, Virgin Mary [genealogy (update)]).*

Chapter 7, Section 3 • God's Theological Perspective • 343

Biblical verse *(Isaiah 45:5-7 KJV, Yeshayahu 45:5/7 Tanakh);*
Query Stack *(author);*
Query Stack *answer (facts);*
Theology *(Christianity, Devil, God [characteristic (de facto Devil, morality), attribute], Judaism, Messianic Judaism, Shekinah [Jesus], Tanakh [Torah], The Bible [New Testament], Trinity [term (origination)]).*

Chapter 7, Section 4 • QS Answer Statistics and Analyses • 349

Biblical verse *(1 John 5:7 KJV, Devarim 5:21 Tanakh, Genesis 1:26 KJV, Isaiah 45:5-8 KJV, John 10:30 KJV, Mishlei 19:5 Tanakh, Shemot 6:3 Tanakh, Shemot 15:18 Tanakh, Shemot 20:13 Tanakh, Shemot 23:1 Tanakh, Tehillim 18:3 Tanakh, Yeshayahu 40:28 Tanakh, Yeshayahu 45:5-8 Tanakh);*
Query Stack *answer (author, characteristic, interpretation, main subject category [David Mivshek, Trinity, God, QS Answer, Commandment (**introduction**)], point of view [first-person, mixed-person, second-person, third-person], punctuation, statistics [composite, inclusivity level, uniqueness level], word ["Dave," (David Mivshek [prophecy]), definition (archaic, obsolete, standard)], word type [adjective (postpositive, prepositive), adverb, conjunction (recurring), contraction, indefinite article (recurring), interjection, noun (alias, attribute, descriptor,*

name, nickname, plural, possessive proper, proper, recurring, singular), pronoun (first-person, recurring, third-person), verb (active participle, base, excised-S [ESV], recurring, standard, third person singular/present tense verb [TPS-PTV])]);

Query Stack guide *(4 [update], 5);*

Query Stack matrix *(row'd word [letter S]);*

Reminder *(word stack vision);*

Theology *(God [attribute, characteristic, morality, origin (individual, self-transformation, trinity), Ten Commandments]).*

Chapter 7, Section 5 • Composite QS Answer Interpretation • 421

Query Stack answer *(interpretation [composite]);*

Languages humans use were manufactured before humans existed, just like the elements which become fused together to make humans existed before humans existed.

NOTES, AGREEMENTS & ARGUMENTS

www.ingramcontent.com/pod-product-compliance
Lightning Source LLC
Chambersburg PA
CBHW081144290426
44108CB00018B/2436